Penguin Education

Penguin Critical Anthologies

General Editor: Christopher Ricks

Henry Fielding

Edited by Claude Rawson

Henry Fielding
A Critical Anthology

Edited by
Claude Rawson
Penguin Education

Penguin Education
A Division of Penguin Books Ltd,
Harmondsworth, Middlesex, England
Penguin Books Inc, 7110 Ambassador Road,
Baltimore, Md 21207, USA
Penguin Books Australia Ltd,
Ringwood, Victoria, Australia

First published 1973
This selection copyright © Claude Rawson, 1973
Introduction and notes copyright © Claude Rawson, 1973

Made and printed in Great Britain by
Hazell Watson & Viney Ltd,
Aylesbury, Bucks
Set in Monotype Bembo

Contents

6 Contents

7 Contents

8 Contents

Part Two The Developing Debate

11 Contents

14   Contents

15 Contents

Part Three Modern Views

Preface

In Part One, I have been greatly helped by both Blanchard and *Critical Heritage*, as well as by Ioan Williams's collection of Fielding's critical writings, *The Criticism of Henry Fielding*, 1970. Blanchard has also been a valuable, though increasingly incomplete, guide in Part Two.

I owe a personal debt to Christopher Betts, John Rignall, George Whalley and several other friends and scholars, and to the University of Warwick library.

A Note on Presentation and Abbreviations

The selection is arranged in chronological order. Texts used are in every case those given in brackets in the heading, and the page references at the end of each extract refer always to the text used. Where no reference to a text used is given in the brackets, I have reprinted the original source as specified in the unbracketed part of the heading.

In passages from Fielding's lifetime and the period immediately after his death, I have normally used authoritative modern editions where these exist, irrespective of whether the passage occurs in *Critical Heritage* or not. Where there is no separate authoritative edition for an extract appearing in *Critical Heritage*, I have normally used *Critical Heritage*, having checked against original editions in selected cases. Extensive minor alterations in the spelling, capitalization, italicization and punctuation of extracts, and in the style of their footnotes and references, have been made by the publishers, however, in conformity with their house practice.

I have used the following abbreviations:

Blanchard	Frederic T. Blanchard, *Fielding the Novelist: A Study in Historical Criticism*, 1926, reprinted 1966
Critical Heritage	Ronald Paulson and Thomas Lockwood (eds.), *Henry Fielding: The Critical Heritage*, 1969
Works	W. E. Henley (ed.), *The Complete Works of Henry Fielding*, 16 volumes, 1903

Table of Dates

1742   Fall of Walpole from power. Fielding's first novel, *The
        History of the Adventures of Joseph Andrews, And of his
        Friend Mr Abraham Adams. Written in Imitation of the
        Manner of Cervantes*. His eldest daughter dies.

1743   Publication of *Miscellanies*, in three volumes. This contains
        poems; plays; essays (including the *Essay on Conversation*
        and the *Essay on the Knowledge of the Characters of Men*);
        A Journey from this World to the Next (an other-worldly
        fiction modelled on Lucian); and *The Life of Mr
        Jonathan Wild the Great* (the anti-Walpole part of this
        work was probably begun in 1740).

1744   Sarah Fielding (Henry's sister) publishes her novel
        David Simple; Henry Fielding writes the Preface to the
        second edition. Fielding's first wife dies.

1745–6 Fielding edits *The True Patriot*, supporting the Hanoverian
        cause against the Young Pretender, Charles Edward
        Stuart. (The main action of *Tom Jones* was later to be
        set in this period of the 1745 Jacobite Rebellion.)

1747   Marries Mary Daniel, his housekeeper and formerly his
        first wife's maid. She later bore him several children.

1747–8 Edits the *Jacobite's Journal*, in the Hanoverian cause.
        Richardson's *Clarissa* published in seven volumes over
        this period. Fielding warmly admired this novel and
        wrote to Richardson saying so.

1748   In October, Fielding becomes Justice of the Peace for
        Westminster; his jurisdiction was later extended to the
        whole of Middlesex.

1749   *The History of Tom Jones, A Foundling* is published.

1751   *An Enquiry into the Causes of the Late Increase of Robbers,
        &c. With some Proposals for Remedying this Growing Evil*,
        an important legal-sociological work, the product of

Fielding's experience as a magistrate. *Amelia*, Fielding's last novel, published in December (though dated 1752).

1752   Fielding edits the *Covent-Garden Journal*, his last periodical.

1753   *A Proposal for Making an Effectual Provision for the Poor, for Amending their Morals, and for Rendering them Useful Members of the Society*, another legal-sociological work.

1754   A new, revised edition of *Jonathan Wild* is published. Fielding's health deteriorates; he resigns his office as a magistrate and leaves for Lisbon. Dies near Lisbon in October.

1755   *The Journal of a Voyage to Lisbon* published posthumously in February and, in a more authentic text, in December.

Part One **Contemporaneous Criticism**

Introduction

The early criticism of Fielding's plays presents a dull picture. Fielding's own comments, in prologues, epilogues and prefaces, assert familiar positions: the author's concern for truth and morality and the time-honoured functions and responsibilities of comedy, and his repudiation of the vices of the age, and of the depraved taste of current theatrical fashions (heroic bombast, vulgar farce, harlequinades, operas, etc.). Fielding's best comments on these things are usually the plays themselves, especially those which use protracted forms of parody and the *Rehearsal*-device of the play-within-the-play. But it is precisely these comments which are impossible to anthologize in short or typical extracts, because their effect makes itself felt obliquely and cumulatively, and depends on context, atmosphere, and an extensive network of allusion. The more hostile reviewers of Fielding's plays accused him of the faults he was satirizing, but the level of critical liveliness and insight remained low.

The interest quickens in 1736 and 1737, when Fielding's political satires caused stormy debate. Fielding was attacked notably in the Government's *Gazetteer* and was defended, by Fielding himself and others, in the Opposition's *Common Sense*. This was founded by Chesterfield and Lyttelton, and took its name from the Queen Common Sense of *Pasquin*, one of the more notorious of Fielding's plays. The debate surrounding these plays is of wider interest because it involved arguments about the need for censorship (on political and moral grounds) and about freedom of expression, and because Fielding's satirical anti-Walpole plays helped to bring about the Stage Licensing Act of 1737, which more or less ended Fielding's career as a playwright. Among the stock accusations levelled at Fielding at this time, and in the ensuing period of editorship of the *Champion*, were several which became part of the Fielding legend: that he was a party hack, a careless and prolific producer of low journalism, an impoverished Grub-Streeter, a loose-living profligate.

These attacks continued throughout Fielding's career as a
novelist, which began in 1742 with the publication of *Joseph
Andrews*. *Joseph Andrews* itself sold well and was reprinted several
times (Parson Adams in particular became a favourite and often-
mentioned figure), but there are relatively few extended
references to it. It was not until after the publication of *Tom Jones*
in 1749 that Fielding became known and seriously discussed as an
important novelist, and comments on *Joseph Andrews* became more
frequent from then on. Among the comments before 1749, the
most interesting are Joseph Warton's report in 1746 that Fielding
valued 'Joseph Andrews above all his writings' (Blanchard, p. 13),
the brief comments by Gray and Shenstone, the fuller comments
of Elizabeth Carter (who was to remain a staunch defender of
Fielding against her own Richardsonian friends), and of the novel's
French translator, Desfontaines. There is also, in the Prologue to
Fielding's play *The Wedding-Day* (1743; *Works*, vol. 12, p. 68) spoken
by Macklin, a friendly admonition that Fielding would have done
better to stick 'to honest Abraham Adams' instead of writing plays,
a remark which suggests that people were already saying that
Fielding had more talent as a novelist than as a playwright. It is
Fielding's own comments on the art of fiction, in the Prefaces to
Joseph Andrews, to the *Miscellanies* and to Sarah Fielding's *David
Simple*, and in his admiring letter of 15 October 1748 to Richardson
about *Clarissa*, which throw the most light, in this period, on his
fiction and his conception of the novelist's art.

Despite Fielding's notoriety as a playwright and a political
controversialist, Richardson was the better-known of the two as a
novelist. By the end of his life, Fielding was widely acknowledged
as a novelist of great distinction, but never quite gained the first
place even then. Before *Tom Jones*, he was nowhere near it, and
Joseph Andrews was itself partly a product of the celebrity of
Pamela. Fielding's earlier and anonymous *Shamela* (1741) was one
of many anti-Pamelaic squibs by various authors in the early 1740s.

But all Fielding's subsequent major writings (*Tom Jones*, *Amelia*, the *Voyage to Lisbon*, and the various periodical essays), reflect in some way a preoccupation – hostile, friendly or mixed – with Richardson's personality and writings.

Between *Joseph Andrews* and *Tom Jones*, Fielding's main publication was a three-volume collection of *Miscellanies* (1743), which included plays, poems, essays, the *Journey from this World to the Next*, and, most important of all, the anti-Walpole satire, *Jonathan Wild*. This set of volumes was handsomely subscribed for, with many prominent political and social figures taking several copies: the Prince of Wales took fifteen, and (ironically) Walpole himself ten. *Jonathan Wild* does not seem to have had much critical attention.

When *Tom Jones* appeared in 1749 it quickly became very popular indeed. 'By the winter of 1749–50 the appellations "Tom Jones" and "Sophia" had acquired something of that popularity which, in a subsequent age, was responsible for "Pickwick" cigars and other Pickwickian commodities' (Blanchard, p. 40). Several 'sequels' and imitations began to appear: *The History of Tom Jones, the Foundling, in his Married State* (1749), *The History of Charlotte Summers, the Fortunate Parish Girl* (1750), and Francis Coventry's *History of Pompey the Little* (1751), whose third edition (1752) contained in addition an Epistle Dedicatory to Fielding. Coventry may also have been the author of *An Essay on the New Species of Writing founded by Mr Fielding*, a pamphlet which was published in 1751. Another work of some length, the *Examen of the History of Tom Jones*, had strongly attacked Fielding the previous year. Comments, friendly and hostile, were many from the start. Personal and political attacks on Fielding continued. His association with Lyttelton (to whom the work is dedicated) provoked further accusations that Fielding was a political hireling. Fielding's appointment as Justice of the Peace for Westminster in 1748 gave added fuel to jibes that Fielding was a party hack. The book was attacked for untidiness, scurrility, lowness, irreligiousness, plagiarism. Richardson wrote many sneering and obsessive things about it in correspondence with his circle of female devotees, and showed discomfiture when one or other of these put in a good word for Fielding. *Tom Jones* overshadowed *Clarissa* in sales. Johnson, a friend of Richardson, devoted *Rambler*, no. 4, 31 March 1750, to an important discussion of the didactic potentialities and dangers of realistic fiction, rebuking authors who painted peccant heroes in too attractive a light. His unnamed targets were Fielding's *Tom Jones* and Smollett's *Roderick Random*. (Smollett himself attacked Fielding in the first edition of his *Peregrine Pickle*, 1751, and again after *Amelia* appeared, but was later to praise Fielding in his *History of England*.) There were many friendly reactions too. The *London Magazine* reviewed the novel warmly. Lady Mary Wortley Montagu (who was related to Fielding, and referred more than once to his works in her letters) is said to have written *Ne plus ultra* in her copy, and Prince Charles Edward, the Pretender, is said to have admired it (a piquant fact, since the novel, written by a staunch Whig, is set in the England of the abortive Jacobite rebellion of 1745). *Tom Jones* was translated into French, in a truncated version, in 1750. It seems to have been temporarily suppressed in France as a result of a legal side-issue, but nevertheless enjoyed a good run in France. News of the French ban, however, gave a further weapon to the book's English enemies.

Although critical discussion of Fielding by his contemporaries became very much more frequent and detailed after the publication of *Tom Jones*, his own critical discussions even at this time remain at least as interesting as those of his other critics. The prefatory chapters to each book of *Tom Jones* contain much of his thinking on the art of narrative, on the moral themes of his work, on the proper relations between the order of art and the facts of life, and on the reader's as well as the narrator's role in his fiction. The irony and playfulness in these chapters give the discussions a certain obliquity, without however impairing their importance as evidence of Fielding's critical attitudes. After *Tom Jones*, Fielding made several other important critical statements, notably in several essays in the *Covent-Garden Journal* (which includes a famous defence of *Amelia*), and in the Preface to the *Voyage to Lisbon* (a document which registers certain interesting changes of emphasis in his critical thinking at the end of his life).

Amelia was published in December 1751 and was said to have sold out the same day. Johnson was to say that it was 'perhaps the only book, which, being printed off betimes one morning, a new edition was called for before night' (Blanchard, p. 79). What was actually issued was a second *impression*. A new edition, with corrections, was prepared by Fielding, but had to await posthumous publication in Murphy's edition of Fielding's *Works* (1762). The success of *Amelia* did not continue. It was favourably reviewed in the *Monthly Review* (by John Cleland, author of *Fanny Hill*), and there were several other friendly reactions, notably from Christopher Smart. But many reacted very harshly, and Fielding had to defend himself in his periodical, the *Covent-Garden Journal*. Bonnell Thornton, in his imitation of Fielding's periodical, the *Drury-Lane Journal*, repeatedly attacked Fielding, printed a mock-advertisement for *Shamelia*, and some amusing parody of Fielding's novel. Richardson had some odious things to say, as usual, and said some of them to Fielding's sister, the novelist Sarah Fielding, who happened also to admire Richardson. Critics found the novel duller than Fielding's other novels, and also accused it of coarseness, immorality and the rest. The accident which broke the heroine's nose gave rise to a stream of jeers to the effect that venereal disease was the cause of the trouble. Johnson said that the book's later sale was impaired by the 'vile broken nose, never cured' (Blanchard, p. 103). Fielding did try to clear this question up in his revised edition, but that was not published until 1762.

The *Voyage to Lisbon*, which appeared soon after Fielding's death, was reviewed not unkindly, but not widely. There was compassion for Fielding in his last illness, which is part of the painful subject-matter of the *Voyage*, and praise of the work as preserving some of Fielding's genius, though in a dimmed form. A nasty jibe came from Horace Walpole, whose letters contain several harsh passages about Fielding.

Fielding does not seem to have dislodged Richardson from his position as the supreme English novelist of the day, although, after *Tom Jones*, he was thought of as a powerful rival and often as an equal, one of the two towering masters of the novel form. He was more readily regarded as an important technical innovator than as a great *moral* novelist, like Richardson. This view, however, did not go unquestioned even at the time, and has been eloquently challenged in later periods.

John Perceval, Earl of Egmont

from *Diary*   24 April 1730 (*Critical Heritage*)

I went to the Haymarket Playhouse and saw a play called *The Author's Farce and the Pleasures of the Town*, with an additional piece called *The Tragedy of Tom Thumb*. Both these plays are a ridicule on poets, and several of their works, as also of operas, etc., and the last of our modern tragedians, and are exceedingly full of humour, with some wit. The author is one of the sixteen children of Mr Fielding, and in a very low condition of purse.

(27)

Henry Fielding

from the Epilogue to *Rape upon Rape*   1730 (*Works*, vol. 9)

Hey, pray, confess, do all your frowns arise
Because so much of Rape and Rape we bawl?
Or is it, that we have no Rape at all?

   Indeed, our Poet, to oblige the age,
Had brought a dreadful scene upon the stage:
But I, perceiving what his Muse would drive at,
Told him the ladies never would connive at
A downright actual Rape – unless in private.

(157)

Henry Fielding

from 'H. Scriblerus Secundus; His Preface',
The Tragedy of Tragedies   1731 (James T. Hillhouse (ed.), 1918)

I shall not presume to determine which of these two styles [meaningless 'big sounding words' or 'bathos, which is the profound of *Scriblerus*'] be properer for Tragedy – It sufficeth, that our author

excelleth in both. He is very rarely within sight through the whole
play, either rising higher than the eye of your understanding can
soar, or sinking lower than it careth to stoop. But here it may perhaps be observed, that I have given more frequent instances of
authors who have imitated him in the sublime, than in the contrary.
To which I answer, first; bombast being properly a redundancy of
genius, instances of this nature occur in poets whose names do more
honour to our author, than the writers in the doggrel, which proceeds from a cool, calm, weighty way of thinking. Instances whereof
are most frequently to be found in authors of a lower class: secondly;
that the works of such authors are difficultly found at all: thirdly;
that it is a very hard task to read them, in order to extract these
flowers from them: and lastly; it is very often difficult to transplant
them at all; they being like some flowers of a very nice nature,
which will flourish in no soil but their own: for it is easy to transcribe a thought, but not the want of one.
(84–5)

Henry Fielding

Prologue to *The Lottery. A Farce*   1732 (*Works*, vol. 8)

As Tragedy prescribes to passion rules,
So Comedy delights to punish fools;
And while at nobler games she boldly flies,
Farce challenges the vulgar as her prize.
Some follies scarce perceptible appear
In that just glass which shows you as you are.
But Farce still claims a magnifying right
To raise the object larger to the sight,
And show her insect fools in stronger light.
Implicit faith is to her poets due,
And all her laughing legends still are true.
Thus when some conjurer does wives translate,
What dull, affected critic damns the cheat?
Or should we see credulity profound,
Give to ten thousand fools, Ten Thousand Pound;

Should we behold poor wretches horse away
The labour of a twelvemonth in a day;
Nay, should our poet, with his muse agog,
Show you an Alley-broker for a rogue,
Though 'tis a most impossible suggestion,
Faith! think it all but Farce, and grant the question.
(267)

Henry Fielding

from the Prologue to *The Modern Husband*   1732 (*Works*, vol. 10)

If then true nature in his scenes you trace,
Not scenes that Comedy to Farce debase;
If modern vice detestable be shown,
(And, vicious as it is, he draws the town;)
Though no loud laugh applaud the serious page,
Restore the sinking honour of the stage:
The stage, which was not for low farce designed,
But to divert, instruct, and mend mankind.
(10)

'Prosaicus'

from *Grub-Street Journal*, no. 127   8 June 1732 (*Critical Heritage*)

I had seen too much in the Playhouse to follow them, and went to a
coffee-house to examine, whether there was any thing in this *Covent-
Garden Tragedy* that could lay the least claim to wit, or deserve any
encouragement from the Town. I must submit it to all men of sense,
whether that can pass for humour, which is only the dull representation of the most obscene characters in life; and humour is the only
thing the poet can pretend to boast. Were it so, I doubt not but every
Drury-lane bully might make a humourous poet: for surely he could
very naturally describe a scene of life in which he was always conversant; nor is there the most stupid wretch but might pass for a wit,

would he gain that name at the expence of all decency, as well as innocence.

Where is the humour of the bawdy-house scene to any but a rake? Or that of Hackabouta and Stormandra to any women, but those of the town? These indeed, may smile to see how naturally the poet enters into their characters; but the joke is entirely lost to all others. – As to the mock heroic, the lines are bad, nor anything to recommend the numerous similies. The success of this piece will determine whether the age is fallen to the lowest ebb; for I should entertain but a bad opinion of the intellects of that man, or chastity of that woman, who would give the least encouragement to the most dull obscene piece, that, I may venture to say, ever appeared on any public stage. (42–3)

'Philalethes' (probably Fielding)

from *Daily Post* 31 July 1732 (*Critical Heritage*)

Why should any person of modesty be offended at seeing a set of rakes and whores exposed and set in the most ridiculous light? Sure the scene of a bawdy-house may be shewn on a stage without shocking the most modest woman; such I have seen sit out that scene in the *Humorous Lieutenant*, which is quoted and commended by one of the finest writers of the last age.

The author is said to recommend whoring and drunkenness; how! Why a rake speaks against matrimony and a sot against sobriety: So Molière in *Don Juan* recommends all manner of vices, and every poet (I am sure every good one) that hath exposed a vicious character, hath by this rule contributed to debauch mankind. . . . I must tell our critic, there is a vein of good humour and pleasantry which runs through all the works of this author, and will make him and them amiable to a good-natured and sensible reader, when the low, spiteful, false criticism of a *Grub-Street Journal* will be forgotten. . . .

P.S. Whether his scurrility on the *Mock Doctor* be just or no, I leave to the determination of the town, which hath already declared loudly on its side. Some particulars of the original are omitted, which the elegance of an English audience would not have endured; and which, if the critic had ever read the original, would have shewn him that the chaste Molière had introduced greater indecencies on the stage than the author he abuses: I may aver he will find more in Dryden, Congreve, Wycherly, Vanbrugh, Cibber, and all our best Writers of Comedy, nay in the writings of almost every genius from the days of Horace, to those of a most witty, learned and reverend writer of our own age [Swift].

(62–4)

'Maevius' (Richard Russel)

from *Grub-Street Journal*, no. 135   3 August 1732 (*Critical Heritage*)

Charg'd with writing of bawdy, this was F—'s reply:
Tis what Dryden and Congreve have done as well as I.
Tis true – but they did it with this good pretence,
With an ounce of rank bawdy went a pound of good sense:
But thou hast proportion'd, in thy judgement profound,
Of good sense scarce an ounce, and of bawdy a pound.

(64)

'Prosaicus'

from *Grub-Street Journal*, no. 138   24 August 1732 (*Critical Heritage*)

As to the *Covent-Garden Tragedy*, I shall ... consider it only in the author's own way, whether 'tis a piece of just humour; and as such to be tolerated on the stage. ... As I layed it down before, that nature must be the basis of humour, Mr F— may say this is just humour, as being a just imitation of nature; and that the characters are drawn from known realities. But humour is to represent the foibles of nature, not its most shocking deformities; and when any thing becomes indecent, it is no longer humour, but ribaldry. Ben Jonson, the greatest humourist, I believe, of any age, never makes any infringement on morals or good manners: That would be only to pretend to an excellence in which a poet might be equalled if not excelled, by any rake or bawdy-house bully. . . .

I . . . have censured [Mr Fielding's] writings, not him: I pay a deference to his birth, but cannot think it a title to wit, any more than it is to a fortune; nor that every man who has had the honour of being scourged at Eton or Westminster is a man of sense: this I mention only that I would have no poet pique himself on his family or his school.
(66–7)

?Jonathan Swift

from *On Poetry: A Rapsody* 1733 (Harold Williams (ed,),
Poems, 2nd edn, vol. 2, 1958)
[It is possible that the insertion of Fielding's name was not
by Swift.]

For Instance: When you rashly think,
No Rhymer can like *Welsted* sink.
His Merits balanc'd you shall find,
That *Feilding* leaves him far behind.
(393–6, p. 654)

Jonathan Swift

from *Memoirs of Mrs Letitia Pilkington, 1712–50* c. 1733
(Iris Barry (ed.), 1928)

The Dean told me he did remember that he had not laughed above twice in his life – once at some trick a mountebank's merry-andrew played, and the other time was at the circumstance of Tom Thumb's killing the ghost; and I can assure Mr Fielding the Dean had a high opinion of his wit, which must be a pleasure to him, as no man was ever better qualified to judge, possessing it so eminently himself.
(414)

Anonymous

from 'A Letter to a Friend in the Country . . .', *The Old Whig*
8 April 1736 (*Critical Heritage*)

Pasquin? 'Tis a dramatic satire now upon the stage that bears the
title; and is full of sarcasm from one end to the other. The humour is
very popular at least, tho' not all equally delicate; It is a representation of a rehearsal of a Comedy and Tragedy. The latter is principally
pointed at the abuses of the law and physick; and priestcraft is
delineated under the character of *Firebrand Tartuffe*, Priest of the
Sun. You would be greatly pleased with the 'panegyric', as Mr
Fustian calls it, on our clergy, who act with views so different from
this heathen priest! I cannot omit observing the delicacy of the poet,
in not introducing the minister of the queen of common sense, who
must be supposed to have advised the checking the ambition and
insolence of this priest: tho' I must at the same time own to you that
the avoiding this compliment to great men led a dull fellow of my
acquaintance to fancy that common sense made use of no minister
at all. There are such strong strokes in this satire, that if it continues to
be followed with the crowded audiences it has now had for above forty
nights together, some gentlemen will feel its influence more effectually,
and be more hurt in the esteem of Mankind than by a thousand
examinations, tho' ever so well writ, to expose their schemes.
(81)

'Pasquin' (probably Fielding)

from *Common Sense: or, the Englishman's Journal*   21 May 1737
(*Critical Heritage*)

To the Author of the Gazetteer of 7 May.
[See *Critical Heritage*, p. 98, for the attack to which this is an answer.]

. . . You set out, Sir, with a pretty panegyric on the lenity of the
administration, whence you draw this conclusion, that it is ungenerous
to attack it, because it will not crush you for so doing. To abuse the

lenity of power, when men know it will not hurt them (say you) is like talking obscenity to a woman who will not defend herself, and *must* hear it. The comparison between the attack of a ministry, and that of a woman, might afford some pleasant remarks; I shall only say, I suppose you do not mean an old woman, seeing, that to talk a little smuttily to such, would be no great insult, if the common saying be true, which however I do not believe, that all old women love B—y.

You are pleased to say, sir, that no argument whatever can be alledged, to support the bringing of politics on the stage. If you mean by politics, those secrets of Government which, like the mysteries of the *Bona Dea*, are improper to be beheld by vulgar eyes, such as Secret Service, etc. I must answer, your caution is unnecessary, at least to me, who cannot expose to others, what I have not found out myself. But if by your Politics, you mean a general corruption (one of the greatest evils (you are pleased to own) our Constitution is subject to) I cannot think such politics too sacred to be exposed. But *Pasquin* was not (as you insinuate) the first introducer of things of this kind; we have several political plays now extant; And had you ever read Aristophanes, you would know that the gravest matters have been try'd this way. A method which a great writer (I think Mr Bayle) seems to approve; where he represents ridicule as a kind of fiery trial, by which truth is most certainly discovered from imposture. Indeed, I believe, there are no instances of bringing politics on the stage 'in those neighbouring nations' where, you say, that 'we may see disguised Informers in almost every public place, with blank *lettres de cachet*, ready to fill up with the names of such as dare barely inquire, in a manner different from the sense of the court, into the state of affairs, and a Bastile always open to receive them:' Nor where you tell us, that 'a Holy Inquisition, and the gallies, offer their service to the State, as well as to religion'.

But pray, Sir, what do you intend by mentioning these? I hope not to threaten us, nor to insinuate that any thing will make it necessary to introduce such damned engines of Tyranny among us.

But you seem to think, Sir, that to ridicule Vice is to serve its cause. And you mention the late ingenious Mr Gay, who, you say, in his *Beggar's Opera* hath made heroes and heroines of highwaymen and whores. Are then impudence, boldness, robbery and picking pockets the characteristics of a hero? Indeed, Sir, we do not always approve what we laugh at. So far from it, Mr Hobbes will tell you that laughter is a sign of contempt. And by raising such a laugh as this against Vice, Horace assures us we give a sorer wound, than it receives from all the abhorrence which can be produced by the gravest and bitterest satire. You will not hardly, I believe, persuade us, how much soever you may desire it, that it is the mark of a great character to be laughed at by a whole kingdom.

I shall not be industrious to deny, what you are so good to declare, that I am buoy'd up by the greatest wits, and finest gentlemen of the Age; and patroniz'd by the great, the sensible, and the witty in the Opposition. Of such patrons I shall be always proud, and to such shall be always glad of the honour of owning an obligation. Nor is it a small pleasure to me, that my heart is conscious of none, to certain persons who are in the Opposition, to those characters by which you have been pleased to distinguish my patrons.... As you are pleased to assert, that I have insinuated that all Government is a *Farce*, and perhaps a damn'd one too, I shall quote the lines on which you ground your assertion; and, I hope, then you will be so good as to retract it.

Wolsey's Self, that mighty Minister,
In the full Height and Zenith of his Power,
Amid a Crowd of Sycophants and Slaves,
Was but (perhaps) the Author of a Farce,
Perhaps, a damn'd one too.
(*Eurydice Hiss'd*, *Works*, vol. 11, p. 298)

I am far from asserting that all Government is a *Farce*, but I affirm that, however the very name of power may frighten the vulgar, it will never be honoured by the philosopher, or the man of sense, unless accompany'd with dignity. On the contrary, nothing can be more burlesque than greatness in mean hands....

I shall only make a remark or two, and conclude. First, I have not ridiculed patriotism, but have endeavoured to show the several obstructions to a proper exerting this noble principle; and that corruption alone is equal to all the rest....

Secondly, I must observe, Sir, that if we are not (as you say) to expose evil or weak measures, for fear of informing our neighbours, this argument will extend in its full force to the Press; and I think I remember to have seen it formerly used on that occasion. But it will not hold in either case; for I do not believe foreign ministers to be so weak, as to remain in an entire stupid ignorance of what we are doing; nor do I think, if well considered, a more ridiculous image can enter into the mind of man than that of all the ambassadors of Europe assembling at the Haymarket Playhouse to learn the character of our Ministry.

Lastly, you insinuate, that the same poet, who (you say) now prostitutes *the Muses* (that is, by laughing at Vice and Folly), may hereafter attack future administrations (tho', by the by, I am far from owning that he hath attacked the present). To this, Sir, I must beg leave to say, without any reflection on our present Ministry, that, I believe, there are now amongst those gentlemen who are styled the Opposition, men in genius, learning and knowledge so infinitely superior to the rest of their countrymen, and of integrity so eminent, that should they, *in process of Time*, be in the possession of power, they will be able to triumph over, and trample upon all the ridicule which any Wit or Humour could level at them: For ridicule, like Ward's Pill, passes innocently through a sound Constitution; but when it meets with a complication of foul distempers in a gross corrupt carcase, it is apt to give a terrible shock, to work the poor patient most immoderately; in the course of which working, it is ten to one but he bes—ts his breeches. I am, Sir,

Your humble (tho' not obliged) Servant,
Pasquin
(102–5)

Voltaire

from *Vie de Molière* 1739 (reprinted in Louis Moland (ed.),
Oeuvres Complètes, vol. 23, 1879; extract translated by
C. J. Rawson)

Shadwell's [translation of Molière's *L'Avare*] is generally despised. Mr Fielding, a better poet and more modest, has translated *L'Avare*, and had it performed in London in 1733. He has genuinely added to

it certain beauties of dialogue peculiar to his nation, and the play had
close to thirty performances, a very rare success in London.
(115)

Colley Cibber

from *An Apology for the Life of Mr Colley Cibber*, ch. 8   1740
(B.R.S. Fone (ed.), 1968)

These so tolerated companies gave encouragement to a broken wit,
to collect a fourth company who, for some time, acted plays in the
Haymarket, which house the united Drury Lane comedians had
lately quitted: this enterprising person, I say (whom I do not choose
to name, unless it could be to his advantage or that it were of importance), had sense enough to know that the best plays with bad
actors would turn but to very poor account; and therefore found it
necessary to give the public some pieces of an extraordinary kind,
the poetry of which he conceived ought to be so strong, that the
greatest dunce of an actor could not spoil it. He knew, too, that, as
he was in haste to get money, it would take up less time to be intre-
pidly abusive than decently entertaining; that to draw the mob after
him he must rake the channel and pelt their superiors; that, to show
himself somebody, he must come up to Juvenal's advice and stand
the consequences:

Aude aliquid brevibus Gyaris, et carcere dignum
Si vis esse aliquis . . .
(Juvenal, *Satires*, 1)

Such, then, was the mettlesome modesty he set out with; upon this
principle he produced several frank and free farces, that seemed to
knock all distinctions of mankind on the head: religion, laws, government, priests, judges, and ministers were all laid flat at the feet of this
Herculean satirist! This *Drawcansir* in wit that spared neither friend or
foe! Who, to make his poetical fame immortal, like another Erostra-
tus, set fire to his stage, by writing up to an act of Parliament to
demolish it. I shall not give the particular strokes of his ingenuity a
chance to be remembered by reciting them; it may be enough to say,

in general terms, they were so openly flagrant that the wisdom of the legislature thought it high time to take a proper notice of them. (155–6)

Henry Fielding

from *Shamela* 1741 (Martin C. Battestin (ed.), *Joseph Andrews and Shamela*, 1961)

[From Parson Oliver's prefatory letter to Parson Tickletext]:

And notwithstanding our author's [i.e. Richardson's] professions of modesty, which in my youth I have heard at the beginning of an epilogue, I cannot agree that my daughter should entertain herself with some of his pictures; which I do not expect to be contemplated without emotion, unless by one of my age and temper, who can see the girl lie on her back, with one arm round Mrs Jewkes and the other round the squire, naked in bed, with his hand on her breasts, etc., with as much indifference as I read any other page in the whole novel. . . .

The true name of this wench was Shamela, and not Pamela, as she styles herself. Her father had in his youth the misfortune to appear in no good light at the Old Bailey; he afterwards served in the capacity of a drummer in one of the Scotch regiments in the Dutch service; where being drummed out, he came over to England, and turned informer against several persons on the late Gin Act; and becoming acquainted with an hostler at an inn, where a Scotch gentleman's horses stood, he hath at last by his interest obtained a pretty snug place in the custom-house. Her mother sold oranges in the play-house; and whether she was married to her father or no, I never could learn.

After this short introduction, the rest of her history will appear in the following letters, which I assure you are authentic. (307–8)

[From Letter VI, Shamela to her mother]:

Mrs Jervis and I are just in bed, and the door unlocked; if my master should come – Odsbobs! I hear him just coming in at the door.

You see I write in the present tense, as Parson Williams says. Well, he is in bed between us, we both shamming a sleep; he steals his hand into my bosom, which I, as if in my sleep, press close to me with mine ...

(313)

Anonymous

from *London Magazine*   June 1741 (*Critical Heritage*)

'To the Author of Shamela'

Admired *Pamela*, till *Shamela* shown,
Appear'd in every colour – but her own:
Uncensur'd she remained in borrow'd light,
No nun more chaste, few angels shone so bright.
But now, the idol we no more adore,
Jervice a bawd, and our chaste nymph a w—
Each buxom lass may read poor *Booby's* case,
And charm a *Williams* to supply his place;
Our thoughtless sons for round-eared caps may burn,
And curse *Pamela*, when they've serv'd a turn.
(116)

Henry Fielding

from *Joseph Andrews*   1742 (Martin C. Battestin (ed.),
Joseph Andrews and Shamela, 1961)

Author's Preface

As it is possible the mere English reader may have a different idea of romance with the author of these little volumes, and may consequently expect a kind of entertainment not to be found, nor which was even intended, in the following pages, it may not be improper to premise a few words concerning this kind of writing, which I do not remember to have seen hitherto attempted in our language.

The Epic, as well as the Drama, is divided into tragedy and comedy. Homer, who was the father of this species of poetry, gave us a pattern of both these, though that of the latter kind is entirely lost; which Aristotle tells us, bore the same relation to comedy which his *Iliad* bears to tragedy. And perhaps, that we have no more instances of it among the writers of antiquity, is owing to the loss of this great pattern, which, had it survived, would have found its imitators equally with the other poems of this great original.

And farther, as this poetry may be tragic or comic, I will not scruple to say it may be likewise either in verse or prose: for though it wants one particular, which the critic enumerates in the constituent parts of an epic poem, namely metre; yet, when any kind of writing contains all its other parts, such as fable, action, characters, sentiments, and diction, and is deficient in metre only, it seems, I think, reasonable to refer it to the epic; at least, as no critic hath thought proper to range it under any other head, or to assign it a particular name to itself.

Thus the *Telemachus* of the Archbishop of Cambray appears to me of the epic kind, as well as the *Odyssey* of Homer; indeed, it is much fairer and more reasonable to give it a name common with that species from which it differs only in a single instance, than to confound it with those which it resembles in no other. Such are those voluminous works commonly called Romances, namely, *Clelia*, *Cleopatra*, *Astræa*, *Cassandra*, the *Grand Cyrus*, and innumerable others, which contain, as I apprehend, very little instruction or entertainment.

Now, a comic romance is a comic epic-poem in prose; differing from comedy, as the serious epic from tragedy: its action being more extended and comprehensive; containing a much larger circle of incidents, and introducing a greater variety of characters. It differs from the serious romance in its fable and action, in this; that as in the one these are grave and solemn, so in the other they are light and ridiculous: it differs in its characters by introducing persons of inferior rank, and consequently, of inferior manners, whereas the grave romance sets the highest before us: lastly, in its sentiments and diction, by preserving the ludicrous instead of the sublime. In the diction, I think, burlesque itself may be sometimes admitted; of which many instances will occur in this work, as in the description of the battles, and some other places, not necessary to be pointed out to the classical reader, for whose entertainment those parodies or burlesque imitations are chiefly calculated.

But though we have sometimes admitted this in our diction, we have carefully excluded it from our sentiments and characters; for there it is never properly introduced, unless in writings of the burlesque kind, which this is not intended to be. Indeed, no two species of writing can differ more widely than the comic and the burlesque; for as the latter is ever the exhibition of what is monstrous and unnatural, and where our delight, if we examine it, arises from the surprising absurdity, as in appropriating the manners of the highest to the lowest, or è converso; so in the former, we should ever confine ourselves strictly to nature, from the just imitation of which will flow all the pleasure we can this way convey to a sensible reader. And perhaps there is one reason why a comic writer should of all others be the least excused for deviating from nature, since it may not be always so easy for a serious poet to meet with the great and admirable; but life everywhere furnishes an accurate observer with the ridiculous.

I have hinted this little concerning burlesque, because I have often heard that name given to performances which have been truly of the comic kind, from the author's having sometimes admitted it in his diction only; which, as it is the dress of poetry, doth, like the dress of men, establish characters (the one of the whole poem, and the other of the whole man), in vulgar opinion, beyond any of their greater excellencies: but surely, a certain drollery in style, where the characters and sentiments are perfectly natural, no more constitutes the burlesque, than an empty pomp and dignity of words, where everything else is mean and low, can entitle any performance to the appellation of the true sublime.

And I apprehend my Lord Shaftesbury's opinion of mere burlesque agrees with mine, when he asserts, 'There is no such thing to be found in the writings of the ancients.' But perhaps I have less abhorrence than he professes for it; and that, not because I have had some little success on the stage this way, but rather as it contributes more to exquisite mirth and laughter than any other; and these are probably more wholesome physic for the mind, and conduce better to purge away spleen, melancholy, and ill affections, than is generally imagined. Nay, I will appeal to common observation, whether the same companies are not found more full of good-humour and benevolence, after they have been sweetened for two or three hours with entertainments of this kind, than when soured by a tragedy or a grave lecture.

But to illustrate all this by another science, in which, perhaps, we shall see the distinction more clearly and plainly, let us examine the works of a comic history-painter, with those performances which the Italians call *Caricatura*, where we shall find the true excellence of the former to consist in the exactest copying of nature; insomuch that a judicious eye instantly rejects anything *outré*, any liberty which the painter hath taken with the features of that *alma mater*. Whereas in the *Caricatura* we allow all licence. Its aim is to exhibit monsters, not men; and all distortions and exaggerations whatever are within its proper province.

Now, what *Caricatura* is in painting, burlesque is in writing; and in the same manner the comic writer and painter correlate to each other. And here I shall observe, that, as in the former the painter seems to have the advantage; so it is in the latter infinitely on the side of the writer; for the Monstrous is much easier to paint than describe, and the Ridiculous to describe than paint.

And though perhaps this latter species doth not in either science so strongly affect and agitate the muscles as the other; yet it will be owned, I believe, that a more rational and useful pleasure arises to us from it. He who should call the ingenious Hogarth a burlesque painter, would in my opinion do him very little honour; for sure it is much easier, much less the subject of admiration, to paint a man with a nose, or any other feature, of a preposterous size, or to expose him in some absurd or monstrous attitude, than to express the affections of men on canvas. It hath been thought a vast commendation of a painter, to say his figures *seem to breathe*; but surely it is a much greater and nobler applause, *that they appear to think*.

But to return. The Ridiculous only, as I have before said, falls within my province in the present work. Nor will some explanation of this word be thought impertinent by the reader, if he considers how wonderfully it hath been mistaken, even by writers who have professed it: for to what but such a mistake can we attribute the many attempts to ridicule the blackest villainies, and, what is yet worse, the most dreadful calamities? What could exceed the absurdity of an author, who should write *The Comedy of Nero, with the Merry Incident of Ripping up his Mother's Belly*? or what would give a greater shock to humanity, than an attempt to expose the miseries of poverty and distress to ridicule? And yet, the reader will not want much learning to suggest such instances to himself.

Besides, it may seem remarkable, that Aristotle, who is so fond and free of definitions, hath not thought proper to define the Ridiculous. Indeed, where he tells us it is proper to comedy, he hath remarked that villainy is not its object: but he hath not, as I remember, positively asserted what is. Nor doth the Abbé Bellegarde, who hath writ a treatise on this subject, though he shows us many species of it, once trace it to its fountain.

The only source of the true Ridiculous (as it appears to me) is affectation. But though it arises from one spring only, when we consider the infinite streams into which this one branches, we shall presently cease to admire at the copious field it affords to an observer. Now, affectation proceeds from one of these two causes, vanity or hypocrisy: for as vanity puts us on affecting false characters, in order to purchase applause; so hypocrisy sets us on an endeavour to avoid censure, by concealing our vices under an appearance of their opposite virtues. And though these two causes are often confounded (for there is some difficulty in distinguishing them), yet, as they proceed from very different motives, so they are as clearly distinct in their operations: for indeed, the affectation which arises from vanity is nearer to truth than the other, as it hath not that violent repugnancy of nature to struggle with, which that of the hypocrite hath. It may be likewise noted, that affectation doth not imply an absolute negation of those qualities which are affected; and, therefore, though, when it proceeds from hypocrisy, it be nearly allied to deceit; yet when it comes from vanity only, it partakes of the nature of ostentation: for instance, the affectation of liberality in a vain man differs visibly from the same affectation in the avaricious; for though the vain man is not what he would appear, or hath not the virtue he affects, to the degree he would be thought to have it; yet it sits less awkwardly on him than on the avaricious man, who *is* the very reverse of what he would *seem* to be.

From the discovery of this affectation arises the Ridiculous – which always strikes the reader with surprise and pleasure; and that in a higher and stronger degree when the affectation arises from hypo-crisy, than when from vanity: for to discover anyone to be the exact reverse of what he affects, is more surprising, and consequently more ridiculous, than to find him a little deficient in the quality he desires the reputation of. I might observe that our Ben Jonson, who of all men understood the Ridiculous the best, hath chiefly used the hypocritical affectation.

Now, from affectation only, the misfortunes and calamities of life, or the imperfections of nature, may become the objects of ridi-cule. Surely he hath a very ill-framed mind who can look on ugliness, infirmity, or poverty, as ridiculous in themselves: nor do I believe any man living, who meets a dirty fellow riding through the streets in a cart, is struck with an idea of the Ridiculous from it; but if he should see the same figure descend from his coach and six, or bolt from his chair with his hat under his arm, he would then begin to laugh, and with justice. In the same manner, were we to enter a poor house and behold a wretched family shivering with cold and lan-guishing with hunger, it would not incline us to laughter (at least we must have very diabolical natures if it would); but should we discover there a grate, instead of coals, adorned with flowers, empty plate or china dishes on the sideboard, or any other affectation of riches and finery either on their persons or in their furniture, we might then indeed be excused for ridiculing so fantastical an appear-ance. Much less are natural imperfections the object of derision; but when ugliness aims at the applause of beauty, or lameness endeavours to display agility, it is then that these unfortunate circumstances, which at first moved our compassion, tend only to raise our mirth.

The poet carries this very far:

None are for being what they are in fault,
But for not being what they would be thought.

Where if the metre would suffer the word Ridiculous to close the first line, the thought would be rather more proper. Great vices are the proper objects of our detestation, smaller faults, of our pity; but affectation appears to me the only true source of the Ridiculous.

But perhaps it may be objected to me, that I have against my own rules introduced vices, and of a very black kind, into this work. To which I shall answer: first, that it is very difficult to pursue a series of human actions and keep clear from them. Secondly, that the vices to be found here are rather the accidental consequences of some human frailty or foible, than causes habitually existing in the mind. Thirdly, that they are never set forth as the objects of ridicule, but detestation. Fourthly, that they are never the principal figure at that time on the scene; and lastly, they never produce the intended evil.

Having thus distinguished *Joseph Andrews* from the productions of romance writers on the one hand, and burlesque writers on the other, and given some few very short hints (for I intended no more) of this species of writing, which I have affirmed to be hitherto unattempted in our language; I shall leave to my good-natured reader to apply my piece to my observations, and will detain him no longer than with a word concerning the characters in this work.

And here I solemnly protest, I have no intention to vilify or asperse anyone; for though everything is copied from the book of nature, and scarce a character or action produced which I have not taken from my own observations and experience; yet I have used the utmost care to obscure the persons by such different circumstances, degrees, and colours, that it will be impossible to guess at them with any degree of certainty; and if it ever happens otherwise, it is only where the failure characterized is so minute, that it is a foible only, which the party himself may laugh at as well as any other.

As to the character of Adams, as it is the most glaring in the whole, so I conceive it is not to be found in any book now extant. It is designed a character of perfect simplicity; and as the goodness of his heart will recommend him to the good-natured, so I hope it will excuse me to the gentlemen of his cloth; from whom, while they are worthy of their sacred order, no man can possibly have a greater respect. They will therefore excuse me, notwithstanding the low adventures in which he is engaged, that I have made him a clergy-man; since no other office could have given him so many opportunities of displaying his worthy inclinations.

(7–12)

From Book 3, Chapter 1

Is not such a book as that which records the achievements of the renowned Don Quixote more worthy the name of a history than

even Mariana's [*History of Spain*]? for, whereas the latter is confined
to a particular period of time, and to a particular nation, the former
is the history of the world in general, at least that part which is
polished by laws, arts, and sciences; and of that from the time it was
first polished to this day; nay, and forwards as long as it shall so
remain.

I shall now proceed to apply these observations to the work before
us. . . . I question not but several of my readers will know the lawyer
in the stage-coach the moment they hear his voice. It is likewise odds
but the wit and the prude meet with some of their acquaintance, as
well as all the rest of my characters. To prevent, therefore, any such
malicious applications, I declare here, once for all, I describe not men,
but manners; not an individual, but a species. Perhaps it will be
answered, Are not the characters then taken from life? To which I
answer in the affirmative; nay, I believe I might aver that I have writ
little more than I have seen. The lawyer is not only alive, but hath
been so these four thousand years; and I hope G— will indulge his
life as many yet to come. He hath not indeed confined himself to one
profession, one religion, or one country; but when the first mean
selfish creature appeared upon the human stage, who made self the
centre of the whole creation, would give himself no pain, incur no
danger, advance no money, to assist or preserve his fellow-creatures;
then was our lawyer born; and, whilst such a person as I have
described exists on earth, so long shall he remain upon it. It is, therefore, doing him little honour to imagine he endeavours to mimic
some little obscure fellow, because he happens to resemble him in one
particular feature, or perhaps in his profession; whereas his appearance in the world is calculated for much more general and noble purposes; not to expose one pitiful wretch to the small and contemptible
circle of his acquaintance; but to hold the glass to thousands in their
closets, that they may contemplate their deformity, and endeavour
to reduce it, and thus by suffering private mortification may avoid
public shame. This places the boundary between, and distinguishes
the satirist from the libeller: for the former privately corrects the
fault for the benefit of the person, like a parent; the latter publicly
exposes the person himself, as an example to others, like an executioner.

There are, besides, little circumstances to be considered; as the drapery of a picture, which though fashion varies at different times, the resemblance of the countenance is not by those means diminished. Thus, I believe, we may venture to say Mrs Tow-wouse is coeval with our lawyer: and, though perhaps, during the changes which so long an existence must have passed through, she may in her turn have stood behind the bar at an inn, I will not scruple to affirm she hath likewise in the revolution of ages sat on a throne. In short, where extreme turbulency of temper, avarice, and an insensibility of human misery, with a degree of hypocrisy, have united in a female composition, Mrs Tow-wouse was that woman; and where a good inclination, eclipsed by a poverty of spirit and understanding, hath glimmered forth in a man, that man hath been no other than her sneaking husband.

I shall detain my reader no longer than to give him one caution more of an opposite kind: for, as in most of our particular characters we mean not to lash individuals, but all of the like sort, so, in our general descriptions, we mean not universals, but would be understood with many exceptions: for instance, in our description of high people, we cannot be intended to include such as, whilst they are an honour to their high rank, by a well-guided condescension make their superiority as easy as possible to those whom fortune chiefly hath placed below them. . . . By those high people . . . whom I have described, I mean a set of wretches, who, while they are a disgrace to their ancestors, whose honours and fortunes they inherit . . . have the insolence to treat those with disregard who are at least equal to the founders of their own splendour.

(158–61)

George Cheyne

from a letter to Samuel Richardson   9 March 1742
(A. D. McKillop, *Samuel Richardson*, 1936)

I had Feilding's [sic] wretched performance, for which I thank you. It will entertain none but porters or watermen.
(77)

Thomas Gray

from a letter to Richard West   8 April 1742
(P. Toynbee and L. Whibley (eds.), *Correspondence*, vol. 1, 1935)

I have myself, upon your recommendation, been reading *Joseph Andrews*. The incidents are ill laid and without invention; but the characters have a great deal of nature, which always pleases even in her lowest shapes. Parson Adams is perfectly well; so is Mrs Slipslop, and the story of Wilson; and throughout he shews himself well read in stage-coaches, country squires, inns, and Inns of Court. His reflections upon high people and low people, and misses and masters, are very good. However the exaltedness of some minds (or rather as I shrewdly suspect their insipidity and want of feeling or observation) may make them insensible to these light things (I mean such as characterize and paint nature), yet surely they are as weighty and much more useful than your grave discourses upon the mind, the passions, and what not. Now as the paradisaical pleasures of the Mahometans consist in playing upon the flute and lying with Houris, be mine to read eternal new romances of Marivaux and Crebillon. (191–2)

Henry Fielding

from *A Journey from this World to the Next*, book 1, chapter 8
c. 1742 (*Works*, vol. 2)

He [Shakespeare, in Elysium] was then interrogated concerning some ... ambiguous passages in his works; but he declined any satisfactory answer: saying, if Mr Theobald had not writ about it sufficiently, there were three or four more new editions of his plays coming out, which he hoped would satisfy every one: Concluding, 'I marvel nothing so much as that men will gird themselves at discovering obscure beauties in an author. Certes the greatest and most pregnant beauties are ever the plainest and most evidently striking; and when two meanings of a passage can in the least balance our judgments which to prefer, I hold it matter of un-

questionable certainty, that neither of them is worth a farthing.'
(248)

Elizabeth Carter

from a letter to Catherine Talbot   1 January 1743
(*Critical Heritage*)

[*Joseph Andrews*] contains such a surprising variety of nature, wit, morality, and good sense, as is scarcely to be met with in any one composition, and there is such a spirit of benevolence runs through the whole, as I think renders it peculiarly charming. The author has touched some particular instances of inhumanity which can only be hit in this kind of writing, and I do not remember to have seen observed any where else. . . .

It must surely be a marvellous wrongheadedness and perplexity of understanding that can make any one consider this complete satire as a very immoral thing, and of the most dangerous tendency, and yet I have met with some people who treat it in the most outrageous manner. . . .
(123)

Henry Fielding

from the Preface to *Miscellanies*   1743 (*Works*, vol. 12)

The poetical pieces which compose the first part of the first volume were most of them written when I was very young, and are indeed productions of the heart rather than of the head. If the good-natured reader thinks them tolerable, it will answer my warmest hopes. This branch of writing is what I very little pretend to, and will appear to have been very little my pursuit, since I think (one or two poems excepted) I have here presented my reader with all I could remember, or procure copies of.

I come now . . . to the *History of Jonathan Wild*. . . . My design is not to enter the lists with that excellent historian, who from authentic papers and records, etc., hath already given so satisfactory an account of life and actions of this great man. I have not indeed the least intention to deprecate the veracity and impartiality of that history; nor do I pretend to any of those lights, not having, to my knowledge, ever seen a single paper relating to my hero, save some short memoirs, which about the time of his death were published in certain chronicles called newspapers, the authority of which hath been sometimes questioned, and in the Ordinary of Newgate his account, which generally contains a more particular relation of what the heroes are to suffer in the next world, than of what they did in this.

To confess the truth, my narrative is rather of such actions which he might have performed, or would, or should have performed, than what he really did; and may, in reality, as well suit any other such great man, as the person himself whose name it bears.

A second caution I would give my reader is, that as it is not a very faithful portrait of Jonathan Wild himself, so neither is it intended to represent the features of any other person. Roguery, and not a rogue, is my subject; and as I have been so far from endeavouring to particularize any individual, that I have with my utmost art avoided it; so will any such application be unfair in my reader, especially if he knows much of the great world, since he must then be acquainted, I believe, with more than one on whom he can fix the resemblance.

In the third place, I solemnly protest, I do by no means intend in the character of my hero to represent human nature in general. Such insinuations must be attended with very dreadful conclusions; nor do I see any other tendency they can naturally have, but to encourage and soothe men in their villainies, and to make every well-disposed man disclaim his own species, and curse the hour of his birth into such a society. . . .

But without considering Newgate as no other than human nature with its mask off, which some very shameless writers have done, a thought which no price should purchase me to entertain, I think we may be excused for suspecting, that the splendid palaces of the great are often no other than Newgate with the mask on. Nor do I know anything which can raise an honest man's indignation higher than that the same morals should be in one place attended with all imaginable misery and infamy, and in the other, with the highest luxury and honour. Let any impartial man in his senses be asked, for which of these two places a composition of cruelty, lust, avarice, rapine, insolence, hypocrisy, fraud and treachery, was best fitted; surely his answer must be certain and immediate; and yet I am afraid all these ingredients, glossed over with wealth and a title, have been treated with the highest respect and veneration in the one, while one or two of them have been condemned to the gallows in the other. . . .

Nothing seems to me more preposterous than that, while the way to true honour lies so open and plain, men should seek false by such perverse and rugged paths: that while it is so easy and safe, and truly honourable, to be good, men should wade through difficulty and danger, and real infamy, to be great, or, to use a synonymous word, villains.

Nor hath goodness less advantage in the article of pleasure than of honour over this kind of greatness. The same righteous judge always annexes a bitter anxiety to the purchases of guilt, whilst it adds a double sweetness to the enjoyments of innocence and virtue: for fear, which all the wise agree is the most wretched of human evils, is, in some degree, always attending on the former, and never can in any manner molest the happiness of the latter.

This is the doctrine which I have endeavoured to inculcate in this history, confining myself at the same time within the rules of probability (for, except in one chapter, which is visibly meant as a burlesque on the extravagant accounts of travellers, I believe I have not exceeded it). And though perhaps it sometimes happens, contrary to the instances I have given, that the villain succeeds in his pursuit, and acquires some transitory imperfect honour or pleasure to himself for his iniquity; yet I believe he oftener shares the fate of my hero, and suffers the punishment, without obtaining the reward.

As I believe it is not easy to teach a more useful lesson than this, if I have been able to add the pleasant to it, I might flatter myself with having carried every point.

But perhaps some apology may be required of me, for having used the world greatness to which the world hath affixed such honourable ideas, in so disgraceful and contemptuous a light. Now if the fact be, that the greatness which is commonly worshipped is really of that kind which I have here represented, the fault seems rather to lie in those who have ascribed to it those honours to which it hath not in reality the least claim.

The truth, I apprehend, is, we often confound the ideas of goodness and greatness together, or rather include the former in our idea
of the latter. If this be so, it is surely a great error, and no less than a
mistake of the capacity for the will. In reality, no qualities can be
more distinct: for as it cannot be doubted but that benevolence,
honour, honesty, and charity, make a good man; and that parts,
courage, are the efficient qualities of a great man, so must it be confessed, that the ingredients which compose the former of these
characters bear no analogy to, nor dependence on, those which
constitute the latter. A man may therefore be great without being
good, or good without being great.

However, though the one bear no necessary dependence on the
other, neither is there any absolute repugnancy among them which
may totally prevent their union so that they may, though not of
necessity, assemble in the same mind, as they actually did, and all in
the highest degree, in those of Socrates and Brutus; and perhaps in
some among us. I at least know one to whom Nature could have
added no one great or good quality more than she hath bestowed on
him.

Here then appear three distinct characters; the great, the good, and
the great and good.

The last of these is the true sublime in human nature. That elevation
by which the soul of man, raising and extending itself above the order
of this creation, and brightened with a certain ray of divinity, looks
down on the condition of mortals. This is indeed a glorious object,
on which we can never gaze with too much praise and admiration.
A perfect work! the Iliad of Nature! ravishing and astonishing, and
which at once fills us with love, wonder, and delight.

The second falls greatly short of this perfection, and yet hath its
merit. Our wonder ceases; our delight is lessened, but our love
remains; of which passion, goodness hath always appeared to me the
only true and proper object. On this head I think proper to observe,
that I do not conceive my good man to be absolutely a fool or a
coward; but that he often partakes too little of parts or courage to
have any pretensions to greatness.

Now as to that greatness which is totally devoid of goodness, it
seems to me in nature to resemble the false sublime in poetry; whose
bombast is, by the ignorant and ill-judging vulgar, often mistaken

for solid wit and eloquence, whilst it is in effect the very reverse. Thus pride, ostentation, insolence, cruelty, and every kind of villainy, are often construed into true greatness of mind, in which we always include an idea of goodness.

This bombast greatness then is the character I intend to expose; and the more this prevails in and deceives the world, taking to itself not only riches and power, but often honour, or at least the shadow of it, the more necessary is it to strip the monster of these false colours, and show it in its native deformity: for by suffering vice to possess the reward of virtue, we do a double injury to society, by encouraging the former, and taking away the chief incentive to the latter.

(237–46)

Henry Fielding

from the Preface to Sarah Fielding, *David Simple*, 2nd edn   1744
(*Works*, vol. 16)

I have attempted, in my Preface to *Joseph Andrews*, to prove, that every work of this kind is in its nature a comic epic poem, of which Homer left us a precedent, though it be unhappily lost.

The two great originals of a serious air, which we have derived from that mighty genius, differ principally in the action, which in the *Iliad* is entire and uniform; in the *Odyssey*, is rather a series of actions, all tending to produce one great end. . . .

In the same manner the comic writer may either fix on one action, as the authors of *Le Lutrin*, the *Dunciad*, etc.; or on a series, as Butler in verse, and Cervantes in prose have done.

Of this latter kind is the book now before us, where the fable consists of a series of separate adventures, detached from and independent on each other, yet all tending to one great end; so that those who should object want of unity of action here, may, if they please, or if they dare, fly back with their objection in the face even of the *Odyssey* itself.

This fable hath in it these three difficult ingredients, which will be found on consideration to be always necessary to works of this kind, viz. that the main end or scope be at once amiable, ridiculous, and natural.

If it be said that some of the comic performances I have above mentioned differ in the first of these, and set before us the odious instead of the amiable; I answer, that is far from being one of their perfections; and of this the authors themselves seem so sensible, that they endeavour to deceive the reader by false glosses and colours, and by the help of irony at least to represent the aim and design of their heroes in a favourable and agreeable light.

I might further observe, that as the incidents arising from this fable, though often surprising, are everywhere natural (credibility not being once shocked through the whole), so there is one beauty very apparent, which hath been attributed by the greatest of critics to the greatest of poets, that every episode bears a manifest impression of the principal design, and chiefly turns on the perfection or imperfection of friendship; of which noble passion, from its highest purity to its lowest falsehoods and disguises, this little book is, in my opinion, the most exact model.

As to the characters here described, I shall repeat the saying of one of the greatest men in this age, – 'That they were as wonderfully drawn by the writer, as they were by Nature herself.' There are many strokes . . . which would have shined in the pages of Theophrastus, Horace, or La Bruyère. Nay, there are some touches which I will venture to say might have done honour to the pencil of the immortal Shakespeare himself.

The sentiments are in general extremely delicate; those particularly which regard friendship are, I think, as noble and elevated as I have anywhere met with . . .

The diction I shall say no more of, than as it is the last and lowest perfection in a writer, and one which many of great genius seem to have little regarded; so I must allow my author to have the least merit on this head; . . . but experience and habit will most certainly remove this objection; for a good style, as well as a good hand in writing, is chiefly learned by practice.

(10–12)

P. F. G. Desfontaines

from 'Lettre d'une Dame Angloise', prefixed to his French
translation of *Joseph Andrews*   1744 (English translation of
'Lettre' from *Critical Heritage*)

This novel . . . is the equal here of *Don Quixote*, and is considerably
superior to all of your French novels, especially the novels of this
century and of the most recent times. . . .

The novel that you are going to read is somewhat in the same vein
as your *Roman comique* by Scarron, which is considered to be a masterpiece in England as well as in France. The author is Mr Fielding, one
of our good dramatic authors, who is at his best mainly in the comic
scene. You will judge his skill in this genre by a large number of
features prevalent in his book, and especially by the dialogues, for
which he possesses talent of the highest order. But you will value
most highly the honesty of all his descriptions and of all his expressions, and the wisdom with which he treats a subject which could have
drawn him into licentious descriptions. . . .

The remarkable thing about this work is that, just as *Don Quixote*
is the picture of Spanish customs, the work at hand is the picture of
English customs, which are hardly known in France. . . . This is
certainly not a book of simple pleasures for the crowd: this is a book
of science and of unadorned morality, available to every one; and in
addition it is a book in which one comes to understand how we live
in *England*.

(128–9)

Anonymous

from a review of Desfontaines' translation of
Joseph Andrews, *Bibliothèque Française*   1744 (English translation of
review from *Critical Heritage*)

If this is the portrayal of English customs, we must acknowledge that,
from the chaos we find there, it does little honour to that nation. . . .
(138)

Henry Fielding

from *True Patriot*, no. 22 1 April 1746 (Ioan Williams (ed.),
The Criticism of Henry Fielding, 1970)

As most great inventions have been owing originally to chance, so I
may be said, by mere accident, to have found out the use of an
instrument, which may properly be styled *The Test of Understanding*
or *The Weather-Glass of Wit*: as it shews the degree of heat or coldness in the understanding, with as much certainty as the common
thermometers do that of the atmosphere. And, by the exactest
observations I have been able to make, it appears that the different
degrees of *sense* are ranged according to the ensuing scale, which,
for that reason, I have affix'd to the thermometer:

- Madness
- Wildness
- True wit, or fire
- Vivacity
- Good-sense
- Gravity
- Pertness
- Dullness
- Stupidity, or folly

If any objection should be made to my placing the different degrees
of understanding at equal distances from each other, I must acquaint
the objector, that it did not proceed from my own invention, but
that it was the result of several long and careful experiments, which I
made of the rising and falling of the spirits in my thermometer.
Whenever I read a plain sensible production of any author, I always
observed that the spirits kept exactly to the middle point. If *good-
sense* was mix'd with here and there a lively stroke, they rose to
vivacity. A degree more of heat raises the thermometer to *fire*;
which is always the more laudable quality in an author, the more

steadily and equably it burns. Too great a degree of fire degenerates into *wildness*, or extravagance, which last is but one degree below *madness*, or the raving point. The lower part of the scale points out the different degrees of *coldness* in the understanding: *good-sense*, by a farther degree of cold is condensed into *gravity*; gravity, as appears from my glass, falling just as much short of good-sense as vivacity does of true wit, or fire; and, as they are but one degree distant from each other, this may probably be the reason why the man of *vivacity* is often mistaken for a *wit*, and the grave man for a man of sense. The next degree below *gravity* is *pertness*. This quality of the mind is oftentimes called *wit*; and indeed they appear, by my scale, to be equally distant from good-sense; but with this difference, that as true wit is two degrees above, so pertness is just as many below that point; for the witty writer borders upon extravagance, but the *pert* one is but one degree above being *dull*.

(127–8)

Henry Fielding

from the Preface to Sarah Fielding, *Familiar Letters between the Principal Characters in David Simple, and Some Others*   1747
(*Works*, vol. 16)

But, in reality, this style of conversation is only proper, at least only necessary, to these, which I have called letters of conversation; and is not at all requisite, either to letters of business, which in after-ages make a part of history, or to those on the subject of literature and criticism.

Much less it is adapted to the novel or story writer; for what difference is there, whether a tale is related this or any other way? And sure no one will contend, that the epistolary style is in general the most proper to a novelist, or that it hath been used by the best writers of this kind. . . .

[After recommending Lyttelton's *Persian Letters* for skilful stylistic variegation, Fielding says:] I know not of any essential difference between this and any other way of writing novels, save only, that by making use of letters the writer is freed from the regular beginnings and conclusions of stories, with some other formalities, in which the reader of taste finds no less ease and advantage than the author himself. . . .

Many touches . . . appear to me in these letters [i.e. Sarah Fielding's *Familiar Letters*] which I cannot help thinking as fine as I have ever met with in any of the authors who have made human nature their subject.

As such observations are generally supposed to be the effects of long experience in and much acquaintance with mankind, it may perhaps surprise many to find them in the works of a woman; especially of one, who, to use the common phrase, hath seen so little of the world. . . .

But in reality the knowledge of human nature is not learnt by living in the hurry of the world. True genius, with the help of a little conversation, will be capable of making a vast progress in this learning; and indeed I have observed, there are none who know so little of men as those who are placed in the crowds either of business or pleasure. The truth of the assertion, that pedants in colleges have seldom any share of this knowledge, doth not arise from a defect in the college, but from a defect in the pedant, who would have spent many years at St James's to as little purpose: for daily experience may convince us, that it is possible for a blockhead to see much of the world, and know little of it.

The objection to the sex of the author hardly requires an answer: it will be chiefly advanced by those who derive their opinion of women, very unfairly, from the fine ladies of the age. . . .

In the conduct of women, in that great and important business of their lives, the affair of love, there are mysteries, with which men are perfectly unacquainted: their education being on this head in constraint of, nay, in direct opposition to truth and nature, creates such a constant struggle between nature and habit, truth and hypocrisy, as introduce often much humour into their characters; especially when drawn by sensible writers of their own sex, who are on this subject much more capable than the ablest of ours.

(19–21)

Henry Fielding

from *Jacobite's Journal*, no. 5   26 December 1747
(Ioan Williams (ed.), *The Criticism of Henry Fielding*, 1970)

How charmed am I . . . when I meet with a new production in the region of Fancy, capable of giving me the same delight which I have received from my most favourite authors at my first acquaintance with them. . . .

When I tell you I have lately received this pleasure, you will not want me to inform you that I owe it to the author of *Clarissa*. Such simplicity, such manners, such deep penetration into nature; such power to raise and alarm the passions, few writers, either ancient or modern, have been possessed of. My affections are so strongly engaged, and my fears are so raised, by what I have already read, that I cannot express my eagerness to see the rest. Sure this Mr Richardson is master of all that Art which Horace compares to witchcraft. . . .

With what indignation do I therefore hear the criticisms made on this performance. Clarissa is undutiful; she is too dutiful. She is too cold; she is too fond. She uses her father, mother, uncles, brother, sister, lover, friend, too ill, too well. In short, there is scarce a contradiction in character which I have not heard assigned from different reasons to this poor girl; who is as much the object of compassion as she can be, and as good as she should be described.

Do pray, Sir, now and then lay aside your politics, and take upon you to correct our critics. Advise these snarlers, of both sexes, to improve their heads a little, before they venture to sit in judgement on the merit of an author. I wish likewise before they read any more of this author, they would amend their hearts; for this, I take it, is an axiom: *that a* bad *heart cannot taste the productions of a* good *one.*
(201–2)

An 'Oxford Scholar'

from *The Parallel; or, Pilkington and Phillips Compared*   1748
(cited by Martin C. Battestin, *Notes and Queries*, vol. 213, 1968)

'Well, Sir, if you don't like *Pamela*, what say you to *Joseph Andrews*?'
I told him I looked upon it as one of the best Pieces in the English
language; that it was much superior to Scarron's *Comical Romance*,
and not at all inferior to *Gil Blas*. 'But for all that,' said he, 'it is very
easy writing.' Quite otherwise, returned I; it is, if you please, very
easy reading, it is just, natural, and lively; a fine picture of Human
Nature, and full of great good sense, and true judgement. 'Well
then,' added my dealer in title pages, 'you can write something like
that?' No indeed, unless I transcribe it.
(451)

Henry Fielding

Letter to Samuel Richardson   15 October 1748 (*Yale Review*,
vol. 38, 1948)

Dear Sir,
I have read over your fifth volume. In all the accounts which Loveless
gives of the transactions at Hampstead, you preserve the same vein
of humour which hath run through the preceding volumes. The
new characters you introduce are natural and entertaining, and there
is much of the true comic force in the Widow Bevis. I have seen her
often, and I promise you, you have drawn her with great exactness.
The character of Loveless is heightened with great judgement. His
former admirers must lose all regard for him on his perseverance,
and as this regard ceases, compassion for Clarissa rises in the same
proportion. Hence we are admirably prepared for what is to follow
– shall I tell you? Can I tell you what I think of the latter part of your
volume? Let the overflowings of a heart which you have filled
brim full speak for me.
    When Clarissa returns to her lodgings at St Clairs the alarm
begins, and here my heart begins its narrative. I am shocked; my

terrors ar[e ra]ised, and I have the utmost apprehensions for the poor betrayed creature – but when I see her enter with the letter in her hand, and after some natural effects of despair, clasping her arms about the knees of the villain, call him her Dear Lovelace, desirous and yet unable to implore his protection or rather his mercy; I then melt into compassion, and find what is called an effeminate relief for my terror, to continue to the end of the scene. When I read the next letter I am thunderstruck; nor can many lines explain what I feel from two.

What I shall [sic] say of holding up the licence? I will say a finer picture was never imagined. He must be a glorious painter who can do it justice on canvas, and a most wretched one indeed who could not do much on such a subject. The circumstance of the fragments is great and terrible; but her [Clarissa's] letter to Lovelace is beyond any thing I have ever read. God forbid that the man who reads this with dry eyes should be alone with my daughter when she hath no assistance within call. Here my terror ends and my grief begins which the cause of all my tumultuous passions soon changes into raptures of admiration and astonishment by a behaviour the most elevated I can possibly conceive, and what is at the same time most gentle and most natural. This scene I have heard hath been often objected to. It is well for the critic that my heart is now writing and not my head. During the continuance of this volume my compassion is often moved but I think my admiration more. If I had received no hint or information of what is to succeed I should perceive you paving the way to load our admiration of your heroine to the highest pitch, as you have before with wonderful art prepared us for both terror and compassion on her account. This last seems to come from the head. Here then I will end: for I assure you nothing but my heart can force me to say half of what I think of *the* Book. And yet what hinders me? I cannot be suspected of flattery. I know the value of that too much to throw it away, where I have no obligation, and where I expect no reward. And sure the world will not suppose me inclined to flatter one whom they will suppose me to hate if the[y] will be pleased to recollect that we are rivals for that coy Mrs Fame. Believe me however if your Clarissa had not engaged my affections more than this Mrs all your art and all your nature had not been able to extract a single tear: for as to this Mrs I have ravished her long ago, and live in a settled cohabitation with her in defiance of that public voice which is supposed to be her guardian, and to have alone the power of giving her away. To explain this riddle. It is not that I am less but more addicted to vanity than others; so much that I can wrap my self up as warmly in my own vanity, as the ancient could involve himself in his virtue. If I have any merit I certainly know it and if the world will not allow it me, I will allow it my self. I would not have you think (I might say know) me *to be* so dishonest as to assert that I despise fame; but this I solemnly aver that I love her as coldly, as most of us do heaven, so that I will sacrifice nothing to the pursuit of her. Much less would I bind my self, as all her passionate admirers do, to harbour in my bosom that monster Envy which of all beings either real or imaginary I most heartily and sincerely abhor. You will begin to think I believe, that I want not much external commendation. I will conclude then with assuring you, that I heartily wish you success; that I sincerely think you in the highest manner deserve it; and that if you have it not, it it [*sic*] would be in me unpardonable presumption to hope for success, and at the same time almost contemptible humility [not?] to desire it.

I am, Dear Sir, yours most affectionately Hen. Ffielding

I beg you to send me immediately the two remaining volumes. (304–6)

Anonymous

'Epitaph' on Fielding's *Jacobite's Journal* and its pseudonymous author, John Trottplaid, in *Old England* 20 November 1748 (*Critical Heritage*)

   Beneath this stone,
    Lies *Trotplaid John*
His length of chin and nose;
    His crazy brain,
    Unhumourous vein
In verse and eke in prose.
    Some plays he wrote,
    Sans wit or plot,

Adventures of inferiors!
  Which, with his lives
    Of *rogues* and *thieves*,
Supply the town's posteriors.
  But ah, alack! He broke his back,
When politics he tried:
  For like a —
  He play'd his part,
Cracked loudly, stunk, and died.
(146)

Henry Fielding

from *Tom Jones*   1749 (R. P. C. Mutter (ed.), 1966)

From Dedication to Lyttelton

I declare, that to recommend goodness and innocence hath been my sincere endeavour in this history. This honest purpose . . . is likeliest to be attained in books of this kind; for an example is a kind of picture, in which virtue becomes as it were an object of sight, and strikes us with an idea of that loveliness, which Plato asserts there is in her naked charms.

Besides displaying that beauty of virtue which may attract the admiration of mankind, I have attempted to engage a stronger motive to human action in her favour, by convincing men, that their true interest directs them to a pursuit of her. For this purpose I have shewn, that no acquisitions of guilt can compensate the loss of that solid inward comfort of mind, which is the sure companion of innocence and virtue; nor can in the least balance the evil of that horror and anxiety which, in their room, guilt introduces into our bosoms. And again, that as these acquisitions are in themselves generally worthless, so are the means to attain them not only base and infamous, but at best incertain, and always full of danger. Lastly, I have endeavoured strongly to inculcate, that virtue and innocence can scarce ever be injured but by indiscretion; and that it is this alone which often betrays them into the snares that deceit and villainy spread for them. A moral which I have the more industriously laboured, as the teaching it is, of all others, the likeliest to be attended with success; since, I believe, it is much easier to make good men wise, than to make bad men good.

For these purposes I have employed all the wit and humour of which I am master in the following history; wherein I have endeavoured to laugh mankind out of their favourite follies and vices. (37–8)

From Book 1, Chapter 1
The Introduction to the Work, or Bill of Fare to the Feast

... The provision ... which we have here made is no other than Human Nature. Nor do I fear that my sensible reader, though most luxurious in his taste, will start, cavil, or be offended, because I have named but one article ... in Human Nature, tho' here collected under one general name, is such prodigious variety, that a cook will have sooner gone through all the several species of animal and vegetable food in the world, than an author will be able to exhaust so extensive a subject.

An objection may perhaps be apprehended from the more delicate, that this dish is too common and vulgar; for what else is the subject of all the romances, novels, plays and poems, with which the stalls abound. Many exquisite viands might be rejected by the epicure, if it was a sufficient cause for his contemning of them as common and vulgar, that something was to be found in the most paultry alleys under the same name. In reality, true nature is as difficult to be met with in authors, as the Bayonne ham or Bologna sausage is to be found in the shops.

But the whole, to continue the same metaphor, consists in the cookery of the author; for, as Mr Pope tells us,

True wit is nature to advantage drest,
What oft' was thought, but ne'er so well exprest.

... the excellence of the mental entertainment consists less in the subject, than in the author's skill in well dressing it up. How pleased therefore will the reader be to find, that we have, in the following work, adhered closely to one of the highest principles of the best cook which the present age, or perhaps that of Heliogabalus, hath produced.

This great man, as is well known to all polite lovers of eating, begins at first by setting plain things before his hungry guests, rising afterwards by degrees, as their stomachs may be supposed to decrease, to the very quintessence of sauce and spices. In like manner, we shall represent Human Nature at first to the keen appetite of our reader, in that more plain and simple manner in which it is found in the country, and shall hereafter hash and ragoo it with all the high French and Italian seasoning of affectation and vice which courts and cities afford. By these means, we doubt not but our reader may be rendered desirous to read on for ever. . . .

(51–3)

From Book 2, Chapter 1
Shewing what Kind of a History this is; what it is like, and what it is not like

Tho' we have properly enough entitled this our work, a history, and not a life; nor an apology for a life, as is more in fashion; yet we intend in it rather to pursue the method of those writers, who profess to disclose the revolutions of countries, than to imitate the painful and voluminous historian, who, to preserve the regularity of his series, thinks himself obliged to fill up as much paper with the detail of months and years in which nothing remarkable happened, as he employs upon those notable æras when the greatest scenes have been transacted on the human stage.

Such histories as these do, in reality, very much resemble a newspaper, which consists of just the same number of words, whether there be any news in it or not. . . .

Now it is our purpose in the ensuing pages, to pursue a contrary method. When any extraordinary scene presents itself (as we trust will often be the case), we shall spare no pains nor paper to open it at large to our reader; but if whole years should pass without producing anything worthy his notice, we shall not be afraid of a chasm in our history; but shall hasten on to matters of consequence, and leave such periods of time totally unobserved. . . .

My reader then is not to be surprised, if, in the course of this work, he shall find some chapters very short, and others altogether as long; some that contain only the time of a single day, and others that comprise years; in a word, if my history sometimes seems to stand still, and sometimes to fly. For all which I shall not look on myself as accountable to any court of critical jurisdiction whatever: for as I am, in reality, the founder of a new province of writing, so I am at liberty to make what laws I please therein. And these laws, my readers, whom I consider as my subjects, are bound to believe in and to obey; with which that they may readily and chearfully comply, I do hereby assure them, that I shall principally regard their ease and advantage in all such institutions: for I do not, like a *jure divino* tyrant, imagine that they are my slaves, or my commodity. I am, indeed, set over them for their own good only, and was created for their use, and not they for mine. Nor do I doubt, while I make their interest the great rule of my writings, they will unanimously concur in supporting my dignity, and in rendering me all the honour I shall deserve or desire. (87–9)

From Book 3, Chapter 1
Containing little or nothing

The reader will be pleased to remember, that, at the beginning of the second book of this history, we gave him a hint of our intention to pass over several large periods of time, in which nothing happened worthy of being recorded in a chronicle of this kind.

In so doing, we do not only consult our own dignity and ease, but the good and advantage of the reader: for besides, that, by these means, we prevent him from throwing away his time, in reading without either pleasure or emolument, we give him, at all such seasons, an opportunity of employing that wonderful sagacity, of which he is master, by filling up these vacant spaces of time with his own conjectures; for which purpose, we have taken care to qualify him in the preceding pages.

For instance, what reader but knows that Mr Allworthy felt, at first, for the loss of his friend, those emotions of grief, which, on such occasions, enter into all men whose hearts are not composed of flint, or their heads of as solid materials? Again, what reader doth not know that philosophy and religion, in time, moderated, and at last extinguished this grief?
(121)

From Book 3, Chapter 4

I would not willingly give offence to any, especially to men who are warm in the cause of virtue or religion. . . .

On the contrary, it is with a view to their service that I have taken upon me to record the lives and actions of two of their false and pretended champions [Thwackum and Square]. A treacherous friend is the most dangerous enemy; and I will say boldly, that both religion and virtue have received more real discredit from hypocrites, than the wittiest profligates or infidels could ever cast upon them. . . .

Indeed, I doubt not but this ridicule will in general be allowed; my chief apprehension is, as many true and just sentiments often came from the mouths of these persons, lest the whole should be taken together, and I should be conceived to ridicule all alike. Now the reader will be pleased to consider, that as neither of these men were fools, they could not be supposed to have holden none but wrong principles, and to have uttered nothing but absurdities; what injustice, therefore, must I have done to their characters, had I selected only what was bad, and how horribly wretched and maimed must their arguments have appeared!

Upon the whole, it is not religion or virtue, but the want of them which is here exposed. Had not Thwackum too much neglected virtue, and Square religion, in the composition of their several systems; and had not both utterly discarded all natural goodness of heart, they had never been represented as the objects of derision in this history. . . .

(130–31)

From Book 4, Chapter 1

We have taken every occasion of interspersing through the whole sundry similes, descriptions, and other kind of poetical embellishments. These are, indeed, designed to supply the place of the said ale, and to refresh the mind, whenever those slumbers which in a long work are apt to invade the reader as well as the writer, shall begin to creep upon him. Without interruptions of this kind, the best narrative of plain matter of fact must overpower every reader; for nothing but the everlasting watchfulness, which Homer hath ascribed to Jove himself, can be proof against a newspaper of many volumes.

We shall leave to the reader to determine with what judgement we have chosen the several occasions for inserting these ornamental parts of our work. Surely it will be allowed that none could be more proper than the present; where we are about to introduce a considerable character on the scene; no less, indeed, than the heroine of this heroic, historical prosaic poem. Here, therefore, we have thought proper to prepare the mind of the reader for her reception, by filling it with every pleasing image, which we can draw from the face of nature. And for this method we plead many precedents. First, this is an art well known to, and much practised by, our tragic poets; who seldom fail to prepare their audience for the reception of their principal characters.

Thus the hero is always introduced with a flourish of drums and trumpets . . . [and] generally ushered on the stage by a large troop of half a dozen scene-shifters. . . .

But there is one instance which comes exactly up to my purpose. This is the custom of sending on a basket-woman, who is to precede the pomp at a coronation, and to strew the stage with flowers, before the great personages begin their procession. The antients would certainly have invoked the goddess Flora for this purpose, and it would have been no difficulty for their priests or politicians to have persuaded the people of the real presence of the deity, though a plain mortal had personated her, and performed her office. But we have no such design of imposing on our reader, and therefore those who object to the heathen theology, may, if they please, change our goddess into the above-mentioned basket-woman. Our intention, in short, is to introduce our heroine with the utmost solemnity in our power, with an elevation of stile, and all other circumstances proper to raise the veneration of our reader. . . .

And now, without any further preface, we proceed to our next chapter.

Book, 4 Chapter 2
A short Hint of what we can do in the Sublime, and a Description of Miss Sophia Western

Hushed be every ruder breath. May the heathen ruler of the winds confine in iron chains the boisterous limbs of noisy Boreas . . . [there

follows a protracted elaboration of mock-grandiloquence, leading to the famous and in itself unrhetorical portrait of Sophia: 'Sophia . . . was a middle-sized woman; but rather inclining to tall.'].
(151–3)

Chapter Heading to Book 4, Chapter 8
A Battle sung by the Muse in the Homerican Stile, and which none but the classical Reader can taste
(172)

From Book 5, Chapter 1
Of the Serious in Writing, and for what Purpose it is introduced

Peradventure there may be no parts in this prodigious work which will give the reader less pleasure in the perusing, than those which have given the author the greatest pains in composing. Among these, probably, may be reckoned those initial essays which we have pre-fixed to the historical matter contained in every book; and which we have determined to be essentially necessary to this kind of writing, of which we have set ourselves at the head.

For this our determination we do not hold ourselves strictly bound to assign any reason; it being abundantly sufficient that we have laid it down as a rule, necessary to be observed in all prosai-comi-epic writing. Who ever demanded the reasons of that nice unity of time or place which is now established to be so essential to dramatick poetry? . . . Or hath anyone living attempted to explain, what the modern judges of our theatres mean by that word *low*; by which they have happily succeeded in banishing all humour from the stage, and have made the theatre as dull as a drawing-room? . . .

Now, in reality, the world have paid too great a compliment to critics, and have imagined them men of much greater profundity than they really are. From this complaisance, the critics have been emboldened to assume a dictatorial power, and have so far succeeded, that they are now become the masters, and have the assurance to give laws to those authors, from whose predecessors they originally received them. . . .

To these encroachments, time and ignorance, the two great

supporters of imposture, gave authority; and thus, many rules for good writing have been established, which have not the least foundation in truth or nature; and which commonly serve for no other purpose than to curb and restrain genius, in the same manner as it would have restrained the dancing-master, had the many excellent treatises on that art, laid it down as an essential rule, that every man must dance in chains.

To avoid, therefore, all imputation of laying down a rule for posterity, founded only on the authority of *ipse dixit*; for which, to say the truth, we have not the profoundest veneration, we shall here waive the privilege above contended for, and proceed to lay before the reader, the reasons which have induced us, to intersperse these several digressive essays, in the course of this work.

And here we shall of necessity be led to open a new vein of knowlege, which, if it hath been discovered, hath not, to our remembrance, been wrought on by any antient or modern writer. This vein is no other than that of contrast, which runs through all the works of the creation, and may, probably, have a large share in constituting in us the idea of all beauty, as well natural as artificial: for what demonstrates the beauty and excellence of anything, but its reverse? . . .

A great genius among us, will illustrate this matter fully. . . . I mean here the inventor of that most exquisite entertainment, called the English pantomime.

This entertainment consisted of two parts, which the inventor distinguished by the names of *the serious* and *the comic*. The serious exhibited a certain number of heathen gods and heroes, who were certainly the worst and dullest company into which an audience was ever introduced; and (which was a secret known to few) were actually intended so to be, in order to contrast the *comic* part of the entertainment, and to display the tricks of Harlequin to the better advantage.

This was, perhaps, no very civil use of such personages; but the contrivance was, nevertheless, ingenious enough, and had its effect. And this will now plainly appear, if instead of *serious* and *comic*, we supply the words *duller* and *dullest*; for the *comic* was certainly duller than anything before shewn on the stage, and could only be set off by that superlative degree of dulness, which composed the serious. So intolerably serious, indeed, were these gods and heroes, that Harlequin (though the English gentleman of that name is not at all related to the French family, for he is of a much more serious disposition) was always welcome on the stage, as he relieved the audience from worse company.

Judicious writers have always practised this art of contrast, with great success. . . .

To say the truth, these soporific parts are so many scenes of *serious* artfully interwoven, in order to contrast and set off the rest; and this is the true meaning of a late facetious writer, who told the public, that whenever he was dull, they might be assured there was a design in it.

In this light then, or rather in this darkness, I would have the reader to consider these initial essays. And after this warning, if he shall be of opinion, that he can find enough of serious in other parts of this history, he may pass over these, in which we profess to be laboriously dull, and begin the following books, at the second chapter.

(199–202)

Book 6, Chapter 1
Of Love

In our last book we have been obliged to deal pretty much with the passion of love; and, in our succeeding book, shall be forced to handle this subject still more largely. It may not, therefore, in this place, be improper to apply ourselves to the examination of that modern doctrine, which certain philosophers, among many other wonderful discoveries, pretend to have found out, that there is no such passion in the human breast.

Whether these philosophers be the same with that surprizing sect, who are honourably mentioned by the late Dr Swift; as having, by the mere force of genius alone, without the least assistance of any kind of learning, or even reading, discovered that profound and invaluable secret, that there was no God: or whether they are not rather the same with those who, some years since, very much alarmed the world, by shewing that there were no such things as virtue or goodness really existing in human nature, and who deduced our best actions from pride, I will not here presume to determine. In reality,

I am inclined to suspect, that all these several finders of truth are the very identical men, who are by others called the *finders of gold*. The method used in both these searches after truth and after gold, being indeed one and the same; viz. the searching, rummaging and examining into a nasty place; indeed, in the former instances, into the nastiest of all places, a bad mind.

But though, in this particular, and perhaps in their success, the truth-finder, and the gold-finder, may very properly be compared together; yet in modesty, surely, there can be no comparison between the two; for who ever heard of a gold-finder that had the impudence or folly to assert, from the ill success of his search, that there was no such thing as gold in the world? Whereas the truth-finder, having raked out that *jakes* his own mind, and being there capable of tracing no ray of divinity, nor anything virtuous, or good, or lovely, or loving, very fairly honestly, and logically concludes, that no such things exist in the whole creation.

To avoid, however, all contention, if possible, with these philosophers, if they will be called so; and to shew our own disposition to accommodate matters peaceably between us, we shall here make them some concessions, which may possibly put an end to the dispute.

First, we will grant that many minds, and perhaps those of the philosophers, are entirely free from the least traces of such a passion.

Secondly, that what is commonly called love, namely, the desire of satisfying a voracious appetite with a certain quantity of delicate white human flesh, is by no means that passion for which I here contend. This is indeed more properly hunger; and as no glutton is ashamed to apply the word love to his appetite, and to say he *loves* such and such dishes; so may the lover of this kind, with equal propriety say, he *hungers* after such and such women.

Thirdly, I will grant, which I believe will be a most acceptable concession, that this love for which I am an advocate, though it satisfies itself in a much more delicate manner, doth nevertheless seek its own satisfaction as much as the grossest of all our appetites.

And, lastly, that this love when it operates towards one of a different sex, is very apt, towards its complete gratification, to call in the aid of that hunger which I have mentioned above; and which it is so far from abating, that it heightens all its delights to a degree scarce imaginable by those who have never been susceptible of any other emotions, than what have proceeded from appetite alone.

In return to all these concessions, I desire of the philosophers to grant, that there is in some (I believe in many) human breasts, a kind and benevolent disposition, which is gratified by contributing to the happiness of others. That in this gratification alone, as in friendship, in parental and filial affection, and indeed in general philanthropy, there is a great and exquisite delight. That if we will not call such disposition love, we have no name for it. That though the pleasures arising from such pure love may be heightened and sweetened by the assistance of amorous desires, yet the former can subsist alone, nor are they destroyed by the intervention of the latter. Lastly, that esteem and gratitude are the proper motives to love, as youth and beauty are to desire; and therefore though such desire may naturally cease, when age or sickness overtake its object, yet these can have no effect on love, nor ever shake or remove from a good mind, that sensation or passion which hath gratitude and esteem for its basis.

To deny the existence of a passion of which we often see manifest instances, seems to be very strange and absurd; and can indeed proceed only from that self-admonition which we have mentioned above: but how unfair is this? Doth the man who recognizes in his own heart no traces of avarice or ambition, conclude therefore that there are no such passions in human nature? Why will we not modestly observe the same rule in judging of the good, as well as the evil of others? Or why, in any case, will we, as Shakespeare phrases it, 'put the world in our own person'?

Predominant vanity is, I am afraid, too much concerned here. This is one instance of that adulation which we bestow on our own minds, and this almost universally. For there is scarce any man, how much soever he may despise the character of a flatterer, but will condescend in the meanest manner to flatter himself.

To those, therefore, I apply for the truth of the above observations, whose minds can bear testimony to what I have advanced.

Examine your heart, my good reader, and resolve whether you do believe these matters with me. If you do, you may now proceed to their exemplification in the following pages; if you do not, you have, I assure you, already read more than you have understood: and it would be wiser to pursue your business, or your pleasures (such as they are) than to throw away any more of your time in reading what you can neither taste nor comprehend. To treat of the effects of love to you, must be as absurd as to discourse on colours to a man born blind; since possibly your idea of love may be as absurd as that which we are told such blind man once entertained of the colour red: that colour seemed to him to be very much like the sound of a trumpet; and love probably may, in your opinion, very greatly resemble a dish of soup, or a sirloin of roast-beef.

(251–3)

From Book 8, Chapter 1

I think, it may very reasonably be required of every writer, that he keeps within the bounds of possibility; and still remembers that what it is not possible for man to perform, it is scarce possible for man to believe he did perform. This conviction, perhaps, gave birth to many stories of the ancient heathen deities (for most of them are of poetical original). The poet, being desirous to indulge a wanton and extra-vagant imagination, took refuge in that power, of the extent of which his readers were no judges, or rather which they imagined to be in-finite, and consequently they could not be shocked at any prodigies related of it. This hath been strongly urged in defence of Homer's miracles; and it is, perhaps, a defence; not, as Mr Pope would have it, because Ulysses told a set of foolish lies to the Phaeacians, who were a very dull nation; but because the poet himself wrote to heathens, to whom poetical fables were articles of faith. . . . I wish . . . with all my heart, that Homer could have known the rule prescribed by Horace, to introduce supernatural agents as seldom as possible. We should not then have seen his gods coming on trivial errands, and often behaving themselves so as not only to forfeit all title to respect, but to become the objects of scorn and derision. A conduct which must have shocked the credulity of a pious and sagacious heathen. . . .

But I have rested too long on a doctrine which can be of no use to a Christian writer: for as he cannot introduce into his works any of that heavenly host which make a part of his creed; so is it horrid puerility to search the heathen theology for any of those deities who have been long since dethroned from their immortality. Lord Shaftesbury observes, that nothing is more cold than the invocation of a muse by a modern; he might have added that nothing can be more absurd. . . .

The only supernatural agents which can in any manner be allowed to us moderns are ghosts; but of these I would advise an author to be extremely sparing. . . .

Nor is possibility alone sufficient to justify us, we must keep likewise within the rules of probability. It is, I think, the opinion of Aristotle; or if not, it is the opinion of some wise man, whose authority will be as weighty, when it is as old; 'that it is no excuse for a poet who relates what is incredible, that the thing related is really matter of fact.' This may perhaps be allowed true with regard to poetry, but it may be thought impracticable to extend it to the historian: for he is obliged to record matters as he finds them; though they may be of so extraordinary a nature as will require no small degree of historical faith to swallow them. Such was the successless armament of Xerxes, described by Herodotus, or . . . the victory of Agincourt obtained by Harry the Fifth. . . .

Such facts, however, as they occur in the thread of the story; nay, indeed, as they constitute the essential parts of it, the historian is not only justifiable in recording as they really happened; but indeed would be unpardonable, should he omit or alter them. But there are other facts not of such consequence nor so necessary, which tho' ever so well attested, may nevertheless be sacrificed to oblivion in complaisance to the scepticism of a reader. . . .

To say the truth, if the historian will confine himself to what really happened, and utterly reject any circumstance, which, tho' never so well attested, he must be well assured is false, he will sometimes fall into the marvellous, but never into the incredible. He will often raise the wonder and surprize of his reader, but never that incredulous hatred mentioned by Horace. It is by falling into fiction therefore, that we generally offend against this rule, of deserting probability, which the historian seldom if ever quits, till he forsakes his character, and commences a writer of romance. In this, however, those historians who relate publick transactions have the advantage of us who confine ourselves to scenes of private life. The credit of the former is by common notoriety supported for a long time; and public records, with the concurrent testimony of many authors, bear evidence to their truth in future ages. Thus a Trajan and an Antoninus, a Nero and a Caligula, have all met with the belief of posterity; and no one doubts but that men so very good, and so very bad, were once the masters of mankind.

But we who deal in private characters, who search into the most retired recesses, and draw forth examples of virtue and vice, from holes and corners of the world, are in a more dangerous situation. As we have no publick notoriety, no concurrent testimony, no records to support and corroborate what we deliver, it becomes us not only to keep within the limits of possibility, but of probability too; and this more especially in painting what is greatly good and amiable. Knavery and folly, though never so exorbitant, will more easily meet with assent; for ill-nature adds great support and strength to faith. . . .

In the last place, the actions should be such as may not only be within the compass of human agency, and which human agents may probably be supposed to do; but they should be likely for the very actors and characters themselves to have performed: for what may be only wonderful and surprising in one man, may become improbable, or indeed impossible, when related of another.

This last requisite is what the dramatic critics call conservation of character, and it requires a very extraordinary degree of judgement, and a most exact knowledge of human nature.

It is admirably remarked by a most excellent writer, that zeal can no more hurry a man to act in direct opposition to itself, than a rapid stream can carry a boat against its own current. I will venture to say, that for a man to act in direct contradiction to the dictates of nature, is, if not impossible, as improbable and as miraculous as anything which can well be conceived. Should the best parts of the story of M. Antoninus be ascribed to Nero, or should the worst incidents of Nero's life be imputed to Antoninus, what would be more shocking to belief than either instance; whereas both these being related of their proper agent, constitute the truly marvellous. -

Our modern authors of comedy have fallen almost universally into the error here hinted at: their heroes generally are notorious rogues, and their heroines abandoned jades, during the first four acts; but in the fifth, the former become very worthy gentlemen, and the latter, women of virtue and discretion: nor is the writer often so kind as to give himself the least trouble, to reconcile or account for this monstrous change and incongruity. There is, indeed, no other reason to be assigned for it, than because the play is drawing to a conclusion; as if it was no less natural in a rogue to repent in the last act of a play, than in the last of his life; which we perceive to be generally the case at Tyburn, a place which might, indeed, close the scene of some comedies with much propriety, as the heroes in these are most commonly eminent for those very talents which not only bring men to the gallows, but enable them to make an heroic figure when they are there. . . .

For tho' every good author will confine himself within the bounds of probability, it is by no means necessary that his characters, or his incidents, should be trite, common, or vulgar; such as happen in every street, or in every house, or which may be met with in the home articles of a newspaper. Nor must he be inhibited from shewing many persons and things, which may possibly have never fallen within the knowledge of great part of his readers. If the writer strictly observes the rules above-mentioned, he hath discharged his part; and is then intitled to some faith from his reader, who is indeed guilty of critical infidelity if he disbelieves him. For want of a portion of such faith, I remember the character of a young lady of quality, which was condemned on the stage for being unnatural, by the unanimous voice of a very large assembly of clerks and apprentices; tho' it had the previous suffrages of many ladies of the first rank; one of whom, very eminent for her understanding, declared it was the picture of half the young people of her acquaintance. (361–7)

From Book 9, Chapter 1

I shall here venture to mention some qualifications, every one of which are in a pretty high degree necessary to this order of historians.

The first is genius, without a rich vein of which, no study, says Horace, can avail us. By genius I would understand that power, or rather those powers of the mind, which are capable of penetrating into all things within our reach and knowledge, and of distinguishing their essential differences. These are no other than invention and judgement; and they are both called by the collective name of genius, as they are of those gifts of nature which we bring with us into the world. Concerning each of which many seem to have fallen into very great errors: for by invention, I believe, is generally understood a creative faculty; which would indeed prove most romance-writers to have the highest pretensions to it; whereas by invention is really meant no more (and so the word signifies) than discovery, or finding out; or to explain it at large, a quick and sagacious penetration into the true essence of all the objects of our contemplation. This, I think, can rarely exist without the concomitancy of judgement: for how we can be said to have discovered the true essence of two things, without discerning their difference, seems to me hard to conceive; now this last is the undisputed province of judgement, and yet some few men of wit have agreed with all the dull fellows in the world, in representing these two to have been seldom or never the property of one and the same person.

But tho' they should be so, they are not sufficient for our purpose without a good share of learning; for which I could again cite the authority of Horace, and of many others, if any was necessary to prove that tools are of no service to a workman, when they are not sharpened by art, or when he wants rules to direct him in his work, or hath no matter to work upon. All these uses are supplied by learning: for nature can only furnish us with capacity, or, as I have chose to illustrate it, with the tools of our profession; learning must fit them for use, must direct them in it; and lastly, must contribute, part at least, of the materials. A competent knowledge of history and of the *belles lettres*, is here absolutely necessary; and without this share of knowledge at least, to affect the character of an historian, is as vain as to endeavour at building a house without timber or mortar, or brick or stone. Homer and Milton, who, though they added the ornament of numbers to their works, were both historians of our order, were masters of all the learning of their times.

Again, there is another sort of knowledge beyond the power of learning to bestow, and this is to be had by conversation. So necessary is this to the understanding the characters of men, that none are more ignorant of them than those learned pedants, whose lives have been entirely consumed in colleges, and among books: for however exquisitely human nature may have been described by writers, the true practical system can only be learnt in the world. . . .

Now this conversation in our historian must be universal, that is, with all ranks and degrees of men: for the knowledge of what is called high-life, will not instruct him in low, nor *e converso*, will his being acquainted with the inferior part of mankind, teach him the manners of the superior. And though it may be thought that the knowledge of either may sufficiently enable him to describe at least that in which he hath been conversant; yet he will even here fall greatly short of perfection: for the follies of either rank do in reality illustrate each other. For instance, the affectation of high-life appears more glaring and ridiculous from the simplicity of the low; and again, the rudeness and barbarity of this latter, strikes with much stronger ideas of absurdity, when contrasted with, and opposed to the politeness which controuls the former. Besides, to say the truth, the manners of our historian will be improved by both these conversations: for in the one he will easily find examples of plainness, honesty, and sincerity; in the other of refinement, elegance, and a liberality of spirit: which last quality I myself have scarce ever seen in men of low birth and education.

Nor will all the qualities I have hitherto given my historian avail him, unless he have what is generally meant by a good heart, and be capable of feeling. The author who will make me weep, says Horace, must first weep himself. In reality, no man can paint a distress well, which he doth not feel while he is painting it; nor do I doubt, but that the most pathetic and affecting scenes have been writ with tears. In the same manner it is with the ridiculous. I am convinced I never make my reader laugh heartily, but where I have laughed before him; unless it should happen at any time, that instead of laughing with me, he should be inclined to laugh at me. Perhaps this may have been the case at some passages in this chapter, from which apprehension I will here put an end to it.

(437–9)

From Book 10, Chapter 1

Reader, it is impossible we should know what sort of person thou wilt be: for, perhaps, thou may'st be as learned in human nature as Shakespear himself was, and, perhaps, thou may'st be no wiser than some of his editors. Now lest this latter should be the case, we think proper, before we go any farther together, to give thee a few whole-some admonitions; that thou may'st not as grossly misunderstand and misrepresent us, as some of the said editors have misunderstood and misrepresented their author.

First, then, we warn thee not too hastily to condemn any of the incidents in this our history, as impertinent and foreign to our main design, because thou dost not immediately conceive in what manner such incident may conduce to that design. This work may, indeed, be considered as a great creation of our own; and for a little reptile of a critic to presume to find fault with any of its parts, without knowing the manner in which the whole is connected, and before he comes to the final catastrophe, is a most presumptuous absurdity. The allusion and metaphor we have here made use of, we must acknowledge to be infinitely too great for our occasion, but there is, indeed, no other, which is at all adequate to express the difference between an author of the first rate, and a critic of the lowest.

Another caution we would give thee, my good reptile, is, that thou dost not find out too near a resemblance between certain characters here introduced; as for instance, between the landlady who appears in the seventh book, and her in the ninth. Thou art to know, friend, that there are certain characteristics, in which most individuals of every profession and occupation agree. To be able to preserve these characteristics, and at the same time to diversify their operations, is one talent of a good writer. Again, to mark the nice distinction be-tween two persons actuated by the same vice or folly is another; and as this last talent is found in very few writers, so is the true discern-ment of it found in as few readers; though, I believe, the observation of this forms a very principal pleasure in those who are capable of the discovery. . . .

In the next place, we must admonish thee, my worthy friend (for, perhaps, thy heart may be better than thy head), not to condemn a character as a bad one, because it is not perfectly a good one. If thou dost delight in these models of perfection, there are books enow written to gratify thy taste; but as we have not, in the course of our conversation, ever happened to meet with any such person, we have not chosen to introduce any such here. To say the truth, I a little question whether mere man ever arrived at this consummate

degree of excellence, as well as whether there hath ever existed a
monster bad enough to verify that

– nulla virtute redemptum
A vitiis –[1]

in Juvenal: nor do I, indeed, conceive the good purposes served by
inserting characters of such angelic perfection, or such diabolical
depravity, in any work of invention: since from contemplating
either, the mind of man is more likely to be overwhelmed with
sorrow and shame, than to draw any good uses from such patterns;
for in the former instance he may be both concerned and ashamed to see
a pattern of excellence, in his nature, which he may reasonably despair
of ever arriving at; and in contemplating the latter, he may be no less
affected with those uneasy sensations, at seeing the nature, of which
he is a partaker, degraded into so odious and detestable a creature.

In fact, if there be enough of goodness in a character to engage the
admiration and affection of a well-disposed mind, though there
should appear some of those little blemishes, *quas humana parum cavit
natura*, they will raise our compassion rather than our abhorrence.
Indeed, nothing can be of more moral use than the imperfections
which are seen in examples of this kind; since such form a kind of
surprize, more apt to affect and dwell upon our minds, than the faults
of very vicious and wicked persons. The foibles and vices of men in
whom there is great mixture of good, become more glaring objects,
from the virtues which contrast them, and shew their deformity; and
when we find such vices attended with their evil consequence to our
favourite characters, we are not only taught to shun them for our own
sake, but to hate them for the mischiefs they have already brought on
those we love.

(467–9)

From Book 12, Chapter 1
*Shewing what is to be deemed Plagiarism in a modern Author, and
what is to be considered as lawful Prize*

The learned reader must have observed, that in the course of this
mighty work, I have often translated passages out of the best ancient

1 Whose vices are not allayed with a single virtue.

authors, without quoting the original, or without taking the least notice of the book from whence they were borrowed. . . .

To fill up a work with these scraps may indeed be considered as a downright cheat on the learned world, who are by such means imposed upon to buy a second time in fragments and by retail what they have already in gross, if not in their memories, upon their shelves; and it is still more cruel upon the illiterate, who are drawn in to pay for what is of no manner of use to them. A writer who intermixes great quantity of Greek and Latin with his works, deals by the ladies and fine gentlemen in the same paultry manner with which they are treated by the auctioneers, who often endeavour so to confound and mix up their lots, that, in order to purchase the commodity you want, you are obliged at the same time to purchase that which will do you no service.

And yet as there is no conduct so fair and disinterested, but that it may be misunderstood by ignorance, and misrepresented by malice, I have been sometimes tempted to preserve my own reputation, at the expence of my reader, and to transcribe the original, or at least to quote chapter and verse, whenever I have made use either of the thought or expression of another. I am indeed in some doubt that I have often suffered by the contrary method; and that by suppressing the original author's name, I have been . . . suspected of plagiarism. . . .

Now to obviate all such imputations for the future, I do here confess and justify the fact. The antients may be considered as a rich common, where every person who hath the smallest tenement in Parnassus hath a free right to fatten his Muse. Or, to place it in a clearer light, we moderns are to the antients what the poor are to the rich. By the poor here I mean, that large and venerable body which, in English, we call The Mob. Now, whoever hath had the honour to be admitted to any degree of intimacy with this mob, must well know that it is one of their established maxims, to plunder and pillage their rich neighbours without any reluctance; and that this is held to be neither sin nor shame among them. . . .

In like manner are the antients, such as Homer, Virgil, Horace, Cicero, and the rest, to be esteemed among us writers, as so many wealthy squires, from whom we, the poor of Parnassus, claim an immemorial custom of taking whatever we can come at. This liberty I demand, and this I am as ready to allow again to my poor neighbours in their turn. All I profess, and all I require of my brethren, is to maintain the same strict honesty among ourselves, which the mob shew to one another. To steal from one another, is indeed highly criminal and indecent; for this may be strictly styled defrauding the poor (sometimes perhaps those who are poorer than ourselves) or, to see it under the most opprobrious colours, robbing the spittal. (551–2)

From Book 13, Chapter 9

In the evening Jones met his lady again, and a long conversation again ensued between them; but as it consisted only of the same ordinary occurrences as before, we shall avoid mentioning particulars, which we despair of rendring agreeable to the reader; unless he is one whose devotion to the fair sex, like that of the Papists to their saints, wants to be raised by the help of pictures. . . .
(639)

From Book 14, Chapter 1
An Essay to prove that an Author will write the better, for having some Knowledge of the Subject on which he writes

As several gentlemen in these times, by the wonderful force of genius only, without the least assistance of learning, perhaps, without being well able to read, have made a considerable figure in the republic of letters; the modern critics, I am told, have lately begun to assert, that all kind of learning is entirely useless to a writer; and, indeed, no other than a kind of fetters on the natural spriteliness and activity of the imagination, which is thus weighed down, and prevented from soaring to those high flights which otherwise it would be able to reach.

   This doctrine, I am afraid, is, at present, carried much too far. . . . I cannot conceive that Homer or Virgil would have writ with more fire, if, instead of being masters of all the learning of their times, they had really been as ignorant as most of the authors of the present age. Nor do I believe that all the imagination, fire and judgement of Pitt could have produced those orations that have made the senate of England in these our times a rival in eloquence to Greece and Rome, if he had not been so well read in the writings of Demosthenes and Cicero, as to have transfused their whole spirit into his speeches, and with their spirit, their knowledge too.

I would not here be understood to insist on the same fund of learning in any of my brethren, as Cicero persuades us is necessary to the composition of an orator. On the contrary, very little reading is, I conceive, necessary to the poet, less to the critic, and the least of all to the politician. For the first, perhaps, Bysshe's *Art of Poetry*, and a few of our modern poets, may suffice; for the second, a moderate heap of plays; and for the last, an indifferent collection of political journals.

To say the truth, I require no more than that a man should have some little knowledge of the subject on which he treats. . . .

I am apt to conceive, that one reason why many English writers have totally failed in describing the manners of upper life, may possibly be, that in reality they know nothing of it.

This is a knowledge unhappily not in the power of many authors to arrive at. Books will give us a very imperfect idea of it; nor will the stage a much better. . . .

A true knowledge of the world is gained only by conversation, and the manners of every rank must be seen in order to be known.

Now it happens that this higher order of mortals is not to be seen, like all the rest of the human species, for nothing, in the streets, shops, and coffee-houses: nor are they shewn like the upper rank of animals, for so much a piece. In short, this is a sight to which no persons are admitted, without one or other of these qualifications, viz. either birth or fortune; or what is equivalent to both, the honourable profession of a gamester. And very unluckily for the world, persons so qualified, very seldom care to take upon themselves the bad trade of writing; which is generally entered upon by the lower and poorer sort, as it is a trade which many think requires no kind of stock to set up with.

Hence those strange monsters in lace and embroidery, in silks and brocades, with vast wigs and hoops; which, under the name of lords and ladies, strut the stage, to the great delight of attornies and their clerks in the pit, and of citizens and their apprentices in the galleries. . . . But to let my reader into a secret, this knowledge of upper life, though very necessary for the preventing mistakes, is no very great resource to a writer whose province is comedy, or that kind of novels, which, like this I am writing, is of the comic class.

What Mr Pope says of women is very applicable to most in this station, who are indeed so entirely made up of form and affectation, that they have no character at all, at least, none which appears. I will venture to say the highest life is much the dullest, and affords very little humour or entertainment. The various callings in lower spheres produce the great variety of humorous characters; whereas here, except among the few who are engaged in the pursuit of ambition, and the fewer still who have a relish for pleasure, all is vanity and servile imitation. Dressing and cards, eating and drinking, bowing and curtseying, make up the business of their lives.

Some there are however of this rank, upon whom passion exercises its tyranny, and hurries them far beyond the bounds which decorum prescribes; of these, the ladies are as much distinguished by their noble intrepidity, and a certain superior contempt of reputation, from the frail ones of meaner degree, as a virtuous woman of quality is by the elegance and delicacy of her sentiments from the honest wife of a yeoman or shopkeeper. Lady Bellaston was of this intrepid character; but let not my country readers conclude from her, that this is the general conduct of women of fashion, or that we mean to represent them as such. They might as well suppose, that every clergyman was represented by Thwackum, or every soldier by ensign Northerton.

There is not indeed a greater error than that which universally prevails among the vulgar, who borrowing their opinion from some ignorant satyrists, have affixed the character of lewdness to these times. On the contrary, I am convinced there never was less of love intrigue carried on among persons of condition, than now. Our present women have been taught by their mothers to fix their thoughts only on ambition and vanity, and to despise the pleasures of love as unworthy their regard; and being afterwards, by the care of such mothers, married without having husbands, they seem pretty well confirmed in the justness of those sentiments; whence they content themselves, for the dull remainder of life, with the pursuit of more innocent, but I am afraid more childish amusements, the bare mention of which would ill suit with the dignity of this history. In my humble opinion, the true characteristick of the present *Beau*

Monde, is rather folly than vice, and the only epithet which it deserves is that of *frivolous*.
(655–8)

From Book 15, Chapter 1

There are a set of religious, or rather moral writers, who teach that virtue is the certain road to happiness, and vice to misery, in this world. A very wholesome and comfortable doctrine, and to which we have but one objection, namely, that it is not true.

... if by virtue is meant ... a certain relative quality, which is ... as much interested in pursuing the good of others as its own; I cannot so easily agree that this is the surest way to human happiness; because I am afraid we must then include poverty and contempt, with all the mischiefs which backbiting, envy, and ingratitude can bring on mankind in our idea of happiness.

... my design was to wipe off a doctrine that lay in my way; since while Mr Jones was acting the most virtuous part imaginable in labouring to preserve his fellow creatures from destruction, the devil, or some other evil spirit, one perhaps cloathed in human flesh, was hard at work to make him completely miserable in the ruin of his Sophia.
(695–6)

From Book 17, Chapter 1

When a comic writer hath made his principal characters as happy as he can; or when a tragic writer hath brought them to the highest pitch of human misery, they both conclude their business to be done, and that their work is come to a period.

Had we been of the tragic complexion, the reader must allow we were now very nearly arrived at this period, since it would be difficult for the devil, or any of his representatives on earth, to have contrived much greater torments for poor Jones, than those in which we left him in the last chapter. ... What then remains to complete the tragedy but a murder or two, and a few moral sentences.

But to bring our favourites out of their present anguish and distress, and to land them at last on the shore of happiness, seems a much harder task; a task indeed so hard that we do not undertake to execute it. ...

This I faithfully promise, that notwithstanding any affection, which we may be supposed to have for this rogue, whom we have unfortunately made our hero, we will lend him none of that super-natural assistance with which we are entrusted, upon condition that we use it only on very important occasions. If he doth not therefore find some natural means of fairly extricating himself from all his dis-tresses, we will do no violence to the truth and dignity of history for his sake; for we had rather relate that he was hanged at Tyburn (which may very probably be the case) than forfeit our integrity, or shock the faith of our reader.

In this the antients had a great advantage over the moderns. Their mythology, which was at that time more firmly believed by the vulgar than any religion is at present, gave them always an oppor-tunity of delivering a favourite hero. Their deities were always ready at the writer's elbow, to execute any of his purposes. . . .

But we have none of these helps. To natural means alone are we confined; let us try therefore what by these means may be done for poor Jones; though, to confess the truth, something whispers me in the ear, that he doth not yet know the worst of his fortune; and that a more shocking piece of news than any he hath yet heard, remains for him in the unopened leaves of fate.
(777–8)

Book 18, Chapter 1
A Farewel to the Reader

We are now, reader, arrived at the last stage of our long journey. As we have therefore travelled together through so many pages, let us behave to one another like fellow-travellers in a stage-coach, who have passed several days in the company of each other; and who, notwithstanding any bickerings or little animosities which may have occurred on the road, generally make all up at last, and mount, for the last time, into their vehicle with chearfulness and good-humour; since, after this one stage, it may possibly happen to us, as it commonly happens to them, never to meet more.

As I have here taken up this simile, give me leave to carry it a little farther. I intend then in this last book to imitate the good company I have mentioned in their last journey. Now it is well known, that all jokes and raillery are at this time laid aside; whatever characters any of the passengers have for the jest-sake personated on the road, are now thrown off, and the conversation is usually plain and serious.

In the same manner, if I have now and then, in the course of this work, indulged any pleasantry for thy entertainment, I shall here lay it down. The variety of matter, indeed, which I shall be obliged to cram into this book, will afford no room for any of those ludicrous observations which I have elsewhere made, and which may sometimes, perhaps, have prevented thee from taking a nap when it was beginning to steal upon thee. In this last book thou wilt find nothing (or at most very little) of that nature. All will be plain narrative only; and, indeed, when thou hast perused the many great events which this book will produce, thou wilt think the number of pages contained in it, scarce sufficient to tell the story.

And now, my friend, I take this opportunity (as I shall have no other) of heartily wishing thee well. If I have been an entertaining companion to thee, I promise thee it is what I have desired. If in anything I have offended, it was really without any intention. Some things perhaps here said, may have hit thee or thy friends; but I do most solemnly declare they were not pointed at them. I question not but thou hast been told, among other stories of me, that thou wast to travel with a very scurrilous fellow: but whoever told thee so, did me an injury. No man detests and despises scurrility more than myself; nor hath any man more reason; for none has ever been treated with more: and what is a very severe fate, I have had some of the abusive writings of those very men fathered upon me, who in other of their works have abused me themselves with the utmost virulence.

All these works, however, I am well convinced, will be dead long before this page shall offer itself to thy perusal: for however short the period may be of my own performances, they will most probably outlive their own infirm author, and the weakly productions of his abusive contemporaries.

(813-14)

Anonymous

from a review of *Tom Jones*, *London Magazine*   February 1749
(*Critical Heritage*)

A book having been lately published, which has given great amusement, and, we hope, instruction to the polite part of the town, we
think ourselves obliged to give our readers some account of it.

It is intitled, *The History of Tom Jones, a Foundling*, by Henry Fielding, Esq.; being a novel, or prose epic composition, and calculated to
recommend religion and virtue, to shew the bad consequences of
indiscretion, and set several kinds of vice in their most deformed and
shocking light. This piece, like all such good compositions, consists of
a principal history, and a great many episodes or incidents; all which
arise naturally from the subject, and contribute towards carrying on
the chief plot or design. Through the whole, the reader's attention is
always kept awake by some new surprising accident, and his curiosity
upon the stretch, to discover the effects of that accident; so that after
one has begun to read, it is difficult to leave off before having read
the whole.
(148)

? Samuel Johnson

from *Gentleman's Magazine*   March 1749 (*Critical Heritage*)

The loose images in these pieces [including *Tom Jones*] perhaps
invite to vice more than the contrast figures alarm us into virtue. . . .
(161)

Captain Lewis Thomas

from a letter to Welbore Ellis   3 April 1749 (*Critical Heritage*)

If my design had been to propagate virtue by appearing publickly in its defence, I should rather have been ye author of *Tom Jones* than of five Folio Volumes of sermons. . . .
(162)

William Shenstone

from a letter to Lady Luxborough   7 April 1749
(Marjorie Williams (ed.), *Letters of William Shenstone*, 1939)

I think as you do that that [*sic*] the plan is by no means easy, but must own at the same time that several parts have afforded me much amusement. There is a good deal of wit dispersed throughout, or rather tied up in bundles at the beginning of every Book. You will conclude my taste to be not extremely delicate when I say I am chiefly pleased with the striking lines of Mr Western's character. It is I fancy a natural picture of thousands of his majesty's rural subjects; at least it has been *my* fortune to see the original pretty frequently. 'Tis perhaps a likeness that is easily taken and moreover he seems to apply it too indiscriminately to country gentlemen in general. But it is the only character that made me laugh; and that is a great point gained, when one is in danger of losing that faculty through disuse. 'Tis moreover a character better worth exposing than his landlords and landladys with which he seemed so delighted – his serjeants and Abigails etc.
(185–6)

Joseph Spence

from a letter to W. B. Massingberd   15 April 1749 (reprinted in
Austin Wright, *Joseph Spence: A Critical Biography*, 1950)

Tom Jones is my old acquaintance, now; for I read it before it was
publisht; and read it with such rapidity, that I began and ended
within the compass of four days; tho' I took a journey to St Albans,
in the same time. He is to me extremely entertaining; and will be so,
I believe, to you. A set of 2500 copies was sold, before it was publisht,
which is perhaps an unheard-of case. That I may not seem to write
riddles, you must know that the way here generally is, to send in their
number of books to each of the booksellers they deal with, four or
five days before the publication; that they may oblige people, who
are eager for a new thing. In this case, 10 February was fixt for
publication; and by the 10th, all the books were disposed of. The
author sold the copy for £100 each volume; and might probably
have got five times as much by it, had he kept the right in his own
hands: but authors at first don't know, whether their works are
good or bad, much less, whether they will sell or not.
 232)

Horace Walpole

from a letter to George Montagu   18 May 1749 (W. S. Lewis
and R. S. Brown (eds.), *Yale Edition of Horace Walpole's
Correspondence*, vol. 9, 1941)

Rigby . . . and Peter Bathurst t'other night carried a servant of the
latter's who had attempted to shoot him, before Fielding, who to
all his other vocations has, by the grace of Mr Lyttelton, added that
of Middlesex justice. He sent them word he was at supper, that they
must come next morning. They did not understand that freedom and
ran up, where they found him banqueting with a blind man, three
Irishmen and a whore on some cold mutton and a bone of ham, both
in one dish, and the cursedest dirty cloth! He never stirred nor asked
them to sit. Rigby, who had seen him so often come to beg a guinea

of Sir Charles Williams, and Bathurst at whose father's he had lived
for victuals, understood that dignity as little, and pulled themselves
chairs, on which he civilized. Millar the bookseller has done very
generously by him; finding *Tom Jones*, for which he had given him
six hundred pounds sell so greatly, he has since given him another
hundred.
(84)

Catherine Talbot

from a letter to Elizabeth Carter   22 May 1749
(*Critical Heritage*)

The more I read *Tom Jones* the more I detest him, and admire
Clarissa Harlowe – yet there are in it things that must touch and
please every good heart, and probe to the quick many a bad one,
and humour that it is impossible not to laugh at.
(166)

'Aretine'

from a letter to 'Selim Slim' (Lyttelton) in *Old England*
27 May 1749 (*Critical Heritage*)

That this motely [*sic*] history of bastardism, fornication and adultery,
is highly prejudicial to the cause of religion, in several parts of it, is
apparent in the gross ridicule and abuse which are wantonly thrown
on religious characters. Who reviles the clergy may be well said to
be upon the very threshold of immorality and irreligion. A contempt
inculcated of the first brings on the last of course. The character of
Thwackum is drawn out in the most odious colours that can possibly
raise detestation in the mind of the reader; and Supple is painted in
the contemptible light of an insignificant formal fool. Is this, Sir, the
sincere endeavours of your author in recommending goodness and
innocence? Or, is the marrying of a Reverend clergyman to a
common harlot his way of *rewarding* virtue? It is amazing, Sir, you

should venture on commending a book so truly profligate, of such evil tendency, and offensive to every chaste reader, so discouraging to Virtue and detrimental to religion!
(168)

Elizabeth Carter

from a letter to Catherine Talbot   20 June 1749 (*Critical Heritage*)

I am sorry to find you so outrageous about poor Tom Jones; he is no doubt an imperfect, but not a detestable character, with all that honesty, good-nature, and generosity of temper. Though nobody can admire Clarissa more than I do, yet with all our partiality, I am afraid, it must be confessed, that Fielding's book is the most natural representation of what passes in the world, and of the bizarreries which arise from the mixture of good and bad, which makes up the composition of most folks. Richardson has no doubt a very good hand at painting excellence, but there is a strange awkwardness and extravagance in his vicious characters.
(169)

Samuel Richardson

from a letter to Aaron Hill   12 July 1749 (John Carroll (ed.), *Selected Letters of Samuel Richardson*, 1964)

While the taste of the age can be gratified by a Tom Jones (dear sir, have you read *Tom Jones*?) I am not to expect that the world will bestow two readings, or one, indeed, attentive one, on such a grave story as *Clarissa*, which is designed to make those think of death who endeavour all they can to banish it from their thoughts. I have found neither leisure nor inclination yet to read that piece; and the less inclination, as several good judges of my acquaintance condemn it, and the general taste together. I could wish to know the sentiments of your ladies upon it. If favourable, they would induce me to open the six volumes; the rather, as they will be so soon read.
(126)

Astraea and Minerva Hill

from a letter to Samuel Richardson   27 July 1749
(*Critical Heritage*)

But the commission you, at present, charge us with tends no farther
than *Tom Jones*: and Tom Jones is not a Clarissa. . . .

Having with much ado got over some reluctance, that was bred
by a familiar coarseness in the title, we went through the whole six
volumes; and found much (masqued) merit in 'em all : a double merit,
both of head and heart. Had there been only that of the last sort, you
love it I am sure, too much, to leave a doubt of your resolving to
examine it – however, if you do, it should be when you can best
spare it your attention – else the author introduces all his sections
(and too often interweaves the *serious* body of his meanings) with
long runs of bantering levity, which his good sense may suffer the
effect of. It is true, he seems to wear this lightness, as a grave head
sometimes wears a feather; which though he and fashion may consider as an ornament, reflection will condemn, as a disguise and
covering.

Girls, perhaps, of an untittering disposition, are improper judges
of what merit there may be in lightness, when (as seems here intended) it endeavours rather at ironic Satire, than encouragement of
folly. But tell us, dear sir, are we in the right or no, when we presume
to own it as our notion, that however well-meant such a motive may
have been, the execution of it must be found distasteful? . . .

Meanwhile, it is an honest pleasure, which we take in adding, that
(exclusive of one wild, detached and independent story of a Man of
the Hill that neither brings on anything, nor rose from anything that
went before it) all the changeful windings of the author's fancy
carry on a course of regular design; and end in an extremely moving
close, where lines that seemed to wander and run different ways,
meet, all, in an instructive centre.

The whole piece consists of an inventive race of disappointments
and recoveries. It excites curiousity, and holds it watchful. It has just
and pointed Satire; but it is a partial Satire and confined too narrowly: it sacrifices to authority, and interest – its *events* reward
sincerity, and punish and expose hypocrisy; shew pity and benevo-

lence in amiable lights and avarice and brutality in very despicable ones. In every part it has humanity for its intention; in too many, it *seems* wantoner than it was meant to be: it has bold shocking pictures; and (I fear) not unresembling ones, in high life and in low – and (to conclude this too adventurous guesswork from a pair of forward baggages) would, everywhere (we think) *deserve* to please – if stript of what the author thought himself most sure to *please by*. (172–4)

Samuel Richardson

from a letter to Astraea and Minerva Hill   4 August 1749
(John Carroll (ed.), *Selected Letters*, 1964)

. . . I must confess, that I have been prejudiced by the opinion of several judicious friends against the truly coarse-titled *Tom Jones*; and so have been discouraged from reading it – I was told, that it was a rambling collection of waking dreams, in which probability was not observed; and that it had a very bad tendency. And I had reason to think that the author intended for his second view (His *first*, to fill his pocket, by accomodating it to the reigning taste) in writing it, to whiten a vicious character, and to make morality bend to his practices. What reason has he to make his Tom illegitimate, in an age where keeping is becoming a fashion? Why did he make him a common – what shall I call it? – and a kept fellow, the lowest of all fellows, yet in love with a Young Creature who was trapsing after him, a fugitive from her father's house? Why did he draw his heroine so fond, so foolish and so insipid? Indeed, he has one excuse – he knows not how to draw a delicate woman – he has not been accustomed to such company – and is too prescribing, too impetuous, too immoral, I will venture to say, to take any other bias than that a perverse and crooked Nature has given him; or evil habits, at least, have confirmed in him. Do men expect grapes of thorns or figs of thistles? But, perhaps, I think the worse of the piece because I know the writer and dislike his principles, both public and private, though I wish well to the *man* and love four worthy sisters of his, with whom I am well acquainted. And indeed should admire him, did he make the use of his talents which I wish him to make; for the vein of humour and ridicule, which he is Master of, if properly turned, do great service to the cause of virtue.

But no more of this gentleman's work after I have said, that the favourable things you say of the piece will tempt me, if I can find leisure, to give it a perusal. . . .

But in an age so dissolute as the present what can be said for the morality (for the morality shall I say?) propagated in *Tom Jones*?

But his judges, by whom I have been governed, are perhaps too severe. I am sure I am disinterested enough, if I do read it, to give it (to the best of my judgement) its due praises, as well as censure. But I thought to have said no more of it till I had run it over. . . .
(127–8)

Lady Mary Wortley Montagu

from a letter to the Countess of Bute   1 October 1749 (Robert Halsband (ed.), *Complete Letters*, vol. 2, 1966)

Falling upon Fielding's works [I] was fool enough to sit up all night reading. I think Joseph Andrews better than his Foundling.
(443)

Tobias Smollett

from a letter to Alexander Carlyle   1 October 1749
(Lewis M. Knapp (ed.), *Letters*, 1970)

If I should pretend to set up in defence of Tom Jones, in those particulars where he is affected by your censure, you would easily discover my affectation and be justly offended at my feigned candour ... even the author's most sanguine adherents confess that there is an evident difference between that part of his book which he wrote for the town, and that which was composed for the benefit of his bookseller.
(11)

Lady Bradshaigh

from a letter to Samuel Richardson   November 1749
(*Critical Heritage*)

As to Tom Jones, I am fatigued with the name, having lately fallen
into the company of several young ladies, who had each a Tom
Jones in some part of the world, for so they call their favourites; and
ladies, you know, are for ever talking of their favourites. Last post
I received a letter from a lady, who laments the loss of her Tom
Jones; and from another, who was happy in the company of her
Tom Jones. In like manner, the gentlemen have their Sophias. A
few days ago, in a circle of gentlemen and ladies, who had their
Tom Jones's and their Sophias, a friend of mine told me he must
shew me his Sophia, the sweetest creature in the world, and immediately produced a Dutch mastiff puppy.
(183)

Samuel Richardson

from a letter to Lady Bradshaigh   November–December 1749
(John Carroll (ed.), *Selected Letters*, 1964)

So long as the world will receive, Mr Fielding will write. Have you
ever seen a list of his performances? Nothing but a shorter life than
I wish him, can hinder him from writing himself out of date. The
Pamela, which he abused in his Shamela, taught him how to write
to please, though his manners are so different. Before his Joseph
Andrews (hints and names taken from that story, with a lewd and
ungenerous engraftment) the poor man wrote without being read,
except when his Pasquins, etc. roused party attention and the legislature at the same time, according to that of Juvenal, which may be
thus translated:

Would'st thou be read, or would'st thou bread ensure,
Dare something worthy Newgate or the Tower.

In the former of which (removed from inns and alehouses) will

some of his next scenes be laid; and perhaps not unusefully; I hope not. But to have done, for the present, with this fashionable author ....
(133–4)

'Orbilius'

from *An Examen of the History of Tom Jones, A Foundling* 1750 (*Critical Heritage*)

John Bunyan perform'd, as it seems, a work infinitely superior and more useful, with much greater ease. And John Bunyan's performance was a work of genius; but John Bunyan *was* a genius, though a grave one. Mr F., on the contrary, is so volatile, that I daresay he never pursued any one thing for a year together; much less such a *skipping* work as this before us; which, though it comprehends an unmeasurable length of time, need not have cost much in writing, if we may guess by the correctness of the style. John Dryden . . . boasted of his having produced a bad play in a fortnight: Mr F., more inconsistently, of having spent *some years* (which others may interpret as *many*) in corrupting youth, i.e. in writing *Tom Jones*. . . .

To Lady Bellaston, suitably to his infamous birth, he performed the offices of a Maskwell, for which she becomes his tributary. In this scandalous and despicable manner does he live with that quality-strumpet, till, having dangerously wounded one FitzPatrick . . . he is thrown into prison, and is in imminent peril of his neck: whence at last he is rescued by the *seasonable* recovery of FitzPatrick, and as *seasonable* arrival of Allworthy, to whom the whole history of his honourable birth is revealed by that very Mrs Waters, who had impersonated his mother, and debauched (if we may use the word of one before debauched) her supposed son. This discovery restores her credit with Allworthy, who had banished her the country on her false confession that she was the mother of Tom; and at the same time ingratiates the latter with his uncle Allworthy. . . .

Sophia herself is with great pomp introduced to the veneration of the reader for her modesty, and other good qualities; but as it is certain, that Mr F. is utterly unable (as we see in all his pieces, but most flagrantly in this) to draw a woman of true virtue and modesty;

so in nothing is she so illustrious as in her partiality to the well-known debaucheries of Jones and in her elopement from her father's house. . . .

And now arrives the time, when our author, being at a loss to contrive ways and means to raise the character of his hero, since he could not in merit, and would not at Tyburn, reconciles him to Allworthy by the means before mentioned; Allworthy reconciles him to Sophia; and the fiddles strike up (not without the Melody of Marrow-bones and Cleavers, we presume) to the joy of every fortune-hunter and rathe-ripe virgin in the Kingdom . . .

[In book 5, chapter 1, Fielding's] question is, 'Hath anyone living attempted to explain what the modern judges of our theatres mean by the word *low*?' Mr F. can best explain it, and seems to be conscious how fitly it has been applied to his works. But his question may be further answer'd by informing him, that *low* characters are those in which Nature is degraded beneath the standard at which it of right ought to be placed, by making them too much, or too little, what they should be. . . .

This calm villain Blifil may have had all the ill qualities ascribed to him; but how is it, that one more vice was not added to the rest, I mean that, which Mr F. had called 'Hungering after Women', chapter 1 of this book? To which he had such excitements in the beauty of Sophia. The author paints him as without desires of this sort; which how he will make agreeable to Nature, I know not. He seems indeed to have this cold temper allotted to him, to detract from the value of the virtue of chastity, by representing it only as constitutional; which is the character of an eunuch; and the contrary vice to be so largely distributed to Jones, to advance in like manner the credit of incontinence, which few, besides, our author, will think at too low an ebb in this age and nation. . . .

As to person, features, youth, health, strength, spirit and good nature in the popular sense . . . they were all possessed perhaps in as eminent a degree by Captain Macheath, as by our hero. Yet Captain Macheath's author was not so conceited as to imagine his infamous hero resembled one of that beatified order, who 'are happier than Mankind, because they're better', but, with the strictest Poetical Justice, dooms him to death for his villainies, tho' the Royal Mercy interposes to save the criminal, and prevent the damnation of Mr Gay's comic opera. And whoever compares that opera (bad as it is) with Mr F.'s production, will find the former infinitely surpass the latter in morality, as well as in *all* that wit and humour with which our author supposes he hath clothed his dirty characters. . . .

Fifty pounds given to Jones for his gallantry is a most excellent instance of Christian charity! Jones's indeed to Anderson is praise-worthy. But this impudent quality-whore's is beneath censure. Can anything be more odious, than for a woman of figure to divest herself of her dignity for a vile satisfaction, and heap on her partner in guilt so ample a reward of his baseness? Where is female decency, that seeks to be courted, even when its own inclination forwards the courtship? Can any *English* lady of quality be so gross a sensualist? Perhaps she may: but is this corrupted scene to be called Nature? And shall an author glory in describing the jakes of an human mind, and say that he drew his character from the 'original Book of Nature'? . . .

That so great a voluptuary as Mr Jones should be alternately committing acts of debauchery and tasting, by conferring, the pleasures of beneficence . . . is an inconsistency in character never before heard of. To earn the wages of iniquity, in order with those wages to merit heaven by acts of disinterested beneficence, may qualify him indeed for a place in the *Roman* Calendar of Saints. . . .

That the author is not of a tragic complexion, he has sufficiently shewn in the most tragical matter in his whole history (book 15, chapter 4) where the intended rape of Sophia affords excellent farce . . . But why should Mr F. so far deride his reader, as to advise him 'not to lose any time in taking a first row' at Tyburn to see Jones's execution, when he knew in his own heart, that he never intended to bring the hero thither? Is not this to affront his reader, by intimating, that he cannot see further than his nose? . . .

Good Mr F., since you are at last come to be plain and serious and to lay aside your jokes and raillery, let me ask you one *plain and serious* question: which is, pray, what *obliged* you to *cram into this book* so great a *variety of matter*? Were you not at liberty to omit any of your episodes, that of the Man of the Hill, that of Mrs FitzPatrick's history, or that of Partridge at *Hamlet*, whichever you thought least entertaining, that so you might have found room to move, and that nevertheless your readers might not have been disappointed in paying for an even six? . . .

'No'orow a father' is Mr Western's dialect here [i.e. book 18, chapter 8]: formerly, as in book 17, chapter 3, we find, used by the same gentleman, 'Narro' woman upon earth would ha' me.' Whence this difference in the 'Zummerzetshire' alphabet? Let Mr Western be constant to his errors at least. . . .

Were it not for the bad morals . . . the author's *counterfeit* wit might have pass'd for true, and dazzled the eyes of our beaux and belles with its tinsel lustre, for anything I should have done to prevent it. But so much notice has been taken of this performance, as an inimitable one that, when I was opposing the author's scheme of morality, I could not avoid lifting up the censorial rod against the other also. Yet have I no personal pique against this gentleman; but admire some irregular touches of wit and morality, which, like the few fertile spots to be seen among the most barren parts of the Alps, may be found in travelling thro' his volumes. But these are . . . overbalanced by their contraries, and by what we have reason to fear (from comparing our author's former works with his latter) of his future degeneracy from the milk of human kindness to the pap of infantile insipidity. . . .

(189–212)

Samuel Richardson

from a letter to Frances Grainger   22 January 1750
(John Carroll (ed.), *Selected Letters*, 1964)

I have taken the liberty to account, elsewhere, for the good reception the character of the weak, the insipid, the runaway, the inn-frequenting Sophia has met with. In that, as in the character of her illegitimate Tom, there is nothing that very common persons may not attain to; nothing that will reproach the conduct or actions of very ordinary capacities, and very free-livers: while Clarissa's character, as it might appear unattainable by them, might be supposed prudish, too delicate, and a silent reproach to themselves. Had I been at leisure to examine *The History of Tom Jones* . . . I should have known

whom by the examination to have called Sophias and whom
Clarissas.
(143)

P. A. de la Place

from the Preface to his French translation of *Tom Jones* 1750
(English translation of Preface from *Critical Heritage*)

If Mr Fielding, I have said, had written for the French, he probably
would have suppressed a large number of passages which are very
excellent in themselves, but which would have seemed out of place
to them. Once heated with the interest that comes from a moving
and skilfully woven plot, they endure impatiently all manner of
digressions, of essays, or of moral treatises, and they consider these
ornaments, however fine they may be, as just so many obstacles to
the pleasure which they are eager to enjoy. I have done what the
author himself would have done.

   Such is, Sir, my full apology, for having dared, not to change, but
to adapt certain parts of your work.
(224)

Anonymous

from 'A Literary Article from Paris', *Gentleman's Magazine*
March 1750 (*Critical Heritage*)

In *France* the ladies would be shocked at the repeated breaches of
faith in Tom Jones to his mistress, and fathers and mothers would
exclaim against that resolute boldness with which Miss Western
abandons her father's house to preserve herself inviolate to her lover.
In *England* they are not so rigorous; every father and mother indeed,
in *London* as well as *Paris*, would be glad to have their children
perfectly obedient to their will; but the love of liberty in the *English*,
renders them generally more disposed to forgive the disobedience of
a daughter, when her obedience might make her miserable. In-

constancy in a lover, will no more be pardoned by an *English* than a *French* woman, but the first will sooner pass by a slight neglect; in general, the *English* ladies are more jealous of a man's sentiments, the *French* of his actions . . . .

The public has not for a long time been entertained with a piece where the principal persons are more engaging or more interesting, the episodes better connected with the principal action, the characters more equally sustained, the incidents more artfully prepared, or more naturally arising one out of another. Miss Western is a truly admirable character; Tom Jones, as much a libertine as he is, engages all sensible hearts by his candor, generosity, humanity, his gratitude to his benefactors, his tender compassion, and readiness to assist the distressed. . . .

(225–6)

Samuel Johnson

from *Rambler*, no. 4   31 March 1750 (W. J. Bate and
Albrecht B. Strauss (eds.), *Yale Edition of the Works of
Samuel Johnson*, vol. 3, 1969)[1]

In the romances formerly written, every transaction and sentiment was so remote from all that passes among men, that the reader was in very little danger of making any applications to himself; the virtues and crimes were equally beyond his sphere of activity; and he amused himself with heroes and with traitors, deliverers and persecutors, as with beings of another species, whose actions were regulated upon motives of their own, and who had neither faults nor excellencies in common with himself.

But when an adventurer is levelled with the rest of the world, and acts in such scenes of the universal drama, as may be the lot of any other man; young spectators fix their eyes upon him with closer attention, and hope by observing his behaviour and success to regulate their own practices, when they shall be engaged in the like part. . . .

It is therefore not a sufficient vindication of a character, that it is

---

1 Johnson's essay is said to have been occasioned by the recent publication of *Roderick Random* (1748) and *Tom Jones* [ed.].

drawn as it appears, for many characters ought never to be drawn. . . .

Many writers, for the sake of following nature, so mingle good and bad qualities in their principal personages, that they are both equally conspicuous; and as we accompany them through their adventures with delight, and are led by degrees to interest ourselves in their favour, we lose the abhorrence of their faults, because they do not hinder our pleasure, or, perhaps, regard them with some kindness for being united with so much merit.
(21-3)

Samuel Richardson

from a letter to J. B. de Freval 21 January 1751 (John Carroll (ed.), *Selected Letters*, 1964)

Tom Jones is a dissolute book. Its run is over, even with us. Is it true, that France had virtue enough to refuse a licence for such a profligate performance?
(175)

Anonymous

from a review of *An Enquiry into the Causes of the Late Increase of Robbers*, *Monthly Review* January 1751 (*Critical Heritage*)

The public hath been hitherto not a little obliged to Mr Fielding for the entertainment his gayer performances have afforded it; but now this gentleman hath a different claim to our thanks, for services of a more substantial nature. If he has been heretofore admired for his wit and humour, he now merits equal applause as a good magistrate, a useful and active member, and a true friend to his country. As few writers have shown so just and extensive a knowledge of mankind in general, so none ever had better opportunities for being perfectly acquainted with that class which is the main subject of this perform-

ance: a class of all others the most necessary and useful to all, yet the most neglected and despised; we mean the labouring part of the people.
(239–40)

Anonymous

from *An Apology for the Life of Mr Bampfylde Moore Carew*
?1751 (*Critical Heritage*)

I am afraid, sir ... that everybody knows what the word *low* means, and that it is likewise very expressive in its signification. I am therefore doubtful that the public will not think, what you have assign'd, sir, a sufficient reason for the disuse of it: I cannot flatter you neither that they will fall in with your sentiments of confining the use of this word to Right Honourables and putting a gag in the mouths of all under that rank, for tho' you, sir, are in too great a station now to suppose the *people* know anything, yet there happens to be two small objections to this opinion of yours; the first is, that the wisest and most learned men, of all ages, have thought directly contrary; the second is, that experience has shown me that the *people* (that is, what you with so just contempt denominate the gentlemen of the Law, apprentices, clerks, etc. and if you had added shoemakers and tailors, it would have made no difference), have always been right in their judgement, unless biass'd and led astray by superior examples. ... I have heard several affirm that your Worship (so far from drawing your characters after Nature) does not know what the word, Nature, means; Nature, say these gentlemen, is the highest degree of perfection, with which that order of beings we are speaking of is generally indued with; or ... the inclinations, faculties, properties, qualities or affections which anything has originally; now, say these critics, it is absurd, because there may chance to be some single characters in life who, by bad example, idleness or drunkenness, have lost all their *original* properties, to draw these at full length and tell us it is Nature as if a painter was to draw any of his principal figures with scald heads and blear eyes and tell us it was Nature, because he had happened to have seen such; or would not an anatomist, say they, be laugh'd at, who shall call a child born with two heads and five legs or any other monstrous birth, Nature, because there has now and then happened to be such brought into the world.

Others are so envious to say, they don't believe there is so stupid and ignorant a character in life (at least, not above the station of a kennel-raker) as your 'Squire Western'....
(256–9)

?Francis Coventry

from *An Essay on the New Species of Writing Founded by Mr Fielding* 1751 (*Critical Heritage*)

Mr Fielding ... who sees all the little movements by which human nature is actuated, found it necessary to open a new vein of humour, and thought the only way to make them lay down *Cassandra* would be to compile characters which really existed, equally entertaining with those chimeras which were beyond conception. This thought produced *Joseph Andrews*, which soon became a formidable rival to the *amazing* class of writers; since it was not a mere dry narrative, but a lively representative of real life. For crystal palaces and winged horses, we find homely cots and ambling nags; and instead of impossibility, what we experience every day....

'Twas thought necessary, to give it a greater air of truth, to entitle it an *History*; and the *dramatis personae* (if I may venture to use the expression) were christened not with fantastic high-sounding names, but such as, tho' they sometimes bore some reference to the character, had a more modern termination....

To enliven it the more, it is sometimes heightened to the mock-heroic, to ridicule the bombast and fustian which obtain'd so much in the romances. Of this kind are his various descriptions of the morning, and his diverting similes occasionally dispers'd thro' the body of his work.... On the subject of the titles to his chapters, perhaps I may convince the reader, these little scraps, if rightly manag'd, conduce more to his entertainment than he is at first aware of. 'Tis quite opposite to the custom of the very best writers in this way, to give too full an account of the contents: it should be just hinted to the reader something extraordinary is to happen in the seven or eight subsequent pages, but what that is should be left for them to discover. Monsieur Le Sage, in his *Gil Blas* (one of the best books of the kind extant), has always pursu'd this method. . . .

At the beginning of the last Book of *Tom Jones* [even more than in *Gil Blas*] the reader is apt to think it an equal chance whether he is to be hanged or married; nor does he undeceive him but by gradual narration of facts: and lest the reader's curiosity should pry too far into the truth, what admirable titles has he invented for his chapters to keep him in the dark! Such as: 'In which the history draws near to a conclusion'; 'In which the history draws nearer to a conclusion', etc., etc., which everybody will own conduces greatly to their entertainment, and a reader of the least discernment will perceive how much more consequence the clever management of these scraps prefix'd to each chapter is of than he at first imagin'd. . . .

These thoughts upon the inscriptions to the chapters were thrown together to shew, that Mr Fielding had another intention besides making the world laugh in the lines prefix'd to each portion of his History. . . . As the works of Mr Fielding are in everybody's hands, there ought not to be a line in them which should cause the modestest lady a blush in the perusal. This delicacy of style and sentiment has been quite neglected in some dialogues between the wanton Lady Booby and most innocent Joseph Andrews . . . tho' the narration is conducted with great spirit, and there are innumerable strokes of Wit and Nature throughout, it is no small derogation to the merit of this work, that the story on which it is founded is not sufficiently interesting. The characters indeed, are equally natural and entertaining with those of *Tom Jones*, but the parts they are allotted engage much less of our attention. In dramatic pieces, where the story must be stretch'd into five Acts, there is some excuse for this inaction, and want of incidents, but in these performances, where the length of the work is left entirely to the discretion of the writer, little can be alledg'd in his defence.

We will here . . . briefly observe what deserves reproof in . . . *Tom Jones*; a performance which on the whole perhaps is the most lively book ever publish'd, but our author has here and there put in his claim to that privilege of being dull. . . . The most glaring in-

stance of this kind in all this author's works is the long unenliven'd
story of the Man of the Hill. . . .
(263–8)

Tobias Smollett

from the first edition of *Peregrine Pickle*, chapter 102   1751
(James L. Clifford (ed.), 1964)

I insist upon it, these [flattery and bribery] are arts which, will never
fail to engage the friendship of Mr Scrag [Lyttelton], which will be
sooner or later manifested in some warm sinecure, ample subscription, post or reversion; and I advise Mr Spondy, to give him the
refusal of this same pastoral: who knows but he may have the good
fortune of being listed in the number of his beef-eaters: in which
case he may, in process of time, be provided for in the customs or
church; when he is inclined to marry his own cook-wench, his
gracious patron may condescend to give the bride away; and finally
settle him in his old age, as a trading Westminster-justice.
(659–60)

John Cleland

from a review of *Amelia*, *Monthly Review*. December 1751
(*Critical Heritage*)

To give a just idea of this his last production, which, from the choice
of his subject, appears to be the boldest stroke that has yet been
attempted in this species of writing, will be sufficient.
  The author takes up his heroine at the very point at which all his
predecessors have dropped their capital personages. It has been heretofore a general practice to conduct the lover and his mistress to the
doors of matrimony, and there leave them, as if after that ceremony
the whole interest in them was at end, and nothing could remain
beyond it worthy of exciting or keeping up the curiosity of the
reader. Instead of which, Mr Fielding, in defiance of this established

custom, has ventured to give the history of two persons already married, but whose adventures, hardships, and distressful situations form a chain of events, in which he has had the art of keeping up the spirit of his narration from falling into that languor and flatness which might be expected from the nature of the subject. . . . The author, however, has interwove such natural situations, such scenes of trial, taken from nature, that the attention is for ever kept on the stretch. . . .

The chief and capital purport of this work is to inculcate the superiority of virtuous conjugal love to all other joys; to prove that virtue chastens our pleasures, only to augment them; and to exemplify, that the paths of vice, are always those of misery, and that virtue even in distress, is still a happier bargain to its votaries, than vice, attended with all the splendor of fortune. So just, so refined a morality, would alone, with a candid and ingenuous reader, compensate for almost any imperfections in the execution of this work, some parts whereof will doubtless appear, amidst its beauties, to stand in need of an apology: for example, where the characters are, however exact copies of nature, chosen in too low, and disgustful a range of it, and rather too often repeated, and too long dwelt upon. The humours of an inn-keeper, an inn-keeper's wife, a gaoler, a highwayman, a bailiff, a street-walker . . . when they occur too often . . . will disgust even those, who, from their distance in rank or circumstances from these subjects, may be curious to have some idea of them, and can only come at it in such descriptions. (304–6)

Lady Orrery

from a letter to Lord Orrery   6 January 1752 (Critical Heritage)

[She has 'a horrid head ach', which] was occasioned by reading so much of Amelia last night till it was very late, which I have finished, but cannot say it has given me equal pleasure with Tom Jones or Joseph Andrews. It certainly is his own history, the love part foolishly fond beneath the dignity of a man. Amelia vastly good, but a little silly. I think she is dead many years in reality. The prison and the baillif scenes very well; the catastrophe of recovering their fortune unnatural; Amelia's conduct in carrying her children to 'my Lord' foolish and indiscreet; Mrs Atkinson's character neither uniform nor natural, the only good stroke in it making so learned a lady also a drunken lady; Miss Matthews the most consistant character in the book. However, his observations on the abuse of laws, and his moral discourses are very well. But all together it is tedious.

(311)

Henry Fielding

from *Covent-Garden Journal*, nos. 7–8   25 and 28 January 1752
(G. E. Jensen (ed.), vol. 1, 1915)

Proceedings at the Court of Censorial Enquiry, Etc.
(*Amelia was set to the Bar.*)

COUNSELLOR TOWN ... The book ... indicted upon the Statute of Dulness, a very ancient Law, and too well known to need much expatiating upon. But it may be necessary to observe, *that that that* is dulness in one age, is not so in another. ...

Now the humour, or manners, of this age are to laugh at everything, and the only way to please them is to make them laugh; nor hath the prisoner any excuse, since it was so very easy to have done this in the present case; what, indeed, more was necessary, than to have turned the ridicule the other way, and, in the characters of Dr Harrison, and Amelia herself, to have made a jest of religion, and the clergy, of virtue, and innocence?

(*Here the Council was hastily stopt by the censor, and desired to proceed to his proofs.*)

COUNCILLOR TOWN We shall prove then, to you, Sir, that the book now at the bar, is *very sad stuff*; that Amelia herself is a *low* character, a *fool*, and a *milksop*; that she is very apt to faint, and apt *to drink water*, to prevent it. That she once *taps a bottle of wine, and drinks two glasses*. That she *shews too much kindness for her children*, and is too apt to *forgive the faults of her husband*. That she exerts, *no manner of spirit*, unless, perhaps, in supporting Afflictions. That *her concealing the* knowledge of her husband's amour, when she knew he had discontinued it, was *low and poor*. That *her not abusing him*, for having lost his money at play, when she saw his heart was already almost broke by it, *was contemptible meanness*. That she *dresses her husband's supper; dresses her children*; and *submits* to the thoughts of every servile office. That she once mentions the devil, and as often swears by her soul. Lastly, that she is a beauty *without a nose*. I say again, *without a nose*. All this we shall prove by many witnesses.

We shall likewise prove that Dr Harrison is a very *low, dull, unnatural,* character . . . in short, not to descend to too many particulars . . . that the whole book is a heap of *sad stuff, dulness, and nonsense*; that it contains no wit, humour, knowledge of human nature, or of the world; indeed, that the fable, moral character, manners, sentiments, and diction, are all alike bad and contemptible. . . .

COUNCILLOR TOWN Call Lady Dilly Dally . . . Mr Censor, we call this young Lady to the character of Amelia, and she will give you an account of all the low behaviour I have opened – Lady Dilly, your Ladyship knows the prisoner at the bar?

LADY DILLY I cannot say I ever saw the creature before . . .

COUNCILLOR TOWN I thought your Ladyship had said that Amelia was sad stuff from beginning to end.

LADY DILLY I believe I might say so – Eh! I don't always remember what I say; but if I did say so, I was told it . . . Dr Dosewell, my physician, told me so – The doctor said, in a great deal of company, that the book, I forget the name of it, was a sad stupid book, and that the author had not a bit of wit, or learning, or sense, or anything else. . . .

(A great number of beaus, rakes, fine ladies, and several formal persons with bushy wigs, and canes at their noses, pushed forward, and offered themselves as witnesses against poor Amelia, when a grave man stood up and begged to be heard; which the court granted, and he spoke as follows.)

'If you, Mr Censor, are yourself a parent, you will view me with compassion when I declare I am the father of this poor girl the prisoner at the bar; nay, when I go farther, and avow, that of all my offspring she is my favourite child. I can truly say that I bestowed a more than ordinary pains in her education; in which I will venture to affirm, I followed the rules of all those who are acknowledged to have writ best on the subject; and if her conduct be fairly examined, she will be found to deviate very little from the strictest observation of all those rules; neither Homer nor Virgil pursued them with greater care than myself, and the candid and learned reader will see that the latter was the noble model, which I made use of on this occasion.

I do not think my child is entirely free from faults. I know nothing human that is so; but surely she doth not deserve the rancour with which she hath been treated by the public. However ... I do ... solemnly declare to you, Mr Censor, that I will trouble the world no more with any children of mine by the same muse.'

(178–86)

Henry Fielding

from *Covent-Garden Journal*, no. 10   4 February 1752
(G. E. Jensen (ed.), vol. 1, 1915)

The present age seems pretty well agreed in an opinion, that the utmost scope and end of reading is amusement only. . . .

Letters, however, were surely intended for a much more noble and profitable purpose than this. Writers are not, I presume, to be considered as mere jack-puddings, whose business it is only to excite laughter: This, indeed, may sometimes be intermixed, and served up, with graver matters, in order to titilate the palate, and to recommend wholesome food to the mind; and, for this purpose, it hath been used by many excellent authors: 'for why,' as Horace says 'should not any one promulgate Truth with a smile on his countenance? Ridicule, indeed, as he again intimates, is commonly a stronger and better method of attacking Vice, than the severer kind of Satire.'

When wit and humour are introduced for such good purposes, when the agreeable *is blended with the useful, then* is the writer said *to have succeeded in every point. Pleasantry* (as the ingenious author of

Clarissa says of a story) *should be made only the vehicle of instruction*;[1] and thus romances themselves, as well as epic poems, may become worthy the perusal of the greatest of men: But when no moral, no lesson, no instruction is conveyed to the reader, where the whole design of the composition is no more than to make us laugh, the writer comes very near to the character of a buffoon. . . .

I cannot fairly, I think, be represented as an enemy to laughter, or to all those kinds of writing that are apt to promote it . . . Few men . . . do more admire the works of those great masters who have sent their satire . . . laughing into the world. Such are that great Triumvirate, Lucian, Cervantes, and Swift. These authors I shall ever hold in the highest degree of esteem; not indeed for that wit and humour alone which they all so eminently possess, but because they all endeavoured, with the utmost force of their wit and humour, to expose and extirpate those follies and vices which chiefly prevailed in their several countries.

I would not be thought to confine wit and humour to these writers. Shakespeare, Molière, and some other authors, have been blessed with the same talents, and have employed them to the same purposes. There are some, however, who tho' not void of these talents have made so wretched a use of them, that had the consecration of their labours been committed to the hands of the hangman, no good man would have regretted their loss: nor am I afraid to mention Rabelais, and Aristophanes himself in this number. For if I may speak my opinion freely of these two last writers, and of their works, their design appears to me very plainly to have been to ridicule all Sobriety, Modesty, Decency, Virtue and religion, out of the world. Now whoever reads over the five great writers first mentioned in this paragraph, must either have a very bad head, or a very bad heart, if he doth not become both a wiser and a better man.

(193–4)

1 Fielding again refers to Richardson's statement at the end of the Preface to *The Journal of a Voyage to Lisbon*; see p. 134 [ed.].

Hester Chapone

from a letter to Elizabeth Carter   11 February 1752
(*Critical Heritage*)

You are a friend to Fielding's Amelia. I love the woman, but for the
book – it must have merit, since Miss Carter and some few more good
judges approve of it. Are not you angry with the author, for giving
his favourite character such a lord and master? and is it quite natural
that she should be so perfectly happy and pleased with such a wretch?
A fellow without principles, or understanding, with no other merit
in the world but a natural good temper, and whose violent love for his
wife could not keep him from injuring her in the most essential
points, and that in circumstances that render him utterly inexcusable.
Can you forgive his amour with that dreadful, shocking monster,
Miss Mathews? Are we to look upon these crimes as the failings of
human nature, as Fielding seems to do, who takes his notions of
human nature from the most depraved and corrupted part of it, and
seems to think no characters natural, but such as are a disgrace to the
human species? Don't you think Booth's sudden conversion a mere
botch to save the author's credit as a moral writer? And is there not a
tendency in all his works, to soften the deformity of vice, by placing
characters in an amiable light, that are destitute of every virtue except
good nature? Was not you tired with the two first volumes? What
think you of Mrs Bennet and her story? . . . The last volume pleased
me very well; Doctor Harrison's character is admirable; the scene
between Colonel James and his lady, excellent; that in which Colonel
James's challenge comes to the hands of Amelia is extremely affecting; the conversation between the Lord and Doctor Harrison, the
doctor's letter, and the comments of the bucks upon it, I also admire
very much. And now, I think, I have mentioned all that I can praise
in the whole book; but it would take up more paper than I have left
to point out one half of the pages that disgusted me.
(318–19)

Bonnell Thornton

from *Drury-Lane Journal* 13 February 1752 *(Critical Heritage)*

A New Chapter in *Amelia*
More witty than the rest, if the Reader has but sense enough to find out the Humour

Amelia, finding her husband did not come home, sat herself down contented to her supper, which consisted of no other variety than a Welch rabbit, and of which I have told my reader she was particularly fond. Her little family were squatted upon the hearth close by her knees, and knawing each of them an huge luncheon of bread and butter, with windows cut upon it, and strew'd with brown sugar. Poor Mrs Atkinson, who had taken too large a sip of the cherry brandy bottle that evening, had loll'd herself back against her chair by the fireside, and sat snoring.

The disconsolate turtle was lamenting the long absence of her mate, when the old decrepit magistrate of the night went his rounds, and with an hearty bounce at the door proclaim'd it – past twelve o'clock, and a frosty morning. Booth was not yet return'd; and Amelia, who was sitting all the while upon tenter-hooks, had enough to do to quiet her babes, who incessantly worried her with, 'Mammy! – where's Pappy? – Mammy! – where's Pappy? – Mammy! – where's Pappy?'

'He's coming presently,' cried the fond mother, 'he's but gone to buy a dilly-cock for pappy's nown children to shy at.' – And she comforted them as well as she could, with singing 'Dance over the Lady Lea', and telling them merry stories about murder.

At length a very violent knocking was heard, which almost beat the door down, and made the house ring again: The children squalled out: Mrs Atkinson started, and endeavouring to get up, fell off her seat sideways: Amelia's gentle spirits were so much agitated, that if she had not gulp'd down some small oats, which she had warm'd in a tin cup at supper, she must infallibly have fainted away. As it was, she had no power to wag, but sat upright in her chair with both arms expanded, stiff and motionless, all the same as if she had been ty'd to a stake, or put into the ducking stool.

Little Betty burst open the door, and ran in, frighten'd out of her seven senses. 'La, Mistress,' says she, 'here's Master com'd home, as drunk as a piper; to be sure, he's in a woundy sad pickle, that sartain: he's all over of a gore of blood, and as nasty! – I wouldn't touch him with a pair of tongs.'

During this, there was a great rumbling upon the stairs; when presently Sergeant Atkinson led the staggering Booth in; and, as he held him out at arms length with one hand, pinched his own nostrils close together between his thumb and fore-finger with the other. Amelia was just going to have her old qualms again, but taking heart and another gulp of beer, she flew into her husband's arms, clasped him round the middle, and immediately fell a whimpering: nor did she perceive the nasty souse he had been swashed in, till her delicate nose scented something about him not very savoury.

'Are you hurt, my dear, any wheres?' cried the tender Amelia. 'Hiccup,' says Booth, and what he had never been guilty of before, belch'd in her lovely face. She then clapped him down upon a chair, and was going to wipe his mouth with her muckender: but what was her consternation, when she found his high-arched Roman nose, that heretofore resembled the bridge of a fiddle, had been beat all to pieces! As herself had before lost the handle to her face, she now truly sympathis'd with him in their mutual want of snout.

But it was more than she could bear, when she came to search his breeches, and found nothing in them: for she had put a crooked shilling (the only one they had in the world, and which had been long kept for luck's sake) into his pocket, before he went out, that he might appear like a gentleman.

Atkinson by this time had raised his wife, who, in the tumble, got a great bump upon her nob, and was gone down to fetch some brown paper and vinegar. As soon as Mrs Atkinson spied the queer figure Booth cut with his flatten'd proboscis, she set up an horse-laugh; and as she is an old dab at Latin, especially when tipsy, she pour'd out the following scraps from Virgil and Horace.

Monstr' horrend' inform' ingens, cui lumen ademptum!
Hoc magis esse velim, quam pravo vivere naso
Spectandum nigris oculis, nigroque capillo.

'Ha' done with your Nasos, and your Negroes,' quoth Amelia in a pet, 'and don't ye laugh at other people's haps.' 'Why, Madam,' replied Mrs Atkinson, a little dumb-founded, 'sure a body may talk Greek, mayn't one, without' – here a hiccup opportunely cut the thread of her sentence. 'God bless you, poor woman!' cries Amelia, and lifted up her hands. 'God bless me!' says Mrs Atkinson, snapping her up; 'God bless you; I have no more need of God's blessing than you, Madam!'

Little Betty, coming in at this instant with a pail of water, put a stop to the dispute, which other wise might have ended in the destruction of caps. Serjeant Atkinson was permitted to apply the plaister to his wife's forehead, which helped to cool her brains. All hands were now aloft in assisting to sweeten poor Booth, who, after having puked awhile, recover'd his senses sufficiently to remember how he came in this condition.

The sum of it is this: Captain Trent had carried him, by main force, to the nobleman's so often mentioned in this history, who plied him so with burgundy and champagne, that Booth crossed the streets all the way in reeling home. He had thought enough to know he could not muster up the dust to pay the hire of a chair, having dispos'd of his last and only hog to the footman at the door – in his way he unfortunately stumbled against a tub, which the nightmen had left standing in the middle of the street; knock'd his nozzle against the brim of it, and fairly (I should rather say, foully) tumbled into it: where he must have been smother'd in the ordure, had they not come to his assistance, and help'd him out. In this stinking condition he swagger'd home by himself, not being able to tell them where he lodg'd.

After they had put Booth to bed, the Sergeant and his crooked rib took themselves away, and retired to rest; Amelia did the same, as soon as she had disposed of her little nursery, who were sent down, and kept below stairs during what has been related in the conclusion of this chapter. She comforted herself with the old proverb, that – *luck was good luck*, as it indeed proved to Booth. But what the good fortune consequent to this accident was, the Reader, if he has any nose at all, may smell out in the next chapter.

N.B. We could have split this into innumerable breaks, according to the example of the original, which would have spun it into two pages

more; but we chuse to crowd as much matter into our numbers as we can, that nobody may complain they have not an exceeding good threepenny-worth for their three-pence.
(321–4)

Samuel Richardson

from a letter to Anne Donnellan 22 February 1752
(John Carroll (ed.), *Selected Letters*, 1964)

Will I leave you to Captain Booth? Captain Booth, Madam, has done his own business. Mr Fielding has over-written himself, or rather *under*-written; and in his own journal seems ashamed of his last piece; and has promised that the same Muse shall write no more for him. The piece, in short, is as dead as if it had been published forty years ago, as to sale.

You guess that I have not read Amelia. Indeed I have read but the first volume. I had intended to go through with it; but I found the characters and situations so wretchedly low and dirty, that I imagined I could not be interested for any one of them; and to read and not to care what became of the hero and heroine, is a task that I thought I would leave to those who had more leisure than I am blessed with.

Parson Young sat for Fielding's Parson Adams, a man he knew, and only made a little more absurd than he is known to be. The best story in the piece, is of himself and his first wife. In his *Tom Jones*, his hero is made a natural child, because his own first wife was such. Tom Jones is Fielding himself, hardened in some places, softened in others. His Lady Bellaston is an infamous woman of his former acquaintance. His Sophia is again his first wife. Booth, in his last piece again himself; Amelia, even to her noselessness, is again his first wife. His brawls, his jarrs, his gaols, his spunging-houses, are all drawn from what he has seen and known. As I said (witness also his hamper plot) he has little or no invention: and admirably do you observe, that by several strokes in his Amelia he designed to be good, but knew not how, and lost his genius, low humour, in the attempt.
(196–7)

Samuel Richardson

from a letter to Lady Bradshaigh   23 February 1752
(John Carroll (ed.), *Selected Letters*, 1964)

I have not been able to read any more than the first volume of Amelia. Poor Fielding! I could not help telling his sister that I was equally surprised at and concerned for his continued lowness. Had your brother, said I, been born in a stable, or been a runner at a sponging-house, we should have thought him a genius, and wished he had had the advantage of a liberal education, and of being admitted into good company; but it is beyond my conception, that a man of family, and who had some learning, and who really is a writer, should descend so excessively low, in all his pieces. Who can care for any of his people? A person of honour asked me, the other day, what he could mean, by saying, in his *Covent Garden Journal*, that he had followed Homer and Virgil, in his Amelia. I answered, that he was justified in saying so, because he must mean Cotton's *Virgil Travestied*, where the women are drabs, and the men scoundrels.
(198–9)

Allan Ramsay

from *A Letter ... Concerning the Affair of Elizabeth Canning*
1753 (*Critical Heritage*)

[*Tom Jones* is the highest type of] an artful story, ... where the incidents are so various, and yet so consistent with themselves, and with nature, that the more the reader is acquainted with nature, the more he is deceived into a belief of its being true; and is with difficulty recall'd from that belief by the author's confession from time to time of its being all a fiction.
(361)

Friedrich Melchior, Baron Grimm

from *Correspondance Littéraire*   1 August 1753
(English translation from *Critical Heritage*)

The English have a kind of domestic novel that is completely unknown to the French. I speak of the novels of an excellent author in
that genre, Mr Fielding, who has just produced a new novel in
English called *Amelia*. This writer, who doubtless deserves a distinguished place among the authors who have added glory to England, is a great and original painter, always truthful and sometimes
as sublime as Molière. . . . At first it seems astonishing that the French,
who have many good novels in their language, have never painted
their domestic customs; but . . . if there are no representations in
this genre, it is not the fault of the painter, but of his models. For
when he paints our *petits maîtres* and *petites maîtresses* he has almost
exhausted the subject.
(363)

Lady Mary Wortley Montagu

from a letter to the Countess of Bute   23 July 1754 (Robert
Halsband (ed.), *Complete Letters*, vol. 3, 1967)

H. Fielding has given a true picture of himself and his first wife in
the characters of Mr and Mrs Booth (some complement to his own
figure excepted) and I am persuaded several of the incidents he
mentions are real matters of fact. I wonder he does not perceive Tom
Jones and Mr Booth are sorry scoundrels. All these sort of books
have the same fault, which I cannot easily pardon, being very
mischievous. They place a merit in extravagant passions, and encourage young people to hope for impossible events to draw them
out of the misery they choose to plunge themselves into, expecting
legacies from unknown relations, and generous benefactors to
distressed virtue, as much out of Nature as fairy treasures. Fielding
has really a fund of true humour, and was to be pitied at his first
entrance into the world, having no choice (as he said himself) but to

be a Hackney writer or a Hackney coachman. His genius deserved a better Fate, but I cannot help blaming that continued indiscretion (to give it the softest name) that has run through his life, and I am afraid still remains. I guessed *R. Random* to be his, though without his name. I cannot think Fadom wrote by the same hand; it is every way so much below it.
(66)

Anonymous

'From Joseph Addison to the Author of *Tom Jones*', letter 16, *Admonitions from the Dead to the Living* 1754 (*Critical Heritage*)

It has grieved me to see so much power to do good as you have possessed, employed to so little purpose as you have employed it. . . .

Wit, the most dangerous weapon in the hands of an ill-natured, or ill, man that could be put into them, you possess, or have possessed in a degree superior to all your contemporaries. But it were well if you had apply'd it to those purposes which it would so happily have answer'd in the hands of a good, or good-natured person. . . .

Ridicule, tho' one of the lowest parts of what deserves the name of wit; nay, humour, which, if there be a yet lower, is that lowest, may be rendered useful; no man has possessed it more perfectly than you have done. Nature joined in you the spirit of the late Rabelais, and of the early Lucian: but you have not employed them as they did. She has given you, with the humour, a double portion of the indelicacy of the Frenchman, and with the wit of the Greek, a tenfold freedom where restraint was necessary. . . .

There are men who deserve all your severity, but they have yet escaped it: there are those who deserve your approbation; be generous, and declare it. But hereafter use more discretion in your praise, and less bitterness in your severity. . . .

Believe that you may err, and carrying that modest opinion always with you, never be positive. . . . The credit the world is ready to pay to what you say, ought to have weight to inspire you doubly with this caution. . . .

Severity of satire, even if it be carried to the height without this stain, yet is, of all things, that for which a judicious writer would least wish to be praised. Because those who praised, would at the same time dread him; and men naturally hate what they fear. . . . Men are ill-natur'd too often, and those who are inclin'd to think the worst, will receive all as Truth, because there is some pretence for supposing he who writes has known it all.

This is the light in which every man will see the satirist, who, with the power of wounding, possesses that badness of heart which will give him pleasure in doing it. All will dread him, and he can never be assured that those with whom he is in the most perfect intimacy, do not in their hearts detest him. We see farther, who are out of the world, than you do who are in it; and, believe a friendly shade, who tells you that this has been the case with many, who have thought themselves happy in their friendships; and this has been the case with you.

(381-5)

Henry Fielding

from the Preface to *Journal of a Voyage to Lisbon*   1754
(Harold E. Pagliaro (ed.), 1963)

There would not, perhaps, be a more pleasant, or profitable study, among those which have their principal end in amusement, than that of travels or voyages, if they were writ, as they might be, and ought to be, with a joint view to the entertainment and information of mankind. If the conversation of travellers be so eagerly sought after as it is, we may believe their books will be still more agreeable company, as they will, in general, be more instructive and more entertaining.

But when I say the conversation of travellers is usually so welcome, I must be understood to mean that only of such as have had good sense enough to apply their peregrinations to a proper use, so as to acquire from them a real and valuable knowledge of men and things; both which are best known by comparison. If the customs and manners of men were every where the same, there would be no office so dull as that of a traveller: for the difference of hills, valleys, rivers; in short, the various views in which we may see the face of the earth, would scarce afford him a pleasure worthy of his labour; and surely it would give him very little opportunity of communicating any kind of entertainment or improvement to others.

To make a traveller an agreeable companion to a man of sense, it is necessary, not only that he should have seen much, but that he should have overlooked much of what he hath seen. Nature is not, any more than a great genius, always admirable in her productions, and therefore the traveller, who may be called her commentator, should not expect to find every where subjects worthy of his notice.

It is certain, indeed, that one may be guilty of omission as well as of the opposite extreme: but a fault on that side will be more easily pardoned. . . .

As there are few things which a traveller is to record, there are fewer on which he is to offer his observations: this is the office of the reader, and it is so pleasant a one, that he seldom chooses to have it taken from him, under the pretence of lending him assistance. Some occasions, indeed, there are, when proper observations are pertinent, and others when they are necessary; but good sense alone must point them out. I shall lay down only one general rule, which I believe to be of universal truth between relator and hearer, as it is between author and reader; this is, that the latter never forgive any observation of the former which doth not convey some knowledge that they are sensible they could not possibly have attained of themselves.

But all his pains in collecting knowledge, all his judgement in selecting, and all his art in communicating it, will not suffice, unless he can make himself, in some degree, an agreeable, as well as an instructive companion. The highest instruction we can derive from the tedious tale of a dull fellow scarce ever pays us for our attention. There is nothing, I think, half so valuable as knowledge, and yet there is nothing which men will give themselves so little trouble to attain; unless it be, perhaps, that lowest degree of it which is the object of curiosity, and which hath therefore that active passion constantly employed in its service. This, indeed, it is in the power of every traveller to gratify; but it is the leading principle in weak minds only. . . .

Why there should scarce exist a single writer of this kind worthy our regard; and whilst there is no other branch of history (for this is history) which hath not exercised the greatest pens, why this alone should be overlooked by all men of great genius and erudition, and delivered up to the Goths and Vandals as their lawful property, is altogether as difficult to determine.

And yet that this is the case, with some very few exceptions, is most manifest. Of these I shall willingly admit Burnet and Addison; if the former was not perhaps to be considered as a political essayist, and the latter as a commentator on the Classics, rather than as a writer of travels; which last title perhaps they would both of them have been least ambitious to affect. . . .

I am not here unapprized that old Homer himself is by some considered as a voyage-writer; and indeed the beginning of his *Odyssey* may be urged to countenance that opinion, which I shall not controvert. But whatever species of writing the *Odyssey* is of, it is surely at the head of that species, as much as the *Iliad* is of another; and so far the excellent Longinus would allow, I believe, at this day.

But, in reality, the *Odyssey*, the *Telemachus*, and all of that kind, are to the voyage-writing I here intend, what romance is to true history, the former being the confounder and corrupter of the latter. I am far from supposing, that Homer, Hesiod, and the other antient poets and mythologists, had any settled design to pervert and confuse the records of antiquity; but it is certain they have effected it; and, for my part, I must confess I should have honoured and loved Homer more had he written a true history of his own times in humble prose, than those noble poems that have so justly collected the praise of all ages; for though I read these with more admiration and astonishment, I still read Herodotus, Thucydides and Xenophon, with more amusement and more satisfaction.

The original poets were not, however, without excuse. They found the limits of nature too strait for the immensity of their genius, which they had not room to exert, without extending fact by fiction; and that especially at a time when the manners of men were too simple to afford that variety, which they have since offered in vain to the choice of the meanest writers. In doing this, they are again excusable for the manner in which they have done it: *Ut speciosa dehinc miracula promant.*

They are not indeed so properly said to turn reality into fiction, as fiction into reality. Their paintings are so bold, their colours so strong, that every thing they touch seems to exist in the very manner they represent it: their portraits are so just, and their landscapes so beautiful, that we acknowledge the strokes of nature in both, without enquiring whether nature herself, or her journeyman the poet, formed the first pattern of the piece.

But other writers (I will put Pliny at their head) have no such pretensions to indulgence: they lie for lying sake, or in order insolently to impose the most monstrous improbabilities and absurdities upon their readers on their own authority ... without ever taking the pains of adapting their lies to human credulity. . . .

There is another fault of a kind directly opposite to this, to which [travel-] writers are sometimes liable, when, instead of filling their pages with monsters which no body hath ever seen, and with adventures which never have nor could possibly have happened to them, waste their time and paper with recording things and facts of so common a kind, that they challenge no other right of being remembered, than as they had the honour of having happened to the author, to whom nothing seems trivial that in any manner happens to himself. Of such consequence do his own actions appear to one of this kind, that he would probably think himself guilty of infidelity, should he omit the minutest thing in the detail of his journal. That the fact is true, is sufficient to give it a place there, without any consideration whether it is capable of pleasing or surprising, of diverting or informing the reader. . . .

Now from both these faults we have endeavoured to steer clear in the following narrative: which, however the contrary may be insinuated by ignorant, unlearned, and fresh-water critics, who have never travelled either in books or ships, I do solemnly declare doth, in my own impartial opinion, deviate less from truth than any other voyage extant; my Lord Anson's alone being, perhaps, excepted.

Some few embellishments must be allowed to every historian: for we are not to conceive that the speeches in Livy, Sallust, or Thucydides, were literally spoken in the very words in which we now read them. It is sufficient that every fact hath its foundation in truth, as I do seriously aver is the case in the ensuing pages; and when it is so, a good critic will be so far from denying all kind of ornament of style or diction, or even of circumstance to his author, that he would be rather sorry if he omitted it: for he could hence derive no other advantage than the loss of an additional pleasure in the perusal.

Again, if any merely common incident should appear in this journal, which will seldom, I apprehend, be the case, the candid reader will easily perceive it is not introduced for its own sake, but for some observations and reflections naturally resulting from it; and which, if but little to his amusement, tend directly to the instruction of the reader, or to the information of the public; to whom if I choose to convey such instruction or information with an air of joke and laughter, none but the dullest of fellows will, I believe, censure it; but if they should, I have the authority of more than one passage in Horace to allege in my defence. . . .

One hint . . . I must give the kind reader; which is, that if he should be able to find no sort of amusement in the book, he will be pleased to remember the public utility which will arise from it. If entertainment, as Mr Richardson observes, be but a secondary consideration in a romance; with which Mr Addison I think agrees, affirming the use of the pastry-cook to be the first; if this, I say, be true of a mere work of invention, sure it may well be so considered in a work founded, like this, on truth, and where the political reflections form so distinguishing a part.

But perhaps I may hear, from some critic of the most saturnine complexion, that my vanity must have made a horrid dupe of my judgment, if it hath flattered me with an expectation of having any thing here seen in a grave light, or of conveying any useful instruction to the public, or to their guardians. I answer with the great man, whom I just now quoted, that my purpose is to convey instruction in the vehicle of entertainment;[1] and so to bring about at once, like the revolution in *The Rehearsal,* a perfect reformation of the laws relating to our maritime affairs: an undertaking, I will not say more modest, but surely more feasible, than that of reforming a whole people, by making use of a vehicular story, to wheel in among them worse manners than their own.

(23–30)

1 For an earlier reference to this remark of Richardson's, see p. 125. [ed.]

Anonymous

from a review of *Journal of a Voyage to Lisbon*,
Gentleman's Magazine   March 1755 (*Critical Heritage*)

This journal [*Voyage to Lisbon*] contains an account of the adventures
and distresses of the author and his family, in a journey from Fordham
to Rotherhithe, on board the ship; thence to the Isle of Wight, and
on shore there, while they were wind bound, at a paltry alehouse,
where, as the best room, they chose to dine in a barn. The captain,
the seamen, the landlady and her husband, and several other characters,
which the particular circumstances of his situation brought under his
notice, are described, with that humour in which he is confessed to
have excelled every other writer of his age. But this little book would
be very valuable for the instruction which it contains, if the entertainment was wanting; the remarks upon his own situation, upon the
manners of others, upon many intollerable inconveniences which
arise either from the defect of our laws, or the ignorance of those by
whom they should be executed, deserve the attention not of individuals only but of the public.
(388)

Horace Walpole

from a letter to Richard Bentley   27 March 1755
(P. Toynbee (ed.), *Letters*, vol. 3, 1903)

... Fielding's *Travels*, or rather an account how his dropsy was
treated and teased by an inn-keeper's wife in the Isle of Wight.
(294)

Lady Mary Wortley Montagu

from a letter to the Countess of Bute   22 September 1755
(Robert Halsband (ed.), *Complete Letters*, vol. 3, 1967)

I am sorry for H. Fielding's death, not only as I shall read no more of his writings, but I believe he lost more than others, as no man enjoy'd life more than he did, tho' few had less reason to do so, the highest of his preferment being raking in the lowest sinks of vice and misery. . . . His happy constitution (even when he had, with great pains, half demolish'd it) made him forget every thing when he was before a venison pasty or over a flask of champaign, and I am persuaded he has known more happy moments than any prince upon earth. His natural spirits gave him rapture with his cookmaid, and cheerfulness when he was fluxing in a garret. There was a great similitude between his character and that of Sir Richard Steele. He had the advantage both in learning and, in my opinion, genius. They both agreed in wanting money in spite of all their friends, and would have wanted it if their hereditary lands had been as extensive as their imagination, yet each of them so form'd for happiness, it is pity they were not immortal. . . .

I desire to have Fielding's posthumous works with his *Memoirs of Jonathan Wild* and *Journey to the Next World*, also the *Memoirs of Verocand a Man of Pleasure*, and those of *A Young Lady*. You will call all this trash, trumpery, etc.
(87–8)

Part Two The Developing Debate

Introduction

The first important study of Fielding after his death was Arthur Murphy's 'Essay on the Life and Genius of Henry Fielding', prefixed to an edition of Fielding's *Works* (1762). Murphy has been made responsible for perpetuating far into the future the old myth of a careless, profligate Fielding. But if the biographical portions of the 'Essay' (which are not included here in any detail) tend to damn the novelist with 'pompous and patronizing' praise (Blanchard, pp. 156–9), there is in the 'Essay' some good discussion of Fielding's *writings*. Murphy's 'Essay' was frequently reprinted or paraphrased throughout the rest of the century.

In the 1760s and later, Fielding's novels became popular in dramatic and operatic adaptations in English, French and German. They were also imitated in several minor fictions. Collected editions and editions of individual works by Fielding appeared frequently in England and abroad. Richardson continued to hold sway in critical opinion, and, for some time, in popular taste. His position was notably maintained at the expense of Fielding's by Dr Johnson and his circle, although Boswell and others defended Fielding, and Fanny Burney clearly admired him despite some recoil from his coarseness. This coarseness was often held to be related to the biographical legend of Fielding's dissolute ways, although there were those, like James Harris, who said that 'Had his life been less irregular . . . his pictures of human kind had neither been so various, nor so natural', a view refreshingly expressed but which looks forward to that special sentimental archness about Fielding that became current among Victorian free spirits like Thackeray.

Fielding's reputation had always suffered from that eighteenth-century cult of 'sensibility' which professed itself too refined for scenes of coarse or low life, and too tender-hearted for satire. That Fielding's celebration of 'good nature' and open-heartedness was in harmony with some of the most valuable and most

fundamental aspects of 'sensibility' was not always recognized.
As fashionable 'sentiment' became more squeamishly respectable
and 'refined', Fielding suffered increasing disrepute in some
quarters. (Richardson and Sterne were more acceptable to
fashionable taste, though they too were found too coarse for some
palates.) But there were also some strong celebrations of Fielding
by George Colman and William Hayley (Blanchard, pp. 208 and
213), by David Garrick, who in 1778 wrote the Prologue to
Fielding's *The Fathers: or, The Good-Natur'd Man*, and by some
others.

Partly related to the sensibilist rejection of Fielding was the
notion, most memorably expressed in the clockwork image used
by Richardson and Johnson, that Fielding was a superficial
observer of human behaviour rather than a profound analyst of
the human heart. Running alongside it was a view, which has
proved very enduring, of Fielding's novels as notable primarily
for their supremely well-articulated plots. This view sometimes,
though by no means always, carries the implication that
Fielding was deficient in more important elements of the novelist's
art. But it also enabled scholarly critics like Beattie and Pye to
celebrate Fielding according to high Aristotelian canons. Pye
anticipates (and outdoes in Fielding's favour) a famous Coleridgean
comparison of the plot of *Tom Jones* to that of the *Oedipus
Tyrannus*, and it is very clear that for Coleridge Fielding was no
mere plot-spinner, but a great artist and a great human being.
The excellence of Fielding's plots was sometimes thought to be
impaired by interpolated narratives, like that of the Man of the
Hill, by the introductory chapters which open each book of *Tom
Jones*, by several other forms of authorial intrusion, and by an
excess of mock-heroic and other stylizations. These features of
Fielding's style have always had their defenders, but, singly or in
combination, have also been attacked from the eighteenth
century onwards not only by hostile critics but by Fielding's

admirers: Monboddo, Cumberland, Scott. The debate anticipates, and is continued into, those post-Flaubertian discussions of 'authorial intrusion' in the novel whose great English examples are the critical writings of James (who nevertheless greatly admired Fielding, intrusions included) and Ford Madox Ford (who disliked Fielding intensely).

To the praise of serious critics like Beattie, Monboddo, Pye and others in the second half of the eighteenth century should be added the celebrated statement of Gibbon about Fielding's immortality. The dramatist and novelist Richard Cumberland paid Fielding the tribute of writing in *Henry* (1795) the most interesting of various eighteenth-century imitations of *Tom Jones*, and of mentioning Fielding repeatedly in its series of Fieldingesque introductory chapters.

The publication by Mrs Barbauld of Richardson's *Correspondence* (1804), with its many hostile and often small-minded comments on Fielding, seems to have caused a revulsion against Richardson on the part of some readers (like Coleridge), and may paradoxically have been a factor in the rise of Fielding in popular and critical esteem. Mrs Barbauld perpetuated or refined on some of the current biographical slanders against Fielding, and the old habit of allowing biographical slurs to colour the criticism of the novels persisted throughout the nineteenth century. But Mrs Barbauld's admiration for Richardson did not prevent her from writing some warmly and acutely appreciative criticism of Fielding in her important fifty-volume collection of *The British Novelists* (1810). Another admirer of Richardson, Sir James Mackintosh, noted a decline in Richardson's popularity and a rise in Fielding's, expressing some qualified admiration of Fielding on his own part (1811 and 1815).

It is interesting to find the more Augustan of the two great novelists becoming very highly and generously esteemed, sometimes at the expense of his more obviously 'pre-Romantic' rival, by some of the greatest figures of the Romantic period: Coleridge (whose first preference had once been for Richardson), Byron, Lamb, Hazlitt, Scott. Hazlitt, in particular, wrote many times about Fielding, celebrating his great moral decency and warmth, his understanding of human nature, his value as a counterweight to the 'respectability' and overnice squeamishness of early nineteenth-century taste, his Englishness, his technical mastery. Hazlitt also acted as an acute, enthusiastic and successful propagandist for Fielding among his literary friends, notably Coleridge and Lamb, and near the end of his life he wrote up an extremely lively set of conversations (part-real, part-fictional) with the painter James Northcote, who is on several occasions presented as an intelligent but severely critical reader of Fielding. Hazlitt's writing is shot through with exhilarating, though not uncritical, loyalty. But Coleridge's tributes (most of which, being in the form of letters, notes, marginalia and the like, did not reach a wide audience at once) are among the most probingly intelligent, as well as the handsomest, ever paid to Fielding. Byron, too, was an acute and warm admirer, who drew particular attention among other things to a political radicalism which he felt to be reflected in *Jonathan Wild*. (Byron also inveighed against the squeamishness of an age which would reject his *Don Juan* whilst being perfectly willing to read older authors like Smollett, Prior, Ariosto and Fielding.)

But it was Scott, whose many comments on Fielding combined generous praise with a few of the old biographical prejudices, who was more widely influential. Scott says many shrewd things about Fielding's artistry, though he has surprised later critics by his tendency, in many important respects, to prefer Smollett. Fielding's rising reputation received a boost from Scott's own novelistic achievement, from *Waverley* (1814) onwards, which helped to raise the status of the novel-form; equally, Scott's novels themselves came often to be more highly rated than Fielding's.

In the late eighteenth century and the first half of the
nineteenth, Fielding was increasingly read and esteemed on the
Continent. He was spoken of in Germany, by Goethe and others,
as one of the great figures of English literature, an influence and a
source of healthy envy and emulation for German writers. He was
translated into Russian, and greatly admired in eighteenth-century
Russia despite a prevailing preference for Richardson.[1] In the 1830s
and 1840s he is mentioned with the highest respect by Gogol and
Pushkin, and later in the century the young Gorki read and
defended his enthusiasm for 'Thomas Jones'.

In France, Fielding's novels were translated early, though usually
in truncated versions intended for the more refined and
classically purer tastes which the French believed themselves to be
blessed with. Voltaire and Diderot refer to Fielding occasionally.
Mme de Staël regarded *Tom Jones* as exceptionally serious among
novels in its moral, philosophical and psychological grasp. The
Marquis de Sade paid Fielding one of the most surprising
compliments he has ever received. But among major French
writers who were interested in Fielding, Stendhal is the most
important and the most fascinating. He began with a certain
dislike of *Tom Jones*, which he read in La Place's translation in
1803 (he bought an English text in 1810 which was found among
his books when he died). But he came to feel in 1825 that it was
'one of the greatest works that modern literature has produced'[2]
and five years before his death said that it was 'to other novels
what the *Iliad* is to epic poems' (1837). He never seems to have
mentioned Fielding's other novels. But his interest in *Tom Jones*
was obsessive. Critics have differed over the nature and extent of
Fielding's influence on Stendhal's novels. But the frequency of

1 See Ernest J. Simmons, *Introduction to Russian Realism*, 1965, pp. 13 and 14.
2 Stendhal, *Selected Journalism from the English Reviews*, ed. Geoffrey
Strickland, John Calder, 1959, p. 35.

F-7

the comments on *Tom Jones* in his diaries, his working notebooks and elsewhere (only a selection is given here), and their subtlety, eloquence and arrestingly idiosyncratic quality, show the intimacy of his engagement in Fielding's novel, and his deep though not of course uncritical interest as a working novelist in Fielding's techniques and achievements.

Among English nineteenth-century novelists, Thackeray was the most deeply and obsessively preoccupied with Fielding. His admiration for Fielding goes back to his boyhood, and at Cambridge he praised him to his undergraduate friends. (For some amusing pencilled illustrations by him in a copy of *Joseph Andrews*, see *Thackerayana*, new edn, n.d., pp. 74–7.) He modelled himself on Fielding in his writings, identified himself with him as an author and as a man, wrote about him unceasingly in his published writings and private correspondence, and had a longing to write a biography of him. There are, as one might expect from such an intimate self-involvement, some ambiguities and vacillations in Thackeray's attitude (for an analysis of differences between the review article of 1840 and the lecture of 1851, see Blanchard, pp. 409 ff.). Like other Victorian authors, he envied Fielding's freedom to portray life frankly, without evading the facts of immorality and low-life (a freedom partly attributed to a more 'free-spoken' age), and noted acutely in 1840 that 'decorous' Victorian treatments of low-life could actually be more immoral and corrupting than Fielding. But he himself recoiled from time to time in censorious embarrassment at some of the things he envied Fielding's ability to portray. He presented a sentimentalized portrait of Fielding as a convivial roisterer, thus consolidating an existing legend which has always been a mixed blessing to Fielding's reputation, but charging the portrait also with a certain guilty and envious self-identification which was Thackeray's own. He differed from time to time in his estimates of *Joseph Andrews*, which he admired at times, yet on one occasion

repudiated not only for being 'coarse and careless' but for the
author's 'absurd brag of his twopenny learning'. His accounts of
Tom Jones and to some extent of *Amelia* also differ in mood. But
he was exceptionally devoted to *Amelia* and its heroine (the
influence of *Amelia* on *Vanity Fair* was considerable), and he did
much to rehabilitate a novel which has not often been very highly
valued. He paid handsome tributes not only to the energy and
gusto of Fielding's writings, but to his careful craftsmanship, and
the lecture of 1851, despite some irritating and silly portions, was
a wholehearted, generous and influential statement. Thackeray's
public championship of Fielding, and the manifest influence of
Fielding on his own novels, gave him the reputation of being 'the
Fielding of the nineteenth century'.[1] Critics frequently compared
the two. Charlotte Brontë passionately admired Thackeray and
disliked Fielding, and was dismayed by the praise contained in
Thackeray's lecture. She also challenged G. H. Lewes for saying
favourable things about Fielding (Lewes was later to change his
mind: compare his views of 1847 and 1860). In more recent times,
Ford Madox Ford was to repudiate the two for authorial intrusion,
gentlemanly posturing and lack of artistic seriousness.

Dickens was not so deeply preoccupied with Fielding as was
Thackeray. But like Thackeray he spoke of him as an author who
had been able to write frankly about life, and appealed to his
example when *Oliver Twist* was accused of coarseness. Occasionally,
he turned to Fielding when considering problems of craftsmanship,
as we can see in the letter to Forster about *Little Dorrit*. In letters
of consolation to friends who had lost a child, Dickens more than
once refers to the episode in Fielding's *Journey from this World to
the Next*, book 1, chapter 8, in which Fielding meets his dead
child in Elysium, on one occasion saying that the author was

1 Gordon N. Ray (ed.), *Thackeray's Letters and Private Papers*, Oxford University
Press, 1945–6, vol. 2, p. 312; vol. 3, p. 184.

'one of the greatest English writers' (13 June 1855). *Tom Jones* was one of the books which, along with several novels by Smollett and others, David Copperfield read and loved as a boy in his father's house. Dickens gave one of his sons the name Henry Fielding. It seems likely, however, that Smollett's work meant more to Dickens than Fielding's.

Among other nineteenth-century novelists who had a high regard for Fielding, George Eliot (who does not seem to have shared the poor view of Fielding which G. H. Lewes expressed in 1860) spoke eloquently in *Middlemarch* about Fielding's 'copious remarks and digressions' and the 'initial chapters' in *Tom Jones*, while refusing to follow the example; and noted in a letter of 1861 that courage to be colloquial and familiar which Fielding shared with Shakespeare, Scott, Balzac 'and indeed every other writer of fiction of the first class' (compare Stendhal, 4 October 1832, on the 'familiarity' of tone in Scott and Fielding).

Other novelists who declared a very high regard for Fielding, and who considered his example in their fiction or their discussions of fiction, are Trollope; Meredith; and Hardy, who is one of the few critics to question the 'artistic form' of *Tom Jones* and to assert Richardson's superiority in this (but no other) respect, and who, like Gosse in 1898, thought of Fielding as a Wessex novelist.

Henry James (who also, but in the name of Flaubertian standards more specialized and exacting than Hardy's, found Fielding deficient in artistic form) was always more sympathetic to, and more interesting about, Fielding than post-Jamesian pundits of the art of fiction like Ford Madox Ford. James discussed Fielding briefly in his first book review (1864) and on several later occasions. He regarded Fielding as one of 'the fine painters of life', together with Shakespeare, Cervantes, Balzac, Dickens and some others,[1] and his tributes combine generosity and subtlety with an exquisitely modulated and uninsulting note of

1 See R. P. Blackmur (ed.), *The Art of the Novel*, p. 67.

patronage (see especially 1864 and 1908). Fielding was for James an example of the moralizing or didactic novelist, but one to whose energy and richness in that mode James was very responsive. He writes interestingly and critically of Fielding's treatment of women and of the quality 'of thought, of generalizing instinct, of *brain*' in his work as contrasted with George Eliot's (in her favour). Like many other nineteenth-century commentators, he notes that novelists of more recent times had to show more reticence in their treatment of sexual love than did Richardson and Fielding, but instead of showing Thackeray's naughty-clubman's mixture of envy and distaste for more 'free-spoken' days, James is able in the course of a masterly exploration to consider freshly and without cant the artistic advantages of such a reticence, once it is naturally imposed (1899).

A novelist more hostile to Fielding was James's close friend Robert Louis Stevenson. The discussion of Fielding and Scott in his essay on Victor Hugo is perhaps the most vivid and searchingly discussed expression of a preference for Scott's (and especially for Hugo's) type of Romantic novel, which had been voiced not infrequently by critics since the publication of *Waverley* in 1814. Among several other interesting statements about Fielding, the argumentative bravura of the 'odd inversion' of June 1888, in which Stevenson claims that Richardson was as a novelist more gentlemanly than Fielding, has particular piquancy (like Trollope, and perhaps following Thackeray, Stevenson expresses a preference for *Amelia* over *Tom Jones*).

Among nineteenth-century authors who were not practising novelists (e.g. Carlyle and Ruskin), the familiar blend of admiration and of moral reservation or recoil comes up again and again. Ruskin's various expressions of this are particularly sharp and vigorous, and often have other interesting things to say as well. Swinburne's admiration was more whole-hearted. He listed Fielding among 'the hundred books which I think I might prefer to keep if compelled to choose',[1] and wrote warmly about him in his sonnet on Dickens (*Poems*, vol. 5, 1905, p. 238), as well as in the essay on Dickens of 1902, where Dickens is rated more highly on some points than Fielding – a preference which was, naturally, not uncommon.

Among Continental readers, *Tom Jones* was a favourite of Karl Marx.[2] But the best-known of what seem to have been very few discussions of Fielding by Continental authors of the mid-century is Taine's portrait of the 'good buffalo' in his *History of English Literature*, an influential but essentially traditional conflation of the images of the carefree roisterer and the John Bull Englishman. An odd touch is the reference to Fielding's 'valiant plebeian heart', which should perhaps be borne in mind alongside James's description of Fielding as 'one of the masses', who 'wrote from the midst of the ... throng' (1864) and Stevenson's paradoxical denial of Fielding's gentlemanliness (1888). Taine writes vividly of Fielding's exposure of hypocrisy and the 'brood of secret passions' which it conceals. His passing comparison of Fielding with Molière, though commonplace, gains status by coming from a Frenchman (see also Gide's comparison in his prefatory notes on *Tom Jones*). His contrast of Fielding with 'the great impartial artists, Shakespeare and Goethe' is well-formulated, and was to elicit some interesting discussion from Leslie Stephen (1882).

Stephen is one of a group of several scholarly critics and editors of Fielding in the second half of the nineteenth century and the earliest years of the twentieth, who helped greatly to rehabilitate Fielding's moral reputation, and showed a desire to play down the more scabrous elements of the biographical legend. In Stephen himself, the legend intermittently held sway, although he recognized

1 See Cecil Y. Lang (ed.), *Letters*, vol. 5, 1962, p. 134.
2 See K. Marx and F. Engels, *Über Kunst und Literatur*, Europäische Verlagsanstalt, Frankfurt; Europa Verlag, Vienna, 1968, vol. 1, pp. 20, 29.

that Fielding was in some ways a great moral writer. Among other learned men of letters who wrote favourably and acutely about Fielding in important works of literary history and criticism, and in introductions to influential editions of Fielding's *Works*, were Henley, Gosse, Raleigh and Saintsbury. Henley partly accepted the old biographical legend, but argued bracingly that it was not to Fielding's discredit. Long before his edition of 1903, however, that legend had come under factual scrutiny. The most important figure in the early history of this factual reappraisal was Austin Dobson, whose volume on *Fielding* (1883) in the English Men of Letters Series, as Henley recognized in a review in the *Athenaeum* at the time (see Blanchard, p. 482), marked a decisive change of attitude, based scrupulously on biographical knowledge; and who subsequently wrote many shorter pieces on Fielding, including 'A New Dialogue of the Dead' (1913), in which Fielding confronts his early biographer, Arthur Murphy (reprinted in *Rosalba's Journal and Other Papers*, 1915). But a good deal of primary biographical investigation had been started in the 1850s, in Frederick Lawrence's *Life of Henry Fielding* (1855), a work which added to the factual record while maintaining some of the old prejudices, and in some articles by Thomas Keightley in *Fraser's Magazine* (1858), which challenged the prejudices themselves. The importance of Keightley's articles was not properly recognized until Dobson used them in 1883. They were collected into a book in 1907 by another scholarly defender of Fielding, Frederick S. Dickson. The tradition of careful documentary research was continued in Miss G. M. Godden's *Henry Fielding. A Memoir* (1910; Blanchard, pp. 538–9, notes the attractive fact that Fielding's 'moral laxity' was powerfully denied by his 'first woman biographer'), and the process culminates in Cross's extremely distinguished *History of Henry Fielding* (1918), still a standard biography.

Between 1871 and 1903, there were six prestigious collected

editions of Fielding: those of J. P. Browne (1871), Leslie Stephen (1882), George Saintsbury (1893), Edmund Gosse (1898–9), W. E. Henley (1903) and G. H. Maynadier (1903). Few scholarly critics attacked him, Sidney Lanier (1881) being a lively exception. Important scholarly work was beginning to take place even outside the biographical domain. Dobson's important edition of the *Voyage to Lisbon* (1892) helped to give this work a new status. His discovery, announced in 1895, of the sale catalogue of Fielding's library gave a fresh understanding of the breadth of Fielding's intellectual interests and the massiveness of his erudition, and helped to undermine the Thackerayan image of the carefree playboy flaunting his 'twopenny learning' (see *Eighteenth-Century Vignettes*, third series, 1896). In 1913, J. E. Wells published a long and important article on the politics of *Jonathan Wild*. In 1915, G. E. Jensen's edition of the *Covent-Garden Journal* appeared, followed in 1918 by James T. Hillhouse's edition of *The Tragedy of Tragedies*: both editions are impressively annotated, and remain standard. Aurélien Digeon's *Les Romans de Fielding* (1923; trs. 1925) is still a good critical introduction, while his study of the text of Fielding's novels (*Le Texte des Romans de Fielding*, 1923), though superseded in some important details by the specialized labours of later experts, remains a useful survey. In ensuing years, there were to be several further contributions from learned critics, among which Sherburn's essay on *Amelia* (1936) stands out. But it was not until after 1945 that the academic floodgates opened, releasing many important additions to the factual record and some of the best-informed academic criticism, along with unprecedented quantities of lugubrious rubbish.

Popular taste ran more or less in line with the learned revival of the late nineteenth century. Fielding's novels were again adapted for the stage in Robert Buchanan's *Sophia* (1886) and *Joseph's Sweetheart* (1888). In 1891, Birkbeck Hill noted that Fielding had ten readers to Richardson's one (Blanchard, p. 508).

It was now being said quite often that it was not only harmless but positively good for young girls to read Fielding's novels, as in the letter reprinted from the *New York Times* of 1904, or in a jaunty coarse-grained dialogue in Jerome K. Jerome's novel *They and I* (1909), pp. 262-3. Much celebration took place in the bicentenary year of Fielding's birth (1907; see Blanchard, pp. 523 ff.). Harold Williams was asserting in 1911 that *Tom Jones* was probably able to claim 'a larger and more imposing consensus of opinion that it is the greatest novel ever written than any other piece of prose-fiction penned by the hand of man' (Blanchard, p. 530).

A good deal of this esteem was reflected among creative writers and artists: see Shaw's startling tribute of 1898, Chesterton's energetic and sane discussion of 'Tom Jones and Morality' (1908), Arnold Bennett's warm admiration (Blanchard, p. 533), the not entirely wholehearted but affectionate respect of D. H. Lawrence (1914-15, 1930), the lively advocacy of J. B. Yeats (1914, 1921), the deeply personal interest of Gide (1911 onwards), and the variously expressed and not uncritical regard of Forster (1927), Graham Greene (1937: see Bibliography) and George Orwell (1940s). There were always dissenting voices, Samuel Butler's expression of boredom (1897) for example, and Ford Madox Ford's lifetime of lively hostility in the name of neo-Jamesian standards of artistic conscience. James himself did not share Ford's hostility. But Fielding was obviously being accused, even before Ford, of a lack of artistic refinement and moral sensibility. Already in 1894, Raleigh was having to defend Fielding against partisans of 'subdued tones in art'; in 1903 Henley was declaiming ironically to the effect that 'There is no more Fielding now. But we have not been idle. Far from it. And there is now an infinite deal of Messrs Howells and James'; and in 1911, H. G. Wells rejoiced at signs that a 'phase of narrowing and restriction' in the novel was over, and that the 'laxer, more spacious form of

novel-writing' associated with *Tom Jones* was beginning to come
back into repute. If Fielding was having to be defended against
charges of falling short of the artistic refinement of one kind of
modern novel, he also had to be defended for seeming to come too
close to the ugly 'realism' of another. Denials that Fielding was a
'realist' in a limiting sense are found as early as Stephen (1882),
and again in Godden (1910). In his book on the novel (1899),
Cross noted that *Amelia* contained the favourite subject-matter 'of
the modern realist', but also a 'tenderness' absent from the works
of such realists, a view which echoes Brunetière's earlier
celebration of the humanity of Fielding and George Eliot in
contrast to the hardness of the *petits naturalistes* of France (1884;
and see 1881).

'Realism' is an all-purpose term, and a freely adaptable notion.
Fielding had boasted his truth to nature himself, and had been
praised for it from his own time to ours: Orwell in 1944 was
remarking on the 'psychological realism' of *Amelia* (Sonia Orwell
and Ian Angus (eds.), *Collected Essays, Journalism and Letters*, vol. 3,
1970, p. 308). In the 1930s, Marxist critics like George Lukács
and Ralph Fox were discussing his 'realism' in another sense.[1]
The applicability of the term was to come under acute and
sophisticated scrutiny in Ian Watt's *The Rise of the Novel* (1957):
but that is to look forward to the next section of this book.

[1] See, in addition to the extracts from Lukács, Fox's *The Novel and the People*,
Lawrence & Wishart, 1937, pp. 52–5, 104–5.

Samuel Richardson

from a letter to Sarah Fielding 7 December 1756 (John Carroll (ed.), *Selected Letters*, 1964)

Well might a critical judge of writing say, as he did to me, that your late brother's knowledge of [the human heart] was not (fine writer as he was) comparable to yours. His was but as the knowledge of the outside of a clockwork machine, while yours was that of all the finer springs and movements of the inside. . . .
(330)

Voltaire

from a letter to Madame du Deffant 13 October 1759 (Louis Moland (ed.), *Oeuvres Complètes*, vol. 40, 1880; extract translated by C. J. Rawson)

[The Old Testament stories] seem to me better than *Tom Jones*, where there is nothing passable but the character of a barber.
(190)

Oliver Goldsmith

from *The Bee*, no. 6 10 November 1759 (Arthur Friedman (ed.), *Collected Works*, vol. 1, 1966)

Instead . . . of romances, which praise young men of spirit, who go through a variety of adventures, and at last conclude a life of dissipation, folly, and extravagance in riches and matrimony, there should be some men of wit employed to compose books that might equally interest the passions of our youth, where such an one might be praised for having resisted allurements when young, and how he at last became Lord Mayor; how he was married to a lady of great sense, fortune, and beauty; to be as explicit as possible, the old story of Whittington, were his cat left out, might be more serviceable to the

tender mind, than either Tom Jones, Joseph Andrews, or an hundred others, where frugality is the only good quality the hero is not possessed of.
(461)

Denis Diderot

from a letter to Sophie Volland   20 October 1760 (Georges Roth (ed.), *Correspondance*, vol. 3, 1957; extract translated by C. J. Rawson)

I shall not be pleased with you or myself if I do not bring you to appreciate the truth of *Pamela*, of *Tom Jones*, of *Clarissa* and of *Grandison*.
(173–4)

Robert Lloyd

from 'A Familiar Epistle. To a Friend who Sent the Author a Hamper of Wine'   ? 1761 (S. Johnson and A. Chalmers (eds.), *Works of the English Poets*, vol. 15, 1810)

O Lucian, sire of ancient wit,
Who wedding humour, didst beget
Those doctors in the laughing school,
Those giant sons of ridicule,
Swift, Rabelais, and that favourite child[1]
Who less eccentrically wild,
Inverts the misanthropic plan,
And hating vices, hates not man . . . .
(129)

1 Fielding [ed.].

Tobias Smollett

from *Continuation of the Complete History of England*, vol. 4   1761
(*Critical Heritage*)

The genius of Cervantes was transfused into the novels of Fielding,
who painted the characters, and ridiculed the follies of life with equal
strength, humour and propriety.
(403)

Arthur Murphy

from 'An Essay on the Life and Genius of Henry Fielding, Esq.',
in *Works of Henry Fielding*, vol. 1   1762 (*Critical Heritage*)

It would lead a great way from the intention of this essay should we
attempt to analyse the several dramatic compositions of this author;
and indeed, as he confessedly did not attain to pre-eminence in this
branch of writing, at least was unequal to his other productions, it
may be sufficient to observe that from the year 1727 to the end of
1736, almost all his plays and farces were written, not above two or
three having appeared since that time; so that he produced about
eighteen theatrical performances, plays and farces included, before
he was quite thirty years old. . . . Though it must be acknowledged
that in the whole collection, there are few plays likely to make any
considerable figure on the stage hereafter, yet they are worthy of
being preserved, being the works of a genius, who in his wildest and
most inaccurate productions, yet occasionally displays the talents of
a master. Though in the plan of his pieces he is not always regular,
yet is he often happy in his diction and style; and in every group,
that he has exhibited, there are to be seen particular delineations that
will amply recompense the attention bestowed upon them. The
comedy of the *Miser*, which he has mostly taken from Molière, has
maintained its ground upon the stage, ever since it was first performed
and has the value of a copy from a great painter by an eminent hand.
If the comedy of *Pasquin* were restored to the stage, it would, perhaps,
be a more favourite entertainment with our audiences than the much

admired *Rehearsal*; a more rational one it certainly would be, as it would undoubtedly be better understood. . . .

The *Pasquin* of Fielding came from the pen of an author in indigence, or, as the late Colly Cibber has contumeliously called him, a broken wit; and, therefore, though its success was considerable, it never shone forth with a lustre equal to its merit; and yet it is a composition that would have done honour to the Athenian stage, when the middle comedy, under the authority of the laws, made use of fictitious names to satyrize vice and folly, however dignified by honours and employments. But the middle comedy did not flourish long at Athens; the archness of its aim, and the poignancy of its satire, soon became offensive to the officers of state; a law was made to prohibit those oblique strokes of wit, and the comic muse was restrained from all indulgencies of personal satire, however humourously drawn, under the appearance of imaginary characters. The same fate attended the use of the middle comedy in England; and it is said that the wit and humour of our modern Aristophanes. Mr Fielding, whose quarry in some of his pieces, particularly the *Historical Register*, was higher game than in prudence he should have chosen, were principal instruments in provoking that law, under which the British theatre has groaned ever since. . . . In all the plays of our author however in some respects deficient, there are strokes of humour and half-length paintings not excelled by some of the ablest artists. The farces written by Mr Fielding were almost all of them very successful, and many of them are still acted every winter with a continuance of approbation. They were generally the production of two or three mornings, so great was his facility in writing; and to this day, they bear frequent repetition, at least as well as any other pieces of the kind. It need not be observed, in justification of their being preserved in this collection of more important works, that farce is deemed by our best critics an appendage of the theatre as well as pieces of a higher nature. . . . The mock tragedy of *Tom Thumb* is replete with as fine parody as, perhaps, has ever been written. . . .

A love of imitation very soon prevailed in Mr Fielding's mind. By imitation the reader will not understand that illegitimate kind, which consists in mimicking singularities of person, feature, voice or manner; but that higher species of representation, which delights in just and faithful copies of human life. . . . It has been already observed

... that distress and disappointments betrayed him into occasional fits of peevishness, and satric humour. The eagerness of creditors, and the fallacy of dissembling friends, would for a while sour his temper; his feelings were acute, and naturally fixed his attention to those objects from whence his uneasiness sprung; of course he became, very early in life, an observer of men and manners. Shrewd and piercing in his discernment, he saw the latent sources of human actions, and he could trace the various incongruities of conduct arising from them. As the study of man is delightful in itself, affording a variety of discoveries, and particularly interesting to the heart, it is no wonder that he should feel delight from it; and what we delight in soon grows into a habit. The various ruling passions of men, their foibles, their oddities, and their humours, engaged his attention; and from these principles he loved to account for the consequences which appeared in their behaviour. The inconsistencies that flow from vanity, from affectation, from hypocrisy, from pretended friendship, and in short, all the dissonant qualities, which are often blended together by the folly of men, could not fail to strike a person who had so fine a sense of ridicule. A quick perception in this way, perhaps, affords as much real pleasure as the exercise of any other faculty of the mind; and accordingly, we find that the ridiculous is predominant through all our author's writings, and he never seems so happy, as when he is developing a character made up of motley and repugnant properties, and shews you a man of specious pretences, turning out in the end the very reverse of what he would appear. To search out and to describe objects of this kind, seems to have been the favourite bent of Mr Fielding's mind, as indeed it was of Theophrastus, Molière, and others; like a vortex it drew in all his faculties, which were so happily employed in descriptions of the manners, that upon the whole he must be pronounced an admirable comic genius.

When I call our author a 'comic genius', I would be understood in the largest acceptation of the phrase, implying humorous and pleasant imitation of men and manners, whether it be in the way of fabulous narration, or dramatic composition. In the former species of writing, lay the excellence of Mr Fielding: but in dramatic imitation he must be allowed to fall short of the great masters in that art. . . . [Fielding's plays lack 'delicacy' which gives 'to good sense an air of urbanity and politeness', and which comedy needs in order to be completely successful.] This want of refinement . . . was principally owing to the woundings which every fresh disappointment gave him, before he was yet well disciplined in the school of life, and hackney'd in the ways of men; for in a more advanced period, when he did not write *recentibus odiis*, with his uneasiness just beginning to fester, but with a calmer and more dispassionate temper, we perceive him giving all the graces of description to incidents and passions, which in his youth he would have dashed out with a rougher hand. . . . Perhaps the asperity of Fielding's muse was not a little encouraged by the practice of two great wits, who had fallen into the same vein before him; I mean *Wycherley* and *Congreve*, who were in general painters of harsh features, attached more to subjects of deformity than grace; whose drawings of women are ever a sort of *Harlot's Progress*, and whose men, for the most part lay violent hands upon deeds and settlements, and generally deserve informations in the king's bench. These two celebrated writers were not fond of copying the amiable part of human life. . . . By making Congreve his model, it is no wonder that our author contracted this vicious turn, and became faulty in that part of his art, which the painters would call *design*. In his style, he derived an error from the same source: he sometimes forgot that humour and ridicule were the two principal ingredients of comedy; and, like his master, he frequently aimed at decorations of wit, which do not appear to make part of the *ground*, but seem rather to be embroidered upon it. It has been observed, that the plays of Congreve *appear not to be legitimate comedies, but strings of repartees and sallies of wit, the most poignant and polite indeed, but unnatural and ill-placed*. . . . The frequent surprises of allusion, and the quickness and vivacity of those sudden turns, which abound in Mr Congreve, breaking out where you least expected them, as if a train of wit had been laid all around, put one in mind of . . . fireworks. . . . The same kind of entertainment our author aimed at, too frequently in his comedies; and as in this he bore a similitude to Wycherley and Congreve, so he also frequently resembled them in the indelicacy, and sometimes the downright obscenity of his raillery; a vice introduced, or at least pampered by the wits of Charles II, the dregs of it, till very lately, not being quite purged away. There is another circumstance respecting the drama, in which Fielding's judgement seems to have failed him: the strength of his genius certainly lay in fabulous narration, and he did not sufficiently consider that some incidents of a story, which, when related, may be worked up into a deal of pleasantry and humour, are apt, when thrown into action, to excite sensations incompatible with humour and ridicule. I will venture to say, that if he had resolved to shape the business and characters of his last comedy (*The Wedding Day*) into the form of a novel, there is not one scene in the piece, which, in his hands, would not have been very susceptible of ornament: but as they are arranged at present in dramatic order, there are few of them from which the taste and good sense of an audience ought not, with propriety, to revolt.... The *Tom Jones* of our author, and the *Gil Blas* of Le Sage, still continue to yield universal delight to their respective readers; but two late attempts to dramatize them, if I may so call it, have demonstrated that the characters and incidents of those applauded performances, which, when figured to us by the imagination only, are found so agreeable and interesting, lose much of their comic force and beauty, when they are attempted to be realized to us on the stage. There are objects and parts of nature, which the rules of composition will allow to be described, but not actually to be produced on the scene, because they are attended with some concomitant circumstances, which in the narrative are overlooked, but, when shown to view, press too hardly on the mind, and become indelicate. . . .

To these causes of our author's failure in the province of the drama, may be added that sovereign contempt he always entertained for the understandings of the generality of mankind. It was in vain to tell him that a particular scene was dangerous on account of its coarseness, or because it retarded the general business with feeble efforts of wit; he doubted the discernment of his auditors, and so thought himself secured by their stupidity, if not by his own humour and vivacity. . . .

If we add to the foregoing remarks an observation of his own, namely, that he left off writing for the stage, when he ought to have begun; and together with this consider his extreme hurry and dispatch, we shall be able fully to account for his not bearing a more distinguished place in the rank of dramatic writers. It is apparent, that in the frame and constitution of his genius there was no defect, but some faculty or other was suffered to lie dormant, and the rest of course were exerted with less efficacy: at one time we see his wit superseding all his other talents; at another his invention runs riot, and multiplies incidents and characters in a manner repugnant to all the received laws of the drama. Generally his judgement was very little consulted. And indeed, how could it be otherwise? When he had contracted to bring on a play, or a farce, it is well known by many of his friends now living, that he would go home rather late from a tavern, and would, the next morning, deliver a scene to the players written upon the papers, which had wrapped the tobacco, in which he so much delighted.

Notwithstanding the inaccuracies, which have arisen from this method of proceeding, there is not a play in the whole collection which is not remarkable for some degree of merit very striking in its kind; in general, there prevails a fine idea of character; occasionally, we see the true comic both of situation and sentiment; and always, we find a strong knowledge of life, delivered indeed with a caustic wit, but often zested with fine infusions of the ridiculous. . . .

A large number of fugitive political tracts, which had their value when the incidents were actually passing on the great scene of business, came from his pen: the periodical paper, called the *Champion*, owing its chief support to his abilities; and tho' his essays in that collection, cannot now be so ascertained, as to perpetuate them in this edition of his works, yet the reputation arising to him at the time of publication was not inconsiderable. It does not appear that he ever wrote much poetry: with such talents as he possessed, it cannot be supposed that he was unqualified to acquit himself handsomely in that art; but correct versification probably required more pains and time than his exigencies would allow. . . .

Our author proceeds [in the Preface to the *Miscellanies*] to give a further account of [*Jonathan Wild*] in a strain which shews, however conversant he might be in the characters of men, that he did not suffer a gloomy misanthropy to take such possession of him, as to make him entertain depreciating ideas of mankind in general, without exceptions in favour of a great part of the species. . . .

But though the merit of the life of *Jonathan Wild* be very considerable yet it must be allowed to be very short of that higher order of composition which our author attained in his other pieces of invention. Hitherto he seems but preluding, as it were, to some great work, in which all the component parts of his genius were to be seen in their full and vigorous exertion; in which his *imagination* was to strike us by the most lively and just colouring, his *wit* to enliven by the happiest allusions, his *invention* to enrich with the greatest variety of character and incident, and his *judgement* to charm not only by the propriety and grace of particular parts, but by the order, harmony, and congruity of the whole: to this high excellence he made strong approaches in the *Joseph Andrews*; and in the *Tom Jones* he has fairly borne away the palm.

In the progress of Henry Fielding's talents there seem to have been three remarkable periods; one, when his genius broke forth at once with an effulgence superior to all the rays of light it had before emitted, like the sun in his morning glory, without the ardour and the blaze which afterwards attend him; the second, when it was displayed with collected force, and a fulness of perfection, like the sun in meridian majesty, with all his highest warmth and splendour; and the third, when the same genius, grown more cool and temperate, still continued to cheer and enliven, but showed at the same time that it was tending to its decline, like the same sun, abating from his ardour, but still gilding the western hemisphere.

To these three epochs of our author's genius . . . there is an exact correspondence in the *Joseph Andrews*, *Tom Jones*, and *Amelia*. *Joseph Andrews*, as the preface to the work informs us, was intended for an imitation of the style and manner of Cervantes: and how delightfully he has copied the humour, the gravity, and the fine ridicule of his master, they can witness who are acquainted with both writers. The truth is, Fielding, in this performance, was employed in the very province for which his talents were peculiarly and happily formed; namely, the fabulous narration of some imagined action, which did occur, or might probably have occurred in human life. Nothing could be more happily conceived than the character of Parson Adams for the principal personage of the work; the humanity, and benevolence of affection, the goodness of heart, and the zeal for virtue, which come from him upon all occasions, attach us to Mr Adams in the most endearing manner; his excellent talents, his erudition, and his real acquirements of knowledge in classical antiquity, and the sacred writings, together with his honesty, command our esteem and

respect; while his simplicity and innocence in the ways of men
provoke our smiles by the contrast they bear to his real intellectual
character, and conduce to make him in the highest manner the object
of mirth, without degrading him in our estimation, by the many
ridiculous embarrassments to which they every now and then make
him liable; and to crown the whole, that habitual absence of mind,
which is his predominant foible, and which never fails to give a
tinge to whatever he is about, makes the honest clergyman almost a
rival of the renowned *Don Quixote*; the adventures he is led into, in
consequence of this infirmity, assuming something of the romantic
air which accompanies the knight errant, and the circumstances of
his forgetfulness tending as strongly to excite our laughter as the
mistakes of the Spanish hero. I will venture to say, that when *Don
Quixote* mistakes the barber's basin for Mambrino's helmet, no reader
ever found the situation more ridiculous and truly comic than
Parson Adams's travelling to London to sell a set of sermons, and
actually *snapping his fingers and taking two or three turns round the room
in exstacy*, when introduced to a bookseller in order to make an
immediate bargain; and then immediately after, not being able to
find those same sermons, when he exclaims, 'I profess, I believe I left
them behind me.' There are many touches in the conduct of this
character, which occasion the most exquisite merriment; and I
believe it will not be found too bold an assertion, if we say that the
celebrated character of an absent man, by La Bruyère, is extremely
short of that true and just resemblance to nature with which our
author has delineated the features of Adams; the former indeed is
carried to an agreeable extravagance, but the latter has the fine
lights and shades of probability. It will not be improper here to
mention that the Rev. Mr Young, a learned and much esteemed
friend of Mr Fielding's, sat for this picture. Mr Young was remarkable for his intimate acquaintance with the Greek authors, and had as
passionate a veneration of *Aeschylus* as Parson Adams; the overflowings of his benevolence were as strong, and his fits of *reverie*
were as frequent. . . . The whole work indeed abounds with situations
of the truly comic kind. . . . But still it is but the sun-rise of our author's
genius. . . . In the plan of the work, Mr Fielding did not form to
himself a circle wide enough for the abundance of his imagination;
the main action was too trivial and unimportant to admit of the variety

of characters and events which the reader generally looks for in such productions. . . .

In the *True Patriot* there was displayed a solid knowledge of the British laws and government, together with occasional sallies of humour, which would have made no inconsiderable figure in the political compositions of an *Addison* or a *Swift*. The *Jacobite Journal* was calculated to discredit the shattered remains of an unsuccessful party, and, by a well-applied raillery and ridicule, to bring the sentiments of the disaffected into contempt, and thereby efface them not only from the conversation, but the minds of men. . . .

Our author by this time attained the age of forty-three; and being incessantly pursued by reiterated attacks of gout, he was wholly rendered incapable of pursuing the business of a barrister any longer. He was obliged therefore to accept an office, which seldom fails of being hateful to the populace, and of course liable to many injurious imputations, namely, an acting magistrate in the commission of the peace for Middlesex. That he was not inattentive to the calls of his duty, and that, on the contrary, he laboured to be a useful citizen, is evident from the many tracts he published, relating to several of the penal laws, and to the vices and malpractices which those laws were intended to restrain. Under this head will be found several valuable pieces. . . . The pamphlet on the *Increase and Cause of Robberies*, has been held in high estimation by some eminent persons who have administered justice in Westminster Hall, and still continue to serve their country in a legislative capacity. . . . *A Proposal for the Maintenance of the Poor*, which, though it is not reprinted in this collection, not being deemed of a colour with works of invention and genius, yet . . . does honour to our author as a magistrate, as it could not be produced without intense application, and an ardent zeal for the service of the community.

Amidst these severe exercises of his understanding, and all the laborious duties of his office, his invention could not lie still; but he found leisure to amuse himself, and afterwards the world, with *The History of Tom Jones*. And now we are arrived at the second grand epoch of Mr Fielding's genius, when all his faculties were in perfect unison, and conspired to produce a complete work. If we consider *Tom Jones* in the same light in which the ablest critics have examined the *Iliad*, the *Aeneid*, and the *Paradise Lost*, namely, with a view to the fable, the manners, the sentiments, and the style, we shall find it standing the test of the severest criticism, and indeed bearing away the envied praise of a complete performance. In the first place, the action has that unity, which is the boast of the great models of composition; it turns upon a single event, attended with many circumstances, and many subordinate incidents, which seem, in the progress of the work, to perplex, to entangle, and to involve the whole in difficulties, and lead on the reader's imagination, with an eagerness of curiosity, through scenes of prodigious variety, till at length the different intricacies and complications of the fable are explained after the same gradual manner in which they had been worked up to a crisis: incident arises out of incident; the seeds of everything that shoots up, are laid with a judicious hand, and whatever occurs in the latter part of the story, seems naturally to grow out of those passages which preceded; so that, upon the whole, the business with great propriety and probability works itself up into various embarrassments, and then afterwards, by a regular series of events, clears itself from all impediments, and brings itself inevitably to a conclusion; like a river, which, in its progress, foams amongst fragments of rocks, and for a while seems pent up by unsurmountable oppositions; then angrily dashes for a while, then plunges under ground into caverns, and runs a subterraneous course, till at length it breaks out again, meanders round the country, and with a clear, placid stream flows gently into the ocean. By this artful management, our author has given us the perfection of fable; which, as the writers upon the subject have justly observed, consists in such obstacles to retard the final issue of the whole, as shall at least, in their consequences, accelerate the catastrophe, and bring it evidently and necessarily to that period only, which, in the nature of things, could arise from it; so that the action could not remain in suspense any longer, but must naturally close and determine itself. It may be proper to add, that no fable whatever affords, in its solution, such artful states of suspense, such beautiful turns of surprise, such unexpected incidents, and such sudden discoveries, sometimes apparently embarrassing, but always promising the catastrophe, and eventually promoting the completion of the whole. . . .

In the execution of this plan, thus regular and uniform, what a variety of humorous scenes of life, of descriptions, and characters has our author found means to incorporate with the principal action; and this too, without distracting the reader's attention with objects foreign to his subject, or weakening the general interest by a multiplicity of episodical events? Still observing the grand essential rule of unity in the design, I believe no author has introduced a greater diversity of characters, or displayed them more fully, or in more various attitudes. Allworthy is the most amiable picture in the world of a man who does honour to his species: in his own heart he finds constant propensities to the most benevolent and generous actions, and his understanding conducts him with discretion in the performance of whatever his goodness suggests to him. And though it is apparent that the author laboured this portrait *con amore*, and meant to offer it to mankind as a just object of imitation, he has soberly restrained himself within the bounds of probability, nay, it may be said, of strict truth; as, in the general opinion, he is supposed to have copied here the features of a worthy character still in being. Nothing can be more entertaining than Western; his rustic manners, his natural undisciplined honesty, his half-enlightened understanding, with the self-pleasing shrewdness which accompanies it, and the bias of his mind to mistaken politicks, are all delineated with precision and fine humour. The sisters of those two gentlemen are aptly introduced, and give rise to many agreeable scenes. Tom Jones will at all times be a fine lesson to young men of good tendencies to virtue, who yet suffer the impetuosity of their passions to hurry them away. Thwackum and Square are excellently opposed to each other.... In short, all the characters down to Partridge, and even to a maid or an hostler at an inn, are drawn with truth and humour: and indeed they abound so much, and are so often brought forward in a dramatic manner, that every thing may be said to be here in action; every thing has manners; and the very manners which belong to it in human life. They look, they act, they speak to our imaginations just as they appear to us in the world. The sentiments which they utter, are peculiarly annexed to their habits, passions and ideas; which is what poetical propriety requires; and, to the honour of the author, it must be said, that, whenever he addresses us in person, he is always in the interests of virtue and religion, and inspires, in a strain of moral reflection, a true love of goodness and honour, with a just detestation of imposture, hypocrisy, and all specious pretences to uprightness.

168 Arthur Murphy

There is, perhaps, no province of the Comic Muse that requires so great a variety of style as this kind of description of men and manners, in which Mr Fielding so much delighted. The laws of the mock-epic, in which this species of writing is properly included, demand that, when trivial things are to be represented with a burlesque air, the language should be raised into a sort of tumour of dignity, that by the contrast between the ideas and the pomp in which they are exhibited, they may appear the more ridiculous to our imaginations. Of our author's talent in this way, there are instances in almost every chapter; and were we to assign a particular example, we should refer to the relation of a battle in the *Homerican style*. On the other hand, when matters, in appearance, of higher moment, but, in reality, attended with incongruous circumstances, are to be set forth in the garb of ridicule, which they deserve, it is necessary that the language should be proportionably lowered, and that the metaphors and epithets made use of be transferred from things of a meaner nature, so that the false importance of the object described may fall into a gay contempt. The first specimen of this manner that occurs to me is in the *Jonathan Wild*: 'For my own part,' says he, 'I confess I look on this death of hanging to be as proper for a hero as any other; and I solemnly declare, that had Alexander the Great been hanged, it would not in the least have diminished my respect of his memory.' [book 4, chapter 8] . . . Things of this nature may be found almost every where in *Tom Jones*, or *Joseph Andrews*. . . . The mock-epic has likewise frequent occasion for the gravest irony, for florid description, for the true sublime, for the pathetic, for clear and perspicuous narrative, for poignant satire, and generous panegyric. For all these different modes of eloquence, Mr Fielding's genius was most happy versatile, and his power in all of them is so conspicuous, that he may justly be said to have had the rare skill, required by Horace, of giving to each part of his work its true and proper colouring. . . . Thus our author being confessedly eminent in all the great essentials of composition, in fable, character, sentiment, and elocution; and as these could not be all united in so high an assemblage, without a rich invention, a fine imagination, an enlightened judgment, and a lively wit, we may fairly here decide his character, and pronounce him the English Cervantes.

It may be added, that in many parts of the *Tom Jones* we find our author possessed the softer graces of character-painting, and of description; many situations and sentiments are touched with a delicate hand, and throughout the work he seems to feel as much delight in describing the amiable part of human nature, as in his early days he had in exaggerating the strong and harsh features of turpitude and deformity. This circumstance breathes an air of philanthropy through his work, and renders it an *image of truth*. . . . And hence it arose, from this *truth of character* which prevails in Tom Jones, in conjunction with the other qualities of the writer, above set forth, that the suffrage of the most learned critic [Warburton] of this nation was given to our author, when he says, 'M. de Marivaux, in France, and Mr Fielding in England stand the foremost among those, who have given a faithful and chaste copy of *life and manners*, and by enriching their romance with the best part of the comic art, may be said to have brought it to perfection.' Such a favourable decision from so able a judge, will do honour to Mr Fielding with posterity; and the excellent genius of the person, with whom he has paralleled him, will reflect the truest praise on the author, who was capable of being his illustrious rival. . . .

. . . The *Paysan Parvenu* seems to be the *Joseph Andrews* of [Marivaux]; and the *Marianne* his higher work, or his *Tom Jones*. They are both, in a very exquisite degree, amusing and instructive. They are not written, indeed, upon any of the laws of composition promulged by *Aristotle*, and expounded by his followers: his romances begin regularly with the birth and parentage of the principal person, and proceed in a narrative of events, including indeed great variety, and artfully raising and suspending our expectation: they are rather to be called *fictitious biography*, than a comic fable, consisting of a *beginning*, a *middle*, and *end*, where one principal action is offered to the imagination, in its process is involved in difficulties, and rises gradually into tumult and perplexity, till, in a manner unexpected, it works itself clear, and comes by natural but unforeseen incidents, to a termination.

In this last-mentioned particular, Fielding boasts a manifest superiority over Marivaux. Uniformity amidst variety is justly allowed in all works of invention to be the prime source of beauty, and it is the peculiar excellence of *Tom Jones*. The author, for the most part, is more readily satisfied in his drawings of character than the French writer; the strong specific qualities of his personages he sets forth with a few masterly strokes, but the nicer and more subtle workings of the mind he is not so anxious to investigate; when the passions are agitated, he can give us their conflicts, and their various transitions, but he does not always point out the secret cause that sets them in motion, or, in the poet's language, 'the small pebble that stirs the peaceful lake'. Fielding was more attached to the *manners* than to the *heart*: in descriptions of the former he is admirable; in unfolding the latter he is not equal to Marivaux. In the management of his story, he piques and awakens curiosity more strongly than his rival of France; when he interests and excites our affections, he sometimes operates more by the force of situation, than by the tender pathetic of sentiment, for which the author of *Marianne* is remarkable; not that it must be imagined that Fielding wanted these qualities; we have already said the reverse of him; but in these particulars Marivaux has the preference. In point of style, he is more unexceptionable than Marivaux, the critics never having objected to him that his figures are forced or unnatural; and in humour the praise of pre-eminence is entirely his. Marivaux was determined to have an air of originality, and therefore disdained to form himself upon any eminent mode of preceding writers; Fielding considered the rules of composition as delivered by the great philosophic critic; and finding that Homer had written a work entitled *Margites*, which bore the same relation to *comedy*, that the *Iliad* or *Odyssey* does to tragedy, he meditated a plan conformable to the principles of a well-arranged fable. Were the *Margites* still extant, it would perhaps be found to have the same proportion to this work of our author, as the sublime epic has to the *Télémaque* of Fénelon. This was a noble vehicle for humorous description; and to insure his success in it, with great judgement, he fixed his eye upon the style and manner of Cervantes, as Virgil had before done in respect to Homer. To this excellent model, he added all the advantages he could deduce from Scarron and Swift; few or no sprinklings of *Rabelais* being to be found in him. His own strong discernment of the foibles of mankind, and his quick sense of the ridiculous being thus improved, by a careful attention to the works of the great masters of their art, it is no wonder that he has been able to raise himself to the top of the *comic character*, to be admired by readers with the most lively sensations of mirth, and by novel-writers *with a despair that he should ever be emulated with success.*

Thus we have traced our author in his progress to the time when the vigour of his mind was in its full growth of perfection; from this period it sunk, but by slow degrees, into a decline; *Amelia*, which succeeded *Tom Jones* in about four years, has indeed the marks of genius, but of a genius beginning to fall into its decay. The author's invention in this performance does not appear to have lost its fertility: his judgment too seems as strong as ever; but the warmth of imagination is abated; and in his landskips or his scenes of life, Mr Fielding is no longer the colourist he was before. The personages of the piece delight too much in narrative, and their characters have not those touches of singularity, those specific differences, which are so beautifully marked in our author's former works: of course, the humour, which consists in happy delineations of the caprices and predominant foibles of the human mind, loses here its high flavour and relish. And yet *Amelia* holds the same proportion to *Tom Jones*, that the *Odyssey* of *Homer* bears, in the estimation of *Longinus*, to the *Iliad*. A fine vein of morality runs through the whole; many of the situations are affecting and tender; the sentiments are delicate; and upon the whole, it is the *Odyssey*, the moral and pathetic work of Henry Fielding. (405–32)

James Beattie

from 'An Essay on Poetry and Music' ?1762 (*Essays*, 1778)

Of the comic epopee we have two exquisite models in English; I mean the *Amelia* and *Tom Jones* of Fielding. The introductory part of the latter follows indeed the historical arrangement, in a way somewhat resembling the practice of Euripides in his *Prologues*, or at least as excusable; but, with this exception, we may venture to say, that both fables would bear to be examined by Aristotle himself, and, if compared with those of Homer, would not greatly suffer in the comparison. This author, to an amazing variety of probable occurrences, and of characters well drawn, well supported, and finely contrasted, has given the most perfect unity, by making them all cooperate to one and the same final purpose. It yields a very pleasing surprise to observe, in the unravelling of his plots, particularly that of *Tom Jones*, how many incidents, to which, because of their apparent minuteness, we had scarce attended as they occurred in the narrative, are found to have been essential to the plot. And what heightens our idea of the poet's art is, that all this is effected by natural means, and human abilities, without any machinery – while his great master Cervantes is obliged to work a miracle for the cure of Don Quixote. Can any reason be assigned, why the inimitable Fielding, who was so perfect in epic fable, should have succeeded so indifferently in dramatic? Was it owing to the peculiarity of his genius, or of his circumstances? To anything in the nature of dramatic writing in general, or of that particular taste in dramatic comedy which Congreve and Vanburgh had introduced, and which he was obliged to comply with?

110–11 n.)

Christopher Smart

'Epitaph on Henry Fielding, Esq.,' from *Poems on Several Occasions* 1763 (reprinted in Norman Callan (ed.), *Collected Poems*, vol. 1, 1949)

The Master of the Greek and Roman page,
The lively scorner of a venal age,
Who made the publick laugh, at publick vice,
Or drew from sparkling eyes the pearls of price;
Student of nature, reader of mankind,
In whom the patron, and the bard were join'd;
As free to give the plaudit, as assert,
And faithful in the practice of desert.
Hence power consigned the laws to his command,
And put the scales of Justice in his hand;
To stand protector of the Orphan race,
And find the female penitent a place.
From toils like these, too much for age to bear,
From pain, from sickness, and a world of care;
From children, and a widow in her bloom,

From shores remote, and from a foreign tomb,
Call'd by the word of life, thou shalt appear,
To *please* and *profit* in a higher sphere,
Where endless hope, unperishable gain,
Are what the scriptures *teach* and *entertain*.
(35–6)

Voltaire

from a review of Frances Brooke's *History of Lady Julia
Mandeville*, *Gazette Littéraire*   30 May 1764 (Louis Moland (ed.),
Oeuvres Complètes, vol. 25, 1879; extract translated
by C. J. Rawson.)

English novels were not read in Europe before *Pamela*. That particular
genre seemed very piquant; *Clarissa* had less success, but deserved
more. Then Fielding's novels presented other scenes, other customs,
another tone: they pleased, because they had truth and gaiety. The
success of both kinds brought about a plethora of poor imitations
which have not caused the originals to be forgotten, but have
appreciably lowered the appetite for them.
(182)

Samuel Johnson and James Boswell

from a conversation   Spring 1768 (G. B. Hill and L. F. Powell,
(eds.), *Boswell's Life of Johnson*, vol. 2, 1934)

'Sir, (continued [Johnson]) there is all the difference in the world
between characters of nature and characters of manners; and *there*
is the difference between the characters of Fielding and those of
Richardson. Characters of manners are very entertaining; but they
are to be understood, by a more superficial observer, than characters
of nature, where a man must dive into the recesses of the human
heart.'
It always appeared to me that he estimated the compositions of

Richardson too highly, and that he had an unreasonable prejudice against Fielding. In comparing those two writers, he used this expression; 'that there was as great a difference between them as between a man who knew how a watch was made, and a man who could tell the hour by looking on the dial-plate.' This was a short and figurative state of his distinction between drawing characters of Nature and characters only of manners. But I cannot help being of opinion, that the neat watches of Fielding are as well constructed as the large clocks of Richardson, and that his dial-plates are brighter. Fielding's characters, though they do not expand themselves so widely in dissertation, are as just pictures of Human Nature, and I will venture to say, have more striking features, and nicer touches of the pencil; and though Johnson used to quote with approbation a saying of Richardson's, 'that the virtues of Fielding's heroes were the vices of a truly good man', I will venture to add, that the moral tendency of Fielding's writings, though it does not encourage a strained and rarely possible virtue, is ever favourable to honour and honesty, and cherishes the benevolent and generous affections. He who is as good as Fielding would make him, is an amiable member of society, and may be led on by more regulated instructors, to a higher state of ethical perfection.
(48–9)

James Beattie

from 'Remarks on the Utility of Classical Learning' ? 1769
(*Essays*, 1778)

If study be detrimental to any faculty of the mind, we might suspect, that a playful imagination, the parent of wit and humour, would be most likely to suffer by it. Yet the history of our first-rate geniuses in this way (Shakespeare always excepted) is a proof of the contrary. There is more learning, as well as more wit, in *Hudibras* than in any book of the same size now extant. In the *Tale of a Tub*, the *Tatler*, and the *Spectator*, the *Memoirs of Martinus Scriblerus*, and in many parts of Fielding, we discover at once a brilliant wit and copious erudition. . . .

The very worst effect that Classical learning can produce on the intelligent mind, is, that it may sometimes transform an original genius into an imitator. Yet this happens not often; and when it does happen, we ought not perhaps to complain. Ingenious imitations may be as delightful, and as useful, as original compositions. . . . Not withstanding the merit of Cervantes, I believe there are few critics in Great Britain, who do not think in their hearts, that Fielding has outdone his master.
(536–8)

Samuel Johnson and Others

from a conversation   6 April 1772 (G. B. Hill and L. F. Powell (eds.), *Boswell's Life of Johnson*, vol. 2, 1934)

Fielding being mentioned, Johnson exclaimed, 'he was a blockhead'; and upon my expressing my astonishment at so strange an assertion, he said, 'What I mean by his being a blockhead is that he was a barren rascal.'

BOSWELL: Will you not allow, Sir, that he draws very natural pictures of human life?

JOHNSON: Why, Sir, it is of very low life. Richardson used to say, that had he not known who Fielding was, he should have believed he was an ostler. Sir, there is more knowledge of the heart in one letter of Richardson's, than in all *Tom Jones*. I, indeed, never read *Joseph Andrews*.

ERSKINE: Surely, Sir, Richardson is very tedious.

JOHNSON: Why, Sir, if you were to read Richardson for the story, your impatience would be so much fretted that you would hang yourself. But you must read him for the sentiment, and consider the story as only giving occasion to the sentiment.

I have already given my opinion of Fielding; but I cannot refrain from repeating here my wonder at Johnson's excessive and unaccountable depreciation of one of the best writers that England has produced. *Tom Jones* has stood the test of publick opinion with such success, as to have established its great merit, both for the story, the

sentiments, and the manners, and also the varieties of diction, so as to leave no doubt of its having an animated truth of execution throughout.
(173–5)

Richard Brinsley Sheridan

from a letter to Thomas Grenville   30 October 1772 (Cecil Price (ed.), *Letters*, vol. 1, 1966)

For my own part when I read for entertainment, I had much rather view the characters of life as I would wish they *were* than as they *are*: therefore I hate novels, and love romances. The praise of the best of the former, their being *natural*, as it is called, is to me their greatest demerit. Thus it is with Fielding's, Smollet's, etc. Why should men have a satisfaction in viewing only the mean and distorted figures of Nature? tho', truly speaking not of *Nature*, but of vicious and corrupt society. Whatever merit the painter may have in his execution, an honest mind is disgusted with the design.
(61–2)

Samuel Johnson

from a conversation   12 April 1776 (G. B. Hill and L. F. Powell (eds.), *Boswell's Life of Johnson*, vol. 3, 1934)

He told us, he read Fielding's *Amelia* through without stopping. He said, 'if a man begins to read in the middle of a book, and feels an inclination to go on, let him not quit it, to go to the beginning. He may, perhaps, not feel again the inclination.'
(43)

Lord Monboddo

from *Of the Origin and Progress of Language*, vol. 3   1776

Mr Fielding, in his comic narrative poem, *The History of Tom Jones*, has mixed with his narrative a good deal of mock-heroic; and, particularly, there is a description of a squabble in a country churchyard wholly in that style. It is, indeed, an excellent parody of Homer's battles, and is highly ridiculous; but, in my opinion, it is not proper for such a work: First, because it is too great a change of style, greater than any work of a legitimate kind, which I think Fielding's is, will admit, from the simple and familiar to the heroic or mock-heroic. It is no better than a patch; and, though it be a shining one, no regular work ought to have any at all. For Horace has very properly given it as a mark of a work irregular, and of ill texture, the having such purple clouts, as he calls them:

. . . Late qui splendeat unus et alter
Assuitur pannus . . .
(*Ars Poetica*)

Secondly, because it destroys the probability of the narrative, which ought to be carefully studied in all works, that, like Mr Fielding's, are imitations of real life and manners, and which, accordingly, has been very much laboured by that author. It is for the probability of the narrative chiefly that I have so much commended *Gulliver's Travels*. Now, I appeal to every reader, whether such a description in those Travels, as that of the battle in the churchyard, would not have entirely destroyed the credibility of them, and prevented their imposing upon anybody, as it is said they did at first. This, therefore, I cannot help thinking a blemish, in a work which has otherwise a great deal of merit, and which I should have thought perfect of the kind, if it had not been for this, and another fault that I find to it, namely, the author's appearing too much in it himself, who had nothing to do in it at all.[1] By this the reader will understand that I

1 The fable of this piece is, I think, an extraordinary effort both of genius and art; for, though it be very complex, taking in as great a variety of matter as, I believe, any heroic fable, it is so simple as to be easily enough comprehended in one view. And it has this peculiar excellency, that every incident of the

mean his reflections, with which he begins his Books, and sometimes
his chapters. . . .
(296–8)

Fanny Burney

from the Preface to *Evelina*   1778 (Edward A. Bloom (ed.), 1968)

However I may feel myself enlightened by the knowledg eof Johnson,
charmed with the eloquence of Rousseau, softened by the pathetic
powers of Richardson, and exhilarated by the wit of Fielding, and
humour of Smollet; I yet presume not to attempt pursuing the same
ground which they have tracked; whence, though they may have
cleared the weeds, they have also culled the flowers, and though they
have rendered the path plain, they have left it barren.
(9)

Samuel Johnson and Others

from Fanny Burney's Diary   August–September 1778
(Charlotte Barrett (ed.), *Diary and Letters of Madame D'Arblay*,
vol. 1, 1876)

'Ay, Miss Burney,' said Mrs Thrale, 'the Holborn beau is Dr John-
son's favourite; and we have all your characters by heart, from Mr
Smith up to Lady Louisa.'
   'Oh, Mr Smith, Mr Smith is the man!' cried [Johnson], laughing

---

almost infinite variety which the author has contrived to introduce into it,
contributes, some way or other, to bring on the catastrophe, which is so artfully wrought up, and brought about by a change of fortune, so sudden and
surprising, that it gives the reader all the pleasure of a well-written tragedy or
comedy. And, therefore, as I hold the invention and composition of the
fable to be the chief beauty of every poem, I must be of opinion, that Mr
Fielding was one of the greatest poetical geniuses of his age; nor do I think that
his work has hitherto met with the praise it deserves.
(298n).

violently. 'Harry Fielding never drew so good a character! – such a fine varnish of low politeness! – such a struggle to appear a gentleman! Madam, there is no character better drawn anywhere – in any book, or by any author.'

I almost poked myself under the table. Never did I feel so delicious a confusion since I was born!

(34)

[Johnson said:] 'Richardson would have been really afraid of her; there is merit in *Evelina* which he could not have borne. No; it would not have done! unless, indeed, she would have flattered him prodigiously. Harry Fielding, too, would have been afraid of her; there is nothing so delicately finished in all Harry Fielding's works as in *Evelina*!'

(48)

'But,' said Mrs Montagu, 'one thing must be considered: Fielding, who was so admirable in novel-writing, never succeeded when he wrote for the stage.'

'Very well said,' cried Dr Johnson; 'that was an answer which showed she considered her subject.'

(75)

Sir John Fielding

from Dedication to Duke of Northumberland of Henry Fielding's posthumous play, *The Fathers: or, The Good-Natur'd Man*   1778 (*Works*, vol. 12)

The author of this play was an upright, useful, and distinguished magistrate for the County of Middlesex; and by his publications laid the foundation of many wholesome laws for the support of good order and subordination in this metropolis, the efforts of which have been, and now are, forcibly felt by the public. His social qualities made his company highly entertaining. His genius, so universally admired, has afforded delight and instruction to thousands. The memory of such a man calls for respect; and to have that respect shown him by the great and praiseworthy must do him the highest honour.

Under these circumstances this little orphan posthumous work, replete with humour and sound sense, looks up to Your Grace for protection. . . .
(153)

David Garrick

from the Prologue to Fielding's *The Fathers*   1778 (Fielding, *Works*, vol. 12)

But who the Author? Need I name the wit,
Whom nature prompted as his genius writ?
Truth smiled on Fancy for each well-wrought story,
Where characters live, act, and stand before ye:
Suppose these characters, various as they are,
The knave, the fool, the worthy, wise, and fair,
For and against the Author pleading at your bar.
First pleads Tom Jones – grateful his heart and warm –
Brave, generous Britons, shield this play from harm;
My best friend wrote it; should it not succeed,
Though with my Sophy blest – my heart will bleed –
Then from his face he wipes the manly tear;
Courage, my master, Partridge cries, don't fear:
Should Envy's serpent hiss, or malice frown,
Though I'm a coward, zounds! I'll knock 'em down:
Next, sweet Sophia comes – she cannot speak –
Her wishes for the play o'erspread her cheek;
In every look her sentiments you read:
And more than eloquence her blushes plead.
Now Blifil bows – with smiles his false heart gilding,
He was my foe – I beg you'll damn this Fielding;
Right! Thwackum roars – no mercy, sirs, I pray –
Scourge the dead Author, through his orphan play.
What words! cries Parson Adams, fie, fie, disown 'em,
Good Lord! – *de mortuis nil nisi bonum*:
If such are Christian teachers, who'll revere 'em –
And thus they preach, the Devil alone shall hear 'em.

Now Slipslop enters – though this scrivening vagrant,
Salted my virtue, which was ever flagrant,
Yet, like black 'Thello, I'd bear scorns and whips,
Slip into poverty to the very hips,
T' exalt this play – may it increase in favour;
And be its fame immortalized for ever!
'Squire Western, reeling, with October mellow,
Tall, yo! – Boys! – Yoax – Critics! hunt the fellow!
Damn 'em, those wits are varmint not worth breeding,
What good e'er came of writing and of reading?
Next comes, brimful of spite and politics,
His sister Western – and thus deeply speaks:
Wits are armed powers, like France attack the foe;
Negotiate till they sleep – then strike the blow!
Allworthy last, pleads to your noblest passions –
Ye generous leaders of the taste and fashions;
Departed genius left his orphan play
To your kind care – what the dead wills, obey:
O then, respect the father's fond bequest,
And make his widow smile, his spirit rest.

(154–5)

Samuel Johnson and Hannah More

from a letter by Hannah More to a sister   *c.* 1780 (*Critical Heritage*)

I never saw Johnson really angry with me but once; and his displeasure did him so much honour that I loved him the better for it. I
alluded rather flippantly, I fear, to some witty passage in *Tom Jones*:
he replied, 'I am shocked to hear you quote from so vicious a book.
I am sorry to hear you have read it: a confession which no modest
lady should ever make. I scarcely know a more corrupt work.' I
thanked him for his correction; assured him I thought full as ill of it
now as he did, and had only read it at an age when I was more
subject to be caught by the wit, than able to discern the mischief. Of
Joseph Andrews I declared my decided abhorrence. He went so far as
to refuse to Fielding the great talents which are ascribed to him, and

broke out into a noble panegyric on his competitor, Richardson; who, he said, was as superior to him in talents as in virtue; and whom he pronounced to be the greatest genius that had shed its lustre on this path of literature.

(443)

James Harris

from *Philological Inquiries*   1781

The celebrated Henry Fielding . . . was a respectable person both by education and birth; having been bred at Eton School and Leyden, and being lineally descended from an Earl of Denbigh.

His *Joseph Andrews* and *Tom Jones* may be called masterpieces in the Comic Epopee, which none since have equalled, though multitudes have imitated; and which he was peculiarly qualified to write in the manner he did, both from his life, his learning, and his genius.

Had his life been less irregular (for irregular it was, and spent in a promiscuous intercourse with persons of *all* ranks) his pictures of humankind had neither been so various nor so natural.

Had he possest less of literature, he could not have infused such a spirit of classical elegance.

Had his genius been less fertile in wit and humour he could not have maintained that uninterrupted pleasantry which never suffers his reader to feel fatigue.

(163–4 n.)

Edward Gibbon

from a footnote in *Decline and Fall of the Roman Empire*, chapter 32   1781 (J. B. Bury (ed.), vol. 3, 1906)

Suidas . . . has given a very unfavourable picture of Timasius. The account of his accuser, the judges, trial, etc. is perfectly agreeable to the practice of ancient and modern courts . . . I am almost tempted to quote the romance of a great master [Fielding's *A Journey from this*

World to the Next, book 1, chapter 10], which may be considered as the history of human nature.
(363)

Fanny Burney

from a letter to Mrs Susan Phillips   3 October 1783
(Charlotte Barrett (ed.), *Diary and Letters of Madame D'Arblay*,
vol. 1, 1876)

My father ... had recourse to *Pasquin*, to put us in better spirits. And so we laughed. But I must own I too frequently meet with disgust in all Fielding's dramatic works, to laugh with a good heart even at his wit, excellent as it is; and I should never myself think it worth wading through so much dirt to get at. Where any of his best strokes are picked out for me, or separately quoted, I am always highly pleased, and can grin most cordially; but where I hear the bad with the good, it preponderates too heavily to suffer my mind to give the good fair play.
(540)

Samuel Johnson

from a conversation with Mrs Thrale (Piozzi), before 1784, in her *Anecdotes of the Late Samuel Johnson*   1786 (G. B. Hill (ed.), *Johnsonian Miscellanies*, vol. 1, 1897)

His attention to veracity was without equal or example: and when I mentioned Clarissa as a perfect character; 'On the contrary (said he), you may observe there is always something which she prefers to truth. Fielding's Amelia was the most pleasing heroine of all the romances (he said); but that vile broken nose never cured, ruined the sale of perhaps the only book, which being printed off betimes one morning, a new edition was called for before night.'
(297)

Georg Christoph Lichtenberg

from a letter to Johann Gottwert Müller   20 December 1784
(Wolfgang Promies (ed.), *Schriften und Briefe*, vol. 4, 1967;
extract trans. John Rignall)

What I do not like are the Sternean digressions [in a work by
Müller], especially those that are occasioned not by the *subject* in
itself, but simply by a *word*. . . . I do not criticize the passages in
themselves – they are very witty – they just sometimes seem to me
to have a bad effect in their context. And that is a shame, for the
reader, who is absorbed in the plot, who has forgotten about himself
and the author, and is only interested in the hero of the piece, is
often unmerciful enough to fail to recognize the beauty that such
passages contain when he comes across one of them. Pearls are cast
before swine. The swine is innocent. Fielding appears to have sensed
this. Thus he keeps his reflections to the beginnings of his Books.
When the reader sees the heading 'Book number so-and-so', he
pauses, as does the author, and even the type-setter, too. The heading
itself is an intermezzo, and now the reader can bear with reflections
that have nothing to do with the subject, in the same way that he
looks at a vignette by Meil.
(594–5)

Horace Walpole

from a letter to John Pinkerton   26 June 1785 (W. S. Lewis *et al.*
(eds.), *Yale Edition of Horace Walpole's Correspondence*, vol. 16, 1951)

Fielding had as much humour perhaps as Addison, but having no
idea of grace, is perpetually disgusting. His innkeepers and parsons
are the grossest of their profession, and his gentlemen are awkward
when they should be at their ease.
(270)

Clara Reeve

from *The Progress of Romance*, vol. 1   1785 (Esther M. McGill
(ed.), 1930)

EUPHRASIA The next Author upon the list, and whom Hortensius
feared I should forget, is Henry Fielding, Esq., whose works are
universally known and admired – as I consider wit only as a
secondary merit, I must beg leave to observe, that his writings are
as much inferior to Richardson's in morals and exemplary characters as they are superior in wit and learning. Young men of warm
passions and not strict principles are always desirous to shelter
themselves under the sanction of mixed characters, wherein virtue
is allowed to be predominant. In this light the character of *Tom
Jones* is capable of doing much mischief; and for this reason a
translation of this book was prohibited in France. On the contrary
no harm can arise from the imitation of a perfect character, though
the attempt should fall short of the original. . . .

HORTENSIUS My objections were in character and yours are so
likewise; as you have defended Richardson, so I will defend
Fielding. I allow there is some foundation for your remarks, nevertheless in all Fielding's works, virtue has always the superiority she
ought to have, and challenges the honours that are justly due to her,
the general tenor of them is in her favour, and it were happy for us,
if our language had no greater cause of complaint in her behalf.

EUPHRASIA There we will agree with you. Have you any further
observations to make upon Fielding's writings?

HORTENSIUS Since you refer this part of your task to me, I will
offer a few more remarks – Fielding's *Amelia* is in much lower
estimation than his *Joseph Andrews*, or *Tom Jones*; which have both
received the stamp of public applause. He likewise wrote several
dramatic pieces of various merits, but these and his other works
have no place in our present retrospect. Lest you should think me
too partial to the merits of this writer, I will give you the sentence
of an historian upon him: 'The genius of Cervantes,' says Dr
Smollet, 'was transfused into the novels of Fielding, who painted
the characters and ridiculed the follies of life with equal strength,
humour and propriety.'

EUPHRASIA We are willing to join with you in paying the tribute due to Fielding's Genius, humour and knowledge of mankind, but he certainly painted Human Nature *as it is* rather than *as it ought to be*.
(136–41)

Sir John Hawkins

from *The Works of Samuel Johnson*, vol. 1   1787 (*Critical Heritage*)

At the head of these [writers of fiction] we must, for many reasons, place Henry Fielding, one of the most motley of literary characters. This man was, in his early life, a writer of comedies and farces, very few of which are now remembered; after that, a practising barrister with scarce any business; then an anti-ministerial writer, and quickly after, a creature of the duke of Newcastle, who gave him a nominal qualification of 100*l*. a year, and set him up as a trading-justice, in which disreputable station he died. He was the author of a romance, intitled *The History of Joseph Andrews*, and of another, *The Foundling, or the History of Tom Jones*, a book seemingly intended to sap the foundation of that morality which it is the duty of parents and all public instructors to inculcate in the minds of young people, by teaching that virtue upon principle is imposture, that generous qualities alone constitute true worth, and that a young man may love and be loved, and at the same time associate with the loosest women. His morality, in respect that it resolves virtue into good affections, in contradiction to moral obligations and a sense of duty, is that of Lord Shaftesbury vulgarized, and is a system of excellent use in palliating the vices most injurious to society. He was the inventor of that cant phrase, 'goodness of heart', which is every day used as a substitute for probity, and means little more than the virtue of a horse or a dog; in short, he has done more towards corrupting the rising generation than any writer we know of.
(446)

Dorothy Wordsworth

from a letter to Jane Pollard   6–7 August 1787 (E. de Selincourt
and Chester L. Shaver (eds.), *Letters of William and Dorothy
Wordsworth*, vol. 1, 1967)

I ha[ve] a very pretty little collection of books from my brothers
which they have given me. I will give you a catalog[ue]. I have the
Iliad, the *Odyssey*, [?] works, Fielding's works, Heyley's poems, *Gil
Blas* (in French), Gregory's *Legacy to his Daughters*, and my Brother
Ric[hard] intends sending me Shakespeare's plays and the *Spec[tator.]*
I have also Milton's Works, Dr Goldsmith's poems, [and] other
trifling things.
(8)

Edward Gibbon

from *Memoirs of My Life*   1788–93 (Georges A. Bonnard (ed.),
1966)

From Chapter 1

Our immortal Fielding was of a younger branch of the Earls of
Denbigh who draw their origin from the Counts of Habsburgh, the
lineal descendants of Eltrico, in the seventh century Duke of Alsace.
Far different have been the fortunes of the English and German
divisions of the family of Habsburgh. The former, the Knights and
Sheriffs of Leicestershire, have slowly risen to the dignity of a peerage:
the latter the Emperors of Germany, and Kings of Spain have
threatened the liberty of the old and invaded the treasures of the new
World. The successors of Charles the Fifth may disdain their brethren
of England: but the romance of *Tom Jones*, that exquisite picture of
human manners, will outlive the palace of the Escurial and the Imperial Eagle of the house of Austria. . . .
(5)

From Notes to Chapter 8

In the first of ancient or modern romances [*Tom Jones*, book 13,
chapter 1] this proud sentiment, this feast of fancy is enjoyed by the

genius of Fielding 'Foretell me that some future maid whose grand-
mother is yet unborn etc.' But the whole of this beautiful passage
deserves to be read.
(196)

William Hazlitt

from 'On Reading Old Books', *London Magazine* February 1820,
referring partly to the early 1790s (reprinted in P. P. Howe (ed.),
Complete Works, vol. 12, 1931)

Give me . . . a volume of *Peregrine Pickle* or *Tom Jones*. Open either
of them any where – at the memoirs of Lady Vane, or the adventures
at the masquerade with Lady Bellaston, or the disputes between
Thwackum and Square, or the escape of Molly Seagrim, or the
incident of Sophia and her muff, or the edifying prolixity of her
aunt's lecture – and there I find the same delightful, busy, bustling
scene as ever, and feel myself the same as when I was first introduced
into the midst of it. Nay, sometimes the sight of an odd volume of
these good old English authors on a stall, or the name lettered on the
back among others on the shelves of a library, answers the purpose,
revives the whole train of ideas, and sets 'the puppets dallying'.
Twenty years are struck off the list, and I am a child again. . . .
   I think of the time 'when I was in my father's house, and my path
ran down with butter and honey', – when I was a little, thoughtless
child, and had no other wish or care but to con my daily task, and
be happy! – *Tom Jones*, I remember, was the first work that broke
the spell. It came down in numbers once a fortnight, in Cooke's
pocket-edition, embellished with cuts. I had hitherto read only in
school-books, and a tiresome ecclesiastical history (with the exception
of Mrs Radcliffe's *Romance of the Forest*): but this had a different
relish with it, – 'sweet in the mouth', though not 'bitter in the
belly'. It smacked of the world I lived in, and in which I was to live –
and shewed me groups, 'gay creatures' not 'of the element', but of the
earth; not 'living in the clouds', but travelling the same road that I
did – some that had passed on before me, and others that might soon
overtake me. My heart had palpitated at the thoughts of a boarding-

school ball, or gala-day at Midsummer or Christmas: but the world I had found out in Cooke's edition of the *British Novelists* was to me a dance through life, a perpetual gala-day. The six-penny numbers of this work regularly contrived to leave off just in the middle of a sentence, and in the nick of a story, where Tom Jones discovers Square behind the blanket; or where Parson Adams, in the inextricable confusion of events, very undesignedly gets to bed to Mrs Slip-slop. Let me caution the reader against this impression of Joseph Andrews; for there is a picture of Fanny in it which he should not set his heart on, lest he should never meet with any thing like it; or if he should, it would, perhaps, be better for him that he had not. It was just like — —! With what eagerness I used to look forward to the next number, and open the prints! Ah! never again shall I feel the enthusiastic delight with which I gazed at the figures, and anticipated the story and adventures of Major Bath and Commodore Trunnion, of Trim and my Uncle Toby, of Don Quixote and Sancho and Dapple, of Gil Blas and Dame Lorenza Sephora, of Laura and the fair Lucretia, whose lips open and shut like buds of roses.
(221–3)

Robert Burns

from a letter to Dr John Moore   28 February 1791 (J. de L. Ferguson (ed.), *Letters of Robert Burns*, vol. 2, 1931)

I have just read over, once more of many times, your Zelucco.... Original strokes, that strongly depict the human heart is your and Fielding's province beyond any other novelist, I have ever perused. Richardson indeed might perhaps be excepted; but unhappily, his dramatis personae are beings of some other world; and however they may captivate the unexperienced, romantic fancy of a boy or a girl, they will ever, in proportion as we have made human nature our study, disgust our riper minds.
(58–9)

Henry James Pye

from *A Commentary Illustrating the Poetic of Aristotle* 1792

We have another writer also, Henry Fielding, who in his comic epopees, is a most accurate delineator of manners. However there is one distinction between him and Shakespear, which, though perhaps it gives his pictures a more striking effect, renders them not equal in real merit to those of our great dramatic poet. Shakespear paints for all ages and all countries; while the portraits of Fielding are generally drawn from local and national circumstances.
(309)

['poetical goodness' is sometimes] in opposition to what may strictly be called moral virtue. That a degree of this poetical goodness is not incompatible even with atrocious crimes, has already been observed; and we may add, that in modern times it frequently depends on acknowledged vices, as a certain degree of gallantry and duelling. In regard to the first, how nearly has Fielding made Joseph Andrews an object of ridicule; and what pains is he obliged to employ to excuse him, by his violent attachment to another woman.
(321)

Allworthy in *Tom Jones* . . . has always appeared to me a striking instance of a character at opposition with himself, though more perhaps in general with that which the author tells you in his own person he is, than with his own conduct in those parts where the author suffers him to act from himself. The author is at great pains to inform us frequently that he is, though no scholar, a man of sense and discernment, with a benevolence almost angelic; and to press this more forcibly on our minds, he has given him a name strongly expressive of his moral goodness, though all his other characters have common names. But how is he really drawn? He is the dupe of every insinuating rascal he meets; and a dupe not of the most amiable kind, since he is always led to acts of justice and severity. The consequence of his pliability is oftener the punishment of the innocent than the acquittal of the guilty; and in such punishment he is severe and implacable. As in the case of Jones himself, his supposed father and

mother, and Black George. He suffers his adopted son and his foundling to be ill treated by an imperious pedagogue ... and to have their principles corrupted by a hypocritical infidel.
(335-6)

What can put both the invention and judgement of the poet to so great an exertion as to contrive his incidents in such a manner that the audience, or the reader, should never once conceive the real situation of his principal character, and yet when his real situation is revealed, it should be confirmed by a retrospect examinate of those incidents?

My most diligent recollection will furnish me with no example ancient or modern of a composition in which this arduous task is strictly and perfectly executed, except that wonderful effort of judgement and imagination the comic epopee of *Tom Jones*. No reader I believe ever guessed that the hero of the piece would turn out to be the nephew of Allworthy and the son of Mrs Bridget, till the moment before the discovery takes place, and yet how natural is the behaviour of those who know the circumstances, when the incidents are examined afterwards. With what nice touches is the conduct of the mother expressed, and especially her partiality to Jones; and Dowling, when he accidentally meets Jones on the road, actually calls Allworthy his uncle without giving the reader the least suspicion of the truth; so inimitable is the art of the poet.

The Oedipus though a masterpiece of this kind is by no means of equal merit. It was impossible, during so long a stay at Thebes, but Oedipus must have heard of the death of Laius, and the exposure of his infant son, so concurrent with the response of the oracle to him, which occasioned his determination not to return to Corinth. Aristotle observed this defect, and he has tried to palliate it by remarking that it occurred prior to the opening of the drama.
(357-8)

Samuel Taylor Coleridge

from 'With Fielding's *Amelia*' *c.* 1792 (E. H. Coleridge (ed.),
Poems, 1961)

Virtues and Woes alike too great for man
  In the soft tale oft claim the useless sigh;
For vain the attempt to realize the plan,
  On Folly's wings must Imitation fly.
With other aim has Fielding here display'd
  Each social duty and each social care;
With just yet vivid colouring portrayed
  What every wife should be, what many are.
(37)

Richard Cumberland

from *Henry*   1795 (reprinted in Sir Walter Scott (ed.),
The Novelist's Library, vol. 9, 1824)

From Book 2, Chapter 1

An eminent author [Fielding], whose talent for novel-writing was
unequalled, and whose authority ought greatly to weigh with all
who succeed him in the same line, furnished his baiting-places with
such ingenious hospitality, as not only to supply his guests with the
necessary remissions from fatigue, but also to recruit them with
viands of a very nutritive, as well as palatable quality. According to
this figure of speech (which cannot be mistaken, as alluding to his
prefatory chapters), he was not only a pleasant, facetious companion
by the way, but acted the part of an admirable host at every one of
the inns. Alas! it was famous travelling in his days. I remember him
full well, and despair of ever meeting his like again, upon that road,
at least.

Others there have been, and one there was [Richardson], of the
same day, who was a well-meaning, civil soul, and had a soft simper-
ing kind of address, that took mightily with the ladies, whom he

contrived to usher through a long, long journey, with their hand-kerchiefs at their eyes, weeping and wailing by the way, till he conducted them, at the close of it, either to a ravishment, or a funeral, or perhaps to a madhouse, where he left them to get off as they could. He was a charming man, and had a deal of custom; but the other's was the house that I frequented.
(533)

From Book 6, Chapter 1

The early practice of weaving story within story should be avoided; the adventures of the Man of the Hill, in *The Foundling*, is an excrescence that offends against the grace and symmetry of the plot: whatever makes a pause in the main business, and keeps the chief characters too long out of sight, must be a defect.
(625)

From Book 8, Chapter 1

If . . . originality of character . . . is now become hardly attainable, discrimination is yet within reach; and by a happy contrast of leading characters, although they shall not be really new, yet all the best effects of novelty may be obtained by an alternate play on each other's humours, by the means of which very comic and amusing situations may be struck out. Amongst our countrymen, the great masters of contrast in our own day are Fielding and Sterne; Square and Thwackum, Western and his sister, the father and the uncle of Tristram Shandy, are admirable instances: Shakespeare had it from nature, Johnson caught it from Aristophanes; Socrates and the Clown Strepsiades, in the comedy of *The Clouds*, is, perhaps, the most brilliant contrast of comic humour in the now-existing records of the stage, ancient or modern.
(672)

Madame de Staël

from *Essai sur les Fictions* 1795 (*Morceaux Divers*, 1820; extracts translated by C. J. Rawson)

[Philosophical novels (e.g. *Candide*), with their improbabilities, etc.] suffer somewhat from the disadvantage of teachers who are disbelieved by their pupils, because they force everything that happens back to the lesson they wish to teach, and because the children, without consciously realizing it, already know that the real march of events is less orderly. But in such novels as Richardson's and Fielding's, where the object is to stay close to life in following exactly the gradations, the unfoldings, the inconsequences of human story, and where the results of experience are nevertheless constantly referred back to the morality of the actions or to the advantages of virtue, the events are indeed invented: but the sentiments are so natural that the reader often feels that he is being written about under another name. . . . (159–60)

Love is the main subject of novels, and characters foreign to love are only included as ancillary. But if we followed another plan, we should discover a multitude of new topics. *Tom Jones* is, of all such works, the one with the most general moral interest; love is presented in this novel as only one of the means of bringing out the philosophic point. To show the uncertainty of judgements based on appearances, to prove the superiority of natural and as it were involuntary qualities over those reputations which are based only on a respect for external proprieties, such is the true object of *Tom Jones*, which is one of the most useful and most justly celebrated of novels. (166–7)

Goethe

from *Wilhelm Meister's Apprenticeship*, book 5, chapter 7   1795–6 (Thomas Carlyle (trans.), vol. 1, 1894)

One evening a dispute arose among our friends about the novel and the drama, and which of them deserved the preference . . .

They conversed together long upon the matter; and in fine, the following was nearly the result of their discussion:

In the novel as well as in the drama, it is human nature and human action that we see. . . .

But in the novel, it is chiefly *sentiments* and *events* that are exhibited; in the drama, it is *characters* and *deeds*. The novel must go slowly forward; and the sentiments of the hero, by some means or another, must restrain the tendency of the whole to unfold itself and to conclude. The drama, on the other hand, must hasten, and the character of the hero must press forward to the end; it does not restrain, but is restrained. The novel-hero must be suffering, at least he must not in a high degree be active; in the dramatic one, we look for activity and deeds. Grandison, Clarissa, Pamela, the Vicar of Wakefield, Tom Jones himself, are, if not suffering, at least retarding personages; and the incidents are all in some sort modelled by their sentiments. In the drama the hero models nothing by himself; all things withstand him, and he clears and casts away the hindrances from off his path, or else sinks under them.

(23–4)

Jane Austen

from a letter to Cassandra Austen   9 January 1796 (R. W. Chapman (ed.), *Letters*, 1964)

Mr Tom Lefroy ... has but *one* fault, which time will, I trust, entirely remove – it is that his morning coat is a great deal too light. He is a very great admirer of Tom Jones, and therefore wears the same coloured clothes, I imagine, which *he* did when he was wounded.

(3)

Johann Gottfried Herder

from *Briefe zu Beförderung der Humanität*, no. 100 1796
(Hans-Joachim Kruse (ed.), vol. 2, 1971; extract translated by
Judy Rawson)

The poetic pantheon of the British troubles me. Where are our
Shakespeares, our Swifts, Addisons, Fieldings, Sternes? ... We
awoke when it was midday everywhere, and in some countries the
sun was already declining. In short, *we came too late*.
(113)

William Godwin

from *The Enquirer* 1797

Fielding's novel of *Tom Jones* is certainly one of the most admirable
performances in the world. The structure of the story perhaps has
never been equalled; nor is there any work that more frequently or
more happily excites emotions of the most elevated and delicious
generosity.

The style, however, is glaringly inferior to the constituent parts of
the work. It is feeble, costive and slow. It cannot boast of periods
elegantly turned or delicately pointed. The book is interspersed
with long discourses of religious or moral instruction; but these have
no novelty of conception or impressive sagacity of remark, and are
little superior to what any reader might hear at the next parish-
church. The general turn of the work is intended to be sarcastic and
ironical; but the irony is hard, pedantic and unnatural. Whoever
will compare the hide-bound sportiveness of Fielding, with the
flowing and graceful hilarity of Sterne, must be struck with the
degree in which the national taste was improved, before the latter
author could have made his appearance. . . .

From the examination of Fielding we proceed to that of Smollet.

The efforts of the first of these writers, in the novel of *Tom Jones*, in
the character of Parson Adams, and a few other instances, are exquisitely meritorious. But, when Fielding delights us, he appears to go

out of himself. The general character of his genius, will probably be found to be jejune and puerile. For the truth of this remark, we may appeal, in particular, to his comedies.

Everything that is the reverse of this may be affirmed of Smollet (462–7)

William Hazlitt

from 'My First Acquaintance with Poets', *Liberal*, no. 3
April 1823, describing Coleridge in 1798 (P. P. Howe (ed.),
Complete Works, vol. 17, 1933)

He liked Richardson, but not Fielding; . . . he was profound and discriminating with respect to those authors whom he liked, and where he gave his judgement fair play; capricious, perverse, and prejudiced in his antipathies and distastes.
(121)

Madame de Staël

from *De la Littérature Considérée dans ses Rapports avec les Institutions Sociales* 1800 (Paul van Tieghem (ed.), vol. 2, 1959; extracts translated by C. J. Rawson)

There is nevertheless in some English writings a kind of gaiety which has all the characteristics of originality and naturalness. The English language has created a word, *humour*, to describe this gaiety, which is a disposition of the blood almost as much as of the mind; it depends on climate and on national *mores*, and would be absolutely inimitable in countries in which these same factors did not bring it out. Certain writings of Fielding and of Swift, *Peregrin Pickle* [sic], *Roderick Random*, but especially the works of Sterne give a complete idea of what is called *humour*.

There is some moroseness, one might almost say sadness, in this gaiety; the man who makes you laugh does not experience the pleasure he is causing. . . .

198 Marquis de Sade

There is some misanthropy in the very joking of Englishmen, and some sociability in that of the French. . . .

What the English are particularly good at depicting are bizarre characters, because there are many such among them. . . .

Tom Jones cannot be considered simply as a novel. The most fertile of philosophical ideas – the contrast between natural qualities and social hypocrisy – is set in motion in that work with infinite artistry; and love, as I have said elsewhere [in *Essai sur les Fictions*, 1795], is merely ancillary to such a subject. But Richardson in the first place, and, after his writings, several novels, many of which are by women, give a perfect idea of this kind of work, of which the interest is inexpressible.

(216–17 and 230)

Marquis de Sade

from 'Idée sur les Romans', prefixed to *Les Crimes de l'Amour*
1800 (reprinted in Jean Fabre and Pierre Klossowski (eds.),
Oeuvres Complètes, vol. 10, 1966; extract translated by
C. J. Rawson)

At last the English novels, the vigorous works of Richardson and Fielding, came to teach Frenchmen that it is not in painting the tedious languors of love, or the boring conversations of the boudoir, that one succeeds in this genre; but in drawing manly characters who are toys and victims of that agitation of the heart called love, and who thus show us both its dangers and its misfortunes; from this alone can one obtain these unfoldings, these passions, so excellently portrayed in English novels. It is Richardson and Fielding who have taught us that the deep study of the human heart (that veritable labyrinth of nature) can alone inspire the novelist, whose work must show us man, not only as he is or as he shows himself (that is the historian's task), but as he might be, as he must become through the transformations of vice and all the upheavals of passion. One must therefore know and use all of these, if one wishes to work in this genre. It is there that we have learnt that it is not always by allowing virtue to triumph that one interests the emotions of the reader. One should certainly tend in this direction as much as possible, but this rule (neither Nature's nor Aristotle's, but merely a rule by which we would wish men to be governed for the sake of our happiness) is in no way essential to the novel and is not even certain to arouse the reader's concern. For when virtue triumphs, things being what they must be, our tears are stanched even before flowing. But if, after the severest ordeals, we finally see virtue crushed by vice, our souls are inevitably torn. The novel having then moved us exceedingly, having, as Diderot put it, stained our hearts with blood, necessarily produces that emotional interest which alone guarantees the laurels.

(12-13)

Alexandre-Louis de Villeterque

from a review of Sade's *Crimes de l'Amour* in *Journal des Arts, des Sciences et de Littérature* 22 October 1800 (Gilbert Lely, *Vie du Marquis de Sade*, in *Oeuvres Complètes*, vol. 2, 1966; extract translated by C. J. Rawson)

Rousseau, Voltaire, Marmontel, Fielding, Richardson etc., you have not written novels. You have depicted manners [*moeurs*], and should have depicted crimes. You arouse a love of virtue, showing that it alone leads to happiness . . . you should have shown *virtue crushed by vice*. . . . We do not see, in your pale writings, mothers strangling their children, children poisoning their mothers and sons raping them. Farewell, Rousseau, Voltaire, Marmontel, Fielding and Richardson, no one will read you any more.

(523)

Marquis de Sade

from *L'Auteur des Crimes de l'Amour à Villeterque, Folliculaire* 1800 (*Oeuvres Complètes*, vol. 10, 1966; extract translated by C. J. Rawson)

A fine invocation concludes the cheap diatribe of our scribbler: 'Rousseau, Voltaire, Marmontel, Fielding, Richardson, you have not

written novels', he cries. 'You have depicted *manners*, and should have depicted *crimes*.' As though crimes were not a part of manners, and as though there were no *criminal manners* as well as *virtuous* ones! ... Be comforted, Villeterque. Rousseau, Voltaire, Marmontel, Fielding and Richardson will always be read; your stupid jokes on the subject will convince no one that I have maligned these great men, when on the contrary I do not cease to present them as models. ...
(514)

Madame de Staël

from the Preface to the first edition of *Delphine*   1802
(vol. 1, 1820; extract translated by C. J. Rawson)

The novels which will forever be admired, *Clarissa*, *Clementina*, *Tom Jones*, *La Nouvelle Héloïse*, *Werther*, etc., have the object of revealing or recounting a host of sentiments from which, in the depths of the soul, the happiness or misery of life are formed; sentiments which we do not utter, because they are bound up with our secrets or our weaknesses, and because men live out their lives with one another without confessing to one another what they feel.
(xxvii)

Stendhal

from a *pensée* relating to 8–11 October 1803 (Henri Martineau (ed.), *Pensées. Filosofia Nova*, vol. 1, 1931; extract translated by C. J. Rawson)

I read *Jones* ... during my illness, which may be lessening my appreciation of its beauties. If one man had made the plan of this novel and another had carried it out, the latter would have almost no merit in my eyes. There is, throughout, a disagreeable tone of perpetual facetiousness. All the conversations and love-letters are botched. In the early books, which ought to be delightful, the author

gives nothing but summaries of conversations, and never shows his characters speaking. In spite of everything which M. de la Place claims to have pruned, there still remains a tedious prolixity in tiniest details, and Fielding never describes the places where his characters are, which often impairs the effect. Mr Western and Pastridge [*sic*] seem to me caricatures rather than characters. But the republican atmosphere of England might nevertheless produce characters which will seem exaggerated to a man spoiled by the courtier's manners [of France]. If it were reduced to two volumes, this novel would seem excellent.
(226)

Stendhal

from a *pensée* of 26 August 1804 (Henri Martineau (ed.), *Pensées. Filosofia Nova*, vol. 2, 1931; extract translated by C. J. Rawson)

The comic poet presents me with a young man similar to myself, who becomes unhappy through an excess of his good qualities, and who becomes happy through these same qualities; this, by showing happiness to my view, interests me and makes me smile. Tom Jones is an example. The greater the distress of the protagonist with whom I have identified myself, the more I reflect profoundly on possible ways of extricating myself from it, the more the protagonist interests me.
(267)

Anna Laetitia Barbauld

from 'Life of Samuel Richardson', prefixed to Richardson's *Correspondence*, vol. 1   1804

It is well known that Fielding, who started in his career of fame soon after Richardson, wrote his *Joseph Andrews* in ridicule of *Pamela*. Joseph is supposed to be the brother of Pamela, and Mr B. is Squire

Booby. Richardson was exceedingly hurt at this; the more so, as they had been upon good terms, and he was very intimate with Fielding's two sisters. He never appears cordially to have forgiven it, (perhaps it was not in human nature that he should) and he always speaks in his letters with a great deal of asperity of *Tom Jones*, more indeed than was quite graceful in a rival author. No doubt he himself thought his indignation was solely excited by the loose morality of the work and of its author, but he could tolerate Cibber. Richardson and Fielding possessed very different excellencies – Fielding had all the ease which Richardson wanted, a genuine flow of humour, and a rich variety of comic character; nor was he wanting in strokes of an amiable sensibility, but he could not describe a consistently virtuous character, and in deep pathos he was far excelled by his rival. When we see Fielding parodying *Pamela*, and Richardson asserting, as he does in his letters, that the run of *Tom Jones* is over, and that it would be soon completely forgotten: we cannot but smile on seeing the two authors placed on the same shelf, and going quietly down to posterity together.

(lxxix–lxxx)

Samuel Taylor Coleridge

from a Notebook   March 1805 (Kathleen Coburn (ed.), *Notebooks*, vol. 2, 1962)

I confess that it has cost and still costs my philosophy some exertion not to be vexed that I must admire – aye, greatly, very greatly, admire Richardson. His mind is so very vile a mind – so oozy, hypocritical, praise-mad, canting, envious, concupiscent – but to understand and draw *him* would be to produce almost equal to any of his own, but in order to do this, 'down proud Heart down!' as we teach little children to say to themselves ... all hatred down! – charity, calmness, an heart fixed on the good parts, tho' the understanding is surveying all – Richardson felt truly the defect of Fielding – or rather what was not his excellence, and made that his defect, a trick of uncharitableness often played chiefly, tho' not exclusively by contemporaries. Fielding's talent was observation not meditation –

But Richardson was not philosopher enough to know the difference –
say rather, to understand and develope it.
(no. 2471)

William Hazlitt

from 'Of Persons one would Wish to have Seen', *New Monthly Magazine*   January 1826, describing one of Charles Lamb's parties, *c.* 1806 (P. P. Howe (ed.), *Complete Works*, vol. 17, 1933)

P[hillips], who was deep in a game of piquet at the other end of the room, whispered . . . to ask if Junius would not be a fit person to invoke from the dead. 'Yes,' said L[amb], 'provided he would agree to lay aside his mask.'

We were now at a stand for a short time, when Fielding was mentioned as a candidate: only one, however, seconded the proposition. 'Richardson?' – 'By all means, but only to look at him through the glass-door of his back-shop, hard at work upon one of his novels (the most extraordinary contrast that ever was presented between an author and his works), but not to let him come behind his counter lest he should want you to turn customer, nor to go upstairs with him, lest he should offer to read the first manuscript of Sir Charles Grandison, which was originally written in eight and twenty volumes octavo, or get out the letters of his female correspondents, to prove that Joseph Andrews was low.'
(129)

William Hazlitt

from 'On the Conversation of Authors', *London Magazine*
September 1820, referring to one of Charles Lamb's evening
parties, sometime before 1808 (P. P. Howe (ed.),
Complete Works, vol. 12, 1931)

L[amb] could not bear *Gil Blas*. This was a fault. I remember the
greatest triumph I ever had was in persuading him, after some
years' difficulty, that Fielding was better than Smollet.
(36)

Samuel Taylor Coleridge

from a lecture on Shakespeare, as reported by H. Crabb Robinson
May 1808 (T. M. Raysor (ed.), *Shakespearean Criticism*, vol. 2,
1960)

C[oleridge] took occasion on mentioning R[ichardson] to express
his opinion of the *immorality* of his novels. 'The higher and lower
passions of our nature are kept through seven or eight volumes in a
hot-bed of interest. Fielding is far less pernicious, for the gusts of
laughter drive away sensuality.'
(15)

Samuel Taylor Coleridge

from *Friend*, no. 3   10 August 1809 (Barbara E. Rooke
(ed.), vol. 2, 1969)

Blifil related accurately Tom Jones's riotous joy during his benefactor's illness, only omitting that this joy was occasioned by the
physician's having pronounced him out of danger. Blifil was not the
less a liar for being an accurate *matter-of-fact* liar. *Tell-truths* in the
service of falsehood we find every where.
(47)

Samuel Taylor Coleridge

from notes in a copy of *Tom Jones*   *c.* 1809–10 (T. M. Raysor
(ed.), *Miscellaneous Criticism*, 1936)

Manners change from generation to generation, and with manners
morals appear to change, – actually change with some, but appear to
change with all but the abandoned. A young man of the present day
who should act as Tom Jones is supposed to act at Upton, with Lady
Bellaston, etc. would not be a Tom Jones; and a Tom Jones of the
present day, without perhaps being in the ground a better man,
would have perished rather than submit to be kept by a harridan of
fortune. Therefore this novel is, and, indeed, pretends to be, no
exemplar of conduct. But, notwithstanding all this, I do loathe the
cant which can recommend Pamela and Clarissa Harlowe as strictly
moral, though they poison the imagination of the young with
continued doses of *tinct. lyttae*, while Tom Jones is prohibited as
loose. I do not speak of young women, but a young man whose heart
or feelings can be injured, or even his passions excited, by aught in
this novel, is already thoroughly corrupt. There is a cheerful, sun-
shiny, breezy spirit that prevails every where, strongly contrasted
with the close, hot, day-dreamy continuity of Richardson. Every
indiscretion, every immoral act, of Tom Jones, (and it must be
remembered that he is in every one taken by surprise – his inward
principles remaining firm –) is so instantly punished by embarrassment and unanticipated evil consequences of his folly, that the reader's
mind is not left for a moment to dwell or run riot on the criminal
indulgence itself. In short, let the requisite allowance be made for
the increased refinement of our manners – and then I dare believe
that no young man who consulted his heart and conscience only,
without adverting to what the world would say – could rise from the
perusal of Fielding's *Tom Jones*, *Joseph Andrews*, or *Amelia*, without
feeling himself a better man – at least, without an intense conviction
that he could not be guilty of a base act.

If I want a servant or mechanic, I wish to know what he does: but
of a friend, I must know what he is. And in no writer is this momen-
tous distinction so finely brought forward as by Fielding. We do not
care what Blifil does; the deed, as separate from the agent, may be

good or ill, but Blifil is a villain; and we feel him to be so from the very moment he, the boy Blifil, restores Sophia's poor captive bird to its native and rightful liberty. . . .

Book 15, Chapter 9
The rupture with Lady Bellaston

Even in the most questionable part of *Tom Jones*, I cannot but think after frequent reflection, than an additional paragraph, more fully and forcibly unfolding Tom Jones's sense of self-degradation on the discovery of the true character of the relation in which he had stood to Lady Bellaston, and his awakened feeling of the dignity of manly chastity, would have removed in great measure any just objections – at all events relatively to Fielding himself, and with regard to the state of manners in his time.

(302–4)

Anna Laetitia Barbauld

from 'Fielding', *The British Novelists*   1810 (new edition, vol. 18, 1820)

It has been matter of surprise to those who contemplated Fielding in the quality of a novelist, that an author whose characteristics are genuine humour and delineation of character should have succeeded so ill in comedy; for what is a comedy but a short story, or novel put into dialogue? and the more of dialogue there is in the novel, the more spirit it possesses; so that they seem to be very kindred modes of writing.

But it must be considered, in the first place, that a dramatic writer, being confined by time and other circumstances belonging to representation on the stage, is obliged to concentrate his powers, and give the effect by a spirited outline, which the novel-writer has leisure to produce by the slow and patient touches of a more leisurely pencil. Comedy also requires much more delicate management. Coarse incidents and language may pass in relation, which would disgust upon the stage, where every thing being in action, an indelicacy or awkwardness becomes much more prominent than when it meets the eye of a solitary reader in the pages of a book; and the least circumstance that provokes a laugh at the piece is sufficient to ruin it for ever. A quicker sense of propriety is exercised on the benches of a theatre than at the desk of the reader. In the drama, moreover, the *author* is not allowed to show himself; by which the wit of Fielding would lose much of its poignancy. He does not dramatize his novel so much as many others have done. The *author's* learning, the *author's* wit appear continually not only in his digressive chapters, but in the representations of the characters and secret views of his personages; and the humour is continually heightened by the contrast between the author's style and his views of things, and the characters he is holding up to ridicule.

But the want of merit in Fielding's comedies may be ascribed to other causes. They were his first productions; and, like most of the productions of youth, rather drawn from what he had read than what he had seen.... The English stage has few models of elegant comedy, and he seems to have taken his from Congreve and Wycherley, and to have imitated their loose and vicious morals without their humour and brilliancy. Most of his pieces also were written in the intervals of pleasures and dissipation, with great rapidity, and upon the spur of the occasion, that is, the occasion for a present supply of money....
(iv–v)

Joseph Andrews, the first of Fielding's novels in the order of publication, has been, and always must be, a most captivating performance to those who have a taste for genuine humour. There is little or nothing in it of story, compared with the elaborate plan of his subsequent work; nor so great a variety of characters: on which account the performance is inferior; but it possesses, in quite an equal degree, the comic spirit of the author. He professes to have written it in the manner of Cervantes; and accordingly the style, where the author himself speaks, is in a kind of mock heroic, particularly in the introductory flourishes, where he ushers in the incidents of a foot-race, or a boxing match between two rustics, in the pompous and lofty phrase which might be used to describe one of

Homer's battles. This manner he has preserved in his other novels: in all of them the *author* is constantly kept in sight, and the grave humour of the piece is heightened by *his* remarks. The plan of Richardson, on the contrary, which was to make his characters tell their own story in letters to each other, necessarily excludes the author: each mode has its advantages, that of Richardson is perhaps the most difficult. The most striking figure in this piece is that of Parson Adams, an original and most diverting character, in which the lights and shades are so admirably blended, and estimable qualities so mixed with foibles and eccentricities, that we love and laugh at him at the same time. . . .

The author has shown great skill in making us laugh so heartily at a character, and yet keeping it above contempt. This could not have been done in the degrading scenes of low life to which he is exposed, if he had not, in addition to his higher qualities, given him great personal courage and an athletic constitution; so that in the scenes in which his poverty exposes him to insult, his Herculean strength and intrepidity make us feel, that though he may be played upon, he is not to be trampled on. . . .

Two other characters of clergymen appear in this work, those of Barnabas and Trulliber. Trulliber feeding his hogs and tyrannizing over his wife is a truly Dutch piece, and worthy the pencil of a Teniers. It is possible a Trulliber might be found in a remote part of the country when the author wrote, but it is to be presumed the race is now extinct. Barnabas is a character of hypocrisy and selfishness, of which the world will always afford specimens. Joseph and Fanny are sufficiently interesting: the latter is drawn with ease and simplicity. Joseph is a hero in virtue, more so perhaps than might naturally have been expected from the free pen of the author, who seems to have been induced to give him this purity of character from a whimsical competition with the author of *Pamela*, against which work there are many sly strokes of satire. It is certain, however, that *Joseph Andrews* is the most unexceptionable in point of morals of any of Fielding's novels. So far as a free exhibition of vicious characters may be objected to on the score of delicacy, perhaps it is not free from blame, but in this it is far less exceptionable than those of Smollet; and there is between them this essential difference, that in

Joseph Andrews the interest is constantly and uniformly thrown on the side of virtue. . . .

The winding up of his novel is the only part in which there is any aim at intricacy; and it may perhaps be thought some disparagement to the invention of the author, that the plot of two of his novels turns upon the discovery of foundling children. As Joseph Andrews is made the brother of Pamela Andrews, and as both are stories in low life, Richardson complained heavily of Fielding that he had followed up the mode of writing which he had opened for him, and made it a vehicle for abusing him; for, in fact, a good deal of ridicule is thrown upon *Pamela*, and *of that* its author might complain. But his manner and that of Fielding are so totally different, that each may be admired as an original writer without interference with the other, and different tastes will be attracted by different talents. *Joseph Andrews* may with more propriety be compared to the *Paysan Parvenu* of Marivaux than to any work of Richardson's.

Joseph Andrews was followed by *Tom Jones*, a novel produced when the author was in the meridian of his faculties, and after he had joined to his natural talents experience of the world, mature judgement, and practice in the art of writing. From these advantages a finished work may be expected; and such, considered as a composition, *Tom Jones* undoubtedly is. There is perhaps no novel in the English language so artfully conducted, or so rich in humour and character. Nor is it without scenes that interest the heart. The story of the highwayman, the distress of Mrs Miller and her daughter in the affair with Nightingale, and many little incidents relating to ones in his childhood, are highly affecting, and calculated to awaken our best feelings. Touches of the pathetic thus starting out in a work of humour, do not lose, they rather gain, from the contrast of sensations, and have a greater air of nature from being mixed with adventures drawn from common life. The conduct of the piece is as masterly as the details are interesting. It contains a story involving a number of adventures and a variety of characters, all of which are strictly connected with the main design, and tend to the development of the plot; which yet is so artfully concealed, that it may be doubted whether it was ever anticipated by the most practised and suspicious reader. The story contains all that we require in a regular epopea, or drama; strict unity of design, a change of fortune, a discovery, punishment and reward distributed according to poetical or rather moral justice.... The peculiar beauty of the plot consists in this; that though the author's secret is impenetrable, the discovery is artfully prepared by a number of circumstances not attended to at the time, and by obscure hints thrown out, which, when the reader looks back upon them, are found to agree exactly with the concealed event....

But intricacy of plot, admirable as this is, is still of secondary merit compared with the exhibition of character, of which there is in this work a rich variety. Of the humorous ones, Squire Western and his sister are the most prominent. They are admirably contrasted. He, rough, blunt, and boorish; a country squire of the last century; fond of his dogs and horses; a bitter Jacobite, as almost all the country squires at that time were; and from both causes averse to lords, and London, and every circumstance belonging to a court. She, a staunch whig, a politician in petticoats, valuing herself upon court breeding, finesse, and management, and not disposed, as Young says in one of his satires, 'to take her tea without a stratagem'. Their opposite though both wrong modes of managing Sophia, their mutual quarrels, and the cordial contempt shown for female pretensions on the one side, and country ignorance on the other, are highly amusing. The character of Western is particularly well drawn: he is quite a worldly man, and strongly attached to money, notwithstanding an appearance of jollity and heartiness, which might seem to indicate a propensity to the social feelings. His extreme fondness for Jones, and his total blindness to the passion between him and his daughter, though he had thrown them continually in each other's way, are very natural, and what we see every day exemplified in real life, as well as the astonishment he expresses that a young lady of fortune should think of falling in love with a young fellow without any. Many parents seem by their conduct to think this as impossible as if the two parties were beings of a different species, and they deservedly suffer the consequences of their incautious folly. His fondness for Sophia too, like that of many parents, is very consistent with the most tyrannical behaviour to her in points essential to her happiness. His leaving the pursuit of his daughter when he hears the cry of the hounds, in order to join a fox chase, is very characteristic and diverting.

It must be admitted that the language and manners of Western have a coarseness which in the present day may be thought exaggerated; and it is to be hoped it would be difficult now to find a breed of country squires quite so unpolished. Perhaps the improvement may be partly owing to their not being so independent as formerly. When they lived insulated, each in his own little domain, and their estates sufficed them to reside among their tenants and dependants in rustic consequence, they supplied such characters as a Western, a Sir Francis Wronghead, the Jacobite esquire in *The Freeholder*; and, of the more amiable sort, a Sir Roger de Coverley; for the drama and the novel; which are now nearly extinct, from the necessity the increasing demands of luxury have occasioned of seeking an increase of fortune in the busy and active scenes of life. Estates are purchased by moneyed men; they bring down the habits of mercantile life from the brewery or the warehouse; a library and a drawing-room take the place of the hall hung with stags' horns and brushes of foxes; the hounds are sold; the mansion is deserted during half the year for London or a watering-place. . . .

Jones is a youth of true feeling, honour and generosity; open and affectionate in his disposition, but very accessible to the temptations of pleasure. Blifil, with great apparent sobriety and decorum of manners, is a mean selfish hypocrite, possessing a mind of thorough baseness and depravity. In characters so contrasted, it is not doubtful to which of them the reader will, or ought to give the preference. To the faults of Blifil the reader has no inclination to be partial. They revolt the mind, particularly the minds of youth. The case is not the same with those more pardonable deviations from morals which are incident to youths of a warm temperament and an impressible heart: these are contagious in their very nature, and therefore the objections which have been made to the moral tendency of this novel are no doubt in some measure just. It is said to have been forbidden in France on its first publication. The faults of Jones are less than those of almost every other person who is brought upon the stage; yet they are of more dangerous example, because they are mixed with so many qualities which excite our affections. Still, his character is of a totally different stamp from the heroes of Smollet's novels. He has an excellent heart and a refined sensibility, though he has also passions of a lower order. In every instance where he transgresses the rules of virtue, he is the seduced, and not the seducer; his youth, his constitution, his unprotected situation after he left Allworthy's, palliate his faults, and in honourable love he is tender and constant. His refusal of the young widow who makes him an offer of her hand does him honour. In one instance only is he *degraded* – his affair with Lady Bellaston.

The character of Sophia was probably formed according to the author's ideas of female perfection: she is very beautiful, very sweet-tempered, very fond and constant to her lover; but her behaviour will scarcely satisfy one who has conceived high ideas of the delicacy of the female character. A young woman just come from reading *Clarissa* must be strangely shocked at seeing the heroine of the tale riding about the country on post-horses after her lover; and the incidents at Upton are hightly indelicate. It is observable that Fielding uniformly keeps down the characters of his women, as much as Richardson elevates his. A yielding easiness of disposition is what he seems to lay the greatest stress upon. Allworthy is made to tell Sophia, that what had chiefly charmed him in her behaviour was the great deference he had observed in her for the opinions of men. Yet Sophia, methinks, had not been extraordinarily well situated for imbibing such reverence. Any portion of learning in women is constantly united in this author with something disagreeable. It is given to Jenny, the supposed mother of Jones. It is given in a higher degree to that very disgusting character Mrs Bennet in *Amelia*; Mrs Western, too, is a woman of reading. A man of licentious manners, and such was Fielding, seldom respects the sex. Of the other characters, Lady Bellaston displays the ease, good-breeding, and impudence of a town-bred lady of fashion, who has laid aside her virtue. The scene where Jones meets Sophia at her house unexpectedly, the confusion of the lovers, and the civil, sly teasings of Lady Bellaston, are very diverting. Mrs Miller is a specimen of a natural character given without any exaggeration. She is warm-hearted, overflowing with gratitude, sanguine, and very loquacious .... The character of Allworthy is not a shining one; he is imposed upon by every body: this may be consistent with goodness, but it is not consistent with that dignity in which an eminently virtuous character, meant to be exhibited as a pattern of excellence, ought to appear. But Fielding could not draw such a character. Traits of humanity and kindness he is able to give in all their beauty; but a religious and strictly moral character was probably connected in his mind with a want of sagacity, which those who have been conversant with the vicious part of the world are very apt to imagine must be the consequence of keeping aloof from it. Besides, it was necessary for the plot that Allworthy should be imposed upon. . . .

Upon the whole, *Tom Jones* is certainly for humour, wit, character, and plot, one of the most entertaining and perfect novels we possess. With regard to its moral tendency we must content ourselves with more qualified praise. A young man may imbibe from it sentiments of humanity, generosity, and all the more amiable virtues; a detestation of meanness, hypocrisy, and treachery: but he is not likely to gain from it firmness to resist temptation, or to have his ideas of moral purity heightened or refined by the perusal. More men would be apt to imitate Jones than would copy Lovelace; and it is to be feared there are few women who would not like him better than Sir Charles Grandison. The greater refinement also and delicacy of the present age, a sure test of national civilization, though a very equivocal one of national virtue, has almost proscribed much of that broad humour which appears in the works of Fielding's times, and we should scarcely bear, in a new novel, the indelicate pictures which are occasionally presented to the imagination. The scenes at inns also are coarse, and too often repeated. The introductory chapters ought not to be passed over; they have much wit and grave Cervantic humour, and occasionally display the author's familiarity with the classics.

Fielding's vein was not yet exhausted; he produced a third novel called *Amelia*. If this has less of the author's characteristic humour, it has more scenes of domestic tenderness. Contrary to the usual practice of novel-writers, the story begins after the marriage of the principal personages. The hero, Mr Booth, is introduced to us in a prison; the distresses of the piece arise from the vicious indulgencies of the husband, combined with unfortunate circumstances; and in the character of Booth, Fielding is generally supposed to have delineated his own. Amelia is such a wife as most men of that stamp would deem the model of female perfection, such a one as a man, conscious of a good many frailties and vices, usually wishes for. Faithful, fond, and indulgent, the prospect of immediate ruin cannot draw from her one murmur against her husband, and she willingly sacrifices to him her jewels and every article in her possession. Booth is represented as good-natured, thoughtless, and extravagant; passionately fond of his wife, notwithstanding occasional breaches of fidelity to her; and very ready to receive the sacrifices she makes, even to the pawning of her clothes and moveables, for the discharge of his gaming debts. Amelia, indeed, is a heroine of affection and obedience, and the impression upon the reader is certainly that of her being a very amiable and interesting woman; but her character exhibits a great degree of weakness, particularly in her behaviour to the nobleman who is endeavouring to seduce her. What woman of any sense could suppose, that a gay nobleman would frequent her house for the sake of amusing himself with her little ones? Her softness and tenderness form a happy contrast with the boldness and daring guilt of Miss Matthews, a character conceived with great strength and spirit. . . .

The prison scenes are strongly drawn. Fielding was well acquainted with rogues and rascals in his judicial, and probably not unfrequently in his private capacity. . . . There is something very touching in the humble love of Atkinson, which is only revealed when he thinks himself on his death-bed; but the author has not used him very kindly in matching him with so disagreeable a personage as Mrs Bennet, whose character throughout is thoroughly disgusting, and seems introduced purely to show the author's dislike to learned women. Learning in women may be inimical to some parts of the feminine character, but certainly does not lead to the vices he has given Mrs Bennet. Probably the coterie of literary and accomplished ladies that generally assembled at his rival's house had its share in fostering this aversion. . . .

There are many good moral maxims in *Amelia*, and much of grave dissertation, but less of humour than in the author's former works. There are also many tender touches of conjugal affection and domestic feeling. There is no great merit, it is true, on Booth's side in receiving graciously the endearments of a beautiful woman who is always in good humour with him, even when he is most faulty. He is pleased with her; he could not well be otherwise; but he denies himself nothing for her sake or his children's. Yet, faulty as he is, the reader is glad when he is extricated from his distresses. That this should be done by the discovery of a forged will, betrays some poverty of invention, as nearly the same incident is made use of in the *dénouement* of *Tom Jones*.

Upon the whole, though *Amelia* must be acknowledged inferior to the author's other two works, it would establish the reputation of a common writer; and the three together present an exhibition of wit, humour, and character, not easy to be paralleled before or since the time when they were published.
(xiii–xxxi)

Charles Lamb

from 'On the Genius and Character of Hogarth' 1811
(E. V. Lucas (ed.), *Works of Charles and Mary Lamb*, vol. 1, 1912)

A little does it, a little of the *good* nature overpowers a world of *bad*. One cordial honest laugh of a Tom Jones absolutely clears the atmosphere that was reeking with the black putrifying breathings of a hypocrite Blifil. One homely expostulating shrug from Strap, warms the whole air which the suggestions of a gentlemanly ingratitude from his friend Random had begun to freeze. One 'Lord bless us!' of Parson Adams upon the wickedness of the times, exorcizes and purges off the mass of iniquity which the world-knowledge of even a Fielding could cull out and rake together. . . .

What heart was ever made the worse by joining in a hearty laugh at the simplicities of Sir Hugh Evans or Parson Adams, where a sense of the ridiculous mutually kindles and is kindled by a perception of the amiable? . . .

I say not that all the ridiculous subjects of Hogarth have necessarily something in them to make us like them; some are indifferent to us, some in their natures repulsive, and only made interesting by the wonderful skill and truth to nature in the painter; but I contend that there is in most of them that sprinkling of the better nature, which, like holy water, chases away and disperses the contagion of the bad. They have this in them besides, that they bring us acquainted with the every-day human face, – they give us skill to detect those gradations of sense and virtue (which escape the careless or fastidious observer) in the countenances of the world about us; and prevent that disgust at common life, that *taedium quotidianarum formarum*, which an unrestricted passion for ideal forms and beauties is in danger

of producing. In this, as in many other things, they are analogous to the best novels of Smollett or Fielding.
(97–101)

Sir James Mackintosh

from 'Remarks on Fiction' in his journal   1 September 1811
(R. J. Mackintosh (ed.), *Memoirs of . . . Sir James Mackintosh*, vol. 2, 1835)

There may be persons now alive who may recollect the publication of *Tom Jones*, at least, if not of *Clarissa*. In that time, probably twelve novels have appeared, of the first rank – a prodigious number, of such a kind, in any department of literature; and the whole class of novels must have had more influence on the public, than all other sorts of books combined. Nothing popular can be frivolous; whatever influences multitudes, must be of proportionable importance. . . .

If fiction exalts virtue by presenting ideal perfection, and strengthens sympathy by multiplying the occasions for its exercise, this must be best done when the fiction most resembles that real life which is the sphere of the duties and feelings of the great majority of men. At first sight, then, it seems that the moralist could not have imagined a revolution in literature more favourable to him, than that which has exalted and multiplied novels. And now I hear a clamour around me: '*Tom Jones* is the most admirable and popular of all English novels, and will Mr Philosopher pretend that *Tom Jones* is a moral book?' With shame and sorrow it must be answered, that it does not deserve the name, and a good man, who finds such a prostitution of genius in a book so likely to captivate the young, will be apt to throw it from him with indignation; but he will still, even in this extreme case, observe, that the same book inspires the greatest abhorrence of the duplicity of Blifil, of the hypocrisy of Thwackum and Square; that Jones himself is interesting by his frankness, spirit, kindness, and fidelity – all virtues of the first class. The objection is the same in its principle with that to the *Iliad*. The ancient epic exclusively presents war – the modern novel love; the one what was most interesting in

public life, and the other what is most brilliant in private, and both with an unfortunate disregard of moral restraint.
(129–30)

Samuel Taylor Coleridge

from a lecture on Shakespeare, as reported by J. P. Collier December 1811 (T. M. Raysor (ed.), *Shakespearean Criticism*, vol. 2, 1960)

I honour, I love, the works of Fielding as much, or perhaps more, than those of any other writer of fiction of that kind: take Fielding in his characters of postillions, landlords, and landladies, waiters, or indeed, of any-body who had come before his eye, and nothing can be more true, more happy, or more humorous; but in all his chief personages, Tom Jones for instance, where Fielding was not directed by observation, where he could not assist himself by the close copying of what he saw, where it is necessary that something should take place, some words be spoken, or some object described, which he could not have witnessed, (his soliloquies for example, or the interview between the hero and Sophia Western before the reconciliation) and I will venture to say, loving and honouring the man and his productions as I do, that nothing can be more forced and unnatural: the language is without vivacity or spirit, the whole matter is incongruous, and totally destitute of psychological truth.
(101)

Samuel Taylor Coleridge

from a lecture on Shakespeare   October 1813 (T. M. Raysor (ed.), *Shakespearean Criticism*, vol. 2, 1960)[1]

In observations of living character, such as of landlords and postillions, Fielding had great excellence; but in drawing from his own heart, and depicting that species of character which no observation could

1 See previous extract [ed.].

teach, he failed in comparison with Richardson, who perpetually placed himself, as it were, in a day-dream. But Shakespeare excelled in both....
(217)

Sir James Mackintosh

from a review of William Godwin, *Lives of Edward and John Philips*, *Edinburgh Review*, vol. 25   October 1815

Richardson has perhaps lost, though unjustly, a part of his popularity at home; but he still contributes to support the fame of his country abroad. The small blemishes of his diction are lost in translation. The changes of English manners, and the occasional homeliness of some of his representations, are unfelt by foreigners. Fielding will for ever remain the delight of his country, and will always retain his place in the library of Europe, notwithstanding that unfortunate grossness which is the mark of an uncultivated taste, and which, if not yet entirely excluded from conversation, has been for some time banished from our writings, where, during the best age of national genius, it prevailed more than in those of any other polished nation.
(485)

Samuel Taylor Coleridge

from *Biographia Literaria*, chapter 22   1817 (J. Shawcross (ed.), vol. 2, 1958)

A poem, where the author, having occasion for the character of a poet and a philosopher in the fable of his narration, had chosen to make him a chimney-sweeper; and then, in order to remove all doubts on the subject, has invented an account of his birth, parentage and education, with all the strange and fortunate accidents which had concurred in making him at once poet, philosopher, and sweep! Nothing but biography can justify this. If it be admissible even in a novel, it must be one in the manner of Defoe's, that were meant to pass for histories, not in the manner of Fielding's: in the life of

Moll Flanders, or Colonel Jack, not in a Tom Jones, or even a
Joseph Andrews. Much less then can it be legitimately introduced in
a poem, the characters of which, amid the strongest individualization,
must still remain representative.... Spite of all attempts, the fiction
will appear, and unfortunately not as *fictitious* but as *false*.
(106–7)

John Keats

from a letter to George and Tom Keats 5 January 1818
(H. E. Rollins (ed.), *Letters*, vol. 1, 1958)

Scott endeavours to th[r]ow so interesting and romantic a colouring
into common and low characters as to give them a touch of the
Sublime – Smollett on the contrary pulls down and levels what with
other men would continue Romance. The grand parts of Scott are
within the reach of more minds than the finest humours in *Humphrey
Clinker* – I forget whether that fine thing of the Sargeant is Fielding's
or Smollett's but it gives me more pleasure that the whole novel of
the Antiquary – you must remember what I mean. Some one says
to the Sargeant 'that's a non sequiter', 'if you come to that', replies
the Sargeant, 'you're another' [*Tom Jones*, Book 9, chapter 6].
(200)

William Hazlitt

from 'On Respectable People', *Edinburgh Magazine* August 1818
(P. P. Howe (ed.), *Complete Works*, vol. 12, 1931)

Respectability means a man's situation and success in life, not his
character or conduct ...

   The country parson may pass his whole time, when he is not employed in the cure of souls, in flattering his rich neighbours, and leaguing
with them to *snub* his poor ones, in seizing poachers, and encouraging
informers; he may be exorbitant in exacting his tithes, harsh to all
his servants, the dread and bye-word of the village where he resides,

and yet all this, though it may be notorious, shall abate nothing of his respectability. It will not hinder his patron from giving him another living to play the petty tyrant in, or prevent him from riding over to the squire's in his carriage and being well-received, or from sitting on the bench of Justices with due decorum and with clerical dignity. The poor curate, in the meantime, who may be a real comfort to the bodies and minds of his parishioners, will be passed by without notice. Parson Adams, drinking his ale in Sir Thomas Booby's kitchen, makes no very respectable figure; but Sir Thomas himself was right worshipful, and his widow a person of honour! A few such historiographers as Fielding would put an end to the farce of respectability, with several others like it. . . .
(363)

William Hazlitt

from a review of *Letters of Horace Walpole*, *Edinburgh Review*
December 1818 (P. P. Howe (ed.), *Complete Works*, vol. 16, 1933)

We may begin with a curious anecdote of Fielding, which is almost as interesting as any thing in the book. Thus it is [see above, 18 May 1749, p. 103]. . . .

It is very certain that the writings of men are coloured by their indolence, their amusements, and their occupations; and this little peep into Fielding's private hours, lets us at once into his course of studies, and is an admirable illustration of his *Tom Jones, Jonathan Wild*, and other novels. We are taken into the artist's workshop, and shown the models from which he works; or rather, we break in upon him at a time when he is copying from the *life*. It is a very idle piece of morality, to lament over Fielding for this low indulgence of his appetite for character. If he had been found quietly at his tea, he would never have left behind him the name he has done. There is nothing of a tea inspiration in any of his novels. They are assuredly the finest things of the kind in the language; and we are Englishmen enough to consider them the best in any language. They are indubitably the most English of all the works of Englishmen.
(147)

William Hazlitt

from *Lectures on the English Comic Writers* 1819 (P. P. Howe (ed.),
Complete Works, vol. 6, 1931)

From Lecture VI, published in an earlier form in 1815

I should be at a loss where to find in any authentic documents of
the same period so satisfactory an account of the general state of
society, and of moral, political, and religious feeling in the reign of
George II as we meet with in the *Adventures of Joseph Andrews and
his friend Mr Abraham Adams*. This work, indeed, I take to be a perfect
piece of statistics in its kind. In looking into any regular history of
that period, into a learned and eloquent charge to a grand jury or the
clergy of a diocese, or into a tract on controversial divinity, we
should hear only of the ascendancy of the Protestant succession, the
horrors of popery, the triumph of civil and religious liberty, the
wisdom and moderation of the sovereign, the happiness of the subject,
and the flourishing state of manufactures and commerce. But if we
really wish to know what all these fine-sounding names come to,
we cannot do better than turn to the works of those, who having
no other object than to imitate nature, could only hope for success
from the fidelity of their pictures; and were bound (in self-defence)
to reduce the boasts of vague theorists and the exaggerations of
angry disputants to the mortifying standard of reality. Extremes are
said to meet: and the works of imagination, as they are called,
sometimes come the nearest to truth and nature. Fielding in speaking
on this subject, and vindicating the use and dignity of the style of
writing in which he excelled against the loftier pretensions of professed historians, says that in their productions nothing is true but
the names and dates, whereas in his every thing is true but the names
and dates. If so, he has the advantage on his side.

I will here confess, however, that I am a little prejudiced on the
point in question; and that the effect of many fine speculations has
been lost upon me, from an early familiarity with the most striking
passages in the work to which I have just alluded. Thus nothing can
be more captivating than the description somewhere given by Mr
Burke of the indissoluble connection between learning and nobility;

and of the respect universally paid by wealth to piety and morals. But the effect of this ideal representation has always been spoiled by my recollection of Parson Adams sitting over his cup of ale in Sir Thomas Booby's kitchen. Echard, *On the Contempt of the Clergy* is, in like manner, a very good book, and 'worthy of all acceptation': but, somehow, an unlucky impression of the reality of Parson Trulliber involuntarily checks the emotions of respect, to which it might otherwise give rise: while, on the other hand, the lecture which Lady Booby reads to Lawyer Scout on the immediate expulsion of Joseph and Fanny from the parish, casts no very favourable light on the flattering accounts of our practical jurisprudence which are to be found in Blackstone or De Lolme. The most moral writers, after all, are those who do not pretend to inculcate any moral. The professed moralist almost unavoidably degenerates into the partisan of a system; and the philosopher is too apt to warp the evidence to his own purpose. But the painter of manners gives the facts of human nature, and leaves us to draw the inference: if we are not able to do this, or do it ill, at least it is our own fault.

The first-rate writers in this class, of course, are few; but those few we may reckon among the greatest ornaments and best benefactors of our kind. There is a certain set of them who, as it were, take their rank by the side of reality, and are appealed to as evidence on all questions concerning human nature. The principal of these are Cervantes and Le Sage, who may be considered as having been naturalized among ourselves; and, of native English growth, Fielding, Smollett, Richardson, and Sterne[1]....
(106–7)

There is very little to warrant the common idea that Fielding was an imitator of Cervantes, except his own declaration of such an intention in the title-page of *Joseph Andrews*, the romantic turn of the character of Parson Adams (the only romantic character in his works), and the proverbial humour of Partridge, which is kept up only for a few pages. Fielding's novels are, in general, thoroughly his own; and they are thoroughly English. What they are most remarkable for, is

1 It is not to be forgotten that the author of *Robinson Crusoe* was also an Englishman. His other works, such as *The Life of Colonel Jack*, etc., are of the same cast, and leave an impression on the mind more like that of things than words.

neither sentiment, nor imagination, nor wit, nor even humour, though there is an immense deal of this last quality; but profound knowledge of human nature, at least of English nature; and masterly pictures of the characters of men as he saw them existing. This quality distinguishes all his works, and is shown almost equally in all of them. As a painter of real life, he was equal to Hogarth; as a mere observer of human nature, he was little inferior to Shakespeare, though without any of the genius and poetical qualities of his mind. His humour is less rich and laughable than Smollett's; his wit as often misses as hits; he has none of the fine pathos of Richardson or Sterne; but he has brought together a greater variety of characters in common life, marked with more distinct peculiarities, and without an atom of caricature, than any other novel writer whatever. The extreme subtlety of observation on the springs of human conduct in ordinary characters, is only equalled by the ingenuity of contrivance in bringing those springs into play, in such a manner as to lay open their smallest irregularity. The detection is always complete, and made with the certainty and skill of a philosophical experiment, and the obviousness and familiarity of a casual observation. The truth of the imitation is indeed so great, that it has been argued that Fielding must have had his materials ready-made to his hands, and was merely a transcriber of local manners and individual habits. For this conjecture, however, there seems to be no foundation. His representations, it is true, are local and individual; but they are not the less profound and conclusive. The feeling of the general principles of human nature operating in particular circumstances, is always intense, and uppermost in his mind; and he makes use of incident and situation only to bring out character.

It is scarcely necessary to give any illustrations. *Tom Jones* is full of them. There is the account, for example, of the gratitude of the elder Blifil to his brother, for assisting him to obtain the fortune of Miss Bridget Allworthy by marriage; and of the gratitude of the poor in his neighbourhood to Allworthy himself, who had done so much good in the country that he had made every one in it his enemy.... There is the gradation in the lovers of Molly Seagrim; the philosopher Square succeeding to Tom Jones, who again finds that he himself had succeeded to the accomplished Will. Barnes, who had the first possession of her person, and had still possession of her heart,

Jones being only the instrument of her vanity, as Square was of her interest.... The moral of this book has been objected to, without much reason [in 1815, Hazlitt had said 'not altogether without reason']; but a more serious objection has been made to the want of refinement and elegance in two principal characters. We never feel this objection, indeed, while we are reading the book: but at other times, we have something like a lurking suspicion that Jones was but an awkward fellow, and Sophia a pretty simpleton. I do not know how to account for this effect, unless it is that Fielding's constantly assuring us of the beauty of his hero, and the good sense of his heroine, at last produces a distrust of both [see also the extract dated November 1827]. The story of *Tom Jones* is allowed to be unrivalled: and it is this circumstance, together with the vast variety of characters, that has given the history of a Foundling so decided a preference over Fielding's other novels. The characters themselves, both in *Amelia* and *Joseph Andrews*, are quite equal to any of those in *Tom Jones*. The account of Miss Matthews and Ensign Hibbert, in the former of these; the way in which that lady reconciles herself to the death of her father; the inflexible Colonel Bath; the insipid Mrs James, the complaisant Colonel Trent, the demure, sly, intriguing, equivocal Mrs Bennet, the lord who is her seducer, and who attempts afterwards to seduce Amelia by the same mechanical process of a concert-ticket, a book, and the disguise of a great coat; his little, fat, short-nosed, red-faced, good-humoured accomplice, the keeper of the lodging-house, who, having no pretensions to gallantry herself, has a disinterested delight in forwarding the intrigues and pleasures of others (to say nothing of honest Atkinson, the story of the miniature-picture of Amelia, and the hashed mutton, which are in a different style), are masterpieces of description. The whole scene at the lodging-house, the masquerade, etc. in *Amelia*, are equal in interest to the parallel scenes in *Tom Jones*, and even more refined in the knowledge of character. For instance, Mrs Bennet is superior to Mrs Fitzpatrick in her own way. The uncertainty, in which the event of her interview with her former seducer is left, is admirable. Fielding was a master of what may be called the *double entendre* of character, and surprises you no less by what he leaves in the dark (hardly known to the persons themselves), than by the unexpected discoveries he makes of the real traits and circumstances in a character with which, till then, you find you were unacquainted. There is nothing at all heroic, however, in the usual style of his delineations. He does not draw lofty characters or strong passions; all his persons are of the ordinary stature as to intellect; and possess little elevation of fancy, or energy of purpose. Perhaps, after all, Parson Adams is his finest character. It is equally true to nature, and more ideal than any of the others. Its unsuspecting simplicity makes it not only more amiable, but doubly amusing, by gratifying the sense of superior sagacity in the reader. Our laughing at him does not once lessen our respect for him. His declaring that he would willingly walk ten miles to fetch his sermon on vanity, merely to convince Wilson of his thorough contempt of this vice, and his consoling himself for the loss of his Aeschylus, by suddenly recollecting that he could not read it if he had it, because it is dark, are among the finest touches of *naïveté*. The night-adventures at Lady Booby's with Beau Didapper, and the amiable Slipslop, are the most ludicrous; and that with the huntsman, who draws off the hounds from the poor Parson, because they would be spoiled by following *vermin*, the most profound. Fielding did not often repeat himself; but Dr Harrison, in *Amelia*, may be considered as a variation of the character of Adams: so also is Goldsmith's Vicar of Wakefield; and the latter part of that work, which sets out so delightfully, an almost entire plagiarism from Wilson's account of himself, and Adams's domestic history.

Smollett's first novel, *Roderick Random*, which is also his best, appeared about the same time as Fielding's *Tom Jones*; and yet it has a much more modern air with it: but this may be accounted for, from the circumstance that Smollett was quite a young man at the time, whereas Fielding's manner must have been formed long before. The style of *Roderick Random* is more easy and flowing than that of *Tom Jones*; the incidents follow one another more rapidly (though, it must be confessed, they never come in such a throng, or are brought out with the same dramatic effect); the humour is broader, and as effectual; and there is very nearly, if not quite, an equal interest excited by the story. What then is it that gives the superiority to Fielding? It is the superior insight into the springs of human character, and the constant development of that character through every change of circumstance. Smollett's humour often arises from the situation of the persons, or the peculiarity of their external appearance; as, from Roderick Random's carrotty locks, which hung down over his shoulders like a pound of candles, or Strap's ignorance of London, and the blunders that follow from it. There is a tone of vulgarity about all his productions. The incidents frequently re-semble detached anecdotes taken from a newspaper or magazine; and, like those in *Gil Blas*, might happen to a hundred other characters. He exhibits the ridiculous accidents and reverses to which human life is liable, not 'the stuff' of which it is composed. He seldom probes to the quick, or penetrates beyond the surface; and, therefore, he leaves no stings in the minds of his readers, and in this respect is far less interesting than Fielding. His novels always enliven, and never tire us: we take them up with pleasure, and lay them down without any strong feeling of regret. We look on and laugh, as spectators of a highly amusing scene, without closing in with the combatants, or being made parties in the event. We read *Roderick Random* as an entertaining story; for the particular accidents and modes of life which it describes have ceased to exist: but we regard *Tom Jones* as real history; because the author never stops short of those essential principles which lie at the bottom of all our actions, and in which we feel an immediate interest – *intus et in cute*. Smollett excels most as the lively caricaturist: Fielding as the exact painter and profound meta-physician. I am far from maintaining that this account applies uni-formly to the productions of these two writers; but I think that, as far as they essentially differ, what I have stated is the general distinc-tion between them. *Roderick Random* is the purest of Smollett's novels: I mean in point of style and description. Most of the incidents and characters are supposed to have been taken from the events of his own life; and are, therefore, truer to nature. There is a rude conception of generosity in some of his characters, of which Fielding seems to have been incapable, his amiable persons being merely good-natured. It is owing to this that Strap is superior to Partridge; as there is a heartiness and warmth of feeling in some of the scenes between Lieutenant Bowling and his nephew, which is beyond Fielding's power of impassioned writing.

(112–16)

From Lecture VII

[Hogarth] was one of the greatest comic geniuses that ever lived, and he was certainly one of the most extraordinary men this country has produced. The wonderful knowledge which he possessed of human life and manners, is only to be surpassed (if it can be) by the power of invention with which he has combined and contrasted his materials in the most ludicrous and varied points of view, and by the mastery of execution with which he has embodied and made tangible the very thoughts and passing movements of the mind. Critics sometimes object to the style of Hogarth's pictures, or to the class to which they belong. First, he belongs to no class, or if he does, it is to the same class as Fielding, Smollett, Vanbrugh, and Molière.... Make what deductions you please for the vulgarity of the subject, yet in the research, the profundity, the absolute truth and precision of the delineation of character; in the invention of incident, in wit and humour; in the life with which they are 'instinct in every part'; in everlasting variety and originality; they never have, and probably never will be surpassed. They stimulate the faculties as well as soothe them. 'Other pictures we see, Hogarth's we read.'...
(133)

The inferiority of Hogarth (be it what it may) did not arise from a want of passion and intense feeling; and in this respect he had the advantage over Fielding, for instance, and others of our comic writers, who excelled only in the light and ludicrous. There is in general a distinction, almost an impassable one, between the power of embodying the serious and the ludicrous; but these contradictory faculties were reconciled in Hogarth, as they were in Shakespeare, in Chaucer....
(144)

From Lecture VIII, printed in an earlier form in 1813

Some theorists ... have been sanguine enough to expect a regular advance from grossness to refinement on the stage and in real life, marked on a graduated scale of human perfectibility, and have been hence led to imagine that the best of our old comedies were no

better than the coarse jests of a set of country clowns – a sort of *comédies bourgeoises*, compared with the admirable productions which might, but have not, been written in our times. I must protest against this theory altogether, which would go to degrade genteel comedy from a high court lady into a literary prostitute. I do not know what these persons mean by refinement in this instance. Do they find none in Millamant and her morning dreams, in Sir Roger de Coverley and his widow? ... Where, in the annals of modern literature, shall we find any thing more refined, more deliberate, more abstracted in vice, than the nobleman in *Amelia*? Are not the compliments which Pope paid to his friends equal in taste and elegance to any which have been paid since? Are there no traits in Sterne? Is not Richardson minute enough? Must we part with Sophia Western and her muff, and Clarissa Harlowe's 'preferable regards' for the loves of the plants and the triangles?
(152-3)

[Fielding's plays] are very inferior to his novels: they are particularly deficient both in plot and character. The only excellence which they have is that of the style, which is the only thing in which his novels are deficient.
(159)

Samuel Taylor Coleridge

from letters to Thomas Allsop   30 March and 8 April 1820
(E. L. Griggs (ed.), *Collected Letters*, vol. 5, 1971)

Walter Scott's poems and novels ... supply both instance and solution of the present conditions and components of popularity, viz. to amuse without requiring any effort of thought and without exciting any deep emotion. The age seems sore from excess of stimulation. ... Even to *admire* otherwise than 'on the whole' – and where 'I admire' is but a synonym for 'I remember I *liked* it very much when I was reading it' – is too much an effort, would be too disquieting an emotion! Compare *Waverley*, *Guy Mannering*, etc. with works that had an immediate run in the last generation –

Tristram Shandy, Roderick Random, Sir Charles Grandison, Clarissa Harlow, and *Tom Jones* (all of which became popular as soon as published and therefore instances fairly in point) and you will be convinced, that the difference of taste is real and not any fancy croaking of my own. . . .
(24–5)

I selected Scott for the very reason, that I do hold him a man of very extraordinary powers; and when I say, that I have read the far greater part of his novels twice, and several three times over with undiminished pleasure and interest . . . I am far from thinking, that *Old Mortality* or *Guy Mannering* would have been less admired in the age of Sterne, Fielding and Richardson, than they are in the present times; but only that Sterne etc. would not have had the same *immediate* popularity in the present day as in their own less stimulated and therefore less languid reading world. . . . My criticism was confined to the *one* point of the higher degree of intellectual activity implied in the reading and admiration of Fielding, Richardson, and Sterne – in moral, or if that be too high and inwardly a word, in *mannerly* manliness of taste the present age and its writers have the decided advantage, and I sincerely trust that Walter Scott's readers would be as little disposed to relish the stupid lechery of the courtship of Widow Wadham [Wadman] as Scott himself would be capable of presenting it. Add, that tho' I cannot pretend to have found in any of these novels a character that even approaches in genius, in truth of conception or boldness and freshness of execution, to Parson Adams, Blifil, Strap, Lieutenant Bowling, Mr Shandy, Uncle Toby and Trim, Lovelace; and tho' Scott's *female* characters will not, even the very best, bear a comparison with Miss Byron, Emily, Clementina in *Sir Charles Grandison*; nor the comic ones with Tabitha Bramble, or with Betty (in Mrs Bennett's *Beggar-Girl*) – and tho' by the use of the Scotch dialect, by Ossianic mock-Highland motley heroic, and by extracts from the printed sermons, memoirs, etc. of the fanatic preachers, there is a good deal of false effect and stage trick; still the number of characters *so good* produced by one man and in so rapid a succession, must ever remain an illustrious phenomenon in Literature. . . .
(33–4)

Sir Walter Scott

from 'Prefatory Memoir to Fielding'   25 October 1820
(*The Novelist's Library*, vol. 1, 1824)

The reader is here presented with the novels of the celebrated
Henry Fielding, in a form at once portable and comprehensive. Of
all the works of imagination, to which English genius has given
origin, these are, perhaps, most decidedly and exclusively her own.
They are not only altogether beyond the reach of translation, in the
proper sense and spirit of the word, but we even question, whether
they can be fully understood, or relished to the highest extent, by
such natives of Scotland and Ireland, as are not habitually acquainted
with the character and manners of Old England. . . .
(i)

Fielding, the first of British novelists, for such he may surely be
termed, has thus added his name to that of Le Sage and others, who,
eminent for fictitious narration, have either altogether failed in their
dramatic attempts, or at least have fallen far short of that degree of
excellence, which might have been previously augured of them. It
is hard to fix upon any plausible reason for a failure, which has
occurred in too many instances to be the operation of mere chance. . . .
Force of character, strength of expression, felicity of contrast and
situation, a well-constructed plot, in which the development is at
once natural and unexpected, and where the interest is kept uni-
formly alive, till summed up by the catastrophe – all these are requisites as essential to the labour of the novelist, as to that of the
dramatist, and, indeed, appear to comprehend the sum of the qualities
necessary to success in both departments. . . . The author of a novel,
in short, has neither stage nor scene-painter nor company of comedians, nor dresser, nor wardrobe, – words applied with the best of his
skill, must supply all that these bring to the assistance of the dramatist.
Action and tone and gesture, the smile of the lover, the frown of the
tyrant, the grimace of the buffoon – all must be told, for nothing can
be shewn. Thus, the very dialogue becomes mixed with the narration;
for he must not only tell what the characters actually said, in which

his task is the same as that of the dramatic author, but must also describe the tone, the look, the gesture, with which their speech was accompanied – telling, in short, all which, in the drama, it becomes the province of the actor to express. It must, therefore, frequently happen, that the author best qualified for a province, in which all depends on the communication of his own ideas and feelings to the reader, without any intervening medium, may fall short of the skill necessary to adapt his compositions to the medium of the stage, where the very qualities most excellent in a novelist are out of place, and an impediment to success. . . . It may thus easily be conceived, that he whose chief talent lies in addressing the imagination only, and whose style, therefore, must be expanded and circumstantial, may fail in a kind of composition where so much must be left to the efforts of the actor, with his allies and assistants the scene-painter and property-man, and where every attempt to interfere with their province, is an error unfavourable to the success of the piece. Besides . . . in fictitious narrative an author carries on his manufacture alone, and upon his own account; whereas, in dramatic writing, he enters into partner-ship with the performers, and it is by their joint efforts that the piece is to succeed. Copartnery is . . . the mother of discord. . . . And he who in a novel had only to fit sentiments, action, and character, to ideal beings, is now compelled to assume the much more difficult task of adapting all these to real existing persons, who, unless their parts are exactly suited to their own taste, and their peculiar capacities, have, each in his line, the means, and not infrequently the inclination to ruin the success of the play. . . .
(iv–vii)

But *Pamela*, to which that irony was applied, is now in a manner forgotten, and *Joseph Andrews* continues to be read, for the admirable pictures of manners which it presents, and, above all, for the inimit-able character of Mr Abraham Adams, which alone is sufficient to stamp the superiority of Fielding over all writers of his class. His learning, his simplicity, his evangelical purity of mind, and benevo-lence of disposition, are so admirably mingled with pedantry, absence of mind, and with the habit of athletic and gymnastic exercise, then acquired at the universities by students of all descriptions, that he may be safely termed one of the richest productions of the Muse of fiction. Like Don Quixote, Parson Adams is beaten a little too much, and too often; but the cudgel lights upon his shoulders, as on those of the honoured Knight of La Mancha, without the slightest stain to his reputation; and he is bastinadoed without being degraded. The style of this piece, is said, in the preface, to have been an imitation of Cervantes; but both in *Joseph Andrews* and *Tom Jones*, the author appears also to have had in view the *Roman Comique* of the once celebrated Scarron. From this author he had copied the mock heroic style, which tells ludicrous events in the language of the classical Epic; a vein of pleasantry which is soon wrought out, and which Fielding has employed so often as to expose him to the charge of pedantry.

Joseph Andrews was eminently successful; and the aggrieved Richardson, who was fond of praise even to adulation, was proportionally offended, while his group of admirers, male and female, took care to echo back his sentiments, and to heap Fielding with reproach. Their animosity survived his life, and we find the most ungenerous reproaches thrown upon his memory, in the course of Richardson's correspondence. . . . Fielding does not appear to have retorted any of this ill-will; so that, if he gave the first offence, and that an unprovoked one, he was also the first to retreat from the contest, and to allow to Richardson those claims which his genius really demanded from the liberality of his contemporaries. In the fifth number of the *Jacobite Journal*, Fielding highly commends *Clarissa*, which is by far the best and most powerful of Richardson's novels. . . . Perhaps this is one of the cases in which one would rather have sympathized with the thoughtless offender, than with the illiberal and ungenerous mind which so long retained its resentment. . . .

Fielding published in, or about, 1743, a volume of Miscellanies, including *The Journey from this World to the Next*, a tract containing a good deal of Fielding's peculiar humour, but of which it is difficult to conceive the plan or purport. *The History of Jonathan Wild the Great* next followed. It is not easy to see what Fielding proposed to himself by a picture of complete vice, unrelieved by any thing of human feeling, and never by any accident even deviating into virtue; and the ascribing a train of fictitious adventures to a real character, has in it something clumsy and inartificial on the one hand, and, on

the other, subjects the author to a suspicion that he only used the title of Jonathan Wild in order to connect his book with the popular renown of that infamous depredator. But there are few passages in Fielding's more celebrated works, more marked with his peculiar genius, than the scene betwixt his hero and the Ordinary, when in Newgate. . . .
(xi–xiii)

Under such precarious circumstances the first English novel was given to the public, which had not yet seen any works of fiction founded upon the plan of painting from nature. Even Richardson's novels are but a step from the old romance, approaching, indeed, more nearly to the ordinary course of events, but still dealing in improbable incidents, and in characters swelled out beyond the ordinary limits of humanity. The *History of a Foundling* is truth and human nature itself, and there lies the inestimable advantage which it possesses over all previous fictions of this particular kind. It was received with unanimous acclamation by the public, and proved so productive to Millar the publisher, that he handsomely added £100 to £600, for which he had purchased the work from the author. . . .

The felicitous contrivance, and happy extrication of the story, where every incident tells upon, and advances the catastrophe, while, at the same time, it illustrates the characters of those interested in its approach, cannot too often be mentioned with the highest approbation. The attention of the reader is never diverted or puzzled by unnecessary digressions, or recalled to the main story by abrupt and startling recurrences; he glides down the narrative like a boat on the surface of some broad navigable stream, which only winds enough to gratify the voyager with the varied beauty of its banks. One exception to this praise, otherwise so well merited, occurs in the story of the Old Man of the Hill; an episode, which, in compliance with a custom introduced by Cervantes, and followed by Le Sage, Fielding has thrust into the midst of his narrative, as he had formerly introduced the History of Leonora, equally unnecessarily and inartificially, into that of *Joseph Andrews*. It has also been wondered, why Fielding should have chosen to leave the stain of illegitimacy on the birth of his hero; and it has been surmised, that he did so, in allusion to his own first wife, who was also a natural child. A better reason may be discovered in the story itself; for had Miss Bridget been privately married to the father of Tom Jones, there could have been no adequate motive assigned for keeping his birth secret from a man so reasonable and compassionate as Allworthy.

But even the high praise due to the construction and arrangement of the story, is inferior to that claimed by the truth, force, and spirit of the characters, from Tom Jones himself, down to Black George the game-keeper, and his family. Amongst these, Squire Western stands alone; imitated from no prototype, and in himself an inimitable picture of ignorance, prejudice, irascibility, and rusticity, united with natural shrewdness, constitutional good humour, and an instinctive affection for his daughter – all which qualities, good and bad, are grounded upon that basis of thorough selfishness, natural to one bred up, from infancy, where no one dared to contradict his arguments, or to control his conduct. In one incident alone, we think Fielding has departed from this admirable sketch. As an English squire, Western ought not to have taken a beating so unresistingly from the friend of Lord Fellamar. We half suspect that the passage is an interpolation. It is inconsistent with the Squire's readiness to engage in rustic affrays. We grant a pistol or sword might have appalled him; but Squire Western should have yielded to no one in the use of the English horsewhip; and as, with all his brutalities, we have a sneaking interest in the honest jolly country gentleman, we would willingly hope there is some mistake in this matter.

The character of Jones, otherwise a model of generosity, openness, manly spirit, mingled with thoughtless dissipation, is, in like manner, unnecessarily degraded by the nature of his intercourse with Lady Bellaston; and this is one of the circumstances which incline us to believe, that Fielding's ideas of what was gentleman-like and honourable had sustained some depreciation, in consequence of the unhappy circumstances of his life, and of the society to which they condemned him.

A more sweeping and general objection was made against the *History of a Foundling* by the admirers of Richardson, and has been often repeated since. It is alleged, that the ultimate moral of *Tom Jones*, which conducts to happiness, and holds up to our sympathy and esteem a youth who gives way to licentious habits, is detrimental to society, and tends to encourage the youthful reader in the practice of those follies, to which his natural passions, and the usual course of the world, but too much direct him. French delicacy, which, on so many occasions, has strained at a gnat, and swallowed a camel, saw this fatal tendency in the work, and by an *arrêt* discharged the circulation of a bungled abridgment by De la Place, entitled a translation. To this charge Fielding himself might probably have replied, that the vices into which Jones suffers himself to fall, are made the direct cause of placing him in the distressful situation, which he occupies during the greater part of the narrative; while his generosity, his charity, and his amiable qualities, become the means of saving him from the consequences of his folly. But we suspect with Dr Johnson, that there is something of cant both in the objection, and in the answer to it. 'Men,' says that moralist, 'will not become highwaymen, because Macheath is acquitted on the stage'; and we add, they will not become. . . . licentious debauchees, because they read *Tom Jones*. The professed moral of a piece is usually what the reader is least interested in. . . . The worst evil to be apprehended from the perusal of novels is, that the habit is apt to generate an indisposition to real history, and useful literature; and that the best which can be hoped is, that they may sometimes instruct the youthful mind by real pictures of life, and sometimes awaken their better feelings and sympathies by strains of generous sentiment, and tales of fictitious woe. Beyond this point they are a mere elegance, a luxury contrived for the amusement of polished life, and the gratification of that half love of literature, which pervades all ranks in an advanced stage of society, and are read much more for amusement, than with the least hope of deriving instruction from them. The vices and follies of Tom Jones, are those which the world soon teaches to all who enter on the career of life, and to which society is unhappily but too indulgent; nor do we believe, that, in any one instance, the perusal of Fielding's novel has added one libertine to the large list, who would not have been such, had it never crossed the press. And it is with concern we add our sincere belief, that the fine picture of frankness and generosity, exhibited in that fictitious character, has had as few imitators as the career of his follies. . . . He has himself said, that there is nothing which can offend the chastest eye in the perusal; and he spoke probably according to the ideas of his time. But in modern estimation, there are several passages at which delicacy may justly take offence; and we can only say, that they may be termed rather jocularly coarse than seductive; and that they are atoned for by the admirable mixture of wit and argument, by which, in others, the cause of true religion and virtue is supported and advanced.

Fielding considered his works as an experiment in British literature; and, therefore, he chose to prefix a preliminary chapter to each Book, explanatory of his own views, and of the rules attached to this mode of composition. Those critical introductions, which rather interrupt the course of the story, and the flow of the interest at the first perusal, are found, on a second or third, the most entertaining chapters of the whole work. . . .

Amelia was the author's last work of importance. It may be termed a continuation of *Tom Jones*; but we have not the same sympathy for the ungrateful and dissolute conduct of Booth, which we yield to the youthful follies of Jones. The character of Amelia is said to have been drawn for Fielding's second wife. If he put her patience, as has been alleged, to tests of the same kind, he has, in some degree, repaid her, by the picture he has drawn of her feminine delicacy and pure tenderness. Fielding's novels shew few instances of pathos; it was, perhaps, inconsistent with the life which he was compelled to lead; for those who see most of human misery become necessarily, in some degree, hardened to its effects. But few scenes of fictitious distress are more affecting, than that in which Amelia is described, as having made her little preparations for the evening, and sitting in anxious expectation of the return of her unworthy husband, whose folly is, in the mean time, preparing for her new scenes of misery. But our sympathy for the wife is disturbed by our dislike of her unthankful husband; and the tale is, on the whole, unpleasing, even though relieved by the humours of the doughty Colonel Bath, and the learned Dr Harrison, characters with such force and precision, as Fielding alone knew how to employ. . . .

Among [those who attacked Fielding at the time of *Amelia* and the *Covent-Garden Journal*], we are sorry to particularize Smollett, although possessed of the most kindred genius to Fielding's which has yet appeared in British literature. The warfare was of brief duration, and neither party would obtain honour by an inquiry into the cause or conduct of its hostilities. . . .

It remains a singular example of Fielding's natural strength of mind that, while struggling hard at once with the depression, and with the irritability of disease, he could still exhibit [in the *Voyage to Lisbon*] a few flashes of that bright wit, which could once set the 'world' in a roar. His perception of character, and power of describing it, had not forsaken him in those sad moments; for the master of the ship in which he sailed, the scolding landlady of the Isle of Wight, the military coxcomb, who visits their vessel, are all portraits, marked with the master-hand which traced Parson Adams and Squire Western. . . .

Thus lived, and thus died, at a period of life when the world might have expected continued delight from his matured powers, the celebrated Henry Fielding, father of the English Novel; and in his powers of strong and national humour, and forcible yet natural exhibition of character, unapproached as yet, even by his successful followers.

(xvii–xxiv)

Lord Byron

from a diary   4 January 1821 (R. E. Prothero (ed.),
Letters and Journals, vol. 5, 1901)

I was out of spirits – read the papers – thought what *fame* was, on reading, in a case of murder, that 'Mr Wych, grocer, at Tunbridge, sold some bacon, flour, cheese, and, it is believed, some plums, to some gipsy woman accused. He had on his counter (I quote faithfully) a book, the *Life of Pamela*, which he was tearing for waste paper, etc. etc. In the cheese was found, etc., and a leaf of *Pamela* wrapt round the bacon'. What would Richardson, the vainest and luckiest of living authors (i.e. while alive), he who, with Aaron Hill, used to prophesy and chuckle over the presumed fall of Fielding (the prose Homer of Human nature) and of Pope (the most beautiful of poets) – what would he have said, could he have traced his pages from their place on the French prince's toilets (see Boswell's *Johnson*) to the grocer's counter and the gipsy-murderess's bacon!!!

(147–9)

Lord Byron

from 'Observations upon "Observations"'. A Second Letter to
John Murray, Esq., on the Rev. W. L. Bowles's Strictures on the
Life and Writings of Pope'   25 March 1821 (R. E. Prothero (ed.),
Letters and Journals, vol. 5, 1901)

Vulgarity is far worse than downright blackguardism; for the latter
comprehends wit, humour and strong sense at times; while the former
is a sad abortive attempt at all things, 'signifying nothing'. It does
not depend upon low themes, or even low language, for Fielding
revels in both; but is he ever vulgar? No. You see the man of education, the gentleman, and the scholar, sporting with his subject – its
master, not its slave.

(592)

Sir Walter Scott

from 'Prefatory Memoir to Smollett'   1 June 1821
(*The Novelist's Library*, vol. 2, 1824)

The manner in which [Smollett] mentions Fielding and Richardson
in the account of the literature of the century, shews how much he
understood, and how liberally he praised, the merit of those, who,
in the view of the world, must have been regarded as his immediate
rivals. 'The genius of Cervantes,' in his generous expression, 'was
transfused into the novels of Fielding, who painted the characters,
and ridiculed the follies of life, with equal strength, humour, and
propriety.' A passage which we record with pleasure, as a proof that
the disagreement which existed betwixt Smollett and Fielding did
not prevent his estimating with justice, and recording in suitable
terms, the merits of the father of the English novel. . . .

    In leaving Smollett's personal for his literary character, it is im-
possible not to consider the latter as contrasted with that of . . .
Fielding. . . . The history, accomplishments, talents, pursuits, and,
unfortunately, the fates of these two great authors, are so closely
allied, that it is scarce possible to name the one without exciting

recollections of the other. Fielding and Smollett were both born in the highest rank of society, both educated to learned professions, yet both obliged to follow miscellaneous literature as the means of subsistence. Both were confined, during their lives, by the narrowness of their circumstances; both united a humorous cynicism with generosity and good nature; both died of the diseases incident to a sedentary life and to literary labour; and both drew their last breath in a foreign land, to which they retreated under the adverse circumstances of a decayed constitution, and an exhausted fortune.

Their studies were no less similar than their lives. They both wrote for the stage, and neither of them successfully. They both meddled in politics; they both wrote travels, in which they shewed that their good humour was wasted under the sufferings of their disease; and, to conclude, they were both so eminently successful as novelists, that no other English author of that class has a right to be mentioned in the same breath with Fielding and Smollett.

If we compare the works of these two great masters yet more closely, we may assign to Fielding, with little hesitation, the praise of a higher and a purer taste than was shewn by his rival; more elegance of composition and expression; a nearer approach to the grave irony of Swift and Cervantes; a great deal more address or felicity in the conduct of his story; and, finally, a power of describing amiable and virtuous characters, and of placing before us heroes, and especially heroines, of a much higher as well as pleasing character than Smollett was able to present.

Thus the art and felicity with which the story of *Tom Jones* evolves itself, is no where found in Smollett's novels, where the heroes pass from one situation in life, and from one stage of society, to another totally unconnected, except that, as in ordinary life, the adventures recorded, though not bearing upon each other, or on the catastrophe, befall the same personage. Characters are introduced and dropped without scruple, and, at the end of the work, the hero is found surrounded by a very different set of associates from those with whom his fortune seemed at first indissolubly connected. Neither are the characters which Smollett designed should be interesting, half so amiable as his readers could desire. The low-minded Roderick Random ... is not to be named in one day with the open-hearted, good-humoured, and noble-minded Tom Jones, whose libertinism (one particular omitted) is perhaps rendered but too amiable by his good qualities. . . . We should do Jones equal injustice by weighing him in the balance with the savage and ferocious Pickle, who, besides his gross and base brutality towards Emilia, besides his ingratitude to his uncle, and the savage propensity which he shews, in the pleasure he takes to torment others by practical jokes resembling those of a fiend in glee, exhibits a low and ungentleman-like tone of thinking, only one degree higher than that of Roderick Random. The blackguard frolic of introducing a prostitute, in a false character, to his sister, is a sufficient instance of that want of taste and feeling which Smollett's admirers are compelled to acknowledge may be detected in his writings. It is yet more impossible to compare Sophia or Amelia to the females of Smollett, who (excepting Aurelia Darnel) are drawn as the objects rather of appetite than of affection. . . .

It follows from this superiority on the side of Fielding, that his novels exhibit, more frequently than those of Smollett, scenes of distress, which excite the sympathy and pity of the reader. No one can refuse his compassion to Jones, when, by a train of practices upon his generous and open character, he is expelled from his benefactor's house under the foulest and most heart-rending accusations; but we certainly sympathize very little in the distress of Pickle, brought on by his own profligate profusion, and enhanced by his insolent misanthropy. We are only surprised that his predominating arrogance does not weary out the benevolence of Hatchway and Pipes, and scarce think the ruined spendthrift deserves their persevering and faithful attachment.

But the deep and fertile genius of Smollett afforded resources sufficient to balance these deficiencies; and when the full weight has been allowed to Fielding's superiority of taste and expression, his northern contemporary will still be found fit to balance the scale with his great rival. If Fielding had superior taste, the palm of more brilliancy of genius, more inexhaustible richness of invention, must in justice be awarded to Smollett. In comparison with his sphere, that in which Fielding walked was limited; and, compared with the wealthy profusion of varied character and incident which Smollett has scattered through his works, there is a poverty of composition about his rival. Fielding's fame rests on a single *chef d'œuvre*; and the art and industry which produced *Tom Jones*, was unable to rise to equal excellence in

Amelia. Though, therefore, we may justly prefer *Tom Jones* as the most masterly example of an artful and well-told novel, to any individual work of Smollett; yet *Roderick Random*, *Peregrine Pickle*, and *Humphry Clinker*, do each of them far excel *Joseph Andrews* or *Amelia*; and, to descend still lower, *Jonathan Wild*, or *The Journey to the Next World*, cannot be put into momentary comparison with *Sir Lancelot Greaves*, or *Ferdinand Count Fathom*.

Every successful novelist must be more or less a poet, even although he may never have written a line of verse. The quality of imagination is absolutely indispensable to him: his accurate power of examining and embodying human character and human passion, as well as the external face of nature, is not less essential; and the talent of describing well what he feels with acuteness, added to the above requisites, goes far to complete the poetic character. Smollett was, even in the ordinary sense, which limits the name to those who write verses, a poet of distinction; and, in this particular, superior to Fielding, who seldom aims at more than a slight translation from the classics. Accordingly, if he is surpassed by Fielding in moving pity, the northern novelist soars far above him in his powers of exciting terror. Fielding has no passages which approach in sublimity to the robber-scene in *Count Fathom*; or to the terrible description of a sea-engagement, in which Roderick Random sits chained and exposed upon the poop, without the power of motion or exertion, during the carnage of a tremendous engagement. Upon many other occasions, Smollett's descriptions ascend to the sublime; and, in general, there is an air of romance in his writings, which raise his narratives above the level and easy course of ordinary life. He was, like a pre-eminent poet of our own day, a searcher of dark bosoms, and loved to paint characters under the strong agitation of fierce and stormy passions. Hence, misanthropes, gamblers, and duellists, are as common in his works, as robbers in those of Salvator Rosa, and are drawn, in most cases, with the same terrible truth and effect. To compare *Ferdinand Count Fathom* to the *Jonathan Wild* of Fielding, would be perhaps unfair to the latter author; yet, the works being composed on the same plan (a very bad one, as we think), we cannot help placing them by the side of each other, when it becomes at once obvious that the detestable Fathom is a living and existing miscreant, at whom we shrink as from the presence of an incarnate fiend, while the villain of Fielding seems rather a cold personification of the abstract principle of evil, so far from being terrible, that, notwithstanding the knowledge of the world argued in many passages of his adventures, we are compelled to acknowledge him absolutely tiresome.

It is, however, chiefly in his profusion, which amounts almost to prodigality, that we recognize the superior richness of Smollett's fancy. He never shews the least desire to make the most either of a character, or a situation, or an adventure, but throws them together with a carelessness which argues unlimited confidence in his own powers. Fielding pauses to explain the principles of his art, and to congratulate himself and his readers on the felicity with which he constructs his narrative, or makes his characters evolve themselves in the progress. These appeals to the reader's judgement, admirable as they are, have sometimes the fault of being diffuse, and always the great disadvantage, that they remind us we are perusing a work of fiction; and that the beings with whom we have been conversant during the perusal, are but a set of evanescent phantoms, conjured up by a magician for our amusement. Smollett seldom holds communication with his readers in his own person. He manages his delightful puppet-show without thrusting his head beyond the curtain, like Gines de Passamonte, to explain what he is doing; and hence, besides that our attention to the story remains unbroken, we are sure that the author, fully confident in the abundance of his materials, has no occasion to eke them out with extrinsic matter. . . .

Fielding is pre-eminent in grave irony, a Cervantic species of pleasantry, in which Smollett is not equally successful. On the other hand, the Scotchman . . . excels in broad and ludicrous humour. His fancy seems to run riot in accumulating ridiculous circumstances one upon another, to the utter destruction of all power of gravity. . . .

We readily grant to Smollett an equal rank with his great rival Fielding, while we place both far above any of their successors in the same line of fictitious composition.

(xxxvi–xlii)

William Hazlitt

from 'Pope, Lord Byron and Mr Bowles', *London Magazine* June 1821 (P. P. Howe (ed.), *Complete Works*, vol. 19, 1933)

To give one more instance or two of what we understand by a natural interest ingrafted on artificial objects, and of the principle that still keeps them distinct. Amelia's 'hashed mutton' in Fielding, is one that I might mention. Hashed mutton is an article in cookery, homely enough in the scale of art, though far removed from the simple products of nature; yet we should say that this common delicacy which Amelia provided for her husband's supper, and then waited so long in vain for his return, is the foundation of one of the most natural and affecting incidents in one of the most natural and affecting books in the world. No description of the most splendid and luxurious banquet could come up to it. It will be remembered, when the *Almanach des Gourmands*, and even the article on it in the last *Edinburgh Review*, are forgotten.

(77)

Lord Byron

from *Don Juan*, IV. 97–8   1821 (reprinted in T. G. Steffan and W. W. Pratt (eds.), *Variorum Edition*, vol. 2, 1971)

Here I might enter on a chaste description,
    Having withstood temptation in my youth,
But hear that several people take exception
    At the first two books having too much truth; ...

'Tis all the same to me; I'm fond of yielding,
    And therefore leave them to the purer page
Of Smollet, Prior, Ariosto, Fielding,
    Who say strange things for so correct an age;
I once had great alacrity in wielding
    My pen, and liked poetic war to wage,

And recollect the time when all this cant
Would have provoked remarks which now it shan't.
(397)

Lord Byron

from 'Detached Thoughts', no. 116   November 1821
(R. E. Prothero (ed.), *Letters and Journals*, vol. 5, 1901)

I have lately been reading Fielding over again. They talk of Radicalism, Jacobinism, etc. in England (I am told), but they should turn over the pages of *Jonathan Wild the Great*. The inequality of conditions, and the littleness of the great, were never set forth in stronger terms; and his contempt for conquerors and the like is such, that, had he lived *now*, he would have been denounced in the *Courier* as the grand mouthpiece and factionary of the revolutionists. And yet I never recollect to have heard this turn of Fielding's mind noticed, though it is obvious in every page.
(465)

Sir Walter Scott

from 'Introductory Epistle' to *The Fortunes of Nigel*   1 April 1822
(*Waverley Novels*, Centenary Edition, vol. 14, 1886)

CAPTAIN [Clutterbuck] – And the story is, I hope, natural and probable; commencing strikingly, proceeding naturally, ending happily – like the course of a famed river, which gushes from the mouth of some obscure and romantic grotto – then gliding on, never pausing, never precipitating its course, visiting, as it were, by natural instinct, whatever worthy subjects of interest are presented by the country through which it passes – widening and deepening in interest as it flows on; and at length arriving at the final catastrophe as at some mighty haven, where ships of all kind strike sail and yard?

AUTHOR ... It would require some one much more like Hercules than I, to produce a story which should gush and glide, and never pause, and visit, and widen, and deepen, and all the rest on't. I should be chin deep in the grave, man, before I had done with my task; and, in the meanwhile, all the quirks and quiddities which I might have devised for my reader's amusement, would lie rotting in my gizzard ... – There never was a novel written on this plan while the world stood.

CAPTAIN Pardon me – *Tom Jones*.

AUTHOR True, and perhaps *Amelia* also. Fielding had high notions of the dignity of an art which he may be considered as having founded. He challenges a comparison between the novel and the epic. Smollett, Le Sage, and others, emancipating themselves from the strictness of the rules he has laid down, have written rather a history of the miscellaneous adventures which befall an individual in the course of life, than the plot of a regular and connected *epopeia*, where every step brings us a point nearer to the final catastrophe. These great masters have been satisfied if they amused the reader upon the road; though the conclusion only arrived because the tale must have an end – just as the traveller alights at the inn because it is evening.

(12)

William Hazlitt

from 'On Criticism', *Table-Talk* 1822 (P. P. Howe (ed.), *Complete Works*, vol. 8, 1931)

Most men's minds are to me like musical instruments out of tune. Touch a particular key, and it jars and makes harsh discord with your own. They like *Gil Blas*, but can see nothing to laugh at in *Don Quixote*: they adore Richardson, but are disgusted with Fielding. Fawcett had a taste accommodated to all these. He was not exceptious. He gave a cordial welcome to all sorts, provided they were the best in their kind. He was not fond of counterfeits or duplicates.

(224–5)

Stendhal

from a review of *Les Cuisinières*,
New Monthly Magazine 1 November 1823

[Stendhal is comparing two French novels, one of which deals with]
the light and transparent froth of high life, and . . . the other, the
opaque and heavy sediment of the lower classes. The middle and
better part of the cup still awaits a French Fielding to describe. . . .
(511)

Thomas Carlyle

from a letter to John A. Carlyle 11 November 1823
(C. R. Sanders *et al.* (eds.), *Collected Letters of Thomas and
Jane Welsh Carlyle*, vol. 2, 1970)

Have you read Fielding's novels? they are genuine things; tho' if
you were not a decent fellow, I should pause before recommending
them, their morality is so loose. Smollett's too are good and bad in
a similar style and degree.
(467)

William Hazlitt

from 'On the Pleasure of Hating' November–December 1823
(P. P. Howe (ed.), *Complete Works*, vol. 12, 1931)

I am half afraid to look into *Tom Jones*, lest it should not answer my
expectations at this time of day; and if it did not, I should certainly
be disposed to fling it into the fire, and never look into another novel
while I lived. But surely, it may be said, there are some works, that,
like nature, can never grow old; and that must always touch the
imagination and passions alike!
(134)

Lord Byron

Don Juan, XIII. 110   1823 (T. G. Steffan and W. W. Pratt (eds.),
Variorum Edition, vol. 3, 1971)

But all was gentle and aristocratic
   In this our party; polish'd, smooth and cold,
As Phidian forms cut out of marble Attic.
   There now are no 'Squire Westerns as of old;
And our Sophias are not so emphatic,
   But fair as then, or fairer to behold.
We have no accomplish'd blackguards, like Tom Jones,
But gentlemen in stays, as stiff as stones.
(409)

Sir Walter Scott

from 'Prefatory Memoir to Richardson'   1 January 1824
(*The Novelist's Library*, vol. 6, 1824)

It was in vain that the mischievous wit of Fielding found a source for
ridicule in that very simplicity of moral and of incident, and gave the
world *Joseph Andrews*, an avowed parody upon the *Pamela* of Richardson. It chanced with that very humorous performance ... that
readers lost sight altogether of the satirical purpose with which it was
written, and were delighted with it on account of its own intrinsic
merit. We may be permitted to regret, therefore, the tone of mind
with which Fielding composed a work, in professed ridicule of such
genius as that of Richardson; but how can we wish that undone,
without which Parson Adams would not have existed?
(xxiii)

Richardson was well qualified to be the discoverer of a new style of
writing, for he was a cautious, deep, and minute examiner of the
human heart, and ... left neither head, bay, nor inlet behind him,
until he had traced its soundings, and laid it down in his chart, with
all its minute sinuosities, its depths, and its shallows. Hence the high,

and, comparatively considered, perhaps the undue superiority assigned by Johnson to Richardson over Fielding, against whom the Doctor seems to have entertained some prejudice. . . . Dissenting as we do from the conclusions to be deduced from Dr Johnson's simile, we would rather so modify it as to describe both authors as excellent mechanics; the time-pieces of Richardson showing a great deal of the internal work by which the index is regulated; while those of Fielding merely point to the hour of the day, being all that most men desire to know. Or, to take a more manageable comparison, the analogy betwixt the writings of Fielding and Richardson resembles that which free, bold, and true sketches bear to paintings which have been very minutely laboured, and, amid their excellence, still exhibit some of the heaviness which almost always attends the highest degree of finishing. . . .

(xlii–xliii)

Walter Savage Landor

from 'Samuel Johnson and John Horne (Tooke)', *Imaginary Conversations*, 1824 (reprinted in T. Earle Welby (ed.), *Complete Works*, vol. 5, 1969)

TOOKE ... I would request you to exert your authority in repressing the term *our hero*. These worthy people [i.e. novelists] seem utterly unaware that the expression turns their narrative into ridicule. Even on light and ludicrous subjects it destroys that illusion which the mind creates to itself in fiction; and I have often wished it away when I have found it in Fielding's *Tom Jones*, although used jocularly. While we are interested in a story we wish to see nothing of the author or of ourselves.

JOHNSON I detest, let me tell you, your difficulties and exceptions, your frivolity and fastidiousness; I have employed the word myself.

(48)

Goethe

from a conversation with J. P. Eckermann   3 December 1824
(J. P. Eckermann, *Conversations with Goethe*, 1935)

The great point ... is to make a capital that will not be exhausted. This you will acquire by the study of the English language and literature. ... You studied the ancient languages but little during your youth; therefore, seek now a stronghold in the literature of so able a nation as the English. And, besides, our own literature is chiefly the offspring of theirs! Whence have we our novels, our tragedies, but from Goldsmith, Fielding, and Shakespeare? And in our own day, where will you find in Germany three literary heroes who can be placed on a level with Lord Byron, Moore, and Walter Scott?
(74)

William Hazlitt

from 'Why the Heroes of Romances are Insipid', *New Monthly Magazine*   November 1827 (P. P. Howe (ed.), *Complete Works*, vol. 17, 1933)

Many people find fault with Fielding's *Tom Jones* as gross and immoral. For my part, I have doubts of his being so very handsome from the author's always talking about his beauty, and I suspect he was a clown, from being constantly assured he was so very genteel. [See *English Comic Writers*, above, p. 224.] Otherwise, I think Jones acquits himself very well both in his actions and speeches, as a lover and as a trencher-man whenever he is called upon. Some persons, from their antipathy to that headlong impulse, of which Jones was the slave, and to that morality of good-nature which in him is made a foil to principle, have gone so far as to prefer Blifil as the prettier fellow of the two. I certainly cannot subscribe to this opinion, which perhaps was never meant to have followers, and has nothing but its singularity to recommend it. Joseph Andrews is a hero of the shoulder-knot: it would be hard to canvass his pretensions too severely, especially considering what a patron he has in Parson Adams. That one character would cut up into a hundred fine gentlemen and novel-heroes! Booth is another of the good-natured tribe, a fine man, a very fine man! But there is a want of spirit to animate the well-meaning mass. He hardly deserved to have the hashed mutton kept waiting for him. The author has redeemed himself in *Amelia*; but a heroine with a broken nose and who was a married woman besides, must be rendered truly interesting and amiable to make up for superficial objections. The character of the Noble Peer in this novel is *not* insipid. If Fielding could have made virtue as admirable as he could make vice detestable, he would have been a greater master even than he was. I do not understand what those critics mean who say he got all his characters out of ale-houses. It is true he did some of them. (250)

William Hazlitt

from 'On Knowledge of the World', *London Weekly Review* 1, 8 and 15 December 1827 (P. P. Howe (ed.), *Complete Works*, vol. 17, 1933)

When it is observed in the *History of a Foundling*, that 'Mr Allworthy had done so many charitable actions that he had made enemies of the whole parish', the sarcasm is the dictate of a generous indignation at ingratitude rather than a covert apology for selfish niggardliness. Misanthropic reflections have their source in philanthropic sentiments; the real despiser of the world keeps up appearances with it, and is at pains to varnish over its vices and follies, even to himself, lest his secret should be betrayed, and do him an injury. Those who see completely into the world begin to play tricks with it, and over-reach themselves by being too knowing: it is even possible to *outcant* it, and get laughed at that way. Fielding knew something of the world, yet he did not make a fortune. (302)

William Hazlitt

from 'Travelling Abroad', *New Monthly Magazine* June 1828
(P. P. Howe (ed.), *Complete Works*, vol. 17, 1933)

One would suppose there had been no such thing as wit or humour
in England, because a French barber is unacquainted with it; we veil
our proud pretensions to the genius of French grimace – in pure
sheepishness and *mauvaise honte*, we give up Fielding and Congreve
as dull Englishmen, or raw beginners. . . .
(341)

William Hazlitt

from *Conversations of James Northcote, Esq., R.A.* 1830;
extracts based on articles of 1829 (P. P. Howe (ed.),
Complete Works, vol. 11, 1932)

From Conversation XVI

NORTHCOTE No; all that can be said against Sir Walter is, that he
has never made a *whole*. There is an infinite number of delightful
incidents and characters, but they are disjointed and scattered.
This is one of Fielding's merits; his novels are regular compositions,
with what the ancients called a *beginning*, a *middle*, and an *end*:
every circumstance is foreseen and provided for, and the conclusion
of the story turns round as it were to meet the beginning. *Gil
Blas* is very clever, but it is only a succession of chapters. *Tom Jones*
is a masterpiece, as far as regards the conduct of the fable.

HAZLITT Do you know the reason? Fielding had a hooked nose,
the long chin. It is that introverted physiognomy that binds and
concentrates.

NORTHCOTE But Sir Walter has not a hooked nose, but one that
denotes kindness and ingenuity. Mrs Abingdon had the pug-nose,
who was the perfection of comic archness and vivacity: a hooked
nose is my aversion.
(280)

From Conversation XX

NORTHCOTE: Both of them [Hogarth and Fielding] were great wits and describers of manners in common life, but neither of them came under the article of painting. What Hogarth had was his own, and nobody will ever have it again in the same degree. But all that did not depend on his own genius was detestable, both as to his subjects and his execution. . . . Cunningham . . . pretends to cry up Hogarth as a painter; but this is not true. He moulded little figures and placed them to see how the lights fell and how the drapery came in, which gave a certain look of reality and relief; but his was not enough to give breadth or grace, and his figures look like puppets after all, or like dolls dressed up. Who would compare any of these little, miserable, deformed caricatures of men and women, to the figure of St Paul preaching at Athens? What we justly admire and emulate is that which raises Human Nature, not that which degrades and holds it up to scorn. We may laugh to see a person rolled in the kennel, but we are ashamed of ourselves for doing so. We are amused with *Tom Jones*; but we rise from the perusal of *Clarissa* with higher feelings and better resolutions than we had before. St Giles's is not the only school of art. It is nature, to be sure; but we must select nature. . . .

(302)

NORTHCOTE The newspaper critic asks with an air of triumph as if he had found a mare's nest: 'What! Are Sophia Western and Allworthy St Giles's?' Why, they are the very ones; they are the Tower-stamp! Blifil, and Black George, and Square are not – they have some sense and spirit in them and are so far redeemed, for Fielding put his own cleverness and ingenuity into them; but as to his refined characters, they are an essence of vulgarity and insipidity. Sophia's a poor doll; and as to Allworthy, he has not the soul of a goose: and how does he behave to the young man that he has brought up and pampered with the expectations of a fortune and of being a fine gentleman? Does he not turn him out to starve or rob on the highway without the shadow of an excuse, or a mere maudlin sermonizing pretext of morality, and with as little generosity as principle? No, Fielding did not know what virtue or refinement meant. As Richardson said, he should have thought his books were written by an ostler; or Sir John Hawkins has expressed it still better, that the virtues of his heroes are the virtues of dogs and horses. . . . That is where Richardson has the advantage over Fielding – the virtues of *his* characters are not the virtues of animals – Clarissa holds her head in the skies, a 'bright particular star'. . . .

(306)

From Conversation XXI

NORTHCOTE I find in the last conversation I saw, you make me an admirer of Fielding, and so I am; but I find great fault with him too. I grant he is one of those writers that I remember; he stamps his characters, whether good or bad, on the reader's mind. This is more than I can say of everyone. . . .

But to say nothing of Fielding's immorality, and his fancying himself a fine gentleman in the midst of all his coarseness, he has oftener described *habits* than *character*. For example, Western is no character; it is merely the language, manners, and pursuits of the country-squire of that day; and the proof of this is, that there is no Squire Western now. Manners and customs wear out, but characters last for ever. . . . Character is the ground-work, the natural *stamina* of the mind, on which circumstances only act. You see it in St Giles's – there are characters there that in the midst of filth, and vice, and ignorance, retain some traces of their original goodness, and struggle with their situation to the last: as in St James's, you will find wretches that would disgrace a halter. *Gil Blas* has character.

HAZLITT I thought he only gave professions and classes, players, footmen, sharpers, courtesans, but not the individual, as Fielding often does, though we should strip Western of his scarlet hunting-dress and jockey phrases. There is Square, Blifil, Black George, Mrs FitzPatrick, Parson Adams; and a still greater cluster of them in the one that is least read, the Noble Peer, the lodging-house-keeper, Mrs Bennett and Colonel Bath.

NORTHCOTE You mean *Amelia*. I have not read that, but will get to it. I allow in part what you say; but in the best there is something, too local and belonging to the time. But what I chiefly object to in Fielding is his conceit, his consciousness of what he is doing, his everlasting recommendation and puffing of his own wit and sagacity. His introductory chapters make me sick.

HAZLITT Why, perhaps, Fielding is to be excused as a disappointed man. All his success was late in life, for he died in 1754; and *Joseph Andrews* (the first work of his that was popular) was published in 1748 [sic]. All the rest of his life he had been drudging for the booksellers, or bringing out unsuccessful comedies. He probably anticipated the same result in his novels, and wished to bespeak the favour of the reader by putting himself too much forward. His prefaces are like Ben Jonson's prologues, and from the same cause, mortified vanity; though it seems odd to say so at present, after the run his writings have had; but he could not foresee that, and only lived a short time to witness it.

NORTHCOTE I can bear anything but that conscious look – it is to me like the lump of soot in the broth, that spoils the whole mess. Fielding was one of the swaggerers.

HAZLITT But he had much to boast of.

NORTHCOTE He certainly was not idle in his time. Idleness would have ruined a greater man.

(311–12)

William Hazlitt

from 'Conversations as Good as Real (2)', *Atlas*
20 September 1829 (reprinted in P. P. Howe (ed.),
Complete Works, vol. 20, 1934)

NORTHCOTE Fielding has tried to describe Sophia as a beauty, but makes a wretched hand of it. He says first she was a beauty; and then to let you know what sort of a beauty she was, that she was like the Venus of Medici; then that her nose inclined to be Roman, which the Venus de Medici's does not; then that she resembled Kneller's portrait of Lady Ranelagh, which is like neither. The truth is, he did not know what she was like; nor that he could not in words give a description of beauty, which is the painter's province.

(272)

William Hazlitt

from 'Trifles Light as Air', *Atlas* 4 October 1829
(P. P. Howe (ed.), *Complete Works*, vol. 20, 1934)

It has been made a subject of regret that in forty or fifty years' time
(if we go on as we have done) no one will read Fielding. What a
falling-off! Already, if you thoughtlessly lend *Joseph Andrews* to a
respectable family, you find it returned upon your hands as an improper book. To be sure, people read *Don Juan*; but *that* is in verse.
The worst is, that this senseless fastidiousness is more owing to an
affectation of gentility than to a disgust at vice. It is not the scenes
that are described at an alehouse, but the *alehouse* at which they take
place that gives the mortal stab to taste and refinement. One comfort
is, that the manners and characters which are objected to as *low* in
Fielding have in a great measure disappeared or taken another shape;
and this at least is one good effect of all excellent satire – that it
destroys 'the very food whereon it lives'. The generality of readers,
who only seek for the representation of existing models, must therefore, after a time, seek in vain for this obvious verisimilitude in the
most powerful and popular works of the kind; and will be either
disgusted or at a loss to understand the application. People of sense
and imagination, who look beyond the surface or the passing folly
of the day, will always read *Tom Jones*.
(280–1)

Alexander Pushkin

from a letter to the editor of *Literary Supplement to the Russian
Invalid* 1831 (Carl R. Proffer (ed. and trans.), *Critical Prose of
Alexander Pushkin*, 1969)

I have just read [Gogol's] *Evenings near Dikanka*. It amazed me.
Here is real gaiety – honest, unconstrained, without mincing, without
primness.... It was told that when the publisher went to the shop
where *Evenings* were being printed, the typesetters began to chortle
and snort, covering their mouths with their hands. The foreman

explained their gaiety, confessing to him that the typesetters were dying of laughter while setting his book. Molière and Fielding would probably have been glad to make their typesetters laugh. I congratulate the public on a truly gay book.

(157)

Sir Walter Scott and William Wordsworth

from a conversation   22 September 1831 (J. G. Lockhart, *Memoirs . . . of Sir Walter Scott*, vol. 10, 1848)

Sitting that evening in the library, Sir Walter said a good deal about the singularity that Fielding and Smollett had both been driven abroad by declining health, and never returned – which circumstance, though his language was rather cheerful at this time, he had often before alluded to in a darker fashion; and Mr Wordsworth expressed his regret that neither of those great masters of romance appeared to have been surrounded with any due marks of respect in the close of life.

(104–5)

Lady Louisa Stuart

from a letter to Louisa Clinton   January 1832 (R. B. Johnson (ed.), *Letters*, 1926)

Madame Roland, one of the heroines of the French Revolution, a virtuous woman, so far as chastity goes, writes her memoirs and tells you what were her sensations towards the other sex in general (without any particular object) at fourteen or fifteen years old! And young ladies were taught to read and admire this who would not have been allowed to open *Tom Jones*, where Fielding certainly does describe *l'amour physique* between Tom and Molly Seagrim, but I daresay would as soon have given Sophia an inclination to commit murder as hinted that she ever had Madame Roland's *sensations*, or even that Tom had them towards her. *Their* passion he studied to refine and ennoble. The French philosophy labours to brutalize and degrade whatever it handles, rakes into the dirt for vile motives. And even supposing it hits right, I should say, as of my dinner, let me eat in peace, do not force me into the kitchen or the slaughter-house to see the nastiness which you say attends the best cookery. The butter looks fresh and good, do not insist upon telling me that perhaps the dairymaid rolled it with dirty hands. ·

(244)

Samuel Taylor Coleridge

a note   27 February 1832 (T. M. Raysor (ed.),
Miscellaneous Criticism, 1936)

Jonathan Wild is assuredly the best of all the fictions in which a villain is throughout the prominent character. But how impossible it is by any force of genius to create a sustained attractive interest for such a groundwork, and how the mind wearies of, and shrinks from, the more than painful interest, the μισητόν of utter depravity – Fielding himself felt and endeavoured to mitigate and remedy by the (on all other principles) far too large a proportion, and too quick recurrence, of the interposed chapters of moral reflection, like the chorus in the Greek tragedy – admirable specimens as these chapters are of profound irony and philosophic satire. Book 2, chapter 6, on Hats, – brief as it is, exceeds any thing even in Swift's *Lilliput*, or *Tale of the Tub*. How forcibly it applies to the Whigs, Tories, and Radicals of our own times.

Whether the transposition of Fielding's scorching wit (as book 3, chapter 14) to the mouth of his hero be objectionable on the ground of *incredulus odi*, or is to be admired as answering the author's purpose by unrealizing the story, in order to give a deeper reality to the truths intended – I must leave doubtful, yet myself inclining to the latter judgement.

(306)

Stendhal

from notes on the writing of *Une Position Sociale*
2 and 4 October 1832 (Henri Martineau (ed.), *Mélanges de Littérature*, vol. 1, 1933; extract translated by C. J. Rawson)

First, absolutely, as relaxation from the serious, a *comic character*. Stendhal must have what it takes to portray such a character, who will be unique: none of the modern boobies has what it takes to do this. Fielding made Squire Western: it isn't *du gros comique*, but is often simply *humour*. . . .

To what lengths should the author who tells the story carry a tone of familiarity? The extreme familiarity of Walter Scott and of Fielding prepares us well to follow the author in his moments of enthusiasm? Isn't the tone of *Rouge* [*et Noir*] too Roman?
(143n.)

Stendhal

from notes on the writing of *Une Position Sociale*
3 and 6 July 1833 (Henri Martineau (ed.), *Mélanges de Littérature*, vol. 1, 1933; extract translated by C. J. Rawson)

The duchess has indeed a sort of duel with Roizand, like Tom Jones with Sophia. Adjoining characters enter into this duel. . . .

The fate of the two lovers affected by something other than the interior movements of their heart. Then, perforce, the reader attends to the characters and their motives, which thus alter, *perforce*, the direction in which the two lovers were heading through their passion.

Thus, Mistress Fitzpatrick, Lady Bellaston, *perforce* influence the fate of Tom Jones, after Tom had gone to the performance of *Hamlet* with Portridge [*sic*].

Thus the cardinal and the comic character, the Falstaff figure, must influence the actions of Roizand and the duchess.
(152–3)

Alexander Pushkin

from 'On the Insignificance of Russian Literature'   1834
(Carl R. Proffer (ed. and trans.), *Critical Prose of Alexander Pushkin*,
1969)

Stunned, enchanted by the glory of French writers, Europe worships
them with servile attention. From the height of their chairs, German
professors proclaim the rules of French criticism. England follows
France in the field of philosophy; Richardson, Fielding, and Sterne
maintain the glory of the prose novel. In the fatherland of
Shakespeare and Milton, poetry becomes dry and insignificant,
as in France; Italy renounces Dante's genius, Metastasio imitates
Racine.
(168)

Samuel Taylor Coleridge

from *Table Talk*   5 July 1834 (new edition, 1905)

What a master of composition Fielding was! Upon my word, I think
the *Oedipus Tyrannus*, *The Alchemist*, and *Tom Jones*, the three most
perfect plots ever planned. And how charming, how wholesome,
Fielding always is! To take him up after Richardson, is like emerging
from a sick room heated by stoves, into an open lawn, on a breezy
day in May.
(332)

Stendhal

from a marginal note in the manuscript of *Lucien Leuwen*
26 September 1834 (Henri Martineau (ed.), *Romans et Nouvelles*,
vol. 1, 1952; extract translated by C. J. Rawson)

Style of *Dominique*. – Feelings about the first twenty-seven pages of
the fifth volume of *Rouge et Noir*: true, but dry. I must adopt a style

more flowery and less dry; it ought to be witty and gay, not like the *Tom Jones* of 1750, but as the same Fielding would be in 1834. (1528)

Stendhal

from a note in the manuscript of *Lucien Leuwen* 14 December 1834 (Henri Martineau (ed.), *Romans et Nouvelles*, vol. 1, 1952; extract translated by C. J. Rawson)

Genius apart . . . the great difference between Fielding and Dominique is that Fielding describes *simultaneously* the feelings and actions of *several* characters, and *Dominique only of one*. Where does Dominique's manner lead? I do not know. Is it a perfecting? Is it a return to the infancy of the art, or rather a drop into the cold style of the philosophic personage?
(1407)

Stendhal

from a comment on an early draft of the opening of *Lucien Leuwen* 9 February 1835 (Henri Martineau (ed.), *Romans et Nouvelles*, vol. 1, 1952; extract translated by C. J. Rawson)

This tone turns to satire instead of being gay and *playful* as a child. Is it that this century drives away all gaiety of tone? Fielding is a facetious joker, full of wit, who tells an interesting story, with some bad habits that derive from the infancy of the art and from the moralizing style made fashionable by Richardson.
(1587)

Stendhal

from *Mémoires d'un Touriste*   18 April 1837 (Louis Royer *et al.*
(eds.), vol. 1, 1968; extract translated by C. J. Rawson)

Have you read Fielding's *Tom Jones*, now so much forgotten? This
novel is to other novels what the *Iliad* is to epic poems, except
that, as with Achilles and Agamemnon, the characters of Fielding
now seem to us too primitive. Good manners have since made
notable progress, and require us all to disguise our natural appetites
rather more. In the eighth book, I think [? actually a misremembered
conflation of book 12, chapter 5 and book 16, chapter 5], a footman
turned exciseman sees a tragedy acted in a barn; he is happy enough
at first, but later finds that the actor who plays the king does not seem
noble enough.
(45)

William Makepeace Thackeray

from a letter to Mrs Carmichael-Smyth   18 January 1840
(Gordon N. Ray (ed.), *Letters and Private Papers*, vol. 1, 1945)

A new Yellowplush addressed to Bulwer has made a great noise and
has hit the Baronet pretty smartly. It is very good-natured however:
but you won't like that either: and it is better that ladies should not
relish such grotesque humour: Rabelais, Fielding and so forth (apart
the indecencies) are not good reading for women, and only for a
small race of men – I don't mean to compare myself to one or the
other mind – but the style of humour is the same.
(412)

Nikolai Gogol

from an article   1840 (cited by F. D. Reeve, *The Russian Novel*, 1967)

Schooled by loneliness, by a harsh, internal life, the artist doesn't have the habit of looking at both sides when he is writing but only involuntarily from time to time casts a glance at the portraits on the wall in front of him – Shakespeare, Ariosto, Fielding, Cervantes, Pushkin – who reflected nature as it is and not as somebody feels it ought to be.

(72)

John Ruskin

from *Letters Addressed to a College Friend*, Letter III   1 September 1840 (E. T. Cook and A. Wedderburn (eds.), *Works*, vol. 1, 1903)

I cannot, for the life of me, understand the feelings of men of magnificent wit and intellect, like Smollett and Fielding, when I see them gloating over and licking their chops over nastiness, like hungry dogs over ordure; founding one half of the laughable matter of their volumes in innuendoes of abomination. Not that I think, as many people do, they are bad books; for I don't think these pieces of open filth are in reality injurious to the mind, or, at least, *as* injurious as corrupt sentiment and disguised immorality, such as you get sometimes in Bulwer and men of his school. But I cannot *understand* the taste. I can't imagine why men who have real wit at their command should *perfume* it as they do.

(418)

William Makepeace Thackeray

from a review of Henry Fielding, *Works*, ed. T. Roscoe, *The Times*
2 September 1840 (Lewis Melville (ed.), *Stray Papers*, 1901)[1]

Here, in a single handsome volume, and a clear distinct type we have
all the works of one of the greatest humorists in our language, and
though there is, to be sure, a great deal of matter in the book that is
not exactly so delicate as the last novel by the last female author of
fashions, and though boys and virgins must read it with caution, we
are very glad to see this great writer's works put forward in a popular
form, and at a price exceedingly low. A man may be very much
injured by perusing maudlin sentimental tales, but cannot be hurt,
though he may be shocked every now and then, by reading works of
sterling humour, like the greater part of these, full of benevolence,
practical wisdom, and generous sympathy with mankind. . . .

Great were his errors, doubtless, and low his tastes. We fear very
much that he did even worse in the course of his hard life than
what Walpole has described of him . . . [see above, p. 103] those,
therefore, who are excessively squeamish and genteel will scornfully
keep away from him; those who have a mind to forgive a little
coarseness for the sake of one of the honestest, manliest, kindest
companions in the world, cannot, as we fancy, find a better than
Fielding, or get so much true wit and shrewdness from any other
writer of our language. . . .

The world does not tolerate now such satire as that of Hogarth
and Fielding, and the world no doubt is right in a great part of its
squeamishness; for it is good to pretend to the virtue of chastity even
though we do not possess it; nay, the very restraint which the hypocrisy lays on a man, is not unapt, in some instances, to profit him.
But any man who has walked through Regent Street of a night, or
has been behind the scenes of the Opera, or has even been to a
theatre, and looked up to that delectable part of the house, the second
tier of boxes, must know that the *Rake's* and *Harlot's Progress* is still
by no means concluded. . . . The same vice exists, only we don't
speak about it; the same things are done, but we don't call them by
their names. Here lies the chief immorality of Fielding, as we take it.

1 See below, 26 June 1851, and Blanchard, pp. 410 ff.

As for Hogarth, he has passed into a tradition; we allow him and Shakespeare to take liberties in conversation that we would not permit to any other man. It is wise that the public modesty should be as prudish as it is; that writers should be forced to chasten their humour. ... But an impartial observer ... knows pretty well that Fielding's men and Hogarth's are Dickens' and Cruikshank's, drawn with ten times more skill and force, only the latter humorists dare not talk of what the elder discussed honestly.

Let us, then, not accuse Fielding of immorality, but simply admit that his age was more free-spoken than ours, and accuse it of the fault (such as it is) rather than him. But there is a great deal of good, on the other hand, which is to be found in the writings of this great man, of virtue so wise and practical, that the man of the world cannot read it and imitate it too much. He gives a strong, real picture of human life, and the virtues which he exhibits shine out by their contrasts with the vices which he paints so faithfully, as they never could have done, if the latter had not been depicted as well as the former.... Tom Jones' sins, and his faults, are described with a curious accuracy, but then follows the repentance which comes out of his very sins, and surely that is moral and touching. Booth goes astray (we do verily believe that many persons even in these days are not altogether pure), but how good his remorse is! ... He married and (though Sir Walter Scott speaks rather slightingly of the novel in which Fielding has painted his first wife) the picture of Amelia, in the story of that name, is (in the writer's humble opinion) the most beautiful and delicious description of a character that is to be found in any writer, not excepting Shakespeare....

Amelia was in her grave when poor Fielding drew this delightful portrait of her; but, with all his faults, and extravagancies, and vagaries, it is not hard to see how such a gentle, generous, loving creature, as Fielding was, must have been loved and prized by her....

When Harry Fielding was writing for the week's bread, we find style and sentiment both careless, and plots hastily worked off. ...

But as soon as he is put out of the reach of this base kind of want, his whole style changes, and, instead of the reckless and slovenly hack-writer, we have one of the most minute and careful artists that ever lived.... Moral or immoral, let any man examine [Tom Jones] as a work of art merely, and it must strike him as the most astonishing production of human ingenuity. There is not an incident ever so trifling, but advances the story, grows out of former incidents, and is connected with the whole. Such a literary *providence*, if we may use such a word, is not to be seen in any other work of fiction ... it is marvellous to think how the author could have built and carried all this structure in his brain, as he must have done, before he began to put it to paper....

In spite of Richardson's prophecies, the piece [*Amelia*] which was dead at its birth is alive a hundred years after, and will live, as we fancy, as long as the English language shall endure. ... Poor Booth's habits and customs are bad indeed, but who can deny the benevolence, and charity, and pity of this simple and kindly being? His vices, even, if we may say so, are those of a man; there is nothing morbid or mawkish in any of Fielding's heroes; no passionate pleas in extenuation, such as one finds in the pseudo-moral romances of the sentimental character; no flashly excuses like those which Sheridan puts forward (unconsciously, most likely) for those brilliant blackguards who are the chief characters of his comedies. Vice is never to be mistaken for virtue in Fielding's honest downright books; it goes by its name, and invariably gets its punishment. See the consequences of honesty! Many a squeamish lady of our time would fling down one of these romances with horror, but would go through every page of Mr Ainsworth's *Jack Sheppard* with perfect comfort to herself. Ainsworth dared not paint his hero as the scoundrel he knew him to be; he must keep his brutalities in the background, else the public morals will be outraged, and so he produces a book quite absurd and unreal, and infinitely more immoral than anything Fielding ever wrote. *Jack Sheppard* is immoral actually because it is decorous. ...

But what is especially worthy of remark is the masterly manner in which the author paints the good part of those equivocal characters that he brings upon his stage; James has his generosity, and his silly wife her good nature; Matthews her starts of kindness; and old Bath, in his sister's dressing-gown, cooking possets for her, is really an amiable object, whom we like while we laugh at him. A great deal of tenderness and love goes along with this laughter, and it was this mixed feeling that our author liked so to indulge himself, and knew so well how to excite in others. Whenever he has to relate an action of benevolence, honest Fielding kindles as he writes it. Some writers

of fiction have been accused of falling in a passion with their bad characters; these our author treats with a philosophic calmness – it is when he comes to the good that he grows enthusiastic; you fancy that you see the tears in his manly eyes, nor does he care to disguise any of the affectionate sympathies of his great simple heart. This is a defect in art, perhaps, but a very charming one.
(103–11)

Charles Dickens

from 'Author's Preface to the Third Edition', *Oliver Twist*
April 1841 (Kathleen Tillotson (ed.), 1966)

If I look for examples, and for precedents [of coarse subject-matter, for which Dickens had been reproached], I find them in the noblest range of English literature. Fielding, Defoe, Goldsmith, Smollett, Richardson, Mackenzie – all these for wise purposes, and especially the two first, brought upon the scene the very scum and refuse of the land. Hogarth, the moralist, and censor of his age – in whose great works the times in which he lived, and the characters of every time, will never cease to be reflected – did the like, without the compromise of a hair's breadth; with a power and depth of thought which belonged to few men before him, and will probably appertain to fewer still in time to come. Where does this giant stand now in the estimation of his countrymen? And yet, if I turn back to the days in which he or any of these men flourished, I find the same reproach levelled against them every one, each in his turn, by the insects of the hour, who raised their little hum, and died, and were forgotten.
(lxiv)

George Borrow

from *The Bible in Spain*, chapter I   1843 (U. R. Burke (ed.), 1901)

Let travellers . . . repair to the English church and cemetery [in Lisbon] . . . , where, if they be of England, they may well be excused

if they kiss the cold tomb, as I did, of the author of *Amelia*, the most singular genius which their island ever produced, whose works it has long been the fashion to abuse in public and to read in secret.
(6)

John Ruskin

from a diary   20 October 1844 (Joan Evans and John Howard Whitehouse (eds.), *Diaries . . . 1835–1847*, 1956)

I had a curious thought in church today respecting the literature of the *Gil Blas* stamp, in which the characters are rather types of a species than individuals. It seems to me that in Smollett, Fielding, and Le Sage, none of the characters have *souls*. They feel and act exactly as animals would do if they had human intellects. They have the affection, the cunning, the rage, jealousy, and all other passions of animals, and that which they appear to want seems to me precisely the part of man which is likely to be immortal. I must think this well over – and *what* the want is.
(318–19)

Patrick Branwell Brontë

from a letter to J. B. Leyland   10 September 1845 (T. J. Wise and J. A. Symington (eds.), *The Brontës: Their Lives, Friendships and Correspondence*, vol. 2, 1932)

My novel is the result of years of thought and if it gives a vivid picture of human feelings for good and evil – veiled by the cloak of deceit which must enwrap man and woman – if it records as faithfully as the pages that unveil man's heart in Hamlet or Lear, the conflicting feelings and clashing pursuits in our uncertain path through life, I shall be as much gratified (and as much astonished) as I should be if in betting that I could jump over the Mersey I jumped over the Irish Sea. It would not be more pleasant to light on Dublin instead of Birkenhead than to leap from the present bathos of fictitious litera-

ture on to the firmly fixed rock honoured by the foot of a Smollett or
Fielding.
(61)

Charlotte Brontë

from the preface to the second edition of *Jane Eyre*   21 December
1847 (Jane Jack and Margaret Smith (eds.), 1969)

I think I see in him [Thackeray] an intellect profounder and more
unique than his contemporaries have yet recognized.... I regard him
as the first social regenerator of the day – as the very master of that
working corps who would restore to rectitude the warped system of
things.... I think no commentator on his writings has yet found the
comparison that suits him, the terms which rightly characterize his
talent. They say he is like Fielding: they talk of his wit, humour,
comic powers. He resembles Fielding as an eagle does a vulture:
Fielding could stoop on carrion, but Thackeray never does. His wit
is bright, his humour attractive, but both bear the same relation to
his serious genius, that the mere lambent sheet-lightning playing
under the edge of the summer cloud, does to the electric death-spark
hid in its womb.
(xxxii)

Charlotte Brontë

from a letter to W. S. Williams   23 December 1847 (T. J. Wise
and J. A. Symington (eds.), *The Brontës: Their Lives, Friendships
and Correspondence*, vol. 2, 1932)

Mr Lewes, with his penetrating sagacity and fine acumen, ought to
be able to do the author of *Vanity Fair* justice. Only he must not
bring him down to the level of Fielding – he is far, far above Fielding.
It appears to me that Fielding's style is arid, and his views of life and
human nature coarse, compared with Thackeray's.
(166)

G. H. Lewes

from 'Recent Novels, French and English', *Fraser's Magazine*
December 1847[1]

Fielding and Miss Austen are the greatest novelists in our language.
Scott has greater invention, more varied powers, a more poetical and
pictorial imagination; but although his delineation of character is
generally true, as far as it goes, it is never deep. . . . Astonishing as
Scott's powers of attraction are, we would rather have written *Pride
and Prejudice* or *Tom Jones*, than any of the Waverley novels.
(687)

Charlotte Brontë

from a letter to G. H. Lewes   12 January 1848 (T. J. Wise and
J. A. Symington (eds.), *The Brontës: Their Lives, Friendships and
Correspondence*, vol. 2, 1932)

What induced you to say that you would have rather written *Pride
and Prejudice* or *Tom Jones*, than any of the Waverley novels?
(179)

William Makepeace Thackeray

from a letter to Mrs Brookfield   1–5 August 1848 (Gordon N. Ray
(ed.), *Letters and Private Papers*, vol. 2, 1945)

I have just got two new novels from the libery [*sic*] by Mr Fielding.
The one is *Amelia* the most delightful portrait of a woman that surely
ever was painted; the other is *Joseph Andrews* which gives me no particular pleasure for it is both coarse and careless, and the author
makes an absurd brag of his twopenny learning upon which he
values himself evidently more than upon the best of his own qualities.
(416)

1 See pp. 286–8.

William Makepeace Thackeray

from a letter to Robert Bell   3 September 1848 (Gordon N. Ray (ed.), *Letters and Private Papers*, vol. 2, 1945)

You have all of you taken my misanthropy to task – I wish I could myself: but take the world by a certain standard (you know what I mean) and who dares talk of having any virtue at all? For instance Forster says after a scene with Blifil, the air is cleared by a laugh of Tom Jones – Why Tom Jones in my holding is as big a rogue as Blifil. Before God he is – I mean the man is selfish according to his nature as Blifil according to his. In fact I've a strong impression that we are most of us not fit for – never mind.
(424)

Charles Dickens

from *David Copperfield*, chapter 4   1849 (Trevor Blount (ed.), 1966)

My father had left a small collection of books in a little room upstairs, to which I had access (for it adjoined my own) and which nobody else in our house ever troubled. From that blessed little room, *Roderick Random*, *Peregrine Pickle*, *Humphrey Clinker*, *Tom Jones*, *The Vicar of Wakefield*, *Don Quixote*, *Gil Blas*, and *Robinson Crusoe*, came out, a glorious host, to keep me company. They kept alive my fancy, and my hope of something beyond that place and time, – they, and the *Arabian Nights*, and the *Tales of the Genii*, – and did me no harm; for whatever harm was in some of them was not there for me; *I* knew nothing of it. It is astonishing to me now, how I found time, in the midst of my porings and blunderings over heavier themes, to read those books as I did. It is curious to me how I could ever have consoled myself under my small troubles (which were great troubles to me), by impersonating my favourite characters in them – as I did – and by putting Mr and Miss Murdstone into all the bad ones – which I did too. I have been Tom Jones (a child's Tom Jones, a harmless creature) for a week together. I have sustained my

own idea of Roderick Random for a month at a stretch, I verily
believe. . . .

This was my only and my constant comfort. When I think of it,
the picture always rises in my mind, of a summer evening, the boys
at play in the churchyard, and I sitting on my bed, reading as if for
life. Every barn in the neighbourhood, every stone in the church,
and every foot of the churchyard, had some association of its own,
in my mind, connected with these books, and stood for some locality
made famous in them. I have seen Tom Pipes go climbing up the
church-steeple; I have watched Strap, with the knapsack on his back,
stopping to rest himself upon the wicket-gate; and I *know* that
Commodore Trunnion held that club with Mr Pickle, in the parlour
of our little village alehouse.

(105–6)

William Makepeace Thackeray

from the preface to *Pendennis*   26 November 1850 (reprinted in
Lady Ritchie (ed.), *Works*, vol. 3, 1910)

Even the gentlemen of our age – this is an attempt to describe one of
them, no better nor worse than most educated men – even these we
cannot show as they are, with the notorious foibles and selfishness of
their lives and their education. Since the author of *Tom Jones* was
buried, no writer of fiction among us has been permitted to depict to
his utmost power a *man*. We must drape him, and give him a certain
conventional simper. Society will not tolerate the natural in our art.

(liv–lv)

William Makepeace Thackeray

from 'Hogarth, Smollett and Fielding' (*English Humourists of the
Eighteenth Century*, 1853), a lecture given 26 June 1851
(reprinted in Lady Ritchie (ed.), *Works*, vol. 11, 1911)[1]

I suppose, as long as novels last and authors aim at interesting their
public, there must always be in the story a virtuous and gallant hero,
a wicked monster his opposite, and a pretty girl who finds a champion; bravery and virtue conquer beauty; and vice, after seeming to
triumph through a certain number of pages, is sure to be discomfited
in the last volume, when justice overtakes him and honest folk come
by their own. There never was perhaps a greatly popular story but
this simple plot was carried through it: mere satiric wit is addressed
to a class of readers and thinkers quite different to those simple souls
who laugh and weep over the novel. I fancy very few ladies, indeed,
for instance, could be brought to like *Gulliver* heartily, and (putting
the coarseness and difference of manners out of the question) to relish
the wonderful satire of *Jonathan Wild*. In that strange apologue, the
author takes for a hero the greatest rascal, coward, traitor, tyrant,
hypocrite, that his wit and experience, both large in this matter,
could enable him to devise or depict; he accompanies this villain
though all the actions of his life, with a grinning deference and a
wonderful mock respect; and doesn't leave him till he is dangling at
the gallows, when the satirist makes him a low bow and wishes
the scoundrel good day.

  It was not by satire of this sort, or by scorn and contempt, that
Hogarth achieved his vast popularity and acquired his reputation.
His art is quite simple; he speaks popular parables to interest simple
hearts, and to inspire them with pleasure or pity or warning and
terror. Not one of his tales but is as easy as *Goody Twoshoes*; it is the
moral of Tommy was a naughty boy and the master flogged him,
and Jacky was a good boy and had plum-cake, which pervades the
whole works of the homely and famous English moralist. And if the
moral is written in rather too large letters after the fable, we must
remember how simple the scholars and schoolmaster both were, and
like neither the less because they are so artless and honest. 'It was a

1 See above, p. 263, and Blanchard, pp. 410 ff.

maxim of Doctor Harrison's,' Fielding says, in *Amelia*, speaking of the benevolent divine and philosopher who represents the good principle in that novel, 'that no man can descend below himself, in doing any act which may contribute to protect an innocent person, *or to bring a rogue to the gallows*.' The moralists of that age had no compunction, you see; they had not begun to be sceptical about the theory of punishment, and thought that the hanging of a thief was a spectacle for edification. Masters sent their apprentices, fathers took their children, to see Jack Sheppard or Jonathan Wild hanged, and it was as undoubting subscribers to this moral law, that Fielding wrote and Hogarth painted. Except in one instance, where, in the mad-house scene in the *Rake's Progress*, the girl whom he has ruined is represented as still tending and weeping over him in his insanity, a glimpse of pity for his rogues never seems to enter honest Hogarth's mind. There's not the slightest doubt in the breast of the jolly Draco....

In that last plate of the London Apprentices, in which the apotheosis of the Right Honourable Francis Goodchild is drawn, a ragged fellow is represented in the corner of the simple, kindly piece, offering for sale a broadside, purporting to contain an account of the appearance of the ghost of Tom Idle executed at Tyburn. Could Tom's ghost have made its appearance in 1847, and not in 1747, what changes would have been remarked by that astonished escaped criminal! Over that road which the hangman used to travel constantly, and the Oxford stage twice a week, go ten thousand carriages every day: over yonder road, by which Dick Turpin fled to Windsor, and Squire Western journeyed into town, when he came to take up his quarters at the 'Hercules Pillars' on the outskirts of London, what a rush of civilization and order flows now! What armies of gentlemen with umbrellas march to banks, and chambers, and counting-houses! What regiments of nursery-maids and pretty infantry; what peaceful processions of policemen, what light broughams and what gay carriages, what swarms of busy apprentices and artificers, riding on omnibus-roofs, pass daily and hourly! Tom Idle's times are quite changed: many of the institutions gone into disuse which were admired in his day. There's more pity and kindness and a better chance for poor Tom's successors now than at that simpler period when Fielding hanged him and Hogarth drew him. . . .

(276–82)

Fielding, too, has described, though with a greater hand, the characters and scenes which he knew and saw. He had more than ordinary opportunities for becoming acquainted with life. His family and education, first – his fortunes and misfortunes afterwards – brought him into the society of every rank and condition of man. He is himself the hero of his books: he is wild Tom Jones, he is wild Captain Booth; less wild, I am glad to think, than his predecessor: at least heartily conscious of demerit, and anxious to amend.

When Fielding first came upon the town in 1727, the recollection of the great wits was still fresh in the coffee-houses and assemblies, and the judges there declared that young Harry Fielding had more spirits and wit than Congreve or any of his brilliant successors. His figure was tall and stalwart; his face handsome, manly, and noble-looking; to the very last days of his life he retained a grandeur of air, and although worn down by disease, his aspect and presence imposed respect upon the people round about him.

A dispute took place between Mr Fielding and the captain of the ship in which he was making his last voyage, and Fielding relates how the man finally went down on his knees, and begged his passenger's pardon. He was living up to the last days of his life, and his spirit never gave in. His vital power must have been immensely strong. Lady Mary Wortley Montagu prettily characterizes Fielding and this capacity for happiness which he possessed, in a little notice of his death when she compares him to Steele, who was as improvident and as happy as he was, and says that both should have gone on living for ever. One can fancy the eagerness and gusto with which a man of Fielding's fame, with his vast health and robust appetite, his ardent spirits, his joyful humour, and his keen and healthy relish for life, must have seized and drunk that cup of pleasure which the town offered to him. Can any of my hearers remember the youthful feats of a college breakfast – the meats devoured and the cups quaffed in that Homeric feast? I can call to mind some of the heroes of those youthful banquets, and fancy young Fielding from Leyden rushing upon the feast, with his great laugh, and immense healthy young appetite, eager and vigorous to enjoy. The young man's wit and manners made him friends everywhere: he lived with the grand Man's society of those days; he was courted by peers and men of wealth and fashion. As he had a paternal allowance from his father,

General Fielding, which, to use Henry's own phrase, any man might
pay who would; as he liked good wine, good clothes, and good
company, which are all expensive articles to purchase, Harry Fielding began to run into debt, and borrow money in that easy manner
in which Captain Booth borrows money in the novel: was in nowise
particular in accepting a few pieces from the purses of his rich
friends, and bore down upon more than one of them, as Walpole
tells us only too truly, for a dinner or a guinea. To supply himself
with the latter, he began to write theatrical pieces, having already,
no doubt, a considerable acquaintance amongst the Oldfields and
Bracegirdles behind the scenes. He laughed at these pieces and scorned
them. When the audience upon one occasion began to hiss a scene
which he was too lazy to correct, and regarding which, when
Garrick remonstrated with him, he said that the public was too
stupid to find out the badness of his work: when the audience began
to hiss, Fielding said with characteristic coolness: 'They have found
it out, have they?' He did not prepare his novels in this way, and
with a very different care and interest laid the foundations and built
up the edifices of his future fame.

Time and shower have very little damaged those. The fashion and
ornaments are, perhaps, of the architecture of that age, but the
buildings remain strong and lofty, and of admirable proportions –
masterpieces of genius and monuments of workmanlike skill.

I cannot offer or hope to make a hero of Harry Fielding. Why hide
his faults? Why conceal his weaknesses in a cloud of periphrases?
Why not show him, like him as he is, not robed in a marble toga, and
draped and polished in an heroic attitude, but with inked ruffles, and
claret stains on his tarnished laced coat, and on his manly face the
marks of good fellowship, of illness, of kindness, of care and wine?
Stained as you see him, and worn by care and dissipation, that man
retains some of the most precious and splendid human qualities and
endowments. He has an admirable natural love of truth, the keenest
instinctive antipathy to hypocrisy, the happiest satirical gift of laughing it to scorn. His wit is wonderfully wise and detective; it flashes
upon a rogue and lightens up a rascal like a policeman's lantern. He
is one of the manliest and kindliest of human beings: in the midst of
all his imperfections, he respects female innocence and infantine
tenderness as you would suppose such a great-hearted, courageous

soul would respect and care for them. He could not be so brave, generous, truth-telling as he is, were he not infinitely merciful, pitiful, and tender. He will give any man his purse – he can't help kindness and profusion. He may have low tastes, but not a mean mind; he admires with all his heart good and virtuous men, stoops to no flattery, bears no rancour, disdains all disloyal arts, does his public duty uprightly, is fondly loved by his family, and dies at his work.

If that theory be – and I have no doubt it is – the right and safe one, that human nature is always pleased with the spectacle of innocence rescued by fidelity, purity, and courage, I suppose that of the heroes of Fielding's three novels, we should like honest Joseph Andrews the best, and Captain Booth the second, and Tom Jones the third.

Joseph Andrews, though he wears Lady Booby's cast-off livery, is, I think, to the full as polite as Tom Jones in his fustian suit, or Captain Booth in regimentals. He has, like those heroes, large calves, broad shoulders, a high courage, and a handsome face. The accounts of Joseph's bravery and good qualities; his voice, too musical to halloo to the dogs; his bravery in riding races for the gentlemen of the county, and his constancy in refusing bribes and temptation, have something affecting in their *naïveté* and freshness, and prepossess one in favour of that handsome young hero. The rustic bloom of Fanny, and the delightful simplicity of Parson Adams, are described with a friendliness which wins the reader of their story; we part from them with more regret than from Booth and Jones.

Fielding, no doubt, began to write this novel in ridicule of *Pamela* for which work one can understand the hearty contempt and antipathy which such an athletic and boisterous genius as Fielding's must have entertained. He couldn't do otherwise than laugh at the puny cockney bookseller, pouring out endless volumes of sentimental twaddle, and hold him up to scorn as a mollcoddle and a milksop. *His* genius had been nursed on sack posset, and not on dishes of tea. *His* Muse had sung the loudest in tavern choruses, had seen the daylight streaming in over thousands of emptied bowls, and reeled home to chambers on the shoulders of the watchman. Richardson's goddess was attended by old maids and dowagers, and fed on muffins and bohea. 'Milksop!' roars Harry Fielding, clattering at the timid shop-shutters. 'Wretch! Monster! Mohock!' shrieks the sentimental author of *Pamela*; and all the ladies of his court cackle out an affrighted chorus. Fielding proposes to write a book in ridicule of the author, whom he disliked and utterly scorned and laughed at; but he is himself of so generous, jovial, and kindly a turn that he begins to like the characters which he invents, can't help making them manly and pleasant as well as ridiculous, and before he has done with them all, loves them heartily every one.

Richardson's sickening antipathy for Harry Fielding is quite as natural as the other's laughter and contempt at the sentimentalist. I have not learned that these likings and dislikings have ceased in the present day: and every author must lay his account not only to misrepresentation, but to honest enmity among critics, and to being hated and abused for good as well as for bad reasons. Richardson disliked Fielding's works quite honestly: Walpole quite honestly spoke of them as vulgar and stupid. Their squeamish stomachs sickened at the rough fare and the rough guests assembled at Fielding's jolly revel. Indeed the cloth might have been cleaner: and the dinner and the company were scarce such as suited a dandy. The kind and wise old Johnson would not sit down with him. But a greater scholar than Johnson could afford to admire that astonishing genius of Harry Fielding; and we all know the lofty panegyric which Gibbon wrote of him, and which remains a towering monument to the great novelist's memory. 'Our immortal Fielding,' Gibbon writes, 'was of the younger branch of the Earls of Denbigh, who drew their origin from the Counts of Hapsburgh. The successors of Charles V may disdain their brethren of England, but the romance of Tom Jones, that exquisite picture of humour and manners, will outlive the palace of the Escurial and the Imperial Eagle of Austria.'

There can be no gainsaying the sentence of this great judge. To have your name mentioned by Gibbon, is like having it written on the dome of St Peter's. Pilgrims from all the world admire and behold it.

As a picture of manners, the novel of Tom Jones is indeed exquisite: as a work of construction, quite a wonder: the by-play of wisdom; the power of observation; the multiplied felicitous turns and thoughts; the varied character of the great comic epic: keep the reader in a perpetual admiration and curiosity. But against Mr Thomas Jones himself we have a right to put in a protest, and quarrel with the esteem the author evidently has for that character. Charles Lamb says finely of Jones, that a single hearty laugh from him 'clears the air' – but then it is in a certain state of the atmosphere. It might clear the air when such personages as Blifil or Lady Bellaston poison it. But I fear very much that (except until the very last scene of the story), when Mr Jones enters Sophia's drawing-room, the pure air there is rather tainted with the young gentleman's tobacco-pipe and punch. I can't say that I think Mr Jones a virtuous character; I can't say but that I think Fielding's evident liking and admiration for Mr Jones shows that the great humourist's moral sense was blunted by his life, and that here, in Art and Ethics, there is a great error. If it is right to have a hero whom we may admire, let us at least take care that he is admirable: if, as is the plan of some authors (a plan decidedly against their interests, be it said), it is propounded that there exists in life no such being, and therefore that in novels, the picture of life, there should appear no such character; then Mr Thomas Jones becomes an admissible person, and we examine his defects and good qualities, as we do those of Parson Thwackum, or Miss Seagrim. But a hero with a flawed reputation; a hero spunging for a guinea; a hero who can't pay his landlady, and is obliged to let his honour out to hire, is absurd, and his claim to heroic rank untenable. I protest against Mr Thomas Jones holding such rank at all. I protest even against his being considered a more than ordinary young fellow, ruddy-cheeked, broad-shouldered, and fond of wine and pleasure. He would not rob a church, but that is all; and a pretty long argument may be debated, as to which of these old types – the spendthrift, the hypocrite, Jones and Blifil, Charles and Joseph Surface – is the worst member of society and the most deserving of censure. The prodigal Captain Booth is a better man than his predecessor Mr Jones, in so far as he thinks much more humbly of himself than Jones did: goes down on his knees, and owns his weaknesses, and cries out, 'Not for my sake, but for the sake of my pure and sweet and beautiful wife Amelia, I pray you, O critical reader, to forgive me.' That stern moralist regards him from the bench (the judge's practice out of court is not here the question), and says: 'Captain Booth, it is perfectly true that your life has been disreputable, and that on many occasions you have shown yourself to be no better than a scamp – you have been tippling at the tavern, when the kindest and sweetest lady in the world has

cooked your little supper of boiled mutton and awaited you all the
night; you have spoilt the little dish of boiled mutton thereby, and
caused pangs and pains to Amelia's tender heart. You have got into
debt without the means of paying it. You have gambled the money
with which you ought to have paid your rent. You have spent in
drink or in worse amusements the sums which your poor wife has
raised upon her little home treasures, her own ornaments, and the
toys of her children. But, you rascal! You own humbly that you are
no better than you should be; you never for one moment pretend
that you are anything but a miserable weak-minded rogue. You do
in your heart adore that angelic woman, your wife, and for her sake,
sirrah, you shall have your discharge. Lucky for you, and for others
like you, that in spite of your failings and imperfections, pure hearts
pity and love you. For your wife's sake you are permitted to go hence
without a remand; and I beg you, by the way, to carry to that angeli-
cal lady the expression of the cordial respect and admiration of this
court.' Amelia pleads for her husband, Will Booth: Amelia pleads
for her reckless kindly old father, Harry Fielding. To have invented
that character is not only a triumph of art, but it is a good action. They
say it was in his own home that Fielding knew her and loved her:
and from his own wife that he drew the most charming character in
English fiction. Fiction! why fiction? why not history? I know
Amelia just as well as Lady Mary Wortley Montagu. I believe in
Colonel Bath almost as much as in Colonel Gardiner or the Duke of
Cumberland. I admire the author of *Amelia*, and thank the kind
master who introduced me to that sweet and delightful companion
and friend. *Amelia* perhaps is not a better story than *Tom Jones*, but
it has the better ethics; the prodigal repents, at least, before forgiveness – whereas that odious broad-backed Mr Jones carries off his
beauty with scarce an interval of remorse for his manifold errors and
shortcomings: and is not half punished enough before the great prize
of fortune and love falls to his share. I am angry with Jones. Too
much of the plum-cake and rewards of life fall to that boisterous,
swaggering young scapegrace. Sophia actually surrenders without a
proper sense of decorum; the fond, foolish, palpitating little creature!
'Indeed, Mr Jones,' she says, 'it rests with you to appoint the day.'
I suppose Sophia is drawn from life as well as Amelia; and many a
young fellow, no better than Mr Thomas Jones, has carried by a

coup de main the heart of many a kind girl who was a great deal too good for him.

What a wonderful art! What an admirable gift of nature was it by which the author of these tales was endowed, and which enabled him to fix our interest, to waken our sympathy, to seize upon our credulity, so that we believe in his people – speculate gravely upon their faults or their excellences, prefer this one or that, deplore Jones's fondness for play and drink, Booth's fondness for play and drink, and the unfortunate position of the wives of both gentlemen – love and admire those ladies with all our hearts, and talk about them as faithfully as if we had breakfasted with them this morning in their actual drawing-rooms, or should meet them this afternoon in the park! What a genius! what a vigour! what a bright-eyed intelligence and observation! what a wholesome hatred for meanness and knavery! what a vast sympathy! what a cheerfulness! what a manly relish of life! what a love of human kind! what a poet is here! watching, meditating, brooding, creating! What multitudes of truths has that man left behind him! What generations he has taught to laugh wisely and fairly! What scholars he has formed and accustomed to the exercise of thoughtful humour and the manly play of wit! What a courage he had! What a dauntless and constant cheerfulness of intellect, that burned bright and steady through all the storms of his life, and never deserted its last wreck! It is wonderful to think of the pains and misery which the man suffered; the pressure of want, illness, remorse which he endured! And that the writer was neither malignant nor melancholy, his view of truth never warped, and his generous human kindness never surrendered.

In the quarrel mentioned before, which happened on Fielding's last voyage to Lisbon, and when the stout captain of the ship fell down on his knees, and asked the sick man's pardon – 'I did not suffer,' Fielding says, in his hearty, manly way, his eyes lighting up as it were with their old fire: 'I did not suffer a brave man and an old man to remain a moment in that posture, but immediately forgave him.' Indeed, I think, with his noble spirit and unconquerable generosity, Fielding reminds one of those brave men of whom one reads in stories of English shipwrecks and disasters – of the officer on the African shore, when disease had destroyed the crew, and he himself is seized by fever, who throws the lead with a death-stricken hand,

takes the soundings, carries the ship out of the river or off the dangerous coast, and dies in the manly endeavour – of the wounded captain, when the vessel founders, who never loses his heart, who eyes the danger steadily, and has a cheery word for all, until the inevitable fate overwhelms him, and the gallant ship goes down. Such a brave and gentle heart, such an intrepid and courageous spirit, I love to recognize in the manly, the English Harry Fielding.
(298–309)

Charlotte Brontë

from a letter to Sydney Dobell   28 July 1851 (T. J. Wise and
J. A. Symington (eds.), *The Brontës: Their Lives, Friendships and
Correspondence*, vol. 3, 1932)

I had already prolonged my stay in London to the furthest available minute for the sake of hearing one more lecture from Mr Thackeray. Nor was I disappointed; on the theme of Fielding – he put forth his great strength – and though I could not *agree*, I was forced to *admire*.
(253)

Charlotte Brontë

from a letter to George Smith   11 March 1852 (T. J. Wise and
J. A. Symington (eds.), *The Brontës: Their Lives, Friendships and
Correspondence*, vol. 3, 1932)

In listening to a lecture you have not time to be angry enough. Mr Thackeray's worship of his Baal-Bel-Bülzebub (they are all one), his false god of a Fielding – is a thing I greatly desire to consider deliberately. In that red book of yours (which I returned long ago) there was a portrait of the author of *Jonathan Wild*. In the cynical prominence of the under-jaw one reads the man. It was the stamp of one who would never see his neighbours (especially his women neighbours) as they *are*, but as they *might* be under the worst circumstances. In Mr Thackeray's own nature is a small seasoning

of this virtue, but it does not (I hope) prevail throughout his whole
being.
(322)

Charlotte Brontë

from a letter to W. S. Williams   May 1853 (T. J. Wise and
J. A. Symington (eds.), *The Brontës: Their Lives, Friendships and
Correspondence*, vol. 4, 1932)

Not that by any means I always agree with Mr Thackeray's opinions,
but his force, his penetration, his pithy simplicity, his eloquence –
his manly, sonorous eloquence – command entire admiration. I deny
and must deny that Mr Thackeray is very good, or very amiable, but
the man is great – great, but mistaken, full of errors – against his
errors I protest, were it treason to do so. I was present at the Fielding
lecture; the hour spent in listening to it was a painful hour. That
Thackeray was wrong in his way of treating Fielding's character and
vices my conscience told me. After reading that lecture I trebly felt
that he was wrong – dangerously wrong. Had Thackeray owned a
son, grown or growing up, and a son brilliant but reckless – would
he have spoken in that light way of courses that lead to disgrace and
the grave? He speaks of it all as if he theorized; as if he had never been
called on, in the course of his life, to witness the actual consequences
of such failings; as if he had never stood by and seen the issue, the
final result of it all. I believe, if only once the prospect of a promising
life blasted at the outset by wild ways had passed close under his eyes,
he never *could* have spoken with such levity of what led to its piteous
destruction. Had I a brother yet living, I should tremble to let him
read Thackeray's lecture on Fielding. I should hide it away from him.
If, in spite of precaution, it should fall into his hands, I should
earnestly pray him not to be misled by the voice of the charmer, let
him charm never so wisely. Not that for a moment I would have had
Thackeray to *abuse* Fielding, or even pharisaically to condemn his
life; but I do most deeply grieve that it never entered into his heart
sadly and nearly to feel the peril of such a career, that he might have
dedicated some of his great strength to a potent warning against its

adoption by any young man. I believe temptation often assails the finest manly natures, as the pecking sparrow or destructive wasp attacks the sweetest and mellowest fruit, eschewing what is sour and crude. The true lover of his race ought to devote his vigour to guard and protect; he should sweep away every lure with a kind of rage at its treachery.

(67)

Thomas de Quincey

from *Autobiography*, chapter 15   1853 (reprinted in D. Masson (ed.), *Collected Writings*, vol. 1, 1896)

With Fielding commenced the practice of systematically traducing our order of country gentlemen. His picture of Squire Western is not only a malicious, but also an incongruous, libel. The squire's ordinary language is impossible, being alternately bookish and absurdly rustic. In reality, the conventional dialect ascribed to the rustic order in general – to peasants even more than to gentlemen – in our English plays and novels, is a childish and fantastic babble, belonging to no form of real breathing life; nowhere intelligible; not in *any* province ... how false and powerless does ... Sir Walter [Scott] become, when the necessities of his tale oblige him at any time to come among the English peasantry! His magic wand is instantaneously broken; and he moves along by a babble of impossible forms, as fantastic as any that our London theatres have traditionally ascribed to English rustics, to English sailors, and to Irishmen universally. Fielding is open to the same stern criticism, as a deliberate falsehood-monger, and from the same cause – want of energy to face the difficulty of mastering a real living idiom. This defect in language, however, I cite only as one feature in the complex falsehood which disfigures Fielding's portrait of the English country gentleman.

(343–4)

William Makepeace Thackeray

from *The Newcomes*, chapter 4   1853 (reprinted in Lady Ritchie
(ed.), *Works*, vol. 12, 1911)

When we asked [Colonel Newcome] his opinion of Fielding: '*Tom
Jones*, sir; *Joseph Andrews*, sir,' he cried twirling his mustachios. 'I read
them when I was a boy, when I kept other bad company, and did
other low and disgraceful things, of which I'm ashamed now. Sir,
in my father's library I happened to fall in with those books; and I
read them in secret, just as I used to go in private and drink beer, and
fight cocks, and smoke pipes with Jack and Tom, the grooms in the
stables. Mrs Newcome found me, I recollect, with one of those books;
and thinking it might be by Mrs Hannah More, or some of that sort,
for it was a grave-looking volume: and though I wouldn't lie about
that or anything else – never did, sir; never, before heaven, have I
told more than three lies in my life – I kept my own counsel; I say,
she took it herself to read one evening; and read on gravely–for she
had no more idea of a joke than I have of Hebrew – until she came to
the part about Lady B— and Joseph Andrews; and then she shut the
book, sir; and you should have seen the look she gave me! I own I
burst out a laughing, for I was a wild young rebel, sir. But she was in
the right, sir, and I was in the wrong. A book, sir, that tells the story
of a parcel of servants, of a pack of footmen and ladies' maids fuddling
in alehouses! Do you suppose I want to know what my kitmutgars
and cansomahs are doing? I am as little proud as any man in the
world: but there must be distinction, sir; and as it is my lot and
Clive's lot to be a gentleman, I won't sit in the kitchen and booze in
the servants' hall. As for that Tom Jones – that fellow that sells himself, sir – by heavens, my blood boils when I think of him! I wouldn't
sit down in the same room with such a fellow, sir. If he came in at that
door, I would say, "How dare you, you hireling ruffian, to sully with
your presence an apartment where my young friend and I are con-
versing together? Where two gentlemen, I say, are taking their wine
after dinner? How dare you, you degraded villain!" I don't mean
you, sir. I – I – I beg your pardon'. . . . [He] continued:

'No, sir, I have no words to express my indignation against such
a fellow as Tom Jones. But I forgot that I need not speak. The great

and good Dr Johnson has settled that question. You remember what he said to Mr Boswell about Fielding?'

'And yet Gibbon praises him, Colonel,' said the Colonel's interlocutor, 'and that is no small praise. He says that Mr Fielding was of the family that drew its origin from the Counts of Hapsburgh; but –'

'Gibbon! Gibbon was an infidel, and I would not give the end of this cigar for such a man's opinion. If Mr Fielding was a gentleman by birth, he ought to have known better; and so much the worse for him that he did not.'

(51–4)

Charles Dickens

from a letter to Mrs Maria Winter   13 June 1855 (W. Dexter (ed.), *Letters*, vol. 2, 1938)

In a book by one of the greatest English writers, called *A Journey from this World to the Next*, a parent comes to the distant country beyond the grave, and finds the little girl he had lost so long ago, engaged in building a bower to receive him in, when his aged steps should bring him there at last. He is filled with joy to see her – so young – so bright – so full of promise – and is enraptured to think that she never was old, wan, tearful, withered. This is always one of the sources of consolation in the deaths of children. With no effort of the fancy, with nothing to undo, you will always be able to think of the pretty creature you have lost, *as a child* in Heaven.

(671)

Charles Dickens

from a letter to John Forster   ? May 1856 (John Forster, *Life of Charles Dickens*, ed. J. W. T. Ley, 1928)

I don't see the practicability of making the History of a Self-Tormentor [in *Little Dorrit*], with which I took great pains, a written narrative. But I do see the possibility ... of making it a chapter by itself, which might enable me to dispense with the necessity of the turned commas. Do you think that would be better? I have no doubt that a great part of Fielding's reason for the introduced story, and Smollett's also, was, that it is sometimes really impossible to present, in a full book, the idea it contains (which yet it may be on all accounts desirable to present), without supposing the reader to be possessed of almost as much romantic allowance as would put him on a level with the writer. In Miss Wade I had an idea, which I thought a new one, of making the introduced story so fit into surroundings impossible of separation from the main story, as to make the blood of the book circulate through both. But I can only suppose, from what you say, that I have not exactly succeeded in this.

(626)

G. H. Lewes and John Blackwood

from an exchange of letters about Lewes's article of March 1860[1]
18, 23 and 25 January 1860 (Gordon S. Haight (ed.),
The George Eliot Letters, vol. 3, 1954)

LEWES: Herewith goes Tom Jones, which I hope you will like – I have rather exaggerated the praise in order not to raise too great a hubbub . . . .

BLACKWOOD: I enclose proof of Tom Jones which I have read twice with great amusement. You make out a most logical case. At page 2 I think 'coarse drollery' is too low a quality to be put forward as Fielding's leading merit. It grated on me a bit in the MS and I still feel it in the proof. As it would turn aside his great admirers whom we wish to read the paper I think you should put some higher estimate first. Coarse drollery is too low a term for humour such as his which has made so many generations of us shout with laughter. At page 7 'shallow circumscribed nature' seems to me a phrase which should not be applied to a man who has done so much as Fielding. I think you would improve the paper by speaking of him throughout as an intensely clever fellow and making it more clear that it is only the very high rank given to him among

1 See p. 287, and also p. 269.

the giants by modern critics that you utterly deny his right to ...
return the proof. Thackeray's laudation of Fielding is most
ludicrous. In fact throughout these lectures on the humorists his
tone is absurd or insincere. He had the lectures to do and I suppose
he did them on the large hearted or the bitterly virtuous view
according to his humour. . . .

LEWES: You will see I have modified the article according to your
suggestions. . . .

(250–53)

G. H. Lewes

from 'A Word about Tom Jones', *Blackwood's Magazine*,
March 1860[1]

In the high and highest qualities of a novelist, Fielding seems to us
quite unworthy to rank beside Scott or Miss Austen. . . . Fielding is
assuredly far below Scott in invention, imagination, humour, and
sympathy; he is also, we think, many degrees below Miss Austen as
an artist and a painter of character (not of characteristics), and even
in humour of the finer sort. . . . A great deal is said about the 'construction' of *Tom Jones*. In this quality it is declared to surpass all
other novels. . . . We very much fear that the critics who have
lavished their praises on the construction of *Tom Jones* would, for
the most part, be totally unable to say in what construction consists.
. . . Whatever is superfluous – whatever lies outside the real feeling
and purpose of the work, either in incident, dialogue, description, or
character – whatever may be omitted without in any degree lessening
the effect–is a defect in construction. . . . Hazlitt says that Fielding's
novels are most . . . remarkable for profound knowledge of human
nature. . . . To be candid, this sentence is almost startling to us, from
the excess of its exaggeration. We find it impossible to ascribe a
profound knowledge of human nature to one so utterly without
seriousness, so ludicrously incompetent to portray any of the deeper
emotional and intellectual forms of life. Knowledge of human
nature is not to be attained through observation, but through
sympathy. . . . Fielding seems to have been a man of acute observation,

1 See p. 286, and also p. 269.

of hearty kindliness, and generous impulse, but of a nature neither deep nor many-sided. He was immensely clever, without a spark of poetical genius.... His knowledge is knowingness.... A painter of manners, and an amusing story-teller, is a valuable possession for any literature; and we do not remember any one whom we should place above Fielding as a painter of manners; but we must burn our pens, and abdicate the judgement-seat altogether, if we are to pronounce him a great artist, or a great painter of human nature.... Indeed, it is to the utter absence of anything like poetry or sentiment that we must ascribe the failure of Fielding to interest women and foreigners. It is not his coarseness alone which keeps Fielding out of the hands of women; certainly it is not that which keeps him out of the hands of foreigners; it is the clumsy incompetence with which he treats every serious scene. In France and Germany we find men ready enough to welcome Goldsmith, Sterne, Richardson – but they have never at any time welcomed Fielding.... We should describe *Tom Jones* as abounding in liveliness, coarse fun, and irony, but not in fine humour. (333–40)

William Makepeace Thackeray

from a letter to the Bishop of St Davids   18 May 1860
(Gordon N. Ray (ed.), *Letters and Private Papers*, vol. 4, 1946)

Think of poor Smollett (an honest hardworking man) dying a pauper at Leghorn; of Fielding leaving England without a friend to shake him by the hand; and of poor Goldsmith's dismal end. I'm afraid the last two were dishonest about money: but what a blessed difference between their time and our's! I for one am rather ashamed of my luck. Some of us are paid like tenor opera singers.... (186–7)

George Eliot

from a letter to François D'Albert-Durade   29 January 1861
(Gordon S. Haight (ed.), *Letters*, vol. 3, 1954)

Balzac, I think, dares to be thoroughly colloquial, in spite of French straitlacing. Even in English this daring is far from being general. The writers who dare to be thoroughly familiar are Shakespeare, Fielding, Scott (where he is expressing the popular life with which he is familiar), and indeed every other writer of fiction of the first class. (374)

H. A. Taine

from *History of English Literature*   1863 (H. van Laun (trans.), vol. 3, 1906)

Disgust, weariness did not affect him; he was too solidly made to have the nerves of a woman. Force, activity, invention, tenderness, all overflowed in him. He had a mother's fondness for his children, adored his wife, became almost mad when he lost her, found no other consolation than to weep with his maid-servant, and ended by marrying that good and honest girl, that he might give a mother to his children; the last trait in the portrait of this valiant plebeian heart, quick in telling all, having no dislikes, but all the best parts of man, except delicacy. We read his books as we drink a pure, wholesome, and rough wine, which cheers and fortifies us, and which wants nothing but bouquet. . . .

The sentiment of nature is a talent, like the understanding of certain rules; and Fielding, turning his back on Richardson, opens up a domain as wide as that of his rival. What we call nature is this brood of secret passions, often malicious, generally vulgar, always blind, which tremble and fret within us, ill-covered by the cloak of decency and reason under which we try to disguise them; we think we lead them, and they lead us; we think our actions our own, they are theirs. They are so many, so strong, so interwoven, so ready to rise, break forth, be carried away, that their movements elude all our reasoning and our grasp. This is Fielding's domain; his art and pleasure like Molière's are in lifting a corner of the cloak; his characters parade with a rational air, and suddenly, through a vista, the reader perceives the inner turmoil of vanities, follies, lusts, and secret rancours which make them move.... Thus unveiled, natural impulse has a grotesque appearance; the people advance gravely, cane in hand, but in our eyes they are all naked. Understand, they are every whit naked; and some of their attitudes are very lively. Ladies will do well not to enter here. This powerful genius, frank and joyous, loves boorish feasts like Rubens; the red faces, beaming with good humour, sensuality, and energy, move about his pages, flutter hither and thither, and jostle each other, and their overflowing instincts break forth in violent actions. Out of such he creates his chief characters. He has none more lifelike than these, more broadly sketched in bold and dashing outline, with a more wholesome colour. If sober people like Allworthy remain in a corner of his vast canvas, characters full of natural impulse, like Western, stand out with a relief and brightness, never seen since Falstaff. Western is a country squire, a good fellow in the main, but a drunkard, always in the saddle, full of oaths, ready with coarse language, blows, a sort of dull carter, hardened and excited by the brutality of the race, the wildness of a country life, by violent exercise, by abuse of coarse food and strong drink, full of English and rustic pride and prejudice.... Nothing holds or lasts with him; he is impulsive in everything; he lives but for the moment. Rancour, interest, no passions of long continuance affect him. He embraces people whom he just before wanted to knock down. Everything with him disappears in the fire of the momentary passion, which floods his brain, as it were, in sudden waves, and drowns the rest. Now that he is reconciled to Tom Jones, he cannot rest until Tom marries his daughter: 'To her, boy, to her, go to her. That's it, little honeys, O that's it.' ... This is pure nature, and no one has displayed it more free, more impetuous, ignoring all rule, more abandoned to physical passions than Fielding.

It is not because he loves it like the great impartial artists, Shakspeare and Goethe; on the contrary, he is eminently a moralist; and it is one of the great marks of the age, that reformatory designs are as decided with him as with others. He gives his fictions a practical aim, and commends them by saying that the serious and tragic tone sours, whilst the comic style disposes men to be 'more full of good humour and benevolence'. Moreover, he satirizes vice; he looks upon the passions not as simple forces, but as objects of approbation or blame. At every step he suggests moral conclusions; he wants us to take sides; he discusses, excuses, or condemns. He writes an entire novel in an ironical style, to attack and destroy rascality and treason. He is more than a painter, he is a judge and the two parts agree in him. For a psychology produces a morality: where there is an idea of man, there is an ideal of man; and Fielding, who has seen in man nature as opposed to rule, praises in man nature as opposed to rule; so that, according to him, virtue is but an instinct. Generosity in his eyes is, like all sources of action, a primitive inclination; like all sources of action, it flows on receiving no good from catechisms and phrases; like all sources of action, it flows at times too copious and quick. Take it as it is, and do not try to oppress it under a discipline, or to replace it by an argument. Mr Richardson, your heroes, so correct, constrained, so carefully made up with their impedimenta of maxims, are cathedral vergers, of use but to drone in a procession. Square or Thwackum, your tirades on philosophical or Christian virtue are mere words, only fit to be heard after dinner. Virtue is in the mood and the blood; a gossipy education and cloistral severity do not assist it. Give me a man, not a show-mannikin or a mere machine, to spout phrases. My hero is the man who is born generous, as a dog is born affectionate, and a horse brave. I want a living heart, full of warmth and force, not a dry pedant, bent on squaring all his actions. This ardent and impulsive character will perhaps carry the hero too far; I pardon his escapades. . . .

To this we reply: You do well to defend nature, but let it be on condition that you suppress nothing. One thing is wanting in your strongly-built folks – refinement; delicate dreams, enthusiastic elevation, and trembling delicacy exist in nature equally with coarse vigour, noisy hilarity, and frank kindness. Poetry is true, like prose; and if there are eaters and boxers, there are also knights and artists. Cervantes, whom you imitate, and Shakspeare, whom you recall, had this refinement, and they have painted it; in this abundant harvest, which you have gathered so plentifully, you have forgotten the flowers. We tire at last of your fisticuffs and tavern bills. You flounder too readily in cowhouses, among the ecclesiastical pigs of Parson

Trulliber. We would fain see you have more regard for the modesty
of your heroines; wayside accidents raise their tuckers too often; and
Fanny, Sophia, Mrs Heartfree, may continue pure, yet we cannot
help remembering the assaults which have lifted their petticoats. You
are so coarse yourself, that you are insensible to what is atrocious.
You persuade Tom Jones falsely, yet for an instant, that Mrs Waters,
whom he has made his mistress, is his own mother, and you leave the
reader during a long time buried in the shame of this supposition.
And then you are obliged to become unnatural in order to depict
love; you can give but constrained letters; the transports of your Tom
Jones are only the author's phrases. For want of ideas he declaims
odes. You are only aware of the impetuosity of the senses, the up-
welling of the blood, the effusion of tenderness, but you are unacquainted with nervous exaltation and poetic rapture. Man, such as
you conceive him, is a good buffalo; and perhaps he is the hero
required by a people which gives itself the nickname 'John Bull'.
(290–300)

Walter Bagehot

from 'Sterne and Thackeray', *National Review*   April 1864
(R. H. Hutton (ed.), *Literary Studies*, vol. 2, 1905)

Those who perceive that this irritable sensibility was the basis of
Thackeray's artistic character, that it gave him his materials, his
implanted knowledge of things and men, and gave him also that
keen and precise style which hit in description the nice edges of all
objects – those who trace these great qualities back to their real
source in a somewhat painful organization, must have been vexed or
amused, according to their temperament, at the common criticism
which associates him with Fielding. Fielding's essence was the very
reverse; it was a bold spirit of bounding happiness. No just observer
could talk to Mr Thackeray, or look at him without seeing that he
had deeply felt many sorrows – perhaps that he was a man *likely* to
feel sorrows – that he was of an anxious temperament. Fielding was
a reckless enjoyer. He saw the world – wealth and glory, the best
dinner and the worst dinner, the gilded *salon* and the low sponging-

house – and he saw that they were good. Down every line of his characteristic writings there runs this elemental energy of keen delight. There is no trace of such a thing in Thackeray. A musing fancifulness is far more characteristic of him than a joyful energy.
(323)

Henry James

from a review of N. W. Senior's *Essays on Fiction*, *North American Review*   October 1864

[Scott] ... was the first English prose story-teller. He was the first fictitious writer who addressed the public from its own level, without any preoccupation of place. Richardson ... is neither a romancer nor a story-teller: he is simply Richardson. The works of Fielding and Smollett are less monumental, yet we cannot help feeling that they too are writing for an age in which a single novel is meant to go a great way. And then these three writers are emphatically preachers and moralists.... To posterity one of the chief attractions of *Tom Jones* is the fact that its author was one of the masses, that he wrote from the midst of the working, suffering mortal throng. But we feel guilty in reading the book in any such disposition of mind. We feel guilty, indeed, in admitting the question of art or science into our considerations. The story is like a vast episode in a sermon preached by a grandly humorous divine; and however we may be entertained by the way, we must not forget that our ultimate duty is to be instructed. With the minister's week-day life we have no concern: for the present he is awful, impersonal Morality; and we shall incur his severest displeasure if we view him as Henry Fielding, Esq., as a rakish man of letters, or even as a figure in English literature. *Waverley* was the first novel which was self-forgetful. It proposed simply to amuse the reader, as an old English ballad amused him. It undertook to prove nothing but facts. It was the novel irresponsible.
(584–5)

George Eliot

from *Middlemarch*, vol. 1, chapter 5   1871

A great historian, as he insisted on calling himself, who had the
happiness to be dead a hundred and twenty years ago, and so to take
his place among the colossi whose huge legs our living pettiness is
observed to walk under, glories in his copious remarks and digressions as the least imitable part of his work, and especially in those
initial chapters to the successive books of his history, where he seems
to bring his armchair to the proscenium and chat with us in all the
lusty ease of his fine English. But Fielding lived when the days were
longer (for time, like money, is measured by our needs), when summer afternoons were spacious, and the clock ticked slowly in the
winter evenings. We belated historians must not linger after his
example; and if we did so, it is probable that our chat would be thin
and eager, as if delivered from a camp-stool in a parrot-house. I at
least have so much to do in unravelling certain human lots, and
seeing how they were woven and interwoven, that all the light I
can command must be concentrated on this particular web, and not
dispersed over that tempting range of relevancies called the universe.
(250–51)

Henry James

from a review of *Middlemarch*, *Galaxy*   March 1873
(Leon Edel (ed.), *The House of Fiction*, 1962)

It is striking evidence of the altogether superior quality of George
Eliot's imagination that, though elaborately represented, Lydgate
should be treated so little from what we may roughly (and we trust
without offence) call the sexual point of view. Perception charged
with feeling has constantly guided the author's hand, and yet her
strokes remain as firm, her curves as free, her whole manner as
serenely impersonal, as if, on a small scale, she were emulating the
creative wisdom itself. Several English romancers – notably Fielding,
Thackeray, and Charles Reade – have won great praise for their

figures of women: but they owe it, in reversed conditions, to a meaner sort of art, it seems to us, than George Eliot has used in the case of Lydgate; to an indefinable appeal to masculine prejudice – to a sort of titillation of the masculine sense of difference. George Eliot's manner is more philosophic – more broadly intelligent, and yet her result is as concrete or, if you please, as picturesque. . . .
(263)

The constant presence of thought, of generalizing instinct, of *brain*, in a word, behind her observation, gives the latter its great value and her whole manner its high superiority. It denotes a mind in which imagination is illumined by faculties rarely found in fellowship with it. In this respect – in that broad reach of vision which would make the worthy historian of solemn fact as well as wanton fiction – George Eliot seems to us among English romancers to stand alone. Fielding approaches her, but to our mind, she surpasses Fielding. Fielding was didactic – the author of *Middlemarch* is really philosophic. These great qualities imply corresponding perils. The first is the loss of simplicity. . . .
(266)

John Ruskin

from *Fors Clavigera*, Letter 34　October 1873
(E. T. Cook and A. Wedderburn (eds.), *Works*, vol. 27, 1907)

The imaginative power always purifies; the want of it therefore as essentially defiles; and as the wit-power is apt to develop itself through absence of imagination, it seems as if wit itself had a defiling tendency. In Pindar, Homer, Virgil, Dante, and Scott, the colossal powers of imagination result in absolute virginal purity of thought. The defect of imagination and the splendid rational power in Pope and Horace associate themselves – it is difficult to say in what decided measures – with foulness of thought. The *Candide* of Voltaire, in its gratuitous filth, its acute reasoning, and its entire vacuity of imagination, is a standard of what may perhaps be generally and fitly termed 'fimetic literature,' still capable, by its wit, and partial truth, of a certain service in its way. But lower forms of modern literature and art – Gustave Doré's paintings, for instance – are the corruption, in national decrepitude, of this pessimist method of thought; and of these, the final condemnation is true – they are neither fit for the land, nor *yet* for the dunghill.

It is one of the most curious problems respecting mental government to determine how far this fimetic taint must necessarily affect intellects in which the reasoning and imaginative powers are equally balanced, and both of them at high level – as in Aristophanes, Shakespeare, Chaucer, Molière, Cervantes, and Fielding; but it always indicates the side of character which is unsympathetic, and therefore unkind (thus Shakespeare makes Iago the foulest in thought, as cruellest in design, of all his villains), but which, in men of noble nature, is their safeguard against weak enthusiasms and ideals. It is impossible, however, that the highest conditions of tenderness in affectionate conception can be reached except by the absolutely virginal intellect. Shakespeare and Chaucer throw off, at noble work, the lower part of their natures as they would a rough dress; and you may also notice this, that the power of conceiving personal, as opposed to general, character, depends on this purity of heart and sentiment. The men who cannot quit themselves of the impure taint, never invent character, properly so called; they only invent symbols of common humanity. Even Fielding's Allworthy is not a character, but a type of a simple English gentleman; and Squire Western is not a character, but a type of the rude English squire. But Sir Roger de Coverley is a character, as well as a type; there is no one else like him; and the masters of Tullyveolan, Ellangowan, Monkbarns, and Osbaldistone Hall, are all, whether slightly or completely drawn, portraits not mere symbols.
(630–31)

Robert Louis Stevenson

from 'Victor Hugo's Romances', *Cornhill Magazine*   August 1874

Fielding has as much human science; has a far firmer hold upon the tiller of his story; has a keen sense of character, which he draws (and

Scott often does so too) in a rather abstract and academical manner; and finally, is quite as humorous and quite as good-humoured as the great Scotchman. With all these points of resemblance between the men, it is astonishing that their work should be so different. The fact is, that the English novel was looking one way and seeking one set of effects in the hands of Fielding; and in the hands of Scott it was looking eagerly in all ways and searching for all the effects that by any possibility it could utilize. The difference between these two men marks a great enfranchisement. With Scott the Romantic movement, the movement of an extended curiosity and an enfranchised imagination, has begun . . . and this enfranchisement, in as far as it regards the technical change that came over modern prose romance, has never perhaps been explained with any clearness.

To do so, it will be necessary roughly to compare the two sets of conventions upon which plays and romances are respectively based. The purposes of these two arts are so much alike, and they deal so much with the same passions and interests, that we are apt to forget the fundamental opposition of their methods. . . . In the drama the action is developed in great measure by means of things that remain outside of the art; by means of real things, that is, and not artistic conventions for things . . . real live men and women move about the stage; we hear real voices; what is feigned merely puts an edge upon what is; we do actually see a woman go behind a screen as Lady Teazle, and, after a certain interval, we do actually see her very shamefully produced again. Now all these things, that remain as they were in life, and are not transmuted into any artistic convention, are terribly stubborn and difficult to deal with; and hence there are for the dramatist many resultant limitations in time and space. . . . But the great restriction is this, that a dramatic author must deal with his actors, and with his actors alone. Certain moments of suspense, certain significant dispositions of personages, a certain logical advance of fable, these are the only means at the disposal of the playwright. It is true that, with the assistance of the scene-painter, the costumier and the conductor of the orchestra, he may add to this something of pageant, something of sound and fury; but these are, for the dramatic writer, beside the mark, and do not come under the vivifying touch of his genius. When we turn to romance, we find this no longer. Here nothing is reproduced to our senses directly. . . .

With the loss of every degree of such realism as we have described, there is for art a clear gain of liberty and largeness of competence.... It is by giving up these childish identities that art gains true strength. And so in the case of novels as compared with the stage. Continuous narration is the flat board on to which the novelist throws everything. And from this, there results for him a great loss of vividness, but a great compensating gain in his power over the subject; so that he can now subordinate one thing to another in importance, and introduce all manner of very subtle detail, to a degree that was before impossible....

This touches the difference between Fielding and Scott. In the work of the latter, true to his character of a modern and a romantic, we become suddenly conscious of the background. Fielding, on the other hand, although he had recognized that the novel was nothing else than an epic in prose, wrote in the spirit not of the epic, but of the drama. This is not, of course, to say that the drama was in any way incapable of a regeneration similar in kind to that of which I am now speaking with regard to the novel. The notorious contrary fact is sufficient to guard the reader against such a misconstruction. All that is meant is, that Fielding remained ignorant of certain capabilities which the novel possesses over the drama; or, at least, neglected and did not develop them. To the end he continued to see things as a playwright sees them. The world with which he dealt, the world he had realized for himself and sought to realize and set before his readers, was a world of exclusively human interest. As for landscape he was content to underline stage directions, as it might be done in a play-book: Tom and Molly retire into a practicable wood. As for nationality and public sentiment it is curious enough to think that *Tom Jones* is laid in the year forty-five, and that the only use he makes of the rebellion is to throw a troop of soldiers into his hero's way. It is most really important, however, to notice the change which has been introduced into the conception of character by the beginning of the romantic movement and the consequent introduction into fiction of a vast amount of new material. Fielding tells us as much as he thought necessary to account for the actions of his creatures; he thought that each of these actions could be decomposed on the spot into a few simple personal elements, as we decompose a force in a question of perfectly abstract dynamics. The larger motives are all unknown to him; he had not understood that the configuration of the landscape or the fashion of the times could be for anything in a story; and so, naturally and rightly, he said nothing about them. But Scott's instinct, the instinct of the man of an age profoundly different, taught him otherwise; and, in his work, the individual characters begin to occupy a comparatively small proportion of that canvas on which armies manoeuvre, and great hills pile themselves upon each other's shoulders. Fielding's characters were always great to the full stature of a perfectly arbitrary will. Already in Scott we begin to have a sense of the subtle influences that moderate and qualify a man's personality; that personality is no longer thrown out in unnatural isolation, but is resumed into its place in the constitution of things....

Scott took an interest in many things in which Fielding took none; and for this reason, and no other, he introduced them into his romances. If he had been told what would be the nature of the movement that he was so lightly initiating, he would have been very incredulous and not a little scandalized. At the time when he wrote the real drift of this new manner of pleasing people in fiction was not yet apparent; and, even now, it is only by looking at the romances of Victor Hugo that we are enabled to form any proper judgement in the matter. . . . When we come to Hugo, we see that the deviation, which seemed slight enough and not very serious between Scott and Fielding, is indeed such a great gulf in thought and sentiment as only successive generations can pass over; and it is but natural that one of the great advances that Hugo has made upon Scott is an advance in self-consciousness. Both men follow the same road; but where the one went blindly and carelessly, the other advances with all deliberation and forethought.
(180–83)

Anthony Trollope

from *An Autobiography*   1876 (Frederick Page (ed.), 1950)

From Chapter 7

The plots of *Tom Jones* and of *Ivanhoe* are almost perfect, and they are probably the most popular novels of the schools of the last and

of this century; but to me the delicacy of Amelia, and the rugged strength of Burley and Meg Merrilies, say more for the power of those great novelists than the gift of construction shown in the two works I have named. . . .
(126)

From Chapter 17

In writing *Phineas Finn* I had constantly before me the necessity of progression in character – of marking the changes in men and women which would naturally be produced by the lapse of years. In most novels the writer can have no such duty, as the period occupied is not long enough to allow of the change of which I speak. In *Ivanhoe*, all the incidents of which are included in less than a month, the characters should be, as they are, consistent throughout. Novelists who have undertaken to write the life of a hero or heroine have generally considered their work completed at the interesting period of marriage, and have contented themselves with the advance in taste and manners which are common to all boys and girls as they become men and women. Fielding, no doubt, did more than this in *Tom Jones*, which is one of the greatest novels in the English language, for there he has shown how a noble and sanguine nature may fall away under temptation and be again strengthened and made to stand upright. But I do not think that novelists have often set before themselves the state of progressive change.
(318–19)

Leslie Stephen

from *English Thought in the Eighteenth Century*   1876
(vol. 2, 1962)

No enchanted light of old romance colours or distorts his fictions; we do not feel that his characters are puppets in the hands of an irresistible destiny, or constituent atoms of a vast organism slowly developing under the action of gigantic forces; there is no tender regret for past forms of society or passionate aspirations for the future. But for insight into the motives of his contemporaries; for a power of seeing things as they are; for sympathy with homely virtues; and contempt for shams and hypocrites, Fielding is as superior to some later writers of equal imaginative force as they are superior to him in width of sympathy and delicacy of perception. His art is thus the most faithful representative of his age; he gives its coarseness and its brutalities, and sometimes with too little consciousness of their evils, though no one ever satirized more powerfully the worst abuses of the time. But he also represents the strong healthy common sense and stubborn honesty of the sound English nature, with a certain massive power of grouping and colouring which is peculiar to himself.

In Fielding and his beloved Hogarth we have the 'prosai-comi-epos' – I use Fielding's phrase – of the middle class of the time. Richardson, though a greater artist, is far inferior in sheer intellectual vigour; and Smollett is comparatively but a caricaturist. Fielding announced that his object is to give a faithful picture of human nature. Human nature includes many faculties which had an imperfect play under the conditions of the time; there were dark sides to it, of which, with all his insight, he had but little experience; and heroic impulses, which he was too much inclined to treat as follies. But the more solid constituents of that queer compound, as they presented themselves under the conditions of the time, were never more clearly revealed to any observer. A complete criticism of the English artistic literature of the eighteenth century would place Fielding at the centre, and measure the completeness of other representatives pretty much as they recede from an approach to his work. Others, as Addison and Goldsmith, may show finer qualities of workmanship and more delicate sentiment; but Fielding, more than anyone, gives the essential – the very form and pressure of the time.

(323)

George Meredith

from *An Essay on Comedy*   1897, first delivered as a lecture on
1 February 1877

How difficult it is for writers to disentangle themselves from bad
traditions is noticeable when we find Goldsmith, who had grave
command of the comic in narrative, producing an elegant farce for
a comedy; and Fielding, who was a master of the comic both in
narrative and in dialogue, not even approaching to the presentable
in farce.

These bad traditions of comedy affect us not only on the stage,
but in our literature, and may be tracked into our social life.
(31)

O for a breath of Aristophanes, Rabelais, Voltaire, Cervantes,
Fielding, Molière! These are spirits that, if you know them well, will
come when you do call. You will find the very invocation of them
act on you like a renovating air – the south-west coming off the sea,
or a cry in the Alps.

No one would presume to say that we are deficient in jokers.
They abound, and the organization directing their machinery to
shoot them in the wake of the leading article and the popular sentiment is good.

But the comic differs from them in addressing the wits for
laughter; and the sluggish wits want some training to respond to it,
whether in public life or private, and particularly when the feelings
are excited. . . .
(64–5)

The comic, which is the perceptive, is the governing spirit,
awakening and giving aim to these powers of laughter, but it is not
to be confounded with them: it enfolds a thinner form of them,
differing from satire, in not sharply driving into the quivering sensi-
bilities, and from humour, in not comforting them and tucking them
up, or indicating a broader than the range of this bustling world to
them.

Fielding's *Jonathan Wild* presents a case of this peculiar distinction, when that man of eminent greatness remarks upon the unfairness of a trial in which the condemnation has been brought about by twelve men of the opposite party; for it is not satiric, it is not humorous; yet it is immensely comic to hear a guilty villain protesting that his own 'party' should have a voice in the Law. It opens an avenue into villains' ratiocination.[1] And the comic is not cancelled though we should suppose Jonathan to be giving play to his humour. I may have dreamed this or had it suggested to me, for on referring to *Jonathan Wild*, I do not find it.[2]

Apply the case to the man of deep wit, who is ever certain of his condemnation by the opposite party, and then it ceases to be comic, and will be satiric.

The look of Fielding upon Richardson is essentially comic. His method of correcting the sentimental writer is a mixture of the comic and the humorous. Parson Adams is a creation of humour. But both the conception and the presentation of Alceste and of Tartuffe, of Célimène and Philaminte, are purely comic, addressed to the intellect: there is no humour in them. . . .
(80–81)

Leslie Stephen

from 'Fielding's Novels', *Cornhill Magazine*   February 1877
(*Hours in a Library*, vol. 2, 1909)

Fielding will not efface himself; he is always present as chorus; he tells us what moral we ought to draw; he overflows with shrewd remarks, given in their most downright shape, instead of obliquely suggested through the medium of anecdotes; he likes to stop us as we pass through his portrait gallery; to take us by the button-hole and expound his views of life and his criticisms on things in general. His

1 The exclamation of Lady Booby, when Joseph Andrews defends himself: '*Your virtue!* I shall never survive it!' etc., is another instance (*Joseph Andrews*). Also that of Miss Mathews in her narrative to Booth: 'But such are the friendships of women' (*Amelia*) [Meredith's note].
2 This sentence did not appear when the essay was first published in 1877 (*New Quarterly Magazine*, vol. 8, p. 30). Meredith is misremembering a passage relating to one of Wild's ancestors in *Jonathan Wild*, book 1, chapter 2 [ed.].

remarks are often so admirable that we prefer the interpolations to the main current of narrative. Whether this plan is the best must depend upon the idiosyncrasy of the author; but it goes some way to explain one problem, over which Scott puzzles himself – namely, why Fielding's plays are so inferior to his novels. There are other reasons, external and internal; but it is at least clear that a man who can never retire behind his puppets is not in the dramatic frame of mind. He is always lecturing where a dramatist must be content to pull the wires. Shakespeare is really as much present in his plays as Fielding in his novels; but he does not let us know it; whereas the excellent Fielding seems to be quite incapable of hiding his broad shoulders and lofty stature behind his little puppet-show. . . .
(169–70)

He is a hearty Whig, but no revolutionist. He has as hearty a contempt for the cant about liberty as Dr Johnson himself, and has very stringent remedies to propose for regulating the mob. The bailiff in *Amelia*, who, whilst he brutally maltreats the unlucky prisoners for debt, swaggers about the British Constitution, and swears that he is 'all for liberty', recalls the boatman who ridiculed French slavery to Voltaire, and was carried off next day by a press-gang. Fielding, indeed, is no fanatical adherent of our blessed Constitution, which, as he says, has been pronounced by some of our wisest men to be too perfect to be altered in any particular, and which a number of the said wisest men have been mending ever since. He hates cant on all sides impartially, though, as a sound Whig, he specially hates Papists and Jacobites as the most offensive of all Pharisees, marked for detestation by their taste for frogs and French wine in preference to punch and roast beef. He is a patriotic Briton, whose patriotism takes the genuine shape of a hearty growl at English abuses, with a tacit assumption that things are worse elsewhere. . . .
(178)

The offences against morality are condoned too easily, and the line between vice and virtue drawn in accordance with certain distinctions which even Parson Adams could scarcely have approved. Vice, he seems to say, is altogether objectionable only when complicated by cruelty or hypocrisy. But if Fielding's moral sense is not very delicate, it is vigorous. He hates most heartily what he sees to be wrong,

though his sight might easily be improved in delicacy of discrimination. The truth is simply that Fielding accepted that moral code which the better men of the world in his time really acknowledged, as distinguished from that by which they affected to be bound. That so wide a distinction should generally exist between these codes is a matter for deep regret. That Fielding in his hatred for humbug should have condemned purity as puritanical is clearly lamentable. The confusion, however, was part of the man, and, as already noticed, shows itself in one shape or other throughout his work. But it would be unjust to condemn him upon that ground as antagonistic or indifferent to reasonable morality. His morality is at the superior antipodes from the cynicism of a Wycherley; and far superior to the prurient sentimentalism of Sterne or the hot-pressed priggishness of Richardson, or even the reckless Bohemianism of Smollett.
(187)

Robert Louis Stevenson

from 'On Falling in Love', *Cornhill Magazine*   February 1877

It is by no means in the way of everyone to fall in love . . . I do not believe that Henry Fielding was ever in love. . . . [Shakespeare, Fielding and Scott are] strong, healthy, high-strung and generous natures, of whom the reverse might have been expected.
(215)

John Ruskin

from *Fors Clavigera*, Letter 82   October 1877
(E. T. Cook and A. Wedderburn (eds.), *Works*, vol. 29, 1907)

. . . Fielding (whom Mr Gale and I agree in holding to be a truly moral novelist, and worth any quantity of modern ones since Scott's death, be they who they may). . . .
(220)

Maxim Gorky

from *My Apprenticeship* 1916, referring to early 1880s
(Margaret Wettlin (trans.), 4th impression, n.d.)

After that we read *Ivanhoe*. Smury liked Richard Plantagenet.

'There's a king for you!' he said impressively. But I found the book boring.

In general our tastes differed. I was fascinated by *The Tale of Thomas Jones*, the old translation of *The History of Tom Jones, a Foundling*.

'Nonsense!' muttered Smury. 'What's that Thomas to me? What do I want with him? There must be other books.'
(163–4).

Sidney Lanier

from *The English Novel* (1883), lectures at Johns Hopkins
University 1881 (Clarence Ghodes and Kemp Malone (eds.),
Works, vol. 4, 1945)

The glory of *Tom Jones* is Squire Allworthy, whom we are invited to regard as the most miraculous product of the divine creation so far in the shape of man; but to your present lecturer's way of thinking the kind of virtue represented by Squire Allworthy is completely summed in the following sentence of the work introducing him in the midst of nature. It is a May morning, and Squire Allworthy is pacing the terrace in front of his mansion before sunrise; 'when,' says Fielding, 'in the full blaze of his majesty up rose the sun, than which one object alone in this lower creation could be more glorious, and that Mr Allworthy himself presented – a human being replete with benevolence meditating in what manner he might render himself most acceptable to his Creator by doing most good to his creatures': that is, in plain commercial terms, how he might obtain the largest possible amount upon the letter of credit which he found himself forced to buy against the inevitable journey into the foreign parts lying beyond the water of death. . . .

I protest that I can read none of these books [the novels of Richardson, Fielding, Smollett, and Sterne] without feeling as if my soul had been in the rain, draggled, muddy, miserable. In other words, they play upon life as upon a violin without a bridge, in the deliberate endeavor to get the most depressing tones possible from the instrument. This is done under pretext of showing us vice.

In fine, and this is the characterization I shall use in contrasting this group with that much sweeter group led by George Eliot, the distinctive feature of these first novelists is to show men with microscopic detail how bad men may be. I shall presently illustrate with the George Eliot group how much larger the mission of the novel is than this: meantime, I cannot leave this matter without recording in the plainest terms that . . . if I had my way with these classic books I would blot them from the face of the earth.

(154–7)

Ferdinand Brunetière

from 'Le Naturalisme Anglais' 17 September 1881 (*Le Roman Naturaliste*, 1896; extract translated by C. J. Rawson)

Imagine for a moment deleting from the historical record the whole of Dutch painting and the whole of the English novel: naturalism then becomes nothing more than a system wandering through metaphysical space; – a system one can accept or a doctrine one can resist; a doctrine one can support or a system one can refute – but a doctrine which in a sense belies itself, and which, because it is unsupported by reality, totters, stumbles and collapses at its first step on this earth. On the other hand, if the Ruysdaëls and the Hobbemas (though suspiciously tainted with poetry), if Hals and even Steen, are masters; if *Tom Jones* and perhaps *Amelia* are masterpieces, and also *Adam Bede* and *The Mill on the Floss*; then the system, with its roots deep in a rich, fertile and incontestably powerful soil, does demand attention; and criticism can no longer be content with formulas which leave out of its hold or jurisdiction an entire half of modern art.

It remains to be seen, of course, whether this Dutch or English naturalism is not as it were vivified by an internal principle lacking hitherto in our French naturalism. The work of George Eliot provides perhaps the most useful place for enquiring into precisely this. . . .

(207–8)

Leslie Stephen

from 'Henry Fielding', prefixed to his edition of Fielding's *Works*, vol. 1,   1882

[Fielding's] moral standard is by no means elevated, and . . . his heroes fail to secure our sympathies as fully as he meant them to do. At the same time, it is equally true that in his novels, at least, Fielding is intentionally a moralist and a very emphatic moralist; so much a moralist that most modern critics would be more apt to condemn his didactic tendencies than his neglect of moral considerations; and that he is as thoroughly in earnest in preaching the virtues in which he really believes as he was during all the later and nobler part of his life, in carrying on the war against thieves and ruffians. His nature, though not free from deplorable taints, is sound at the core. . . .

(lxxviii)

If Adams be Fielding's masterpiece, we are still more attracted to Fielding himself by his heroines in *Tom Jones* and *Amelia*. Fielding's notions of feminine excellence are not, indeed, in all respects the highest, and we can understand why Richardson and his feminine *côterie* considered him as showing a disrespect for the sex in the ridicule which he bestows upon their classical acquirements. The exemplary Amelia is carefully confined to English reading, to a play of Farquhar's, and a sermon of Barrow's upon Sunday. The question, indeed, of the propriety of classical education for ladies, is one upon which Richardson himself gives a rather uncertain sound. We are evidently not in the period of women's rights and the equality of the sexes. But, however restricted may be the sphere, we undoubtedly feel – to take a tolerably stringent test – that we should be much more disposed to fall in love with Sophia or Amelia than with the

exemplary Clarissa or Miss Byron; and not only because they are more human, but because we can sympathize more unreservedly with the kind of homage which they receive. . . .
(lxxxiii–lxxxiv)

I do not wish ... to argue against M. Taine [see pp. 290 ff., 1863] ... I am certainly not disposed to deny Fielding's inferiority to the 'great impartial artists'. Only I do not think that it consists precisely in an absence of this impartiality. A great artist, and even a small artist, ought clearly to be impartial in one sense; he should not lose his temper with his villains, or misrepresent the facts of life; he blunders if he tries to be moral by inflicting arbitrary punishment upon his scoundrels, or again, if he makes them impossible in the attempt to make them hateful. He should describe vice as impartially as a physiologist describes a disease; and exhibit its real nature and development as a man of science in presence of any disagreeable phenomenon. And, so far, it seems to me that Fielding is hardly less impartial than Shakespeare. Fielding undoubtedly speaks as a moralist when he describes a Jonathan Wild or a Blifil. He wishes to show us a thoroughly hateful character, and he expects us to hate what he hates. But in this he is doing nothing more than Shakespeare when he described Richard III or Iago or Shylock. Shakespeare clearly expected his audience to detest his villains; and his impartiality is evident only in this, that he describes the villains as they really were. He makes Shylock, for example, intelligible instead of making him a mere monster like Marlowe's Jew of Malta; because his moral sense does not blind his insight or lead him to libel even a villain. This, undoubtedly, is a proof of Shakespeare's genius, but it would be absurd to infer that it was a proof of moral indifference. If anything it is the contrary, for it is a practical application of the familiar sentiment that vice 'to be hated needs but to be seen', and artistic morality consists in showing the essential quality of vice as of everything else described.

Now Blifil is perhaps Fielding's nearest approach to a kind of partiality which is both unscientific and inartistic. He hated a sneak and a hypocrite so heartily that he could hardly describe him fairly. But we feel that this is an exception to Fielding's ordinary method. As a rule, he is really anxious to insist upon the inconsistency of human nature in a good as well as a bad sense, and to exhibit freely the good impulses which remain even in a thoroughpaced scoundrel. And I doubt whether, even after this admission, we could show that Fielding's Blifil shows more of the objectionable kind of partiality than Shakespeare's Iago.... The inferiority of Blifil (and it is no shame to Fielding that he should have come short of one of the greatest achievements of the greatest of dramatists) is of a different and indeed a more obvious kind. It is simply that he has not Shakespeare's astonishing imaginative intensity, his power of concentrated and vivid presentation, or so profound an insight into the psychology of his characters. He is comparatively superficial, and, in short, is not a great poet, though he is a very keen observer of life and character. And this inferiority is indicated by another shortcoming which no doubt must lead us to place Fielding on a distinctly lower platform than the highest attained by the human intellect. It may be expressed briefly by saying that Shakespeare and Goethe had philosophic intellects and that Fielding emphatically had not. I do not mean of course ... to say that Shakespeare and Goethe owed their excellence to the appreciation of philosophical systems, but simply that they were at home in the highest regions of thought, and that their writings provide concrete symbols for the ideas which might in different minds give birth to a philosophy. Shakespeare is never more himself than when he is commenting on his own text, that our 'little lives are rounded by a sleep'; showing us man as the poor player who frets and struts his hour upon the stage; and the world as an atom suspended in the infinite abysses of space. So Goethe makes us hear the roaring loom of time; the world is to him the living raiment of God; and all history is the slow evolution corresponding to the gradual revelation of a divine idea. The greatest men show their greatness by rising to the summits of speculation from which this planet takes its place as a 'grain of sand', an infinitesimal fragment, in a boundless and mysterious universe. Their 'impartiality', again, manifests itself in this, that from such a point of view, the vices and follies of mankind represent themselves as mere details in an infinite system. It is impossible to be angry with such an insect as man, even as man at his greatest.

It is enough to indicate the kind of reflections by which the

highest minds are preoccupied, to see how entirely they are alien to such a writer as Fielding. . . .
(lxxxvi–lxxxviii)

Fielding . . . was . . . something of a fatalist. Men, he thought, were governed by their passions; and this must be taken to mean that . . . a man's character is practically unalterable. You may fill his mind with excellent reasoning, you may persuade him to clothe his purposes in different languages, but the great springs of action remain unaltered. The villain remains a villain, though he may be turned into a hypocritical villain; the benevolent man remains benevolent though he may have blundered into a thousand errors. Religious people may talk about conversions, and probably Fielding would not deny that such a phenomenon might occur now and then; or at any rate had occasionally occurred in a distant historical epoch. But when, with his own eyes, he saw a mean-spirited tradesman converted by a Methodist preacher, we may be pretty clear as to what the judgement would be. The man, he would say, is not going to give better measure or put less sand in his sugar; he is only going to whine out a few cant phrases and to pacify his conscience by acquiring a very orthodox set of dogmas for use on Sundays. He has not really acquired new motives, but he has learnt a new dodge for cheating the devil. . . . A man must be born with an instinct or he will never acquire it; you can no more create benevolence than you can make the proverbial silk purse from the sow's ear.

This sentiment is not . . . peculiar to Fielding. Character, we are told, has in modern tragedy taken the place of fate in the ancient. Shakespeare's heroes and villains are fully as much the creatures of passion as Fielding's. And, indeed, it is rather difficult to see how any vivid presentation of character is compatible with any other assumption. The dramatist or novelist who allows his character to go through any sudden change, is either writing a tract and allowing his perceptions to be modified by his didactic purposes, or else he has a very inadequate grasp of the situation. Poetic truth demands that the character should be firmly and forcibly drawn, and that the actions should be the natural manifestation of the character; it is very difficult, to say the least, to comply with this requirement, and yet to give the impression of any capacity for modification. With Fielding, however,

the doctrine becomes permanent for another reason. It is not that he wishes to make effective situations: nor is it because he has any general theory as to fate and free will. Such difficulties as he felt upon that matter, and we see that he had felt difficulties, were in all probability suggested not by any speculative refinements, but by his actual experience of life. There is a well-known letter in which one of Richardson's correspondents beseeches him to save Lovelace's soul. Richardson's answer, if he had sincerely expressed his reasons, would probably have been that by saving Lovelace's soul, he would have lost an edifying catastrophe. If any one had asked Fielding to do the same good office for Blifil, his answer would have been that – as a matter of fact – Blifil did go to hell and deserved it. To his question, How do you know that? he would have replied, If you have any doubts on the matter, just act for a short time as a police magistrate in London; when you really know what a rogue is made of, what is the intimate composition of Jonathan Wild, what is the sort of article that serves for a soul to the inmates of the Fleet Prison, or even, if you please, what is the real nature of a man about town, you will understand why most people are certain to be damned. The clergy ... will talk about deathbed conversions which may be very satisfactory ... but in real life, in the actual stress and struggle of human passions which concerns magistrates and constables and men of business, we may take for granted at once that men do not, and cannot, change.... And in this matter I am inclined to think that the opinions of the first police magistrates we might meet at the present day would be very apt to coincide with Fielding's. How far they would be right is a matter which I need not discuss, though, for my part, I should find it hard to say much in answer....
(xcii–xciv)

The relation between realism and idealism is not one of mutual exclusion. The novelist has to represent life, and of course to represent it faithfully. The more profound his insight, the more accurately and fully he will represent the facts of human nature. But he is an idealist in so far as he expresses ideas, or in other words, has to embody in visible types his conception of the world, and therefore again to exhibit those 'laws' of human nature which are generalized statements of the facts. The feebler kind of idealist is the observer who disregards truth and tries to bend the facts into conformity with some preconceived theory. And Fielding is radically hostile to such an idealism, which in his time was represented by the strained senti-mentalism of Richardson and Marivaux. Men, according to him, are made of flesh and blood, and not of fine phrases. But he is equally opposed to the coarser kind of realism which either confines itself to merely superficial representations, and is content to give the outside view of affairs without troubling itself about the real springs of conduct, or which becomes cynical by refusing to believe in any but the grossest and most tangible sentiments. Fielding has most emphatic-ally a very definite and very forcible conception of human nature; he has a distinct psychology if he has no particular philosophy; and making allowance for the want of elevation or of the romantic sentiment, in the higher sense of the phrase, it is the psychology of a very keen and of a very generous observer.... His morality – what-ever its shortcomings – is not the superficial one which rewards his virtuous heroes with extrinsic and arbitrary prizes, but which stimu-lates our sympathies by showing the intrinsic lovableness of the higher qualities of character. And his idealism, again, consists in this, that he gives us types of character which we cannot understand without gaining more insight into the class to which they belong; which could only have been drawn by a reflective and sympathetic mind; and which show – not by formal preaching, but with the force of vivid portraiture of concrete realities – what is his ideal of excellence. (ciii–civ)

Austin Dobson

from *Fielding*   1883 (second edition, 1889)

That he who was prodigal as a lad was prodigal as a man may be conceded; that he who was sanguine at twenty would be sanguine at forty (although this is less defensible) may also be allowed. But, if we press for 'better assurance than Bardolph', there is absolutely no good evidence that Fielding's career after his marriage materially differed from that of other men struggling for a livelihood, hampered with ill-health, and exposed to all the shifts and humiliations of necessity.

If any portrait of him is to be handed down to posterity, let it be the last rather than the first; – not the Fielding of the green-room and the tavern – of Covent Garden frolics and 'modern conversations'; but the energetic magistrate, the tender husband and father, the kindly host of his poorer friends, the practical philanthropist, the patient and magnanimous hero of the *Voyage to Lisbon*. If these things be remembered, it will seem of minor importance that to his dying day he never knew the value of money, or that he forgot his troubles over a chicken and champagne. And even his improvidence was not without its excusable side.

(187)

Ferdinand Brunetière

from 'Les Petits Naturalistes'   1 July 1884 (*Le Roman Naturaliste*, 1896; extract translated by C. J. Rawson)

Both the great and the small [naturalists], from Flaubert to M. de Maupassant, are very hard on the poor, I mean on the comicality and (if they insist) the nastiness which poverty engenders. In this, they are the very opposite of English naturalism, from Fielding to George Eliot, which is so forbearing, so compassionate, so human.
(316–17)

Thomas Hardy

from 'The Profitable Reading of Fiction', *Forum*   March 1888 (Harold Orel (ed.), *Personal Writings*, 1967)

Tom Jones is usually pointed out as a near approach to perfection in this as in some other characteristics; though, speaking for myself, I do not perceive its great superiority in artistic form over some other novels of lower reputation. . . .

   Herein lies Richardson's real if only claim to be placed on a level with Fielding: the artist spirit that he everywhere displays in the structural parts of this work and in the interaction of the personages, notably those of *Clarissa Harlowe*. However cold, artificial even, we may, at times, deem the heroine and her companions . . ., however numerous the twitches of unreality in their movements across the scene beside those in the figures animated by Fielding, we feel, nevertheless, that we are under the guidance of a hand which has consummate skill in evolving a graceful, well-balanced set of conjectures, forming altogether one of those circumstantial wholes which, when approached by events in real life, cause the observer to pause and reflect, and say, 'What a striking history!' . . .

I have dwelt the more particularly on this species of excellence, not because I consider it to rank in quality beside truth of feeling and action, but because it is one which so few non-professional readers enjoy and appreciate without some kind of preliminary direction.

(121–2)

Robert Louis Stevenson

from 'Some Gentlemen in Fiction', *Scribner's Magazine* June 1888

In *Tom Jones*, a novel of which the respectable profess that they could stand the dullness if it were not so blackguardly, and the more honest admit they could forgive the blackguardism if it were not so dull – in *Tom Jones*, with its voluminous bulk and troops of characters, there is no shadow of a gentleman, for Allworthy is only ink and paper. In *Joseph Andrews*, I fear I have always confined my reading to the parson; and Mr Adams, delightful as he is, has no pretension 'to the genteel'. In *Amelia*, things get better; all things get better; it is one of the curiosities of literature that Fielding, who wrote one book that was engaging, truthful, kind, and clean, and another book that was dirty, dull, and false, should be spoken of, the world over, as the author of the second and not the first, as the author of *Tom Jones*, not of *Amelia*. And in *Amelia*, sure enough, we find some gentlefolk; Booth and Dr Harrison will pass in a crowd, I dare not say they will do more. It is very differently that one must speak of Richardson's creations . . . Lovelace – in spite of his abominable misbehavior – Colonel Morden and my Lord M— are all gentlemen of undisputed quality.... The

best of Fielding's gentlemen had scarce been at their ease in M—
Hall. . . .

So that here . . . we have an odd inversion, tempting to the cynic.
(766)

Walter Raleigh

from *The English Novel*   1894 (Popular (fifth) edition, 1904)

Whether regarded for its art or for its thought, whether treated as
detached scenes of the human comedy, as an example of plot-
architecture, or as an attempt at the solution of certain wide problems
of life, no truer, saner book has ever been written. Indeed, to borrow
the words of the American poet, 'this is no book; who touches this
touches a man'. Through all the motley scenes of life with which its
pages are crowded, the reader finds that keener than his delight in the
wealth of scenery and character that is displayed before him is his
delight in the strength and excellence of the companionship that
guides and befriends him. The very qualities that have been foremost
in finding Fielding enemies (if those who waste their time in apologizing for him, allowing him the benefit of the age in which he lived,
and pitying him, may be so called) have also found him the warmest
friends. His splendid candour, his magnanimity, his tolerance, spring
from no ignorance or indifference; he is keenly sensitive to minute
traits of character, and merciless to meanness. Under what precise set
of conditions, and exactly by what persons, he is to be read, is a
question that need trouble no one long. Books are written to be read
by those who can understand them; their possible effect on those
who cannot is a matter of medical rather than of literary interest.
Some literary critics, it is true, with a taste for subdued tones in art,
have found some of Fielding's loudest notes too strident for enfeebled
ears, but not to the great musician can the whole range of the
orchestra, not to the great painter can the strongest contrast of
colours, profitably be denied. . . .

If terms borrowed from literary criticism could be applied to
morals, it might truly be said that Richardson is a classic, and Fielding
a romantic moralist. Richardson lays most stress on code, conformity

to the social standard, and judges by the deed done; Fielding lays most on native impulse, goodness of heart, the individual's conformity to his better self, and uses a novelist's privilege in judging his creatures by their motives. . . .
(170–72)

Samuel Butler

from a notebook   1897 (H. F. Jones (ed.), *Note-Books*, 1912)

I know that I could read the whole of *The Pilgrim's Progress* (except occasional episodical sermons) without being at all bored by it, whereas, having spent a penny upon Mr Stead's abridgement of *Joseph Andrews*, I had to give it up as putting me out of all patience. I then spent another penny on an abridgement of *Gulliver's Travels*, and was enchanted by it. What is it that makes one book so readable and another so unreadable? Swift, from all I can make out, was a far more human and genuine person than he is generally represented, but I do not think I should have liked him, whereas Fielding, I am sure, must have been delightful. Why do the faults of his work overweigh its many great excellences, while the less great excellences of the *Voyage to Lilliput* outweigh its more serious defects?

I suppose it is the prolixity of Fielding that fatigues me. Swift is terse, he gets through what he has to say on any matter as quickly as he can and takes the reader on to the next, whereas Fielding is not only long, but his length is made still longer by the disconnectedness of the episodes that appear to have been padded into the books – episodes that do not help one forward, and are generally so exaggerated, and often so full of horse-play as to put one out of conceit with the parts that are really excellent.

Whatever else Bunyan is he is never long.
(190–91)

Thomas Hardy

from a note   24 June 1898 (Florence Emily Hardy, *Life of Thomas Hardy*, vol. 2, 1933)

Fielding as a local novelist has never been clearly regarded, to my mind: and his aristocratic, even feudal, attitude towards the peasantry (e.g. his view of Molly as a 'slut' to be ridiculed, not as a simple girl, as worthy a creation of Nature as the lovely Sophia) should be exhibited strongly. But the writer could not well be a working novelist without his bringing upon himself a charge of invidiousness. [Hardy was 'declining to write an Introduction to a proposed Library Edition of Fielding's novels'.]
(74)

Edmund Gosse

from the Introduction to Henry Fielding *Works*, vol. 1   1898

Between Fielding and all his contemporaries there rose a wall of imperfect sympathy. He was not as they were; his ideals were different, his aims contradicted theirs. To the comparatively wholesome and manly generation of the age of Anne, there had succeeded a race much reduced in its animal and mental vigour. It was the age of tears that had dawned with Fielding's childhood; it was the generation which meditated with Young and Blair among the tombs, that combined the lachrymose with the sentimental, that wrapped itself, sighing, in a genteel mantle of melancholy. . . .

While his contemporaries turned their faces away from everything that was loud and rank, Fielding descended into the crowd. He loved the 'low' forms of humour which he met with among porters, chambermaids, farm-boys, and thieves. As he said himself, he described 'not men but manners, not an individual, but a species'. Above all, doubtless, he studied, with such loving care as had never been given to them before, the farmers, huntsmen, and dairymaids of his own Wessex, pointing the road, with a broad smile of welcome, to that son of his who is our living glory, the author of *Tess of the*

D'Urbervilles and *The Trumpet Major*. The result was, as we can never too emphatically reassert, a wholly new departure.
(xxxviii–xxxix)

George Bernard Shaw

from the preface to *Plays Unpleasant* 1898 (reprinted, 1951)

In 1737, Henry Fielding, the greatest practising dramatist, with the single exception of Shakespear, produced by England between the Middle Ages and the nineteenth century, devoted his genius to the task of exposing and destroying parliamentary corruption, then at its height. Walpole, unable to govern without corruption, promptly gagged the stage by a censorship which is in full force at the present moment. Fielding, driven out of the trade of Molière and Aristophanes, took to that of Cervantes; and since then the English novel has been one of the glories of literature, whilst the English drama has been its disgrace.
(xii–xiii)

Henry James

from 'The Future of the Novel' 1899 (Leon Edel (ed.), *The House of Fiction*, 1962)

As the novel is at any moment the most immediate and, as it were, admirably *treacherous* picture of actual manners – indirectly as well as directly, and by what it does not touch as well as by what it does – so its present situation, where we are most concerned with it, is exactly a reflection of our social change and chances, of the signs and portents that lay most traps for most observers, and make up in general what is most 'amusing' in the spectacle we offer. Nothing, I may say, for instance, strikes me more as meeting this description than the predicament finally arrived at, for the fictive energy, in consequence of our long and most respectable tradition of making it defer supremely, in the treatment, say, of a delicate case, to the inexperience of the young. The particular knot the coming novelist, who shall prefer not simply to beg the question, will have here to untie may represent assuredly the essence of his outlook. By what it shall decide to do in respect to the 'young' the great prose fable will, from any serious point of view, practically see itself stand or fall. What is clear is that it has, among us, veritably never chosen – it has, mainly, always obeyed an unreasoning instinct of avoidance in which there has often been much that was felicitous. While society was frank, was free about the incidents and accidents of the human constitution, the novel took the same robust ease as society. The young then were so very young that they were not table-high. But they began to grow, and from the moment their little chins rested on the mahogany, Richardson and Fielding began to go under it. There came into being a mistrust of any but the most guarded treatment of the great relation between men and women, the constant world-renewal, which was the conspicuous sign that whatever the prose picture of life was prepared to take upon itself, it was not prepared to take upon itself not to be superficial. Its position became very much: 'There are other things, don't you know? For heaven's sake let *that* one pass!' And to this wonderful propriety of letting it pass the business has been for these so many years – with the consequences we see today – largely devoted. These consequences are of many sorts, not a few altogether charming. One of them has been that there is an immense omission in our fiction – which, though many critics will always judge that it has vitiated the whole, others will continue to speak of as signifying but a trifle. One can only talk for one's self, and of the English and American novelists of whom I am fond, I am so superlatively fond that I positively prefer to take them as they are. I cannot so much as imagine Dickens and Scott *without* the 'love-making' left, as the phrase is, out. They were, to my perception, absolutely right – from the moment their attention to it could only be perfunctory – practically not to deal with it. In all their work it is, in spite of the number of pleasant sketches of affection gratified or crossed, the element that matters least.

(55–6)

Wilbur L. Cross

from *The Development of the English Novel* 1899 (reprinted 1906)

Indeed, the main situation in *Amelia* is the favorite one of the modern realist. . . . It is the story of the hard lot of a woman of high breeding who has married for love a poor lieutenant. Owing to the husband's passion for gambling, and the wrongs of others, they are thrown upon London with a lieutenant's half-pay as their only income. Its scenes, described in stern and hard reality, are those of the miserable lodging-house, the sponging-house, the pawn-shop, Newgate, and the homes of the disreputable London aristocracy. . . . The wretched family sink lower and lower into poverty and squalor; the last guinea and the jewels and dresses of Amelia have gone to pay gambling debts, and Booth is confined to the bailiff's house, when they are rescued by the good Dr Harrison, the *deus ex machina* of the drama, and restored to their rightful fortune; and all who have wronged them are duly punished. Had Fielding worked out his situation to its logical conclusion; had he transported Booth to the West Indies; had he turned Amelia with her children into the street, or given her over as mistress to Colonel James – all of which he suggests in the course of his story – he would have anticipated the relentless *débâcle* of naturalism. The infinite tenderness of Fielding, soon to bid a most pathetic farewell to his children and then to life, was mightier than the logic of art. (56-7)

George Sturt

from a journal 8 March 1901 (E. D. Mackerness (ed.), *Journals*, vol. 1, 1967)

And like us moderns, [Henry Harland] is much more pagan than those his two predecessors. The world he loves is that of visual beauty . . . Jane Austen and Fielding . . . were intellectual; moral: and for these qualities their books are great, and would be still undiminished in greatness, were their artistic ineptitudes and crudities

doubled and trebled. It is Fielding's untroubled sane masculine man-of-the-world intellect, and it is Jane Austen's sensitive penetrating feminine one, shining through their books, that give the value. But Mr Harland charms us, by the things he has *seen* with his eyes, and the emotions they have occasioned to him.
(347)

Henry James

from 'Gustave Flaubert', a Preface to *Madame Bovary*   1902
(Leon Edel (ed.), *The House of Fiction*, 1962)

Madame Bovary, Salammbô, Saint-Antoine, L'Éducation are so written and so composed (though the last-named in a minor degree) that the more we look at them the more we find in them, under this head, a beauty of intention and of effect; the more they figure in the too often dreary desert of fictional prose a class by themselves and a little living oasis. So far as that desert is of the complexion of our own English speech it supplies with remarkable rarity this particular source of refreshment. So strikingly is that the case, so scant for the most part any dream of a scheme of beauty in these connections, that a critic betrayed at artless moments into a plea for composition may find himself as blankly met as if his plea were for trigonometry. He makes inevitably his reflections, which are numerous enough; one of them being that if we turn our back so squarely, so universally to this order of considerations it is because the novel is so preponderantly cultivated among us by women, in other words by a sex ever grace-fully, comfortably, enviably unconscious (it would be too much to call them even suspicious) of the requirements of form. The case is at any rate sharply enough made for us, or against us, by the circum-stance that women are held to have achieved on all our ground, in spite of this weakness and others, as great results as any. The judge-ment is undoubtedly founded: Jane Austen was instinctive and charming, and the other recognitions – even over the heads of the ladies, some of them, from Fielding to Pater – are obvious; without, however, in the least touching my contention. For signal examples of what composition, distribution, arrangement can do, of how they intensify the life of a work of art, we have to go elsewhere; and the value of Flaubert for us is that he admirably points the moral. (206–7)

Algernon Charles Swinburne

from 'Charles Dickens', *Quarterly Review* July 1902

David Copperfield, from the first chapter to the last, is unmistakable by any eye above the level and beyond the insight of a beetle's as one of the masterpieces to which time can only add a new charm and an unimaginable value. The narrative is as coherent and harmonious as that of *Tom Jones*; and to say this is to try it by the very highest and apparently the most unattainable standard. But I must venture to reaffirm my conviction that even the glorious masterpiece of Fielding's radiant and beneficent genius, if in some points superior, is by no means superior in all. Tom is a far completer and more living type of gallant boyhood and generous young manhood than David; but even the lustre of Partridge is pallid and lunar beside the noontide glory of Micawber. Blifil is a more poisonously plausible villain than Uriah: Sophia Western remains unequalled except by her sister heroine Amelia as a perfectly credible and adorable type of young English womanhood, naturally 'like one of Shakespeare's women', socially as fine and true a lady as Congreve's Millamant or Angelica. But even so large-minded and liberal a genius as Fielding's could never have conceived any figure like Miss Trotwood's, any group like that of the Peggottys. As easily could it have imagined and realized the magnificent setting of the story, with its homely foreground of street or wayside and its background of tragic sea. (26)

W. E. Henley

from 'Henry Fielding', prefixed to Henry Fielding, *Works*,
vol. 16   1903

Was there a lady Bellaston in his life? Who knows? Yet the chances
are that there was? Who cares? Did he smoke so furiously that he
needed nothing but the wrappings of his tobacco for the manuscript
paper of the very solid five volumes of *Théâtre* contained in this
edition? Was he commonly drunk, always begrimed with snuff, and
ever bending the stiles along his path up Parnassus' Hill with no
better dunnage than a yard of clay and a flask of champagne?
Thackeray's charming but (in the circumstances) really rascally
discovery of him made strongly for these last conclusions; for
Thackeray, you see, knew all about the eighteenth century, and was
good at Grub Street, and had all but published with Lintot and Cave.
So the middle-Victorian feeling against the author of *Tom Jones*
was strong: so strong that Lord Houghton (himself a man with an
idiosyncrasy which demanded privacy), writing of Thackeray dead,
could actually refer to him as 'Fielding without the manners' dross'.
It sounds incredible; yet so it is. And, for my part, I cannot be emphatic enough in my praise of them that have done what they
could to discredit this affecting perversion of life, and character, and
fact.
(vi–vii)

He was certainly no bibulous and futile wastrel that spent 'some
thousands of hours' over *Tom Jones*. That book is the work of a great
and serious artist; and I hold that the Fielding of these years of study
and comparison is different in no single particular from the diligent
and apprehensive writer to whom we owe our greatest novel. Lady
Mary, and 'Horry' Walpole, and Arthur Murphy after them, and
after him the brilliant W. M. T. knew something, and guessed more;
but they did not know enough, and they guessed backwards; and
none has ever suggested a means of reconciling their 'views' of Fielding with the strength, the majesty, the stately undiminishing serenity
of Fielding's four great books. . . .

All these things [i.e. some early writings] are journalism, and

Fielding, though in a manner of speaking he died writing for the Press, is by this time something better, something vastly more considerable, than the best journalist that ever lived. In effect, in 1742, this scandalous rake, idler, and tippler, produced his *Joseph Andrews*; and the English novel, started rather poorly by Nashe in *Jack Wilton*, brutified and stultified by the Head of *The English Rogue*, half-visioned, yet never seriously attempted, by Defoe, touched in a pretty futile way by Mrs Behn – the English novel, I say, became a living, breathing, working fact. . . .

To Harry Fielding: who, for one thing, knew the worth of a wench's humour, and for another how the noble Mr B. should have done by Pamela, and would assuredly have done by Pamela, had he not been the creation of a vegetarian, who knew nothing of life, and wrote of women only from their own report of themselves: to Harry Fielding, I say, *Pamela* appeared (as in fact it is) so much strained, unhealthy, and unnatural rubbish. That being the case, he began upon a parody . . . as a person of consequence in letters once said to me, 'In *Joseph Andrews* the Old Man' – (he talked of Fielding *aetat* 35, as 'the Old Man!') – 'got his hands right into the guts of life.' That says anything there is left to say about this gamesome and delightful epic of the road.[1] . . .

1743 was the year of the *Miscellanies*: included in which, with much in prose and verse which is interesting to us only because Fielding

---

1 'Tis a pleasure to record that it began as the success it is. It had not, one gathers, so instant and so splendid a triumph as *Pamela*; but there were editions; and now, I take it, for one that reads the story of Mr B. and the sublime Miss Richardson (for that, and nothing else, that is what Miss Pamela Andrews is) some sixty read the story of Joseph and Fanny. For the rest, it may be noted that fornication, the sole unpardonable sin in English fiction, is but a detail (as it is in life) in *Joseph Andrews*; but in much of *Pamela* it is the staple of the book. In the work done by the man who knew the world there is My Lady, there is Betty, there is the fair and desperate Slipslop, there are Didapper and Tow-wouse. But they are but circumstances: they fit in well enough, but they are nothing like the whole. Now, in *Pamela*, none is permitted to fornicate; yet the theme of the novel is fornication. Mr B. is always hovering round in a most dreadful and indecent state; and Pamela is always praying to be protected from a kind of walking phallus (as in a Kaulbach allegory), terribly menacing and ever ineffectual, or resisting its approaches, or writing to her parents to tell them that it has had no luck, and that she is still their virgin child. Which is the more moral writer? Which the more buxom book?

thought it worth printing, are a *Journey to the Next World*, that odd, clever half-success in the manner of Lucian; and *Mr Jonathan Wild the Great*; that tremendous achievement in pure irony, that masterpiece in a mode in which none save Swift has excelled this author.[1] The *Journey to the Next World* is ingenious and clever; but it is not to be named in the same breath with *Jonathan Wild*. . . .

When he sailed for Lisbon, his work was over; and he knew it. Still, he had enough of life and energy left to enact and write the circumstances of his pilgrimage; and, as I think, 'tis in this book, this *Voyage to Lisbon*, that we find the true Fielding. Modest, patient, suffering, ever dignified, perfectly wholehearted, perfectly cheerful, perfectly resigned: in fact, the great Englishman, whose ghost, if he have a ghost, has pretty certainly put Thackeray's on its knees long since, very much as in his real body he put his Captain on his marrowbones in the cabin of that *Queen of Portugal* in which he sailed for Lisbon. Lisbon and Death. . . . There is no more Fielding now. But we have not been idle. Far from it. And there is now an infinite deal of Messrs Howells and James.

Of all the definitions that ever were defined Taine's definition of Fielding as 'a good buffalo' strikes me as one of the most absurd. But Taine, man of genius as he was born, and *savant* as he made himself, was at all times the prey of any theory that happened to commend itself to his imaginative yet very logical mind; and either this, his theory of Harry Fielding, was one of the unluckiest he ever developed, or you can pay no man a higher compliment than to call him a Good Buffalo. For consider what, in Fielding's case, is comprehended in the term. Here is a man brave, generous, kind to the nth

1 And has he, has Swift himself, done better? I cannot think so. . . . The truth is, the book is an exemplar, and the best we have, of a certain mode in letters; and the mode which it examples is irony: a mode in which few Englishmen have excelled, and in whose practice even Mr Meredith has come, at times, to hopeless grief. And for this reason it is isolated in English Letters. It is given to few to love irony for its own sake; to still fewer to delight in the ironical presentation of life and character, which in this book Fielding essays with complete success. What did the vulgar think of it? What but that they have always thought of what they could not understand?

Some Plays he wrote sans Wit or Plot,
    Adventures of Inferiors,
'Which with his lives of rogues and thieves
    Supply the Town's —.'

degree; a man with a great hatred of meanness and hypocrisy, and a strong regard for all forms of *virtus*, whether natural and impulsive or an effect of culture and reflection; an impassioned lover, a devout husband, a most cordial and careful father; so staunch a friend that his books are so many proofs of his capacity for friendship; of so sound a heart, of so vigorous a temperament, of so clear-eyed and serene a spirit, that years and calamities and disease do not exist for him, and he takes his leave of the world in one of the most valiant and most genial little books that ever was penned; distinguished among talkers by a delightful gaiety, a fine and gracious under-standing, an inalienable dignity; withal of an intelligence at once so vigilant and so penetrating, at once so observant and so laborious and exacting, that, without hurry as without noise, patient ever and ever diligent, a master of life, a master of character, a master of style, he achieved for us the four great books we have, and, in achieving them, did so nobly by his nation and his mother tongue that he that would praise our splendid, all-comprehending speech aright has said the best he can of it when he says that it is the speech of Shakespeare and Fielding. If to be a Good Buffalo be all that (and in Harry Fielding's case it is all that, and more), why, then, I can't help wishing that the breed were more prolific; and even that M. Henri [*sic*] Taine had himself belonged to it.

I shall say nothing about the four great books, for the very simple reason that everything there is to say about them has been said. Like Dickens's work, and Scott's, but, as is inevitable and natural, to a still greater extent, as yet they are as essential a component in the mighty fabric of our literature as the plays and poems of Shakespeare, or the poetry of Spenser and Milton, and Gibbon and John Bunyan, and Defoe's half-failures, and Mr Boswell's biography. And when I say that to consider them: in all their stately shapeliness of plan, their admirable completeness of structure, their reasoned prodigality of detail and adornment: is for me about the same, neither more nor less, than considering St Paul's, which I esteem the piece of architec-ture the nearest to perfection these eyes of mine have seen, it will be apprehended, I hope, that I keep not silence out of irreverence. (xxxii–xl)

New York Times

from a letter of 3 September 1904 (cited by Blanchard)

If I had a daughter, I should certainly give her the works of Fielding. I should be sorry, of course, that she would have to make the acquaintance of many severe facts with which Fielding deals, but she would have to learn these things at one time or another, and I do not think she could learn them in a better way than by reading *Amelia*. It is a true study of human nature on robust lines, and the moral Fielding draws is invariably sound and reasonable. Unreasonable novels do enormous harm.

(520-21)

Henry James

from the preface to *The Princess Casamassima*   1908
(R. P. Blackmur (ed.), *The Art of the Novel*, n.d.)

It is very true that Fielding's hero in *Tom Jones* is but as 'finely', that is but as intimately, bewildered as a young man of great health and spirits may be when he hasn't a grain of imagination: the point to be made is, at all events, that his sense of bewilderment obtains altogether on the comic, never on the tragic plane. He has so much 'life' that it amounts, for the effect of comedy and application of satire, almost to his having a mind, that is to his having reactions and a full consciousness; besides which his author – *he* handsomely possessed of a mind – has such an amplitude of reflexion for him and round him that we see him through the mellow air of Fielding's fine old moralism, fine old humour and fine old style, which somehow really enlarge, make every one and every thing important.

(68)

G. K. Chesterton

from 'Tom Jones and Morality', *All Things Considered*   1908

There seems to be an extraordinary idea abroad that Fielding was in some way an immoral or offensive writer. I have been astounded by the number of the leading articles, literary articles, and other articles written about him just now in which there is a curious tone of apologizing for the man. One critic says that after all he couldn't help it, because he lived in the eighteenth century; another says that we must allow for the change of manners and ideas; another says that he was not altogether without generous and humane feelings; another suggests that he clung feebly, after all, to a few of the less important virtues. What on earth does all this mean? Fielding described Tom Jones as going on in a certain way, in which, most unfortunately, a very large number of young men do go on. It is unnecessary to say that Henry Fielding knew that it was an unfortunate way of going on. Even Tom Jones knew that. He said in so many words that it was a very unfortunate way of going on; he said, one may almost say, that it had ruined his life; the passage is there for the benefit of any one who may take the trouble to read the book. There is ample evidence (though even this is of a mystical and indirect kind), there is ample evidence that Fielding probably thought that it was better to be Tom Jones than to be an utter coward and sneak. There is simply not one rag or thread or speck of evidence to show that Fielding thought that it was better to be Tom Jones than to be a good man. All that he is concerned with is the description of a definite and very real type of young man; the young man whose passions and whose selfish necessities sometimes seemed to be stronger than anything else in him.

The practical morality of Tom Jones is bad, though not so bad, *spiritually* speaking, as the practical morality of Arthur Pendennis or the practical morality of Pip, and certainly nothing like so bad as the profound practical immorality of Daniel Deronda. The practical morality of Tom Jones is bad; but I cannot see any proof that his theoretical morality was particularly bad. There is no need to tell the majority of modern young men even to live up to the theoretical ethics of Henry Fielding. They would suddenly spring into the stature of archangels if they lived up to the theoretic ethics of poor Tom Jones. Tom Jones is still alive, with all his good and all his evil: he is walking about the streets; we meet him every day. We meet with him, we drink with him, we smoke with him, we talk with him, we talk about him. The only difference is that we have no longer the intellectual courage to write about him. We split up the supreme and central human being, Tom Jones, into a number of separate aspects. We let Mr J. M. Barrie write about him in his good moments, and make him out better than he is. We let Zola write about him in his bad moments, and make him out much worse than he is. We let Maeterlinck celebrate those moments of spiritual panic which he knows to be cowardly; we let Mr Rudyard Kipling celebrate those moments of brutality which he knows to be far more cowardly. We let obscene writers write about the obscenities of this ordinary man. We let puritan writers write about the purities of this ordinary man. We look through one peephole that makes men out as devils, and we call it the new art. We look through another peephole that makes men out as angels, and we call it the New Theology. But if we pull down some dusty old books from the bookshelf, if we turn over some old mildewed leaves, and if in that obscurity and decay we find some faint traces of a tale about a complete man, such a man as is walking on the pavement outside, we suddenly pull a long face, and we call it the coarse morals of a bygone age.

The truth is that all these things mark a certain change in the general view of morals; not, I think, a change for the better. We have grown to associate morality in a book with a kind of optimism and prettiness; according to us, a moral book is a book about moral people. But the old idea was almost exactly the opposite; a moral book was a book about immoral people. A moral book was full of pictures like Hogarth's 'Gin Lane' or 'Stages of Cruelty', or it recorded, like the popular broadsheet, 'God's dreadful judgement' against some blasphemer or murderer. There is a philosophical reason for this change. The homeless scepticism of our time has reached a sub-conscious feeling that morality is somehow merely a matter of human taste – an accident of psychology. And if goodness only exists in certain human minds, a man wishing to praise goodness will naturally exaggerate the amount of it that there is in human minds or the number of human minds in which it is supreme. Every confession that man is vicious is a confession that virtue is visionary. Every book which admits that evil is real is felt in some vague way to be admitting that good is unreal. The modern instinct is that if the heart of man is evil, there is nothing that remains good. But the older feeling was that if the heart of man was ever so evil, there was something that remained good – goodness remained good. An actual avenging virtue existed outside the human race; to that men rose, or from that men fell away. Therefore, of course, this law itself was as much demonstrated in the breach as in the observance. If Tom Jones violated morality, so much the worse for Tom Jones. Fielding did not feel, as a melancholy modern would have done, that every sin of Tom Jones was in some way breaking the spell, or we may even say destroying the fiction of morality. Men spoke of the sinner breaking the law; but it was rather the law that broke him. And what modern people call the foulness and freedom of Fielding is generally the severity and moral stringency of Fielding. He would not have thought that he was serving morality at all if he had written a book all about nice people. Fielding would have considered Mr Ian Maclaren extremely immoral; and there is something to be said for that view. Telling the truth about the terrible struggle of the human soul is surely a very elementary part of the ethics of honesty. If the characters are not wicked, the book is.

This older and firmer conception of right as existing outside human weakness and without reference to human error, can be felt in the very lightest and loosest of the works of old English literature. It is commonly unmeaning enough to call Shakespeare a great moralist; but in this particular way Shakespeare is a very typical moralist. Whenever he alludes to right and wrong it is always with this old implication. Right is right, even if nobody does it. Wrong is wrong, even if everybody is wrong about it.

(261–6)

Thomas Hardy

from a speech written for the Society of Dorset Men in London
1908 (Harold Orel (ed.), *Personal Writings*, 1967)

There are many others from the same little shire who have stepped or
ridden up to this City by the old road which comes through High
Street, Kensington, and on to Hyde Park Corner. One might almost
include Henry Fielding, who was a London magistrate as well as a
writer of novels and plays. Though not born in the county, he was
closely associated with North-East Dorset, having settled for some
time at East Stower. That he knew Dorset like a native is apparent
to any Dorset man who makes himself familiar with this keen observer's humorous scenes and dialogues.
(224)

Ford Madox Ford

from 'The Critical Attitude: English Literature of Today',
English Review November 1909 (*The Critical Attitude*, 1915)

We think we have proved that, in the case of such writers as Mr
James, Mr Conrad and Mr George Moore, the great mainstream of
European international literature is cultivating still in England the
muses upon a little thin oatmeal. The temperamentally British novel,
the loose, amorphous, genial and easy-going thing that was represented by Fielding, by Dickens and by Thackeray, and with more art
and less geniality by Anthony Trollope – this thing that is as essentially
national as is the English pudding – is a little more difficult to discern.
But Mr Wells has his spiritual kinship with Dickens: Mr Kipling is,
or perhaps we should say was, a less discursive Thackeray. And have
we not Mr William de Morgan?
(107–8)

G. M. Godden

from *Henry Fielding: A Memoir* 1910

This capacity of Fielding for relegating circumstance to its true level. the detached idealism that moulded his genius, are, indeed, shown once and for all in the fact that the exquisite picture of virtue, the whole-hearted attack on vice, the genial humour, the sunny portraits of humanity, the splendid cheerfulness of *Tom Jones*, that 'Epic of Youth', came from a man in middle age, immersed in disheartening struggles, and fighting recurrent ill health. Superficial critics have called Fielding a realist because his figures are so full-blooded and alive that we feel we have met them but yesterday in the street; to eyes so shortsighted life itself must seem merely realistic. As none but an idealist could have conceived Parson Adams, so the creator of Sophia again announced himself an idealist in the Dedication of *Tom Jones*. Here, in a language of pure symbolism, he contends that the ideal virtues such as goodness and innocence, may most effectively be presented to men in a figure, for 'an example is a kind of picture, in which Virtue becomes as it were an object of sight, and strikes us with an idea of that loveliness, which Plato asserts there is in her naked charms.' To the man who could write thus, and who, in later pages of his great 'Epic' could humbly desire of Genius 'do thou kindly take me by the hand, and lead me through all the mazes, the winding labyrinth of Nature. Initiate me into all those mysteries which profane eyes never beheld.' To this man the material surroundings of life must have seemed of little greater import than the fittings of that narrow box to the occupation of which he looked forward with so calm a foresight. . . .
(180–81)

Such were the noble purposes to which Fielding consciously dedicated his genius in *Tom Jones*, and such was the careful restraint with which he exercised his chosen methods of wit and humour. That these purposes, executed by a supreme genius in the language and scenes of his own day, should ever have laid their author open to a charge of immorality is perhaps one of the most amazing pieces of irony in the whole history of English literature. But as this charge of moral laxity has been seriously brought against the pages of *Tom Jones*, and is perhaps not yet quite exploded, it cannot be wholly disregarded. The imputation amounts, briefly, to a too easy forgiveness for the youthful sins of Jones, and the involving that engaging youth in too deep a degradation. The answers to these charges are, firstly, that Fielding held strongly, and here exhibits, the humane and wise doctrine that a man should be judged, not by what he sometimes does, but by what he *is*. And, secondly, that as Sir Walter Scott pointed out, when dealing with this very matter, 'the vices into which Jones suffers himself to fall are made the direct cause of placing himself in the distressful situation which he occupies during the greater part of his narrative; while his generosity, his charity, and his amiable qualities become the means of saving him from the consequences of his folly'. Fielding was not wholly concerned with the acts of a man; to him the admission of the penitent thief into Paradise, at the eleventh hour, could have been no stumbling block. And, further, Tom Jones not only suffers for his ill doing, but wins no heaven until he wholly purges himself from the sin which did so easily beset him.

(187–8)

H. G. Wells

from 'The Contemporary Novel' 1911 (Leon Edel and Gordon N. Ray (eds.), *Henry James and H. G. Wells*, 1958)

Following on the days of Dickens, the novel began to contract, to subordinate characterization to story and description to drama . . . but I rejoice to see many signs today that that phase of narrowing and restriction is over, and that there is every encouragement for a return towards a laxer, more spacious form of novel-writing. The movement is partly of English origin, a revolt against those more exacting and cramping conceptions of artistic perfection to which I will recur in a moment, and a return to the lax freedom of form, the rambling discursiveness, the right to roam, of the earlier English novel, of *Tristram Shandy* and of *Tom Jones*; and partly it comes from

abroad, and derives a stimulus from such bold and original enterprises as that of Monsieur Rolland in his *Jean Christophe*. . . .
(137-8)

Richardson wrote deliberately for edification, and *Tom Jones* is a powerful and effective appeal for a charitable, and even indulgent, attitude towards loose-living men. But excepting Fielding and one or two other of those partial exceptions that always occur in the case of critical generalizations, there is a definable difference between the novel of the past and what I may call the modern novel. It is a difference that is reflected upon the novel from a difference in the general way of thinking. It lies in the fact that formerly there was a feeling of certitude about moral values and standards of conduct that is altogether absent today. It wasn't so much that men were agreed upon these things – about these things there have always been enormous divergences of opinion – as that men were emphatic, cocksure, and unteachable about whatever they did happen to believe to a degree that no longer obtains. This is the Balfourian age, and even religion seeks to establish itself on doubt.
(144-5)

André Gide

from a letter to Arnold Bennett   21 July 1911 (Linette F. Brugmans (ed.), *Correspondance André Gide–Arnold Bennett*, 1964; extract translated by C. J. Rawson)

 am rereading *Tom Jones*. Yes, indeed, it is stunning.
66)

J. B. Yeats

from a letter to W. B. Yeats   10 May 1914 (Joseph Hone (ed.),
Letters to his Son, 1944)

I see that Stephens denounces Fielding as not much better than an after-dinner speaker. What nonsense! He says the profoundest things – and besides he was a man attended by visions. . . .

I used to say that Meredith had the cruelty of the sedentary man, as George Eliot had that of the old maid and I compared him with the kindly and the FEARLESS Fielding – people don't realize and don't remember that Christ was a man *tempted in all things*. Of how few men could this be said? Certainly not of Meredith or of George Eliot and yet it would be true of Fielding.

(179)

D. H. Lawrence

from *Study of Thomas Hardy*, chapter 9   1914–15 (Edward D. McDonald (ed.), *Phoenix: The Posthumous Papers of D. H. Lawrence*, 1936)

And, because they were afraid of the unknown, and because they wanted to retain the full-veined gratification of self-pleasure, men have kept their women tightly in bondage. But when the men were no longer afraid of the unknown, when they deemed it exhausted, they said, 'There are no women; there are only daughters of men' – as we say now, as the Greeks tried to say. Hence the 'Virgin' conception of woman, the passionless, passive conception, progressing from Fielding's Amelia to Dickens's Agnes, and on to Hardy's Sue.

(493)

André Gide

from a journal   9 May 1918 (*Journal 1889–1939*, 1951;
extract translated by C. J. Rawson)

The interest of Fielding's *Amelia*, which I'm reading aloud to Em., is
flagging somewhat. Wanting to find a possible relation to *Gil Blas*
(or rather, a similarity of tone), I reread in the latter the story of
Scipio, and am above all surprised to find it better.
(653)

Wilbur L. Cross

from *The History of Henry Fielding*   1918 (vol. 3, 1963)

James Russell Lowell, I have heard, shocked Harriet Beecher Stowe
by suggesting to the author of *Uncle Tom's Cabin* that she might improve her art by reading *Tom Jones*. . . .
(230)

I do not mean to enrol Henry Fielding among the saints of this
world, for their rigid discipline and circumspection bored him; their
lives lacked colour and variety; and many of them, he discovered,
were hypocrites. He was a gentleman who flourished in the reign of
George the Second, and it would be hazardous to give any gentleman
of that period a clean bill. One may argue, as Dobson has argued,
that a man of Fielding's temperament must have been often over-
powered by the sex instinct; that there must have been, as Henley
has said, many 'accidental women' in the course of his career. But
this conclusion is not necessarily true. Against it stands the fact that
there is no evidence that Fielding ever consorted with lewd women.
His name was never associated with any woman of questionable
character. The sex instinct, however strong and imperious, may
manifest itself quite differently from the ways surmised by Dobson
and Henley. Among the prime characteristics which Murphy gave
Fielding was unusual constancy in his attachments. So far as anyone
knows, what overmastered Fielding was the vehemence of his

passion at a given time for a particular woman.... But no dishonour can be attached to his conduct. No woman, picked up and discarded, has yet been discovered in his life; nor any attempt to steal away the wife of a friend. What Wordsworth did or what Thackeray did, has never been recorded of Fielding.

Fielding's memory should also be eased somewhat of that heavy burden of poverty which it has had to bear. It has always been taken for granted that the playwright worked and slept a good deal of the time in a garret. His poems addressed to Walpole are of course the source of the legend.... Fielding's lines were ... playful. In his time the garret was the abode of literary hacks in the employ of book-sellers. Fielding was not of them; they were his butt throughout his entire literary career. Had Fielding really written his lines to Walpole in a garret, we may be certain that the fact would never have been embodied in the poem. He merely placed himself in a garret as a point of vantage for taking the Prime Minister to task for his utter neglect of letters.
(269–70)

J. B. Yeats

from a letter to W. B. Yeats 30 June 1921 (Joseph Hone (ed.), *Letters to his Son*, 1944)

When is your poetry at its best? I challenge all the critics if it is not when its wild spirit of your imagination is wedded to concrete fact. Had you stayed with me and not left me for Lady Gregory, and her friends and associations, you would have loved and adored concrete life for which as I know you have a real affection. What would have resulted? Realistic and poetical plays – poetry in closest and most intimate union with the positive realities and complexities of life.... Not idea but the game of life should have been your preoccupation, as it was Shakespeare's and the old English writers', notably the kinglike Fielding. ... Whistler was too arrogant or rather too insolent – and insolence I do not love, it makes me think of the nobleman's footman. So he had not the patience to become the student and lover of life itself. Carlyle the man was to him nothing except an

occasion for an artistic picture. In Shakespeare's time that kind of insolence was not known among the poets. France had not ennobled and decorated them, they were little better than noblemen's servants or servants to the public – so that there was nothing to prevent their making a close study of life itself – and they had not despised their fellow creatures as did the Puritan and does the modern English gentleman. For this kind of study you have by nature every natural qualification – your conversation shows it. Never are you happier and never more felicitous in words than when in your conversation you describe life and comment on it. But when you write poetry you as it were put on your dress coat and shut yourself in and forget what is vulgar to a man in a dress coat.
(280–81)

J. B. Yeats

from a letter to W. B. Yeats   5 July 1921 (Joseph Hone (ed.), *Letters to his Son*, 1944)

My mother's family, of English extraction, worshipped force and so did the Pollexfens and all the English. Force means courage and honesty.

   In the eighteenth century, this kind of preference meant a frank and unbridled animalism, with cock fighting and bull baiting and boxing and every kind of blasphemy. It meant Hogarth and Fielding, and solemn hilarious old Johnson, and the portrait painters like Gainsborough who 'loved' the women they painted, or honoured and worshipped them like Reynolds.
(282)

André Gide

from *Journal des Faux-Monnayeurs*   21 August 1921
(translated by J. O'Brien)

Why try to conceal it? The form that tempts me is the epic. The epic tone alone suits me and has the power to satisfy me; it alone can free the novel from its realistic rut. For a great many years it was possible to think that Fielding and Richardson occupied opposite poles. Actually one is as realistic as the other. Until now the novel in every country has always clung to reality. Our great literary period found it possible to carry out its effort toward idealization only in the drama. *La Princesse de Clèves* is without a successor; when the French novel really launches out, it does so in the direction of the *Roman bourgeois*.

(29)

André Gide

from *Journal des Faux-Monnayeurs*   1 November 1922
(translated by J. O'Brien)

In the seventeenth century, tragedy and comedy attained a magnificent purity – (and purity, in art as elsewhere, is what matters) – and in addition almost all the *genres*, big and little: fables, maxims, sermons, memoirs, letters. Lyric poetry, purely lyrical . . . and not the novel? (No, do not make too much of *La Princesse de Clèves* – it is chiefly a marvel of tact and taste . . .).

As for this *pure* novel, no one has produced it since either – not even that admirable Stendhal, who of all novelists perhaps approached it the closest. But is it not remarkable that Balzac, possibly our greatest novelist, is beyond doubt the one who mingled with the novel, annexed to it and amalgamated with it, more heterogeneous and inherently indigestible elements than anyone else? Hence the very bulk of one of his books is simultaneously one of the most powerful, but also one of the most turgid, most imperfect, and most dross-laden things in all our literature. It is worthy of note that the English, who have never known how to *purify* their drama in the sense that Racine's tragedy is purified, yet achieved at the very outset a much greater purity in the novels of Defoe, Fielding, and even Richardson.

(31–2)

André Gide

'Notes en Manière de Préface' to *Tom Jones*, *c*. 1924 (William B. Coley, 'Gide and Fielding', *Comparative Literature*, vol. II, 1959; extract translated by C. J. Rawson)

He loves only spontaneous virtue; all effort to perfection, if it is not naturally generated by love, is exacted by pride and at the price of making us unnatural. His slender regard for saintliness relates him to Molière. I do not say that either of them was incapable of admiring a saint. But none of their protagonists aspires to become better, to conquer himself, to treat harshly the 'rags' that are his flesh – to self-maceration, in short. The worst lapses of Tom are never followed by remorse or repentance; if he regrets them, it is because they have given pain to Sophia:

> Good-nature is that benevolent and amiable temper of mind,
> which disposes us to feel the misfortunes, and enjoy the
> happiness of others; and, consequently, pushes us on to
> promote the latter, and prevent the former; and that without
> any abstract contemplation on the beauty of virtue, and
> without the allurements or terrors of religion . . .

> For admitting, that laughing at the vices and follies of
> mankind is entirely innocent (which is more, perhaps, than
> we ought to admit), yet, surely, their miseries and misfortunes
> are no subjects of mirth; and with these *Quis non vicus
> abundat*? the world is so full of them, that scarce a day
> passes without inclining a truly good-natured man rather to
> tears than merriment.[1]

The character of Allworthy: some doubts. It is always dangerous for an author to thrust a paragon upon us: Grandison – even Mishkine is almost compromised and all the profound tack of Dostoyevsky was needed to save him. It is in any case noteworthy that Fielding, who dislikes perfect creatures (whether they are perfect in good or in evil), should have blended Allworthy's goodness with some foolishness; in spite of all the theoretical wisdom which is attributed to

1 'Essay on the Characters of Men', *Works*, XIV, pp. 285–6.

Allworthy, he is constantly duped. He tends to believe that others are as good as he is. He cannot protect himself from tricks and calumnies of which he himself is incapable, for we truly understand only those feelings of which we have at least the germ in our own hearts.

Moreover, and especially, Allworthy is a portrait. He had a living model, to whom Fielding meant to pay a debt of gratitude. If Allen, the model, was, as is reported, flattered to recognize himself in the portrait, he was doubtless not as perfect as all that.

Nowadays, knowing too well that the devout man is not always a hypocrite, the portraits of – affect us less.

But isn't it odd that Fielding described only the hypocritically pious, and that true virtue is never in his novels accompanied by piety? (But perhaps I am going a little too far on this point; check very carefully.)

From the very beginning, we see Tom Jones stealing. But he steals for others, not for himself. He gets the reproaches and the beating; the family of his friend the gamekeeper gets the stolen fruit and the duck.

Soon after, we find him lying; but he does this to protect the same gamekeeper and to take sole responsibility for an illegal act which they committed together. Fearing the threatened punishment, Tom has a sleepless night; but we are told at once that he is not afraid of the pain, but of the risk of being unable to endure it and of admitting under the whip the secret which he feels bound in honour and friendship to keep, i.e. the name of his accomplice (who, it is amusingly disclosed, also has a sleepless night, tormented by similar fears, but even more concerned for the boy's honour than for his skin). Tom, however, persists: he 'was contented to be flead rather than betray his friend or break the promise he had made'.

Allworthy, who ordered the whipping, feels that it is in excess of the crime, because, after all, he considers Tom's obstinate silence as merely 'a mistaken point of honour'.

'Honour,' cries X [Thwackum], who is the executioner, 'can honour teach anyone to tell a lie, or can any honour exist independent of religion?' [*Tom Jones*, book 3, chapter 2.]

Fielding lets his reader into secrets about certain characters, asking him on the one hand not to abuse this trust, and warning him on the other that he is:

much deceived, if he imagines, that the most intimate
acquaintance which he himself could have had with that
divine, would have informed him of those things which we,
from our inspiration, are enabled to open and discover. . . .

If the event happened contrary to his expectations, this
possibly proceeded from some fault in the plan itself; which
the reader hath my leave to discover, if he can: for we do
not pretend to introduce any infallible characters into this
history; where we hope nothing will be found which hath
never yet been seen in human nature. . . .
(Book 3, chapter 5)

In reality, tho', she certainly hated her own son; of which,
however monstrous it appears, I am assured she is not a
singular instance. . . .
(Book 3, chapter 6)
(8–10)

André Gide

from *Journal des Faux-Monnayeurs*   14 February 1924
(translated by J. O'Brien)

I find myself again confronted with my *Faux-Monnayeurs*; but this
brief plunge into Fielding [he had been considering writing a preface
to a French translation of *Tom Jones*, and has just decided not to
because the translation sent to him by the publisher turned out to be
poor; see previous extract, eventually published as the Preface to a
translation in 1938] has enlightened me as to the insufficiencies of my
book. I am wondering whether I shouldn't expand the text, intrude
myself (in spite of what Martin du Gard says), make comments. I
have lost touch.
(41–2)

E. M. Forster

from *Aspects of the Novel* 1927

From Chapter 4

May the writer take the reader into his confidence about his characters? Answer has already been indicated: better not. It is dangerous,
it generally leads to a drop in the temperature, to intellectual and
emotional laxity, and worse still to facetiousness, and to a friendly
invitation to see how the figures hook up behind. 'Doesn't A look
nice – she always was my favourite.' 'Let's think of why B does that
– perhaps there's more in him than meets the eye – yes, see – he has a
heart of gold – having given you this peep at it I'll pop it back – I
don't think he's noticed.' 'And C – he always was the mystery man.'
Intimacy is gained but at the expense of illusion and nobility. It is like
standing a man a drink so that he may not criticize your opinions.
With all respect to Fielding and Thackeray it is devastating, it is bar-
parlour chattiness, and nothing has been more harmful to the novels
of the past. To take your reader into your confidence about the
universe is a different thing. It is not dangerous for a novelist to
draw back from his characters, as Hardy and Conrad do, and to
generalize about the conditions under which he thinks life is carried
on. It is confidences about the individual people that do harm, and
beckon the reader away from the people to an examination of the
novelist's mind. Not much is ever found in it at such a moment, for
it is never in the creative state: the mere process of saying 'come
along, let's have a chat' has cooled it down.
(111–12)

From Chapter 6

Among the devices in my list I mentioned 'parody' or 'adaptation'
and would now examine this further. The fantasist here adopts for
his mythology some earlier work and uses it as a framework or
quarry for his own purposes. There is an aborted example of this in
Joseph Andrews. Fielding set out to use *Pamela* as a comic mythology.
He thought it would be fun to invent a brother to Pamela, a pure-

minded footman, who should repulse Lady Booby's attentions just as Pamela repulsed Mr B's, and he made Lady Booby Mr B's aunt. Thus he would be able to laugh at Richardson, and incidentally express his own views of life. Fielding's view of life however was of the sort that only rests content with the creation of solid round characters, and with the growth of Parson Adams and Mrs Slipslop the fantasy ceases, and we get an independent work. *Joseph Andrews* (which is also important historically) is interesting to us as an example of a false start. Its author begins by playing the fool in a Richardsonian world, and ends by being serious in a world of his own – the world of *Tom Jones* and *Amelia*.

(156)

D. H. Lawrence

from *A Propos of Lady Chatterley's Lover*   1930 (Warren Roberts and Harry T. Moore (eds.), *Phoenix II*, 1968)

In the old England, the curious blood-connection held the classes together. The squires might be arrogant, violent, bullying and unjust, yet in some ways they were *at one* with the people, part of the same blood-stream. We feel it in Defoe or Fielding. And then, in the mean Jane Austen, it is gone. Already this old maid typifies 'personality' instead of character, the sharp knowing in apartness instead of knowing in togetherness, and she is, to my feeling, thoroughly unpleasant, English in the bad, mean, snobbish sense of the word, just as Fielding is English in the good, generous sense.

(513)

Ford Madox Ford

from *The English Novel*   1930

It is impossible to absolve such writers as Defoe, Fielding or Thackeray from the charge of deliberately writing with their tongues in their cheeks passages of virtuous aspirations that were in no way any

aspirations of theirs and that in consequence very seriously detracted from the value of their works as art. . . .
(58)

Before . . . considering Diderot, Stendhal, Chateaubriand, and Flaubert, all avowed followers of the author of *Clarissa*, it might be as well to think a little about Fielding – as at once a dreadful example of how not to do things and as the begetter of Thackeray and the product that it is convenient to call the nuvvle as opposed to the novel. . . .

Were it not that they were avowed moralizers of a middle-to-lower-middle-class type, the Fielding-to-Thackeray lineage of writers might also be regarded as purveyors of the Literature of Escape, but their continually brought-in passages of moralizations are such a nuisance that they cannot be ignored. Though they were both amateurs in the sense that neither knew how to write or cared anything about it, Thackeray at times projected his scenes so wonderfully that now and then he trembles dreadfully excitingly on the point of passing from the stage of purveyor of the nuvvle to that of the real novelist. And it is to be said for Fielding that although *Tom Jones* contains an immense amount of rather nauseous special-pleading, the author does pack most of it away into solid wads of hypocrisy at the headings of Parts or Chapters. These can in consequence be skipped and the picaresque story with its mildly salacious details can without difficulty be followed. One might indeed almost say that Fielding was a natural story-teller, whereas Thackeray was none at all. Fielding at least, like a story-teller in a school dormitory, does manage to lose himself in details of people running into and out of each others' bedrooms in hotel corridors at night – something like that. But Thackeray never could: the dread spectre of the Athenaeum Club was for ever in his background . . . .
(76–8)

The trouble with the English nuvvelist from Fielding to Meredith is that not one of them cares whether you quite believe in their characters or not. If you had told Flaubert or Conrad in the midst of their passionate composings that you were not convinced of the reality of Homais or Tuan Jim, as like as not they would have called you out and shot you, and in similar circumstances Richardson would have showed himself extremely disagreeable. But Fielding, Thackeray, or Meredith would have cared relatively little about that, though any one of them would have knocked you down if they could, supposing you had suggested that he was not a 'gentleman'. So would any English novelist today. . . .

The lot of the novelist is, in fact, hard – but not harder than that of any other man. If you put it to bakers, tram-conductors, politicians, or musicians that they must be first bakers and the rest and then gentlemen, they will sigh, but admit it. It is almost only the English novelist who will aspire at being first gentleman and then craftsman – or even not craftsman at all since it is not really gentlemanly to think of being anything but a gentleman.

This is an incisive way of putting a truth that might perhaps be more wrapped up in social or material generalizations, but it is none the less a hard truth, and if you consider the case of Fielding, connected with the best families, placeman and diplomatist in a small way, and compare him with Smollett who was, socially nothing at all with no chance of a change, you will see that truth all the more clearly.

God forbid that I should say anything really condemnatory of any book by any brother-novelist, alive or dead. One is here to commend all that one can commend and to leave the rest alone. But there are few books that I more cordially dislike than *Tom Jones*. That is no critical pronouncement but merely a statement of a personal prejudice: one may dislike grape-fruit and yet acknowledge its admirable qualities, or one may, as I do, dislike the quality of goose-flesh that reading Mr George Moore will confer on one's skin and yet acknowledge Mr Moore as easily the greatest of living technicians.

But as regards *Tom Jones* my personal dislike goes along with a certain cold-blooded, critical condemnation. I dislike Tom Jones, the character, because he is a lewd, stupid, and treacherous phenomenon; I dislike Fielding, his chronicler, because he is a bad sort of hypocrite. Had Fielding been in the least genuine in his moral aspirations it is Blifil that he would have painted attractively and Jones who would have come to the electric chair, as would have been the case had Jones lived today.

Of course that is merely saying that Fielding liked a type that I dislike – but what appalls me in view of the serious, cynical foreigner that I have postulated our taking about with us is the extremely thin nature of all the character-drawing, of all the events and of all the catastrophes. Is it to be seriously believed that Tom Jones's bene-factor would have turned upon him on the flimsy nature of the evidence adduced against him, or, equally, is it to be believed that Tom Jones's young woman would have again taken up with him after all the eye-openers she had had, she being represented as a girl of spirit? It simply isn't in any world of any seriousness at all. The fact, in short, is that Tom Jones is a papier-mâché figure, the catas-trophes the merest invention without any pretence at being con-vincing, and even the mere morality of the most leering and disastrous kind.

For myself, I am no moralist: I consider that if you do what you want you must take what you get for it and that if you deny yourself things you will be better off than if you don't. But fellows like Fielding, and to some extent Thackeray, who pretend that if you are a gay drunkard, lecher, squanderer of your goods and fumbler in placket-holes you will eventually find a benevolent uncle, concealed father or benefactor who will shower on you bags of tens of thousands of guineas, estates and the hands of adorable mistresses – those fellows are dangers to the body politic and horribly bad constructors of plots.

It is all very well to say that such happy endings were the conven-tion of the day.... But the really great writer is not bound by the conventions of his day, nor, if he desires to give his reader a happy ending, need he select a wastrel like Jones as the recipient of his too easily bestowed favours.

If, in short, we are to regard Fielding as a serious writer writing for grown-up people, we must regard him also as a rather intolerable scoundrel with perhaps *Jonathan Wild* to his credit. But *Jonathan Wild* is of another category and, neither winking nor leering, might be regarded as the finger on the wall, pointing out what happens to the Tom Joneses of the world if their case is regarded with any seriousness.

But the fact is that for a century and a half after the death of Field-ing nothing in the Anglo-Saxon world was further from anyone, either novelist or layman, than the idea that the novel could be taken seriously....

(89–94)

It would ... undoubtedly be absurd to suggest to the public that Smollett was a greater artist or a greater novelist than either Fielding or Dickens: and yet, if the novel is to be regarded as a rendering of life, there is not much way out of it.
(98–9)

George Lukács

from 'Tolstoy and the Development of Realism'   1936
(Edith Bone (trans.), *Studies in European Realism*, 1950)

The world depicted by Tolstoy is a world much less *bourgeois* than the world of the eighteenth-century English novelists, but – especially in *Anna Karenina* – it is a world in which the process of capitalist development is more strongly apparent than in the English novels which nearly always depict only one particular phase of it. In addition, the great English novelists of the eighteenth century lived in a *post-revolutionary* period, and this gave their works (especially those of Goldsmith and Fielding) an atmosphere of stability and security and also a certain complacent shortsightedness.
(149–50)

George Lukács

from *The Historical Novel*   1937 (Hannah and Stanley Mitchell (trans.), 1969)

From Chapter I

... Even the great realistic social novel of the eighteenth century, which in its portrayal of contemporary morals and psychology accomplished a revolutionary breakthrough to reality for world literature, is not concerned to show its characters as belonging to any concrete time. The contemporary world is portrayed with unusual plasticity and truth-to-life, but is accepted naïvely as something given: whence and how it has developed have not yet become problems for the writer. This abstractness in the portrayal of historical time also affects the portrayal of historical place. Thus Lesage is able to transfer his highly truthful pictures of the France of his day to Spain and still feel quite at ease. Similarly, Swift, Voltaire and even Diderot set their satirical novels in a 'never and nowhere' which nevertheless faithfully reflects the essential characteristics of contemporary England and France. These writers, then, grasp the salient features of their world with a bold and penetrating realism. But they do not see the specific qualities of their own age historically.

This basic attitude remains essentially unchanged despite the fact that realism continues to bring out the specific features of the present with ever greater artistic power. Think of novels like *Moll Flanders*, *Tom Jones*, etc. Their broad, realistic portrayal of the present takes in here and there important events of contemporary history which it links with the fortunes of the characters. In this way, particularly in Smollett and Fielding, time and place of action acquire much greater concreteness than was customary in the earlier period of the social novel or in most contemporary French writing. Fielding indeed is to some extent aware of this development, this increasing concreteness of the novel in its grasp of the historical peculiarity of characters and events. His definition of himself as a writer is that of an historian of bourgeois society.

(15–16)

Scott's artistic faithfulness to history is an extension and application to history of the creative principles of the great English realist writers of the eighteenth century. And not only in the sense of a broadening of theme, an assimilation of historical material to the great tradition of realism, but in the sense of portraying men and events historically. What, for instance, was only latent in Fielding, becomes with Scott the driving spirit of literary portrayal. Scott's 'necessary anachronism' consists, therefore, simply in allowing his characters to express feelings and thoughts about real, historical relationships in a much clearer way than the actual men and women of the time could have done. But the content of these feelings and thoughts, their relation to their real object, is always historically and socially correct.

(69)

From Chapter 2

The new relationship between individual and society, between individual and class, creates a new situation for the modern novel. It is only very conditionally and in special cases that individual action has a direct and social aim. Indeed, as the novel develops, more and more important works arise which neither have nor can have any concrete aim at all. This is true already of *Don Quixote* where the hero's aim is not more than a general one to revive chivalry and seek adventure. But this cannot possibly be called an aim in the same sense as Odysseus' intention to return home. It is the same with important novels like *Tom Jones*, *Wilhelm Meister*, etc. In *Wilhelm Meister*, indeed, the peculiarity of the new novel is clearly stated in the conclusion: the hero realizes that he has achieved something quite different from what he set out to achieve on his wanderings.
(174)

From Chapter 4

When Marx says that the economic categories are 'forms of existence, determinants of existence', he is not only defining the material character of economic categories philosophically; he is also providing a key to the literary portrayal of economic determination. That is, the economic categories must not be seen fetishistically as abstractions – as in the vulgar economics of the bourgeoisie or in Menshevism and vulgar sociology – but as immediate forms of existence of human life, forms in which the metabolism of every individual person with nature and society takes place.

And to observe this concretely, as a writer, one does not need to be a Marxist. Defoe or Fielding, Scott or Cooper, Balzac or Tolstoy in most cases grasped this living side of economy correctly and deeply. And this portrayal of the basis of life could produce extraordinarily accurate and profound pictures of society, even when the writers concerned drew economic conclusions which were entirely false. This falseness remained as it were (in the case of Balzac or Tolstoy) the private falseness of the writer, a false commentary upon a picture of life in which the real interaction between the economic and spiritual-moral life of men has been correctly portrayed and corresponds with objective truth.

But for this the writer must have deep ties with popular life in its most varied ramifications, with the real life of all classes in society. And should the correct observations then give birth to false theories artistic truth is not likely to be endangered. The reverse position is well-nigh impossible: that is, to penetrate to the concrete problems of popular life from the standpoint of abstract, though correct, economic truths. (354–5)

André Gide

from 'Travels in English Literature' 1938 (Dorothy Bussy (trans.), *Verve*, Spring 1938)

Carried away by my admiration of *Tom Jones*, I set to work to read Fielding's other works, and could not, I confess, take much pleasure in them. The interest of *Amelia* seemed to flag. I liked *Jonathan Wild* without being altogether enraptured. The *Voyage to Lisbon* disappointed me. In his *Joseph Andrews* Fielding seems to me greatly inferior to Richardson whom he parodies; but I cannot really judge of this book as I gave it up after the first quarter (whereas I read to the end and without skipping a word the five volumes of *Clarissa Harlowe*) and I have been told that *Joseph Andrews* improves as it goes on. As for *Tom Jones*, I consider it a masterpiece. At times Fielding, by his power of simplification and what Nietzsche calls 'the erosion of contours', takes his place beside Molière. What sureness of touch! What health! What delightful gaiety! A little heavy, it is true, but with a foot so firmly planted on the soil! Not the amused dancing of wit but real solid intelligence. I once made some notes in view of a Preface to *Tom Jones* which Dent asked me to write for a new translation he was proposing to publish. The scheme fell through, however, because I was not satisfied with the translation. But I shall bring out these notes later on [see above, p. 343]. They put forward a number of psychological truths on which my heart is set and which are not generally recognized. I was glad to rediscover them in Fielding.

When I read *Clarissa Harlowe* later on, how much astonished I was by the antagonistic position which contemporary criticism assigned to these two rival novelists – Fielding representing realism and Richardson idealism. This is really too much of a misconception and the religious point of view has distorted the whole question. Fielding is anti-religious, but Richardson, though religious, or appearing to be so, is far more of a realist than he. His case is perhaps unique in literature; amongst great writers there is not one whose work was more applauded when it first appeared (1748) and who is less read today; nor one who, himself neglected, has left more illustrious descendants. (15)

Ford Madox Ford

from *The March of Literature* 1938 (first English edition, 1939)

The extremely tiring harangues ... of Alemán's *Guzman d'Alfarache* ... are only paralleled in nauseous prurience and hypocrisy by the introductions to chapters of Fielding's *Tom Jones*. Fielding, indeed, would appear to have been almost more than Defoe, Alemán's direct successor, though he did not flourish until a hundred and fifty years after Alemán's death.... It was not until nearly a hundred years after the death of Fielding that with *Madame Bovary* the novel really appeared as a complete work of art, having at once *progression d'effet*, *charpente*, *façade*, *cadences*, *mots justes* – and all the other accoutrements and attributes of a work of art in its glory, for which the English language has no name. Till then the novel had to be content to be the patient Cinderella of all the seven arts....

It will be observed that all these narrations [Spanish picaresque tales] are set down in the spirit of complete and remorseless observation of effects and cause. The rogue is neither sentimentalized over as in the case of *Tom Jones* – which has always seemed to the writer to be one of the most immoral books ever written – or glorified as is the case with the toughs and gangsters of today's Anglo-Saxon novel. No, the *picaro* is a poor creature gifted with certain mean shortnesses and a metropolitan courage in facing adversities brought about by scoundrelism. He is the son of a man born to be hanged and he himself is predestined to the same fate. So that you have in these works

enjoined upon you the great truth today too much obscured that the fox may run but he's caught at last.
(497-8)

It is impossible that the gorge should not rise at the mere wrongness of the vital outlooks of a Fielding or a Sterne. Who, indeed, would not be concerned if he thought the views of the values of life of the young person of today and tomorrow or the morals of any spiritual pastor of a flock should anywhere or at any time be guided by that police magistrate or that dissolute, brandified and atheistic parson? It is obviously not our province here to be moralists. But the high mission of the novelist and the high function of the novel in the republic is so to draw life that from their pages the public may learn at least that life is first of all governed by cause and effect – that if you are lousy, and I use the word on purpose, you will live like a louse and, if there is a hell, go to hell. And what other word could describe Tom Jones – the miserable parasite who was forever wreathed, whining about his benefactor's knees, whose one idea of supporting himself was to borrow money simultaneously from his heart's adored and two mistresses, and who was such a miserable hero of romance that in a duelling age he could not even handle a rapier? ... For – and this is what is so lamentably puzzling – if you will read the best and most benevolent of the orthodox critics on the subject of those lamentable productions, you will find them bursting into paeans of lachrymose praise. This is a queer instance of obscured moralizing that follows. Some years ago this writer wrote a little history of the English novel in which in the course of a much milder scarification of Fielding than what is above written he had occasion to quote a late librarian of the House of Lords and great official Anglo-Saxon accepted critic as saying that *Tom Jones* came into the stuffy scene of ordinary life like the pure breath of a May morning! And for this, if you please, this writer was stigmatized as 'vitriolic' – nothing less! – by (and that is what is extraordinary!) the chief Roman Catholic organ of the United States.... So hard will *l'homme moyen sensuel* fight for his right to his *menus plaisirs*....
(572-3)

This *charpente*, this *progression d'effet* and certainly that kind of *coup de canon* are lamentably absent from the novels of Defoe, Fielding and

Smollett. But Richardson, having always at the back of his mind the happy ending of *Pamela* and the tragedy of *Clarissa* – and having as novelist a genius and common sense all his own – certainly got into his work at least such a cumulation of effect that as – in serial form – *Clarissa* neared her end he set all Europe screaming with apprehension. But his genius was very special. He stands, as it were, apart with Jane Austen and Trollope; and the influence of the happy ending on the novel form showed itself only very gradually. . . .

Mr Austin Dobson in one of his unbuttoned moments commits himself to the dictum that *Tom Jones* has been the model of all *manly* British fiction since his day. But it is difficult to think of any writers later than Thackeray who can have been much under the influence of Fielding. And it is at once the glory and the bane of Thackeray that for a considerable portion of his career he played the sedulous ape to the author of *Amelia*. But it is pretty safe to advance that during the lives and after the deaths of those two writers – during, that is to say, the whole of the first half century of the reign of Victoria – the British novel took to itself a sort of stereotyped but loose form in which, on its way to the wedding bells, the novelist dropped his moralizing and his digressions occasionally, and gave some attention to shoving his story forward. To that we must return. . . .

It is remarkable how one-voiced all these novelists are in taking that line [i.e. that they are moralists] about their productions. . . . Fielding in perhaps the most sober paragraph that he ever wrote – the beginning of the Dedication of *Amelia* – states succinctly that:

The following book is sincerely designed to promote the cause of virtue and to expose some of the most glaring evils, as well public as private, which at present infect the country.

Tom Jones, on the other hand, makes in its Preface no claim at all to moralizing aims. On the contrary, the author announces that all his skill has been devoted in this book to delighting the reader – as if he had been at a banquet. As thus, in a paragraph that gives much more the quality of Fielding's prose than the one quoted above:

The excellence of the entertainment consists less in the subject than in the author's skill in well dressing it up. How

pleased, therefore, will the reader be to find that we have, in
the following work, adhered closely to one of the highest
principles of the best cook which the present age, or perhaps
that of Heliogabalus, hath produced. This great man, as is
well known to all polite lovers of eating, begins at first by
setting plain things before his hungry guests, rising afterwards
by degrees as their stomachs may be supposed to decrease,
to the very quintessence of sauce and spices. In like manner,
we shall represent human nature at first to the keen appetite
of our reader, in that more plain and simple manner in
which it is found in the country, and shall hereafter hash and
ragout it with all the high French and Italian seasoning of
affectation and vice which courts and cities afford. By these
means, we doubt not but our reader may be rendered desirous
to read on forever, as the great person just mentioned is
supposed to have made some persons eat.

From that one might deduce that Fielding not only paid attention to
his technique but actually had the ambition to produce in his work
a cumulative effect. That is true enough, but the technique to which
he paid attention was that of eighteenth-century wit and the cumulative effect he sought after was that of introducing his shapely person,
with whisking skirts and whirling, clouded cane, more and more
prominently on to the stage of his novel. Until there should be no
soul in the audience that should not cry: 'A damned clever fellow,
this author,' with all the ladies inscribing as fast as they may his *bons
mots* on their tablets.

From the earliest days, as we have remarked in one of our earlier
chapters, two schools of writers in successive periods have flourished
and given way, the one before the other. There are those who seek
by every hypnotizing device known to them to snatch their readers
from earth into the ambience of their rendering of stories or affairs . . .
and then those who by every trick of verbal juggling and mental
smart-aleckery seek to delight their readers, not caring at all whether
their tales or poems convince or carry away. At times they will interrupt their tale-telling for, as it were, weeks, and wander off into hun-
dreds of miles of digression and into not so much sub-plot but a perfectly different story from the one on which they begin and end.

Each school finds for a period its public, the public of the jugglers being as a rule aristocratic, that of the engrossed tale tellers being more plebeian or more all-embracing. As witness the age of the troubadours when the knights and ladies took delight in metrical felicities, the groundlings finding hypnotic escape from their surroundings in the illusions of the primitive *conte-fable* of the market place. . . . Or the matter may be more comprehensibly put by a speech addressed to the present writer early in this century by a young lion then expecting to supersede him in the public favor. Said he:

Old fogeys like you and Conrad and Henry James go to
unending troubles to kid the public into the idea that you
provide them with vicarious experience. You efface
yourselves like ostriches, never let yourselves appear through
a whole long, blessed story, go to enormous trouble to get
in atmospheres, to invent plausible narrators – old colonels,
ships' captains, priests, surgeons – what do I know all . . .
oh, yes, 'above all to make you *see*'. . . . But that sort of
stuff will never succeed. It isn't what the public wants.
What the public wants is to see monstrous clever fellows –
[and here he slapped himself on the cheek] – monstrous
clever fellows like *me*. . . . Handsome, elegant figures,
striding, posturing, pirouetting, moustache-twisting, cane-
twirling, gold-ball juggling, tight-rope dancing trapezists. . . .
You're all done with, I tell you. To me the far-flung future. . . .

Well, Fielding might have said as much to Defoe and Richardson . . . even to Smollett.

But, to certain minds, writing like that of *Tom Jones* is teasing and worrying in the extreme. Even in the relatively sober *Amelia*, over which Fielding must have taken much more pains, the note of fussing over the narrative as a hen fusses over her chicks is almost insupportable. It is a good story. Critics of the older fashion would have called it 'spirited'; but we may seem to trace in it a certain anxiousness . . . perhaps a certain fatigue caused by his duties as a magistrate and the earlier stages of the long illness that three years after was to finish his career. Or we may well imagine that his duties as a police magistrate may have added to his views of the values of life a certain ballast of seriousness. It was not for nothing that *Tom Jones* was published and its author appointed a justice of the peace for Westminster in the same year – 1748.

At any rate, *Amelia* contains a good story. One is anxious to know what will become of Captain Booth, who is a poor sort of a hero, and still more anxious about Amelia, who is almost the perfect wife for a hero who was rather a poor sort of man. In fact, compared with the rather tinny note of heartlessness of *Tom Jones*, the note of *Amelia* is one of compassion and concern for poor humanity ... and we know that as a magistrate in a horrible epoch Fielding showed himself very conscientious, a quality that in a magistrate calls most of all for compassion and concern. But even at that, *Amelia* is – not so much ruined – as turned into a sort of unceasing obstacle race by the continual intrusions of Mr Fielding. Reading it for the story, one is perpetually forced to run around or jump over interminable pages of digressions – digressions for the interminable biographies of newly introduced characters, for the display of Fielding's knowledge of the criminal heart, of law, of divinity, of classical scholarship. And what is more trying still, be you the most skilled skipper in the world, Mr Fielding will foil you – and that more in *Amelia* than in any of his other works. For *Amelia*, being a good story, one is anxious not to miss any detail of the unwinding of the tale. But Fielding will sandwich three lines indispensable to the comprehension of that story between two passages, each ten pages long, of theological discussions between the book's chief benefactor and a young Anglican seminarist. And that is a serious defect. You are, for instance, for quite a long time left under the impression that the matchless Amelia is a shade insensitive, so little emotion does she show at the revelation of her Mr Booth's infidelity with Miss Matthews. And then, casting back a hundred and twenty pages, you discover, between two tirades of classical erudition by Mrs Atkinson, that she has already had the news of that infidelity in a blackmailing letter from Miss Matthews some weeks before, so that she has had time to get used to the fact. ... A serious defect.

Fielding, indeed, tries that trick at the very beginning of the book. After his first chapter called 'Exordium', in which Fielding displays himself as something less man-of-the-worldish and more serious than the author of *Tom Jones*, he sets, with spirit, out upon his story. As, thus, in the first paragraph of chapter two:

On the first of April in the year – the watchmen of a certain parish (I know not particularly which) within the liberty of Westminster brought several persons whom they had apprehended the preceding night before Jonathan Thrasher Esq., one of the justices of the peace for that liberty.

And you will observe that Fielding has not gone fifteen words of his journey before the necessity to introduce himself into it becomes overwhelming. He *has* to inform the reader, that, as author, Mr Fielding does not 'particularly' know in what parish his Mr B oth was arrested. That is a kind of insouciance that may show the reader that Mr Fielding was too much of a great gentleman to bother about details. An author ought to be omniscient as far as his tale is concerned or he has no right to write his tale. And it is an untruth too because Fielding *must* have known in what parish his Mr Booth was arrested . . . or he cannot have read his own book. For the reader will observe that Mr Booth, as an insolvent debtor, had taken lodgings in the 'verges' – the sanctuary of Westminster Abbey, which was then included in the parish of St Margaret's Westminster. And Mr Fielding is careful afterwards to inform us that Mr Booth had not ventured outside the verges for fear of arrest for debt. . . . Nor is that sufficient.

Having got in his five lines of the tale you would think that Fielding would have gone on with it for a page or two. Not a bit of it. In the very next paragraph after the words 'of the peace for that liberty' he has to begin:

But here, reader, before we proceed to the trials of these offenders, we shall, after our usual manner, premise some things which it may be necessary for thee to know.

It hath been observed, I think, by many, as well as the celebrated writer of three letters, that no human institution is capable of consummate perfection. An observation which perhaps that writer at least gathered from discovering some defects in the polity even of this well-regulated nation. And indeed if there should be any such defect in a constitution

which my Lord Coke long ago told us 'the wisdom of all
the wise men in the world, if they had all met together at
one time, could not have equalled . . .'. [And so on
interminably.]

These are serious mismanagements in a story teller and we will
reconsider them in a minute or two because they are all the more
serious in that in *Amelia* Fielding shows that he really was a story
teller of some skill and more genius. In the case of *Tom Jones*, the
story is so negligible and the incidents are invented with such list-
lessness that we have to regard the tale as a mere string on which are
threaded the pearls of Mr Fielding's – cousin to the Right Honorable
the Earl of Denbigh – Mr Fielding, the man about town's, wit. As
such, for people who like the sort of thing, *Tom Jones* may well pass
as a masterpiece – perhaps only of the second rank, this being an
order of criticism of which we have little the habit. It is then less
ebullient than Rabelais, less obscenely divergent than *Tristram
Shandy*, less lewd in cruelty than the *Sentimental Journey*, less humane
than *Don Quixote*, less ferociously realist than the *Satyricon*, which in
its determination to 'make you see' gives you a night in the streets
of Rome that once read can never fade from the memory . . . and it
is less profuse in moralizations than Fielding's own *Amelia*.

It is, in its own form, a neatly performed job. It begins with a
chapter 1 which, being headed 'The introduction to the work or a
bill of fare to the feast', warns the reader at once that the story as such
is not to hypnotize him with its reality. For no author with a real
passion for his coming projection will begin his novel with an
exordium calling attention to the artificiality of his convention any
more than any author with any passion for what he has projected
will end up his novel with snufflingly calling attention to the fact that
the tale is only a tale. Consider, in this respect, Thackeray; how,
directly imitating Fielding, he ruins whole books of his by their
introductions or their last paragraphs – those last paragraphs in which
the real novelist strains every nerve to add reality to his closing so
that the reader, rising from the book in the actual atmosphere of a
West Chester library, goes about for an hour or so still beneath the
palms of Malaysia or the lower reaches of the Thames. But what must
Mr Thackeray do but begin or end up his books with paragraphs

running: 'Reader, the puppet play is ended; let down the curtain; put the puppets back into their boxes, sweep up the programmes and orange peels from the sawdust.' . . . and the whole effect of the long book is dispelled. . . . But the truth is that both Thackeray all his life and Fielding in *Tom Jones* were intent first of all on impressing on their readers that they were not real novelists . . . but gentlemen.

It is curious to consider how the mind when thinking on *Tom Jones* considers it as a wilderness of interpolations. Yet actually it is a matter of a hundred and six closely printed pages before Fielding interrupts his story for the first time. And when he does so he indicates plainly enough that it is only through sheer incapacity to carry on his story as a story . . . or out of a fear that the moral of that story has not made itself plain. He commits himself, therefore, suddenly to a number of platitudinous statements to the effect that: 'Prudence and circumspection are necessary to the best of men', and the like, and then makes the avowal of want of skill thus:

I ask pardon for this short appearance, by way of chorus, on the stage. It is in reality for my own sake, that, while I am discovering the rocks on which innocence and goodness often split, I may not be misunderstood to recommend the very means to my worthy readers, by which I intend to show them they will be undone. And thus, as I could not prevail on any of my actors to speak, I was obliged to declare myself.

Fielding, in fact, had intended to make his *Joseph Andrews* a mere parody of Richardson's *Pamela* and then afterwards, finding that the story was going very well, turned the rest of the book into a straight and spirited narration. In the same way he had intended to make of *Tom Jones* a straight and spirited narration until he found that he could not swing it and, against his will, introduced himself into his own pages. A man of common sense and of great reading from Cicero to Le Sage, he probably felt that the introduction of himself spoiled, to some extent, the reader's illusion. Or, perhaps, it was merely that he knew that moralizing was not to the taste of *l'homme moyen sensuel* to whom principally he addressed himself. But having tried it in the passage we have just read, he must have found that he could compound a brand of moralizing such that neither the man of the world, of the town, nor yet of the street would by it be incommoded to the extent of cutting down his *menus plaisirs* – his lecheries, bibulousnesses, amorous deceits, borrowing from mistresses and all the manly exercises that rendered tolerable the lives of gentry of his kidney. And having satisfied himself that his self-introduction would give no offence, from that moment onwards Fielding gave himself *carte blanche* and pirouetted and winked across his pages whenever – and that was often enough – the mood occurred to him.

Nor is it to be said that these digressions in themselves make disagreeable reading. Such a passage as what follows is sprightly and pleasant and well-calculated to prove that Fielding as writer was a monstrous clever prestidigitator. And one would be curmudgeonly, indeed, if one grudged as much to the clever and full-blooded. It is merely that – as Mr Stalin lately remarked of Mr Trotsky – his practices were not in themselves wrong save in that they were untimely. In any other form but that of the novel this passage would make agreeable reading, but coming as it does at the very crisis of one of the only two at all excitingly rendered passages in the book it is *per se* simply disastrous:

As in the season of *rutting*, an uncouth phrase by which *the vulgar denote* that *gentle dalliance*, which in the well-wooded forest of Hampshire, passes between lovers of the *ferine kind*, if, while *the lofty-crested stag* meditates the *amorous sport*, a couple of puppies, or any other beasts of hostile note, should wander so near the temple of Venus Ferina that the *fair hind* should shrink from the place, touched with that somewhat, either of fear or frolic, of nicety or skittishness, with which *nature hath bedecked all females*, or hath at least instructed them how to put it on; lest, through the *indelicacy of males*, the *Samean mysteries* should be pryed into by *unhallowed eyes*: for, at the *celebration of these rites*, the female priestess cries out with her in Virgil (who was then, probably, hard at work on such a celebration) –

Procul, o procul este, profani,
Proclamat vates, totoque absistite loco.

Far hence be souls profane,
The sibyl cry'd, and from the grove abstain. (Dryden)

(The words italicized above are not so italicized in the original.)[1]

This sort of thing continues for some time more and then Mr Fielding remembers his story and, thus, continues it:

Thus, and more terrible, when he perceived the enemy's approach, leaped forth our hero. Many a step advanced he forwards, in order to conceal the *trembling hind*, and, if possible, to *secure her retreat*. And now Thwackum, having first *darted some livid lightning* from his *fiery eyes*, began to thunder forth, 'Fie upon it! Fie upon it! Mr Jones. Is it possible you should be the person?' – 'You see,' answered Jones, 'it is possible I should be here.'

It must, in short, be apparent to the most unpracticed reader that this adventure of Mr Jones made a lively scene and that, by cutting it up in the middle, Fielding effectually scotched it.

Let us then quote the end of the book.

To conclude, as there are not to be found a worthier man and woman, than this *fond couple*, so neither can any be imagined more happy. They preserve the *purest and tenderest affection* for each other, an affection daily increased and confirmed by *mutual endearments* and *mutual esteem*. Nor is their conduct towards their relations and friends less amiable than towards one another. And such is their condescension, their indulgence, and their beneficence to those below them, that there is not a neighbour, a tenant, or a servant, who doth not most gratefully bless the day when Mr Jones was married to his Sophia.

It is a mere statement of facts and as such carries relatively little or no conviction. Had Mr Fielding done, as many of his successors had the skill to do – namely, put in a little picture of children and New-foundland dogs tumbling together on a lawn he would have done much more to assure us that his Sophia really did achieve a measure of wedded bliss. Or had he done as Smollett did in ending his *Roderick Random* – pictured the wedding night lusciously and then almost as lusciously the nature of the 'settlements'; or had he, as he

1 Ford's comment [ed.].

himself subsequently did in *Amelia* – a book that grows and grows on one the more one reads *Tom Jones* – had he rendered the desperate, bitter straits to which poverty can reduce even heroines... had he, that is to say, showed us Sophia forced to such expedients as poor Amelia in whom mortification was added to the disaster of the theft when she found that the underclothing that had cost her thirty shillings was sold by the thief for a mere five ... why, then, we might believe that the subsequent settlements might have brought her not merely contentment but a measure of soft bliss ... in a really happy ending.

But that paragraph carries neither picture nor conviction. We gather from it no belief at all that merely by listening to the pious conversation of Mr Allworthy – of which in his unredeemed condition he must already have had enough and to spare – that merely by that listening he would be converted from a rather crawling rake to a finely erect specimen of *homo sapiens Europaeus* ... and 'the best of husbands'. We *know* that Jones, driven to desperation by the conventional periods of his uncle and benefactor, must one day seize his hat, rush out of the house, and so betake himself to the house of some Miss Matthews or other. Indeed, if we imagine that in writing the adventures of Mr Booth of *Amelia* Fielding was merely continuing the post-marital career of Tom Jones we need not be too cynically in the wrong. Obviously marital bliss is possible to the wives of the worst of rakes and to the rakes themselves. But to convince us that that is the lot of one or other of his characters the writer must take much more trouble ... and write much better.
(580–91)

From Chapter 7

On top of the complete materialism and sentimentality that overwhelmed Anglo-Saxondom with the coming of the Hanoverian kings, two other changes contributed to giving both English prose and verse a very altered character. In the first place the Georges imported professional musicians from Germany so that native music died. Secondly, the unit of English prose and thought became not the word but the phrase. This has had a very serious and very disastrous effect upon English prose. It operated in the first place towards loose expression of thought and in the second place towards the almost necessitated use of the cliché phrase. It is necessitated because if a man's vocabulary is small and he employs his words in groups of three or four, the number of expressions at his disposal will be proportionately limited and in consequence he will have to use – and all his fellows around him will have to use – the same phrase so often that it will finally become nauseating or ridiculous. The tendency began at the beginning of the Elizabethan period with poets like Spenser and the numerous sonneteers. Their inspiration was exclusively from books. Their language had no connection with the Franco-Teutonic common speech but was founded on a non-comprehension of the spirit of the robust tongue of the Romans. Their habitations were ivory towers. They were the first men of letters and turned their backs on life. Their line ran from Spenser through Milton and Dryden to culminate in Pope and to continue in the crowd of hack verse writers of the eighteenth century. The Elizabethan dramatists, the metaphysical poets and the great prose writers lived full lives and wrote much as they spoke. The change as far as prose was concerned came with Fielding's catering to the taste of the wits of his day.

If you will give yourself the trouble to examine the passages from Fielding that we have lately quoted you will notice, being helped by the italicized phrases, the great number of ready-made groups of words that he uses. Yet the prose of *Tom Jones* is rather good prose for the eighteenth century. But only compare it with the passage from the *Compleat Angler* quoted previously [not reproduced here] in which microscopic scrutiny will not discover one single cliché phrase unless it be 'tempestuous seas'. And Walton may well have been the first to use that conjunction of words. You will then well see how one passage of prose may be artificial, pompous, unduly grandiose and ordinary. That will be because of its writer's use of linked words that have already over again been linked. But another passage of prose will have, indeed, the sparkle of dewdrops on a May morning, simply because its author sought for the simplest words and the most frugally exact adjectives and similes, having the exact eye and the passion above all to make you see. When, in short, you read Fielding – as when you read Virgil – it is as if you looked at an admirable but conventionalized tapestry. But when you read Walton you are sitting beside that author in the shade of a tree and all the landscape is plain before you. That is the difference between great artistry and even the most consummate virtuosity. . . .

You have to think of an intelligent, sophisticated and, perhaps, somewhat cynical foreigner and consider which of your national novels you would with confidence present to him. For, however little of a jingo one may be, it must be disagreeable to one to see the *rictus* of sardonic derision spread over a foreigner's face as he peruses one of one's treasured home-baked products. Of this one need have no fear in the case of Richardson and James, and, indeed, of Jane Austen, Smollett, Trollope and the book of Mrs Gaskell. . . . And possibly also of Fielding. . . . Possibly also of Joseph Conrad. At any rate, they all wrote of topics fit for the attention of grown-up men with a skill sufficient not to disgust the reasonably lettered adult. That is as much as one can ask.

(592–5)

Barry Lyndon . . . published in 1844, is a direct pastiche after the manner of Fielding's *Jonathan Wild*, and, since Thackeray was infinitely the more skillful of the two, it is a work much more sinister.

(812)

The superior intelligences of the day do not usually – and they are quite wrong – apply themselves to the mystery story. Yet the great novels of the world, whether of the romantic, the classical or the realistic modern schools, have all – and this is no paradox – been mystery stories. *Vanity Fair* is a mystery story, worked from the inside instead of from the out. So is *Madame Bovary*; so is Conrad's *The Secret Agent*; so, for the matter of that, is *Tom Jones* with its working up to the triumphant exposure of young Mr Blifil; so is *The Vicar of Wakefield*; so, substituting psychological for material values, is almost every novel of Henry James.

(832)

Part Three Modern Views

Introduction

In the last fifty years, and more especially since the last war,
Fielding, like other authors, has been taken over by the academics.
The bulk of critical writing, good and bad, now comes from the
universities, and this section reflects the change. The exceptions
are few: Orwell, Amis, Rebecca West. Of these, Orwell and Amis
provide brief incidental passages rather than sustained studies;
Amis was, at the time, a nniversity teacher anyway; and Rebecca
West's essay was part of a series of lectures delivered at Yale.
Among a few significant non-academic discussions not reprinted
here the best is Middleton Murry's fine essay in *Unprofessional
Essays* (1956).

There has been both loss and gain. One regrets the thinning out
of a strong earlier tradition of informal but often deeply engaged
comment by working novelists (and it seems that most English
novelists of distinction felt the need to think and talk about
Fielding and to clarify for themselves their attitude to him). One
misses also the very high standards of reviewing and essay-
writing by non-academic men of letters, writing to an informed
but not yet mainly *specialist* audience: Hazlitt, G. H. Lewes,
Bagehot, Chesterton.

But the gains have been real also. Knowledge has increased.
Earlier work on the biography has been supplemented. Many
things are now known, or more exactly and clearly understood
than before, about the text and the canon of Fielding, about the
literary and political background to his works, about his theatrical
career and the theatre of his day, about his religious and
philosophical views and his political alignments, and about many
of the contemporaries, friendly or unfriendly, with whom he
came into contact (most recently, for example, major biographies of
Hogarth and of Richardson have appeared). The factual
investigations of scholars like Battestin, Coley, Miller and others
are outside the immediate scope of a critical anthology of this
sort, although it has to be said that the scholars I have named have

all produced interpretative work of great distinction, and that
Henry Knight Miller's *Essays on Fielding's Miscellanies*: *A
Commentary on Volume One* (1961), despite the apparent narrowness
of its topic, is in fact an invaluable and very central guide to many
important aspects of Fielding studies. These scholars are also
engaged in the great Wesleyan edition of Fielding's *Works*, of
which two volumes have already appeared, and whose texts and
commentaries will bring together, and into live relation with
Fielding's writings themselves, the results of researches in many
fields.

Such a collaborative enterprise is one of the benefits of the
professionalizing of literary study and scholarship. There is also
greater communication among researchers, and among the
universities and other learned societies to which they belong. This
has made it easier to identify areas of incomplete knowledge or
of particular interest, and to plan research more systematically and
with less danger of wasteful repetition or overlap. Many things
are as a result more precisely understood. It has, for example,
always been known that there were important affinities between
the work of Hogarth and Fielding, as well as a personal friendship
between them. But the detailed exactitude with which the question
is presented in Paulson's recent life of Hogarth is at least in part
the product of several scholarly discussions since the last war, in
a book by R. E. Moore,[1] in various learned articles, and in some
separate studies of both Hogarth and Fielding.

One of the disadvantages of scholarly specialization, however,
has been a partial loss of the broader perspectives of the cultivated
amateur. Students engaged in a specific investigation into Fielding
often showed little awareness of major figures on Fielding's
immediate periphery. An earlier, less professional critic would be
likely to possess, and to assume in his readers, a general

1 R. E. Moore, *Hogarth's Literary Relationships*, University of Minnesota Press,
1948.

acquaintance with Hogarth (or Lucian, or Cervantes) which some university-trained experts nowadays lack. It is possible that some of this breadth is being recovered, and placed at the same time on surer foundations of factual knowledge. There is now in many branches of acacemic study a tendency to question existing subject-boundaries and to pursue interdisciplinary interests. This is partly a reaction against narrowness, but partly also the product of a feeling that more specialized inquiries have now made possible certain forms of synthesis for which an earlier state of knowledge was inadequate. Paulson is remarkable in being, in a primary sense, a distinguished student of Fielding and other writers of the period, as well as of Hogarth. But he is not the only recent critic who has been willing and well-equipped to say new things about Fielding in the light of Hogarth in particular, and of art history in general. In this anthology, Ian Donaldson on the plays, Robert H. Hopkins on *Jonathan Wild*, and D. S. Bland on description in the novels, show an ability to use the visual arts to make points, whether of detail or of large import, about Fielding's writings.

Another important interdisciplinary aspect of Fielding studies concerns his views on social, political and economic affairs. The rich humanity of the novels has traditionally given the impression that Fielding was a radical reformer in outlook, and that his reforming ideals were subsequently put into practice when he became a magistrate and a social administrator. More exact study of his legal and sociological works in the light of contemporary legal, social and economic doctrines has shown, in Zirker's book on *Fielding's Social Pamphlets* (1966), that he was on the contrary a conservative and rather severe social thinker. Zirker's book is often careless and loosely argued, but its basic conclusions seem right. The task of relating these conclusions to the novels, which, as Zirker points out, show much warmer and more flexible feelings on the subject of crime, punishment and law-enforcement, largely remains to be done. I have not reprinted any part of Zirker's study because it seemed difficult to find an extract of manageable size and succinctness, but it is nevertheless an essential book for a proper understanding of Fielding.

The isolating of ideas and attitudes from their full creative expression in the novels is perhaps an essential preliminary to full understanding. Its risks are those of a partial view, of a false equation of the work of art with its ideological content, of undue systematizing, with its desire for a ship-shape coherence and its tendency to resist the notion that authors, like other human beings, are sometimes inconsistent, moody, or ambiguous in their feelings. Some of these faults, singly or in combination, and sometimes despite cautions on the subject by the authors themselves, occur in the very best studies of Fielding's attitudes: J. A. Work's 'Henry Fielding, Christian Censor' (1949); Sherburn's 'Fielding's Social Outlook' (1956); and Battestin's *Moral Basis of Fielding's Art* (1959). No student of Fielding can ignore these works, and no informed reader would suppose their authors to be unaware of the many-sidedness of a work of art. But the emphasis of these background writings has sometimes misled more inexpert readers. It seemed preferable to print William Empson's essay on *Tom Jones*, which may not give us in the same precise detail the ideological content of Fielding's Christian doctrine or of his attitudes on society and divisions of rank, but which does vividly render the essential flavour of the doctrine and attitudes within the total context of *Tom Jones*, taking full account of its rich subtleties of tone, its hauteurs, its humanity, its witty fervour, its firm standards of value and its refusal to apply these standards too crudely or rigidly.

A great deal of good criticism has been written in the last thirty years about the qualities of Fielding's *style* as they reflect his moral and social outlook. A. R. Humphreys's study of Fielding's irony (1942), which demonstrates how this irony differs from the more radical irony of Swift, and expresses solidarity with rather than a subversion of the society it satirizes, is one of the earliest formal studies of its kind, and remains one of the best despite the subsequent appearance of several articles and at least three books on the subject (by Eleanor N. Hutchens, G. R. Levine and Glenn W. Hatfield: the latter a good special study focused on Fielding's preoccupation with language and abuses of language). The comedy of formalization which Humphreys draws attention to is simultaneously a mockery of rigid formality, and the expression of a sense of order. Dorothy Van Ghent's essay on *Tom Jones* is one of the earliest of several studies which see in the 'Palladian' architecture of the novel as a whole, as well as in the shaping of individual passages (notably the syntactical order of Fielding's sentences), a stylistic expression of a whole outlook. Martin Price's chapter on 'Fielding: The Comedy of Forms' is an exposition of the deep interpenetration of style and moral outlook, paying a tribute to Fielding's rich generosity of spirit through an analysis of the artistic conventions relevant to his work, and of his patterns of stylization and his displays of artifice (on the role of artifice in *Tom Jones*, see also several pieces in the Bibliography, notably those by F. W. Hilles and Michael Bell).

There has from the beginning been much dispute among Fielding's critics about some of Fielding's 'ornamental' intrusions into his novels, about the mock-heroic routines, the 'initial' chapters, and above all Fielding's constant sign-posting of the fact that such stylizations are taking place, and that he, the author, has no wish to pretend otherwise or to efface himself in any way. If this matter has always been variously controversial, there has been a particular tendency among modern critics to examine it systematically and in depth, and to assert, on the whole, that such 'self-conscious' intrusions are not essentially 'ornamental', whether in a good or bad sense, but radical to the whole meaning, including the moral meaning, of the novels. R. S. Crane's essay on the plot of *Tom Jones* (1950), and some important paragraphs in

Booth's *Rhetoric of Fiction* (1961), have taught us not to see properties of manner or form as merely formal (Crane's essay demonstrated that the traditional emphasis on the excellence of *Tom Jones*'s plot as a mere skilful interweaving of incident was misleading and damaging to the novel as a whole), and that the stylized authorial presence established a relation with the reader which was essential to the novel in much more than a narrowly aesthetic sense. If I do not reprint these statements, it is because so much in them has now been taken for granted. Ehrenpreis's analysis of the authorial presence in *Tom Jones* is in many ways an application of, and an advance on, their principles, while John Preston's essay on the reader's role in *Tom Jones*, part of a highly original recent book on the figure and role of the 'reader' in eighteenth-century fiction, extends their argument in a very important fresh direction.

Few critics would now claim that Fielding's intrusions and gestures of artifice are unconnected with the most fundamental qualities of the novels, including their entire moral outlook. Ian Watt, a critic relatively unsympathetic to Fielding's intrusive narration and to his lack of that 'realism of presentation' which Watt celebrates in Defoe and Richardson, nevertheless thinks of *Tom Jones* as possessing a 'realism of assessment' which was also urgently needed for the proper evolution of the novel-form, and which depends in Fielding on the controlling presence and authority of the narrator.

That presence makes itself felt not only through direct authorial commentary, but through stylizations both playful and serious, of which the most important are various forms of parody and burlesque, notably the mock-heroic. Fielding inclined in the Preface to *Joseph Andrews* to think of such things as essentially 'ornamental', pieces of extra fun for the 'classical reader'. Not all critics are convinced that the mock-heroic flights in *Joseph Andrews* and *Tom Jones* can be as lightly disposed of as Fielding's comment suggests. But it is certain that in other writings of Fielding, and in other major Augustan writers, mock-heroic was a radical rather than merely decorative or playful element of serious literary expression. Pope's *Dunciad*, with its application of mock-heroic to satiric concerns which transcend not only the fun of the joke but any mere desire to deride bad or pompous writers, taught Fielding some of the ways in which parody could be turned into a primary and fundamental idiom of social satire, and how it could be used in particular to express that Augustan vision, which Fielding shared with Pope, of impending cultural disintegration. Ian Donaldson's chapter on Fielding's plays brings out some aspects of this question, and for a revealing two-way traffic between Fielding's plays and Pope's *Dunciad* in the 1730s an important article by George Sherburn should be consulted: 'The *Dunciad*, Book Four', *Studies in English*, University of Texas, 1944, pp. 174–90. In *Jonathan Wild*, the mock-heroic or anti-heroic formula largely detaches itself from the ostensible literary objects of the parody, and turns into a satire on government. The strengths and weaknesses of this highly formulaic work are brought out in Arnold Kettle's brief discussion. He and A. E. Dyson show some of the ways in which the good/great schematism undermines itself, so that the bad 'great' Wild can become oddly engaging, while the 'good' Heartfree altogether fails to come to life. An essay by Allan Wendt on 'The Moral Allegory of *Jonathan Wild*' (see Bibliography) has argued, on the basis of a passage in the Preface to the *Miscellanies*, that Fielding meant seriously to expose some insufficiencies in the character of the 'good' Heartfree. This essay has become influential, but seems to me misguided in its attempt to replace the admittedly awkward schematism of the novel by the tidier schematism of the Preface (I discuss this more fully in my book, *Henry Fielding and the Augustan Ideal under Stress*, 1972, chapters 4–7). But despite the tendency of the mock-heroic scheme to undermine some of its own purposes, the whole burlesque framework is clearly a fundamental rather than a merely 'ornamental' part of the moral and political satire, and probably contains a critique of the heroic ethos itself, not merely of its modern, Walpolian manifestations.

In the Preface to *Joseph Andrews* Fielding claimed to turn away from such radical exploitation of mock-heroic, arguing as we have seen that in his 'comic epic in prose' the burlesque flights were to be thought of as incidental entertainments for the 'classical reader'. He may have intended to distinguish *Joseph Andrews* from *Jonathan Wild* (probably finished or well-advanced by then, though not published until 1743), as well as from *Shamela* and the burlesque plays. Certainly he wished it to be clear that 'comic epic' was not synonymous with epic parody or mock-heroic. The discussion by W. L. Renwick suggests some of the things Fielding was trying to evoke by describing his type of novel as 'comic epic', while Ian Watt is concerned to play down the validity of the phrase as a description of Fielding's novels. But while 'comic epic' emphatically does *not* mean 'parody', many readers would not accept Fielding's own claim that the mock-heroic routines in *Joseph Andrews* (or *Tom Jones*) are simply separable from the main concerns of the fiction, if only because these routines are such characteristic manifestations of authorial presence, of that delight in stylistic interference and ironic mimicry which enable Fielding to declare his domination over the fictional world and his playfully detached superiority to it. In *Amelia*, however, mock-heroic turns 'serious'. There is an avowed imitation of 'serious' epic form, and an ironic exploitation of Virgilian resonances, which anticipate Joyce, as Sherburn and others have pointed out. Robert Alter's many-sided discussion of that novel has some valuable (and commendably cautious) things to say on this, as on much else.

Mock-heroic is not the only important form of parody in Fielding. A good deal of anti-Richardsonian parody is scattered in several of his writings, most notably, of course, in *Shamela* and *Joseph Andrews*. While *Shamela* is obviously shot through with parody from beginning to end, however, *Joseph Andrews* is a more problematical case. A traditional notion that Fielding began his novel simply as another anti-*Pamela*, but found it growing miraculously in his hands into a work of imagination in its own right, has sometimes been challenged by recent critics, who argue that *Joseph Andrews* was conceived from the start as an 'autonomous' fictional creation, fully articulated in all its parts, and was not the accidental product of a parodic impulse. On this reading, *Joseph Andrews* is an 'alternative' to, rather than a parody of, *Pamela*. There is much to be said for any description which implies that parody in a narrow sense hardly accounts for the novel as a whole, but there has been a misleading tendency among some over-zealous commentators to claim that the presence of *Pamela* in *Joseph Andrews* is altogether nugatory. For this reason, Robert Alan Donovan's argument that Fielding's novel in some ways remains continuously preoccupied with Richardson's, not merely in order to parody it, but as a foil against which Fielding can explore and assert his own deepest values, is salutary. (This tendency to restore *Pamela* to *Joseph Andrews* is also reflected in an essay of 1967 by Douglas Brooks (see Bibliography).) Donovan also argues that *Tom Jones* is an anti-*Pamela* (*The Shaping Vision*, pp. 243–6); and it has more than once been said that Richardson seemed to Fielding what the Grub Street hacks and dunces seemed to Swift and Pope, a disorderly, self-important, 'individualist' and typically 'modern' threat to Augustan values of order, politeness and taste. That this feeling remained in Fielding to the end, despite his admiration for Richardson's achievement in *Clarissa*, is shown in the closing words of the Preface to the *Voyage to Lisbon*, which must be among the last words Fielding ever wrote.

George Orwell

from 'Autobiographical Note' 17 April 1940
(Sonia Orwell and Ian Angus (eds.), *Collected Essays, Journalism and Letters*, vol. 2, 1970)

The writers I care most about and never grow tired of are Shakespeare, Swift, Fielding, Dickens, Charles Reade, Samuel Butler, Zola, Flaubert and, among modern writers, James Joyce, T. S. Eliot and D. H. Lawrence. But I believe the modern writer who has influenced me most is Somerset Maugham, whom I admire immensely for his power of telling a story straightforwardly and without frills. (39)

A. R. Humphreys

from 'Fielding's Irony: Its Methods and Effects', *Review of English Studies*, vol. 18 1942

Practical criticism, as applied to the novel, is still in the stage of experiment. The critic who is dealing with modern novelists of a highly developed sensibility, has no difficulty in proving the delicacy of their perceptions through the analysis of representative passages of their prose, by looking for degrees of subtlety and precision not very different from those expected in poetry. But criticism of most of the eighteenth- and nineteenth-century novelists still proceeds in terms of character, plot, and *mise-en-scène*, the established counters of critical discussion. It is still somewhat of an adventure to explore a novelist's qualities of mind through the local alertness of his writing.

Fielding's work, satirical and serious, gives, as Sir Leslie Stephen said, 'quite a peculiar impression of solidity and reality'. It does so for various reasons, mainly perhaps through the vigorous humour of its character-drawing and its sturdy forthrightness of style, but more generally and fundamentally because in its habits of thought and its social attitudes it is organically related to its century. His irony, far from being radically disturbing like that of Swift, is, in intention, corrective and orthodox; it undermines deviations from a healthy, sensible, social morality, it prunes society of perversions. Unlike the irony of Gibbon or Samuel Butler II, it does not unsettle traditional ethics and Christian orthodoxy – it is the irony of integration rather than disintegration.

This suggests, perhaps, a certain philosophical simplicity about Fielding's irony, and it is true that in comparison with many of the other great ironists he appears to launch his attacks in no very subtle manner. His strategy is frontal and conceived in daylight, the am-biguities between what is said and what is intended are clear on the surface, and do not attempt to spring surprises and betrayals. Swift, Gibbon, Butler, and Shaw imply, perhaps, a certain good-humoured contempt for the reader, and invite him to realize his own stupidity by engaging his assent to propositions embodying his current prejudices, which then prove themselves to be preposterous. Fielding wishes merely to stand on a sensible, neighbourly, decent ethic, and (at least up to the time of *Amelia*) is unconcerned with any funda-mental ills. His work has the characteristic virtues and drawbacks inherent in so organic a relationship to its century. Many types of experience are alien to it, many of its judgements little more than contemporary prejudices. On the other hand, the native assurance typical of its age, the sense of knowing just where one is and of grounding oneself on the sturdy principles of commonsense, aware of a vigorous social order and a reasonable, if limited, religious ortho-doxy – these advantages are obvious on every page. Similar per-spicacities and blind spots are widely shared by Fielding's generation. In particular, his irony reinforces the scorn for 'theory' and subtle ratiocination so typical of his empirical and practical age. Johnson, we remember, 'refuted' Berkeley by kicking his foot against a stone. It was the sort of proof Fielding himself liked, and any deviations from commonsense, whether prompted by sincere Christian zeal or by hypocrisy, are chastened by the most forthright, unsubtle, ironic devices. Parson Adams, after reproaching Joseph for the strength of his worldly attachment to Fanny, bursts into lamentations when his son is reported drowned; the philosopher of stoic virtue, Square, is found cowering in Molly Seagrim's bedroom.

Such orthodox irony, in support of so sensible a frame of mind, might be supposed to have lost interest after the passage of two centuries and the transition from a four-square world to a disintegrating one. Yet it has not done so. Folly, one supposes, being perennial, can never be too much chastised, and commonsense, being infrequent, can never be too much reinforced. That being so, the technique of this irony which has for two centuries poured scorn on hypocrisy deserves some attention. At first one is puzzled to account for its effectiveness – or rather, for the fact that despite its crudity of outline it appears so mature. Fielding's practice with the drama – one remembers the slapdash success of *Pasquin, The Author's Farce* and *Tom Thumb* – might give his satire decisiveness and energy, but the reasons why it has had so long a success involve an examination of his whole outlook and temper of mind.

One may assume, perhaps, that the severest exercise of the ironist's art is not to give the game away. In that respect, irony differs from sarcasm. The most outrageous things are to be said with a straight face, with unbroken seriousness of demeanour: the poise is so consistently maintained that the reader is forced to realize the real inner meaning the more keenly by discovering it for himself. If intelligent, he succeeds; if stupid, he is taken in – the ironist's great triumph. But Fielding's art is not severe in this fashion. He is not writing for a very experienced audience, but for the eighteenth century's 'common reader', and he is not trying to score off that reader but to reinforce his native tendency towards good sense. *Jonathan Wild* could not suffer the fate of Butler's *Fair Haven*, which some reputable reviews took to be serious. Behind the vigorous sparring is the fighter who stands firmly on a sensible orthodoxy. In comparison with Swift, his irony is less intellectual, more muscular, less subtly integrated, more vehement, proceeding less from a profound inner organization of mind, more from the zeal of the practical reformer. Although the first of the following passages does not represent Swift at his best, tailing off as it does from irony into open sarcasm, it affords a close enough parallel to the second to stimulate one into drawing some comparisons:

(a) I had the curiosity to enquire, in a particular manner, by what methods great numbers had procured to themselves high titles of honour and prodigious estates; . . . perjury, oppression, subornation, fraud, pandarism and the like infirmities were among the most excuseable arts they had to mention, and for these I gave, as it was reasonable, due allowance. But when some confessed they owed their greatness and wealth to vice, others to the betraying their country or their prince; some to poisoning, more to the perverting of justice in order to destroy the innocent; I hope I may be pardoned, if these discoveries inclined me a little to abate of that profound veneration which I am naturally apt to pay to persons of high rank, who ought to be treated with the utmost respect due to their sublime dignity by us, their inferiors.

(*Gulliver's Travels*, chapter 8, 'Laputa')

(b) He was none of those half-bred fellows who are ashamed to see their friends when they have plundered and betrayed them; from which base and pitiful temper many monstrous cruelties have been transacted by men, who have sometimes carried their modesty so far as to the murder or utter ruin of those against whom their consciences have suggested to them that they have committed some small trespass, either by debauching a friend's wife or daughter, belying or betraying the friend himself, or some other such trifling instance. In our hero there was nothing not truly great; he could, without the least abashment, drink a bottle with the man who knew he had, the moment before, picked his pocket; and when he had stripped him of everything he had, never desired to do him any further mischief; for he carried good nature to that wonderful and uncommon height, that he never did a single injury to man or woman, by which he himself did not expect to reap some advantage.

(*Jonathan Wild*, book 1, chapter 11)

The qualities of feeling are somewhat different. Swift's 'grave verisimilitude' is different from the ready exaggeration, the macabre caricature, of Fielding. Swift tends relentlessly and unremittingly in one calculated direction; Fielding leaps from posture to posture. Swift has the inner and outer consistency of unruffled logic; Fielding the brilliant manifold brandishings of cut-and-parry debate – one never detects him in the same stance two sentences running. 'Half-bred' suggests supercilious scorn for those not brazened in rascality, whether in Wild's or Walpole's circles (where bad manners would arouse more disgust than bad morals); the forcefulness of 'plundered and betrayed' proceeds from another criterion – that of the outraged moralist; 'base and pitiful temper' shifts again – to Wild's diabolic scorn for the promptings of shame; 'monstrous cruelties' might be Wild hypocritically deprecating superfluous villainy, or it might be the outraged moralist stating a fact; 'carried their modesty' is pure sarcasm; 'murder or utter ruin' is again the moralist stating a fact; 'consciences' is a sneer; 'small trespass . . . debauching a friend's wife or daughter . . . trifling instance' is angry sarcasm; 'nothing not truly great' is ironic (and, implies Fielding, a statement of fact, the pun in 'great' reminding us of the Court-Crime equation); 'without the least abashment' is ironic praise; 'never desired to do him any further mischief' is ironic praise by the standards of normal morality, but real praise in comparison with the vindictiveness of less 'magnanimous' criminals; 'good nature' is sarcasm; 'wonderful and uncommon height' is both sarcasm and, Fielding implies, an actual statement of fact; while 'expect to reap some advantage' is again ironic praise by the standards of normal morality, but real praise in comparison with Wild's meaner fellows. The interplay of different tones throughout is so alive that almost any phrase seems to shift its ground the more one looks at it.

When Swift groups 'perjury, oppression, subornation, fraud, pandarism and the like infirmities', the effect is very different. The even litheness of tone prevents the cool ingenious understatement from being too insistent. The abstract terms *conceal* the contrast between mere infirmities and the crimes mentioned. Perjury, oppression, and the rest are 'infirmities' because they are commonly treated as venial offences, but even more, Swift implies, because they are essential frailties of human nature. One would be surprised by their absence, not by their presence. The common view holds them as mere trifles. Fielding, specifying debauchery of a friend's wife or daughter, by this very coarseness makes its discrepancy from a 'small trespass' broad and obvious. By implication, therefore, only those taking the diabolic point of view could condone it. Beyond the momentary sardonic belittlement, there is the strongest hint that normal morals would condemn such an act. Throughout *Jonathan Wild*, the praise or condoning of treachery is too blunt to persuade us that it is more than a pose: the reader automatically supplies the corrective of practical decency, as Fielding intended he should. The very tone and technique of the irony anchor him to orthodoxy, and because of this firmness, this central stability, he can allow himself to indulge apparently cynical or immoral points of view on the clear understanding, implied in his relationship to his reader, that it is all make-believe. The differences between Swift and Fielding in the implications of their irony define the different views they hold about human nature. Both envisage as a standard of comparison a sane moral order from which deviations can be judged; but by the perfect suavity of his tone Swift engages the reader to see it only as an abstract superhuman idea, practised only in the fictional world of Brobdingnag or the Houyhnhnms (the King of Brobdingnag's Olympian dismissal of humanity as 'the most pernicious race of little odious vermin that Nature ever suffered to crawl upon the surface of the earth' is characteristic), and supplanted in practice by an ortho-doxy based on observed behaviour and therefore essentially selfish and immoral. Fielding limits his denunciations to cases, admittedly numerous, of hypocrisy and ill-nature, which are always recognized as deviations from a healthy social conscience existing in the here and now, embodied not only in shadows like Heartfree and Mr Allworthy, but in creatures of flesh and blood like Adams, Tom Jones, Sophia, and Amelia.

Fielding's irony, then, in comparison with Swift's, represents the social stability of its age, and instead of undermining reinforces orthodox morality. Consistently with this, it lacks philosophical and verbal complexity. This does not mean that it is a waste of time to attend to its small details, even though the reward is not so startling as it can be in the case of Swift, but simply that such 'ambiguities' as there are are soon exhausted. The reader must be awake to what Fielding is saying, since whatever his practice as a playwright he was extremely careful as a novelist. But the close significance is that of perfect aptness to define and delimit the subject rather than, as with

Swift, Gibbon and Samuel Butler, to refer it through wide ranges of implication to a large context of moral scepticism. There is in Fielding's irony a superb felicitousness of detail – Miss Laetitia Snap, for instance, 'often confessed to her female confidantes, if she could ever have listened to the thought of living with any one man, Mr Bagshot was he', where the whole effect depends on the intrusive 'one' – but in most cases of innuendo or *double-entendre* (Fielding's favourite types of ambiguity) the possible meanings are sharply limited and soon exhausted. The typical *double-entendre* or pun is marked by its flatly clear and separable components – as, for example, in *Jonathan Wild*, 'that final exaltation which . . . is the most proper and becoming end of all great men' – representing the matter-of-fact definition of central eighteenth-century prose with its concern for plain meanings.

Fielding's irony illuminates the whole temper of his mind. It has been a commonplace of criticism to dub him a realist, and his subject-matter justifies the label; but he shares the real strength of eighteenth-century realism in the imposition on his material of a firm and controlled pattern. The very stiltedness of style in which the more impassioned speeches are written is a mark of this (largely instinctive) formalization. The formal elaboration of speech, though to eighteenth-century taste it engaged the reader's emotions more strongly than it can do today, maintained a certain distance and decorum. Tom Jones's addresses to Sophia, for example, are rooted in the good sense which the *Spectator* had made such an integral part of the century's social behaviour. The most familiar difference between Richardson and Fielding is that the former, by every device in his power, invites the reader to indulge in strained and excessively stimulated states of feeling, while the latter, the master of the comic, preserves his own status, and that of the reader, as an observer. The rhythmical assurance, the grip over movement, the cogency and unobtrusive symmetry of the sentence, are indices of Fielding's real temper, though at present I can only refer to them in passing as the most potent means of implying the artist's self-control and self-possession.

In the sphere of irony, this quality of disciplined formalization shows itself in the elaborate preparation of simple deductions, the scrupulous proof of the obvious, the frankly prepared bathos. It also has close affinities with the deliberate pattern which, for the purposes

of comedy, is imposed on characters' behaviour ... – a type of formalization designed to sharpen outlines and to reduce the complex spontaneity of an individual's behaviour to the clearly apprehensible definiteness beloved of the cartoonist.
(183–9)

George Orwell

from articles in *Tribune*   July–December 1944 (Sonia Orwell and Ian Angus (eds.), *Collected Essays, Journalism and Letters*, vol. 3, 1970)

People pay lip service to Fielding and the rest of them, of course, but they don't read them, as you can discover by making a few inquiries among your friends. How many people have ever read *Tom Jones*, for instance?
(210)

'Realism', a much abused word, has at least four current meanings, but when applied to novels it normally means a photographic imitation of everyday life. A 'realistic' novel is one in which the dialogue is colloquial and physical objects are described in such a way that you can visualize them. In this sense almost all modern novels are more 'realistic' than those of the past, because the describing of everyday scenes and the construction of natural-sounding dialogue are largely a matter of technical tricks, which are passed on from one generation to another, gradually improving in the process. But there is another sense in which the stilted, artificial novelists of the eighteenth century are more 'realistic' than almost any of their successors, and that is in their attitude towards human motives. They may be weak at describing scenery, but they are extraordinarily good at describing scoundrelism. This is true even of Fielding, who in *Tom Jones* and *Amelia* already shows the moralizing tendency which was to mark English novels for a hundred and fifty years. But it is much truer of Smollett, whose outstanding intellectual honesty may have been connected with the fact that he was not an Englishman. . . .

Smollett's influence on subsequent English writers has not been as great as that of his contemporary, Fielding. Fielding deals in the same

kind of boisterous adventure, but his sense of sin never quite leaves him. It is interesting, in *Joseph Andrews*, to watch Fielding start out with the intention of writing a pure farce, and then, in spite of himself as it were, begin punishing vice and rewarding virtue in the way that was to be customary in English novels until almost yesterday. Tom Jones would fit into a novel by Meredith, or for that matter by Ian Hay, whereas Peregrine Pickle seems to belong to a more European background. The writers nearest to Smollett are perhaps Surtees and Marryat, but when sexual frankness ceased to be possible, picaresque literature was robbed of perhaps half of its subject-matter. The eighteenth-century inn where it was almost abnormal to go into the right bedroom was a lost dominion.
(282–6)

English writers from Chaucer onwards have found it very difficult to resist burlesque, but as soon as burlesque enters the reality of the story suffers. Fielding, Dickens, Trollope, Wells, even Joyce, have all stumbled over this problem. Thackeray, in the best of his short pieces, solves it by making *all* his characters into caricatures.
(344)

F. R. Leavis

from *The Great Tradition* 1948

It is necessary to insist, then, that there are important distinctions to be made, and that far from all of the names in the literary histories really belong to the realm of significant creative achievement. And as a recall to a due sense of differences it is well to start by distinguishing the few really great – the major novelists who count in the same way as the major poets, in the sense that they not only change the possibilities of the art for practitioners and readers, but that they are significant in terms of that human awareness they promote; awareness of the possibilities of life.

To insist on the pre-eminent few in this way is not to be indifferent to tradition; on the contrary, it is the way towards understanding what tradition is. 'Tradition', of course, is a term with many forces

– and often very little at all. There is a habit nowadays of suggesting that there is a tradition of 'the English Novel', and that all that can be said of the tradition (that being its peculiarity) is that 'the English Novel' can be anything you like. To distinguish the major novelists in the spirit proposed is to form a more useful idea of tradition (and to recognize that the conventionally established view of the past of English fiction needs to be drastically revised). It is in terms of the major novelists, those significant in the way suggested, that tradition, in any serious sense, has its significance.

To be important historically is not, of course, to be necessarily one of the significant few. Fielding deserves the place of importance given him in the literary histories, but he hasn't the kind of classical distinction we are also invited to credit him with. He is important not because he leads to Mr J. B. Priestley but because he leads to Jane Austen, to appreciate whose distinction is to feel that life isn't long enough to permit of one's giving much time to Fielding or any to Mr Priestley.

Fielding made Jane Austen possible by opening the central tradition of English fiction. In fact, to say that the English novel began with him is as reasonable as such propositions ever are. He completed the work begun by the *Tatler* and the *Spectator*, in the pages of which we see the drama turning into the novel – that this development should occur by way of journalism being in the natural course of things. To the art of presenting character and *moeurs* learnt in that school (he himself, before he became a novelist, was both playwright and periodical essayist) he joined a narrative habit the nature of which is sufficiently indicated by his own phrase, 'comic epic in prose'. That the eighteenth century, which hadn't much lively reading to choose from, but had much leisure, should have found *Tom Jones* exhilarating is not surprising; nor is it that Scott, and Coleridge, should have been able to give that work superlative praise. Standards are formed in comparison, and what opportunities had they for that? But the conventional talk about the 'perfect construction' of *Tom Jones* (the late Hugh Walpole brought it out triumphantly and you may hear it in almost any course of lectures on 'the English Novel') is absurd. There can't be subtlety of organization without richer matter to organize, and subtler interests, than Fielding has to offer. He is credited with range and variety and it is true that some episodes take place in the country and some in town, some in the churchyard and some in the inn, some on the high-road and some in the bed-chamber, and so on. But we haven't to read a very large proportion of *Tom Jones* in order to discover the limits of the essential interests it has to offer us. Fielding's attitudes, and his concern with human nature, are simple, and not such as to produce an effect of anything but monotony (on a mind, that is, demanding more than external action) when exhibited at the length of an 'epic in prose'. What he *can* do appears to best advantage in *Joseph Andrews. Jonathan Wild*, with its famous irony, seems to me mere hobbledehoydom (much as one applauds the determination to explode the gangster-hero), and by *Amelia* Fielding has gone soft.

We all know that if we want a more inward interest it is to Richardson we must go. And there is more to be said for Johnson's preference, and his emphatic way of expressing it at Fielding's expense, than is generally recognized. Richardson's strength in the analysis of emotional and moral states is in any case a matter of common acceptance; and *Clarissa* is a really impressive work. But it's no use pretending that Richardson can ever be made a current classic again ... his immediately relevant historical importance is plain: he too is a major fact in the background of Jane Austen.

(10–13)

Kingsley Amis

from *I Like It Here*   1958

Bowen thought about Fielding. Perhaps it was worth dying in your forties if two hundred years later you were the only non-contemporary novelist who could be read with unaffected and whole-hearted interest, the only one who never had to be apologized for or excused on the grounds of changing taste. And how enviable to live in the world of his novels, where duty was plain, evil arose out of malevolence and a starving wayfarer could be invited indoors without hesitation and without fear. Did that make it a simplified world? Perhaps, but that hardly mattered beside the existence of a moral

seriousness that could be made apparent without the aid of evangelical puffing and blowing.
(185)

Rebecca West

from 'The Great Optimist', *The Court and the Castle:
A Study of the Interactions of Political and Religious Ideas in
Imaginative Literature*   1958

He [Fielding] became infatuated with the idea of good government and saw it in the simplest terms, in Shakespearean terms: as a movement of honest people against First, Second and Third Murderers, who, when Banquo said, 'It will be rain tonight,' answered, 'Let it come down', and stabbed him. Such crime had for him associations which evoked his deep personal emotion, and so did its remedy, politics. That can be seen in the strange book, *The Life of Jonathan Wild the Great*: strange in that it is written with a passion that one would think that no man could lavish on any but his own child. Yet the theme is the parallel between the famous thieftaker Wild and the prime minister, Sir Robert Walpole, and this was not his own – it had already been done to death by the Grub Street pamphleteers. It was as if he liked to contemplate the equal corruption of the despised and the honoured, as if he had that appetite for eating earth which doctors used to call pica. The dark life of the London streets, with their runnels of sewage, and their parallel streams of violent acts, the hideous rough-house fun of Newgate Prison, where even the minister of Christ might be a drunken humbug and a buffoon, the death on the scaffold that was as lonely and graceless as if it were a rat that died; all these were to him that reality which was, to use the word in its literal sense, charming, which compelled his attention, which insisted on being the medium of his action and his thought. . . .
(81)

It is to be remembered that he several times specifically rejects the doctrine of total depravity. This quality of good nature is a human

achievement, and it is conditional on intelligence; for Fielding comes
to the conclusion:

That, as good-nature requires a distinguishing faculty, which
is another word for judgement, and is perhaps the sole
boundary between wisdom and folly; it is impossible for a
fool, who hath no distinguishing faculty, to be good-
natured.

This explains the importance he attaches to classical studies, which he
believed would make men's minds exact, just as many people today
hope that scientific studies will perform the same task. Obviously,
the more intelligent a man was, the more good-natured he would be.
So in his argument with Shakespeare his position was that something,
but not everything, was wrong with the court of Elsinore, and that
Hamlet would certainly be able to set it right because he was the
most intelligent person there.

   Shakespeare disagreed, and showed it once and for all by making
Hamlet send unshriven men to their death. But neither settled the
argument, and it is continuing today. Graham Greene is even now
pursuing Pelagianism round the landscape with an axe, and might
very well write a modern version of *Amelia*, with Billy Booth and
his brother officers and Miss Matthews translated into civil servants;
Amelia would be presented as the really bad person in the book,
because by her beautiful cultivation of the natural affections she was
disguising the advanced putridity of life, while Jonathan Wild would
be borrowed from his volume to play the part of the sort of human
being who does not do that disservice to God, Who could certainly
not be represented as the best-natured Being in the universe. This
reflection forces on our attention the essential impurity of literature.
For we know that in this contention the victory goes to Shakespeare,
against Henry Fielding and Graham Greene, because his plays are
greater than their works, and that as between Henry Fielding and
Graham Greene, a victory lies with Fielding because, though
Brighton Rock and *The Heart of the Matter* and *The Quiet American* are
good novels, *Joseph Andrews* and *Tom Jones* and *Amelia* are better
still. It is obvious, however, that this is only one sort of 'victory',
and there are other victories to be won in other fields. Quite apart
from their aesthetic merit, in the conduct of this argument the

authors score different degrees of success in approaching the truth in their argument about the salvation of man. Yet, again, their books as obviously owe their importance in great part to the fact that they are engaged in this argument . . . .

But even as we read Fielding's happy defence of the new form, knowing how triumphantly he and many others were to use it, the proof appears of its inferiority to the poetic drama, its incapacity to produce an equal faith. Prose keeps so close to the utilitarian use of language that it constantly arouses in both writer and reader associations with the real world which draw them away from the imaginary world where they should remain. It was bound to happen that Fielding constantly interrupted his analysis of the experiences of Tom Jones and Billy Booth in order to tell us about the routine of the gaming-house, the defects of the bail bond system, and that everything practical in the reader should join in the distraction. The novel is always ambushed by the temptation to become informative on matters of fact, and this is not as great a disability as its comparative failure to give information on more relevant matters. We must note again that a prose writer is under a grave handicap because he can create a character only by describing him or her and making him perform actions and utter expressions congruous with his nature, and cannot underline his conception of that nature as a poet can, by suggestions arising from the music of verse. A still greater handicap is the loss of the poetic soliloquy, which is uniquely potent as a revelation of the inner self. Dialogue can rarely go as deep, for what any person says in the presence of others is to some degree conditioned by his relationship with them, and is thus deflected from candour. Skilful dialogue may achieve candour by implication, but that is a sleight-of-hand performance which is apt to lack seriousness. The writer's comment is too remote; and the interior monologue, has, except in the hands of one great writer, failed to achieve intensity and has too often appeared as a droning reverie. None of these resources can convince with the power of a soliloquy, a self-analysis forced out of character at a moment which poetry certifies to be of supreme importance.

If writers know that the form they are using will not permit them to express the deepest truth about their characters' natures, it may well be that they will not trouble to find out what that deepest truth

is. Thus a limitation is imposed on the novelist which narrows his genius, and limits the area of his 'reach and knowledge', often at the point where he must carry conviction to his readers. For it often appears to readers that a man is acting in 'direct contradiction to the dictates of his nature' for the reason that they have not sufficient information about that nature. They think that an Antoninus is being saddled with a Nero's story because they have falsely identified characters with Antoninus and Nero; and the author must be hampered, by comparison with the poetic dramatist, in furnishing them with sufficient information to correct their error, because his more slender resources have actually left him knowing less than he should. It is the special defect of the novel that it often does not wield the requisite authority.
(85–9)

Leslie A. Fiedler

from *Love and Death in the American Novel*   1960 (Paladin, 1967)

The Gothic strain, which in America had fed the fancy of C. B. Brown and was to inspire Poe, and which in Germany had become an essential ingredient of the first part of *Faust*, progressed in England no further than the extravagances of *The Monk*. The tragic elements of the Faustian theme, implicit from the first, remained undeveloped or travestied, until they were utterly rejected by the genteel male novelists who founded the historical romance. These founding fathers turned back, not inappropriately, to the example of Fielding, who had at the very start of the bourgeois novel provided (first in *Joseph Andrews*, then more spectacularly in *Tom Jones*) an anti-tragic alternative to Richardsonianism.

Fielding's example cues first of all a literature of masculine protest, an attempt to rescue prose fiction from the bourgeois ladies, who were in fact Richardson's chief, though by no means only, readers. For the heroine, Fielding proposed to substitute the hero; for the boudoir, the out-of-doors; for an obsessive concern with seduction and marriage, a more varied interest in social relations of all kinds; for what he took to be Richardson's hypocritical prurience, an easy

tolerance of promiscuity and a general candour in dealing with sex. Fielding, however, went further than this, identifying as feminine – and therefore to be avoided – not only conventional Christian piety, but sensibility itself, and, indeed, any analytic concern with the 'heart'. The fear of not seeming manly enough haunts him everywhere, inhibiting reflection and delicacy and subtlety alike; and leading to that exaggerated heartiness, bluffness and downright crudity of manner required in a society where the male has continually to prove that he is one of the boys.
(157)

D. S. Bland

from 'Endangering the Reader's Neck: Background Description in the Novel', *Criticism*, vol. 3   1961 (Philip Stevick (ed.), *The Theory of the Novel*, 1967)

Professor Watt's point about the localization of the setting in the pioneer English novels is perfectly valid; but description is put to other uses than this, and it is with the development of these uses that I am concerned. Localization is a practical matter of placing the characters in an environment within which they can act out their stories. It is equivalent of both the dramatically presented description and the stage scenery of the drama. Thus the interest attaching to Crusoe's island is that of seeing what he can make of it. It is far from being a romantic Treasure Island or Blue Lagoon. In Pamela's case we must be made aware that Mr B's house has closets to which she can retire to write her letters or avoid a rape. And in *Joseph Andrews* and *Tom Jones* a distinction must be made between a good inn and a bad one, between Allworthy's orderly house and Squire Western's free-and-easy one. The nearest we come in Fielding's work to a piece of natural description for its own sake is a short passage in *Joseph Andrews*:

Adams continued his subject till they came to one of the
beautifullest spots of ground in the universe. It was a kind
of natural amphitheatre, formed by the winding of a small

rivulet, which was planted with thick woods, and the trees rose gradually above each other by the natural ascent of the ground they stood on; which ascent as they hid with their boughs, they seemed to have been disposed by the design of the most skilful planter. The soil was spread with a verdure which no paint could imitate; and the whole place might have raised romantic ideas in elder minds than those of Joseph and Fanny, without the assistance of love (book 3, chapter 5).

But even this, as we shall see, is not 'pure' description, though it will appear to be alongside the picture we are given in *Tom Jones* of Allworthy's house and estate, which is much more in line with eighteenth-century taste in landscape description:

It stood on the south-east side of a hill, but nearer the bottom than the top of it, so as to be sheltered from the north-east by a grove of old oaks which rose above it in a gradual ascent of near half a mile, and yet high enough to enjoy a most charming prospect of the vale beneath.

In the midst of the grove was a fine lawn, sloping down towards the house, near the summit of which rose a plentiful spring, gushing out of a rock covered with firs, and forming a constant cascade of about thirty feet, not carried down a regular flight of steps, but tumbling in a natural fall over the broken and mossy stones until it came to the bottom of the rock, then running off in a pebbly channel, that with many lesser falls winded along, till it fell into a lake at the foot of the hill, about a quarter of a mile below the house on the south side, and which was seen from every room in the front. Out of this lake, which filled the centre of a beautiful plain, embellished with groups of beeches and elms, and fed with sheep, issued a river, that for several miles was seen to meander through an amazing variety of meadows and woods till it emptied itself into the sea, with a large arm of which, and an island beyond it, the prospect was closed.

On the right of this valley opened another of less extent, adorned with several villages, and terminated by one of the

towers of an old ruined abbey, grown over with ivy, and part
of the front, which remained still entire.

The left-hand side presented the view of a very fine park,
composed of very unequal ground, and agreeably varied,
with all the diversity that hills, lawns, wood, and water, laid
out with admirable taste, but owing less to art than to nature,
could give. Beyond this, the country gradually rose into a
ridge of wild mountains, the tops of which were above the
clouds (book 1, chapter 4).

The significance of the chapter-heading here should not be overlooked: 'The reader's neck brought into danger by a description'.
Here Fielding is appparently warning us to expect something
unusual, but what in fact he offers us is something to which no good
Augustan would take exception. Allworthy's estate displays the
expected taste of an eighteenth-century landowner who has accepted
the changes in landscape gardening brought about by the influence of
painters such as Poussin and Claude. What Fielding gives us is not a
piece of natural description for its own sake (this *would* have brought
the reader's neck into danger in the middle of the century) but the
panorama of a situation in which nature is so manipulated as to form
a setting for man.[1] We are here at a transitional stage between the
complete formality of the continental garden of the seventeenth
century, and the appreciation of *natural* nature that is to be a characteristic of the Romantic movement. It is on the principles of this
transitional stage that Pope laid out his five-acre plot at Twickenham,
and the river that meanders through Allworthy's estate is at one with
Hogarth's 'line of beauty', the serpentine line that has given its
name to the ornamental water in Hyde Park. How transitional the
situation was can be seen by comparing the close of the passage from
Tom Jones with the paragraph from *Joseph Andrews*. In the latter the
trees are approved of because 'they seemed to have been disposed by

1 Mr Christopher Hussey has suggested that 'the man-made humanized
landscape' of the eighteenth century is 'England's greatest contribution to the
visual arts of the world'. See his introduction to Margaret Jourdain, *The
Work of William Kent* (1948, p. 15). His introduction to the companion
volume, Dorothy Stroud, *Capability Brown* (1950, rev. edn., 1957), should also
be consulted. The two together form an excellent analysis of the aesthetics
of landscape gardening.

the design of the most skilful planter', whereas in *Tom Jones* the left-hand scene pleases because it owes *less* to art than to nature.

Fielding's object in going into such detail should now be obvious. By this means he both places Allworthy on the social map and displays his character, that of a quiet-living man of taste, in contrast to Squire Western, of whose estate we get no such picture. In *Joseph Andrews* the description is used for another purpose. The charm of the natural 'amphitheatre chimes in with and underlines the romantic mood of the lovers, and this, the use of 'mood' landscape, is the next stage in the development of description in the novel. In each case, however, the reader is being invited to participate by being reminded of visual experiences with which Fielding supposes him to be familiar, experiences derived from his acquaintance with neo-classical landscape painting and the garden-design based on it.
(316–19)

Martin Price

'Fielding: The Comedy of Forms', *To the Palace of Wisdom:
Studies in Order and Energy from Dryden to Blake*   1964
(Anchor Books, 1965)

You see the man of education, the gentleman, and the
scholar, sporting with his subject – its master, not its slave.
Byron, of Fielding

What an absurd thing, that fear of the self in literature: fear
of talking of oneself, of being interested in oneself, of
showing oneself. (Flaubert's need of mortification made him
invent that false, that deplorable virtue.)
André Gide

The Energies of Virtue

Unlike Defoe and Richardson, Fielding shows no desire to achieve minute realism. He does not provide the illusion of actuality that allows the reader to participate immediately in the lives of his characters. We may sympathize with Fielding's characters, but we are always aware of them as characters and of the novels as novels. Whatever we see in Fielding's world is filtered through his own telling; his arrangement, his commentary, and his idiom control our awareness throughout. Coleridge speaks of Fielding's 'unrealizing his story in order to give a deeper reality to the truths intended'. 'Unrealizing' is a good term. It reminds us that Fielding was not a primitive, clumsily extending the periodical essay into the novel; he was almost what we would call today an anti-novelist, playing games with an already established art of realistic narrative – in Byron's words, 'sporting with his subject – its master, not its slave'. A great writer finds his peculiar subject through his form, and Fielding's games are what bring his subject into existence. That subject is the problematic nature of human goodness: the puzzles and confusions involved in defining it, the deceptions made possible by the inwardness of virtue, the curiously anti-heroic nature of its power, dependent on Fortune for its worldly success, easily hood-winked and slandered, generously reckless in its refusal to obey the world's law of succeeding by becoming its opposite.

Fielding is an Augustan writer first of all. He moves in a new direction; but more than any other figure he provides the fulcrum for the century. He is less intense and original than Swift before him or Sterne later, but he holds in remarkable balance the virtues of both. The central theme in Fielding's work is the opposition between the flow of soul – of selfless generosity – and the structures – screens, defenses, moats of indifference – that people build around themselves. The flow is the active energy of virtuous feeling; the structures are those forms that are a frozen travesty of authentic order. Fielding's satire builds upon the beautiful demonstrations by Swift and Pope of the logic of forms. *A Tale of a Tub* gives us a world of dress, in which the soul has dwindled to a suit of clothes worn with slavish adherence to the rules of fashion. *The Dunciad* gives the empire of vacuity, the usurpation of true order by a goddess who exists only because she is worshipped. Fielding rarely elevates his theme to this level of mythical generality and dignity; he gives us, instead, a world of artifice and easy rationalization whose quintessence (as we see in both *Tom Jones* and *Amelia*) is the masquerade. Nor does this world require great villains. It is a disenchanting world where moral triviality can account for the horrors we commonly ascribe to demonic forces.

In his presentation of generosity Fielding goes beyond the typical balance of the Augustans. There are intimations of Fielding's theme in Gay's Macheath; and Pope – particularly in the *Horatian Epistles* – dramatizes 'the flow of soul'. But Fielding celebrates feeling in a more radical and unguarded manner. He takes from Shaftesbury the defense of a natural goodness in man that needs no threats or bribes and the celebration of an image of God as perfect goodness rather than as unsearchable mystery, formidable power, or irascible judgement. But Fielding frees Shaftesbury's neo-Stoic vision of its anti-clerical or deistic implications. Instead, he fuses it with the views of those Latitudinarian churchmen who rejected Hobbes and offered a vision of man naturally delighting in good ('virtuously voluptuous', as Isaac Barrow put it) and strengthening his faith in the practical exertions of charity. 'That man believes the gospel best', Archbishop Tillotson preached, 'who lives most according to it.'[1]

Fielding appeals to this natural goodness in man, but he also recognizes that man needs the sanctions of Christian revelation to give his good nature stability and confidence. Divine punishment and reward are not so much threat and bribe as the necessary corrective to the apparently meaningless injustice of the world. They justify goodness rather than coerce it. And once Fielding has established the radical simplicity of charity, he san say, in effect, with Pascal, 'truth apart from charity is not God, but His image and idol, which we must neither love nor worship' (*Pensées*, trans. W. F. Trotter, no. 582).

Fielding wants to show that man is naturally prepared to lead a Christian life. A life of charity may make the severest demands upon him, but it makes its demands upon *him*; that is, upon man as he is

1 Cited from Sermon 228 by Martin C. Battestin in *The Moral Basis of Fielding's Art*, Wesleyan University Press, 1959. The background of Fielding's ethical thought is presented in this book and in Henry Knight Miller's *Essays on Fielding's Miscellanies*, Princeton University Press, 1961. Extremely valuable and different in emphasis is William B. Coley, 'The Background of Fielding's laughter', *ELH*, vol. 26, 1959. I am indebted to William Empson, '*Tom Jones*', *Kenyon Review*, vol. 20, 1958, and to J. Middleton Murry, 'In Defence of Fielding,' *Unprofessional Essays*, Jonathan Cape, 1956. Much of this material is to be found in Ronald Paulson (ed.), *Fielding: A Collection of Critical Essays*, Prentice-Hall, 1962.

naturally constituted and not as he becomes through some violence upon his nature or through some heroic sacrifice that only a few can hope to achieve. Therefore Fielding vehemently attacks those rigorists who make the possibility of achieving goodness seem remote or hopeless. (Mandeville seems to take sardonic pleasure in insisting upon the impossibility of attaining virtue, whereas Swift, as we have seen, tries to mitigate, through politics, the difficulty of meeting its inescapable obligation.) Those who 'preach up mortification and self-denial', Fielding writes, 'may insinuate that a man cannot be good and happy at the same time, and may deny all merit to all actions which are not done in contradiction to nature; but I say, with Dr Barrow, *Let us improve and advance our nature to the utmost perfection of which it is capable*, I mean by doing all the good we can; and surely that nature which seems to partake of the divine goodness in this world is the most likely to partake of the divine happiness in the next. To speak a solemn truth, such natures alone are capable of such beatitude' (*Covent-Garden Journal*, ed. G. E. Jensen, New Haven, 1915, no. 29, p. 309).

This seems genial and optimistic, and to an extent it is. But the effect of it is to remove those pretexts by which men postpone accepting the clear injunctions of the gospels. 'The camel has been discussed', André Gide once wrote, 'the eye has been discussed, the needle has been discussed, and people have above all discussed to find out to what degree the rich man could or could not approach the kingdom of God. Yet what is more luminous than the word of the Gospel.'[1] Like the Augustan satirists, Fielding sees the preposterousness of this evasion of goodness. And the methods of evasion are his constant object of scrutiny: the withdrawal into legality and dogma, the sophistry of bad faith, the careful preservation of a code too exalted to use. All these forms of self-justification Fielding renders with ironic courtesy; he is detached enough to make us see through them with ease, but he is attentive enough to their logic to make us respect its formal rigor. His subject is what Hazlitt calls 'the farce of respectability', but the farce touches, too, in its elaboration of a mock order, on the Augustan theme of the tragedy of mind.

It is in the energy of virtue that Fielding finds men's fulfilment.

1 *Pretexts*, trans. Justin O'Brien, Delta, 1959, p. 346. See also William B. Coley 'Gide and Fielding', *Comparative Literature*, vol. 11, 1959.

'*In the energy itself* of virtue (says Aristotle) *there is great pleasure*; and this was the meaning of him who first said, *that virtue was its own reward* ... we may extend the observation of Aristotle to every human passion: for in what but in the energies themselves, can the pleasures of ambition, avarice, pride, hatred, and revenge be conceived to lie?' Their reward lies in 'the labor itself', and why should this not be true, Fielding asks, of benevolence too. 'Why should this most lovely of all mistresses be pursued, not for her native charm, but for the fortune which she is to bring us?' (*Covent-Garden Journal*, no. 29, I, p. 308.) This Shaftesburian emphasis does not, as I have said, preclude Fielding's belief in Christian doctrine. But, significantly, the Christian doctrine may only confirm the unlimited openness of virtue: 'a glorious consideration to the virtuous man,' Fielding wrote earlier (*Champion*, 4 March 1739–40, *Works*, XV, p. 230), 'is that he may rejoice even in the never attaining that which he so well deserves, since it furnishes him with a noble argument for the certainty of a future state.' Or, again, good-nature is 'the only affection of the human mind which can never be sated' (*Works*, XV, p. 260). Fielding regards good-nature or charity much as his contemporaries were beginning to regard the creative imagination: as a force in itself more precious than any of its acts, and a force that could never be satisfied with those limited performances in which it expressed itself. The acts of goodness are essential, for Fielding, as a check upon hypocrisy or self-deception: the sentiments are not enough, for they fester into pride if they are not constantly put to practice. Yet it is not acts themselves that are the ultimate value but 'the strong energies of a good mind' (*Tom Jones*, book 13, chapter 1).[1]

This openness of virtue makes all morality problematic. Motives are hard to penetrate, even for their possessors. The existence of laws tempts men to self-righteous adherence to their letter rather than a generous pursuit of their spirit. What I have spoken of, in connection with Pope's *Essay on Man*, as the fluidity of relatedness is precisely what the existence of structures of order tends to block. Like Pope, Fielding finds a solution in the idea of the duty to the Whole. While he sees no necessary correspondence between rank and virtue, Fielding does accept the hierarchies of an existing social structure. His interest

1 *Works* refers to the so-called W. E. Henley edition, Heinemann, 1903. The novels are cited, where necessary, by abbreviations.

lies not in reordering society but in re-establishing the basis of its conduct. If men were genuinely subject each to the other, they would find their interest in the common good and would regard the powers of rank only as a greater responsibility to serve. The freezing of men into status (professions, classes) or the massing of them into mobs blocks this sense of oneness and mutual subjection. The task, as always, is to hold them to the claims they are so easily tempted to evade.[1]

But this solution, while essential in Fielding's thinking, does not hold the center of his attention. The problematic nature of morality does. His novels, whether or not he meant them to, shocked many of his contemporaries by disturbing their moral assurance. Miss Mulso (later Mrs Chapone) writes with comparative assurance at first: 'Is there not a tendency in all his works to soften the deformity of vice, by placing characters in an amiable light that are destitute of every virtue except good nature?' 'Precisely,' one can imagine Fielding replying. But Miss Mulso has a more fundamental difficulty – he is unsettling: 'Fielding contrives to gloss over gross and monstrous faults in such a manner that even his virtuous readers shall call them frailties.' We know that Lady Mary Wortley Montagu and Dr Johnson were troubled too. William Cobbett, in 1829, could ask: 'How is it possible for young people to read such a book [as Tom Jones], and to look upon orderliness, sobriety, obedience, and frugality, as virtues?'[2] The point, of course, is that each of these virtues can become a vice and does (they are an admirable catalogue of the qualities of Fielding's rogues) – so long as it is not informed by generosity and benevolence. Fielding has attempted nothing less than a fundamental redefinition of virtue – and to redefine it, he must dissociate the inessentials.

Fielding insists upon the difficulties. He demands that we take the full risk of dissociating true charity from moral conventionality. This becomes sharpest in his treatment of love. Presenting figures of innocence and goodness who are young, careless, naïve, and spontaneous – free of all the impostures of their graver elders – he insists, like Gay, upon the relationship between sexual warmth and charitable

1 This draws on George Sherburn, 'Fieldings' Social Outlook', *Philological Quarterly*, no. 35, 1956.
2 For these quotations see F. T. Blanchard, *Fielding the Novelist*, 1926, pp. 96, 101, 358.

love. His fundamental concern is with generosity, and he builds up a contrast between the cold tight self-love of Blifil or the calculating debauchery of Colonel James and the natural vigor that, like the heart itself, outruns the control of prudence. Joseph Andrews preserves his chastity, but with more difficulty in the case of Fanny than of Lady Booby. Tom Jones does not. Booth falls into adultery. But what is common to all these instances is the motif that is so clear in Dryden's heroic plays and *All for Love*: only the man of strong feeling can achieve the generosity of spirit that rejects the partial and restrictive views of more cautious or selfish men. This feeling need not take a sensual form, as we see in Parson Adams or Amelia (neither of whom disdains sexual pleasure, it should be noted); but in the young hero it naturally does. Such vigor is a lesser force than the fury of Almanzor or the towering splendor of Antony, but it is also fresher and more attractive – in Tom Jones, at least – than its counterpart in Mirabell or Macheath. Fielding has transposed scale once more by introducing an element not too far above the mock-pastoral rusticity of Gay's *Shepherd's Week*. Joseph and Tom may turn out to be gentlemen after all, or nature's noblemen, but they are at home in the pasture and they fight best with fist or cudgel.

Fielding is, like the Augustans, trying to define an ideal order of mind. It is in the order of mind, existing as it does within that field of contrary attractions, between the order of flesh and the order of charity, that the human situation must be most clearly faced. If it can bring into harmony these seemingly disjunct orders, it will make possible a morality that is both of this world and beyond it. The typical Augustan problem, as for Pascal, is to destroy the self-sufficient rationalism that abstracts from experience those principles of which an elegant logical structure can be built. Such rationalism becomes a source of pride that cuts man off from the pieties and the sentiments that are rightly his, and its critics posit a subtler, more intuitive order of mind that is at once head and heart, thought and feeling. As Sterne preached later, 'What divines say of the mind, naturalists have observed of the body; that there is no passion so natural to it as love – which is the principle of doing good' (*Sermons*, Shakespeare Head Edition, Oxford, 1927, vol. I, p. 63). Nowhere do these puzzles become sharper than in the nature of love, at once self-seeking and self-transcending, predatory and generous, passionate and contemplative. Its capacity for conversion, from desire to disinterested reverence, has been the stuff of myth and philosophic metaphor at least since Plato.

Fielding's treatment of love is another attempt to find an inclusive view of man's nature. Like Pope, he sees the reconciliation of self-love and the generous, outflowing love of mankind. In his famous chapter, 'Of Love', in *Tom Jones* (book 6, chapter 1), he judiciously sifts the elements that make up the 'passion of Love'. It is telling that he reclaims the term 'passion' (as elsewhere he speaks of 'the glorious lust of doing good' or 'the heart that hungers after goodness') and separates the passion of *love* from 'the desire of satisfying a voracious appetite with a certain quantity of delicate white human flesh'. He grants that love, as he conceives it, will 'call in the aid of that hunger' and that love heightens 'all its delights to a degree scarce imaginable' to men who have mere sensual appetite alone. Love, moreover, seeks 'its own satisfaction as much as the grossest of all our appetites'. These concessions to the 'mixed' nature of the passion of love go far beyond the emphasis we find in Shaftesbury (although not beyond Shaftesbury's full, balanced views) and are close in spirit to the inclusiveness we find in Pope's *Essay on Man*.

In return for these concessions, Fielding establishes his claims for the conversion of appetite. There exists 'in some (I believe many) human breasts a kind and benevolent disposition, which is gratified by contributing to the happiness of others'. This disinterested benevolence is a cause of 'great and exquisite delight', which may be 'heightened and sweetened by the assistance of amorous desires', but need not be. 'Esteem and gratitude' fuse with the amorous desires and give them stability that can outlive youth and beauty (we may think here of Swift's poems to Stella). Fielding's argument is a homely version of the old reconciliation of the terrestrial and the celestial Venus; its emphasis is not the original Platonic one on the falling away of the lower order of appetite as the soul ascends, but on the fusion in the active business of life of these orders. Shaftesbury had insisted upon man's natural capacity for the disinterested love of goodness and argued for it in the facts of aesthetic experience. Pope had shown man's inherent capacity for social love awakened by the necessities of forming a social order to curb his selfishness. This empirical bent is the reply to the Hobbesian or Mandevillian attempt to reduce all benevolence or seeming disinterestedness to a refinement or sublimation of appetite. Fielding, like his predecessors, insists upon a genuine duality, and having established that to his satisfaction, he can accept and celebrate the mixture of disparate elements. Even more, he can draw upon the animal vigor of the barnyard and extend the esteem and gratitude to an acceptance of the teachings of the Gospels, and he can play ironically upon the lowness of both these extremes. Each affronts the self-righteous view of worldly respectability, for each confronts it with spontaneity and warmth, with a 'passion' that needs no recourse to principles or argument.

Love, then, becomes one of the principal empirical tests Fielding uses to challenge the unthinking recourse to forms and principles. It is not, as Sir John Hawkins claimed, that he is 'teaching that virtue upon principle is imposture, that generous qualities alone constitute true worth', but rather that principle without the generous qualities is readily subverted – wrested, like Scripture, and turned, like the will in *A Tale of a Tub*, to travesty.

The Subversion of Forms

Fielding the novelist is consistent with Fielding the moralist. The novelist plays against forms just as much as the moralist. 'Playing against' may need a word of explanation. The comic writer and the comic actor achieve some of their best effects by maintaining the traditional forms of heroism or morality – which provide their world with a stable and secure familiar meaning – but treating them with an excess of gravity, a curiously upsetting literalness, a pleasure in the dilemmas they pose. The high rhetoric invites this touch of fatuity by its very height, as I have tried to show in discussing the Augustan mock form; and the systematic embarrassment of the traditional view is the stuff of comedy. In *The Tragedy of Tragedies* Fielding subverted forms with a high-spirited extravagance, but the forms he subverted were extremely susceptible to this treatment. The same may be said of *Shamela*, where he reduces Richardson's *Pamela* to a trollop with a simple-minded delight in her cunning. On one level or another this subversion of forms runs through Fielding's work; even when it is not used primarily as a comic technique, it represents a saving skepticism, a readiness to examine every possible imposture, even those that his heroes assume.

Let me illustrate. In *Jonathan Wild* the burden of the irony is carried by the villainy of Wild and his rapacious colleagues (as well as their counterparts in the high life of court). But once the innocent Heartfrees escape Wild's exploitation and are reunited with great joy, Mrs Heartfree takes up her astonishing recital of her adventures. Her account is a parody of romance literature, but it also reveals the awakened vanity of a simple woman who has discovered her power over men. We can perhaps acquit her of deliberately torturing her husband with protracted accounts of attempts upon her virtue, but she tends to dwell on the compliments she has received.

'If I mistake not, I was interrupted just as I was beginning to repeat some of the compliments made me by the hermit.' 'Just as you had finished them, I believe, madam,' said the justice. 'Very well, sir,' said she; 'I am sure I have no pleasure in the repetition. He concluded then with telling me, though I was in his eyes the most charming woman in the world, and might tempt a saint to abandon the ways of holiness, yet my beauty inspired him . . . ' (book 4, chapter 11).

And she goes on, unsparingly, apparently anxious to relive those moments of unfamiliar glory.

Something like this occurs in *Amelia* when Mrs Atkinson tells her story to Amelia. Having raised her listener to a high pitch of curiosity, Mrs Atkinson begins the long torture of delay and apology, pleased with her power over her audience, sure of the appeal of her subject. The tale reveals a good deal of pettiness in the teller, and the flood of emotions that are released demands draughts of cordial, glasses of water, and at least one violent convulsion fit that lasts 'the usual time' (book 7, chapter 8).

This constant ironic reservation and readiness to overthrow whatever has grown suspect through hardening into formality link Fielding with some of our contemporary novelists. Kingsley Amis has spoken of his humor as 'closer to our own than that of any writer before the present century,' and has found 'a Fielding revival' in the rejection by contemporaries of 'the novel of consistent tone, moving through a recognized and restricted cycle of emotional keys.' These novelists are comparable to Fielding in their attempt 'to combine the violent and the absurd, the grotesque and the romantic, the farcical and the horrific within a single novel.'[1] Amis overlooks the appeal of Fielding to writers like Stendhal and Gide, who achieved in considerable measure what the post-war English novel has attempted. But his point is important, and it is the kind of critical view that deserves the closest attention because it comes out of the problems of new literary creation.

The kind of writing that most closely resembles Fielding's today is the comic picaresque novel, like Amis's own *Lucky Jim*, in which the hero makes up in honesty for what he lacks in respectability. His inability to live as prudently as others who are less honest and simply less alive produces a series of farcical scrapes. These are often painful, but they are so extravagantly elaborate and so ingeniously invented that our sympathy is displaced into laughter. The laughter is not without its edge – Lucky Jim's desperate efforts to save appearances are a tribute to the power of the conventions he has to live by in order to live at all. But the picaresque hero is at once a moral critic (like the satirist posing as *naïf* or *ingénu*), a careless innocent, and – in his comic resilience – a man saved by luck. Picaresque heroes are necessary whenever we wish to celebrate those virtues that cannot be – or simply haven't been – embodied in our morality. These heroes may be socially mobile men in an age of outgrown establishments, or they may be champions of values that society, by its very organization, necessarily represses. The resilience and survival of the picaresque hero is a survival of the values he stands for, values too closely involved with action to be put to sleep in Avalon. They must be seen in their readiness and their openness, and the picaresque work often concludes with the arc of a new gesture about to be made.

Yet it is not the picaresque hero alone that gives Fielding's novels their distinctive note, but the combination of naïve hero and sophisticated narrator. The fluid shifts of tone that we see in recent picaresque novels are produced by heroes (usually narrators as well) who are open to each new experience, variable and unpredictable, often self-mocking. In these novels the reader is left without a clear guide; he follows along as he can, prepared only for surprise. But in Fielding's

1 *New York Times Book Review*, 7 July 1957.

novels the case is different. Tom Jones may be spontaneous and improvident, but he surprises himself more than he does the reader. We see him through the narrator's commentary, in a series of events that are clearly calculated and tellingly repetitive – so that he becomes a comic figure fixed in a limited pattern of response. We count on Tom's goodness and on his carelessness. It is the novelist, instead, who engages our curiosity. How will he bring it all off? How will he extricate his hero and, even more, his values? The novelist's relationship with the reader – itself, as Wayne Booth has suggested,[1] a sub-plot in the novel – is carefully modulated between doubt and trust, ironic aloofness and warm solidarity. The characters, hero and all, play out their roles within the space that Fielding creates and encloses in his relationship with the reader.

What is this relationship? Here we meet the problem we find in all Augustan irony. Ultimately, behind the work we see the historical author, the real personality behind the mask. In some cases, like Pope's late satires, where the author has become a public figure, our recognition of his actual traits may be essential. But generally before we come at that figure, we have the mask itself to meet. The Fielding who appears in his novels is, like Swift and Pope, a shifting series of personae; he is engaged in a constant dance of ironic postures. Behind them we may recognize a personality we can trust and accept, but we know him through his performance.

Let us consider a single instance of this. In the opening chapter of *Joseph Andrews* the author praises the power of example as opposed to mere precept: 'A good man . . . is a standing lesson to all his acquaintance, and of far greater use in that narrow circle than a good book.' This we can take on trust: 'a standing lesson' is a little chilling and might seem an invitation to self-righteousness, but it need not trouble us. Fielding goes on, then, to consider the problem of making such a lesson available to the world at large, beyond the small circle of a good man's personal acquaintance; it is the writer who can achieve this end, and 'by communicating such valuable patterns to the world, he may perhaps do a more extensive service to mankind, than the person whose life originally afforded the pattern'. Again, this is plausible enough (Pope has done more for mankind than the Man of Ross), but it is disconcerting: the good man is now opposed

1 *The Rhetoric of Fiction*, University of Chicago Press, 1962, p. 216.

to the writer of his history, and heroic goodness is made a less 'extensive service to mankind' than the art of the biographer. We seem to be confusing values, and a phrase like 'service to mankind' carries the seeds of the confusion. What, we ask, would the biographer have to represent without the 'standing lesson' itself? The outside – the representation, the biography or legend – seems to be supplanting the active goodness that is so rare.

The subversion becomes clear as we move on to some examples of this 'service to mankind': 'John the Great, who, by his brave and heroic actions against men of large and athletic bodies, obtained the glorious appellation of the Giant-Killer.' The nursery tales and romances are solemnly offered as the means by which 'the reader is almost as much improved as entertained'. This may be true; nursery tales do instill moral awareness. But the pompous claims begin to strike a false note.

This false note is now carried over to the two works Fielding offers as an 'admirable pattern of the amiable' – Colley Cibber's *Apology* and Richardson's *Pamela*. All the implicit self-advertising of the 'biographer or historian' is now lightly dropped on the shoulders of Richardson, who pretended to be working 'from authentic papers and records'. And Colley Cibber embodies the complete subversion of the relationship of 'standing lesson' and 'biographer'. He is both at once, and 'is by many thought to have lived such a life only in order to write it'. The point of all this is that appearance and pretension have swallowed up the goodness they claim to serve, and Fielding has set the satirical keynote for his novel in the opening paragraphs.

Fielding is addressing his reader at two levels. He is speaking to the perceptive and good-natured man, but he is constantly teasing him with the possibility that he is not up to this candor. Readers, like other men, are conventional, snobbish, hypocritical; and, in any case, the morality of Fielding's novels is designed to unsettle accepted attitudes. If the reader is to achieve the flexibility and discrimination that Fielding's morality demands, he must be teased into a full exercise of his wits. Just as Fielding so often maintains an ironic courtesy toward his characters and hesitates over which motive to ascribe to them (meanwhile, of course, exposing the worst), so he is often embarrassingly tactful to his readers. His tact is the sort that makes its victim aware of how tenderly he must be treated, or, in other words, how little he can be trusted. The man who deserves to be trusted needs no tact; the banter of friends can be free and playful, and the author's irony will then only confirm his solidarity with the reader. But, in the process, there are few readers whose feelings are not tested and whose wit is not sharpened.

The structure of Fielding's major novels is a distinctive combination of elements. His comic plots are elaborate and contrived, but within them there is room for the casualness of picaresque incident; they have the artificiality of stage comedy and the leisurely looseness of a more realistic form. His heroes engage our feelings, surely, but they do not have enough consciousness to allow us to inhabit their minds very long or live there very fully. They do not stretch our awareness or offer the sense of limitlessness our own experience does. They have the measure of reality we confer upon many childhood memories: we can feel ourselves back into that simpler mind and know what it was like, but we cannot suppress our sense of what was not yet there. Tom Jones has traditionally been taken as a somewhat autobiographical character. Whether or not he was in fact, the book presents the effect of the mature author contemplating himself when younger – somewhat more equably than Byron does in *Don Juan* – with detachment but with warmth.

The presence of the author is an element that affects all the rest. He presents us with a microcosm to be contemplated, puzzled over, studied. As he puts it in *Tom Jones* (book 10, chapter 1), 'This work may . . . be considered as a great creation of our own; and for a little reptile of a critic to presume to find fault with any of its parts, without knowing the manner in which the whole is connected . . . is a most presumptuous absurdity.' This is a defense of the literary structure, but Fielding's deliberate echo of Pope's *Essay on Man* is telling: he points in the next paragraph to the 'nice distinctions' – Pope calls them gradations – 'between two persons activated by the same vice or folly as another'. Fielding's novel is a world to be studied as God's creation is studied in the *Essay on Man*, and his diction throughout the book creates categories of discursive thought. We are made to apprehend Fielding's world conceptually. This device is often playful; the concepts are too inclusive to do more than mock the sorry things they denote. But we are always told as well as shown, or told as we are shown. Fielding keeps us constantly aware of the problem we have in coming to terms with a fluid world and an elusive spontaneous goodness by means of the concepts our minds have to make do with. Significantly, Fielding's minor characters talk a great deal; and they reveal in the process the treacherous nature of conceptual language.

Not only the language, but the arrangement of parts in Fielding's novels has a discursive form. Again and again characters are paired off to present false extremes. Or a cast of characters is led past Tom's bedside (as he recovers from the injury he sustained in rescuing Sophia) to cheer him or berate him, to exhibit different shades of love, benevolence, malice, or vindictiveness. Or all the characters execute a dance of attitudes around a single concept – love in *Tom Jones*, charity in *Joseph Andrews*. Characters are created to fill out a moral spectrum, and each gains from the presence of the rest: 'the follies of either rank do in reality illustrate each other,' as Fielding tells us (*Tom Jones*, book 9, chapter 1). We are teased and challenged once more by the problem of arranging these characters. Where shall we place Squire Western in any scale that runs from Allworthy to Blifil? But all these discursive effects would have little interest if they were not constantly played off against the narrative movement and our sympathies with the characters. Fielding is neither essayist nor realistic novelist, nor both in turn. He is rather both at once and therefore something different from either.

In such novels as Fielding writes, neither characters nor action can be allowed to escape the author's control. Fielding controls his characters by limiting them. In general, his heroes have more energy than reflectiveness, although all have their moments of dignified eloquence. The villains, in turn, are so transparent (but not to men like Allworthy) and so compulsive that we are left with an impression of moral shallowness more than depravity. There are bullies and braggarts, misers and hypocrites, but no one to say, 'Evil, be thou my good'. These characters are all dependent upon the social forms that give them a guise of respectability, and the forms – or dogmas or twisted meanings – become as responsible as the people who use them. Fielding brings this out through his symmetrical arrangements. He boasts, for example, of his description of 'the different operations of this passion of love in the gentle and cultivated mind of the Lady

Booby, from those which it effected in the less polished and coarser disposition of Mrs Slipslop' (*Joseph Andrews*, book 1, chapter 7). Again in the second book of *Tom Jones* he gives us 'scenes of matrimonial felicity in different degrees of life'. Here Mrs Partridge's uncontrolled suspicions of her husband's relations with Jenny Jones produce Punch-and-Judy farce, while the hatred of Captain Blifil and his wife has a savage intensity that is possible only with a more refined etiquette. The Blifils' marriage is summed up in the widow's mourning:

[She] conducted herself through the whole season in which
grief is to make its appearance on the outside of the body
with the strictest regard to all the rules of custom and
decency, suiting the alterations of her countenance to the
several alterations of her habit: for as this changed from
weeds to black, from black to gray, from gray to white, so
did her countenance change from dismal to sorrowful, from
sorrowful to sad, and from sad to serious, till the day came in
which she was allowed to return to her former serenity
(book 3, chapter 1).

The word 'allowed', ironic as it is, reminds us that, while the depth of malice may be directly proportionate to the complexity of forms, the forms themselves exercise a tyranny over the man who lives by them. We see something much like this in Restoration comedy; the case of Fainall in *The Way of the World* comes to mind, and the way in which Mirabell seizes the forms and turns them to a better purpose. Fielding's heroes do not attempt what Mirabell so handsomely carries off – or rather they bring new difficulties upon themselves when they do attempt it. Tom's proposal of marriage to Lady Bellaston succeeds in freeing him of a demanding mistress, but it rebounds against him when Sophia learns of it. Amelia sends Mrs Atkinson to the masquerade in her place and eludes her would-be seducer, but she gives Mrs Atkinson's indiscretion occasion to create new difficulties.

Another severe limitation Fielding places upon his characters is the importance that rumor and gossip play in determining their fate. We see Tom pursued along the road by malicious reports; Tom and Sophia kept at odds by the petty jealousy of their servants, Partridge and Honour. (Only rarely does the reverse work out, as when Tom's kindness to Anderson, the desperate highwayman, becomes known to Mrs Miller and ultimately to Allworthy.) What gives Fielding's world its peculiar quality is that so much happens with so little design. There is a great deal of triviality – the snobbery of a Mrs Graveairs, the weak swagger of a Beau Didapper, the autumnal lust of Mrs Slipslop – some of it disarmingly grotesque, too mechanically incongruous to seem very menacing, but all of it building up through a crisscross of coincidence and a steady accumulation to formidable proportions. When Jack Nightingale seduces Nancy Miller, Tom must spell out to Nightingale the meaning of what he has done: 'I do not imagine you have laid a regular premeditated scheme for the destruction of the quiet of a poor little creature, or have even foreseen the consequence: for I am sure thou art a very good-natured fellow, and such a one can never be guilty of a cruelty of that kind; but at the same time you have pleased your vanity, without considering that this poor girl was made a sacrifice to it' (book 14, chapter 4).

Fielding's interest, then, lies less in the moral struggles within characters than in the ways in which selfishness finds refuge in forms. Lady Booby and Black George are both shown in formal deliberation, balancing alternatives with all the scruples of a high tragic character; but the formal deliberation also provides a comfortable disguise – from themselves – of the meanness of their motives. Fielding has taken over from Mandeville the close study of the way in which social forms are learned. His delightful account of the young girl's schooling in coquetry (*Joseph Andrews*, book 4, chapter 7) derives from *The Fable of the Bees* and turns all Mandeville's cruel insights upon Richardson's Pamela as well as Lady Booby. Fielding can use Mandeville's reductive analysis of motives to good purpose so long as he is treating vanity and folly; it is Mandeville's similar account of the origin of moral virtue that he indignantly rejects.

Like Mandeville, Fielding has a detached appreciation of the artistry of our vanities and passions, particularly as they make use of social forms. One example will serve. Squire Western's sister is a woman of shallow vanity, tall, ugly, unloved, who has found her compensations not in prudery, like Bridget Allworthy, but in a studious devotion to the fashionable world. She has 'acquired all that knowledge which the said world usually communicates; and was a perfect mistress of manners, customs, ceremonies, and fashions.' She has studied her plays and romances, her historical memoirs and political pamphlets; she has mastered 'the doctrine of Amour' and the latest gossip – 'a knowledge which she the more easily attained, as her pursuit of it was never diverted by any affairs of her own' (book 6, chapter 2). It is a wonderful picture of an empty woman feeding upon externalities and vicarious excitement. And, of course she speaks a dreadful gibberish of court lingo, diplomatic jargon, and military terms. The gibberish gives away her innocent incomprehension of all she imagines she knows, even as her pride in devious subtlety makes her parrot the cynicism of the town. When Squire Western remarks, 'Allworthy is a queer b—ch, and money hath no effect o' un,' she can reply, 'Do you think Allworthy hath more contempt for money than any other man because he professes more? Such credulity would better become one of us weak women, than that wise sex which Heaven hath formed for politicians.' She is, of course, the most credulous of creatures herself. But all her affection for her brother and niece, all her fundamental goodness ('a very extraordinary good and sweet disposition') can produce, under the influence of fashionable forms upon her vanity, is the astonishing advice that Sophia marry Blifil so that she may have Tom safely as a lover (book 6, chapter 5).

Such innocent depravity as Mrs Western's – and it is not much different from Jack Nightingale's or Lord Fellamar's – shows the diffusion of responsibility Fielding creates in his world. Actions follow from small vanities as often as from deliberate evil. They may be the product of a chance meeting of characters who are in themselves ineffectual but become imposing in combination. Thus, when Sophia and Tom almost meet at Upton, they are kept apart by a series of accidents – yet in retrospect all that happens follows from the nature of the participants. Sophia's maid, Honour, exhibits all her pretensions in the inn kitchen as she loftily allows Partridge, who has come with Tom, to remain: 'you look somewhat like a gentleman, and may sit still if you please: I don't desire to disturb anybody but mob' (book 10, chapter 4). When Honour is sent by Sophia to call Tom, Partridge struts in turn: 'One woman is enough at once for a reasonable man.' His manner enrages Honour, who at once reports Tom's infidelity to Sophia and gives it as ugly a turn as possible. To make matters worse, Susan the chambermaid can relay Partridge's boasts 'that your ladyship was dying for love of the young squire, and that he was going to the wars to get rid of you'. This formidable array of pettiness provides a constant store of motives Fielding can bring into play with the slightest twist of coincidence. The result is that the coincidences that entrap the central characters seem only special cases of the prevailing conditions that surround them. This enables Fielding to use the most flagrant artifice without our losing touch with a plausible social reality.

Fielding's subversion of forms, at work throughout his novels, becomes most apparent in his comic resolutions, which can still outrage moralistic critics by their disdain for the full consequences of the heroes' frailties. Yet the artifice that resolves the near-catastrophe is the same as the artifice that creates it. Fielding weaves together blind and confused motives to bring his heroes to the brink of disasters they hardly merit. And the excess of these disasters makes them ludicrous, morally as well as dramatically. Fielding sharpens this by inventing, in both *Joseph Andrews* and *Tom Jones*, a travesty of the prototypical tragic nemesis, the dark mystery of unknowing incest. His point is that these terrors are not for such heroes as these; the incursion of the terrible into this world of limited consciousness and limited consequences is brilliantly unreal.

When Joseph and Fanny learn that they are apparently brother and sister, Fielding crowds the discovery scene with noisy emotion that suggests panic in a barnyard when a fox has entered. Joseph and Fanny grow faint and pallid, but little Dicky Adams roars and Parson Adams falls to his knees to ejaculate many thanksgivings (book 4, chapter 12). And Adams himself is to undergo, in the night farce of mistaken bedrooms, the test of being discovered by Joseph naked in bed with Fanny ('Hath he offered any rudeness to you?' Joseph asks in a rage). The novel never relaxes long enough to take the threat of incest seriously or to make more than ridiculous the resolutions with which it is met. Adams's advice is feeble enough, and it is followed by the vow of Joseph and Fanny of 'perpetual celibacy'. They plan, poor fools, 'to live together all their days, and indulge a Platonic friendship for each other'.

In *Tom Jones*, once the seeming fact that Tom has slept with his

mother is revealed, we have tragic postures and a near-tragic speech:
'But why do I blame Fortune? I am myself the cause of all my misery.'
But at this point the author intrudes to remind us how artfully he had
managed the ninth book to prevent Partridge from meeting Mrs
Waters there. We are reminded not only of the fictionality of character and event, but of the absurdly intensified causality Fielding has
created: 'Instances of this kind we may frequently observe in life,
where the greatest events are produced by a nice train of little circumstances; and more than one example of this may be discovered
by the accurate eye, in this our history.' Once more in *Amelia*, when
the bailiff apprehends Booth outside Miss Matthews's lodgings just
before he can return to Amelia, our attention is directed to the artifice
that runs through all these novels and tightens causality to the point
where it verges on the farcical:

... there is no exercise of the mind of a sensible reader
more pleasant than tracing the several small and almost
imperceptible links in every chain of events by which all the
great actions of the world are produced (book 12, chapter 1).

We are made securely aware of the novelist in control, and we
recognize that the terrible has been prepared as deftly and artificially
as it will be overturned.

Is this cheating moral seriousness? Fielding has so arranged matters
that there is no Thwackum-like punitive nemesis; he has subverted
the form in which men have traditionally embodied their sense of
guilt: their fear of the price that greatness must exact, their sense of
the exposure to irretrievable error that comes of each new assertion
of power or will. Tom has approached a tragic role throughout the
last part as he assumes responsibility at each turn for what he has
done. So here: 'I am myself the cause of all my misery.' And we can
admire this, but we recognize the disproportion between the act and
its consequences. Only a sinister deity would design such punishment,
the kind of deity who invites prostration or defiance rather than trust.
The fact that the tragic discovery is traditional does not, in short,
make it appropriate; Fielding shrugs off the great tragic forms with
a Christian cheerfulness. Dr Harrison, when he writes to Booth and
Amelia about their loss of her mother's fortune, congratulates them
upon their happiness in each other. 'A superstitious heathen,' he

goes on, 'would have dreaded the malice of Nemesis in your situation; but as I am a Christian, I shall venture to add another circumstance to your felicity ... that you have ... a faithful and zealous friend' (book 3, chapter 10).

The result has its own kind of moral seriousness. Fielding insists upon the weight of folly and triviality that impedes the best and worst intentions. In the preface to his sister's *David Simple*, Fielding speaks of 'the mazes, windings, and labyrinths, which perplex the heart of man to such a degree that he is himself often incapable of seeing through them' (*Works*, XVI, 10). In his own novels, his typical method is to place heroes of transparent and spontaneous goodness (they may have innocent follies and affectations, like Adams) amidst the mazes and windings of others' selfishness. These heroes need not succeed, and they come to recognize this fact; but they need not fail, either, in a world where evil often becomes self-defeating and Fortune seems to rule. Fortune is the name we give to the impenetrable intricacy of those 'nice trains of little causes' or 'small and almost imperceptible links in every chain of events'. The links are, in most cases, the trivial obsessions of others, the inevitable accidents of countless jostling egos.

Fielding can reward his heroes because they do not seek a reward. He wishes to free our faith in order, as Pope does, from any simple-minded expectation that goodness will find its reward on earth. The only reward it can find there is that it pays to itself: the pleasure it finds in doing good and in sustaining its integrity. Beyond that it seeks nothing, and, in seeking nothing, it has earned the reward the author confers. The comic resolutions are not devices for saving these heroes from facing moral consequences but rewards for their having done so. That the reward is externalized and paid in solid pudding rather than praise need not alter the point. That, too, is a way of reminding us that the malignant Fortune that hounds these characters and the comic providence that extricates them are only two aspects of the author himself, as they are of a benevolent deity. Those characters who can act as if there were such a God of course find Him:

Earth smiles around, with boundless bounty blest,
And Heaven beholds its image in his breast.[1]

1 *Essay on Man*, IV, ll. 371–2.

Low and High

It would have been useless for our Lord Jesus Christ to come
like a king, in order to shine forth in His kingdom of
holiness. But He came there appropriately in the glory of His
own order.

   It is most absurd to take offence at the lowliness of Jesus
Christ, as if His lowliness were in the same order as the
greatness which He came to manifest. If we consider this
greatness . . . we shall see it to be so immense that we shall
have no reason for being offended at a lowliness which is not
of that order (*Pensées*, 793).

These are solemn words to bring to Fielding's novels; yet their import is essential to an understanding of his lowness. I have argued for
his constant subversion of forms, his deliberate overturning of rigid
stances or systematized attitudes. Even the attitudes he espouses and
the characters he admires submit to this untiring alertness to pretense.
It is not simply the hypocritical or affected he attacks but the insensible
conversion of active feeling into formal structure. The lowness of
Fielding's heroes – the fact that in one sense or another they are
dispossessed or disinherited – thrusts them into a situation where they
have no props of status. The nakedness of Joseph, as he lies at the
roadside after the robbery, is itself an extreme instance of the un-
protectedness of these characters.

   Not only are the characters without recourse to position; they are,
by their nature, unable to foresee the malice of others. This inability
is both worldly folly and the wisdom of charity. Parson Adams, we
are told, 'never saw farther into people than they desired to let him'.
Hypocrites like Peter Pounce were 'a sort of people whom Mr
Adams never saw through'. Allworthy, of course, carries on the
pattern, and Dr Harrison is no more beyond it than Booth and
Amelia. In contrast, the selfish count on finding their own devious-
ness in others and often as a result overshoot their mark, like Fainall
and Mrs Marwood in *The Way of the World*. Fielding is insisting upon
the fact that goodness cannot be recognized unless it is first felt
within. This is a counterpart of the traditional Christian view that
one cannot know God until one loves Him. Until that love is felt,
one's knowledge remains fixed in categories of another order. There

is no way of grasping the order of charity, one might say, with the categories of the order of mind. The kind of awareness upon which characters act seems deficient when it is interpreted in the terms of another order. Dr Harrison charges Booth with abusing him by calling him wise: 'You insinuated slily,' says the doctor, 'that I was wise, which, as the world understands the phrase, I should be ashamed of; and my comfort is that no one can accuse me justly of it' (*Amelia*, book 9, chapter 4). Characters speak to each other in foreign tongues, although the words they use are the same. It is Fielding himself who can entertain all these levels of discourse at once, who can perceive how men think in each order of being, and who can embody a harmony of orders within himself.

Fielding's strategy is to dissociate orders – to give us figures who upset our conventional expectations of 'goodness and innocence.' In the preface to *Joseph Andrews* he sets forth a doctrine of the 'comic epic in prose' that steers a course between the conventional high heroism of romance and the monstrous parodies of burlesque. He offers us 'low' characters, and among them, 'the most glaring in the whole', Parson Adams, 'a character of perfect simplicity' whose goodness of heart 'will recommend him to the good-natured.' As Stuart M. Tave has shown (in *The Amiable Humorist*, Chicago University Press, 1960), Fielding's profession to write 'in imitation of the manner of Cervantes author of *Don Quixote*' is deceptive to the modern reader, for Fielding is one of the pioneers in the gradual recognition of the dignity of the foolish Quixote. Parson Adams is a challenge to the reader to discern an essential goodness within a sententious, vainly bookish, short-sighted country clergyman. It is only near the close of the novel that he can rise to the dignity of self-assertion in his reply to Lady Booby:

Madam . . . I know not what your ladyship means by the terms master and service. I am in the service of a master who will never discard me for doing my duty. . . . Whilst my conscience is pure, I shall never fear what man can do unto me (book 4, chapter 2).

The contrasts that run through *Joseph Andrews* are less sharp than those of *Jonathan Wild*, the dissociations less overtly satirical and emphatic. The strain of pastoral allows Fielding to use his setting as commentary; it reaches its culmination in Mr Wilson's garden, where the freshness and vitality of the country (already so evident in Joseph and Fanny) take on dignity and serenity:

No parterres, no fountains, no statues, embellished this little garden. Its only ornament was a short walk, shaded on each side by a filbert-hedge, with a small alcove at one end; whither in hot weather the gentleman and his wife used to retire and divert themselves with their children, who played in the walk before them. But though vanity had no votary in this little spot, here was variety of fruit, and every thing useful for the kitchen; which was abundantly sufficient to catch the admiration of Adams, who told the gentleman, he had certainly a good gardener. Sir, answered he, that gardener is now before you: whatever you see here is the work solely of my own hands (*Joseph Andrews*, book 3, chapter 4).

When the visitors leave, Adams declares 'that this was the manner in which the people had lived in the Golden Age', an echo of his obsession with classical learning, but also of Pope on pastoral poetry: 'pastoral is an image of what they call the Golden Age. So that we are not to describe our shepherds as shepherds at this day really are, but as they may be conceived then to have been, when the best of men followed the employment.' What gives *Joseph Andrews* its striking quality is that Fielding mixes this Virgilian note with the Theocritean of Gay's mock pastorals. The low energies of nature are given their animal vigor (though carefully distinguished from the urgencies of Lady Booby or Slipslop, let alone Beau Didapper), but they are made continuous with the warmth and generosity of a pastoral golden age and of the Christian charity that has drawn so much of its imagery from the life of the shepherd.

In *Tom Jones* the pastoral motive is also present, with the mock pastoral centering in Molly Seagrim and Squire Western. Western is the most startling creation in the novel; perhaps the finest English comic character to have emerged after Falstaff. He is a great baby, frankly selfish and uncontrolled, imperious in his whims, cruelly thoughtless, with the tyranny of a demanding child but none of the capacity to spin out of his appetites subtle schemes of domination or revenge, like Blifil and Lady Bellaston. When he bursts into the

London scene, he brings with him the simplicity of the flesh at its most fleshly. He breaks through the code of honor, that most elaborate and attractive of worldly substitutes for goodness, as he breaks through the delicate modesty of Sophia ('To her, boy, to her, go to her'). Early in the novel we see his simplicity achieve the same ends as real astuteness. Thwackum and Square compete in praising Blifil, who has maliciously released Sophia's bird; Square sees in him another Brutus, Thwackum an exemplary Christian. 'I don't know what you mean, either of you,' Western breaks in, 'by right and wrong. To take away my girl's bird was wrong in my opinion' (book 4, chapter 4). And it is he who defends Tom's effort to recapture the bird for Sophia. 'I am sure I don't understand a word of this,' he says to Square and Thwackum, still debating their moral doctrine.

> It may be learning and sense for aught I know; but you
> shall never persuade me into it. Pox! you have neither of you
> mentioned a word of that poor lad who deserves to be
> commended; to venture breaking his neck to oblige my girl
> was a generous-spirited action; I have learning enough to see
> that. D—n me, here's Tom's health! I shall love the boy for
> it the longest day I have to live (book 4, chapter 4).

It is only to be expected that Squire Western cannot sustain this noble intention. He has as little mind as any man can have; he lives in bursts of enthusiasm, maudlin affection, barbarous willfulness, sheer physicality. He pairs off with his sister – she all Whig politics and would-be townish smartness, he the typical hard-drinking Tory country squire. But Fielding does more with him than that. He uses him to embody animal energy without either the selfish cunning that builds upon appetites in some or the generous charity that fuses with appetite (and transforms it) in others. Tom stands between Western and Allworthy, able to participate in the worlds of both – an innocent carnality in Western and a rational charity in Allworthy – and to bring them together. It would be hard, in fact, to conceive of Tom without the presence of both Allworthy and Western in the novel.

One should observe as well how Jenny Jones, who is something of a prig at the outset, mellows into the generous, if irregular, Mrs Waters of the later parts – in marked contrast to the vain and shallow

Harriet Fitzpatrick. The progression of Tom's temptresses is significant. Molly Seagrim is coarse but pretentious, Lady Bellaston is
refined and vindictive. Mrs Waters strikes a balance between Molly's
unmitigated (and slightly corrupt) low and Lady Bellaston's inverted
high. She is capable – in the case of Tom – of a robust and unfastidious
appetite:

> The beauty of Jones highly charmed her eye; but as she could
> not see his heart, she gave herself no concern about it. She
> could feast heartily at the table of love, without reflecting that
> some other already had been, or hereafter might be, feasted
> with the same repast (book 9, chapter 6).

But she is also capable – in the case of Northerton – of 'that violent
and apparently disinterested passion of love, which seeks only the
good of its object' (Book 9, chapter 7). Fielding allows her only a
strong sensuality in her relations with Tom, but he makes her a
woman who squares her passions with her conscience more boldly
than the hypocrites around her. She defends, in Allworthy's presence,
an attachment that has constancy without legal sanctions, and she
values Tom's virtue at a greater rate than his freedom from vices.
And, all the while, she retains her deep gratitude to Allworthy and
recognizes in his goodness something that 'savored more of the
divine than human nature' (book 18, chapter 8). Fielding discriminates
carefully between moral laxity and moral obliviousness – or, as
Coleridge puts it, between what a man does and what he is.

Amelia is a weaker novel than *Tom Jones*, but it is clearly moving in
a new direction. The fact that Billy Booth has a family depending
upon him makes his irregularities less appealing than Tom's. His only
sexual infidelity takes place at the opening of the novel, before our
concern for his family has grown too strong. For the rest of the story
he is suffering from remorse and the threat of Miss Matthews'
revenge; we see more of the hangover than the intoxication. He is
guilty of less attractive vices than Tom's; he is vain about keeping a
coach, and he gambles disastrously when his family is near starvation.
He is also older and shabbier than Tom; and he can do little for himself in the course of the novel. The center of attention is Amelia, his
wife. Fielding makes their marriage the object of the world's attack,

and Booth's moral dependence upon Amelia gives the marriage all the more significance. Amelia is as close as Fielding comes to a pure embodiment of the order of charity; she has traces of vanity, and she is sometimes handled with irony, but she is never made so ridiculous as Mrs Heartfree. Still, Fielding seems to have gone back to the Heartfrees, that 'family of love', reworked them in a new way, and perhaps offered them finally as a further qualification of the ethical doctrines of *Tom Jones*.

It is Amelia's Christian goodness – selfless, warm, readily forgiving – that sets the tone of the book. We hardly see Booth acting well on his own – except on the battlefield – as we see Tom Jones refuting the Gulliver-like misanthropy of the Man of the Hill, keeping Partridge in check, advising Nightingale, resisting the kind proposal of Mrs Hunt. In this novel the generosity of goodness is much more strictly limited to the forgiveness of Amelia and the benevolence of that harsher, less amiable version of Adams, Dr Harrison. And goodness is heavily beleaguered; under the stress of difficulties, Amelia tells her children hard truths. Good people will show love, 'but there are more bad people, and they will hate you for your goodness' (book 4, chapter 3).

More than this, Fielding brings to the surface and faces what he cannot escape in the Heartfrees; the sentimentalism of Booth and Amelia in their innocence. The book opens with the savage injustices perpetrated by Justice Thrasher and the moral chaos of the prison itself. But it moves on at once to the two narratives of Miss Matthews and Booth. Miss Matthews is a brilliant instance of sentimental vanity; she is capable of stabbing her betrayer, and we have few doubts about her strength of will, but she voluptuates in a vision of herself as the creature of helpless passion. She can describe her method quite coolly in the case of her father. The kind old man had once caused Miss Matthews to miss a ball, and she fanned this memory until it could be revived at will in full strength. 'When any tender idea intruded into my bosom, I immediately raised this phantom of an injury in my imagination, and it considerably lessened the fury of that sorrow which I should have otherwise felt for the loss of so good a father, who died within a few months of my departure from him' (book 1, chapter 9). As Booth tells his own story, with torrents of tears, he inflames Miss Matthews' passion for him; and it bursts out

in her brilliantly funny interruptions. But he is totally involved in
his tale of how Amelia recovered from the accident wherein 'her
lovely nose was beat all to pieces'.

Amelia's nose has become famous because Fielding failed, in the
first edition of the novel, to make explicitly clear that it was restored,
and the image of a noseless Amelia danced before critics' eyes. Even
if we allow for an unfortunate oversight, the choice of a nose seems
singularly inept. Amelia's suffering consists of having to hear false
friends say that 'she will never more turn up her nose at her betters';
and surely no author of Fielding's skill brought this kind of difficulty
upon himself unintentionally. We can pity Amelia, but we cannot
take her accident with quite the solemnity that Booth does. There is
an undernote of laughter in more than Miss Matthews' sublime
remarks ('a cottage with the man one loves, is a palace'). And there
is surely laughter as well as pathos in Booth's account of his departure
from Amelia:

... clinging round my neck, she cried, 'Farewell, farewell for
ever; for I shall never, never see you any more.' At which
words the blood entirely forsook her lovely cheeks, and she
became a lifeless corpse in my arms.
    Amelia continued so long motionless, that the doctor, as
well as Mrs Harris, began to be under the most terrible
apprehensions; so they informed me afterwards, for at that
time I was incapable of making any observation. I had
indeed very little more use of my senses than the dear
creature whom I supported. At length, however, we were
all delivered from our fears; and life again visited the
loveliest mansion that human nature ever afforded it (book 3,
chapter 2).

Booth's sentimentalism helps explain his belief that man could act
only 'from the force of that passion which was uppermost in his
mind, and could do no otherwise' (book 1, chapter 3). Just as his
sister Nancy dies, he learns that he may lose Amelia to someone else.
'I now soon perceived how superior my love for Amelia was to
every passion; poor Nancy's idea disappeared in a moment; I quitted
the lifeless corpse, over which I had shed a thousand tears, left the
care of her funeral to others, and posted, I may almost say flew, back

to Amelia . . .' (book 2, chapter 5). It is necessary for Colonel James, his superior officer, to warn him – when he seems dangerously wounded – against going back to Amelia. James can appreciate 'the comfort of expiring in her arms', but he points out the cruelty, too: 'You would not wish to purchase any happiness at the price of so much pain to her' (book 2, chapter 5). The danger of Booth's temperament is obvious; as Fielding says, he is 'in his heart an extreme well-wisher to religion . . . yet his notions of it [are] very slight and uncertain'. He comes close to the error Dr Johnson found in his friend Savage: 'he mistook the love for the practice of virtue, and was indeed not so much a good man as the friend of goodness.'

Amelia, far more than Booth, grows stronger under the stress of suffering. Fielding has designed the novel so that, at each point, we see Amelia – so much a human embodiment of pure charity – assailed by those who cannot understand her nature. She lives with a landlady who is little more than a procuress. She is tried by the designs of two rakes who have no comprehension of the sanctity of 'wedded love'. When Booth, too, seems to have lost all sense of the meaning of Amelia's love, she is close to despair. Amelia can, however, be freed from the temptations of sentimentality by devoting herself to others. When she joins Booth 'she could not so far command herself as to refrain from many sorrowful exclamations against the hardships of their destiny; but when she saw the effect they had upon Booth she stifled her rising grief [and] forced a little cheerfulness into her countenance' (book 12, chapter 2).

Fielding allows Amelia's purity of character to emerge from the test of ridicule. Amelia is constantly seen in contrast with Mrs Atkinson, who is good but vain and touchy, and whose story of her life exhibits a certain amount of partiality and self-justification. The angelic selflessness of Amelia is her primary quality, and it can afford to be seen in lights that make others ridiculous. Amelia's pathos is heightened by the very kind of extended simile that was once used to overwhelm a Deborah Wilkins or to mock a naïve Tom Jones; Amelia's quiet goodness can wear it with grace.

(286–312)

Ronald Paulson

from *Hogarth: His Life, Art and Times* 1971

From Volume 1

Much more important, however, was the influence the *Harlot's Progress* exerted on Henry Fielding, whose next farce, *The Covent Garden Tragedy*, was played on 1 June [1732]. *The Covent Garden Tragedy* shows at once the impact and the popularity of the *Harlot*. Like Hogarth, Fielding includes a Mother Needham character: Mother Punchbowl, who makes her relationship to Needham obvious by rehearsing her sad end in the pillory. Stormandra summons up Plate 1 when she cries, 'dost think I came last week to town, / The waggon straws yet hanging to my tail?' Lovegirlo recalls Plate 2:

I'll take thee into keeping, take the room
So large, so furnish'd, in so fine a street,
The mistress of a Jew shall envy thee;
By Jove, I'll force the sooty tribe to own
A Christian keeps a whore as well as they.

Plate 3 is alluded to when Stormandra reminds Bilkum of all she has done for him: 'Did I not pick a pocket of a watch, / A pocket pick for thee?' And the fourth plate is evoked by various mentions of hemp-beating, as when Mother Punchbowl observes that 'The very hemp I beat may hang my son.' Even the Harlot's funeral is in the air when news is brought in of Stormandra's 'death':

Stormandra's gone!
Weep all ye sister-harlots of the town;
Pawn your best clothes, and clothe yourself in rags.

There may also have been allusion in the sets and costumes. The *Grub-Street Journal* noticed the similarity when, in its customary unsympathetic discussion of Fielding's new play, it linked Stormandra with Hackabouta as whores Fielding paraded on his stage; and in his introduction to the printed text of his play, Fielding added 'A criticism on the *Covent Garden Tragedy*, originally intended for the *Grub-Street Journal*', in which he refers to 'several very odd names in this piece, such as Hackabouta, etc.' Either the *Grub-Street Journal* introduced the Harlot's name as a hint that Fielding was playing on Hogarth's popularity, or Fielding had actually used the name in his play but changed it in the printed text.[1]

It is significant that in *The Covent Garden Tragedy*, Fielding for the first time has his characters consistently alluding to their social superiors as models. He employs the same simile that serves for a passing reference in his earliest plays: 'our affair is grown dull as a chancery suit' (*Love in Several Masques*, I, 1). By 1732, in *The Modern Husband*, the idea was becoming more insistent: Lord Richly explains how he gave Mrs Bellamant a hundred-pound note for the payment of six. 'And how did she receive it?' asks Mrs Modern. 'With the same reluctancy that a lawyer or physician would a double fee, or a court-priest a plurality' (IV, 2): thus extending the satire to lawyers, doctors, and clergymen. But in these plays, he puts the analogies in the mouths of the great (or at least respectable) themselves, and they sound like conventional satiric elaboration; there is no sign of approbation on the part of the speaker. Only with *The Welsh Opera*, first produced 22 April 1731, are the low viewed as analogues of the great, and by then Hogarth had the *Harlot* well enough along to have started his subscription. Even in *The Welsh Opera* not much is made of the idea: the Apshinkens are of the country gentry, and the only low characters are the servants, Robin the butler, William the coachman, John the groom, and Thomas the gardener (equalling Walpole, Pulteney, etc.). Their language, though in general patterned after that of their masters, is more mock-pastoral than anything else; Fielding makes no attempt to suggest that these characters behave as they do in imitation of the royal family, the prime minister, and so forth. This idea becomes explicit only in *The Covent Garden Tragedy*, with the bawds, whores, and their clients assuming the poses and diction of their superiors without their superiors' success. Mother Punchbowl sets the tone with her opening speech:

Who'd be a bawd in this degenerate age!
Who'd for her country unrewarded toil!

1 *Grub-Street Journal*, 8 June 1732; see also R. E. Moore, *Hogarth's Literary Relationships*, 1948, pp. 97–9.

Not so the statesman scrubs his plotful head,
Not so the lawyer shakes his unfee'd tongue,
Not so the doctor guides the doleful quill.

Whether Fielding is puffing the *Harlot's Progress* or benefiting from it, the presence is heavily felt, and it remains in the poor characters who follow Fashion and imitate 'greatness' in *Pasquin*, *Eurydice*, and the later farces, even more in *Jonathan Wild*, and in a modified form in *Joseph Andrews*.[1]

The relationship between the two men goes back at least to 1728, and to Fielding's first published work, *The Masquerade*, a poem informed if not inspired by Hogarth's *Masquerade Ticket*. Although Fielding's first plays were Congrevian intrigue comedies, produced between 1728 and 1729, he very soon learned new techniques from Pope's *The Dunciad*, and probably from Hogarth's emblematic, stage-like representations. In *The Author's Farce* and his subsequent 'farces', he brought *The Dunciad* to the stage. The two may have known each other personally by this time. Hogarth was a prodigious theatergoer, a denizen of the Covent Garden area, and he would certainly have pursued Fielding's dramatic career and soon made his acquaintance. On 24 April 1730 the immensely popular *Tom Thumb* appeared, and a year later, for the revised printed version, Hogarth supplied a design for a frontispiece, as later in the year in which the *Harlot* appeared he furnished designs for two of the plays in the bilingual edition of Molière with which Fielding was involved (published on 8 December 1732).

If Fielding's imitation in *The Covent Garden Tragedy* was in some sense a recognition of what Hogarth was up to, his actual formulation of this theme did not occur until the *Champion* essay of June 1740 and the preface to *Joseph Andrews* in 1742. The earliest indication that Hogarth's intention was recognized by contemporaries is James Ralph's essay on painting in his *Weekly Register*, no. 112, 3 June 1732. . . .

(291–3)

[In 'The Laughing Audience', the subscription ticket for *Southwark Fair* and *A Rake's Progress*,] only the audience is visible, implying perhaps that the stage will be supplied by the prints themselves, and

1 See R. Paulson, *Satire and the Novel*, Yale University Press, 1967, pp. 78–85.

the members of the audience are distinguished by their expressions and gestures: the pleased lower-class denizens of the pit, the sour-faced critic, and the bored fops (aristocrats, but the allusion is not obtrusive) of the boxes. The effect parallels Fielding's schematic description fifteen years later of the audience he presupposed for the actors within *Tom Jones* and for the novel itself. One of Hogarth's links with Fielding is, of course, his constant playing on the artificial, feigned quality of a literary work....

(324)

Later in 1740, Samuel Richardson's *Pamela* appeared; in 1741 Fielding responded with his parody *Shamela*, and 1742 at greater length with *Joseph Andrews*. In his preface Fielding defines the 'comic epic in prose' he projects in terms of the extremes it avoids – of romance and burlesque, two different ways in which reality may be distorted, to glamorize and to vilify. He is, of course, reacting against *Pamela*, which he equates with the romances of *Jack the Giant Killer* and *Guy of Warwick*; but he is also steering clear of burlesques like his own early plays. By 'burlesque', he means 'the Exhibition of what is monstrous and unnatural': a Shamela, a Pistol in *The Author's Farce*, or a Queen Ignorance in *Pasquin*. Burlesque, he finds (perhaps recalling Somerville's attribution of burlesque to Hogarth), is the literary equivalent of caricature. In order to make his point clear, he uses Hogarth's works as an analogy. 'Let us examine the works of a comic history-painter,' he begins, 'with those performances which the Italians call *Caricatura*....' The one involves 'the exactest copying of Nature; insomuch, that a judicious eye instantly rejects any thing *outré*; any liberty which the painter hath taken with the features of that *Alma Mater*' (he is probably remembering *Boys Peeping at Nature*). But the aim of caricature is 'to exhibit monsters, not men, and all distortions and exaggerations whatever are within its proper province'.

Now, what *Caricatura* is in painting, burlesque is in writing; and in the same manner the comic writer and painter correlate to each other. And here I shall observe, that as in the former, the painter seems to have the advantage; so it is in the latter infinitely on the side of the writer: for the Monstrous is much easier to paint than describe, and the Ridiculous to describe than paint.... He who should call the

ingenious Hogarth a burlesque painter [as Somerville had
done], would in my opinion do him very little honour:
for sure it is much easier, much less the subject of
admiration, to paint a man with a nose, or any other feature
of a preposterous size, or to expose him in some absurd or
monstrous attitude, than to express the affections of men
on canvas. It hath been thought a vast commendation of a
painter, to say his figures *seem to breathe*; but surely, it is a
much greater and nobler applause, *that they appear to think*.

Hogarth had replaced the exaggeration of traditional history painting on one side and grotesque emblematic satire on the other with a
more restrained delineation, closer to experience, and reliant on
'character' rather than 'caricature', on the variety rather than the
exaggeration of expression. Fielding wished to do something similar
in prose.

   This is the only specific mention of Hogarth in the preface, but his
presence hovers over the whole, and one senses that in other ways
than 'character' he offered Fielding the best model for what he
intended in *Joseph Andrews*. Fielding's famous definition, 'The only
source of the true ridiculous (as it appears to me) is affectation'
(referring to that middle area between the behavior of paragon and
devil which he says will be his subject), corresponds to the subject of
Hogarth's progresses (the girl from the country affecting the airs of a
lady, or the merchant's son of a gentleman). At one point, Fielding
seems to allude to *The Distressed Poet*:

. . . were we to enter a poor house, and behold a wretched
Family shivering with cold and languishing with hunger,
it would not incline us to laughter (at least we must have
very diabolical natures, if it would:), but should we
discover there a grate, instead of coals, adorned with
flowers, empty plate or china dishes on the sideboard, or
any other affectation of riches and finery either on their
persons or in their furniture; we might then indeed be
excused, for ridiculing so fantastical an appearance.

Both men are concerned with those ordinary people who act according to inappropriate ideas of themselves.

By calling Hogarth's productions 'comic history painting', and his own 'comic epic in prose', Fielding is trying as Hogarth had done, to secure a place in the classical (and contemporary) hierarchy of genres higher than satire, the grotesque, or the comic would command. Hogarth never seems to have used the term 'comic history painting' himself. Putting his thoughts on paper in the 1760s, he frequently called attention to the uniqueness of the form he had invented ('this uncommon way of painting', 'a field unbroke up in any country or any age'), which often echoed Fielding's similar claims for his form; referring to its combination of comic and moral qualities and its use of contemporaneity, he called his works instead 'modern moral subjects'. His closest approach to Fielding's term was in references to his new genre as occupying an area between the accepted categories of sublime and grotesque. He commented sadly that painters and writers 'never mention, in the historical way of any intermediate species of subjects for painting between the sublime and the grotesque', whereas he believes that the 'subject[s] of most consequence are those that most entertain and improve the mind and are of public utility', and that 'true comedy' is a more economical and difficult genre, closer to reality, than highflown tragedy, which he tended to associate with sublime history painting.[1]

All the evidence points to the influence running from Hogarth to Fielding before 1742, and to Fielding's subsequent influence on Hogarth relating primarily to the verbalization of his theories. In 1726, before he even met Fielding, he had produced his polemical frontispiece to *Hudibras*, which sets forth his aesthetic intention in relation to history painting (very similar to Fielding's in relation to the epic), and in 1731 he issued a second print to explain his intention in the *Harlot's Progress*. Only with *Characters and Caricaturas* in 1743 did he adopt Fielding's terminology and begin to add commentary ('for a farther explanation ... see the Preface to *Joseph Andrews*'), and by the time he engraved *The Bench* (1758) the commentary filled more space than the graphic design.

Fielding's immediate effect on Hogarth was perhaps to galvanize him into producing another series to prove the claims made in the preface to *Joseph Andrews*, and certainly to make the particular

1 Hogarth, 'Autobiographical Notes', *Analysis of Beauty*, ed. Joseph Burke, 1955, pp. 208, 212, 215, 216.

subscription ticket dealing with caricature; in the long run, Fielding's influence may indeed have made Hogarth more self-conscious and defensive, more verbal and polemical than he had been before.

In *Joseph Andrews* Fielding begins the complimentary allusions to Hogarth that continue through the remainder of his fiction (and were echoed by other novelists). Explaining the impossibility of describing Lady Booby's appearance after Joseph proclaims his love of virtue, he adds, 'no, not from the inimitable pencil of my friend *Hogarth*, could you receive such an idea of surprise', and Mrs Tow-wouse is so striking 'that *Hogarth* himself never gave more Expression to a picture.'[1] Once he alludes to another aspect of Hogarth – the painter; though perhaps even here keeping in mind the relationship between Hogarth's comic, and other painters' sublime or bathetic, histories. In book 3, chapter 6, he has Joseph link Hogarth's name with homophones of Italian 'masters': 'Ammyconni' for Amigoni, whose success may have led Hogarth to turn to sublime history, carries overtones of 'cony', and perhaps less presentable puns; 'Paul Varnish' for Veronese, with the suggestion that his paintings were valued by Englishmen primarily because of their varnishing; and 'Hannibal Scratchi' for Annibale Carracci, which speaks for itself. (Such corruptions were every day apparent in the auction lists in the papers which advertised works by Hannibal Carrots, and indeed Paul Varnish.) And in this dubious company Joseph puts the Italianate form of Hogarth's name, 'Hogarthi'. Although Fielding is having his little joke, joining Hogarth with his *bêtes noires*, and giving them names that indicate Hogarth's reservations about the old masters, it is proper to see this as a compliment parallel to the praise of other English contemporaries in the same chapter – John Kyrle (the 'Man of Ross') and Ralph Allen of Bath.

Fielding could be alluding to Hogarth's conversation pictures and portraits, which Joseph might have seen in Lady Booby's house.[2] Joseph, as a man about London, could also, however, have seen his histories at St Bartholomew's – *The Pool of Bethesda* and above all the *Good Samaritan*, which may have suggested, and certainly supports, the paradigm for charity that informs the central part of *Joseph*

1 Book 1, chapters 8, 14.
2 According to W. B. Coley, 'Fielding, Hogarth and three Italian Masters', *Modern Language Quarterly*, vol. 24, 1963, pp. 386–391.

Andrews. Even some of the modern moral subjects, like *The Christening* and *The Denunciation*, were in private collections, as well as unengraved ones like Lord Boyne's *Night Encounter* and Miss Edwards' *Taste à la Mode*. Whatever the pictures referred to, W. B. Coley is correct in his conclusion that Fielding was complimenting Hogarth 'by implying that he alone among English painters could breach the foreign monopoly in the arts.'[1] . . .

Even in *Characters and Caricaturas* [with its 'variety of . . . expressions', its 'cloud of faces' suggesting 'infinite possibilities' of variety] the various heads only derive meaning from the contrast with idealized and caricatured heads beneath. Hogarth always includes the heroic shape *and* the grotesque in order to help define the middle area of 'character'. In short, while Fielding defines an intermediate genre between romance and burlesque – the comic – and between extremes of goodness and evil – the ridiculous – Hogarth defines his intermediate genre between sublime history painting and burlesque, the idealized and the caricatured, called 'character'.

These are the distinctive features of both Hogarth's and Fielding's work. The ideals of good and evil are presented as the externalization of mental states: in Hogarth's early progresses they appear in the portraits on the walls which offer standardized, usually inappropriate alternatives of action, and which the characters allow to dominate them. In *Joseph Andrews* they appear in the 'examples' of the Cibbers and Pamelas on the one hand, and the biblical Joseph and Abraham on the other; all, however different qualitatively, amount to external patterns the characters allow to dominate and distort them. Joseph and Parson Adams act and are defined in relation to the stereotypes of both extremes.[2] All of the characters in the novel are defined in terms of these conflicting qualities, the natural inclination *v.* the fashionable or prescribed code – whether Lady Booby's dedication to poses of heroic love, Joseph's to ideals of chastity learned from his sister Pamela, or Parsons Adams' to the authority of the Church Fathers. Throughout, Nature continues to assert her rights: it is 'that violent repugnancy of nature' with which the hypocrite must

1 op. cit., p. 388.
2 See R. Paulson, 'The Pilgrimage and the Family: Structures in the Novels of Fielding and Smollett', in *Tobias Smollett: Bicentennial Essays Presented to Lewis M. Knapp*, Oxford University Press, 1971.

'struggle', and even Joseph adds after Lady Booby's last assault, 'But I am glad she turned me out of the Chamber as she did: for I had almost forgotten every word Parson Adams had ever said to me.' As Fielding put it in *Tom Jones*, 'if we shut nature out at the door, she will come in at the window'.[1]

This is essentially the theme which makes *Marriage à la Mode* part of a cluster including *Strolling Actresses*, *Taste à la Mode*, and the works of Fielding that appeared in the interim. In this new series, the forces of society and fashion are played against the natural impulses of the individual: the fathers, chaining together their two children as two nearby dogs are chained, are symbolic of the social strait-jackets and fashionable assumptions that force the children to disown their natural selves. The artificial *v.* the natural becomes Hogarth's main theme, and he takes the side of the natural against fashion in all its forms, which comes to include art in general.
(468–75)

[In *Marriage à la Mode*] art has become an integral part of Hogarth's subject matter: it is here for itself, a comment on itself, and also on its owners and on the actions that go on before it. In no other series is the note so insistent: it permeates the *Harlot*, Plate 2, or the *Rake*, Plate 2, to a degree, but here it dominates every room, every plate. The old masters have come to represent the evil that is the subject of the series: not aspiration, but the constriction of old, dead customs and ideals embodied in bad art. Both biblical and classical, this art holds up seduction, rape, compulsion, torture, and murder as the ideal, and the fathers act accordingly and force these stereotypes on their children.

The trends toward art as theme and reader as active participant are further underlined by the importance placed on viewing. In Plate 1 the Medusa looks down in horror on the scene. In Plate 2 the steward turns away, and his disdainful face is repeated in the Roman bust on the mantle, even to the broken nose of the one and the pug nose of the other. One is turning away from the scene with pious horror, the other is regarding it. . . .

These trends began with the change, noticeable in the prints of the late 1730s, from the protagonist as chooser to the reader as chooser; more complex reactions are expected of him as he pursues and tries

1 *Tom Jones*, book 12, chapter 2.

to understand the meaning, the visual puns and allusions, and as he is linked with observers like Medusa and St Luke within the scenes. Very similar is the elaborately contrived and underlined author-reader relationship in Fielding's novels of this decade. . . .
(489)

From Volume 2

Something of the effect Hogarth wished to achieve with his 'popular' prints can be seen in Fielding's efforts in the same direction. *Industry and Idleness* appeared in October 1747, and on 28 March 1748 Fielding opened a puppet theater in Panton Street, just a block from Leicester Fields, which operated with great popular success until he closed it in June.[1] Fielding had expressed in the *True Patriot* of 11–18 February 1746 his desire for a return from sophisticated modern plays to the vigor of the ancient Punch and Judy show (specifically, he adds, as a vehicle for satire). With the success of Hogarth's 'George Barnwell' morality play before him, he opened his theater, which to evade the Licensing Act he passed off as entertainment accompanying 'breakfast'. His fare consisted of the old puppet plays seen by generations of Londoners at the fairs: *Bateman, Fair Rosamond,* and *Whittington and his Cat* – plus, significantly, a revival of his own *Covent Garden Tragedy.* The whole subject came up again in book 12, chapter 5 of *Tom Jones,* where Tom argues for the truth and vigor of Punch and Judy shows as against the *Provok'd Husbands* of today. Hogarth may have had these matters in mind a few years later when he introduced a Punch and Judy show on the signboard in the second plate of *The Election.*

In 1747–8 Fielding edited a pro-Pelham periodical, the *Jacobite's Journal,* for which Hogarth is said to have designed the headpiece.[2] Then in the winter of 1748–9 he became a Westminster magistrate.

1 Fielding's advertisements ran in the *General Advertiser* from 7 March off and on until 2 June; for a full account of the affair, see Martin Battestin, 'Fielding and "Master Punch" in Panton Street', *Philological Quarterly,* vol. 45, 1966, pp. 191–208.
2 W. B. Coley ('Hogarth, Fielding, and the Dating of the March to Finchley', *Journal of the Warburg and Courtauld Institutes,* vol. 30, 1967, pp. 317–26) makes a case against the authenticity of this drawing (in the Royal Collection, Oppé, cat. no. 67).

Tom Jones, which he was still writing as he took up his puppet theater and his police duties, came out at the end of the year, with its quota of Hogarth references.[1] But Fielding was now devoting himself wholeheartedly to the business of presiding over the Bow Street police court and his efforts to reform the community. His last novel, *Amelia*, reflects this experience; in the meantime he was writing tracts urging practical solutions to the problem of crime in London.

Fielding faced criminals day after day in his courtroom. Hogarth's personal contact with the encroachments of poverty, crime and violence in the metropolis was less direct. He lived in a respectable and elegant square. . . . [Writing on gin-drinking in the *Enquiry into the Causes of the late Increase of Robbers*, Fielding] sounds as if he is recalling the gin-seller's baby in *The March to Finchley*, emaciated and evidently nourished only on its mother's wares: 'What must become of the infant who is conceived in gin? with the poisonous distillations of which it is nourished both in the womb and at the breast.'[2] In *Gin Lane* Hogarth has one mother pouring gin into her baby's mouth and another (the central figure) with exposed breasts that suggest she has been feeding her child, who is now falling to its death (in a later state Hogarth gave the child a gin-ravaged face).

As *The March to Finchley* was being engraved by Sullivan, Hogarth must have been working on his equivalent to Fielding's *Enquiry*. In the *London Evening Post* of 14–16 February he announced:

> *This Day are publish'd, Price 1s. each.*
> Two large Prints, design'd and etch'd by Mr Hogarth, call'd
> BEER-STREET and GIN-LANE
> A Number will be printed in a better Manner for the
> Curious, at 1s. 6d. each.
> And on Thursday following will be publish'd four Prints
> on the Subject of Cruelty, Price and Size the same.

1 The most famous of the allusions to Hogarth appear when Fielding describes Bridget Allworthy's face by referring the reader to the prude in *Morning* (book 1, chapter 11), Mrs Partridge to the bunter in *Harlot*, Plate 2 (book 2, and chapter 3), and Square to the warden in *Harlot*, Plate 4 (book 3, chapter 6). But there are many others: Jenny Jones' neighbors think of her 'beating hemp in a silk gown', and Molly Seagrim wears Sophia's finery and is attacked for this by the women in the churchyard; both instances (book 1, chapter 9) recall *Harlot*, Plate 4. See also book 14, chapters 1 and 8.
2 *Works*, ed. Henley, XIII, p. 35.

> N.B. As the Subjects of these Prints are calculated to reform
> some reigning Vices peculiar to the lower Class of People, in
> hopes to render them of more extensive use, the Author has
> publish'd them in the cheapest Manner possible.

(96–9)

Sterne, though producing something less immediately recognizable as Hogarthian than Fielding's works, is revealed as the inheritor of Hogarth's method as well as his theory. The closest Fielding comes to the Hogarth of the *Analysis* and the 'chase' through his prints is his chapter on contrast in *Tom Jones*. Fielding and Hogarth share the presentation of shifting characters within an architectural solidity of plot; Sterne's point of departure is the *Analysis*, and he produces an aesthetic for Hogarth's prints through the Line of Beauty and the doctrine of intricacy that sums up Hogarth's achievement at the end of his career as neatly as Fielding did at the beginning.

As the description of Trim's stance shows, the Line of Beauty represents to Sterne the natural and vital versus the rigid and geometrical, as dully conveyed in straight lines. However, as the passage also suggests, defined too precisely the Line of Beauty itself becomes ludicrous. Everything in the world of *Tristram Shandy*, from hobby-horses to the Line of Beauty, appears one way one moment and differently the next.

(305)

The Plays

Ian Donaldson

from 'High and Low Life: Fielding and the Uses of Inversion',
The Word Upside-Down, chapter 8   1970

Behold, the Lord maketh the earth empty, and maketh it
waste, and turneth it upside down, and scattereth abroad
the inhabitants thereof. And it shall be, as with the people,
so with the priest; as with the servant, so with his master;
as with the maid, so with her mistress; as with the buyer,
so with the seller; as with the lender, so with the borrower;
as with the taker of usury, so with the giver of usury to
him. The earth shall be utterly emptied and spoiled; for the
Lord hath spoken this word.
Isaiah xxiv 1–3

Hogarth completed his last print, *Tailpiece, or the Bathos*, a few
months before his death in 1761. In the background of the picture
stand two bare trees, a gibbet, a ruined tower on which is a clock
which has no hands. Falling diagonally across the picture is an inn-
sign of 'the World's End', on which is depicted the world in flames.
Phaeton's chariot falls from the sky, while on a distant sea one last
ship performs the gentle art of sinking. In the foreground Father
Time breathes his last word: 'Finis'. His scythe, his hour-glass, and
his pipe are all broken; and scattered in front of him lie a broken bell,
a broken column, a broken bottle, a broken crown, a broken musket,
and a broken palette. A statute of bankruptcy, inscribed 'H. Nature
bankrupt', and stamped with the seal of a rider on a pale horse, lies
amidst the broken fragments. Beneath it is a play-book open at its
last page, showing the words *Exeunt Omnes*.

The print is likely to remind one of the ending of the fourth book
of *The Dunciad*, where, with a similar use of fine detail, Pope presented a similar picture of the ultimate cosmic 'bathos', the ruin of

the civilization of his time. Like Hogarth, Pope had depicted his apocalypse in terms of the ending of a play, which leaves the theatre of the world in final darkness and disarray:

Thy hand, great Anarch! lets the curtain fall;
And Universal Darkness buries all.

'They showed the age involved in darkness', wrote Dr Johnson aptly of Pope and Swift.[1] It is always a little surprising to realize that the peace of the Augustans, as Saintsbury cheerfully called it, should have been ruffled by this myth of *fin du monde*, though perhaps a myth of this kind is a natural companion to such a highly systematic myth of order as Pope was at pains to formulate in *An Essay on Man*:

The least confusion but in one, not all
That system only, but the Whole must fall.
(1, ll. 249–50)

The more elaborate and delicate you imagine the cosmic mechanism to be, the more you may fear the consequences of its slightest derangement. And similarly, perhaps, the stronger and more specific your conception of the ideal society is, the fiercer and darker your castigation of departures from that ideal may be. Certainly it is remarkable that another apocalyptic myth grew up amongst the writers who so deeply admired the age of Augustus; a myth concerning the advent of a new age which parodied, and would finally obliterate, the values of the first, true Augustan age.[2] This myth necessitated an elaborate comparison between the present age and the great age of Roman civilization. The Emperor Augustus was praised by Horace; George II, christened George Augustus, was praised by the Reverend Laurence Eusden. The first Augustan age had produced Virgil and his *Aeneid*; the new Augustan age had produced Blackmore and his *Creation*. Culture in that age was patronized by Maecenas; culture in this age was neglected by Walpole. *The Dunciad* is an extended ironical celebration of the new Augustan age, in which Pope sounds a mocking echo to Virgil's messianic notes:

1 In G. B. Hill (ed.), *Lives of the Poets*, Oxford University Press, 1905, vol. 3, pp. 61–2.
2 See Aubrey Williams, *Pope's 'Dunciad'*, 1955; James W. Johnson, 'The Meaning of "Augustan"', *J.H.I.*, vol. 19, 1958, pp. 507–22.

This, this is He, foretold by ancient rhymes,
Th'Augustus born to bring Saturnian times.
(1728, III, ll, 317–18)

The reign of Augustus Caesar was said to restore the original harmony
of the Golden Age; but the reign of the new Augustus will bring
'Saturnian times' of anarchy and disorder.

For Pope and his circle, such anarchy and disorder could already be
seen in the theatre of their day, which – in a traditional figure –
might be taken as an emblem of the real world. The absurd entertainments presented in the theatres seemed to reflect the absurdity of the
age itself. Phoebe Clinket, the heroine of *Three Hours After Marriage*,
a comedy by Pope, Gay and Arbuthnot presented at Drury Lane in
1717, is busily engaged in writing a tragedy of her own entitled,
appropriately, *The Deluge*; a tragedy which depicts, with a wonderful confusion of images, the monstrous and inverted world of the
flood. Such fare, it is implied, is well suited to the theatres of the day:

Swell'd with a Dropsy, sickly Nature lies,
And melting in a Diabetes, dies . . .
The roaring Seas o'er the tall Woods have broke,
And Whales now perch upon the sturdy Oak.

In the third book of *The Dunciad* Pope gives a similar, though more
intensely detailed, picture of the activities of the theatres of his day,
whose artificers seem to have brought into being a new and topsy-
turvy creation:

Thence a new world, to Nature's laws unknown,
Breaks out refulgent, with a heav'n its own:
Another Cynthia her new journey runs,
And other planets circle other suns:
The forests dance, the rivers upward rise,
Whales sport in woods, and dolphins in the skies;
And last, to give the whole creation grace,
Lo! one vast Egg produces human race.
(ll. 237–44)

Pope's image of this *new world* – wild, lawless, parodic – brilliantly
coordinates a number of traditional and contemporary notions. Like

the passage from Phoebe Clinket's play, it reaches back to Ovid's account of the deluge in Book One of the *Metamorphoses*, glancing at the same time at Horace's remarks about monstrosities in art (some painters give us a dolphin in the woods, a boar in the flood). At the centre of the image is the idea of the poet as a little god, whose activities imitate, in a humble way, the greater powers of the Creator himself: 'and *a new world* leaps out at his command' (*An Essay on Criticism*, l. 486).[1] Behind the passage, too, lies a long tradition which we glanced at in chapter 4, of a fantastic 'new world' discovered in the sun or moon or in a remote area of the earth: a tradition variously represented by Jonson's *News from the New World Discovered in the Moon*, by Cyrano's *L'Autre Monde*, and by Durfey's *Wonders in the Sun*. The image is further sharpened by an implied reference to a topic of some contemporary interest, that of the *pluralité des mondes*. Man was allowed to live in one world and to know one world, Pope had written in *An Essay on Man*; that was as far as his knowledge was permitted to reach. It was for God alone to

See worlds on worlds compose one universe,
Observe how system into system runs,
What other planets circle other suns ...
(ll. 24–6)

What has happened in the theatres can happen in society at large. Man may presumptuously reject the old world in which God has placed him, and create for himself a new world which parodies the old, and follows its own unnatural laws. What looks like creation turns out to be apocalypse.

How seriously Pope and his group believed in all this it is impossible to tell. There is an obvious playfulness about the way in which the apocalyptic ideas are handled, an obvious enjoyment in the use of such lavish hyperbole, yet the vision is far from comic. It is implied, as in satire it traditionally is implied, that things are unlikely ever to improve. The comic artist, as a rule, lets you know that the chaos is likely to settle a bit in the course of time. The satirist, as a rule, lets you know that it's no good: all we can do is sit about lamenting,

1 On this concept see M. H. Abrams, 'The Poem as Heterocosm', in *The Mirror and the Lamp*, New York, 1953, pp. 272–85.

inveighing, possibly even joking, but always waiting for the end. The distinction is one which may be clarified as we move from the work of the Scriblerians to that of Henry Fielding.

Fielding came to London in 1727, the year of George Augustus's coronation. Pope, Swift, and Gay were at the height of their powers: *Gulliver's Travels* had been published the year before, and Pope was at work on *The Dunciad*, which was published in May of the following year; Gay was busy writing *The Beggar's Opera*, which was to open at Lincoln's Inn Fields just a fortnight before Fielding's own first play, *Love in Several Masques*, was presented at Drury Lane in February 1728. Gay's opera, Fielding confessed, 'engrosses the whole talk and admiration of the town'.[1] In March of 1728 another Scriblerian work was to appear: *Peri Bathous*, the mock 'Art of sinking in poetry', written as early as 1713-14 by Pope, Swift, Gay, Parnell, Oxford, and Arbuthnot, and now rewritten almost entirely by Pope, was published in the third volume of Pope's and Swift's *Miscellanies*. It is scarcely surprising that a young writer just up from the West Country and barely into his twenties should have found the influence of Pope, Swift, Gay, and their circle quite irresistible, and that he should soon be writing under the name of Scriblerus Secundus.

From this older generation of writers Fielding learnt many of the tactics of irony and of satire. From them, too, he picked up a fashionable way of lamenting the times. We live (he declared in one of his poems) in 'no Augustan age';[2] rather, Fielding often implied, it is an age which seems about to disintegrate in farcical disorder. One theme in particular strongly caught Fielding's imagination. Throughout the work of the Scriblerians there recurs, with countless variations, the notion of a ludicrous and sometimes tragic merger of the 'high' and the 'low'. The merger can occur in literature, where (as *Peri Bathous* had shown) the high style is in constant danger of collapsing into the low; it can occur in education – the boast of the pedants in *The Dunciad* is that they bring 'to one dead level ev'ry mind' – it can occur in society as a whole: one of the 'great ends' of Dulness, Pope wrote, was to blot out 'the distinctions between high and low

1 Preface to *Love in Several Masques*, in *Works, Plays and Poems*, ed. W. E. Henley, VIII, p. 9.
2 'Of True Greatness', in *Works, Plays and Poems*, ed. W. E. Henley, XII, p. 255.

in society'.[1] The levelling of high and low becomes, too, one of the most persistent ideas in Fielding's work, yet with a significant difference of emphasis. As time goes by Fielding gradually converts the Tory satirists' despondent myth of a civilization falling to ruins to more optimistic comic ends; his mood becomes, on the whole, lighter and more amiable, and the levelling tends to be seen not with the savage energy of a satirist who proclaims the approach of the end of the world, but with the gentleness of a comic artist who reminds us of the artificiality of such distinctions in the first place.

The conversion of the idea does not occur all at once. *Tom Thumb*, one of Fielding's earliest and best-known plays (April 1730, revised and enlarged March 1731), is still very much under the Scriblerian spell. 'Tragedy', wrote Fielding in the Preface of 1731, 'hath of all writings the greatest share in the bathos, which is the profound of Scriblerus.' Yet Fielding goes a step further than the Scriblerians, literalizing their metaphor and giving us, instead of the expected herculean hero of 'high' tragedy, the lowest hero ever to walk the English stage. One wonders if Fielding remembered Dryden's observations about the difficulty of bringing heroic literature to the stage: that 'the prowess of Achilles or Aeneas would appear ridiculous in our dwarf heroes of the theatre';[2] or Addison's ridicule, in *Spectator* 42, of the popular stage conventions of heroic tragedy: 'The ordinary method of making an heroe, is to clap a huge plume of feathers upon his head, which rises so very high, that there is often a greater length from his chin to the top of his head, than to the sole of his foot. One would believe, that we thought a great man and a tall man the same thing.' Like Addison, Fielding brings into ironic confusion the literal and metaphorical meanings of 'great', 'high', and 'low'. The joke kept playing in Fielding's mind; years later in his 'Modern Glossary' (*Covent-Garden Journal*, no. 4) he was to define the word 'great' as follows: 'Applied to a thing, signifies bigness; when to a man, often littleness or meanness'; at a time when Robert Walpole was popularly known as 'the Great', everyone knew what the point of the joke was. In *Tom Thumb* Fielding does not merely ridicule the conventions of heroic tragedy in the way Buckingham

1 *The Dunciad* (1742), IV, l. 268; 14 n.
2 'Dedication to the Aeneis', *Essays*, ed. W. P. Ker, Oxford University Press, 1900, ii. p. 161.

had done sixty years before; he implies also that the contemporary uncertainty on theatrical matters may be paralleled by our uncertainty on moral and political matters; in each case we have not sufficiently considered the true meaning of greatness: hence on the theatrical stage and on the stage of public life a dwarf may pass as a hero. Thus the images of wild cosmic turbulence and disaster in *Tom Thumb* have suggestions beyond their immediate point of parody, for they serve as fitting emblems of the actual confusion of the times.

Noodle. Sure, Nature means to break her solid chain,
Or else unfix the world, and in a rage
To hurl it from its axletree and hinges;
All things are so confus'd . . .
(II. 10)

But although the play has such implications as these, Fielding's use of the apocalyptic myth differs from Pope's even at this stage in that it remains fundamentally genial and amusing. Swift – who, if Dr Johnson is to be believed, 'stubbornly resisted any tendency to laughter' throughout his life – was reported to have laughed outright on seeing the play.[1] Later, in his Preface to *Joseph Andrews*, Fielding was to reject as 'monstrous and unnatural' the simple inversion device on which *Tom Thumb* and some of his other plays rest – 'appropriating the manners of the highest to the lowest, or *è converso*'; yet he pleaded in favour of this burlesque mode, its power of arousing laughter, sweetness, good humour, and benevolence. If, as Fielding argued, burlesque was not the same thing as true comedy, it was nevertheless closer to comedy than it was to satire, being designed not to unsettle and disturb but primarily to amuse and entertain.

Fielding's burlesque plays often depict society in a state of collapse. In ridiculing the popular theatrical entertainments of the day Fielding, like Pope, was quick to bring out the occasional unintentional appropriateness of subject-matter of such plays. In *Tumble-Down Dick* in April 1736, for instance, Fielding ridiculed John Rich's pantomime *The Fall of Phaeton*, highlighting the aptness of the theme which Rich had chosen: the fall of Phaeton presaged the end of the

1 G. B. Hill (ed.), *Lives of the Poets*, Oxford University Press, 1905, iii, p. 56; Laetitia Pilkington, *Memoirs* 1754, iii, p. 155.

world; Rich's own theatrical nonsense seemed to have 'turned all nature topsy-turvy', and seemed also to presage some final cataclysm; such scenes as Rich depicted were fitting emblems and portents of the age. Some weeks earlier in *Pasquin* Fielding had brought out even more explicitly the symbolic relationship which Rich's entertainments bore to the age. The second half of *Pasquin* presents the rehearsal of a tragedy called *The Life and Death of Common-Sense*. Rich's shows at Covent Garden are once more held up to ridicule; the play-within-the-play reaches its climax with the invasion from Europe of Queen Ignorance with her troupe of 'singers, fiddlers, tumblers, and rope-dancers', and with her assassination of the native Queen Common-Sense. As Common-Sense expires she utters her last prophecy, that the world will now be turned upside-down:

Henceforth all things shall topsy-turvy turn;
Physic shall kill, and Law enslave the world;
Cits shall turn beaux, and taste Italian songs,
While courtiers are stock-jobbing in the city.
Places, requiring learning and great parts,
Henceforth shall all be hustled in a hat,
And drawn by men deficient in them both.
Statesmen – but oh! cold death will let me say
No more – and you must guess *et caetera*.
[*Dies.*]

Like *The Dunciad*, *Pasquin* portrays a widespread and ludicrous series of reversals in human relationships, beginning inside the theatres and radiating out into society at large; it is the final 'bathos', the sinking of the social order, the blotting out of 'distinctions between high and low in society'. Yet although the debt to Pope is clear enough in passages such as these, it is equally clear that Fielding is once again using the apocalyptic myth in a significantly different way. *Pasquin* does not end in universal darkness but instead with a rolling back of the clouds. The ghost of Queen Common-Sense revives:

The coast is clear, and to her native realms
Pale Ignorance with all her host is fled.

The ending of *The Dunciad* is the traditional ending of satire: we are shown the world falling in ruins about our ears, and are offered no comfort or relief, but are permitted to hear only the bitter protests of the world's solitary honest man. The ending of *Pasquin*, on the other hand, is the ending traditional to comedy: though the world seems to be falling in ruins about our ears, it turns out, miraculously, that things are not as confused as they look, and common sense finally triumphs over the forces of disorder.

A play written some years earlier, *The Author's Farce* (March 1730, revised 1734), must serve as a final example of Fielding's methods of inversion in this period, and of his way of moving from satire into comedy; this time we are likely to be reminded not only of the work of Pope but also of that of Ben Jonson. *The Author's Farce* is about a struggling writer named Luckless, who is in debt to his landlady, in love with his landlady's daughter, and unsuccessful in his attempts to sell his plays to the theatre managers. His friend Witmore tells him that the fault lies not with him but with the age. In this age, says Witmore, values are inverted:

But now, when party and prejudice carry all before them, when learning is decried, wit not understood, when the theatres are puppet-shows and the comediens are ballad singers, when fools lead the town would a man think to thrive by his wit? If you must write, write nonsense, write operas, write entertainments, write *Hurlothrumbos*, set up an *Oratory* and preach nonsense, and you may meet with encouragement enough. If you would receive applause, deserve to receive sentence at the Old Bailey; and if you would ride in your coach, deserve to ride in a cart.

Ben Jonson, who often spoke of his own age in somewhat similar terms, implied in *Bartholomew Fair* what Witmore implies here: that theatrical nonsense is all that such an age deserves to get. Luckless writes a puppet-play about just that: nonsense. The scene is the Court of Nonsense, situated in a kind of Lucianic underworld; the presiding Goddess of Nonsense is visited by a number of figures – a Poet and a Bookseller, Punch and Judy, Signior Opera, Don Tragedio, Sir Farcical Comic, and Mrs Novel – who report on the progress of cultural affairs in the other world. 'My Lord Mayor has shortened the time of Bartholomew Fair in Smithfield,' announces the Poet, 'and so they are resolved to keep it all the year round at the other end of the town.' In *Bartholomew Fair* Jonson had suggested that the mischievous, Saturnalian values of Smithfield were spreading across London, infecting the groundlings at the Hope Theatre on the Bankside. Pope may have recalled Jonson's play as he ironically celebrated in *The Dunciad* the progress of 'the Smithfield Muses to the ear of Kings', the triumphant extension of the unruly holiday entertainments of Smithfield beyond their natural time and place to invade 'the theatres of Covent-Garden, Lincoln's-Inn-Fields, and the Haymarket, to be the reigning Pleasures of the Court and Town'.[1] *The Pleasures of the Town* is the title of Luckless's play; Fielding's echo of Pope's phrase shows how close to *The Dunciad* he was working. Like Pope and like Jonson, Fielding dramatizes the threat of a kind of perpetual Saturnalia; like them, he pictures a world in which true drama has had to give way to puppet-shows, in which the role of the 'master-poet' has been usurped by the poetaster, a disordered world which has been left to the mercy of noise and nonsense.

Such at least are Fielding's evident intentions, but *The Author's Farce*, like Fielding's other dramatic burlesques, turns out finally to be a good-natured romp. The play's satirical intentions are mild, and ultimately somewhat muddled. Though the present age, we are told, is one which 'would allow Tom Durfey a better poet than Congreve or Wycherley', Fielding never makes it clear whether Luckless is to be regarded as a Durfey or as a Congreve; if, as it seems, he is a mere hack like Durfey, then it is impossible to feel indignant over the initial rejection of his work by the managers of the theatres or over the later interruption of *The Pleasures of the Town* by a character named Murdertext, who demands, like Zeal-of-the-Land Busy and with equal lack of success, that the show must stop.[2] Fielding was never really able to regard scribblers fiercely as a social menace in the way that Jonson and Pope evidently did, and *The Author's Farce* is written not so much out of satirical contempt as out of a more tolerant and compassionate interest in the difficulties of surviving at

---

1 *The Dunciad* (1729), I, 2 n. The relationship between Fielding's plays and the fourth book of *The Dunciad* is explored by George Sherburn in '*The Dunciad*, Book Four', *Studies in English*, University of Texas, 1944, pp. 174–90.
2 It is to Jonson's credit that he keeps a similar contradiction well concealed at the end of *Bartholomew Fair*; he holds no brief for the kind of puppet-show which Busy wants to stop.

all in Grub Street: hence the sympathetic and almost Dickensian scenes with Dash and Blotpage, Quibble and Scarecrow in the house of Mr Bookweight. And it is significant that *The Author's Farce*, like *Pasquin*, does not end in lamentation over the darkness of the age, but moves instead into lavish and wholesale farce. Though the transition from satire to farce has none of the fine control which Jonson shows in *Bartholomew Fair*, Fielding's confidence once he has actually reached that final mode shows clearly where his real skill lay, not in satire but in the more exuberant traditions of stage comedy. The comic resolution of *The Author's Farce* anticipates the comic resolution of *Joseph Andrews*; in each case the final rapid sequence of accidents and coincidences does not so much suggest that life is an absurd farce as that life is watched over by a benign providence which will finally set straight all confusions, bringing rewards to the innocent and luck to the luckless.

Even at this early stage in Fielding's career, then, his work shows a significantly different emphasis from that of Pope and his fellow-Scriblerians; and the differences become more apparent when, after the Licensing Act of 1737, Fielding turns his attention to the longer and more complex form of the novel, gradually abandoning his favourite tactics of burlesque inversion. In his novels Fielding continues to depict society in a state of fluidity in which 'the distinctions between high and low' have been dissolved, in which unexpected social reversals and equations occur, yet his art now becomes even more decisively comic in nature. . . .
(183–95)

We are used to the notion that comedy ends in lovers' meetings, with promises of marriage and the arrival of unexpected fortunes, with general reconciliations and forgivenesses, with dances, feasting, and widely bestowed goodwill. Fielding's work, as we have seen, characteristically moves to a conclusion of this kind, a conclusion which is normally devoid of major irony or pessimism or sense of imminent doom. Yet as we have also seen, the generally happy ending of comedy may also at times barely manage to conceal another harsher feeling, of returning sobriety and returning awareness of the demands of law and order, of the fact that the levelling and revelling must soon come to a stop, that the world must move once more the right way up. In Fielding's work the 'sense of an ending' is often of this kind: though events move magically towards their resolution, the hard paradoxes remain; benevolence is good, but so is prudence; mercy is good, but so is judgement; all men are flesh and blood, all men are brothers, but some must rule over others. Two incompatible worlds continue to exert their sharply different attractions for us right to the end.

(206)

Jonathan Wild

Arnold Kettle

from *An Introduction to the English Novel*, vol. 1   1951

[Human indignation] is Fielding's weapon, too [i.e. as in Swift], in *Jonathan Wild* which is sometimes referred to as a picaresque novel because the chief character happens to be a rogue, but which is in fact a moral fable. For there is no doubt about Fielding's moral intention or the moral pattern which shapes the book: indeed it may well be argued that this moral pattern is *too* insistent; certainly the story cannot be said to have that haphazard quality which we have seen to be typical of the picaresque tradition. It is all most carefully planned and controlled.[1]

The theme of *Jonathan Wild* is the antithesis between greatness and goodness. 'No two things can possibly be more distinct from each other, for greatness consists in bringing all manner of mischief on mankind and goodness in removing it from them.'

It is this abstract antithesis that informs the whole novel and makes it into the kind of thing it is, and unless the reader quickly realizes the kind of book he is dealing with his reactions to it are likely to be always a shade off-centre, his criticisms a trifle irrelevant. *Jonathan Wild* is not a psychological study nor even an exposure of criminality.[2]

1 I do not think that the fact that *Jonathan Wild* is based on a real person (a criminal hanged in 1725) and actual events should affect our attitude to it as fiction any more than the knowledge that most of Henry James's novels were suggested by true anecdotes.

2 Perhaps a useful comparison is with the early plays of Bernard Shaw (e.g., *Widowers' Houses*; *Mrs Warren's Profession*) or with Chaplin's *Monsieur Verdoux*. Mrs Warren and Verdoux are seen not as individual 'cases' but as symbols of and participants in a social situation rotten at the very foundations. Unlike most 'socially conscious' literature the object here is not to expose to our pity what frightful things a bad society does to individual people. We are not invited to pity but to think. It is the implications of Mrs Warren's profession, not merely its existence, that must give us pause. Fielding is not so consciously radical as Shaw or Chaplin (in a very real sense he is perfectly at home in his society and feels no urge to look beyond it), but his method is similar.

The characters are all relevant to the basic pattern of the book, the antithesis already mentioned. It is not Wild himself in glorious isolation, that interests Fielding, not simply Wild the super-criminal who lives by exploiting other criminals, but Wild as a representative symbol. The chief protagonists of the contending camps, the great and the good, are Wild and Heartfree, the innocent jeweller; but the novel is not *about* Wild and Heartfree, it is about eighteenth-century society. The great are the successes of that society, not just the Wilds but the Robert Walpoles, the politicians, the rulers, the exploiters; the good are not just the Heartfrees but all those who put human values, the values of the heart, above such success.

Because the generalized moral intention of such a book as *Jonathan Wild* is so basic to it, does this mean that it is by its intention, by the truth of the generalized moral, that it should be judged? Certainly not. The test of a moral fable is not whether the moral is true but whether the fable convinces. Clearly it will not convince unless it *is* true (so we cannot dismiss the truth behind it as irrelevant); but we must be particularly careful in the case of the moral fable not to confuse performance with intention. Because in analysing such a book as *Jonathan Wild* one is bound willynilly to be dealing in general moral principles it is tempting to judge the principles rather than the novel.

Fielding makes quite clear the nature of his intention in *Jonathan Wild*. It is no part of his method to leave us in any doubt as to what his story is about. When Bagshot the highwayman innocently expects a half-share in the booty he has by his own efforts obtained (Wild's only part has been to tip him off as to the traveller worth robbing) Wild philosophizes on the relation of rulers and ruled:

It is well said of us, the higher order of mortals, that we are born only to devour the fruits of the earth; and it may well be said of the lower class that they are born only to produce them for us. Is not the battle gained by the sweat and danger of the common soldier? Are not the honour and fruits of the victory the general's who laid the scheme? Is not the house built by the labour of the carpenter and the bricklayer? Is it not built for the profit only of the architect and for the use of the inhabitant, who could not easily have placed one brick upon another? Is not the cloth or the silk, wrought in its

form, and variegated with all the beauty of colours, by those
who are forced to content themselves with the coarsest and
vilest part of their work, while the profit and enjoyment of
their labours fall to the share of others?
(Book 1, chapter 8)

It is this generalized moral concern which gives force to the particular
touches of satirical description in the book, touches which would
otherwise seem often crude and heavy-handed. When, for instance,
in the highway robbery mentioned above, the Count La Ruse has
been robbed (through the agency of Wild) of the money he has just
won by dishonesty at the gambling table, Fielding's comment is:

The Count was obliged to surrender to savage force what he
had in so genteel and civil a manner taken at play. . . .

The irony that comes into play here extends far beyond the particular
situation. It is not merely that the Count was in fact scared stiff so that
Bagshot had to use no force, nor that he had in fact cheated at play:
what Fielding is bringing to our attention here is the utter inadequacy
of the normal eighteenth-century polite, literary use of such concepts
as 'force' and 'civility'. It is not the Count but the whole genteel
tradition that is being held up to criticism.

Almost every aspect of bourgeois society is satirized in *Jonathan
Wild*. Whigs and Tories, the party system itself, the corruption of
office, all are transported to Newgate jail where, in the fantastic world
of conscious criminals and unfortunate debtors, everything is seen
with a new and piercing clarity. An election is fought in the jail
between two parties of rogues. Both use the same catch-phrase, 'the
liberties of Newgate', which, remarks Fielding, 'in cant language
signifies plunder'.

The force of *Jonathan Wild* comes from Fielding's social vision,
which is what puts life into the great passages of the book. The conversations between Wild and his cronies, the Newgate scenes, the final
grotesque, appalling journey to the gallows, these are what capture
the imagination. Many of the descriptions (such as that of Miss Tishy
Snap [book 1, chapter 9]) have a ruthless realism which even Swift
does not surpass. Here there is more than a precise sordidness, more
than a determination to leave no horror unspoken. And when Fielding

speaks of Tishy as 'dishonouring the human species' one realizes how much of humanity as well as of bitterness lies in this strange book. Fielding is not without positive values. You cannot dishonour the human species unless there is honour there. The picture of women in *Jonathan Wild*, either, like Mrs Heartfree, so constantly at the mercy of men that life becomes one long battle for the retention of virtue, or else, like the Snap sisters, almost totally degraded by the world they live in, this picture throws a not irrelevant light on all the Pamelas and Molls of eighteenth-century fiction.

But for all its power and its extraordinary insight *Jonathan Wild* is not quite a great novel and its weaknesses as well as its strength derive from Fielding's social vision. There are, I think, three major weaknesses in the book: Heartfree; a too-insistent reiteration of the ironical antithesis of 'great' and 'good'; and certain compromises – embedded in the plot – which betray inadequacies in Fielding's own moral attitude.

The weakness of Heartfree is important because, as the chief representative of 'goodness' in the novel, he is essential to its pattern. Only once in the book does Heartfree truly come to life, in the interesting, satirical and yet moving soliloquy (book 3, chapter 2) which is a kind of eighteenth-century 'to be or not to be'. And even here his weakness as a symbolic figure is revealed in the feebleness of his final positive affirmation: 'I will do my utmost to lay the foundations of my children's happiness; I will carefully avoid educating them in a station superior to their fortune, and for the event trust to that Being in whom whoever rightly confides must be superior to all worldly sorrows.' Because in a fable like *Jonathan Wild* the vitality of the characters is wholly dependent on their part in the moral pattern one cannot separate what Wild or Heartfree 'stands for' from what he is. Wild and the rogues are vital characters (not, in Mr Forster's sense, 'round' characters, but nevertheless alive in the way they must be) because all that they stand for is fully realized.

Heartfree is not vital because Fielding castrates him as a moral agent and yet at the same time makes him bear the positive values of the fable on his shoulders. Therefore it is precisely Heartfree's passive acceptance, in the sentence I have just quoted, of the inevitability of class society (which Fielding has, through Wild, with such ruthless honesty dissected) and the commonplaces of conventional religion that makes him unfit to be the hero of the book, morally and therefore aesthetically. When Heartfree tells us that 'what we seek in this world is vanity' our hearts sink and the vital tension of the book is weakened, not because the philosophy he is expressing is in the abstract true or untrue, but because we know perfectly well that what Heartfree is seeking is not vanity, but a happy marriage and a decent living.

And if in the conception of Heartfree there is a core of defeatism which makes him an inadequate hero, this same defeatism emerges also in Fielding's prose. The irony, after the first pages, becomes a little too insistent. The reiteration of the good–great antithesis comes after a time somewhat to pall. Is not Fielding protesting, perhaps, too much? And is not his insistence, like the player queen's, a mark for suspicion? Repetition of this kind reveals not full confidence but an underlying doubt, a problem not fully realized, something hollow somewhere.

If we probe the weaknesses of *Jonathan Wild* our examination always leads us toward the same diagnosis. In the last chapter of book 1 there is one of the fullest and richest of Fielding's analyses of the great ('Mankind are first properly to be considered under two grand divisions – those that use their own hands, and those who employ the hands of others . . . etc.'), but out of the vigorous clarity emerges one unresolved ambiguity, his attitude to the 'middle' and particularly the professional class. Again, one notices a tendency (the only hint of sentimentality in Fielding's attitude towards Wild) to treat the villain of the piece as his own worst enemy. This tends to blur the central pattern; if Wild is the victim of a delusion his force as a typical symbol is weakened. Finally, there is in this novel a critical weakness in the resolution of the plot which involves more than once the production of a *deus ex machina* – the 'good magistrate' – who ultimately ensures that right prevails (and, incidentally, runs the 'rational' Utopian city that Mrs Heartfree finds in Africa).

It is the good magistrate (it is perhaps not irrelevant to recall that Fielding was one himself) who saves Heartfree and brings down Wild. He is above party, above class and therefore does not fit into the world of the novel, the world of 'the two grand divisions'. And for this reason he weakens the book and blurs the full powers and horror of it. For the real horror of the *Jonathan Wild* world, as Fielding has already convinced us, is that the Wilds do not inevitably end on the gallows and that the Heartfrees, inadequately armed as they are seen to be, may well be themselves corrupted. And from this final horror Fielding averts his eyes, consoling us with the spectacle of the good magistrate administering an impartial justice. And it is precisely owing to the presence of the magistrate that the 'good' characters in the novel remain passive and unalive, are neither corrupted nor transformed by their participation in the *Wild* world. For if they were corrupted the magistrate could not save them and if they were transformed, made rebels, he would not need to.

The basic weakness of *Jonathan Wild*, to which the various details I have mentioned all contribute, is that no one on the 'good' side actually fights for human values (as Tom Jones, for instance, does). This is why as far as the success and vitality of the book go, the rogues have all the life. And the weakness is not an abstractable 'aesthetic' weakness. It is a weakness which springs direct from the limitations of Fielding's social vision.

I have dwelt in some detail on an analysis of *Jonathan Wild* because it is a typical example of the moral fable and there is no other way of indicating the kind of approach relevant to this kind of book. If we encounter *Jonathan Wild*, or any novel with a serious moral structure, with the preconception that what is most important in a novel is 'character' (in the Dickensian sense) or 'story' (of the kind Stevenson does well) or 'atmosphere' (as in Hardy) or 'plot-construction' (as in Wilkie Collins), then we shall make little of Fielding's wonderful book. That is not to say that 'character', etc., are not important. But it is to say that such terms can only be discussed in relation to the central core and purpose of each particular book. (45–51)

A. E. Dyson

from 'Fielding: Satiric and Comic Irony', a revised version of an essay of 1957, *The Crazy Fabric*, chapter 2   1965

The mingling of good humour with seriousness is bound to reveal itself as a literary infirmity of purpose in passages where satire rather than comedy is the aim: in *Jonathan Wild* it becomes a source of structural weakness throughout. By the consistency and intensity of its irony, this work clearly announces itself as a satire in the tradition of *Gulliver*. But the Swiftian façade is related only fitfully to a genuine disgust; Fielding has as much insight into evil as Swift, but none of the misanthropy which sustains Swift in a gradually mounting indictment of humanity. As a result, the *jeu d'esprit* works against the total artistic purpose rather than for it. Instead of intensifying the satire, it produces a quite alien note of honest mirth.

I am not suggesting, however, that *Jonathan Wild* fails as a work, or anything so simple. Its very lapses from satire are the occasion for that health and vitality which are the true qualities by which Fielding survives. Nor am I suggesting, as I have already made clear, that Fielding is incapable of depicting evil as it really is. His sense of the depravity of the corrupted soul was a profound one, and none the less so for its refusal to become assimilated to a prevailing misanthropy. The real point that has to be made is that Fielding depicts Wild skilfully, but without ultimate conviction; there is even a hint of glamour in the portrait, of the kind that one associates with street ballads of the time. It is hard for us to believe that Wild is very relevant to the life of ordinary men; far from being alarmed on behalf of the species to which he belongs (as we are alarmed on behalf of the species to which the supposed author of Swift's *Modest Proposal* belongs) we must regard him as an interesting exception. He is little more than a puppet, flawless in performance, but curiously abstract in the quality of his crime. There is even a certain monotony about his techniques. First he will try to gain his ends by a brilliant and persuasive rhetoric, which itself implies a Hobbesian view of human nature; when this fails he resorts to open violence, with immediate and predictable success. But his progress in crime is a mere accumulation of incidents, not a deepening insight into the nature of evil. He has used all his best methods, and Fielding has expounded his best irony upon them, before a quarter of the novel is through. So the rest tends to be unsatisfying; well executed in its way, but increasingly tedious by repetition.

(21-2)

Robert H. Hopkins

from 'Language and Comic Play in Fielding's *Jonathan Wild*',
Criticism, vol. 8   1966

The most bestial (and potentially obscene) simile or metaphor is an
implied one, hitherto unnoticed, which relies for its comic effect on
our recognizing its referent in the orgy scene of the Rose Tavern in
Hogarth's *A Rake's Progress*. This metaphor begins at the end of
book 2, chapter 8, when Wild's passion for Mrs Heartfree is equated
with 'the kind of affection which, after the exercise of the dominical
day is over, a lusty divine is apt to conceive for the well-dressed sirloin
or handsome buttock which the well-edified squire in gratitude set
before him, and which, so violent is his love, he devours in imagination
the moment he sees it' (*Works*, II, 81–2). So Wild, after casting his eyes
'on that charming dish' (Mrs Heartfree), plots how he can best devour
her. This simile is extended to the opening paragraph of chapter 9:

When first Wild conducted his flame (or rather his dish, to
continue our metaphore [sic]) from the proprietor, he had
projected a design of conveying her to one of those eating-
houses in Covent Garden, where female flesh is deliciously
dressed and served up to the greedy appetites of young
gentlemen; but, fearing lest she should not come readily
enough into his wishes, and that by too eager and hasty a
pursuit, he should frustrate his future expectations, and luckily
at the same time a noble hint suggesting itself to him by
which he might almost inevitably secure his pleasure, together
with his profit, he contented himself with waiting on Mrs
Heartfree home. . . .

Most readers have no doubt recognized a rather general allusion here
to Covent Garden bawdy houses and have accepted the conventional
equation of food and sex imagery so that the figurative language
would seem to be only figurative. But it is here that Fielding's superb
comic play in *Wild* reveals itself most strikingly in a kind of meta-
phoric double-reverse in which the figurative language can be taken
literally! Hogarth's painting of the Rose, Plate 3 of *A Rake's Progress*,
is described as follows by Peter Quennell:

... among the amusements provided by the Rose were
exhibitions of the sort with which every well-organized
brothel attempts to whet its customers' appetite. Leather-coat
is the master of ceremonies. Musicians have been recruited
from the street; and he is holding the large pewter dish that
an habitué of Covent Garden would at once have recognised.
The 'posture woman' is undressing on the left, with the
patient and practised movements of a mercenary who
thoroughly understands her trade; and, as soon as she has
stripped, she will mount on the platter, 'to whirl herself
round, and display other feats of indecent activity'.[1]

As Christopher Hibbert writes: 'Having undressed she lay naked on
her back on an enormous pewter plate, her knees drawn up to her
chin, her hands clasped under her thighs in the attitude of a trussed
chicken....'[2] This incredible literalization of the food-sex simile at
the Rose Tavern is reinforced in Hogarth's painting by the replacing
of one of the portraits of the Twelve Caesars with a portrait of
Pontac, the renowned chef! The metaphor in *Wild* actually has a
literal referent; female flesh really is 'served up' on a platter to
'greedy appetites'; and the obscenity of the posture woman's activity
perfectly depicts the inner bestiality of Jonathan Wild's mind at even
considering taking Mrs Heartfree to Covent Garden.
(220–21)

1 *Hogarth's Progress*, New York, 1955, pp. 130–31.
2 *The Road to Tyburn: The Story of Jack Sheppard and The Eighteenth-Century
London Underworld*, Cleveland, 1957, p. 56.

Shamela

Martin C. Battestin

from his 'Introduction' to *Joseph Andrews and Shamela* 1961

Early in 1741, Fielding interrupted his work as journalist for the
Patriots to write the first, and by far the best, of the anti-*Pamela*s –
as the spate of 'spoofs' and satires and criticisms spawned in reaction
to Richardson's novel has come to be called. Published pseudony-
mously on 4 April[1] the full title of this brilliant and bawdy parody
suggests the line of attack that he hilariously pursues:

An Apology for the Life of Mrs Shamela Andrews. In
which, the many notorious Falsehoods and
Misrepresentations of a Book called *Pamela*, Are exposed and
refuted; and all the matchless Arts of that young Politician,
set in a true and just Light. Together with a full Account of
all that passed between her and Parson Arthur Williams;
whose Character is represented in a manner something
different from what he bears in *Pamela*. The whole being exact
Copies of authentic Papers delivered to the Editor.
Necessary to be had in all Families. By Mr Conny Keyber.

By the time the burlesque has run its course, the absurdities and
pretensions of *Pamela* have been exposed once and for all. Fielding's
skill at this delightful bathetic art had been developed and sharpened
on several previous occasions and in several different genres: in the
drama, for example, there were *The Covent-Garden Tragedy* and *The
Tragedy of Tragedies*; in poetry there were the mock-epic *Vernoniad*

1 It was not until well into this century that Fielding's authorship of *Shamela*
was established beyond any reasonable doubt. The story of the accumulation
of evidence that has led to the general acceptance of the work as Fielding's is
interesting in itself, but too long to rehearse here. The best single discussion of
the subject is Charles B. Woods' article 'Fielding and the Authorship of
Shamela', *Philological Quarterly*, vol. 25, 1946, pp. 256–72.

and *Juvenal's Sixth Satire Modernised in Burlesque Verse*; and in *The Champion*, more crudely, there were amusing imitations of the 'ultra sublime' style of Colley Cibber's *Apology*. With *Shamela* Fielding brought the art of parody near to perfection. What he provides, in some seventy pages, is a comic abridgement, down to the smallest details, of the very form and substance of *Pamela*. Richardson, for example, maintained the ruse of posing as an editor of Pamela's letters; so Fielding has his Parson Oliver purvey the 'authentic' correspondence of Shamela, of which Richardson's version is said to be the grossest misrepresentation. Richardson had indulged his vanity by prefixing to the second edition of his novel some twenty-four pages of commendatory letters and a poem; so Fielding includes his own 'puffs', one, appropriately enough, from the editor to himself. Richardson, at times somewhat clumsily and at the expense of probability, had his heroic servant maid relate her adventures in long, detailed, and quite literate letters, often employing the present tense for greater immediacy of effect; so Shamela – her pen, even in bed, never out of hand – tells her story in the same epistolary fashion, but eschewing (with a vengeance!) her rival's delicacy of phrase. Richardson's best scenes are all here, but they are impudently imaged in the parodist's fun-house mirror. Pamela's mock drowning to cover her attempted escape from Mrs Jewkes now becomes Shamela's device to divert attention from an amorous tryst with Parson Williams. In the novel Mr B., out for a drive with his bride-to-be and her father, comes upon Williams taking a solitary walk and reading in a book, and thereupon, in a magnanimous gesture of reconciliation with the man who has interfered with the progress of his libertinism, he invites him to enter the carriage and sit beside Pamela; in the parody Williams is caught poaching hares in the squire's meadow, but Booby, choking down his ire in fear of a display of tears from his wife, relinquishes his place in the coach to her lover and takes to his horse. Best of all, of course, is the rough and uproarious handling of the bedroom scenes. Indeed, at every turn Fielding has taken his cue from his original: already in the novel, for instance, there is Mr B's suspicion that Parson Williams' interest in Pamela is not entirely dutiful; there is Pamela's happy knack of fainting away whenever the emergency requires; there is, despite her prodigious virtue, Pamela's own embarrassment at her secret admiration for the handsome rake who has been trying to ravish her; and she ends, after all, by consenting to marry the villain on her own terms.

Fielding's mimicry is complete and it is devastating. By changing the perspective of vision – by taking a hostile and sardonic view of Richardson's triumphant virgin, seeing her chastity (so wonderfully profitable to her!) as artful rather than innocent – he has inverted, and subverted, Richardson's whole design. Take, for instance, the bedroom scenes, two episodes that point to the real cause of Fielding's quarrel with his rival. Fielding has caught the contradiction implicit in the presence of such 'inflaming descriptions' in a book professedly intended to inculcate 'the principles of virtue and religion'. In these scenes, to use the phrase of the appreciative Parson Tickletext, he saw *Pamela*, girl and novel both, 'with all the pride of ornament cast off': what is revealed is the sham of Richardson's whole pose and performance, and the Sham, as the theory of the Ridiculous set forth in the Preface to *Joseph Andrews* attests, was Fielding's special province as a satirist. Delighted to catch the prude staging a peep show, Fielding has turned Richardson's drama into a bawdy game of cat and mouse – exchanging only the identity of the predator! Worst of all, of course, was the naïve moral assumption that underlies the novel and glares forth garishly from the subtitle: the notion that virtue is rewarded, not in the Christian hereafter, but in the here and now, and with pounds and social position – a comfortable doctrine, Fielding observed in *Tom Jones*, 'to which we have but one objection, namely, that it is not true'. A morality based on such mercenary motives was a kind of prostitution masquerading as virtuousness. As Shamela wryly declares to her mother: 'I thought once of making a little fortune by my person. I now intend to make a great one by my vartue.' With such absurdities already latent in the novel, the distorted image mirrored in the parodist's glass is somehow closer to the truth than the original.

But Richardson and *Pamela* are not the only game that come under fire in *Shamela*, and most of these targets are fixed again in *Joseph Andrews*. There are hits, for example, at Fielding's old adversary, Colley Cibber, whose autobiography, *An Apology for the Life of Mr Colley Cibber, Comedian* (1740), not only offended Fielding's taste by the violence it committed upon the English language, but also revived their old quarrel by calling him names. The title of *Shamela* humorously mimics that of Cibber's book, and the pseudonym, Conny Keyber, was sure to call him to mind.[1] Conny was also meant to evoke Conyers Middleton, whose *Life of Cicero* (published in February, little more than a month before *Shamela*) had disparaged the work of Fielding's friend, George Lyttelton. In his own Dedication, Fielding mocks Middleton's, which was fulsomely addressed to the effeminate Lord Hervey, a political ally of Walpole and a man known to his enemies, since Pope's famous gibe, as 'Lord Fanny'. In John Puff's letter, Walpole (or '*his Honour*') himself comes in for some rather indelicate abuse in reference to the prime minister's inability to keep his wife at home. All these cuts add to the fun and variety of Fielding's satire.

More pervasive and significant, however, is the irreverent treatment accorded the clergy, whose critical social function in preserving the public morality made them the special objects of Fielding's concern, defending them when they were unjustly contemned, rebuking them when they failed in their office. The importance of this theme in *Shamela* explains why Fielding chose to frame his story in an exchange of letters between two clergymen, one the naïve Parson Tickletext, the other the wise Parson Oliver, who corrects his friend's misapprehensions about *Pamela* and supplies him with the 'genuine' papers; and it further accounts for the prominence of Parson Williams, to whom Richardson had assigned a relatively minor role. More than anything else, what seems to have set Fielding to work in this vein was the crass enthusiasm of clergymen like Dr Slocock, who encouraged that 'epidemical phrenzy' raging in town over a silly and immoral book by making it, in Tickletext's words, their 'common business here, not only to cry it up, but to preach it up likewise'. By so doing, they were, however unwittingly, betraying their public trust and giving cause to that regrettable contempt of their order which was 'the fashionable vice of the times'. In the spring of 1740, Fielding had published in *The Champion* a series of leaders which he called an 'Apology for the Clergy', four essays designed to correct the general contempt of the priesthood and to define the qualities of

---

1 Conny, a colloquialism for dupe, looks and sounds like Colley; and in the *Apology* Cibber had alluded to himself as 'Minheer Keiber', a name given him in *Mist's Weekly Journal*.

the true and the false clergyman. The same motives are evident in *Shamela* and, as we shall see, in *Joseph Andrews*.

The substance of Fielding's satire of the clergy in *Shamela* is embodied in Parson Williams, who is the very type of the false divine: as Oliver admonishes his brethren, 'if a clergyman would ask me by what pattern he should form himself, I would say, Be the reverse of Williams.' A consummate hedonist and hypocrite, Williams has every vice imaginable, but Fielding has given his portrait special point by making this scoundrel an admirer of the fiery evangelist, George Whitefield, who, along with John Wesley, was just then founding a new sect, Methodism. Fielding, himself an Anglican of the latitudinarian school that made religion a matter rather of the performance of good works than of belief or ceremony, distrusted Methodism from the start and continued to attack it throughout his career. He saw in its Antinomian emphasis upon salvation through grace and faith and the imputed righteousness of Christ a doctrine potentially pernicious to social morality. In general, he was among those who were appalled by what seemed to be the import of Whitefield's message: 'So you say you believe in the Lord Jesus Christ, you may live the life of devils.' Thus, with the aid of Whitefield's works and Williams' counsel, Shamela rationalizes her frequent fornication – the pleasures of which, 'tho' not strictly innocent, are ... to be purged away by frequent and sincere repentance' – and her paramour is made to preach upon the text, 'Be not righteous over-much', the subject of a sustained and heated controversy between Whitefield and Dr Joseph Trapp. Into Williams, Fielding poured all the faults of which the Methodists were popularly accused – in particular, their alleged claims of a special dispensation of grace, exempting them from good works and excusing sinful self-indulgence since salvation was a matter of confidence, not performance. Thus Shamela relates the gist of Williams' casuistry:

Well, on Sunday Parson Williams came, according to his
promise, and an excellent sermon he preached; his text was,
Be not righteous over-much; and, indeed, he handled it in a very
fine way: he showed us that the Bible doth not require too
much goodness of us, and that people very often call things
goodness that are not so. That to go to church, and to pray,

and to sing psalms, and to honour the clergy, and to repent,
is true religion; and 'tis not doing good to one another, for
that is one of the greatest sins we can commit, when we don't
do it for the sake of religion. That those people who talk of
vartue and morality, are the wickedest of all persons. That
'tis not what we do, but what we believe, that must save us,
and a great many other good things; I wish I could
remember them all.

Later, as they ride together in the coach, the learned parson subtly
expatiates to Shamela on the matrimonial implications of the
separateness of the Spirit and the Flesh, demonstrating with a supple
logic the moral justification of adultery. An extension of the campaign begun in *The Champion*, Williams stands as the embodiment
of the corrupt priest, not as an indictment of his whole order, as
some readers, mistaking Fielding's motives, suppose – Parson Oliver,
we recall, has in effect the last word and laugh – but as an object
lesson of abuses to be avoided and corrected.

Shamela is superbly the inspiration of Fielding's antic muse: the
jester's spirit, and something of his very mode, prevails in the droll
mimicry of this brilliant burlesque. But if Fielding preferred the cap
and bells to the preacher's somber gown, he wore them wisely – like
Shakespeare's clowns – and in the service of truth. There is bite and
purpose in his laughter. One after another, Richardson, Cibber,
Middleton, Walpole, Whitefield, the corrupt or incompetent among
the clergy – all feel the sting of the satirist's lash. To speak of such a
coarse and bawdy book as serving the cause of morality and good
taste may seem a contradiction to the fastidious, but Fielding's sexual
comedy is free and open and hearty, unlike the pornographic
melodrama of Richardson's bedroom scenes, for example, in which
a sensual leer hides beneath the mask of gravity. Of all the remedies
against a hyperactive libido, there is none better than laughter.
Though one can scarcely imagine its being recommended from the
pulpit, there is something essentially healthier in *Shamela's* lusty good
humor than in the prurient sobriety of *Pamela*. In its own right and of
its kind, *Shamela* is a remarkable performance – perhaps even, as
Sheridan Baker would have it, 'the best parody in English literature'.
It enjoys, furthermore, the distinction of being, so far as we know,

the first prose fiction that Fielding wrote, the work that began his transformation from a second-rate playwright and hackney scribbler to one of the greatest of novelists. It stands as a kind of fulcrum between *Pamela* and *Joseph Andrews*, the two works that gave direction and shape to the English novel.
(xi–xvi)

'Comic Epic in Prose'

W. L. Renwick

'Comic Epic in Prose', *Essays and Studies by Members of the English Association*, vol. 32   1946

Every examination candidate has picked up the phrase, worn smooth in the brook of lectures that goes on for ever, carries it in the same pouch with *the age of prose and reason – in the depths, on the heights – unified sensibility – the return to nature –* to sling it in due season at the thrice-battered heads of his examiners. The only defence, for ourselves and for the original whence it came, is to pick it up and look at it carefully so that we may see something of what has been lost in the process of attrition.

Even without the warning *in prose* it is obvious that Fielding is not announcing another burlesque like *The Battle of the Frogs and the Mice*, or *The Gymnasiad*, or even *The Rape of the Lock*. The references are not to one set of literary examples but to a whole body of criticism. *Comic* does not mean 'funny', nor *epic* 'exciting and dangerous', as it does in newspaper headlines. The terms have not yet, in 1742, suffered their modern degradation. Nor is *in prose* merely a tag to fill out the phrase. Each word carries the full weight of the critical tradition from which it derives the force of established authority.

The continuity of the tradition was broken by 1800. The terms are no longer the familiar currency of discussion and argument. We have to go back to them deliberately and self-consciously, so that, if less authoritative and less evocative, they are more clearly defined – or at least focused in the epidiascope. For us indeed the focusing is over-conscious; we are tempted to 'research'. But we must resist the temptation to seek our documents always in hidden corners. Fielding was an educated man of the world writing for educated men of the world, with a good average notion of the common sources and arguments in his head and expecting the same of his readers. They gossiped of 'the Rules', 'correctness', 'the Kinds' as we gossip of 'complexes' and 'inhibitions', rather vaguely, out of the same casual acquaintance – or lack of acquaintance – with the original documents. To avoid false relations and false emphases it is often safest to keep to the obvious, as I do here.

Comic: that is, partaking of the nature and purposes of Comedy; and Comedy means *entrer comme il faut dans le ridicule des hommes, et ... rendre agréablement sur le théâtre les défauts de tout le monde*:

> Deedes and language such as men do use:
> And persons, such as *Comoedie* would chuse,
> When she would shew an Image of the times,
> And sport with humane follies, not with crimes.

We could work back from Shaftesbury to Aristotle himself, but there is no great need, and though it would be well to remember Falstaff and Dogberry, these scraps of Molière and Jonson, all the more cogent that they come from two practising playwrights, one a notorious theorist and the other a notorious sceptic, will suffice.

Molière's *sur le théâtre* is cancelled out by *epic*, which demands narrative, for the noun must prevail over the adjective. The form of Comedy disappears; the motives remain. First (and very important it is), pleasure – Fielding will sport *agréablement*: it is a promise. Next, realism, or, since the term is compromised by a later fashion, proximity – the scene is the world, that is the world of all of us, and the actions are neither remote nor fantastical, nor unique. Then, the range of interest – *humane follies, le ridicule*: we are not to expect tragic emotion nor exploration of the darker and more desperate experiences of the human soul. Sorrow is the common lot of mankind, but tragedy, in its true critical sense and not in the hasty usage of journalism, does in fact lie outside the common experience of ordinary men – grows indeed, *ex hypothesi*, out of *les défauts* of rare and exalted souls. This denial of tragic interest (to digress for a moment) might be counted timidity in Fielding, but the tragic novel is so rare to this day that it seems doubtful whether prose narrative can really carry off pure tragedy; anyhow the dramatic form is more economical and therefore more powerful.

Epic was a little more dangerous. In prescribing narrative it is obviously useful, but it might suggest to critical dilettanti or critical pedants the conventions of form – the not beginning *ab ovo* and so on

– exalted personages, heroic actions, supernatural machinery, and the rest of the Receipt to Make an Epic Poem. The prefixed *comic* cuts out a good deal, but vestiges of expectation might remain – and did remain, since Fielding indulges them in casual bursts of mock-heroic. The mock-heroic, however, appears in chapter-headings and fragments of commentary, rarely in the story, and then only as one of many literary tricks. It would seem as if the narrative form were the only epic characteristic – since any story must have a hero of sorts, or at least a heroine. But *epic* does carry weight. An epic is not merely a narrative; it is a narrative largely conceived and of grave and serious import. The ethical content of *comic* is extended: Fielding will treat of human follies, but human follies are important matters – so long, that is, as they are not mere personal eccentricities, but follies *de tout le monde*.

The conclusion *in prose* cuts out certain other implications of *epic*, and particularly the prescription of style. Comedy embodies itself in *language such as men do use*; prose is not subject to the prescriptions of diction and ornament imposed upon the heroic, or even the comic poet. Nor does prose demand that elevation of spirit, the *furor* any more than the *curiositas*. In 1742 men might not echo Ronsard, who 'disoit ordinairement que tous ne devoient témérairement se mesler de poésie; que la prose estoit le langage des hommes, mais la poésie estoit le langage des dieux', but the idea lingered: it was and is a well-understood principle that poetry is proper to the expression of the more elevated thoughts and passions, and the celebration of the great occasion, above the stretch of the ordinary day-to-day goings-on of life. *In prose* plants us firmly down, once and for all, in the ordinary world. And it leaves all rhetorical questions open. Here also Fielding pays tribute to the epic principles he has forgone, by the rhetorical mock-elevation of style in his dithyrambic invocations and travesties of 'apparatus'; and these also he keeps out of the story except at its broadest and most farcical turns, where anybody might have used them.

Taking the phrase as a whole, and allowing that its members, checking and cross-reflecting on one another, do give a notion of the novel as Fielding conceived it, we may yet ask why he troubled with such elaborate allusion to critical theory. The answer is, that Fielding had made a discovery, and an important and delightful one. He had gone out to chase an ass, and found a kingdom. His quick appreciation of the situation is the mark of his greatness, but however delightful the situation, it presented its difficulties. What was this form that was growing under his hand? It was a literary form, and by all the habits of literature as he had been taught them, and as men at large accepted them, it had to be defined. There were no terms *ad hoc*, and in any case the unknown has to be defined in terms of the known. Fielding's kingdom was unexplored and uncharted. If we refer to Aristotle's original triangulation, we find that the non-dramatic equivalent of comedy is lampoon, of tragedy, epic. With a new track opening before him and leading across new country, Fielding takes cross-bearings on the old landmarks: and his choice of base-points is as brilliant as it is crucial. *In prose* gives him a third bearing, and his triangulation is complete. He has left the old tracks, but he is not lost.

He had to do it first for his own sake, and in his directions to readers he betrays his delight and excitement. Of course there were precedents: Richardson who set him on the exemplification of ethical principles in a familiar contemporary setting; Cervantes who set his hero on the road and exploited the ironic treatment of incidents of travel; Defoe who infused humane emotion into the underworld tradition that runs from Harman and Greene to Bampfylde Fuller and Head and Kirkman, and in so doing lifted the whole tradition into the upper world. But these were all limited – one-bearing travellers who, however much they might see as they went, marched on the fixed point they had selected in advance. And of course it was Parson Adams who burst upon Fielding's sight as upon ours; but character is not a novel. Knowledge of the world, understanding and enjoyment of the world, do not make a book. The creative technical understanding had to be added, the joy of life to be fused with the joy of making. In that great phrase Fielding evoked the critical tradition, claimed its authority, asserted the right of his new discovery to the craft of comedy and dignity of epic, and assumed the moral responsibilities of both along with the freedom of prose.

People are asking nowadays whether the novel will last much longer. That is because the novel has become a habit, and habits grow stale, or are lost because they are unconscious. Fielding saw the novel as a literary kind, a new one but as authentic as the rest. The doctrine

of the kinds is forgotten, but the Kinds exist, and always will. The doctrine helped Fielding to find his power. He might help a new generation to recover theirs.
(40–3)

Ian Watt

from *The Rise of the Novel* 1957

Fielding, then, eventually came to see his own society as offering sufficient interest and variety to make possible a literary genre exclusively devoted to engaging the reader in a closer scrutiny of 'nature' and of modern 'manners' than had ever been attempted before: and his own literary development was certainly in this direction. *Amelia* is, as has often been said, much closer to Richardson's close study of domestic life than his previous works; and although Fielding did not live long enough to embody his reorientation in another novel, there seems to be no doubt that he had become conscious of the fact that his earlier applications of the epic analogy had been responsible for his most obvious divergencies from the role proper to the faithful historian of the life of his time – a realization, incidentally, which is implicit in his ironical defence of the epic diction in *Tom Jones* which was introduced, he explained, so that it 'might be in no danger of being likened to the labours of [modern] historians'.[1]

At the same time the extent of the influence of the epic analogy on Fielding's earlier novels must not be exaggerated. He called *Tom Jones* 'A History', and habitually described his role as that of historian or biographer whose function was to give a faithful presentation of the life of his time. Fielding's conception of this role, it is true, was different from that of Defoe or Richardson, but the difference is mainly connected, not with his attempt to imitate epic, but with the general influence of the neo-classical tradition on every aspect of his work. The most specific literary debt manifest in *Tom Jones*, indeed, is not to epic but to drama: not so much because his main critical source, Aristotle's *Poetics*, was primarily concerned with drama and

1 Book 4, chapter 1. On this see Robert M. Wallace, 'Fielding's Knowledge of History and Biography', *SP*, vol. 44, 1947, pp. 89–107.

gave epic a secondary place, as because Fielding had been a dramatist himself for over a decade before attempting fiction. The remarkable coherence of the plot of *Tom Jones* surely owes little to the actual example of Homer or Virgil, and little more to Aristotle's insistence that 'in the Epic as in Tragedy, the story should be constructed on dramatic principles';[1] it is very palpably the product of Fielding's experience as a practising dramatist. It is also highly likely, incidentally, that some of the other features of his novels, such as the coincidences and discoveries which provide surprise at the cost of a certain loss of authenticity, are also a legacy from the drama rather than from the epic; and even the burlesque and mock-heroic elements had appeared long ago in many of his plays, such as *Tom Thumb, a Tragedy* (1730).

Why, then, it may be asked, has the formula of the comic epic in prose so 'obsessed critics of novels', to use George Sherburn's phrase?[2] It no doubt makes an immediate appeal to those who, like Peacock's Dr Folliott, habitually manifest 'a safe and peculiar inaccessibility to ideas except such as are recommended by an almost artless simplicity or a classical origin',[3] and this perhaps gives a clue both to the reason why Fielding was led to invent the formula and to why it later flourished.

In 1742 the novel was a form in grave disrepute, and Fielding probably felt that to enlist the prestige of epic might help win for his first essay in the genre a less prejudiced hearing from the *literati* than might otherwise have been expected. In this Fielding was actually following the example of the French writers of romance a century earlier; they, too, had laid claim to the epic filiation in prefatory asseverations which were not so much accurate analyses of their achievement as attempts to assuage their own anxieties and those of their readers about the uncanonized nature of what was to follow in the text. Nor have such attempts to dissipate the odour of unsanctity in which prose fiction seems destined to have its being ceased even in our day – F. R. Leavis's 'The Novel as Dramatic Poem' would seem to be an analogous attempt to smuggle the novel into the critical pantheon under the disguise of an ancient and honoured member.

At the same time, however, the fact that the formulae both of

1 *Poetics*, chapter 23.
2 'Fielding's *Amelia*', *ELH*, vol. 3, 1936, p. 2.
3 Carl van Doren, *Life of Thomas Love Peacock*, Dent, 1911, p. 194.

470 Glenn W. Hatfield

Fielding and of Leavis connect the novel with major poetic forms
suggests an effort to put the genre into the highest possible literary
context. Obviously both the creation and the criticism of the novel
cannot but gain from this, and it is indeed likely that the most positive
gain which Fielding derived from thinking about his narrative in
terms of epic was that it encouraged him to as intense and serious a
travail as the loftiest literary forms were presumed to demand.

Apart from this it is likely that the epic influence on Fielding was
very slight, mainly retrograde, and of little importance in the later
tradition of the novel. To call Fielding, as Ethel Thornbury does in
her monograph on the subject, 'the founder of the English prose epic'[1]
is surely to award him a somewhat sterile paternity; Fielding's greatest
followers, Smollett, Dickens and Thackeray, do not, for example,
imitate the very few specifically epic features in his work. But, as we
have seen, the idea of the 'comic epic in prose' is by no means Fielding's major claim on our attention: its main function was to suggest
one of the high standards of literary achievement which he wished to
keep in mind when he began in his new path in fiction; it was
certainly not intended as yet another of the innumerable eighteenth-
century 'Receits to make an Epick Poem'; and this is fortunate, for,
in literature at least, the nostrum killeth but the nostalgia may give
life. . . .

(257–9)

Glenn W. Hatfield

from *Henry Fielding and the Language of Irony* 1968

Burlesque diction, Fielding argues in the Preface to *Joseph Andrews*,
does not debase the characters and sentiments of the comic epic poem
in prose any more than clothes, except 'in vulgar opinion', make the
man. On the contrary, to understand the mock-heroic and other
ironic passages we must in effect separate style from content, and
this creates the illusion that we are independent of the verbal medium,
that we have seen through it to the objective truth underneath. But
it also conditions us to accept the surrounding language of straight-

[1] *Henry Fielding's Theory of the Comic Prose Epic*, 1931, p. 166.

forward narration, in which style and content appear harmonious, as above suspicion. The ironic vocabulary and the burlesque diction are verbal sacrifices offered up to the reader's (and Fielding's) distrust of language so that his 'ordinary style' (as he himself calls it after one of the mock-heroic interludes in *Joseph Andrews*) (Book 3, chapter 6) may have by contrast all the force of plain-spoken truth.
(200)

Joseph Andrews

Robert Alan Donovan

'*Joseph Andrews* as Parody', *The Shaping Vision: Imagination in the English Novel from Defoe to Dickens*, chapter 4   1966

> So the whole thing has a happy ending! How calm and
> peaceful would our life be always if a messenger came from
> the king whenever we wanted![1]

Shamela is such a devastating parody of *Pamela* that one wonders why Fielding was impelled to attempt in *Joseph Andrews* yet another attack on the same work. For all its brevity *Shamela* is comprehensive; it parodies virtually every aspect of its original – except perhaps its tediousness. There is the apparatus of laudatory epistles (two such letters had appeared in the first edition of *Pamela*, and others in the second edition of 14 February 1741), the sententious garrulity of the heroine, the admonitions of her mother, and the impotent railing of the squire when his desires are frustrated. The events of the story correspond to those in *Pamela* in remarkable detail, though of course the compass is much smaller. Shamela's ordeal, like Pamela's, is punctuated by an abduction into Lincolnshire, an attempt at suicide, the proffer of a written contract of concubinage, and an abrupt dismissal by the squire, and (again like Pamela's) it terminates in the squire's abject surrender. Even Pamela's charitable offices toward her former fellow servants find their counterpart in Shamela's calculated generosity. All this is brilliantly effective, and it would seem that any attempt to improve on *Shamela's* pungent hilarity would be in vain.

Yet Fielding returned to the assault on *Pamela* in the following year with *Joseph Andrews*, in which the first ten and the last thirteen chapters constitute an explicit parody of Richardson's novel. Commentary has generally focused, however, on the central chapters of the novel, which contain no overt reference to *Pamela* at all. The opening

1 B. Brecht (1929), *The Threepenny Opera*, trans. E. Bentley and D. Vesey, Methuen, 1955.

and closing chapters have proved something of an embarrassment to those who, like Irvin Ehrenpreis, would prefer to regard *Joseph Andrews* as 'autonomous'.[1] The usual way of accounting for these embarrassing chapters is to assume that Fielding 'forgot', during the central portion of the novel, that he was writing a parody and allowed the characters to take matters temporarily into their own hands.[2] In spite of an impressive weight of opinion on this point, I think it might be fruitful to explore the contrary assumption that Fielding, far from forgetting the design of making fun of *Pamela*, pursues that objective continuously throughout the novel, though my concern is less with Fielding's intention than with the coherence, or lack of it, in the imaginative vision which shapes the novel. It is the novel itself that I propose to examine.

Fielding's detestation of Richardson, as Digeon long ago pointed out, is centered upon Richardson's 'devout admiration' (*admiration béate*) of his own heroine and the moral vision she displays.[3] Fielding's

1 Irvin Ehrenpreis, 'Fielding's Use of Fiction: The Autonomy of *Joseph Andrews*,' in C. Shapiro (ed.), *Twelve Original Essays on Great English Novels*, Detroit, 1960, pp. 23–41.
2 This view of the novel has been so often repeated that I shall not attempt to record all the statements of it. The earliest formulation I have found is by Frederick Lawrence: 'It is very evident that, as Fielding proceeded, he thought less of his original design, as he became more attached to those excellent beings whom his fancy had called into existence – good Parson Adams, honest Joseph Andrews, and beautiful, tender-hearted Fanny. As it has been said of Cervantes, so it may be said of his English follower, that he came 'at last to love the creations of his marvellous power, as if they were real familiar personages; and if at the outset he thought only of ridiculing Richardson, and throwing in a sly sarcasm at Cibber, as he advanced in his narrative he ceased to think of those personages or their works' (*The Life of Henry Fielding*, London, 1855, p. 160). That this view, or one very like it, is still current is suggested by Ehrenpreis and by Maurice Johnson in *Fielding's Art of Fiction*, 1961, pp. 47–8. Martin Battestin, on the other hand, takes a quite different position, but one equally removed from my own. He argues, in his introduction to the Riverside edition of *Joseph Andrews and Shamela*, that Fielding did not change his mind, but that parody was never a significant part of his intention (*Joseph Andrews and Shamela*, ed. Martin Battestin, 1961, p. xviii).
3 'Ce qui est irritant et parfois exaspérant, ce n'est point l'héroïne, mais c'est l'admiration béate de l'auteur pour elle' (Aurélien Digeon, *Les Romans de Fielding*, Paris, 1923, p. 71). And later: 'On le sent clairement en lisant Fielding, c'est contre l'état d'esprit de l'auteur, contre son affectation constante de vertu qu'il s'insurge, beaucoup plus que contre le roman lui-même' (p. 72).

474 Robert Alan Donovan

technique in *Shamela* was to assume the events of *Pamela* while he rejected the moral vision which ordered them. Pamela, in other words, emerges as Shamela, with her 'true' motives revealed, not only to us, but to herself. Every line of her story embodies the recognition that her whole bearing toward the squire is hypocritical:

> The poor booby frightened out of his wits, jumped out of
> bed, and, in his shirt, sat down by my bed-side, pale and
> trembling, for the moon shone, and I kept my eyes wide
> open, and pretended to fix them in my head. Mrs Jervis
> apply'd lavender water, and hartshorn, and this, for a full
> half hour; when thinking I had carried it on long enough,
> and being likewise unable to continue the sport any longer,
> I began by degrees to come to my self.[1]

Our delight in all this arises out of the awareness that the events described in Richardson's novel can be accounted for by radically different assumptions about character and motive from those which Richardson asks us to make. All we need to do is to assume that instead of being a pure and virtuous maiden Pamela is really an ambitious trollop, and the same pattern of events can be expected to follow.

Joseph Andrews employs exactly the contrary technique. Instead of adopting the events and rejecting the moral vision, Fielding ironically adopts the moral vision and refashions the events as a consequence of that adoption. For this reason the satiric technique of *Joseph Andrews* is less confining than the one employed in *Shamela*, and it opens up a much greater variety of comic possibilities. *Joseph Andrews* emerges as a novel which is perfectly capable of standing alone as a comic masterpiece in its own right, but at the same time it is continuously enriched by its relation to *Pamela* – a relation which begins in the simplest and most obvious devices of parody, but which unfolds into an extraordinarily subtle and far-reaching commentary on Richardson's ethical assumptions. The result is a more durably funny parody of *Pamela*, as well as a more searching critique of its morality, than we can get from *Shamela*.

Parody, in its most literal sense, is the imitation of a literary work for the purpose of ridicule. It reveals itself most obviously in the structure

1 *An Apology for the Life of Mrs Shamela Andrews*, Augustan Reprint Society Publication, no. 57, Los Angeles, 1956, p. 16.

of a work, for in a parody the structure derives from the work imitated. But what is more significant for my own analysis, parody reveals itself continuously in the texture of the style, which exposes at every point the absurd disparity between the informing idea of the original and that of the parody. The parody which announces its presence in both structure and inner form may be taken to constitute a distinctive literary genre, one to which *Shamela* obviously belongs. The parody which is a matter only of inner form, in which the overt pattern of imitation disappears, is rather more difficult to recognize and define. Nevertheless, I believe that the expectations which Fielding establishes by the explicit parody in the first ten chapters of *Joseph Andrews* are not simply held in abeyance during the central forty-one chapters, to be met, finally, in the last thirteen. It seems to me both more natural and more useful to assume that the explicit and unmistakable comparison between *Joseph Andrews* and *Pamela* which is invited in the opening chapters of the former novel draws the reader's attention to that disparity between Fielding's moral vision and Richardson's which, in my view, most sharply defines the inner form of the entire novel. The double shift is thus not a betrayal of Fielding's satirical purpose; it is only a structural modification which permits the inner form to be more fully and effectively displayed. To test this assumption, I must begin with the explicit parody.

Pamela's simple-minded ethic is preserved intact in her brother, the titular hero of *Joseph Andrews*,[1] but it is made ridiculous by several devices. Most important, of course, is the fact that male chastity, though not inherently ridiculous, becomes absurd when it is insisted upon in apparent forgetfulness that it is not subject to the same threat of forcible privation as female chastity. A man who lives in fear of rape is inherently ridiculous. In the second place, Joseph's posture toward Lady Booby (and later Mrs Slipslop) is both ridiculous and faintly, pathetically chivalrous because neither lady is equipped by nature for the role of seductress. Finally, there is the absurd sententiousness of Joseph's language when he declares that he will never allow his

1 Dick Taylor, Jr, argues that Joseph is the real hero of the novel, but he seems to me to press the point too hard. Joseph undoubtedly becomes much more than the pasteboard simulacrum of his sister he seems at the beginning, but it is Adams who is not only the center of interest, but also, according to the view advanced here, the thematic center of the novel ('Joseph as Hero in *Joseph Andrews*', *Tulane Studies in English*, vol. 7, 1957, pp. 91–109).

inclinations to get the better of his virtue. The climax of the encounter in which Lady Booby forces him from an eminently sane and reasonable stance into a ridiculous one is worth quoting in full:

Your virtue! (said the lady recovering after a silence of two minutes) I shall never survive it. Your virtue! Intolerable confidence! Have you the assurance to pretend, that when a lady demeans herself to throw aside the rules of decency, in order to honour you with the highest favour in her power, your virtue should resist her inclination? That when she had conquered her own virtue, she should find an obstruction in yours? 'Madam,' said Joseph, 'I can't see why her having no virtue should be a reason against my having any: or why because I am a man, or because I am poor, my virtue must be subservient to her pleasures.' 'I am out of patience,' cries the lady: 'did ever mortal hear of a man's virtue! Did ever the greatest, or the gravest men pretend to any of this kind! Will magistrates who punish lewdness, or parsons, who preach against it, make any scruple of committing it? And can a boy, a stripling, have the confidence to talk of his virtue?' 'Madam,' says Joseph, 'that boy is the brother of Pamela, and would be ashamed, that the chastity of his family, which is preserved in her, should be stained in him.'[1]

Fielding squeezes all the juice out of this ironic inversion, but it is clear that so simple a device of parody cannot very well sustain a two-volume novel, and he quickly enlarges the scope of the novel by abandoning the confining pattern of imitation. But though the open references to Richardson's novel disappear, at least for the time being, its moral assumptions remain at the focus of Fielding's satiric humor.

The most significant indication that Fielding is ready to drop the brilliant but not very subtle technique of having Joseph defend his virtue against the threats posed by his lascivious mistress is that he now (book 1, chapter 11) provides Joseph with a genuine human motive for his moral stance; we discover that Joseph's resistance to Lady Booby is not a prudish affectation of virtue after all, but the

[1] *The History of the Adventures of Joseph Andrews*, Shakespeare Head Edition, Oxford, 1926, book 1, chapter 8. All quotations follow the text of this edition.

natural and laudable consequence of his being in love with Fanny.[1] But the same stroke which humanizes Joseph dulls his edge as an instrument of satire by depriving him of the rigidities of attitude and behavior which made the ridiculous inversion of the opening chapters effective. From this point in the novel Joseph's role is altered; now he is to become the romantic lead (though his simplicity remains functional both as comedy and as satire), and the main comic part is to be filled by Parson Adams. The reshuffling of roles here is doubtless a principal reason for the common supposition that Fielding has abandoned his original intention of ridiculing *Pamela*, but that intention is now to be achieved in a subtler, less direct way. The quixotic Adams, who comes to the fore in chapter 14 of book I, is the key to the transition.

Adams's derivation from Don Quixote is obvious and has often been analysed.[2] Both Adams and Quixote are naïve idealists in a hostile world, a world that systematically frustrates their expectations and generally subjects them to indignities, or physical violence, or both. Both subscribe to ideals which are at once lofty and impracticable, and both have taken their ideals and their notions of the world from books. It should be noted, however, that Adams and Quixote are distinguished in at least one important way: Quixote's ideal is that of knight errantry, a manifest anachronism in the realistic seventeenth-century world that Cervantes provides him, but Adams's ideal is simply Christianity, as it was not only understood but professed by everyone in the novel. What makes Adams a quixotic figure is his unconsciousness of the disparity between professing Christianity and practicing it, a difference almost as wide, Fielding ironically suggests, as that between the romantic ideal of chivalry and the grubby materialism of the world Don Quixote really lives in. Like his literary prototype, Adams combines sublime dignity with ridiculous simplicity; he is simultaneously the patriarch whose role as pastor and paterfamilias charges him with the responsibility of giving spiritual guidance and counsel to others, and the naïve innocent whose

1 This highly significant shift of tone was noticed and explained by Digeon, p. 73.
2 See, for example, Wilbur L. Cross, *The History of Henry Fielding*, New Haven, 1918, vol. I, pp. 322–4.

ignorance of real evil makes him as virginal as Pamela.[1] In fact, Adams's character is in several important respects comparable to Pamela's. The essence of their likeness is that they both confront the world with an unbelievably simple set of moral axioms or formulas which they naïvely expect will open all doors and solve all difficulties for them. Adams is as literal-minded and unsophisticated in his acceptance of Christianity as Pamela can possibly be in her espousal of technical chastity. The difference, of course, is just that Pamela's formulas work and Adams's do not, and therein lie the main possibilities for parody which Fielding exploits in the central section of *oseph Andrews*, for Adams is to become the principal instrument of Fielding's *reductio ad absurdum* of the moral view exemplified by Pamela. I do not want to suggest that Adams is a comic or satiric pastiche of Pamela; he is obviously a great deal more. My point is that having referred directly in the opening chapters to Pamela's moral posture, Fielding now seeks to discredit that posture by displaying to us in the character of Adams a moral literalism and simplicity that transcend Pamela's own, and at the same time a warm humanity that is at constant odds with the literalism and simplicity of his doctrinaire Christianity.

The similarity between the moral axioms of Parson Adams and those of Pamela is more than a matter of their simplicity. Both Adams and Pamela are committed to a doctrine of salvation by works. In this respect, of course, Pamela differs sharply from Shamela, who, it will be remembered, favored a sermon of Mr Williams called 'Be Not Righteous Overmuch', and who had studied the works of Mr Whitefield. Adams and Pamela also share a naïve faith in Providence. Pamela recoils from the idea of suicide by reflecting on its impiety:

This act of despondency, thought I, is a sin, that, if I
pursue it, admits of no repentance, and can therefore hope
no forgiveness. – And wilt thou, to shorten thy transitory
griefs, *heavy* as they are, and *weak* as thou fanciest thyself,
plunge both body and soul into everlasting misery!
Hitherto, Pamela, thought I, thou art the innocent, the

1 The dualism of Abraham Adams's nature is implicit, of course, in his name, which combines connotations of patriarch and *ingénu* (Johnson, p. 81).

suffering Pamela; and wilt thou, to avoid thy sufferings, be the guilty aggressor? And, because wicked men persecute thee, wilt thou fly in the face of the almighty, and distrust his grace and goodness, who can *still* turn all these sufferings to benefits?[1]

Similarly, Adams repeatedly admonishes Joseph when Joseph seems inclined to despair. At one point, when the two men are bound back to back to the bedpost of an inn, and Fanny has been carried off by a lecherous squire, Joseph threatens to do violence to himself, and Adams remonstrates:

You are to consider you are a Christian; that no accident happens to us without the divine permission, and that it is the duty of a man, much more of a Christian, to submit. We did not make ourselves; but the same power which made us, rules over us, and we are absolutely at his disposal; he may do with us what he pleases, nor have we any right to complain. A second reason against our complaint is our ignorance; for as we know not future events, so neither can we tell to what purpose any accident tends; and that which at first threatens us with evil, may in the end produce our good (book 3, chapter 11).

It is difficult to avoid the conclusion that Adams's recommendation of the comfortable doctrine of divine providence is an ironic commentary on Pamela's dramatization of her own pathetic innocence. The thrust becomes unmistakable when Adams, toward the end of the novel, once again reproves Joseph for his lack of patience under adversity but reveals his inability to accept his own teaching a moment later when he is told (erroneously, as it turns out) of his son's drowning. Only sorrow which is half affectation, Fielding implies, can find comfort in such facile reflections; real human sorrow is expressed less self-consciously. Both Adams and Pamela are extraordinarily literal-minded in their acceptance of moral precepts. To Pamela the injunction to live chastely conveys a perfectly precise meaning, one that can never be clouded by sophistries about the

1 *Pamela or, Virtue Rewarded*, Shakespeare Head Edition, Oxford, vol. 1, 1929, pp. 235–6.

letter and the spirit. That Adams, too, accepts moral injunctions literally is attested by his disputes with Barnabas (book 1, chapter 17) and Peter Pounce (book 3, chapter 13), by the simple and irrefutable logic which leads him to ask Trulliber for money (book 2, chapter 14), and above all by the whole quixotic cast of his mind which blurs for him the distinction between appearance and reality. It is one of Adams's most conspicuous and characteristic traits that he is never able to distinguish between pretense and sincerity. Thus he is repeatedly deceived, by the 'courageous' hunter who would have all cowards hanged but who takes to his heels at the first hint of danger (book 2, chapter 9), by the 'generous' squire whose extravagant promises even the simple Joseph sees through (book 2, chapter 16), and by the humor-loving squire who takes advantage of Adams's simplicity to amuse his company with practical jokes (book 3, chapter 7). The fact is that Adams, being utterly devoid of guile, always believes literally everything he is told, and he is quite incapable of detecting even the most conventional literary artifice, as is suggested by his childlike response to the narratives of the lady in the coach or of Mr Wilson. The former story, the fictitious 'Leonora, or the Unfortunate Jilt', Adams accepts at face value, making no distinction between fact and fancy, for he has no disbelief to suspend. His interruptions reveal his own absorption in the story and his entirely uncritical acceptance of it, as well as a Pamelesque concern with appearances. 'Madam,' he cries at one point, 'if it be not impertinent, I should be glad to know how this gentleman was drest' (book 2, chapter 4), and it is Adams who most vehemently desires to hear the full text of the letters exchanged by Horatio and Leonora (book 2, chapter 4). Mr Wilson's story is 'true', but the events are relatively remote in time and place. Still, Adams's lively sympathies are actively evoked, and he cannot forbear his groans at the catalogue of Wilson's youthful follies (book 3, chapter 3).

That Pamela's moral tenets, simply held and rigorously followed, prove triumphantly superior to the accidents of existence, while Adams's conspicuously fail to do so, stems from the radically different assumptions made by Richardson and Fielding about the nature of the world in which moral precepts must be rendered operative. Pamela's simple-minded morality will work only – or so Fielding's satire proclaims – in the artificial and unreal world of Richardson's novel. Surely one of the most striking features of Pamela's ordeal is that it takes place in actual isolation – physical as well as moral – from the rest of the world. After the preliminary skirmishing and drawing of lines in Bedfordshire, the action is transferred to Mr B's Lincolnshire estate where Pamela is effectively isolated from other human contact. She does, of course, encounter other people, but these people all belong to the social hierarchy of which Mr B is the pinnacle, and they are therefore solidly aligned on his side, except for the unhappy and unfortunate Williams. Under such artificial conditions, in such an arbitrarily restricted universe, Pamela's trial and triumph occur. The moral dilemma is further simplified in Richardson's novel by the conspicuous lack of guile in all the characters, except perhaps Pamela herself. This is, then, a closed world in which unexpected encounters seldom occur and in which vice rarely masquerades as virtue. Pamela, unlike Adams, is rarely deceived about anyone, and her moral choices are made easy by the fact that good and evil almost always wear their own semblance, uncomplicated by vanity or hypocrisy.

It is Fielding's principal device of parody to send a character armed with moral precepts as simple as Pamela's own into a world like the real one, at least insofar as it offers the possibility of random and unexpected encounters with other human beings, and insofar as it makes moral choices difficult because vice is most often concealed under affectation. This degree of realism seems to me perfectly consistent with Fielding's use of the picaresque tradition; indeed the picaresque setting provides just the right milieu for the testing of pamelesque virtue. Fielding is careful to delineate this world before he introduces Adams into it. After his dismissal by Lady Booby, Joseph sets out on foot to rejoin Fanny in London, but he is at once set upon by robbers, beaten, and left naked in a ditch. Just at this moment a stagecoach arrives on the scene, and the postilion, hearing Joseph's groans, pulls up his horses, but the coachman orders him to drive on, because the coach is 'confounded late'. A lady passenger, hearing the groans, inquires into the matter, but upon being informed that they come from a naked man she recoils in horror and asks the coachman to drive on. Two other passengers interest themselves in the matter; an old gentleman calls for the coachman to go on because he is fearful of the robbers, but a young lawyer points out that the law may hold them responsible for the young man's death, which observation puts a slightly different complexion on the affair. Still, the coachman refuses to admit Joseph to the coach unless someone will pay his fare, which of course no one offers to do, and the lady renews her objections to riding with a naked man. The lawyer's view finally prevails, however, and Joseph is permitted to enter the coach, though now his own modesty prevents him, and he refuses to enter unless someone will lend him a coat. The account continues:

Though there were several great coats about the coach, it was not easy to get over this difficulty which Joseph had started. The two gentlemen complained they were cold and could not spare a rag; the man of wit saying, with a laugh, that charity began at home; and the coachman, who had two great coats spread under him refused to lend either, lest they should be made bloody; the lady's footman desired to be excused for the same reason, which the lady herself, notwithstanding her abhorrence of a naked man, approved: and it is more than probable, poor Joseph, who obstinately adhered to his modest resolution, must have perished, unless the postilion (a lad who hath been since transported for robbing a hen-roost), had voluntarily stript off a great coat, his only garment, at the same time swearing a great oath (for which he was rebuked by the passengers), 'That he would rather ride in his shirt all his life, than suffer a fellow-creature to lie in so miserable condition' (book 1, chapter 12).

Here is a world of casual encounters and ambiguous personal relations, one in which moral judgements are hard to make. Different moral precepts make conflicting demands; modesty, for example, gets in the way of charity. The courageous decision is made upon pusillanimous motives, and the same moral agent is capable of both virtuous and vicious acts. The postilion who alone obeys the Christian admonition to clothe the naked turns out to be a thief. And people are swayed by other motives than the ones they profess; the lady's fastidiousness, for example, proves fraudulent when we discover that the bottle which was supposed to contain Hungary water is in fact filled with brandy (book 1, chapter 12). In such a complicated and misleading world as this the moral judgement of a Parson Adams or a Pamela is ludicrously inadequate.

The world of *Joseph Andrews* exceeds that of *Pamela* in another way, too. It is not only infinitely more complex, it is much wider. The movement of the novel from London to Somerset offers a parallel to the movement in *Pamela* from Bedfordshire to Lincolnshire, but Fielding expands our horizon in other ways than by the mere change of scene. By far the greater part of the novel has a rural setting – the road, especially, with its alehouses and inns, but also an occasional country house, the seat of a squire or rural magistrate. But Fielding provides a fuller spectrum of life than the limited movement of the characters allows by introducing narratives which display other facets of life than those observable by the traveler. The Leonora story, though not particularized in time and place (the names of characters – Leonora, Horatio, Bellarmine – suggest a convention far removed from realism, reminiscent of the novellas in *Don Quixote*), obviously depicts a stylized, artificial, and therefore urban, pattern of life, and Wilson's own autobiographical narrative deals in concrete and Hogarthian terms with the life of a London rake. One inference to be drawn from all this is that vanity and hypocrisy are not specifically rural affectations, but that the whole of society is similarly afflicted.[1] A more important point, however, is that the dimensions of Fielding's world constitute our most convincing proof that the moral life is a difficult and demanding one because we see something of the magnitude both of the forces arrayed against it and of the sheer inertia that all moral activity must combat.

Confronted by the manifold evil and duplicity of this world, simple idealism, even so sturdy a variety as Adams's, is bound to fail. Still, 'failure' is a relative term, and we may well inquire in what way Adams may be said to fail. Certainly he does not fail in any purely spiritual sense; his simple Christian morality receives no taint from the evil which surrounds him (this is part of what I meant when I said he was as 'virginal' as Pamela), and he remains as committed as before to the Christian life. But Richardson himself pro-

1 I. B. Cauthen, Jr, accounts for the four principal 'digressions' in very much these terms ('Fielding's Digressions in *Joseph Andrews*', *College English*, vol. 17, 1956, 372–82).

484 Robert Alan Donovan

vides the license for judging the success or failure of any ethical system by its temporal consequences, and it is clear that Adams derives no benefit of this kind from his constancy to his principles.[1] His goodness, in fact, has exactly the contrary effect of involving him in difficulties of all kinds, and of condemning him to be as often misunderstood by others as they are misunderstood by him. His virtue and his absent-mindedness between them relegate him to the position of the perennial butt.

But though Adams is quite clearly ludicrous as a virtuous man in a wicked world, he is just as clearly an admirable and lovable person, perhaps even more so than his literary prototype, Don Quixote. In this respect, however, he differs more or less conspicuously from Pamela, perhaps because by his very failure to live successfully he acquires the regard which Pamela forfeits by her worldly success. But if Adams's moral stance is to function as a burlesque of Pamela's, the difference must be explored. It is clear, I think, that whatever admiration or affection we may feel toward Adams rests not so much upon his moral perfection as upon his imperfection. The human quality in him that we respond to is, ironically, his very hypocrisy. The parson who has written a sermon against vanity arouses neither liking nor antipathy, but the parson who is proud of his sermon on vanity wins us at once. And the case is the same with Adams's 'hypocrisy' toward the end of the novel when he completely disregards his own injunctions to Joseph to bear affliction with fortitude and then breaks down at the news of his own misfortune. Mrs Adams's comment is revealing, too, when she interrupts her husband as he inveighs against excessive marital devotion:

I hope, my dear, you will never preach any such doctrine as that husbands can love their wives too well. If I knew you had such a sermon in the house, I am sure I should burn it; and I declare, if I had not been convinced you had loved me as well as you could, I can answer for myself I should have hated and despised you. Marry come up! Fine doctrine indeed! A wife hath a right to insist on her husband's loving

1 It is true, of course, that at the end of the novel Adams is presented by Mr Booby with a living of the value of one hundred thirty pounds per annum, but as I shall presently attempt to demonstrate, the distribution of rewards in the final chapter must be taken as ironic.

her as much as ever he can; and he is a sinful villain who doth
not. Doth he not promise to love her, and to comfort her,
and to cherish her, and all that? I am sure I remember it
all, as well as if I had repeated it over but yesterday, and
shall never forget it. Besides, I am certain you do not preach
as you practise; for you have been a loving and a cherishing
husband to me, that's the truth on't (book 4, chapter 8).

The fact is that the natural man is stronger than the doctrinaire
Christian, and the natural man proves to be entirely unselfconscious
about asserting his humanity, either by his innocent vanity or by
his love for his wife and child. Yet even in its differences Adams's
character reflects upon Pamela's, for what is most repulsive in her is
not her virtue but the self-consciousness and complacency with which
she regards it.

   It will be objected, I suppose, that having declared Adams sympathetic for his failure to live up to his own principles and Pamela
contemptible for her fidelity to hers, I have aligned Fielding on the
side of sin. But Fielding, it need hardly be said, is not opposed to
virtue as such; he objects only to a concept of virtue which makes it
wholly self-regarding, and he objects to the comfortable assumptions
that virtue is an easy choice or that providence rewards the virtuous
in some very simple and material way. Pamela's ideal falls considerably below Adams's, because it is self-regarding. Like the lady in the
coach whose modesty prevented her from being charitable, Pamela
allows her virtue to become a form of self-indulgence. Adams, on the
other hand, though he cannot heed his own stoical adjurations to
Joseph, does really devote his life to the service of others. But that
he himself falls short of the Christian ideal he would be the first to
admit, and that he is imperfect – which is to say human – is not
Fielding's way of saying that virtue is a lost cause, but that the moral
life is hard. Morality for Fielding is much more than obedience to a
set of perfectly simple prescriptive rules; it is a complex and precarious ordering of often conflicting obligations which is made more
difficult by the fact that the world is so big and complicated and
confusing.

   In the final chapters of *Joseph Andrews* Fielding reverts to a more
overt and explicit kind of parody of *Pamela*, a change signaled by

Pamela's own appearance at Booby-Hall. The irony with which she advises Joseph against a union with Fanny because of Fanny's humble rank is obvious but effective:

'Brother,' said Pamela, 'Mr Booby advises you as a friend; and, no doubt, my papa and mamma will be of his opinion, and will have great reason to be angry with you for destroying what his goodness hath done, and throwing down our family again, after he hath raised it. It would become you better, brother, to pray for the assistance of grace against such a passion, than to indulge it.' – 'Sure, sister, you are not in earnest; I am sure she is your equal at least.' – 'She was my equal,' answered Pamela, 'but I am no longer Pamela Andrews, I am now this gentleman's lady, and as such am above her – I hope I shall never behave with an unbecoming pride; but at the same time, I shall always endeavour to know myself, and question not the assistance of grace to that purpose' (book 4, chapter 7).

The satire here is directed not only against Pamela's social snobbery but, even more importantly, against the moral egotism that enables her to see herself as the recipient of divine grace. I do not believe that Fielding questions her sincerity, as he did in *Shamela*, but he offers a powerful rebuke to her spiritual pride, a pride which suggests the arrogance of the Calvinist divine proclaiming his own election. We see overtly displayed the spiritual pride which was satirized implicitly by Adams's selflessness and humility.

But a good many scenes and events in the fourth book which do not include Pamela or her husband recall Richardson's novel and take on satiric pungency when they are referred to events or situations in that novel. The main business of *Pamela*, of course, is the often riotous assault on Pamela's virtue by Mr B, an archetypal situation which is mirrored frequently, though in miniature, in the concluding chapters of *Joseph Andrews*. I shall pass over the hilarious episode in which Adams mistakes Fanny's bed for his own, a staple device of farce,[1]

---

1 Mark Spilka finds a deeper significance in this chapter of accidents ('Comic Resolutions in Fielding's *Joseph Andrews*, *College English*, vol. 15, 1953, pp. 11–19).

and consider here only the ludicrous attempts of Beau Didapper to ravish Fanny, which lead up to Adams's comedy of errors. The language of the beau's first encounter with Fanny is very much like that of countless such scenes in *Pamela*:

He stopt his horse, and swore she was the most beautiful
creature he ever beheld. Then instantly alighting, and
delivering his horse to his servant, he rapt out half a dozen
oaths that he would kiss her; to which she at first submitted,
begging he would not be rude: but he was not satisfied with
the civility of a salute, nor even the rudest attack he could
make on her lips, but caught her in his arms, and endeavoured
to kiss her breasts, which with all her strength she resisted,
and, as our spark was not of the Herculean race, with some
difficulty prevented (book 4, chapter 7).

That Beau Didapper is not 'of the Herculean race' (he is, Fielding tells us, 'about four foot five inches in height') is crucial to the effect here, for it not only explains why Adams entering the fracas between Beau Didapper and Mrs Slipslop in the dark, mistakes Didapper for the female in distress and Mrs Slipslop for the would-be ravisher, it enables us to see Fanny's successful defense of her virtue as a *reductio ad absurdum* very much like the inversion of the first book, when Joseph was called upon to defend his virtue against Lady Booby. And Fanny's conduct throughout contrasts sharply with the absurdities of Pamela's in a similar situation. Fanny is less 'nice' than Pamela, readily admitting the beau's salute, and the inference is that Pamela's scruples are absurd and excessive. In any case we have no doubts of Fanny's essential dignity and wholesomeness; as Digeon acutely observed, she is to be opposed to Pamela as an example of 'authentic' chastity.[1] And in the second place, Fanny responds to the assault on her chastity by vigorously (and successfully) defending herself instead of resorting to the passive technique of fainting, as Pamela habitually does. The contest is also significant in that it pits the health and high spirits of the country girl against the degenerate and impotent passions

1 'En Fanny sa fiancée Fielding a peut-être déjà voulu opposer à la fausse ingénue Pamela la peinture d'une jeune fille authentiquement chaste. . . . C'est une belle campagnarde bien en chair, qui aime assez goulûment son Joseph. Elle ignore les raffinements de Pamela et ses "vapeurs d'honneur" ' (Digeon, p. 77).

which we have already (in Mr Wilson's tale, for example) learned to associate with the town beau.

The dénouement, which Fielding effects with a magnificently absurd double discovery, has generally been regarded as owing more to the traditions of theater or of romance than to a sentimental moral fable like *Pamela*, but even here I think we can discern the hand of the parodist.[1] The whole point of Richardson's novel was that virtue was to be rewarded, that providence, moving in its own mysterious ways, sought out and bestowed its blessing upon the virtuous. Ehrenpreis attributes much the same view of providence and the law of compensation to Fielding by declaring that 'it is well known that Fielding's profuse employment of coincidence is his deliberate way of teaching us to trust in Providence'.[2] All right. But does Fielding expect Providence to operate according to a prearranged timetable or to put a price on virtue in pounds, shillings, and pence? It would seem to me far more likely that he uses the absurd piling up of coincidence at the end of *Joseph Andrews* to ridicule the notion that the cosmos so patly rewards virtue and punishes vice. The contrived ending of this novel – the opportune arrival of the peddler and of Mr Wilson, their sensationally improbable disclosures, the stale device of the birthmark – is a final ironic commentary on the world of *Pamela*, a world which suffers no injustice to triumph, where patient merit, though it must take for a while the spurns of the unworthy, is always rewarded in the end. But the satiric effect of the ending depends on its relation to the rest of the novel, for if we had been made to regard such events as commonplace we could hardly respond to them as violations of the cause and effect sequence that the first part of the novel had taught us to regard as normal. Every novel establishes, most often implicitly, its own canons of probability, so that an event which appears wildly improbable in one tale will be perfectly ordinary in another. The ending of *Joseph Andrews*, as I have suggested, would offend no one who was conditioned to the normal artifices either of stage comedy or of sentimental fiction, but because it is superimposed on a story in which the moral assumptions are

1 'The dénouement . . . is in gay imitation of a common type of the drama known since Aristotle's time as that of "discovery and revolution" ' (Cross, vol. I, p. 319; cf. Ehrenpreis, p. 35).
2 Ehrenpreis, pp. 35–6.

realistic and the ordering of events as chaotic as life itself, the improbability is magnified to the point of ludicrousness. Fielding has turned his story inside out, as it were, by grossly violating the sense of probability he has instilled in us. *The Threepenny Opera* illustrates exactly the same technique turned to a somewhat different purpose, for where Brecht bitterly assails the sentimental complacency of the public, Fielding directs the main thrust of his satire against the naïve and unrealistic assumptions of Richardson's novel.

There can be no quarrel with the judgement that *Joseph Andrews* is a more nearly self-contained, as well as a richer, novel than *Shamela*. *Joseph Andrews* is, as Fielding's preface proclaims, an experiment in the comic, and as such its humor is largely independent of its relation to *Pamela*, but grows instead out of the universalized attributes of its characters. Reading *Pamela* is not a prerequisite to the enjoyment of *Joseph Andrews*. *Shamela*, on the other hand, can pretend to no autonomy at all; the reader who has not also read *Pamela* will miss the whole point, for the joke depends on the closeness with which Fielding has imitated Richardson. The technique, as we have seen, is an absurdly simple one; by altering a single assumption, the assumption of Pamela's moral naïveté, Fielding succeeds in charging Richardson's book with a new significance, in realizing a layer of meaning which is only latent in *Pamela*. It is nevertheless true that the incongruity, the likeness in difference, can only be perceived by the reader who is simultaneously aware of the motives assigned by Richardson and of their perversion at the hand of Fielding. As comedy, which deals at least in part with universals, *Shamela* does not work; as parody it does all that can be done with the technique of close imitation.

Yet it seems to me fruitful to regard *Joseph Andrews* as parody too, of a different, less pointed, but more comprehensive kind. *Shamela* is a work which never transcends the limitations imposed on it by the book it is attacking; Fielding's assault comes from within, so to speak, and the weight of his animus falls wholly on Pamela, the character. *Joseph Andrews*, however, establishes its own vantage point from which to observe the world of *Pamela*, and the absurdities that Fielding finds there are laid to the charge of Richardson himself. Furthermore, parody is not simply one of a number of ingredients which make up the novel *Joseph Andrews*, for in Fielding's irrepressible impulse to ridicule *Pamela* and Richardson, I believe, can be found the novel's unifying perspective or inner form. If we fail to recognize that impulse the novel becomes fragmented and incomplete, and the best evidence of this is that the critics who ignore or undervalue the element of parody most often find fault with the novel's structure. The suggestions most frequently offered as unifying principles – the spectrum of town and country life, or the journey from London into Somersetshire – are not really principles at all, but arbitrary patterns, which themselves derive point and emphasis from Fielding's persistent, if not altogether systematic, efforts to subject to ridicule the proposition at the heart of *Pamela*, that the choice between good and evil is simple. I have no concern here with the positive implications of this point, although it is essential to recognize that Fielding is doing more than sweeping away the rubbish of Richardson's morality; he is expounding his own morality. That the novel is Christian and moralizing in its tendency, however, has been ably and fully argued,[1] and I do not intend to trace Fielding's principles to their source, or even to characterize his religious and moral position. My concern is rather with the negative proposition that I take to be, if not the most important idea, at any rate the shaping idea of *Joseph Andrews*, that the morality which Richardson offers is worthless as an ideal and fraudulent as a policy.

To argue that *Joseph Andrews* is given form by Fielding's impulse to parody is not to diminish its claims to greatness. On the contrary, to assert, as I have done, that the novel is a consistent parody of *Pamela* is to establish an additional claim. Parody and comedy are doubtless to be regarded as distinct modes, but they do not get in each other's way at all. The characters and incidents of *Joseph Andrews*, which are richly comic in their own right, simply take on satirical point by being referred always to Richardson's simple-minded assumptions about the world. And it can scarcely amount to a derogation of Fielding's genius to defend him from the imputation that he found no adequate form to contain his comic matter, or that

---

1 See especially James A. Work, 'Henry Fielding, Christian Censor', *The Age of Johnson: Essays Presented to Chauncey Brewster Tinker*, New Haven, 1949, pp. 139–48; and George Sherburn, 'Fielding's Social Outlook', *Philological Quarterly*, vol. 35, 1956, pp. 1–23. The most specific and exhaustive account of the moral assumptions of *Joseph Andrews* is in Martin Battestin, *The Moral Basis of Fielding's Art: A Study of 'Joseph Andrews'*, 1959.

he started out to do one thing, then twice changed his mind. The most remarkable thing about *Joseph Andrews*, I believe, is that it should be simultaneously a coherent parody of another work and an authentic comic masterpiece in its own right.

(68–88)

Tom Jones

Dorothy Van Ghent

from 'On *Tom Jones*', *The English Novel: Form and Function*   1953

In *Clarissa Harlowe*, the 'plot' appears under the aspect of fatality, as a movement from one point on a circle, around the circle and back to its beginning: from Clarissa's passion for purity, through its exaltation as a passion for death, down to the closing of the circle where purity and death become one. Not fatality but Fortune rules events in *Tom Jones* – that chance which throws up event and counter-event in inexhaustible variety. Tom himself is a foundling, a child of chance. In the end, because he is blessed with good nature, he is blessed with good fortune as well. Mr Allworthy, we are told, 'might well be called the favourite of both Nature and Fortune': from Nature 'he derived an agreeable person, a sound constitution, a sane understanding, and a benevolent heart', and from Fortune 'the inheritance of one of the largest estates in the county'. Good nature 'had always the *ascendant* in his mind': a metaphor derived from astrology, the science of the influence of the stars over man's life and fortune. The reader might be interested in tracing other metaphors of this kind in Fielding's diction, and in relating them to his view of human life. By chance or fortune, acting occultly, the curtain falls down in Molly's room, exposing the philosopher Square. An obsolete meaning of the word 'square' is that of 'rule' or 'principle'. Significant in Square's situation in this incident is Fortune's or accident's treacherous play with 'squared' (straight-edged) principles, philosopher's rules, dogmatic formulas; for nothing that the philosopher Square might say, to 'square' his position, would alter the ignominy of his exposure. Fortune, capricious as it is, has some occult, deeply hidden association with Nature (in Fielding); therefore, in the long run, good nature does infallibly lead to good fortune, bad nature to bad fortune.

The signature of Fortune's favor is wealth. Tom's blessings, at the end of the book, are not dissociable from the fact that he is All-worthy's heir: this is the center and fulcrum of all the rest of his good fortune. In *Moll Flanders*, the signature of the favor of Providence was also wealth, but the wealth had to be grubbed for with insect-like persistence and concentration; to obtain wealth, even with the help of Providence, one had to work for it and keep one's mind on it. In *Clarissa Harlowe*, again, wealth was to be worked for and schemed for: the Harlowe males work as hard and concentratedly, after their fashion, to acquire Solmes's wealth and the title it will buy for them, as Moll does for her gold watches, her bales, cargoes, and plantations. But in *Tom Jones*, wealth is not got by work or calculation or accumu-lation or careful investment. Blifil, who works shrewdly to obtain it, fails of his ends; Tom, who never thinks of it, is richly endowed with it. The benefits of money are as candidly faced by Fielding as they are by Defoe, or as they will later be by Jane Austen: people need money in order to live pleasantly, and though to be good and to be in love and loved are fine things, the truly harmonious and full life is possible only when one is both good and rich. Fielding is a man of the same century as Defoe and Richardson, the same society and culture (in the anthropological sense of 'culture'), but his outlook toward the getting of wealth is radically different. V. S. Pritchett has described one eighteenth-century attitude in this matter: 'Fortune,' he says,

the speculator's goddess – not money – pours out its plenty from the South Sea bubbles and the slave trade in the eighteenth century. Sacks of gold descend from heaven by fantastic parachute, and are stored in the gloating caves, and trade is still spacious and piratical.[1]

Obviously these statements have not much applicability to the attitudes of Defoe or Richardson, but they do cast some light on Fielding's. Also, we find in Fielding the more traditional, aristocratic attitude toward wealth: one simply has wealth – say, in landed properties, like Squire Allworthy – and how one got it is Fortune's business, a mysterious donation of free gifts to the worthy. But what we are fundamentally interested in here is the coherence of this

1 V. S. Pritchett, *The Living Novel*, Chatto & Windus, 1947, p. 110.

attitude with other elements in the book: that is, the aesthetic coherence and integrity of the whole. We have considered the plot under the aspect of the surprise plays of Fortune, occultly working out its game with Nature, and it is clear that Tom's unsought blessing of financial good fortune in the end is consistent with, all-of-a-piece with, the other activities of Fortune that are exhibited in the action.

There is a certain distortion involved in the attempt to represent a book by a visual figure, but sometimes a visual figure, with all its limitations, helps us to grasp a book's structure. We have spoken of *Clarissa* as making the simple figure of a circle, a figure of fatality. We may think of *Tom Jones* as a complex architectural figure, a Palladian palace perhaps: immensely variegated, as Fortune throws out its surprising encounters; elegant and suavely intelligent in its details (many of Fielding's sentences are little complex 'plots' in themselves, where the reader must follow a suspended subject through a functional ornament of complications – qualifying dependent clauses and prepositional phrases and eloquent pauses – to the dramatic predication or dénouement); but simply, spaciously, generously, firmly grounded in Nature, and domed with an ample magnitude where Fortune shows herself as beneficent artisan. The structure is all out in the light of intelligibility; air circulates around and over it and through it. Since Fielding's time, the world has found itself not quite so intelligible. Though intelligence has been analytically applied to the physical nature of things in our time much more thoroughly than eighteenth-century scientific techniques allowed, our world is tunneled by darkness and invisibility, darknesses of infantile traumata in the human mind, neurotic incalculabilities in personal and social action, fission in the atom, explosion in the heavens. We may feel, then, that there was much – in the way of doubt and darkness – to which Fielding was insensitive. Nevertheless, our respect is commanded by the integrity and radiance of the building that he did build.

(78–81)

Ian Watt

from *The Rise of the Novel* 1957

As far as most modern readers are concerned it is not Fielding's moral but his literary point of view which is open to objection. For his conception of his role is that of a guide who, not content with taking us 'behind the scenes of this great theatre of nature',[1] feels that he must explain everything which is to be found there; and such authorial intrusion, of course, tends to diminish the authenticity of his narrative.

Fielding's personal intrusion into *Tom Jones* begins with his dedication to the Honourable George Lyttleton, a dedication, it must be admitted, which goes far to justify Johnson's definition of this form of writing – 'a servile address to a patron'. There are numerous further references in the body of his work to others among Fielding's patrons, notably Ralph Allen and Lord Chancellor Hardwicke, not to mention other acquaintances whom Fielding wished to compliment, including one of his surgeons, Mr John Ranby, and various innkeepers.

The effect of these references is certainly to break the spell of the imaginary world represented in the novel: but the main interference with the autonomy of this world comes from Fielding's introductory chapters, containing literary and moral essays, and even more from his frequent discussions and asides to the reader within the narrative itself. There is no doubt that Fielding's practice here leads him in completely the opposite direction from Richardson, and converts the novel into a social and indeed into a sociable literary form. Fielding brings us into a charmed circle composed, not only of the fictional characters, but also of Fielding's friends and of his favourites among the poets and moralists of the past. He is, indeed, almost as attentive to his audience as to his characters, and his narrative, far from being an intimate drama which we peep at through a keyhole, is a series of reminiscences told by a genial raconteur in some wayside inn – the favoured and public locus of his tale.

This approach to the novel is quite consistent with Fielding's major intention – it promotes a distancing effect which prevents us

1 Book 7, chapter 1.

from being so fully immersed in the lives of the characters that we lose our alertness to the larger implications of their actions – implications which Fielding brings out in his capacity of omniscient chorus. On the other hand, Fielding's interventions obviously interfere with any sense of narrative illusion, and break with almost every narrative precedent, beginning with that set by Homer, whom Aristotle praised for saying 'very little *in propria persona*', and for maintaining elsewhere the attitude either of a dispassionate narrator, or of an impersonator of one of the characters.[1]

Few readers would like to be without the prefatory chapters, or Fielding's diverting asides, but they undoubtedly derogate from the reality of the narrative: as Richardson's friend, Thomas Edwards, wrote, 'we see every moment' that it is Fielding who 'does *personam gerere*', whereas Richardson is 'the thing itself'.[2] So, although Fielding's garrulity about his characters and his conduct of the action initiated a popular practice in the English novel, it is not surprising that it has been condemned by most modern critics, and on these grounds. Ford Madox Ford, for instance, complained that the 'trouble with the English nuvvelist from Fielding to Meredith, is that not one of them cares whether you believe in their characters or not';[3] and Henry James was shocked by the way Trollope, and other 'accomplished novelists', concede 'in a digression, a parenthesis or an aside' that their fiction is 'only make-believe'. James went on to lay down the central principle of the novelist's attitude to his creation, which is very similar to that described above as inherent in formal realism: Trollope, and any novelist who shares his attitude, James says,

admits that the events he narrates have not really happened, and that he can give the narrative any turn the reader may like best. Such a betrayal of a sacred office seems to me, I confess, a terrible crime; it is what I mean by the attitude of apology, and it shocks me every whit as much in Trollope as it would have shocked me in Gibbon or Macaulay. It implies that the novelist is less occupied in looking for the truth (the truth of

1 *Poetics*, chapters 24, 3.
2 A. D. McKillop, *Richardson*, p. 175.
3 *English Novel*, Constable, 1930, p. 89 [see above, p. 346, (ed.)].

course I mean, that he assumes, the premises that we must grant him, whatever they may be) than the historian, and in so doing it deprives him at a stroke of all his standing room.[1]

There is not, of course, any doubt as to Fielding's intention of 'looking for the truth' – he tells us indeed in *Tom Jones* that 'we determined to guide our pen throughout by the directions of truth'. But he perhaps underestimated the connection between truth and the maintenance of the reader's 'historical faith'. This, at least, is the suggestion of a passage towards the end of *Tom Jones* when he proclaims that he will let his hero be hanged rather than extricate him from his troubles by unnatural means 'for we had rather relate that he was hanged at Tyburn (which may very probably be the case) than forfeit our integrity, or shock the faith of our reader'.[2]

This ironical attitude towards the reality of his creation was probably responsible in part for the main critical doubt which *Tom Jones* suggests. It is, in the main, a very true book, but it is by no means so clear that its truth has, to quote R. S. Crane, been 'rendered' in terms of the novel.[3] We do not get the impressive sense of Fielding's own moral qualities from his characters or their actions that we do from the heroic struggles for human betterment which he conducted as a magistrate under the most adverse personal circumstances, or even from the *Journal of a Voyage to Lisbon*; and if we analyse our impression from the novels alone it surely is evident that our residual impression of dignity and generosity comes mainly from the passages where Fielding is speaking in his own person. And this, surely, is the result of a technique which was deficient at least in the sense that it was unable to convey this larger moral significance through character and action alone, and could only supply it by means of a somewhat intrusive patterning of the plot and by direct editorial commentary. As Henry James put it: Tom Jones 'has so much "life" that it amounts, for the effect of comedy and application of satire, almost to his having a mind'; almost but not quite, and so it was necessary that 'his author – *he* handsomely possessed of a mind – [should have] such an

1 'The Art of Fiction', 1884; cited from *The Art of Fiction*, ed. Bishop, p. 5.
2 Book 3, chapter 1; book 17, chapter 1.
3 'The Concept of Plot and the Plot of *Tom Jones*', *Critics and Criticism Ancient and Modern*, Chicago, 1952, p. 639.

amplitude of reflection for him and round him that we see him through the mellow air of Fielding's fine old moralism. . . .'[1]

All this, of course, is not to say Fielding does not succeed: *Tom Jones* is surely entitled to the praise of an anonymous early admirer who called it 'on the whole . . . the most lively book ever published'.[2] But it is a very personal and unrepeatable kind of success: Fielding's technique was too eclectic to become a permanent element in the tradition of the novel – *Tom Jones* is only part novel, and there is much else – picaresque tale, comic drama, occasional essay.

On the other hand, Fielding's departure from the canons of formal realism indicated very clearly the nature of the supreme problem which the new genre had to face. The tedious asseveration of literal authenticity in Defoe and to some extent in Richardson, tended to obscure the fact that, if the novel was to achieve equality of status with other genres it had to be brought into contact with the whole tradition of civilized values, and supplement its realism of presentation with a realism of assessment. To the excellent Mrs Barbauld's query as to the grounds on which he considered Richardson to be a lesser writer than Shakespeare, Coleridge answered that 'Richardson is *only* interesting'.[3] This is no doubt unfair as a total judgement on the author of *Clarissa*, but it indicates the likely limits of a realism of presentation: we shall be wholly immersed in the reality of the characters and their actions, but whether we shall be any wiser as a result is open to question.

Fielding brought to the genre something that is ultimately even more important than narrative technique – a responsible wisdom about human affairs which plays upon the deeds and the characters of his novels. His wisdom is not, perhaps, of the highest order; it is, like that of his beloved Lucian, a little inclined to be easy-going and on occasion opportunist. Nevertheless, at the end of *Tom Jones* we feel we have been exposed, not merely to an interesting narrative about imaginary persons, but to a stimulating wealth of suggestion and challenge on almost every topic of human interest. Not only so: the stimulation has come from a mind with a true grasp of human reality, never deceived or deceiving about himself, his characters or

1 Preface, *The Princess Casamassima*, Scribner, 1908.
2 *Essay on the New Species of Writing Founded by Mr Fielding*, 1751, p. 43.
3 Blanchard, p. 316.

the human lot in general. In his effort to infuse the new genre with something of the Shakespearean virtues Fielding departed too far from formal realism to initiate a viable tradition, but his work serves as a perpetual reminder that if the new genre was to challenge older literary forms it had to find a way of conveying not only a convincing impression but a wise assessment of life, an assessment that could only come from taking a much wider view than Defoe or Richardson of the affairs of mankind.

So, although we must agree with the tenor of Johnson's watch simile, we must also add that it is unfair and misleading. Richardson, no doubt, takes us deeper into the inner workings of the human machine; but Fielding is surely entitled to retort that there are many other machines in nature besides the individual consciousness, and perhaps to express his surprised chagrin that Johnson should apparently have overlooked the fact that he was engaged in the exploration of a vaster and equally intricate mechanism, that of human society as a whole, a literary subject which was, incidentally, much more consonant than Richardson's with the classical outlook which he and Johnson shared.

(285–9)

William Empson

'*Tom Jones*', *Kenyon Review*, vol. 20   1958

I had been meaning to write about *Tom Jones* before, but this essay bears the marks of shock at what I found said about the book by recent literary critics, and my students at Sheffield; I had to consider why I find the book so much better than they do. Middleton Murry was working from the same impulse of defence in the chief of the *Unprofessional Essays* (1956) written shortly before he died; I agree with him so much that we chose a lot of the same quotations, but he was still thinking of Fielding as just 'essentially healthy' or something like that, and I think the defence should be larger. Of American critics, I remember a detailed treatment of the plot by a Chicago Aristotelian, who praised what may be called the calculations behind the structure; I thought this was just and sensible, but assumed the basic impulse behind the book to be pretty trivial. English critics tend to bother about *Tom Jones* more than American ones and also to wince away from it more, because it is supposed to be so frightfully English, and they are rightly uneasy about national self-praise; besides, he is hearty and they tend to be anti-hearty. What nobody will recognize, I feel, is that Fielding set out to preach a doctrine in *Tom Jones* (1749), and said so, a high-minded though perhaps abstruse one. As he said after the attacks on *Joseph Andrews* (1742) that he would not write another novel, we may suppose that he wouldn't have written *Tom Jones* without at least finding for himself the excuse that he had this important further thing to say. Modern critics tend to assume both (1) that it isn't artistic to preach any doctrine and (2) that the only high-minded doctrine to preach is despair and contempt for the world; I think the combination produces a critical blind spot, so I hope there is some general interest in this attempt to defend *Tom Jones*, even for those who would not mark the book high anyhow.

Fielding, then, is regarded with a mixture of acceptance and contempt, as a worthy old boy who did the basic engineering for the novel because he invented the clockwork plot, but tiresomely boisterous, 'broad' to the point of being insensitive to fine shades, lacking in any of the higher aspirations, and hampered by a style which keeps his prosy common-sense temperament always to the fore. Looking for a way out of this clump of prejudices, I think the style is the best place to start. If you take an interest in Fielding's opinions, which he seems to be expressing with bluff directness, you can get to the point of reading *Tom Jones* with fascinated curiosity, baffled to make out what he really does think about the filial duties of a daughter, or the inherent virtues of a gentleman, or the Christian command of chastity. To leap to ambiguity for a solution may seem Empson's routine paradox, particularly absurd in the case of Fielding; but in a way, which means for a special kind of ambiguity, it has always been recognized about him. His readers have always felt sure that he is somehow recommending the behaviour of Tom Jones, whether they called the result healthy or immoral; whereas the book makes plenty of firm assertions that Tom is doing wrong. The reason why this situation can arise is that the style of Fielding is a habitual double irony; or rather, he moves the gears of his car up to that as soon as the road lets it use its strength. This form, though logically rather complicated, needs a show of lightness and carelessness whether it is being used to cheat or not; for that matter, some speakers convey it all the time by a curl of the tongue in their tone of voice. Indeed, I understand that some Americans regard every upper-class English voice as doing that, however unintentionally; to divide the national honours, I should think the reason for the suspicion is that every tough American voice is doing it too. Single irony presumes a censor; the ironist (A) is fooling a tyrant (B) while appealing to the judgement of a person addressed (C). For double irony A shows both B and C that he understands both their positions; B can no longer forbid direct utterance but I think can always be picked out as holding the more official or straight-faced belief. In real life this is easier than single irony (because people aren't such fools as you think), so that we do not always notice its logical structure. Presumably A hopes that each of B and C will think 'He is secretly on my side, and only pretends to sympathize with the other'; but A may hold some wise balanced position between them, or contrariwise may be feeling 'a plague on both your houses'. The trick is liable to be unpopular, and perhaps literary critics despise its evasiveness, so that when they talk about irony they generally seem to mean something else; but a moderate amount of it is felt to be balanced and unfussy. The definition may seem too narrow, but if you generalize the term to cover almost any complex state of mind it ceases to be useful. I do not want to make large claims for 'double irony', but rather to narrow it down enough to show why it is peculiarly fitted for *Tom Jones*.

There it serves a purpose so fundamental that it can come to seem as massive as the style of Gibbon, who seems to have realized this in his sentence of praise. He had already, in chapter 32 of the *Decline and Fall*, describing a Byzantine palace intrigue, compared it in a footnote to a passage of *Tom Jones*, 'the romance of a great master, which may be considered the history of human nature'.[1] This would be about 1780; in 1789, discussing ancestors at the beginning of his *Autobiography*, for example the claim of Fielding's family to be related to the Hapsburgs, he said, 'But the romance of *Tom Jones*, that exquisite picture of human manners, will outlive the palace of

1 See above, pp. 182–3. Actually, Gibbon is referring not to *Tom Jones* but to *A Journey from this World to the Next* [ed.].

the Escurial and the imperial eagle of the House of Austria.' This has more to do with Fielding than one might think, especially with his repeated claim, admitted to be rather comic but a major source of his nerve, that he was capable of making a broad survey because he was an aristocrat and had known high life from within. I take it that Gibbon meant his own irony not merely to attack the Christians (in that use it is 'single') but to rise to a grand survey of the strangeness of human affairs. Of course both use it for protection against rival moralists, but its major use is to express the balance of their judgement. Fielding is already doing this in *Joseph Andrews*, but there the process seems genuinely casual. In *Tom Jones* he is expressing a theory about ethics, and the ironies are made to interlock with the progress of the demonstration. The titanic plot, which has been praised or found tiresome taken alone, was devised to illustrate the theory, and the screws of the engine of his style are engaging the sea. That is, the feeling that he is proving a case is what gives *Tom Jones* its radiance, making it immensely better, I think, than the other two novels (though perhaps there is merely less discovery about proving the sad truths of *Amelia*); it builds up like Euclid. Modern critics seem unable to feel this, apparently because it is forbidden by their aesthetic principles, even when Fielding tells them he is doing it; whereas Dr Johnson and Sir John Hawkins, for example, took it seriously at once, and complained bitterly that the book had an immoral purpose. It certainly becomes much more interesting if you attend to its thesis; even if the thesis retains the shimmering mystery of a mirage.

Consider for example what Fielding says (book 12, chapter 8) when he is reflecting over what happened when Sophia caught Tom in bed with Mrs Waters at the Upton Inn, and incidentally telling us that that wasn't the decisive reason why Sophia rode away in anger, never likely to meet him again:

I am not obliged to reconcile every matter to the received notions concerning truth and nature. But if this was never so easy to do, perhaps it might be more prudent in me to avoid it. For instance, as the fact before us now stands, without any comment of mine upon it, though it may at first sight offend some readers, yet, upon more mature consideration, it must please all; for wise and good men may consider

what happened to Jones at Upton as a just punishment for
his wickedness in regard to women, of which it was indeed
the immediate consequence; and silly and bad persons may
comfort themselves in their vices by flattering their own
hearts that the characters of men are owing rather to
accident than to virtue. Now, perhaps the reflections which
we should be here inclined to draw would alike contradict
both these conclusions, and would show that these incidents
contribute only to confirm the great, useful, and uncommon
doctrine which it is the whole purpose of this work to
inculcate, and which we must not fill up our pages by
frequently repeating, as an ordinary parson fills up his
sermon by repeating his text at the end of every paragraph.

He does, as I understand, partly tell us the doctrine elsewhere, but
never defines it as his central thesis; perhaps he chooses to put the
claim here because book 12 is a rather desultory book, fitting in
various incidents which the plot or the thesis will require later, and
conveying the slowness of travel before the rush of London begins
in book 13. To say 'the fact before us' makes Fielding the judge, and
his readers the jury. He rather frequently warns them that they may
not be able to understand him, and I think this leaves the modern
critic, who assumes he meant nothing, looking rather comical.
Perhaps this critic would say it is Empson who fails to see the joke of
Fielding's self-deprecating irony; I answer that the irony of the book
is double, here as elsewhere. Fielding realizes that any man who puts
forward a general ethical theory implies a claim to have very wide
ethical experience, therefore should be ready to laugh at his own
pretensions; but also he isn't likely to mean nothing when he jeers
at you for failing to see his point. Actually, the modern critic does
know what kind of thing the secret is; but he has been badgered by
neo-classicism and neo-Christianity and what not, whereas the
secret is humanist, liberal, materialist, recommending happiness on
earth and so forth, so he assumes it is dull, or the worldly advice of a
flippant libertine.
    Nobody would want to argue such points who had felt the tone of
the book; it is glowing with the noble beauty of its gospel, which
Fielding indeed would be prepared to claim as the original Gospel.

The prose of generalized moral argument may strike us as formal, but it was also used by Shelley, who would also appeal to the Gospels to defend a moral novelty, as would Blake; an idea that the Romantics were original there seems to confuse people nowadays very much. When Fielding goes really high in *Tom Jones* his prose is like an archangel brooding over mankind, and I suppose is actually imitating similar effects in Handel; one might think it was like Bach, and that Handel would be too earth-bound, but we know Fielding admired Handel. I admit that the effect is sometimes forced, and strikes us as the theatrical rhetoric of the Age of Sentiment; but you do not assume he is insincere there if you recognize that at other times the effect is very real.

A moderate case of this high language comes early in the book when Squire Allworthy is discussing charity with Captain Blifil (book 2, chapter 5). The captain is trying to ruin young Tom so as to get all the estate for himself, and has just remarked that Christian charity is an ideal, so ought not to be held to mean giving anything material; Allworthy falls into a glow at this, and readily agrees that there can be no merit in merely discharging a duty, especially such a pleasant one; but goes on:

To confess the truth, there is one degree of generosity (of charity I would have called it), which seems to have some show of merit, and that is where, from a principle of benevolence and Christian love, we bestow on another what we really want ourselves; where, in order to lessen the distresses of another, we condescend to share some part of them, by giving what even our necessities cannot well spare. This is, I think, meritorious; but to relieve our brethren only with our superfluities –

– to do one thing and another, go the balanced clauses, 'this seems to be only being rational creatures.' Another theme then crosses his mind for the same grand treatment:

As to the apprehension of bestowing bounty on such as may hereafter prove unworthy objects, merely because many have proved such, surely it can never deter a good man from generosity.

This too is argued with noble rhetoric, and then the captain inserts his poisoned barb. Now, the passage cannot be single irony, meant to show Allworthy as a pompous fool; he is viewed with wonder as a kind of saint (e.g. he is twice said to smile like an angel, and he is introduced as the most glorious creature under the sun), also he stood for the real benefactor Allen whom Fielding would be ashamed to laugh at. Fielding shows a Proust-like delicacy in regularly marking a reservation about Allworthy without ever letting us laugh at him (whereas critics usually complain he is an all-white character). Allworthy is something less than all-wise; the plot itself requires him to believe the villains and throw Tom out of Paradise Hall, and the plot is designed to carry larger meanings. The reason why he agrees so eagerly with the captain here, I take it, apart from his evidently not having experienced what he is talking about, is a point of spiritual delicacy or gentlemanly politeness – he cannot appear to claim credit for looking after his own cottagers, in talking to a guest who is poor; that was hardly more than looking after his own property, and the reflection distracts him from gauging the captain's motives. What is more important, he speaks as usual of doing good on principle, and here the central mystery is being touched upon.

One might think the answer is: 'Good actions come only from good impulses, that is, those of a good heart, not from good principles'; the two bad tutors of Jones make this idea obvious at the beginning (especially book 3, chapter 5). Dr Johnson and Sir John Hawkins denounced the book as meaning this, and hence implying that morality is no use (by the way, in my *Complex Words*, p. 173, I ascribed a sentence of Hawkins to Johnson, but they make the same points). Fielding might well protest that he deserved to escape this reproach; he had twice stepped out of his frame in the novel to explain that he was not recommending Tom's imprudence, and that he did not mean to imply that religion and philosophy are bad because bad men can interpret them wrongly. But he seems to have started from this idea in his first revolt against the *ethos* of Richardson which made him write *Shamela* and *Joseph Andrews*; I think it was mixed with a class belief, that well-brought-up persons (with the natural ease of gentlemen) do not need to keep prying into their own motives as these hypocritical Nonconformist types do. As a novelist he never actually asserts this idea, which one can see is open to misuse, and in *Tom Jones* (1749) he has made it only part of a more interesting idea; but, after he had been attacked for using it there, he arranged an ingenious reply in the self-defensive *Amelia* (1751). He gave the opinion outright to the silly Booth, a free-thinker who disbelieves in free-will (book 3, chapter 5); you are rather encouraged to regard Booth as a confession of the errors of the author when young. When he is converted at the end of the novel (book 12, chapter 5) the good parson laughs at him for having thought this a heresy, saying it is why Christianity provides the motives of Heaven and Hell. This was all right as an escape into the recesses of theology; but it was the Calvinists who had really given up free-will, and Fielding could hardly want to agree with them; at any rate Parson Adams, in *Joseph Andrews*, had passionately disapproved of salvation by faith. Fielding was a rather special kind of Christian, but evidently sincere in protesting that he was one. Adams is now usually regarded as sweetly Anglican, but his brother parson (in book 1, chapter 17) suspects he is the Devil, after he has sternly rejected a series of such doctrines as give a magical importance to the clergy. I take it Fielding set himself up as a moral theorist, later than *Joseph Andrews*, because he decided he could refute the view of Hobbes, and of various thinkers prominent at the time who derived from Hobbes, that incessant egotism is logically inevitable or a condition of our being. We lack the moral treatise in the form of answers to Bolingbroke which he set out to write when dying, but can gather an answer from *Tom Jones*, perhaps from the firm treatment of the reader in book 6, chapter 1, which introduces the troubles of the lovers and tells him that no author can tell him what love means unless he is capable of experiencing it. The doctrine is thus: 'If good by nature, you can imagine other people's feelings so directly that you have an impulse to act on them as if they were your own; and this is the source of your greatest pleasures as well as of your only genuinely unselfish actions.' A modern philosopher might answer that this makes no logical difference, but it clearly brings a large practical difference into the suasive effect of the argument of Hobbes, which was what people had thought worth discussing in the first place. The most striking illustration is in the sexual behaviour of Jones, where he is most scandalous; one might, instead, find him holy, because he never makes love to a woman unless she first makes love to him. Later on (book 13, chapter 7) we find he thinks it a point of honour to accept such a challenge from a woman, no less than a challenge to fight from a man (and that is the absolute of honour, the duel itself); but in his first two cases, Molly Seagrim and Sophia, he is unconscious that their advances have aroused him, and very grateful when they respond. Fielding reveres the moral beauty of this, but is quite hardheaded enough to see that such a man is too easily fooled by women; he regards Tom as dreadfully in need of good luck, and feels like a family lawyer when he makes the plot give it to him. He is thus entirely sincere in repeating that Tom needed to learn prudence; but how this relates to the chastity enjoined by religion he does not explain. We may however observe that nobody in the novel takes this prohibition quite seriously all the time; even Allworthy, when he is friends again, speaks only of the imprudence of Tom's relations with Lady Bellaston (book 18, chapter 10). In any case, the sexual affairs are only one of the many applications of the doctrine about mutuality of impulse; I think this was evidently the secret message which Fielding boasts of in *Tom Jones*, a book which at the time was believed to be so wicked that it had caused earthquakes.

We need not suppose he was well up in the long history of the question, but I would like to know more about his relations to Calvin; Professor C. S. Lewis, in his *Survey of Sixteenth-Century Literature*, brings out what unexpected connections Calvin can have. He maintained that no action could deserve Heaven which was done in order to get to Heaven; hence we can only attain good, that is non-egotist, motives by the sheer grace of God. In its early years the doctrine was by no means always regarded as grim; and it has an eerie likeness to the basic position of Fielding, that the well-born soul has good impulses of its own accord, which only need directing. At least, a humble adherent of either doctrine may feel baffled to know how to get into the condition recommended. However, I take it this likeness arises merely because both men had seriously puzzled their heads over the Gospel, and tried to give its paradoxes their full weight. Fielding never made a stronger direct copy of a Gospel Parable than in *Joseph Andrews*, when Joseph is dying naked in the snow and an entire coach-load finds worldly reasons for letting him die except for the post-boy freezing on the outside, who gives Joseph his overcoat and is soon after transported for robbing a hen-roost.

But I think he felt the paradoxes of Jesus more as a direct challenge after he had trained and practised as a lawyer, and had come into line for a job as magistrate; that is, when he decided to write *Tom Jones*. He first wrote in favour of the Government on the 1745 Rebellion, in a stream of indignant pamphlets, and this was what made him possible as a magistrate; he was horrified at the public indifference at the prospect of a Catholic conquest, from which he expected rack and fire. He must then also be shocked at the indifference, or the moon-eyed preference for the invader, shown by all the characters in *Tom Jones*; nor can he approve the reaction of the Old Man of the Hill, who thanks God he has renounced so lunatic a world. To realize that Fielding himself is not indifferent here, I think, gives a further range to the vistas of the book, because all the characters are being as imprudent about it as Tom Jones about his own affairs; and this at least encourages one to suppose that there was a fair amount going on in Fielding's mind.

Tom Jones is a hero because he is born with good impulses; indeed, as the boy had no friend but the thieving gamekeeper Black George among the lethal hatreds of Paradise Hall, he emerges as a kind of Noble Savage. This is first shown when, keen to shoot a bird, he follows it across the boundary and is caught on Squire Western's land; two guns were heard, but he insists he was alone. The keeper had yielded to his request and come too; if Tom says so, the keeper will be sacked, and his wife and children will starve, but Tom as a little gentleman at the great house can only be beaten. 'Tom passed a very melancholy night' because he was afraid the beating might make him lose his honour by confessing, says Fielding, who adds that it was as severe as the tortures used in some foreign countries to induce confessions. The reader first learns to suspect the wisdom of Allworthy by hearing him say (book 3, chapter 2) that Tom acted here on a mistaken point of honor; though he only says it to defend Tom from further assaults by the bad tutors, who discuss the point with splendid absurdity. Whether it was 'true', one would think, depended on whether the child thought Allworthy himself could be trusted not to behave unjustly. I have no respect for the critics who find the moralizing of the book too obvious; the child's honour really is all right after that; he is a fit judge of other ideas of honour elsewhere. Modern readers would perhaps like him better if they realized his basic likeness to Huck Finn; Mark Twain and Fielding were making much the same protest, even to the details about duelling. But Mark Twain somehow could not bear to have Huck grow up, whereas the chief idea about Tom Jones, though for various reasons it has not been recognized, is that he is planned to become awe-strikingly better during his brief experience of the world. You are first meant to realize this is happening halfway through the book, when the Old Man of the Hill is recounting his life, and Tom is found smiling quietly to himself at a slight error in the ethical position of that mystical recluse (book 8, chapter 13). Old Man is a saint, and Fielding can provide him with some grand devotional prose, but he is too much of a stoic to be a real Gospel Christian, which is what Tom is turning into as we watch him.

All critics call the recital of Old Man irrelevant, though Saintsbury labours to excuse it; but Fielding meant to give a survey of all human experience (that is what he meant by calling the book an epic) and Old Man provides the extremes of degradation and divine ecstasy which Tom has no time for; as part of the structure of ethical thought he is essential to the book, the key-stone at the middle of the arch. The critics could not have missed understanding this if they hadn't imagined themselves forbidden to have intellectual interests, as Fielding had. For that matter, the whole setting of the book in the 1745 Rebellion gets its point when it interlocks with the theory and practice of Old Man. So far from being 'episodic', the incident is meant to be such an obvious pulling together of the threads that it warns us to keep an eye on the subsequent moral development of Tom. As he approaches London unarmed, he is challenged by a highwayman; removing the man's pistol, and inquiring about the motives, he gives half of all he has to the starving family – rather more than half, to avoid calculation. Fielding of course knew very well that this was making him carry out one of the paradoxes of Jesus, though neither Fielding nor Tom must ever say so. The first time he earns money by selling his body to Lady Bellaston, a physic-ally unpleasant duty which he enters upon believing at each step that his honour requires it (and without which, as the plot goes, he could probably not have won through to marrying Sophia), he tosses the whole fifty to his landlady, Mrs Miller, for a hard luck-case who turns out to be the same highwayman, though she will only take ten;

when the man turns up to thank him, with mutual recognition, Tom congratulates him for having enough honour to fight for the lives of his children, and proceeds to Lady Bellaston 'greatly exulting in the happiness he has procured', also reflecting on the evils that 'strict justice' would have caused here (book 13, chapter 10). His next heroic action is to secure marriage for his landlady's daughter, pregnant by his fellow-lodger Nightingale, thus 'saving the whole family from destruction'; it required a certain moral depth, because the basic difficulty was to convince Nightingale that this marriage, which he greatly desired, was not forbidden to him by his honour. We tend now to feel that Tom makes a grossly obvious moral harangue, but Nightingale feels it has pooh-poohed what he regards as the moral side of the matter, removing his 'foolish scruples of honour' so that he can do what he prefers (book 14, chapter 7). Indeed the whole interest of the survey of ideas of honour is that different characters hold such different ones; no wonder critics who do not realize this find the repetition of the word tedious. These chapters in which the harangues of Tom are found obvious are interwoven with others in which his peculiar duty as regards Lady Bellaston has to be explained, and we pass on to the crimes which poor Lord Fellamar could be made to think his honour required. Critics would not grumble in the same way at Euclid, for being didactic in the propositions they have been taught already and immoral in the ones they refuse to learn. The threats of rape for Sophia and enslavement for Tom, as the plot works out, are simply further specimens of the code of honour; that danger for Tom is settled when Lord Fellamar gathers, still from hearsay, that the bastard is really a gentleman and therefore ought not to be treated as a kind of stray animal – he is 'much concerned' at having been misled (book 18, chapter 11). There is a less familiar point about codes of honour, indeed it struck the Tory critic Saintsbury as a libel on squires, when we find that Squire Western regards duelling as a Whig townee corruption, and proposes wrestling or single-stick with Lord Fellamar's second (book 16, chapter 2); but Fielding means Western to be right for once, not to prove that the old brute is a coward, and had said so in his picture of country life (book 5, chapter 12). When you consider what a tyrant Western is on his estate, it really does seem rather impressive that he carries no weapon.

Fielding meant all this as part of something much larger than a picture of the ruling-class code of honour; having taken into his head that he is a moral theorist, he has enough intelligence to be interested by the variety of moral codes in the society around him. A tribe, unlike a man, can exist by itself, and when found has always a code of honour (though not police, prisons and so forth) without which it could not have survived till found; such is the basis upon which any further moral ideas must be built. That is why Fielding makes Tom meet the King of the Gypsies, who can rule with no other force but shame because his people have no false honours among them (book 12, chapter 12) – the incident is rather forced, because he is obviously not a gypsy but a Red Indian, just as Old Man, with his annuity and his house-keeper, has obviously no need to be dressed in skins like Robinson Crusoe; but they make you generalize the question. By contrast to this, the society which Fielding describes is one in which many different codes of honour, indeed almost different tribes, exist concurrently. The central governing class acts by only one of these codes and is too proud to look at the others (even Western's); but they would be better magistrates, and also happier and more sensible in their private lives, if they would recognize that these other codes surround them. It is to make this central point that Fielding needs the technique of double irony, without which one cannot express imaginative sympathy for two codes at once.

It strikes me that modern critics, whether as a result of the neo-Christian movement or not, have become oddly resistant to admitting that there is more than one code of morals in the world, whereas the central purpose of reading imaginative literature is to accustom yourself to this basic fact. I do not at all mean that a literary critic ought to avoid making moral judgements; that is useless as well as tiresome, because the reader has enough sense to start guessing round it at once. A critic had better say what his own opinions are, which can be done quite briefly, while recognizing that the person in view held different ones. (As for myself here, I agree with Fielding and wish I was as good.) The reason why Fielding could put a relativistic idea across on his first readers (though apparently not on modern critics) was that to them the word 'honour' chiefly suggested the problem whether a gentleman had to duel whenever he was huffed; one can presume they were already bothered by it, because it was stopped a generation or two later – in England, though not in the America of Huckleberry Finn. But Fielding used this, as he used the Nightingale marriage, merely as firm ground from which he could be allowed to generalize; and he does not find relativism alarming, because he feels that to understand codes other than your own is likely to make your judgements better. Surely a 'plot' of this magnitude is bound to seem tiresome unless it is frankly used as a means by which, while machining the happy ending, the author can present all sides of the question under consideration and show that his attitude to it is consistent. The professional Victorian novelists understood very well that Fielding had set a grand example there, and Dickens sometimes came near it, but it is a hard thing to plan for.

All the actions of Tom Jones are reported to Allworthy and Sophia, and that is why they reinstate him; they are his judges, like the reader. Some readers at the time said it was wilful nastiness of Fielding to make Tom a bastard, instead of discovering a secret marriage at the end; and indeed he does not explain (book 18, chapter 7) why Tom's mother indignantly refused to marry his father when her brother suggested it (Fielding probably knew a reason, liking to leave us problems which we can answer if we try, as Dr Dudden's book shows, but I cannot guess it). But there is a moral point in leaving him a bastard; he is to inherit Paradise Hall because he is held to deserve it, not because the plot has been dragged round to make him the legal heir. Lady Mary Wortley Montagu, a grand second cousin of Fielding who thought him low, said that *Amelia* seemed to her just as immoral as his previous books, and she could not understand why Dr Johnson forgave it, because it too encouraged young people to marry for love and expect a happy ending. She had enjoyed the books, and thought that Richardson's were just as immoral. I take it that, after a rather uncomfortable marriage for money, she found herself expected to give a lot of it away to her poor relations, so she thought they all ought to have married for money. Wrong though she may have been, the eighteenth-century assumption that a novel has a moral seems to me sensible; *Tom Jones* really was likely to make young people marry for love, not only because that is presented as almost a point of honour but because the plot does not make the gamble seem hopeless. The machinery of the happy ending derives from the fairy tale, as Fielding perhaps recognized, as well as wanting to sound like Bunyan, when he called the house Paradise Hall. The third son seeking his fortune gives his crust to the withered crone and thus becomes a prince because she is Queen of the Fairies; the moral is that this was the right thing to do, even if she hadn't been, but the tale also suggests to the child that maybe this isn't such a bad bet as you might think, either. The mind of Fielding, as he gets near in the actual writing to the end of a plot which he is clearly following from a complete dated skeleton, begins to play round what it means when an author, as it were, tosses up to see whether to give his characters joy or sorrow; he is the creator here, he remarks, but he will promise not to work miracles, and so forth. Rather earlier, he positively asserts that generous behaviour like Tom's is not rewarded with happiness on earth, indeed that it would probably be unchristian to suppose so. This is in one of the introductory chapters of literary prattle (book 15, chapter 1); it is answered in book 15, chapter 8, after a joke about whether Tom has selfish motives for a good action (and the reader who remembers book 4, chapter 11 may well brace himself to hear a new scandal about Tom), by a firm assertion that the immediate results of such behaviour are among the greatest happinesses that earth can provide. However, this play of mind does not arrive at telling us what the happy ending means, and indeed could not, as its chief function is to make the suspense real even for a thoughtful reader. I take it that the childish magic of the fairy tale, and its elder brother, the belief that good actions ought to be done because they will be rewarded in Heaven, are reinforced in this novel by a practical idea which would not always apply; the outstanding moral of *Tom Jones*, if you look at it as Lady Mary did but less sourly, is that when a young man leaves home he is much more in a gold-fish bowl than he thinks. The reader is to be influenced in favour of Tom's behaviour by seeing it through the eyes of Allworthy and Sophia, whom one might think sufficiently high-class and severe. But the end conveys something much more impressive than that these examiners give him a pass degree; he has become so much of a Gospel Christian that he cannot help but cast a shadow even on them. Against all reason and principle, and therefore to the consternation of Allworthy, he forgives Black George.

George robbed him, just after he was cast out, of the money Allworthy had given him to save him from degradation, for example, being pressed to sea as a vagabond, which nearly occurred. The gamekeeper was an old friend rather than a remote peasant, had become comfortable solely through the efforts of Tom to get him a job, and one would also think, as Tom's supposed natural-father-in-law, must have had an interest in letting him even now have a sporting chance. Fielding rated friendship specially highly, and always speaks of this betrayal in the tone of sad wonder he keeps for desperate cases. He says nothing himself about Tom forgiving George, but makes Allworthy give a harangue calling it wicked because harmful to society. We are accustomed in Fielding to hear characters wriggle out of the absolute command by Jesus to forgive, comically bad ones as a rule, and now the ideal landlord is saddled with it. The time must clearly come, if a man carries through a consistent programme about double irony, when he himself does not know the answer; and here, as it should do, it comes at the end of the novel. The practical lawyer and prospective magistrate would have to find the Gospel puzzling on this point; it is quite fair for Fielding still to refuse to admit that Allworthy is in the wrong, because he may well suspect that the command of Jesus would bring anarchy. To be sure, this is not one of the impressive tests of Tom; he is merely behaving nicely, just when everything is falling into his hands, and would lose our sympathy if he didn't; it comes to him naturally, which not all the previous cases did. But still, we have been moving through a landscape of the ethic of human impulses, and when Tom rises above Allworthy he is like a mountain.

There is already a mystery or weird pathos about George when he is first worked back into the plot (book 15, chapter 12). Partridge is overjoyed, after all their troubles in London, to meet someone who loves Tom so much:

Betray you indeed! why I question whether you have a better
friend then George upon earth, except myself, or one that
would go further to serve you.

The reader is bound to take this as single irony at first, but Fielding is soon cheerfully explaining that George really did wish Tom well, as much as a man could who loved money more than anything else; and then we get him offering money to Tom in prison. Though not allowed to be decisive for the plot, he is useful in smuggling a letter to Sophia and trustworthy in hiding it from his employer. As to his love of money, we should remember that we have seen his family starving (book 3, chapter 9) after a bad bit of eighteenth-century administration by Allworthy. I think Fielding means to play a trick, just after the theft, when he claims to put us fully inside the mind of George; acting as go-between, George wonders whether to steal also the bit of money sent by Sophia to the exile, and decides that would be unsafe (book 6, chapter 13). No doubt we are to believe the details, but Fielding still feels free, in his Proust-like way, to give a different picture of the man's character at the other end of the novel; I take it he refused to believe that the 'inside' of a person's mind (as given by Richardson in a letter, perhaps) is much use for telling you the real source of his motives. George of course has not reformed at the end; he has arranged to come to London with his new employer, Western, the more safely to cash the bill he stole, though, as he chooses the lawyer who is the father of Nightingale, the precaution happens to be fatal. I think the mind of Fielding held in reserve a partial justification for George, though he was careful with it and would only express it in the introductory prattle to book 12, where both the case of George and its country setting are particularly far from our minds; indeed, I had to read the book again to find where this comment is put. While pretending to discuss literary plagiarism, Fielding lets drop that the villagers on these great estates consider it neither sin nor shame to rob their great neighbours, and a point of honour to protect any other villagers who have done so. George might assume, one can well imagine, that Tom was going to remain a grandee somehow whatever quarrels he had; in fact, Tom at the time is so much wrapped up in his unhappy love affair that he seems hardly to realize himself how much he will need money. On this view, it would be shameful for George to miss a chance of robbing Tom; for one thing, it would be robbing his own family, as the soldier reflects in book 7, chapter 14. I agree that, so far from advancing this argument, Fielding never weakens the tone of moral shock with which he regards the behaviour of George (who was right to be so ashamed that he ran away); but I think he means you to gather that the confusion between different moral codes made it intelligible. This background I think adds to the rather thrilling coolness with which Tom does not reply to the harangue of Allworthy denouncing his forgiveness; it is in any case time for him to go and dress to meet Sophia.

Sophia has the same kind of briefing as a modern Appointments Board; thus she does not waste time over his offer of marriage to Lady Bellaston; Sophia holds the document, but understands that this was merely the way to get rid of Lady Bellaston, so it joins the list of points already cleared. The decisive question in her mind is whether he has become a libertine, that is, whether his impulses have become corrupted; if they have, she is quite prepared again to refuse to unite by marriage the two largest estates in Somersetshire. Fielding has been blamed for making the forgiveness of Tom too easy, but I think his training as a bad playwright served him well here, by teaching him what he could throw away. A reader does not need to hear the case again, and Fielding disapproved of women who argue, indeed makes Allworthy praise Sophia for never doing it; and he himself has a certain shyness about expressing his doctrine, or perhaps thought it dangerous to express clearly. Beastly old Western comes yelling in to say for the average reader that we can't be bothered with further discussion of the matter, and Sophia decides that she can allow it to have settled itself. The fit reader, interested in the doctrine, is perhaps meant to feel rather disappointed that it is not preached, but also that this is good taste in a way, because after all the man's impulses have evidently not been corrupted. Even so, it is nothing like the view of Flaubert, Conrad and so forth, that a novelist is positively not allowed to discuss the point of his novel.

I want now, though there is so much else to choose from in this rich book, to say something about the thought of incest which terrifies Jones in prison; both because it affects the judgement of Sophia and because it has been a major bond of contention among other critics. Dr F. H. Dudden, in his treatise *Henry Fielding*[1], though concerned to do justice to an author whose morals have been maligned, admits that he had a rather nasty habit of dragging fear of incest into his plots (it also comes into *Joseph Andrews*); but decides that he means no harm by it, and that it was probably just an effect of having to write bad plays when he was young. On the other hand a *Times Literary Supplement* reviewer, quoted with indignation by Middleton Murry

1 Clarendon Press, 2 volumes, 1952.

in *Unprofessional Essays*, had thought this frightening of Jones a specially moral part of the plot. When he goes to bed with Mrs Waters at Upton, says the reviewer, Fielding

> seems to be making light of it, or even conniving at it. Yet
> it is the first step in a moral progress downhill. . . . And
> then, much later in the book, evidence comes to light
> which suggests [that she was his mother]. . . . Fielding's
> connivance was a pretence. He has sprung a trap on Tom
> and us; he has made us realize – as a serious novelist always
> makes us realize, and a frivolous novelist often makes us
> forget – that actions have their consequences. . . . It is this
> sense of the moral structure of life that makes Fielding
> important.

I could have quoted more sanctimonious bits, but this was the part which Middleton Murry found perverse:

> What to a more normal sensibility constitutes the one
> doubtful moment in the book – the one moment at which
> we feel that Fielding *may* have sounded a wrong note, by
> suggesting an awful possibility outside the range of the
> experience he invites us to partake – becomes in this vision
> the one thing which makes the book considerable.

The reviewer of course was trying to speak up for Fielding, and make him something better than a flippant libertine; and it is in favour of his view that the Upton incident is the one place where Fielding says in person that casual sex is forbidden by Christianity as expressly as murder (book 9, chapter 3). Dr Dudden might be expected to agree with the reviewer; he maintains you have only to attend to the text to find that Fielding always not only denounces sin but arranges to have it punished 'inexorably and terribly'. This indeed is one half of what Fielding intended, though the adverbs hardly describe the purring tone of the eventual forgiveness of Tom, as when we are told that he has, 'by reflection on his past follies, acquired a discretion and prudence very uncommon in one of his lively parts'. Instead, we find that Dr Dudden agrees with Middleton Murry; they are more in sympathy with Fielding than the reviewer, but feel they have to confess that the incest trick is rather bad; chiefly

I think, because they like him for being healthy, and that seems clearly not.

I think the basic reason why Fielding twice uses this fear is that he had a philosophical cast of mind, and found it curious that those who laugh at ordinary illicit sex take incest very seriously. As to *Joseph Andrews*, the starting-point is that Fielding is to parody Richardson's Pamela, a servant who made her master marry her by refusing to be seduced. He had already done this briefly and fiercely in *Shamela*, where an ex-prostitute acts like Pamela out of conscious calculation – the moral is that Pamela is *un*consciously calculating, and that girls ought not to be encouraged to imitate this minx. He is now to do it by swapping the sexes; a footman would be cowardly, or have some other low motive, if he refused a lady, and a lady would be lacking in the delicacy of her caste if she even wanted a footman. Thus the snobbish Fielding, in opposition to the democratic Richardson, can prove that the class structure ought not to be disturbed. Or rather, he did not actually have to write this stuff, because he could rely on his readers to imagine he had, as they still do. It is false to say, as is regularly said, that Fielding started on his parody and then wrote something else because he found he was a novelist; he did not start on it at all. From the first words, he treats his story with an almost over-refined, a breathless delicacy; and by the time Lady Booby has offered marriage, and Joseph, though attracted by her, still refuses her because he wants to marry his humble sweetheart, most of the laughing readers should be pretty well outfaced. No doubt Fielding himself, if the story had been outlined at his club, would have laughed as heartily as the others; but he is concerned in this novel, where he is rather oddly safe from being thought a hypocrite, to show that his sympathy is so broad that he can see the question all round, like a judge. I think he did discover something in writing it, but not what is usually said; he discovered how much work he could leave the public to do for him. One type of reader would be jeering at Joseph, and another admiring him, and feeling indignant with the first type; and both of them would hardly notice what the author was writing down. You can understand that he might want to take some rather firm step, towards the end, to recover their attention. What he is really describing is the chastity of the innocent Joseph, adding of course the piercing simplicity of his criticisms of the great world; Parson Adams, whom Fielding certainly does not intend us to think contemptible, preaches to him a rather over-strained doctrine of chastity all along. Just as all seems ready for the happy ending with his humble sweetheart, a twist of the plot makes them apparently brother and sister; they decide to live together chastely, as Parson Adams had always said they should be able to do. Here the clubmen who form Type A of the intended readers no longer dare to jeer at Joseph for believing he has a duty of chastity; the opposed groups are forced to combine. I thus think that this turn of the plot is entirely justified; for that matter, I think that modern critics are rather too fond of the strategic device of claiming to be embarrassed.

In *Tom Jones*, I can't deny, the trick is chiefly used to heighten the excitement at the end of the plot – Tom must go either right up or right down. I agree with *The Times Literary Supplement* reviewer that it marks a change in the attitude of hero, but it comes only as an extra at the end of a gradual development. Saintsbury defended Tom's relations with Lady Bellaston by saying that the rule against a gentleman taking money from a mistress had not yet been formulated; certainly it doesn't seem to have hampered the first Duke of Marlborough, but Tom comes to suspect of his own accord that some such rule has been formulated. He felt it when he first met Sophia in London (book 13, chapter 11); 'the ignominious circumstance of his having been kept' rose in his mind when she began to scold him, and stopped his mouth; the effect of this was good, because her actual accusations came as a relief and were the more easy to argue off convincingly. It is not till book 15, chapter 9 that Nightingale, as a fair return for the teaching of basic morals, warns him that he is liable to become despised by the world, and explains that the way to break with Lady Bellaston is to offer her marriage. Learning that he is one of a series makes Tom feel free to break with her, which he thought before would be ungrateful. By the way, I take it Fielding admired her firmness about marriage, as a protest against unjust laws on women's property; her criminal plot against the lovers is chiefly meant as a satire against the worldly code – she can be taken as sincere in telling Lord Fellamar that the intention is to save her ward Sophia from ruin, and Fielding only means to describe her Unconsciousness when he adds in Book 16, chapter 8

that women support this code out of jealousy. Tom refuses to marry
a rich widow immediately afterwards (book 15, chapter 11); this is
the sternest of his tests, and he is 'put into a violent flutter', because
he suspects it is a duty of honour to accept this fortune so as to release
Sophia from misery. He seems like Galahad when he rejects the point
of honour for love, and it does prove that in learning 'prudence',
which is how Fielding and Allworthy describe his moral reform, he
is not falling into the opposite error of becoming a calculating type.
We next have him refusing to make love to Mrs FitzPatrick, while
easily rejecting her spiteful advice to make love to Sophia's aunt
(book 16, chapter 9). Both she and Lady Bellaston are affronted by
his frank preference for Sophia and yet find their passions excited by
its generosity – 'strange as it may seem, I have seen many instances.'
The last of the series is his refusal to go to bed with Mrs Waters when
she visits him in jail with the news that her supposed husband is not
dying, so that he is safe from execution (book 17, chapter 9); this
might seem ungenerous rather than reformed, but he has just heard
from Mrs Miller that Sophia has become determined to refuse him
because of his incontinency. The next and final book opens with the
supposed discovery that Mrs Waters is his mother, so that he committed incest with her at Upton. This throws him into a state of
shaking horror which serves to illustrate his courage; we realize
how undisturbed he was before at the prospect of being hanged for
an act of self-defence. It is thus not the case that Tom was shocked
into disapproving of his previous looseness by the thought that it
might cause accidental incest, because this fear came after he had
become prudent; still less that the fear of death and the horror of
incest were needed together to crack such a hard nut as the conscience
of Tom, because he has been freed from the fear of death just before
the other alarm arrives. (I understand he was technically in danger
under ecclesiastical law, but prosecution was very unlikely; in any
case the question never occurs to him.) Fielding as a magistrate,
surely, would think it contemptible to cheat a prisoner into reform
by this trick, whereas *The Times Literary Supplement* reviewer seems
to assume it would be moral. What one can say is that the shock puts
Tom into a grave frame of mind, suitable for meeting Sophia; and
Sophia really does need winning over, with some extra moral solemnity however acquired, because she is quite pig-headed enough to fly

in the face of the world all over again, and start refusing Tom just because he has become the heir.

My own objection to this bit about incest has long been something quite different, which I should think occurs oftener to a modern reader; and I think the book feels much better when it is cleared up. I thought the author was cheating in a way that whodunit authors often do, that is, he put in a twist to make the end more exciting though the characters would not really have acted so. Those who dislike Fielding generally say that he makes his characters so obvious, especially from making them so selfish, that they become tiresome like performing toys; but the reason why Mrs Waters gets misunderstood here is that here as always she is unusually generous-minded. A penniless but clever girl, she learned Latin under Partridge when he was a village schoolmaster and did so well that he kept her on as an assistant, but she learned too much Latin; a fatal day came (book 2, chapter 3) when he jovially used Latin to ask her to pass a dish at dinner, and 'the poor girl smiled, perhaps at the badness of the Latin, and, when her mistress cast eyes upon her, blushed, possibly with a consciousness of having laughed at her master.' This at once made Mrs Partridge certain not only that they were lovers but that they were jeering at her by using this code in her presence; and such is the way most of us fail to understand her final letter. A ruinous amount of fuss goes on, and it becomes convenient for her to work with Allworthy's sister in the secret birth of Jones, acting as her personal servant at the great house and paid extra to take the scandal of being his mother before leaving the district. The story is improbable, but as Fielding arranges it you can call it credible. Allworthy gives her a grand sermon against illicit love when she confesses to the bastard, but is impressed by the honour and generosity of her replies; he sends her an allowance, but stops it when he hears she has run off with a sergeant. We next see her when Jones saves her life (book 9, chapter 2); the villain Northerton is trying to murder her for what money she carries, and it is startling for the reader to be told, what Jones is too delicate to ask her (book 9, chapter 7), that she was only wandering about with this man to save him from being hanged, and only carrying the money to give it to him. She had expected to rejoin Captain Waters after his winter campaign against the rebels, but meanwhile Lieutenant Northerton was afraid of being hanged for murdering

Jones (whereas it had been very lucky for Jones that the drunken assault removed him from the army), and needed to be led across hill country to a Welsh port. Fielding always admires women who can walk, instead of being tight-laced and townee, and though he tends to grumble at learned women he had evidently met a variety of them; he can forgive Mrs Waters her Latin. She need not be more than thirty-six when she meets Tom, and the struggle has exposed her breasts, which it appears have lasted better than her face. She stops Tom from hunting for Northerton,

earnestly entreating that he would accompany her to the town whither they had been directed. 'As to the fellow's escape,' said she, 'it gives me no uneasiness; for philosophy and Christianity both preach up forgiveness of injuries. But for you, sir, I am concerned at the trouble I give you; nay, indeed, my nakedness may well make you ashamed to look me in the face; and if it were not for the sake of your protection, I would wish to go alone.'

Jones offered her his coat; but, I know not for what reason, she absolutely refused the most earnest solicitation to accept it. He then begged her to forget both the causes of her confusion.

He walks before her all the way so as not to see her breasts, but she frequently asks him to turn and help her. The seduction is entirely free from any further designs on him; she is as foot-loose as a character in *The Faerie Queene*, though perhaps her happening to fall in with FitzPatrick next morning at the Upton Inn is what saves Jones from finding her even a momentary responsibility. Even so, her capacity to handle FitzPatrick is rather impressive; the only occupation of this gentleman is to hunt for the woman he cheated into marriage in the hope of bullying her out of what little of her money is secured from him by the law, after wasting the rest; one would hardly think he was worth milking, let alone the unpleasantness of his company, so that she had better have gone back to her officer. Perhaps she wanted to get to London; the only story about her is that she is independent. We are told at the end that she eventually married Parson Shuffle.

When Fielding says he doesn't know the reason he always means it is too complicated to explain. Walking with her lifesaver Jones she liked to appear pathetic, and she wanted to show her breasts, but also she really could not bear to let him take his coat off, not on such a cold night. The decision becomes a nuisance when they get to the inn because it makes her almost unacceptable, but this is got over; and she gathers from the landlady that Jones is in love with a younger woman:

The awkward behaviour of Mr Jones on this occasion convinced her of the truth, without his giving a direct answer to any of her questions; but she was not nice enough in her amours to be particularly concerned at the discovery. The beauty of Jones highly charmed her eye; but as she could not see his heart she gave herself no concern about it. She could feast heartily at the table of love, without reflecting that some other had been, or hereafter might be, feasted with the same repast. A sentiment which, if it deals but little in refinement, deals, however, much in substance; and is less capricious, and perhaps less ill-natured and selfish, than the desires of those females who can be contented enough to abstain from the possession of their lovers, provided that they are sufficiently satisfied that nobody else possesses them.

This seems to me a particularly massive bit of double irony, worthy to outlast the imperial eagles of the House of Austria, though I take it Fielding just believed what he said, and only knew at the back of his mind that the kind of man who would otherwise complain about it would presume it was irony.

Such is our main background information about Mrs Waters when she visits him in prison, assures him that her supposed husband is recovering fast so that there is no question of murder, and is rather cross with him for refusing to make love to her. Then her entirely unexpected letter arrives, which I must give in full (book 18, chapter 2):

Sir – Since I left you I have seen a gentleman, from whom I have learned something concerning you which greatly surprises and affects me; but as I have not at present leisure to communicate a matter of such high importance, you

must suspend your curiosity till our next meeting, which
shall be the first moment I am able to see you. Oh, Mr
Jones, little did I think, when I passed that happy day at
Upton, the reflection upon which is like to embitter all my
future life, who it was to whom I owed such perfect
happiness. – Believe me to be ever sincerely your unfortunate
J. Waters.

P.S. I would have you comfort yourself as much as
possible, for Mr Fitzpatrick is in no manner of danger; so
that, whatever other grievous crimes you may have to repent
of, the guilt of blood is not among the number.

Partridge, who happened not to see Mrs Waters at Upton, has seen
her visit the prison and eavesdropped on her talk with Jones, so he
has just horrified Jones by telling him she is his mother; they think
this letter confirms the belief, and certainly it is hard to invent any
other meaning. We are not told who the gentleman was till book 18,
chapter 8, when she tells Allworthy that the lawyer Dowling had
visited her, and told her that

if Mr Jones had murdered my husband, I should be assisted
with any money I wanted to carry on the prosecution, by
a very worthy gentleman, who, he said, was well apprised
what a villain I had to deal with. It was by this man I
discovered who Mr Jones was . . . I discovered his name by
a very odd accident; for he himself refused to tell it to me;
but Partridge, who met him at my lodgings the second time
he came, knew him formerly at Salisbury.

She assumed it was Allworthy who was persecuting Jones in this
relentless manner, whereas Allworthy knows it must be Blifil, whom
Dowling hopes to blackmail; and since she greatly revered Allworthy,
though herself some kind of freethinker, she assumed that Jones had
done something to deserve it – this explains the postscript 'whatever
other grievous crimes'. 'The second time' is an important detail; the
second time Dowling came must have been after she wrote the letter,
and was the first time Partridge came. As soon as Partridge saw her
he would tell her Jones's fear of incest and she would dispel it; but
Partridge has to come, to meet Dowling and tell her his name

(otherwise the plot of Blifil could not be exposed). We have next to consider how she knew, when she wrote the letter, about the anger of Sophia; but Jones would tell her this himself, when she visited him in prison, because he would feel he had to offer a decent reason for refusing to go to bed with her. A deep generosity, when she has thought things over after the unpleasant talk with Dowling, is what makes her write down that if Sophia refuses to marry Tom it will embitter all the rest of her life. The delusion about incest is the kind of mistake which is always likely if you interpret in selfish terms the remarks of a very unselfish character. Certainly, the coincidences of the plot are rigged almost to the point where we reject them unless we take them as ordained by God; Fielding would be accustomed to hearing pious characters call any bit of luck a wonderful proof of Providence, and might hope they would feel so about his plot – as Partridge encourages them to do (e.g. book 12, chapter 8). But the reaction of the character to the plot is not rigged; she behaves as she always does.

I ought finally to say something about his attitude to the English class system, because opinions about what he meant there seem often to be decisive for the modern reader. What people found so entertaining at the time, when Fielding attacked Richardson in a rather explosive class situation (the eager readers of Richardson in French were presumably heading towards the French Revolution), was that the classes seemed to have swapped over. The printer's apprentice was the gentlemanly expert on manners, indeed the first English writer to be accepted as one by the polite French; whereas if you went to see Fielding, they liked to say at the time, you would find him drunk in bed with his cook and still boasting he was related to the Hapsburgs. His answer to Richardson was thus: 'But I know what a gentleman is; I am one.' The real difference was about the meaning of the term; Fielding thought it should mean a man fit to belong to the class which actually rules in his society, especially by being a just judge. His behaviour eventually made a lot of people feel he had won the argument, though not till some time after his death. To die poor and despised while attempting to build up the obviously needed London Police Force, with obvious courage and humanity, creating astonishment by his refusal to accept the usual bribes for such dirty work, and leaving the job in hands which continued it – this became too hard to laugh off; he had done in the heart of London what empire-builders were being revered for doing far away. He provided a new idea of the aristocrat, with the added claim that it was an older tradition; and he did seem to clear the subject up rather – you could hardly deny that he was a better idea than Lord Chesterfield. An impression continued that, if you are very rude and rough, that may mean you are particularly aristocratic, and good in an emergency; I doubt whether, without Fielding, the Victorian novelists (however much they forbade their daughters to read his books) would have retained their trust in the rather hidden virtues of the aristocracy.

Much of this was wished onto Fielding later, but we have a series of jokes against the current idea of a gentleman during Tom's journey to London. The remarks in favour of the status are perhaps what need picking out. Tom leaves Old Man because he hears cries for help; he thus saves the life of Mrs Waters from the villain Northerton, who might seem to justify the contempt for mankind of Old Man. This is at the beginning of Book 9; at the very end of it, after the reader has learned how bad the case is, Fielding urges him not to think he means to blame army officers in general:

Thou wilt be pleased to consider that this fellow, as we
have already informed thee, had neither the birth nor the
education of a gentleman, nor was a proper person to be
enrolled among the number of such. If, therefore, his baseness
can justly reflect on any besides himself, it must be only on
those who gave him his commission.

We learn incidentally, from this typical rounding on an administrator, that Fielding presumed men ought to be promoted to the ruling class, as a regular thing; the point is merely that the system of promotion should be adequate to save it from contempt. The exalted cynicism of Old Man (who by the way did not try to help Mrs Waters, though he and not Tom had a gun) might make one suspect that adequate members of such a class cannot be found, and Fielding has kept in mind the social question of how you should do it. I have known readers think Fielding wanted to abolish gentlemen, and indeed the jokes against them are pretty fierce; but he had planted another remark at the beginning of book 9, in the chapter of introductory prattle, which is clearly meant to fit the last words of that book. An author needs to have experienced both low life and high life, he is saying; low life for honesty and sincerity; high life, dull and absurd though it is, for

> elegance, and a liberality of spirit; which last quality I have myself scarce ever seen in men of low birth and education.

The assertion seems moderate, perhaps hardly more than that most men don't feel free to look all round a question unless their position is comfortable enough; but 'liberality of spirit' feels rather near to the basic virtue of having good impulses. Of course, he does not mean that all gentlemen have it; the total egotism of young Blifil, a theoretically interesting case, with a breakdown into sadism, which critics have chosen to call unlifelike, is chiefly meant to make clear that they do not. But it seems mere fact that Fielding's society needed a governing class, however things may work out under universal education; so it is reasonable of him to take a Reformist view, as the Communists would say, and merely recommend a better selection.

Indeed, it is perhaps flat to end this essay with an example which yields so placid a solution to a build-up of 'double-irony'; nor is it a prominent example, because after we get to London the ironies are about honour rather than gentility. But I suspect that today both halves of the puzzle about gentlemen are liable to work against him; he gets regarded as a coarse snob, whose jovial humour is intended to relax the laws only in favour of the privileged. This at least is unjust; no one attacked the injustices of privilege more fiercely. His position was not found placid at the time, and there is one class paradox which he repeatedly laboured to drive home; though to judge from a survey of opinions on him (Blanchard, 1926) this line of defence never gave him any protection in his lifetime. 'Only low people are afraid of having the low described to them, because only they are afraid of being exposed as themselves low.' The paradox gives him a lot of powerful jokes, but so far from being far-fetched it follows directly from his conception of a gentleman, which was if anything a literal-minded one. He means by it a person fit to sit on the bench as a magistrate, and naturally such a man needs to know all about the people he is to judge; indeed, the unusual thing about Fielding as a novelist is that he is always ready to consider what he would do if one of his characters came before him when he was on the bench. He is quite ready to hang a man, but also to reject the technical reasons for doing so if he decides that the man's impulses are not hopelessly corrupted. As to the reader of a novel Fielding cannot be bothered with him unless he too is fit to sit on a magistrate's bench, prepared, in literature as in life, to handle and judge any situation. That is why the reader gets teased so frankly. The same kind of firmness, I think, is what makes the forgiveness by Tom at the end feel startling and yet sensible enough to be able to stand up to Allworthy. I think the chief reason why recent critics have belittled Fielding is that they find him intimidating.

(217–49)

Irvin Ehrenpreis

from *Fielding: Tom Jones* 1964

Toward the middle of the eighteenth century there was a period when a deeply thoughtful Englishman could believe in a doctrine that had looked very doubtful to his predecessors and that was to grow as doubtful again to his successors during the next two centuries. This was the doctrine that all the essential impulses of a good man can be happily reconciled with one another – that none of his real tendencies need inevitably work against the rest. It was a period when love and honour, faith and reason, providence and fortune could be made to appear complementary; and before a necessary opposition seemed established between the individual and society, or between science and religion. During the 1730s and 1740s a poem like the *Essay on Man* could be defended by so orthodox a figure as Warburton; and in the *Analogy of Religion* Butler could suppose himself to be showing the agreement of nature with revelation.

To this time *Tom Jones* belongs, capturing, like no other of its author's works, the confident mood of a man who feels sure that private virtues mean public benefits. It is this confidence that infuses the novel with the hopefulness that even a corrupted native of the mid-twentieth century must admire. Whether we sympathize with him or not, Fielding shows the generous manner of a public benefactor who, having discovered a saving truth, wishes to share it with the world.

In the most obvious peculiarity of its form the novel suggests this attitude; for the author stands as obtrusively as possible between his readers and his story, showing the events to the onlookers like a surgeon in an operating theatre, who reveals not only the ailment that afflicts the sufferer but also how one should get at it. His authority validates the truth of his account. This extraordinary obtrusiveness is a feature I wish to examine in some detail, going next to the personality behind it. Fielding obtrudes himself most deliberately through the initial essays of his eighteen 'books', because these 'head' chapters sound like so many prefatory speeches or dramatic prologues, and as such are addressed directly by the author to a listener. But he also freely interrupts the narrative of events during the rest of the novel, in order to deliver a moralizing commentary; or else he adds a sentence or clause of analysis to an otherwise impersonal report.

This feature may seem odd in a novel, but it has many antecedents in other genres. It reminds one, for example, of the chorus in a Greek comedy, stepping forward and commenting on the episodes; and of the mock-annotator of a book like the *Dunciad Variorum*, playing with the implications of the text. Most directly, I think, it recalls the device used in the Restoration farce, *The Rehearsal*, and imitated by Fielding in satirical farces of his own – the device of representing a play under rehearsal, with the playwright explaining it to visitors who happen to come in and watch. In this form the scheme usually becomes a method of ridicule, with the playwright-within-the-play unintentionally exposing the absurdities in both his own work and the society it deals with.

When Fielding applies the scheme to *Tom Jones*, however, his most pervasive effect is not the punitive satire of the 'rehearsal' plays; for unlike the dramatists, the novelist elaborates and lingers on his own positive beliefs. We are given to understand that he is a frank speaker, eager to back up his work of fiction with supplementary evidence. Not only, it seems, may we trust him; we cannot accept the story unless we take him along with it. 'If you can't cotton on to me,' Fielding hints, 'you will misunderstand my novel.' The author-as-person becomes a character witness for the author-as-historian.

Repeatedly through the narrative we are flung back on a confidence in this obtrusive author. When a detail seems trifling, Fielding assures us that if we trust him, we will expect its pertinence to be finally made clear. When characters act in ways that contradict our knowledge of them, Fielding insists that his own observation of human nature will supply us with cases exactly parallel. Above all, at the most improbable turns of the plot, when coincidences crowd on us and gods drop from machines, Fielding argues that if we will rely on his experience, we can believe that life moves along just such tracks. In all these operations he seems to make his slogan, No author, no novel.

If Fielding did not give peculiar depth and substance to his personality, these effects would remain unconvincing. One is not likely to feel swayed emotionally or intellectually by vague hints issuing from an indeterminate mask. Furthermore, the special means by which he achieves his solidity are irresistibly simple. They depend on the fact that the ordinary narrative of *Tom Jones* stays outside the characters who are involved. Motives are often abstracted and analysed; feelings are often defined; conscious principles are endlessly expounded through dialogue. Seldom, however, are we treated to a free, detailed rendering of the unspoken thoughts, the unexpressed feelings, that lie behind the numerous, elaborate episodes of his story. Especially at moments of crisis, Fielding likes to repeat not the immediate emotions but the speeches and external gestures of his characters. In fact, it is partly on account of such 'externalization' that we do not find even the genuinely distressful scenes pathetic. Throughout the novel, Fielding is perfectly willing to mention the physical features of his characters, or articles of their clothing, or the furniture of their rooms. But he shies away from directly displaying the minute changes of their internal being.

It is just the contrary with the author's own self. Once in a great while we may come across some physical reference to his appearance or surroundings, such as the famous 'little parlour in which I sit at this instant' (book 13, chapter 1). Normally, however, we know only his opinions, judgements, reflections. We know what he has read but not what he wears. His existence seems almost wholly 'internalized'; it seems to be a moral and intellectual constitution but nothing more tangible. Even his emotions span such a narrow range that they almost escape attention.

This principle has interesting consequences for the structure of the novel. Fundamentally, it sets the author off as belonging to a different mode of existence from the persons of his story – a placid, objective mode, connotative of impartial truth. We are in direct, continual communication with him but hardly ever see him. We meet the others repeatedly, practically head on, but are seldom admitted to their confidence. The author therefore stands easily apart from the events, however closely he may comment on them. Rarely do we want any overt warning that he is about to switch from an opinion of his own to a deed of the actors in his production. More distinctly than any explanation, the simple change in mode tells us that the switch is taking place. And though his interventions are innumerable, they never block our power to separate him from his creation; but instead, his constant lurking sets the narrative by contrast in peculiarly high relief. This sort of clarity Richardson and Sterne denied themselves, the one unwillingly, confined by his epistolary form; the other deliberately, as part of his campaign against narrative structure – for the reader of *Tristram Shandy* is constantly teased into confusing the voice of Tristram with the voice of some other person.

But the separation of modes also succeeds in giving the author a deeper moral reality than anybody else. Not only must the intention of the characters normally be deduced from their behaviour, and therefore often remain controversial; but in addition those intentions, when revealed, are found to be unsteady:

Or puzzling contraries confound the whole,
Or affectations quite reverse the soul.

Bridget's affection for Tom drives her not to protect the boy from punishment but to urge his tutors to chastise him for misconduct (book 3 chapter 6). Hatred turns Blifil not away from Sophia but towards her. Loyalty and avarice, love and fear, alternate in the motives of a Black George or a Bellaston. During the course of the history we can rarely feel sure of our ground when we judge the blamefulness or innocence of a particular person.

With the narrator, however, we enjoy precisely the opposite relation. Through our intimacy with him we learn to appreciate the subtlety of his insights and the steadiness of his principles – two paradoxically related qualities. Thus again and again Fielding corrects our misinterpretations, points out details we have missed, reproaches us for our shallowness. It is he who insists that Allworthy's misunderstanding of Tom's actions is no reflection on the squire's sagacity, or that Sophia's anger at her admirer is not due simply to his philandering. The novelist is always refining, seeing possibilities we have over-looked; and we can only admire his subtlety. Now I think this reaction itself bears directly upon the technique of *Tom Jones*. Our admiration for Fielding's subtlety must be as great today as it would have been two centuries ago, because there is nothing clumsy or weak in his analyses of the deceptions men can practise on themselves. No novelist has shown more shrewdly than he that:

Oft in the passions' wild rotation tost,
Our spring of action to ourselves is lost.

In turn this display of shrewdness operates to ease our acceptance of the author's conventional moral views. It's true that his ingeniousness in advancing those views makes a prior appeal to our consent, and that their consistency in many different circumstances makes another. But his acute, unsentimental, 'realistic' judgement of the characters' failings and deceptions is probably the greatest source of Fielding's power to infuse us (while we read) with his radiant benevolence. So caustic an observer is the most persuasive recommender of a soft-hearted morality.

Ultimately, one should admit, the novelist's morality appeals on its own behalf. Few readers in any age really want to dismiss an assurance that virtue and happiness, reason and love, can be mutually strength-ening. In yielding to such an assurance we may be bowing rather to hope than experience; but the inclination is there before we pick up *Tom Jones*, and gathers force as we go through it.

The danger remains that so outspoken an author will sound pompous. It is bad enough that Fielding should have a doctrine to propagate. It would be much worse if he seemed to nag us with his principles. We might sit down with the impression that a tiresome moralist was trying to convert us to an over-familiar creed. In solving this problem of how to recommend a serious doctrine without appear-ing to take oneself seriously, Fielding shows the value of his training as a playwright; for he does not follow Sterne's method – which would be a mistake here – of laughing covertly at the propositions he wishes us to agree with. Rather, he expounds them with complete candour. But at the same time, this attitude does not require him to act dour or solemn about his character as an author. On the contrary, the playfulness of the author as such provides an exhilarating relief to the earnestness of the teacher. It is, in fact, through a parody of the vain, self-defensive author – say, of Richardson in the postscript to *Clarissa* – that Fielding undercuts the censure of readers who would resent any smugness on his own part. By the same tone he associates his sober argument with a cheerful sensibility, suggesting that the route to virtue is the way of good humour; one says of him what was said (by Steele) of his predecessor in this technique, i.e. Swift: 'The man writes much like a gentleman, and goes to Heaven with a very good mien.'

If, then, the truth of the story depends on the reality of the narrator, it behoves Fielding not to let the reader forget he is there. By reappearing at regular and irregular intervals, he makes us aware of a private voice, sometimes discussing matters of personal interest which do not hinge on the story, but always preventing us from immersing ourselves in the events. So steady a presence necessarily changes our view of those events. Since many of them would, in direct action, be scenes of distress, we have to thank the author for removing them, through the screen of his intervention, to a distance that makes them bearable if not enjoyable.

In the most regular of his interventions, viz. the essays prefatory to each book, Fielding divides his materials along the lines I have been sketching, between ironical literary criticism and moral implication, with the author either pointing humorously to evidence of his literary art or else warning us not to misread his message. The transition from the one concern to the other is easily seen in a passage that will serve as well to illustrate several of my other remarks; this is Fielding's argument that many English writers (especially dramatists) have 'failed in describing the manners of upper life' through the accident of possessing no experience of it:

Now it happens that this higher order of mortals is not to be seen, like all the rest of the human species, for nothing, in the streets, shops, and coffee-houses; nor are they shown, like the upper rank of animals, for so much apiece. In short, this is a sight to which no persons are admitted without one or other of these qualifications, viz. either birth or fortune, or, what is equivalent to both, the honourable profession of a gamester. And, very unluckily for the world, persons so qualified very seldom care to take upon themselves the bad trade of writing; which is generally entered upon by the lower and poorer sort, as it is a trade which many think requires no kind of stock to set up with.

Hence those strange monsters in lace and embroidery, in silks and brocades, with vast wigs and hoops; which, under the name of lords and ladies, strut the stage, to the great delight of attorneys and their clerks in the pit, and of the citizens and their apprentices in the galleries; and which are no more to be found in real life than the centaur, the chimera, or any other creature of mere fiction. But to let my reader into a secret, this knowledge of upper life, though very necessary for preventing mistakes, is no very great resource to a writer whose province is comedy, or that kind of novel which, like this I am writing, is of the comic class.

What Mr Pope says of women is very applicable to most in this station, who are, indeed, so entirely made up of form and affectation, that they have no character at all, at least none which appears. I will venture to say the highest life is much the dullest, and affords very little humour or entertainment. The various callings in lower spheres produce the great variety of humorous characters; whereas here, except among the few who are engaged in the pursuit of ambition, and the fewer still who have still a relish for pleasure, all is vanity and servile imitation. Dressing and cards, eating and drinking, bowing and courtseying, make up the business of their lives.

Some there are, however, of this rank upon whom passion exercises its tyranny, and hurries them far beyond the bounds which decorum prescribes; of these the ladies are as much distinguished by their noble intrepidity, and a certain superior contempt of reputation, from the frail ones of meaner degree, as a virtuous woman of quality is by the elegance and delicacy of her sentiments from the honest wife of a yeoman and shopkeeper. Lady Bellaston was of this intrepid character; but let not my country readers conclude from her that this is the general conduct of women of

fashion, or that we mean to represent them as such. They
might as well suppose that every clergyman was
represented by Thwackum, or every soldier by ensign
Northerton.

There is not, indeed, a greater error than that which
universally prevails among the vulgar, who, borrowing their
opinion from some ignorant satirists, have affixed the
character of lewdness to these times. On the contrary, I am
convinced there never was less of love intrigue carried on
among persons of condition than now. Our present women
have been taught by their mothers to fix their thoughts only
on ambition and vanity, and to despise the pleasures of love
as unworthy of their regard; and being afterwards, by the
care of such mothers, married without having husbands,
they seem pretty well confirmed in the justness of those
sentiments; whence they content themselves, for the dull
remainder of life, with the pursuit of more innocent, but I
am afraid more childish amusements, the bare mention of
which would ill suit with the dignity of this history. In my
humble opinion, the true characteristic of the present beau
monde is rather folly than vice, and the only epithet which it
deserves is that of frivolous (book 14, chapter 1).

For clarity and ease without banality, the style of this passage would
be hard to match. There are no dark places in the writing, and we feel
little doubt that we have grasped both the manifest sense of the
remarks and the deliberate implications of the author. In the shape of
the paragraphs there is a careful symmetry, each one starting with an
open, forward-looking statement that receives a brief development
(in two or three central sentences) through an ironical shift of viewpoint, after which follows a summary apothegm making a distinct
close: the careful form of the whole novel seems epitomized in these
paragraphs. Clauses, sentences and other units of thought are distinctly marked off; and all their joints and hinges show. Fielding
makes much use of connectives, little use of the kind of verbal wit
that might suggest insincerity. Scarcely broken by parentheses or
digressions, the forward movement of meaning is steady and continuous, assisted by an unobtrusive employment of parallelism and

antithesis. Although the changes of tone give the writing unusual liveliness, they are as decorous as the variations in sentence structure. Nothing sounds eccentric or forced. When the mood deepens, the irony grows more insistent, as if to compensate for the weight of the moral censure. But apart from such irony there are few figures of speech, for the author appears to be simply uttering his sentiments. In its transparency, continuity and effortlessness, the style seems to reflect the author's candour.

When Fielding proceeds, in this perspicuous way, from a discourse on the comic writer to a judgement of the comic writer's subjects, he shows how differently he handles the dignity of authorship and the dignity of moral instruction, because his ironic humour is addressed to the profession of letters, but scorn is the tone he uses against vice and frivolity. The explicit theme of the whole essay is that an author ought to know something about the matter of his writing. So Fielding implies that a playwright with no rich experience of the variety of human life can become only a mediocre dramatist. But the argument works as well in reverse. Thus Fielding also insists (like his master Cervantes) that a properly designed work of literary art will be more edifying than an ill-made work. Merely as artist, and regardless of his subject, the *miglior fabbro* stands morally above the hack.

In the paragraphs dealing with high life, therefore, Fielding is touching on the parallel between vicious persons and unskilled authors. To consider the high life more interesting than the low is the blunder committed as much by corrupt men of fashion as by inept playwrights. Similarly, just as Grub Street does not know how to write, the *beau monde* does not know how to live. We are consequently given to understand that Fielding judges himself to be properly equipped in both these respects, or else he would not be offering us his novel. Nevertheless, his attitude toward his 'bad trade' remains mockingly self-deprecating. However he may separate his own writing from that of the hacks, he must come under the same genial ridicule that affects them. His role as a moralist remains free from any such qualification. Rather he strengthens this when he goes on to expose the specious appeals of the high life; for thus he demonstrates not only an ethical code superior to the vanity of both the hacks and the men of fashion but also a shrewdness of psychological insight that deepens one's respect for his judgement.

Finally, the surprising close of the essay triply enriches our impression of the author. From its intimacy of tone the paragraph sounds like the immediate message of a real person. Its bitterness suggests a strength of blame hardly to be found in the traditional representations of a bland hearty Fielding. But, what is more important, the meaning distinguishes him as not at all a conventional thinker: Fielding did believe that a good man was passionate and a bad man was not; *no* passion seemed to him worse than *any* passion; and the preference he expresses for deep but conscious sinners over weak evaders of moral issues comes out of a realism of moral analysis that ironically connects him with the same 'upper' class he is denouncing. For though this preference was bound to seem either foolish or wicked to many of his readers, he felt the gentleman's freedom to tell them precisely what he believed. No other novelist of the century could have written that paragraph.

(7-15)

John Preston

'*Tom Jones* and the "Pursuit of True Judgment"',
Journal of English Literary History, vol. 33   1966 (reprinted in
The Created Self, 1970)

The plot of *Tom Jones*, then, may be best understood in terms of the way it is read. Its structure is the structure of successive responses to the novel. It exists in the reader's attention rather than in the written sequences. This means that its effect is epistemological rather than moral. It helps us to see how we acquire our knowledge of human experience; it is a clarification of the processes of understanding. It presents life as a fortuitous sequence of events, as the play of Fortune, and traces the ways in which we come to see these events as a pattern. This certainly does not in any direct way establish a moral sense in the novel. Take, for instance, Tom's affair with Molly Seagrim. His remorse, prompting him to make amends to her, leads him to find her in bed with Square and then to discover that she had been first seduced by Will Barnes. His generous impulse leads to the knowledge that will release him: 'Jones was become perfectly easy by possession of this secret with regard to Molly' (book 5, chapter 6). But this is luck, not morality. His remorse pays dividends, but not because it *is* remorse. To centre the plot on Fortune is to lift the moral burden from the behaviour of the characters, with the unexpected effect at times of sharpening their conscience. At the point when Tom is least to blame he reproaches himself most bitterly. Hearing of his supposed incest he first exclaims against Fortune and then blames himself: ' "Fortune will never have done with me, 'till she hath driven me to distraction. But why do I blame Fortune? I am myself the cause of all my misery. All the dreadful mischiefs which have befallen me, are the consequences only of my own folly and vice" ' (book 18, chapter 2). This is absurd. Yet there is a truth in it: he *is* responsible in an essential way. But this moral discovery cannot be made through the plot as such.

It is natural to assume that what the plot cannot do will have to be done by the author's explicit comments. Thus Ian Watt holds that Fielding's technique was 'deficient at least in the sense that it was unable to convey this larger moral significance through character and action alone' that *Tom Jones* 'is only part novel'.[1] This kind of distinction between 'showing' and 'telling' has, at least since the publication of *The Rhetoric of Fiction*, come to seem much less secure. But it is as well to note that in Fielding's time it would have been widely accepted. It was in fact confirmed by just that epic theory that Fielding appealed to. Le Bossu himself, the approved interpreter of Aristotle,[2] takes up the assertion that the poet who speaks in his own person is no imitator: he should seek for 'une manière de rendre la Narration agissante'.[3] The orator, but not the poet, may enter into a direct relation with his audience. What makes the narrative convincing in an epic poem is the 'rapport que le poète met entre ses auditeurs et ses personnages'.[4] Thus, as Shaftesbury notes in his 'Advice to an Author', the advantages of the Platonic Dialogue are that 'the author is annihilated, and the reader, being no way applied to, stands for nobody. . . . You are not only left to judge coolly and

---

1 *The Rise of the Novel*, Chatto & Windus, 1957, p. 287.
2 See Ethel M. Thornbury, *Henry Fielding's Theory of the Comic Prose Epic*, University of Wisconsin Studies in Language and Literature, 1931, pp. 56ff.
3 *Traité du Poëme Epique*, p. 239.
4 ibid., p. 207.

with indifference of the sense delivered, but of the character, genius, elocution, and manner of the persons who deliver it.' But this un-happily is not the way of the modern writer: 'he suits himself on every occasion to the fancy of his reader, whom, as the fashion is nowadays, he constantly caresses and cajoles.' This is 'the coquetry of a modern author ... to draw attention from the subject, towards himself.'[1]

In this light Fielding's narrative looks like a planned flouting of decorum; he aligns himself with the vain, egotistical 'modern' author, in the manner of Swift, but with a more subtle ironic inten-tion. Swift apes the bad writer in order to demolish him; Fielding chooses 'bad' art in order to unseat the bad reader. Whilst appearing to ingratiate himself in the 'modern' manner, he is actually trying to school the reader, to induce him to attend more closely and to judge well. Fielding is very far from being defeated by his medium. Rather he employs his narrative method with calculated effect, as a means to draw the reader into the action of the book and so clarify its meaning. His method is, in fact, as William J. Farrell has shown, the proper method for a 'history'.[2] We have seen how Fielding presents the shape of history as a dilemma for the reader; it is important to recognize that conventionally the historian's mode of address also expects the reader's participation. 'The narrator-to-audience observa-tions,' writes Mr Farrell, 'invariably bring into the work a fairly well-defined character called "the reader".'[3] In Fielding's novels, of course, the device is used not to authenticate 'historical' truth but to enforce 'the believability of [the] narrator through whom the reader sees the entire action'.[4] Certainly the rhetorical basis of the novels needs this kind of support; in so far as Fielding successfully projects the persona of his narrator we shall be prepared to accept that 'telling' is after all a kind of 'showing'. But an equally important use for the device is to make the reader's role clear. The reader has his responsi-bility also: he must try to judge well. To encourage him to do so is itself a part of the subject of the book. That is, the book is *about* judgement, and the understanding necessary for good judgement. This is where the moral sense is located, in the analysis and evaluation of

1 *Characteristics*, i, p. 131.
2 'Fielding's Familiar Style', *ELH*, vol. 34, no. 1, March 1967, p. 65.
3 ibid., p. 73.   4 ibid., p. 76.

diverse judgements. It is epistemological in this way also. It focuses attention, not only on events, but on the mind which perceives and judges them. Fielding is quite aware that his fiction has the same aims as Locke's *Essay*. In one of the *Champion* papers he quotes from Locke's opening chapter: '*The understanding, like the eye* (says Mr Lock), *whilst it makes us see and perceive all other things, takes no Notice of itself; and it requires art and pains to set it at a distance and make it its own object*' (1 March 1739–40). But, Fielding continues, the analogy is not perfect, 'for the eye can contemplate itself in a glass, but no narcissus hath hitherto discovered any mirrour for the understanding', and self-knowledge may too easily slide into 'self love'. To provide such a mirror, to guard against such error is the purpose of *Tom Jones*. To effect it Fielding must establish his relationship with the reader.

In his first chapter he shows what this is to be. 'On the image which Fielding produces just here,' says Andrew Wright of the offered 'bill of fare', 'the meaning of the novel depends.'[1] This is true, but not, I think, in the way he explains it, as an invitation 'to take *Tom Jones* in a festive spirit'. We know Fielding's opinion of innkeepers and are hardly surprised that when he poses as one his invitation lacks cordiality. Like 'one who keeps a public ordinary, at which all persons are welcome for their money', he is quite prepared to find that the critical reader will be ill-mannered. 'Men who pay for what they eat, will insist on gratifying their palates, however nice and even whimsical these may prove; and if every thing is not agreeable to their Taste, will challenge a right to censure, to abuse, and to d—n their dinner without controul' (book 1, chapter 1). This is why he publishes his bill of fare: prospective customers may decide either to stay or 'depart to some other ordinary better accommodated to their taste'. This is explicitly not an 'eleemosynary treat'.[2] Fielding thus

1 *Henry Fielding, Mask and Feast*, Chatto & Windus, 1965, p. 32.
2 Perhaps Fielding is echoing Burton: '– *ut palata, sic judicia*, our censures are as various as our palates. . . . Our writings are as so many dishes, our readers guests. . . . What shall I doe in this case? As a Dutch host, if you come to an inne in *Germany*, & dislike your fare, diet, lodging, &c. replies in a surly tone, *aliud tibi quaeras diversorium*, if you like not this, get you to another inne: I resolue, if you like not my writing, goe read something else.' *The Anatomy of Melancholy*, 6th edn, 1632, pp. 9–10.

establishes mutual rights of criticism: if my reader is to be allowed freedom of censure, I must be permitted to make fun of him; in this way we may come to respect each other. Empson, taking his cue from Fielding's work as magistrate rather than his role in the book, puts the matter admirably:

The unusual thing about Fielding as a novelist is that he is always ready to consider what he would do if one of his characters came before him when he was on the bench. . . . As to the reader of a novel, Fielding cannot be bothered with him unless he too is fit to sit on a magistrate's bench, prepared, in literature as in life, to handle and judge any situation. That is why the reader gets teased so frankly.[1]

Actually Fielding's way of envisaging this relationship has less to do with inns and law-courts than with the theatre, and especially with the audience. The usual analogy between the world and the stage is not enough for him: 'None, as I remember, have at all considered the audience at this great drama' (book 7, chapter 1). He imagines the reactions of the world's upper-gallery, pit and boxes to the scene in which Black George steals Tom's £500. Some are abusive, some offended, some tolerant and others 'refused to give their opinion 'till they had heard that of the best judges. . . . As for the boxes, . . . most of them were attending to something else' (book 7, chapter 1). He is interested more in the audience than the play, as we see also from several other passages in the novel. Part-ridge, for instance, is seen in the gallery at a performance of *Hamlet*. 'Jones . . . expected to enjoy much entertainment in the criticisms of Partridge' (book 16 chapter 5). On another occasion Fielding inserts the story of the murderer of Mr Derby, one Fisher, who also went to see *Hamlet*, 'and with an unaltered countenance heard one of the ladies, who little suspected how near she was to the person, cry out, "Good God! if the man that murdered Mr Derby was now present!" Manifesting in this a more seared and callous Conscience than even Nero himself' (book 8, chapter 1).

This manoeuvre, in which the audience becomes the centre of interest, exposed to the author's criticism as he was to theirs, is brilliantly illustrated by Hogarth's etching 'The Laughing Audience'.

1 '*Tom Jones*', *Kenyon Review*, vol. 20, 1958, p. 249.

The ten laughing people are rendered with a touch both subtle and vigorous, both sympathetic and caustic. There is an infectious gaiety in their laughter and at the same time a delicate observation of their different temperaments. We feel a harshness in the drawing and yet a pleasure in the simplicity and naturalness depicted. The one 'critic' among them, who is not watching the stage and sits in contemptuous isolation, is made to seem absurdly out of place. In the boxes and unobserved by anyone in the picture there is a scene of foppish affectation and gallantry, theatrical in appearance and more amusing, Hogarth implies, than anything the audience could be laughing at. Who is laughing at whom? This brilliant and complex design, cutting across the usual distinctions between subject and object, observer and observed, is an exact parallel to Fielding's procedure in *Tom Jones*. For he is not, as Andrew Wright suggests, drawing attention primarily to the artificiality of life, trying to make us see it as a play. On the contrary, as Partridge's naïveté reminds us, the best acting is that which most resembles life. And the consummate 'actor' who appears in the very next chapter is Blifil, the hypocrite. No, if Fielding is watchful of his readers, interested in the way they take his story, this is because their judgement is in the long run part of that story.

But Fielding is not content merely to observe his audience; he wants to teach them. He looks for intelligent readers. We have already seen his attitude to the ill-natured critic. It remains constant throughout the book: 'I must desire all those critics to mind their own business . . .' (book 1, chapter 2); 'a little reptile of a critic' (book 10, chapter 1); 'if we judge according to the Sentiments of some Critics, and of some Christians, no author will be saved in this world, and no man in the next' (book 11, chapter 1). Why does Fielding adopt this petulant tone? It looks as if he is trying to keep up the role of the bad writer to whom all critics are a nuisance. But there is a better use for it. The critic's 'hungry appetite for censure' (book 16, chapter 1) is an extreme example of 'judgement' in the wrong sense, 'in which it is frequently used as equivalent to condemnation' (book 11, chapter 1). This applies in life as well as literature: the critic is a type of the 'common slanderer, . . . a person who prys into the characters of others, with no other design but to discover their faults, and to publish them to the world' (book 11, chapter 1). He means to remind us of Blifil of course; but the remarks are actually referred to our own response as readers. He is expecting the reader to know how to judge with generosity, in T. S. Eliot's words to 'compose his differences with as many of his fellows as possible, in the common pursuit of true judgment'.[1] 'All beauty of character, as well as of countenance, and indeed of every thing human, is to be tried in this manner' (book 11, chapter 1). This sounds very generalized; but we have seen how it grows out of an imagined situation, out of what Wayne Booth calls 'the "plot" of our relationship with Fielding-as-narrator'.[2] To make us serve his purpose Fielding appropriates us to the world of his fiction.

He also reverses the process and contrives in many ways to suggest that his fictional world is available to us in reality. We could follow Tom's route and, in that case, Fielding would recommend us to stay at the Bell, Gloucester, 'an excellent house indeed' (book 8, chapter 8. And we may, says Fielding, 'have the pleasure of riding in the very coach, and being driven by the very coachman, that is recorded in this history' (book 10, chapter 6). He always writes as if we were present at the events narrated: 'the reader will, I believe, bear witness for him' (book 2, chapter 4); 'I question not but the surprise of the reader will be here equal to that of Jones' (book 5, chapter 5); 'Reader, if thou hast any good wishes towards me, I will fully repay them, by wishing thee to be possessed of this sanguine disposition of mind (i.e. like Tom's), ... which puts us, in a manner, out of the reach of fortune' (book 13, chapter 6). We are not insulated. We are not only to watch, it seems, but to be subjected to the same hazards as the characters themselves. Fielding does not set us apart from them; indeed *they* are often made to seem more like audience than actors. Some, like Square and Thwackum, are created just to be observers, to offer opinions. And the design of the story gives equal weight to action and to the discussion it provokes. A transparent example of this is in book 4, chapter 4 when the episode of Sophia's little bird is debated by Square, Thwackum, Western, Allworthy and a 'Gentleman of the Law, who was present'. But hardly anything happens in the novel that does not create its ripples of

1 T. S. Eliot, 'The Function of Criticism', *Selected Essays*, p. 25.
2 *The Rhetoric of Fiction*, University of Chicago Press, 1961, p. 216.

comment, discussion and conflicting judgements. The reader and even the narrator are, in these situations, on an equal footing with the actors. In other words the story, as distinct from the plot, is really a system of stories within stories, like the house that Jack built. Thus the tale told by the Man of the Hill, often thought to be digressive and disruptive, is actually firmly embedded in the whole design. And, as if to emphasize this, Fielding arranges it in symmetry with the parallel story told by Mrs Fitzpatrick to Sophia.

Reactions to an event are themselves events. In the same way some of the most important acts in the novel are acts of judgement. We discover and express ourselves in judging others; our moral existence consists in our ability to form moral judgements. Hence the importance of that chapter (book 7, chapter 1) in which we have seen 'the great audience's' reactions to Black George's theft. For Fielding there goes further than Hogarth, who merely shows the audience its own image. He uses the analogy to discover something about the nature of moral judgements. This audience's opinions are worthless. Theirs is the judgement of the 'mob' (i.e. 'persons without virtue, or sense, in all stations', book 1, chapter 9). They judge superficially and casually, that is on the isolated scene enacted before them. This is why we must go 'behind the scenes of this great theatre of nature' where we shall learn the true character of a man. 'A single bad act no more constitutes a villain in life, than a single bad part on the stage.' This is often taken to mean that we may overlook faults where virtues predominate. But this is certainly not what Fielding intends:

Indeed, nothing can be of more moral use than the
Imperfections which are seen in examples of this kind; since
such form a kind of surprise, more apt to affect and dwell
upon our minds, than the faults of very vicious and
wicked persons ... when we find such vices attended with
their evil consequence to our favourite characters, we are
not only taught to shun them for our own sake, but to hate
them for the mischiefs they have already brought on those
we love (book 10, chapter 1).

So Tom has in the end to face himself. Sophia insists on this, and her insistence has more moral rigour than Allworthy's balancing of 'his faults with his perfections' (book 4, chapter 11). ' "I think, Mr Jones," said she, "I may almost depend on your own Justice, and leave it to yourself to pass sentence on your own conduct" ' (Book 18, chapter 12). One must be harsh with oneself, charitable and compassionate to others. Faults will not go undetected but 'will raise our compassion rather than our abhorrence' (book 10, chapter 1); and, Fielding concludes, having been permitted to look behind the scenes 'the man of candour and of true understanding is never hasty to condemn. . . . The worst of men generally have the words *Rogue* and *Villain* in their mouths' (book 7, chapter 1).

The book, then, is not concerned with judgements made in detachment and isolation. Shaftesbury's ideal reader, judging 'coolly and with indifference', will, Fielding implies, only be sinking deeper into his own illusions. For if our judgements are an expression of our own moral identity, they are also an expression of community, of our attitude to others. Any flaw in this feeling for others will imply a flaw in our own being. This is, of course, nominally Shaftesbury's argument also: 'That to have the natural, kindly, or generous affections strong and powerful towards the good of the public, is to have the chief means and power of self-enjoyment, . . . to want them is certain misery and ill'.[1] Thus Shaftesbury bids 'self-love and social be the same'. What he does not allow for is the difficulty, the stress of living up to these principles. Fielding has to test Shaftesbury's ideals in the thick of life. He puts the matter with a quite different emphasis: '[Tom] was never an indifferent spectator of the misery or happiness of any one; and he felt either the one or the other in greater proportion as he himself contributed to either' (book 15, chapter 8).

Initially, to be sure, Fielding seems to align himself more closely with Shaftesbury. His book, a tribute to Lyttleton and Ralph Allen (the model for his 'Picture of a truly benevolent Mind', [Dedication]), is also a kind of tribute to Shaftesbury, whose image of the Deity has many of the features we discern in Allworthy: '. . . a Deity who is considered as worthy and good, and admired and reverenced as such, . . . In such a presence, 'tis evident that as the shame of guilty actions must be the greatest of any, so must the honour be of well-doing, even under the unjust censure of a world'.[2] But Fielding

1 *Characteristics*, i, p. 292. 2 op. cit., i, p. 268.

cannot sustain such confidence, as we may gather from his scepticism about the Gipsy King's benevolent despotism. As he says, it has the one defect that it is difficult to find 'any man adequate to the office of an absolute monarch' (book 12, chapter 12). From the start, there-fore, there is something unreal about Allworthy: 'a human being replete with benevolence, meditating in what manner he might render himself most acceptable to his creator, by doing most good to his creatures' (book 1, chapter 4). We can hardly credit that this could be meant seriously, and Fielding does in fact give it an ironic twist: 'Reader, take care, I have unadvisedly led thee to the top of as high a hill as Mr Allworthy's, and how to get thee down without breaking thy neck, I do not well know. However, let us e'en venture to slide down together' (book 1, chapter 4).

Allworthy has always seemed one of the puzzles of the book. Henry James Pye, writing in 1792, notes him as 'a character at opposition with himself, though more perhaps in general with that which the author tells you in his own person he is, than with his own conduct in those parts where the author suffers him to act from him-self'. The trouble, as Pye sees it, is that Allworthy, offered as 'a man of sense and discernment, with a benevolence almost angelic', is actually 'the dupe of every insinuating rascal he meets; and a dupe not of the most amiable kind, since he is always led to acts of justice and severity. The consequence of his pliability is oftener the punish-ment of the innocent than the acquittal of the guilty; and in such punishment he is severe and implacable.'[1] Andrew Wright sees more clearly that he could never have been intended as the 'moral centre' of the book[2] but errs, I think, in claiming that the existence in the novel of Western is 'the strongest of all reasons' for thinking so. No doubt Western is 'full of vitality, [and] also playful', but we need not conclude that either Fielding or the reader finds this combination of qualities 'irresistible'. There is surely some severity in Fielding's comment that 'Men over-violent in their dispositions, are, for the most part, as changeable in them' (book 18, chapter 9). Western is erratic, undependable and tyrannical. A full view of him must include the harsh ironies of book 7, chapter 4, in which his love for Sophia is

1 *A Commentary Illustrating the Poetic of Aristotle* (London, 1792), reprinted in *Aristotle's Poetics and English Literature*, ed. E. Olson, pp. 39–40.
2 op. cit., pp. 159–62.

measured against his hatred of his neglected and abused wife. Yet, it appears, Allworthy's detachment and impartiality are not in themselves a protection against profound error. One important way of establishing this is by comparison, not with Western or another character, but with the reader himself.

In book 4, chapter 11 Allworthy is at first represented as somewhat arbitrary and harsh in his treatment of Molly Seagrim: 'I question, as here was no regular Information before him, whether his Conduct was strictly regular'. When Tom pleads for the girl, Allworthy's moral indignation is deflected ('I own, indeed, [the guilt] doth lie principally upon you, and so heavy it is, that you ought to expect it should crush you'). Allworthy fails to see how this rebuke reflects on his judgement of Molly: should he not from the beginning have directed his anger against the principal offender? Fielding has insinuated, in any case, that the house of correction is an ineffectual punishment. And when he seems to wish to salvage Allworthy's reputation for impartiality it is with a curious effect: 'he was not so blinded by [the offence], but that he could discern any virtue in the guilty person, as clearly, indeed as if there had been no mixture of vice in the same character'. This, Fielding asserts, indicates that he has come to 'the same opinion of this young fellow which, we hope, our reader may have conceived'. But he has not in fact been encouraging us to estimate Tom in terms of this kind of 'moral arithmetic'. And its inadequacy emerges as soon as it is challenged. Thwackum, admittedly, cannot sway Allworthy. But Square, 'a much more artful Man', has no difficulty at all in persuading him that Tom's generosity is the mark of 'a depraved and debauched appetite': 'he supported the father, in order to corrupt the daughter, and preserved the family from starving, to bring one of them to shame and ruin.' To Allworthy these 'considerations' (not, we note, new evidence but a new interpretation of the evidence) are 'too plausible to be absolutely and hastily rejected' and stamp in his mind 'the first bad impression concerning Jones'. His judgement throughout the episode is as wrong as it can be. If the arguments advanced by Square have any force, Allworthy should himself have reckoned with them in reaching his first judgement; if they do not, he should not have been affected by them. But his moral failure here is made more glaring by contrast with the kind of judgement Fielding expects

from the reader. Before Square states his case, the reader is given the same evidence as Allworthy himself is given. 'The reader must remember the several little Incidents of the partridge, the horse, and the Bible, which were recounted in the second book.' They had first enlisted Allworthy's approval. 'The same, I believe, must have happened to him with every other person who hath any idea of friendship, generosity, and greatness of spirit; that is to say, who hath any trace of goodness in his mind.' The reader will not easily forfeit his claim to such qualities, and Square's speech need not persuade him to do so. But Allworthy, by contrast, is blinded and confused; his very judiciousness saps his power to judge aright.
confused; his very judiciousness saps his power to judge aright.

Furthermore, Allworthy's detachment and impartiality, fallible enough in themselves, all too often forsake him altogether. When he banishes Tom, for instance, we find him unexpectedly egocentric: it becomes obvious to the reader that what most sways him is Tom's supposed disrespect towards him. As this is just what he cannot admit openly, his censure of Tom looks motiveless: 'nay, indeed, (Tom) hardly knew his accusation: for as Mr Allworthy, in recounting the drunkenness, etc., while he lay ill, out of modesty sunk every thing that related particularly to himself, which indeed principally constituted the crime, Jones could not deny the charge' (book 6, chapter 11). In fact his judgements are almost always prejudiced: 'the poor game-keeper was condemned, without having any opportunity to defend himself' (book 3, chapter 10); Molly was to be committed to Bridewell without a hearing; the evidence that Jenny might have given in support of Partridge 'would have deserved no credit', and, when he continues to protest his innocence, 'Mr Allworthy declared himself satisfied of his guilt, and that he was too bad a Man to receive any encouragement from him' (book 2, chapter 6). Allworthy is quick to blame, more aware of guilt than innocence. Mrs Miller finds in Tom 'one of the most humane tender honest hearts that ever man was blessed with', though he is marred by 'faults of wildness and of youth' (book 17, chapter 2). Allworthy maintains rather that there are 'few characters so absolutely vicious as not to have the least mixture of good in them' (book 17, chapter 7). He is, accordingly, slow to see through Blifil, though quick to dismiss Tom.

Allworthy *should* have seen through Blifil. As Fielding says in his

'Essay on the Knowledge of the Characters of Men', 'the truth is, nature doth really imprint sufficient marks in the countenance, to inform an accurate and discerning eye' (*Works*, ed. A. Murphy, 1771, vol. 8, p. 166). And in fact Mrs Miller's simplicity is more penetrating than Allworthy's deliberate and patient judgement: '"Guilty!"', she exclaims, on seeing the change in Blifil's face, ' "Guilty, upon my honour! Guilty, upon my soul!"' (book 18, chapter 5). With this in mind it is difficult not to suspect Fielding of irony when he appears to be defending Allworthy against possible criticism: 'Of readers who ... condemn the wisdom or penetration of Mr Allworthy, I shall not scruple to say, that they make a very bad and ungrateful use of that knowledge which we have communicated to them' (book 3, chapter 5). Must we take this to mean that there are no grounds for condemning Allworthy's judgements? Surely it is intended rather as a sharp reminder that but for Fielding's help we would fare no better ourselves. If Allworthy fails, his failure reflects no credit on us. It should in fact engage our admiration. There is something heroic in Allworthy. If Tom is the comic hero, always acting and always in the dark, Allworthy, never allowed to withhold judgement or to be less than his best, is the book's most admired yet poignant figure, its tragic hero in fact. It is through his high-minded failures that we gain some of our clearest impressions of the difficulty of judging well. Yet, in our respect for the stubborn excellence of Allworthy, we are not to reconcile ourselves to judging like him. We are expected to go 'behind the scenes', to do in fact what the author has been doing for us. There is no credit in ignorance.

Not that Fielding simply recommends 'penetration' and keen discernment. Indeed it is obvious he likes the opposite qualities – the credulity of Mrs Miller, or the simplicity of Sophia. Mrs Western's penetration on the other hand, or the 'sagacity' of the reader, or the innkeeper who thought that Sophia was Jenny Cameron, are comical. Yet, as he argues elsewhere, 'Good-nature requires a distinguishing faculty, which is another word for judgement, and is perhaps the sole boundary between wisdom and folly; it is impossible for a fool, who hath no distinguishing faculty, to be good-natured' (*Champion*, 27 March 1740). Simplicity is not good-natured (and here we recall Partridge) unless it is combined with keen penetration. But, as we have seen, penetration is often a kind of blindness and folly. We can perhaps resolve the dilemma by recalling the distinction Fielding makes between the two degrees of suspicion. One, arising from the heart, imagines evil where none exists; the other, arising from the head, the understanding, is 'no other than the faculty of seeing what is before your eyes, and of drawing conclusions from what you see' (book 11, chapter 10). Whilst this is a way of detecting guilt, the former can only harm the innocent. But again this is a rather mechanical formula. To see a more vital connection between good nature and understanding, simplicity and discernment, we must turn to Tom.

Tom's good nature is described in terms which ought to apply to Allworthy; the moral principle which governs his conduct is a judicial one, 'like the Lord High Chancellor of this kingdom in his court; where it presides, governs, directs, judges, acquits, and condemns according to merit and justice; with a knowledge which nothing escapes, a penetration which nothing can deceive, and an integrity which nothing can corrupt' (book 4, chapter 6). And this is an 'active principle', not arbitrating in remote detachment, not content 'with knowledge or belief only', but prompting good actions and restraining from bad. Here, surely, is the hub of the book's meaning. All that Fielding has to show of the nature of judgement centres here, in these rare moral qualities. They place before us, as a constant point of reference in the book, the high ideal which, in Butler's sermons, is called conscience.

But there is a superior principle of reflection or conscience
in every man, which distinguishes between the internal
principles of his heart, as well as his external actions: which
passes judgement upon himself and them; ... which, without
being consulted, without being advised with, magisterially
exerts itself, and approves or condemns him the doer of
them accordingly. ... It is by this faculty, natural to man,
that he is a moral agent, that he is a law to himself.[1]

Thus our approval of Tom is meant to lead us to challenging moral issues. There is much more to him than a good heart and a healthy appetite. What we are to appreciate in his nature is something like the discernment and judgement we ourselves are expected to display

1 *Works*, Oxford, 1896, ii, p. 59.

in our reading of the novel. The book, by making us conscious of ourselves as readers, by exercising our critical faculties, is contributing no less than Butler himself to a philosophical process. Indeed the terms in which the eighteenth century derived its ethical principles, from the earlier reactions to Hobbes,[1] are strikingly relevant to the novel. Thus Richard Cumberland in 1672, in the act of refuting Hobbes, anticipates many of Fielding's remarks:

Shall I not reckon among the perfections of the human understanding, that it can reflect upon it self? Consider its habits, as dispositions arising from past actions? Remember and recollect its own dictates, and compare them with its actions? Judge which way the mind inclines? And direct it-self to the pursuit of what seems fittest to be done? Our mind is conscious to it self of all its own actions, and both can, and often does, observe what counsels produced them; it naturally sits a judge upon its own actions, and thence procures to it self either tranquillity and joy, or anxiety and sorrow. In this power of the mind, and the actions thence arising, consists the whole force of conscience by which it proposes laws to it self, examines its past, and regulates its future conduct.[2]

Here, as Baumrin points out, we find the 'terms and ideas which will become part of the conceptual hardware of rationalism';[3] Fielding not only shows himself familiar with them, he takes full possession of them in the imaginative world of his novel. And the reader, whose role in that world is so important, is in a position to possess them in the same way.

It may seem, in fact, that it is only in this way and not through the rendering of character and behaviour that such a meaning is established. Though Tom's moral sense certainly becomes more urgent as the story unfolds, yet his conduct with Lady Bellaston, for instance, calls for more self-reproach than he can command, and its moral

1 See B. H. Baumrin, the New Introduction to Selby-Bigge, *British Moralists*, Dover, 1964, pp. x et seq.
2 *De Legibus Naturae* (1672), chapter 2, section 12, cited in Selby-Bigge, *British Moralists*, p. xxiii.
3 ibid., p. xxiv.

implications remain unresolved. Yet Fielding does drive the narrative to a conclusion where Tom comes face to face with conscience. However lightly, Fielding at last indicates that the book has a religious dimension. Sophia demands of Tom this kind of awareness: ' "Sincere repentance, Mr Jones," answered she, "will obtain the pardon of a sinner, but it is from one who is a perfect judge of that sincerity" ' (book 18, chapter 12). After what we have seen of Fielding's sustained attention to the question of judgement, this ultimate appeal does not seem forced. It provides a way of estimating Allworthy's Shaftes-buryan benevolence, and it anchors Tom's conduct firmly to the tougher principles of conscience: 'conscience naturally and always of course goes on to anticipate a higher and more effectual sentence, which shall hereafter second and affirm its own.'[1]

Yet after all it is by no means because he is morally impeccable that Tom is to be set against Allworthy. Fielding needs someone who can do wrong in order to bring out the hollowness of Allworthy's rectitude. A man who cannot act badly has no business to be judging others. It is in fact Tom, his own affairs tangled and squalid, who is able to persuade Nightingale to do what is right. It seems absurd that he should now 'preach', just as earlier Allworthy had read him 'a very severe lecture on chastity'. Nightingale is ready to scoff: 'Thou wilt make an admirable parson' (book 14, chapter 4). But it is because Tom is what he is that he can reply with authority and force: ' "Lookee, Mr Nightingale," said Jones, "I am no canting hypocrite, nor do I pretend to the gift of chastity, more than my neighbours. I have been guilty with women, I own it; but am not conscious that I have ever injured any – nor would I, to procure pleasure to myself, be knowingly the cause of misery to any human being." ' Not even, we are sure, to procure the pleasure of being in the right.

'Judge not, that ye be not judged': the injunction is often in Fielding's mind. *Tom Jones* shows, though, that we cannot choose not to judge. Nor can we avoid being judged, however 'prudent' our lives. But we can and should learn to judge with knowledge, that is with full experience and full sympathy; above all we have to learn how to forgive. The last thing to learn is that all this is part of a great

1 Butler, op. cit., ii, p. 59.

comedy: if Fielding anywhere sets out his intentions in the book it is in his invocation to his genius, the genius of comedy:

Teach me, which to thee is no difficult task, to know mankind better than they know themselves. Remove that mist which dims the intellects of mortals, and causes them to adore men for their art, or to detest them for their cunning in deceiving others, when they are, in reality, the objects only of ridicule, for deceiving themselves ... fill my pages with humour; 'till mankind learn the good-nature to laugh only at the follies of others, and the humility to grieve at their own (book 13, chapter 1). (114-32)

Glenn W. Hatfield

from *Henry Fielding and the Language of Irony*   1968

Mrs Western, in *Tom Jones*, is associated throughout the novel with the language of politics. 'Parliamentary language has been used without doors,' wrote Richard Cambridge in an essay on 'Fashionable and Court Phrases' in the *World* five years after the publication of *Tom Jones*. 'Our country squires made treaties about their game, and ladies negotiated a meeting of their lap-dogs.'[1] Aunt Western is a perfect example. She manages Sophia's affairs like a cynical diplomat, reading her lectures on 'matrimonial politics' (book 16, chapter 7), persuading the squire that his daughter should not 'be treated with such arbitrary power,' and demanding his 'full ratification of all the concessions stipulated' since he is himself clearly 'not qualified for these negotiations. All your whole scheme of politics is wrong' (book 16, chapter 4). He accuses her of speaking a 'Hanoverian linguo' which he cannot understand, but he recognizes her claim to superior political skill and soon 'a league was struck (to borrow a phrase from the lady) between the contending parties' (book 15,

1 Quoted by William Matthews, 'Polite Speech in the Eighteenth Century', *English*, vol. 1, 1937, p. 502. I am indebted to Robert M. Wallace, 'Henry Fielding's Narrative Method', University of North Carolina doctoral thesis, 1945, p. 408, for pointing out the relevance of this passage to the speech of Mrs Western.

chapter 6). But Mrs Western's affectation of 'parliamentary language' is more than just a comic 'humour.' It is symptomatic of the extent to which the political corruption of words has infected the language at large and rendered it suspect. When Squire Western tells her that Allworthy, despite the obvious advantage to both families, may disapprove of the proposed match between Sophia and Blifil because 'money hath no effect o' un,' Mrs Western replies, 'Brother, . . . your politics astonish me. Are you really to be imposed on by professions? Do you think Mr Allworthy hath more contempt for money than other men because he professes more? Such credulity would better become one of us weak women, than that wise sex which Heaven hath formed for politicians. Indeed, brother, you would make a fine plenipo to negotiate with the French. They would soon persuade you that they take towns out of mere defensive principles' (book 6, chapter 2). The 'Use of Speech' has been corrupted indeed when even an Allworthy cannot speak without suspicion of insincerity and equivocation.
(92–3)

Amelia

Robert Alter

'Fielding's Problem Novel', *Fielding and the Nature of the Novel*, chapter 5 1968

Fielding's last work of fiction can be thought of as a problem novel in much the same way that the troubled comedies of Shakespeare's middle period are often regarded as problem plays. One gets a disconcerting sense that the tone of the writing is not always fully under the writer's control, and the whole fiction threatens at times to slip down between the two literary stools on which it is precariously perched. John Coolidge is surely right in attributing much of the artistic uncertainty of *Amelia* to a vacillation between the old manner of *Tom Jones* and a new novelistic manner toward which Fielding was groping with only an intuitive sense of direction.[1] I do not think, though, that all the peculiar ambiguities of *Amelia* can be explained through that formula, and it seems to me important to get a clear notion at the outset of precisely what Fielding meant to accomplish in his last novel.

Knowledge of the literary model Fielding had in mind is helpful in this case, not because it can really serve as a guide to reading *Amelia*, but because it suggests the tenor of Fielding's intentions. Fielding himself, in the *Covent-Garden Journal* for 28 January 1752, called attention to his use of Virgil as the 'noble model' for his novel, a connection which he trusted 'the candid and learned reader' would be able to see on his own. It is clear that *Amelia* is patterned after the *Aeneid* in a much more intricate and ambitious way than *Tom Jones* and *Joseph Andrews* can be said to be modeled on the *Odyssey*, to which both these novels may be broadly referred as comic epics of the arduous voyage home. Fielding in fact takes some pains to remind us of the presence of Virgil's epic within *Amelia*: his novel is amply

1 'Fielding and "Conservation of Character"', *Modern Philology*, vol. 57, 1960, pp. 245–59.

sprinkled with quotations from the Latin and Greek poets, often un-translated, and Virgil, apparently the favorite poet of the learned Mrs Bennet, is the most frequently quoted or alluded to. George Sherburn first made the observation that *Amelia* includes some paral-lels to the *Aeneid* of veritably Joycean ingenuity. Thus, in the opening section, Booth is cast into Newgate by chance just as Aeneas at the beginning of Virgil's poem is tossed by fate into Dido's palace. After recounting in prison to Miss Matthews – in the manner of Aeneas to Dido – all that has befallen him in the past seven years, Booth spends a week of bittersweet adulterous pleasure with her in her cell, just as Dido and Aeneas consummate their passion in a Carthaginian cave and pass a brief winter of furtive love together. Sherburn is cautious and tactful in suggesting an anticipation in *Amelia* of the technique Joyce would later make famous; two more recent critics have trampled tact and caution underfoot in running to ground all conceivable parallels to Virgil in Fielding's novel.[1] I tend to doubt whether Fielding actually attempted to sustain the elaborate-ness of the connection between Booth's story and Aeneas' after the first three books. In any case, the interesting critical question here is not the deciphering of a Virgilian code in Fielding's novel but the problem of why he chose to use an epic model at all in this way, and why the *Aeneid* in particular.

Although Fielding's adaptation of the classic epic is by no means so ambitious as Joyce's, his invention of the technique is a response to an aesthetic challenge which he envisages basically in the same way as Joyce. The novel has often been described, with more portentousness than precision, as the epic of modern life, or of bourgeois society, though it is clear that in any responsible use of the term epic this is simply not true for most novels. The juxtaposition of novel and epic, however, does point toward a fundamental difficulty for the novel as a genre. The subject of the novel, by and large, is banality itself, and so the task that confronts the novelist is to redeem banality through art. How does a writer take that which is so familiar as to be cliché,

1 See George Sherburn, 'Fielding's *Amelia*: An Interpretation', *ELH*, vol. 3, 1936, pp. 3–4; and compare L. H. Powers, 'The Influence of the *Aeneid* on Fielding's *Amelia*', *Modern Language Notes*, vol. 71, 1956, pp. 330–36 and Maurice Johnson, *Fielding's Art of Fiction*, University of Pennsylvania Press, 1961, pp. 139–56.

which reeks of the sordid tedium and triviality of everyday life, and by representing it in art stir the imagination and speak to the condition of many men for all time? One rather special strategy for coping with this difficulty has been the serious parody of traditional myth. Joyce gives larger significance to his down-at-the-heels advertising agent whose life is a patchwork of tawdry daydreams and pathetic frustrations by inviting us to see him as a modern Ulysses, a resilient, resourceful wanderer in search of a son, an exile looking for home. Similarly, Fielding tries to make the muddled failures of a half-pay captain, cheating on his wife and running into debt through weakness and naïveté, seem more important by suggesting analogies between the moral role Booth must play and that of Virgil's Aeneas.

This difficulty with which the novelist, in contrast to the epic poet, is faced might also be stated in terms of the relationship between public and private experience. The sense of magnitude communicated by the epic derives in part from the fact that the epic generally deals with significant collective events, and its heroes, however sharply individual, are collective heroes: the fate of nations, and cultures, hangs upon the delicate and terrible balance of the epic hero's sword, and that is surely one reason why we feel that something vastly important is transpiring through the action of the epic. The characteristic subjects of the novel, on the other hand, have no wider public significance than those depressingly repetitious notations in the back pages of a daily newspaper – the bankruptcy of a respectable businessman, a wedding between a local clergyman and a genteel young lady, the suicide of a provincial doctor's wife. The greatest novelists have generally found ways of using such familiar private events as seismographs which are capable of registering the most subtle tremors running through the whole social structure and the most critical pressures exerted by the historical moment. An early and striking example of this kind of achievement is the fiction of Jane Austen: her world, which consists of daughters of the landed gentry looking for suitable husbands, is notoriously circumscribed, but her perception of the definition of character and values by social forces is so fine that the little world beautifully catches the significant reverberations of the larger world to which it belongs.

It is clear that Fielding did not possess the kind of delicate apparatus of observation that could enable him to present a subtle interplay of social forces in fictional relationships. Richardson perhaps comes closer to it, though it is not really an excellence one finds in eighteenth-century novelists, whether in England or in France. Fielding's characters, on the whole, are either bizarrely, and delightfully, idiosyncratic, or broadly representative, with only occasional glimpses of the kind of character whose closely observed individuality reveals the social matrix of individual experience. For this reason, a panoramic structure, instead of a tight involvement of personalities at close quarters, is entirely appropriate for his two comic novels. In *Amelia*, however, he sought to make the concerns of the novel at once more private and more public than they had been in either *Tom Jones* or *Joseph Andrews*, and this is finally, I think, the reason for his introducing the *Aeneid* into the story of the domestic difficulties of one William Booth. In the very first sentence of his Dedication, Fielding announces that it is his purpose 'to expose some of the most glaring evils, as well public as private, which at present infest this country', and one of the major problems of his novel is the technical means of relating public to private experience. The general allusion to the *Aeneid* reflects Fielding's desire to establish this connection, though it does not really solve his artistic difficulties for him.

Fielding's awareness of the special challenge of *Amelia*, and the special relevance of the epic to that challenge, is nicely expressed in the flat declaration with which he begins the novel: 'The various accidents which befell a very worthy couple after their uniting in the state of matrimony will be the subject of the following history.' Fielding, as always, is highly conscious of his role as pioneer: with the partial and uncomfortably didactic exception of the continuation of *Pamela*, no novel as yet had attempted to deal with what happens to two people *after* they unite in the state of matrimony, when, in place of the adventures or tensions of courtship, they must bear the heavy and multifarious responsibilities of making a life together. The first sentence of *Amelia* is also the *arma virumque*, the epic proposition of the novel, as George Sherburn observes in his comment on Virgilian allusions. The vicissitudes of this particular young couple are announced at the outset as a subject of the broadest relevance and the gravest moral dignity; and so the narrator immediately goes on to implicate the history of the Booths in the activity of Fortune, just as Aeneas in the first lines of Virgil's poem is seen driven from the shores of Troy by a grand and inexorable *fatum*. Fortune is of course also the subject of much teasing banter by the ostentatiously manipulative narrator of *Tom Jones*, but in *Amelia*, from the very beginning, it is instead seriously discussed, as an idea that shapes men's lives, and part of the philosophical argument of the novel is to refute the pagan concept of Fortune through the action and dialogue.

Amelia is Fielding's one extended attempt to create that figure with which so many Renaissance writers struggled unsuccessfully – the Christian hero. Tom Jones is not, in any clearly indispensable way, Christian in such heroism as he possesses, and Parson Adams is not really a hero, but Booth is a man of heroic qualities, compromised by bad judgement and a dangerous malleability, who must learn as a husband and father to live a Christian life in a pagan world. In this central respect, the *Aeneid* is most relevant as a model, for it is the great epic of duty, the very epic, in fact, sometimes thought of by Christian tradition itself as a sort of proto-Christian poem. Both Aeneas and Booth are soldiers by calling, men who have to perform duties, submit to a rigorous discipline; and the quality of *pietas* – reverent loyalty, implicit obedience to the gods as they work out their purpose in human lives – associated with Aeneas involves a series of painful renunciations which enable him to become a perfect instrument for the divine plan in history. Fielding, to be sure, is not concerned in his novel with the larger reaches of history, but he does want to draw attention to the effect of providential design in individual lives, and his hero, whom we first see mouthing arrant deism and then in dalliance with a modern-day Dido, must learn to renounce his 'unRoman' weakness of conviction – his belief in an insuperable Ruling Passion which provides him an excuse for moral flaccidity – in order to assume the responsibilities of his destiny as the worthy mate of the true Christian wife, Amelia. Booth's role as Christian soldier, incidentally, explains the attention given in the novel to the polemic against dueling – a pagan conception of honor, or love and honor, must be exorcised before an authentically Christian hero can come into being.

This identification between a pristine Roman society and pristine Christianity is characteristically Augustan. As in the weightiest of Augustan satire – notably Swift and the later Pope – the atmosphere of the novel is filled with darkening shadows, is suffused with a sense that the true Roman, or Christian, values have slipped away in a process of disastrous cultural and moral decline. The point is made explicit in an exchange between Dr Harrison and the lord whose aid he futilely attempts to enlist to get Booth a commission:

'Indeed, doctor,' cries the lord, 'all these notions are obsolete and long since exploded. To apply maxims of government drawn from the Greek and Roman histories to this nation is absurd and impossible. But, if you will have Roman examples, fetch them from those times of the republic that were most like our own. Do you not know, doctor, that this as corrupt a nation as ever existed under the sun? And would you think of governing such a people by the strict principles of honesty and morality?'

'If it be so corrupt,' said the doctor, 'I think it is high time to amend it: or else it is easy to foresee that Roman and British liberty will have the same fate; for corruption in the body politic as naturally tends to dissolution as in the natural body' (book 11, chapter 2).

Rome after the period of high achievement of the empire is clearly associated in the novel with England after the abandonment of the moral imperatives of Christianity. As Dr Harrison observes else-where (book 9, chapter 5), in a phrase reminiscent of *Joseph Andrews*, 'I no more esteem this nation to be . . . a Christian society . . . than I do any part of Turkey.' But the treatment of the Christian–pagan opposition is qualitatively different in the two novels. In *Joseph Andrews*, the Christianity of the protagonists is a given thing, un-affected – indeed, unalterable – by experience. In *Amelia* Fielding attempts to show how an unchristian society prevents a man from being a Christian, and how he may manage to behave as a Christian nevertheless. To put this difference in terms of a moral psychology, Fielding in the earlier novels had presented human nature in what might almost be thought of as a Manichean split, humanity con-genitally divided into children of light and children of darkness, men of Good Heart and Mean Spirit, with, however, some interesting cases in between. In *Amelia*, on the other hand, the old dichotomy of good and bad nature is partly replaced by another one of human nature and society. Even a scheming lecher like Colonel James, Dr

Harrison suggests in the passage just quoted, could have been a good man had he lived in a Christian society. 'Bad education,' Harrison argues, 'bad habits, and bad customs, debauch our nature, and drive it headlong . . . into vice. The governors of the world, and I am afraid the priesthood, are answerable for the badness of it.'

Amelia, then, is among other things an embryonic novel of social protest. In the earlier novels, corruption is a predictable consequence of human nature which tends to center in the city, and which is known, condemned, and at last avoided, more or less, by a prudent retreat to the country. One can guess that Fielding's deep involvement in his work as police magistrate had led him, by the time he wrote *Amelia*, to a new concern for the ways in which corruption was endemic to a particular social, political, and legal system. It is the cold, unyielding, arbitrary force of the corrupt system that one feels in *Amelia* at many of the novel's most persuasive moments. Thus the action begins with the nocturnal arraignment of Booth by Justice Thrasher, a figure who in his rapacious greed, savage arbitrariness and arrogant ignorance of the law, makes the obtuse justices of the peace in *Joseph Andrews* and *Tom Jones* look like paragons of judiciary wisdom and rectitude. Shortly after Booth is brought into Newgate, the narrator devotes an entire chapter (book 1, chapter 4) to a darkly satiric panorama of victims of the law: in a manner and mood that look forward to the mature Dickens, we see how the most innocent individuals are ruthlessly crushed by an insane system while the worst scoundrels continue to commit their crimes with impunity.

The terrible wrongness of the system is most painfully apparent in the predicament of Booth. The power to arrest debtors is used against him by the rich would-be seducers of his wife simply to clear him out of the conjugal bed. No matter how many avenues of influence he explores, his efforts to obtain a commission in the army are hopeless; and while he, an experienced officer of proved valor, starves with his family on half-pay, footmen and noblemen's pimps are appointed to positions of command, and spoiled boys, with the first fuzz of puberty on their cheeks, are advanced to captaincies. It is no wonder that the crowd breaking into the bailiff's house at the end of the novel is compared to the ocean inundating the land when the dikes give way in Holland: although Fielding the conservative would have been shocked at any drawing of revolutionary inferences from his work, we at times get a sense in the novel of a system so utterly corrupt that nothing will do for it but to sweep it away in a great cataclysm.

Fielding had sought to expose vice in his earlier novels but he had never before attempted actually to indict the social system. He came closest to it in *Jonathan Wild*, but his strategy of attack there was that of formal satire, through a generalizing rhetorical design and highly schematized narrative pattern. In *Amelia*, on the other hand, he tries to carry out the indictment through novelistic means, showing how the lives of particularized, credible individuals are entangled in the insidious mesh of a pervasively venal social order. His basic problem, then, in his last work of fiction is how to go about doing something new for him and, really, new for the novel as a genre. The procedures he developed in his two previous novels could help him in some ways to deal with his problem, but they could also lead him astray, since much of his technique of comic fiction was wholly inappropriate for a novel more seriously engaged in exposing the institutionalized malfunctions of contemporary life.

The use of formal theme, elaborated through reiteration and variation, which we saw in the comic novels, does lend a strength of assertion and a breadth of social perspective to the moral argument of *Amelia*. The central theme of marriage is firmly announced in the first of the two epigraphs, and the entire novel can be seen as a panorama of unions, marital and extramarital, good and bad, though mostly the latter. Marriage is conceived as the basic institution of both private life and Christian society – making a good home takes on the kind of importance in this novel that the founding of the empire is given in Virgil's poem – so that the prevalent neglect, violation, and loveless manipulation of marriage become measures of the failure of Christian values in society at large.

The first extended narrative in the novel is concerned with an illicit union, Miss Matthews' story of her ill-considered liaison with the unscrupulous Hebbers. This is followed by Booth's account of his true love match with Amelia, which ironically ends up being the prelude to his week-long adulterous connection with Miss Matthews. After Booth is freed from prison, we have an opportunity to see the mutual loyalty and affection of his marriage with Amelia, while over against the Booths are set the Jameses, a Fashionable Couple out of the pages of Restoration comedy, each spouse heartily despising the other and at least one of them always on the lookout for amorous intrigues. Colonel James's description of a tolerable wife rings with echoes of the sundry Dorimants and Rhodophils and Fainalls of the Restoration stage, those jaded hedonistic spokesmen of a thoroughly unChristian society: 'With the spirit of a tigress I would have her be a prude, a scold, a scholar, a critic, a wit, a politician, and a jacobite; and then, perhaps, eternal opposition would keep up our spirits; and, wishing one another daily at the devil, we should make a shift to drag on a damnable state of life, without much spleen or vapors' (book 5, chapter 9). The poetic justice administered to Colonel James at the end of the novel is nicely adjusted to his contemptuous abuse of the married state: divorced at last from his wife, he takes Miss Matthews into keeping and comes to dote on her, while she, grown fat and ugly, uses him ruthlessly as a kind of servile retainer.

Another military couple, the Trents, who appear late in the novel, are a more tawdry, visibly degraded version of the Jameses. Their initial passion for each other has quickly cooled, and Trent then establishes himself in the world by selling his entirely amenable wife to the Noble Lord and afterward becoming chief procurer for that lecherous gentleman. In contrast to these corrupt unions, the first and second marriages of Mrs Bennet are models of faithful affection, though more imperfect than the marriage of Amelia and Booth: the happiness of her first union is poisoned by her own weakness in succumbing to the scheming peer, and her subsequent marriage with Atkinson is somewhat flawed by the wife's sense of intellectual superiority to the husband. Finally, hovering above all these married figures as the spirit of anti-matrimony in the novel is the shadowy presence of the Noble Lord. A sinister descendant of the ubiquitous Horners of Restoration comedy, his main object in life is seducing virtuous wives, and his notion of a relationship with a woman is to use her body for a night, or at best for a week or two.

It should be noted that in all this Fielding is moving toward a new kind of integration of narrative and thematic materials, a first anticipation of the masterful interlocking of separate lives through shared situation that gives *Middlemarch* such remarkable structural coherence. The accounts of the respective unions of Miss Matthews and Hebbers, of the Booths, the Jameses, the Bennets, the Trents, are all narrative regressions, but they all relate to the principal thematic concern of the novel more directly than the interpolated tales of *Joseph Andrews* and *Tom Jones*, and they are connected with each other bodily, as it were, not just thematically. The body that does most of the connecting is the Noble Lord's: Fielding's attempt to make him work as a figure at once peripheral and absolutely central to the major action is an interesting, though not altogether successful, technical experiment.

The key to the anomalous status of this promiscuous peer is, I think, his peculiar anonymity. We normally expect a novelist to give individual names to his personages because we look in the novel not for a summary or abstraction of experience but for a persuasive recreation of the world as we know it, in all its stubborn and prickly particularity. That is why *Moll Flanders*, with its cast of nameless figures whose identity is exhausted in the role they play *vis à vis* Moll, is only rudimentarily a novel. Some critics have argued that the distinctive approach of the novel to fictional character is reflected in its choice of names that could have been lifted – as in fact they sometimes are – straight out of the city directory. This is partly true and partly misleading. Fielding's own practice in *Joseph Andrews* and *Tom Jones* is to assign obviously symbolic names to many of his characters, and a great many novelists, from Dickens and Dostoyevsky to Joyce and Nabokov, have adopted the same method, though usually with a greater attempt at camouflage. Fielding uses symbolic names in his first two novels in order to hold his characters at a comic distance, as elements of a conscious artifice, and because each of the characters is conceived as a particular embodiment of some general moral (or social) role, posture, value. In *Amelia*, on the other hand, the writer exhibits a new empiric openness in imagining his characters, and so all of them, with the exception of Justice Thrasher and Bailiff Bondum, who are the subjects of incidental satirical vignettes, are given quite neutral, realistic names – Booth, Matthews, James, Robinson, Harrison, Trent, Ellison, and so forth. The moral identity of these characters is, to begin with, uncertain, and they will be whatever we can make of them by closely following their words and deeds.

The Noble Lord, however, is left without a name, for Fielding means him to be a vague and generalized presence, almost always kept offstage, the ubiquitous spirit of corruption of a degenerate aristocracy, manipulating the lives of the weak through a chain of underlings and procurers, ready to carry out that nasty little piece of business wherever an innocent woman in England leaves herself vulnerable. The trouble is that a figure so conceived scarcely belongs in the fictional world of this novel. For the general tendency of *Amelia*, however intermittently pursued, is toward a more psychologically individual realization of character, while the Noble Lord is a psychological vacuity of a sort one scarcely finds in either *Joseph Andrews* or *Tom Jones*. He owes something, perhaps, to the satirically generalized figures of *Jonathan Wild*, the schematically designed personages of a mode of fiction alien to that of *Amelia*. Where we might hope for a representative individual who could dramatize the complexities of an obsessional concern with the sexual exploitation of innocence, we get instead a mysterious absence which looks at times almost comical, and that is surely a serious weakness in the novel.

In any case, the Noble Lord serves as the exemplar of that way of life in which adultery is the chief activity, and adultery itself is a kind of paradigm of all that is wrong in a society where Christian values have been discarded. 'It includes in it,' Dr Harrison writes of adultery in the letter to Colonel James which is the object of such ridicule at the masquerade, 'almost every injury and every mischief which one man can do to, or can bring upon, another' (book 10, chapter 2). Adultery, that is to say, is the perfect expression of a ruthlessly egoistic hedonism, a cynically exploitative, utterly disengaged relationship to humanity which makes a man willing to inflict all kinds of suffering on others for the sake of his own momentary gratification. In *Tom Jones* all the sexual liaisons, with the single exception of Mrs Fitzgerald's, are merely promiscuous, not adulterous, for what 'prudence' mainly implies in that novel is an individual's moral responsibilities to himself. In *Amelia*, on the other hand, Fielding is more deeply concerned with the individual's responsibilities to others and to society, and with society's responsibilities to the individual, and so he makes almost all the illicit unions in the novel adulterous. Adultery, it is clear, is a kind of sexual indulgence that often impinges painfully on the lives of others, on the very institution of the family; and a general commitment to the relentless pursuit of adulterous pleasures serves as an apt symbol for a morally irresponsible social system. Fielding chose his subject, then, with a sound sense of strategic appropriateness, but because he had no previous experience or direct models in writing a novel of social indictment, he tends to waver in his treatment of the subject between novelistic and unfortunately homiletic methods.

On the novelistic side, he takes up the familiar theme of mask and disguise from *Tom Jones* and makes it reverberate with a new amplitude through the world of *Amelia*, where a whole society is dedicated to keeping up false appearances and using them to gain illegitimate ends. At the very beginning of the action (book 1, chapter 2), we are told of Justice Thrasher, the symbolic representative of a corrupt system, that he had 'too great an honor for truth to suspect that she ever appeared in sordid apparel'. Though this reverence for the outward forms of wealth – 'virtue' construed as power – is shared by many characters in both *Joseph Andrews* and *Tom Jones*, it immediately has graver implications here because Thrasher's vital professional responsibility is to discriminate truth from falsehood, and because he also has the power, as we see at once, to act swiftly and arbitrarily on his venal impulses. The sundry seducers of innocence in the novel are all skilled in putting on virtuous appearances: Dr Harrison is a little staggered that Colonel James could hide such villainy 'under the appearance of so much virtue' (book 9, chapter 5), and the narrator comments to the same effect on 'that noble art' which enables the colonel to look delighted at an unexpected, and dismaying, meeting with Amelia's husband: 'By this [art], men are enabled to dress out their countenances as much at their own pleasure as they do their bodies, and to put on friendship with as much ease as they can a laced coat' (book 9, chapter 2). In the light of such observations, we can see why the action of the novel begins on April Fool's Day, a pointedly appropriate juncture at which to introduce us to a world of deceivers and contrived illusions.

It is almost inevitable that the central rite of such a society should be the masquerade. Fielding here alludes to literary tradition as well as to social practice: the significance of the masquerade in *Amelia* looks back to the moral meaning of the masquerade in Restoration comedy – most appositely, in Dryden's *Marriage à la Mode* – where assuming the mask is an invitation to saturnalian release, a means not merely of deception but of escape from the responsibilities of personality. At the masquerade, at least as it appears in Restoration literature and as it is used in this novel, hungry sexual egos go stalking after ready partners, everyone hiding behind a glittering facade that protects him from involvement, allows him to forget in a relationship between masks and bodies the commitments of relationships between persons, the limitations and obligations imposed by family and society in ordinary maskless life. It is therefore symbolically right that the Noble Lord should make his conquest of Mrs Bennet's virtue upon returning with her from a masquerade, and that he should attempt to do the same favor for Amelia by inviting her to another masked ball. The spectacle of a crowd of insolent young rakes at the masquerade making a mockery of Dr Harrison's sermon-letter on adultery nicely dramatizes the central opposition of the novel – a true Christianity preached with desperate insistence to an unheeding pagan world of brazen hearts and masked faces.

One of Fielding's most significant innovations in *Amelia*, though he fails to carry it out consistently, is his translation of this sense of a masked humanity into a new method of characterization. The pervasive feeling in *Tom Jones* that Nature will eventually peep out from even the most elaborate disguise is attenuated in *Amelia*: a principal reason for the drastic curtailment of authorial intervention in the latter novel is that the narrator does not want to suggest he holds Nature, or that part of it which relates to his personages, within the secure round of his cunningly cupped hands, to be revealed when he sees fit. John Coolidge has aptly described the new mode of presenting character which begins to emerge in *Amelia*: 'People come into the story in the same way that people come into our lives. ... Our knowledge of a person's character is always provisory, pending further discovery. A new word or act may bring a new revelation, causing a shift in our interpretation and evaluation of a person's character.'[1] This is, perhaps, more a description of the unrealized paradigm toward which Fielding was moving than of his actual practice throughout the novel, for the characterization, even in the more interesting of the major personages, seems to wobble between the old 'high priori way' of the two comic novels and the new method of progressive discovery.

Although the new technique is applied unevenly, it does im-

1 Coolidge, op. cit., p. 250.

plicate the reader directly in the experience of a world where any smiling face may turn out to be a mask, where, indeed, the face behind the mask may sometimes prove to be but another mask. Though the writer seems to settle in the end for a simple view of his own characters, his method of presentation makes us alive to the essential trickiness – the elusiveness as well as the duplicity – of human nature. Thus Colonel James at first really seems to be the most generous and loyal of friends, but we gradually learn that the gold he showers on Booth is intended to buy his way to Amelia's bed. Nevertheless, there is a teasing uncertainty in James's transition from stalwart friend to dastardly villain. On the evidence of the later chapters, I would assume that Fielding finally conceived him as he had conceived Blifil – a thorough scoundrel to be unmasked in the end. The initial impression, however, of James as a sincere benefactor is strong enough not to be easily dissipated. Perhaps Fielding meant us to conclude that the Colonel's initial generosity to Booth was solely the result of his designs on Amelia, but that is not altogether clear: the inferential method of presenting character leaves us room to wonder whether a man may not, after all, be an admirable, honestly disinterested friend, until he takes too close a look at the fair figure of his friend's wife and so converts his friendship into a contemptible instrumentality. As with Miss Matthews, Mrs Atkinson, Mrs Ellison, even Mrs James, the characterization of the colonel would appear to point toward complexities and ambiguities which Fielding himself was not quite ready to confront or follow out.[1]

Fielding's growing concern, then, with the opacities of human nature and with the threatening moral murkiness of contemporary society is in some ways effectively translated into the method of elaborating theme and presenting character. As for the authorial voice of *Amelia*, because its more shrilly hortatory tones are likely to linger uncomfortably in the ear of the imagination, it needs to be stressed that Fielding also succeeds in working out in some passages of the novel a new, trenchant kind of irony, skillfully adjusted to the new earnestness of moral and social criticism. The narrator stays half-hidden in the wings much of the time, but his occasional appearances

1 Morris Golden makes a related observation about the new treatment of character in *Amelia*, and about its sporadic application to both the Jameses, in *Fielding's Moral Psychology*, University of Massachusetts Press, 1966, pp. 70–71.

before the proscenium arch, in a manner quite different from that of *Tom Jones*, are revealing. At the end of a chapter, for example, in which we see one of the first great instances of the munificence of Colonel James to Booth, the narrator steps forward, ostensibly to point the moral:

Here, reader, give me leave to stop a minute, to lament that so few are to be found of this benign disposition; that, while wantonness, vanity, avarice, and ambition are every day rioting and triumphing in the follies and weakness, the ruin and desolation of mankind, scarce one man in a thousand is capable of tasting the happiness of others. Nay, give me leave to wonder that pride, which is constantly struggling, and often imposing on itself, to gain some little pre-eminence, should seldom hint to us the only certain as well as laudable way of setting ourselves above another man, and that is, by becoming his benefactor (book 4, chapter 4).

This is shrewd irony, but to rather a different purpose than that of the comic novels. The plea for altruism and the condemnation of a viciously selfish society in the first sentence are quite serious, yet they also provide a false lead to draw us into the ironic trap of the sentence that follows. As we begin to nod in complacent assent – or boredom – to the proper moral cadences of the sermonic narrator, he quickly concedes that overweening pride is the universal spring of action, and, contrary to all Christian doctrine on charity, he invites us to give unto others – so that we may affirm our own towering superiority to them. There is no certain indication that this egotistic motive is meant to apply to the beneficence of Colonel James, of whom we were told just a moment earlier that 'generous he really was to the highest degree', but I think the ambiguity is intentional. We have not yet been given any hint of the colonel's interest in Amelia: when we eventually learn of that, the serious and ironic defense of generosity here is compounded by a graver doubt, a further possibility of irony.

In *Tom Jones*, the doubleness of the irony is an invitation to suspend judgement, or delicately balance contradictory claims, to step back from humanity and survey it in the round, in all the perplexities and piquant or pathetic self-delusions of its motives. The strategies of *Amelia*, on the other hand, generally lead us toward a closer involvement in the moral predicaments of the novel, and, to a lesser degree, in the lives of the characters. The irony in the passage we have been considering is contrived to snap shut on the reader at the end, to produce not bemused contemplation but an unsettling confrontation, forcing us to face up to the terribly compromised nature of all men's motives, our own included.

The presence of this kind of authorial irony in *Amelia* suggests that it would have been possible for Fielding to have retained a successfully subdued version of his self-conscious narrator while making his readers confront the moral action with a new kind of troubled personal involvement. His desire, however, to conduct an urgent moral argument through his novel leads him in many instances to adopt what I have referred to as homiletic procedures. In the prefatory sections of his two comic novels, he had spoken about using fiction as a means of offering to the reader a variety of moral exempla, but fortunately he never carried out that promise with the singleness of purpose we encounter at some points in *Amelia*. Thus, in book 4, chapter 3, in the first of a series of moral tableaux of domestic life, Booth, ridden with debts and the guilty consciousness of his recent adultery, is given new testimony of Amelia's loving confidence in him, even amidst the hardships of poverty, and he prostrates himself at her feet. At this juncture, the narrator raises his didactic pointer to the two posed figures, and comments: 'Such is ever the fortitude of perfect innocence, and such the depression of guilt in minds not utterly abandoned.' One does not want to begrudge Amelia her virtue, but the explicit moralizing is uncomfortably insistent, and, throughout the novel, the contrast between husband and wife is often heavily overdrawn.

Action and dialogue as well as authorial comment are palpably contrived so that this contrast will stand out. We see Amelia depriving herself and her young ones of food, pawning her only valuable possessions, while Booth squanders fifty pounds at a time over the card table. When Booth, visited by Amelia at the bailiff's after his second arrest for debt, learns that she all along has known of – and forgiven – his affair with Miss Matthews, the narrator's underscoring of the all-too-obvious moral contrast is almost embarrassing: 'Amelia never shined forth to Booth in so amicable and great a light; nor did his own unworthiness ever appear to him so mean and contemptible as at this instant' (book 12, chapter 2).

To view the novel gastronomically, there are lumps of undigested didactic matter in *Amelia* that sometimes block the flow of fictional reality. It would seem that Fielding, anxious to show the cogency of a practical ethical doctrine, did not know quite how to get it all into novelistic terms. So it is that he incorporates into the novel formal debates on religious and philosophical questions, which are connected to the surrounding narrative solely by the ideas discussed. At the bailiff's, Booth encounters a gentleman (book 8, chapter 10) who is unnamed, uncharacterized, unrelated to the main action, whose only purpose is to engage Booth in a dialogue on stoic fortitude in adversity and the power of the Ruling Passion. The two debates (book 9, chapters 8 and 10) between Dr Harrison and the young clergyman – again, symptomatically, a character without a name – are static interruptions of the novel's progress, with none of the cunning counterpoint of interpolation and main narrative that one finds in *Joseph Andrews* and *Tom Jones*. While the tribulations of Amelia and Booth must patiently wait their turn for our attention, the good doctor and the young clergyman conduct a learned argument, matching quotations and the commentators thereon, about the proper Christian attitude toward one's enemies and the role of a clergyman in a society devoid of Christian values. The revelation at the end of the second debate that the young man's father has been merely feigning agreement with the doctor, out of worldly interest, is an attempt to relate satirically these disquisitions on moral theory to the novel's dramatized world of self-seeking hypocrisy. Both chapters, however, remain heavily expository, with only perfunctory attempts to sustain the novelistic life of realized personalities responding to one another.

Similarly, even in the less theoretical exchanges between the principal characters, speech is sometimes formalized and generalized in an unnatural way to point a moral. Booth is not content to tell his story to Miss Matthews but must call attention to what his story teaches: 'In this dreadful situation we were taught that no human condition should inspire men with absolute despair' (book 3, chapter 4); and Amelia at times sounds more like a moral essayist than a wife comforting her husband in distress: 'How many thousands abound in affluence whose fortunes are much lower than ours! for it is not from nature, but from education and habit, that our wants are chiefly derived' (book 4, chapter 3).

A small but most significant symptom of this whole didactic weakness in *Amelia* is the fact that at one point (book 9, chapter 1) the narrator turns to a particular segment of his audience, 'my young readers', before beginning a homiletic *excursus*. In *Tom Jones*, we recall, the assumed reader was an intelligent man of the world with whom the narrator could share sly hints, innuendos, cunning ironies, tempered judgements of moral acts. The reader at this point in *Amelia*, however, begins to look suspiciously like that bloodless figure with a mind as innocent and unsubstantial as a lily petal, the Young Person of Victorian literature, for whom so much bland and emptily self-righteous stuff was written. It is such 'young readers' who are the proper subject for moral instruction uncomplicated by any ironic awareness, as in the sermon in two paragraphs here on the unguessed perils of temptation in woman's beauty. Fortunately, such passages are not altogether typical: Fielding's sense of audience, so essential to the achievement of *Joseph Andrews* and *Tom Jones*, is simply uneven in this novel. At some points, he reflects a subtle consciousness of a sophisticated audience with serious moral concerns; sometimes, as here, he credits his readers with too little experience and sometimes, as we shall see, with too much.

The didacticism of *Amelia*, which results in exhortations to the reader from both narrator and personages, also has a damaging effect on some of the characterization, particularly in the two exemplary figures of the novel, Dr Harrison and Amelia. The dialectic irony which qualified the virtuous characters in the two comic novels is nowhere in evidence here; Fielding seems afraid to do anything that might undermine or mitigate the exemplariness of his models of virtue. In the case of Dr Harrison, the gap between the author's own promise and performance is instructive. Although we are told (book 9, chapter 5) that 'the doctor was one of the best companions in the world, and a vein of cheerfulness, good humour, and pleasantry, ran through his conversation, with which it was impossible to resist being pleased', there are scarcely two attempts in the whole novel to show us Harrison's good-humored jocularity, and one is hard put to think of a character in fiction whose supposed charm is easier to resist.

This is especially remarkable because Fielding, of all eighteenth-century novelists, surely had the ability to create an engagingly witty character; but he apparently was unwilling to relent for a moment from reminding us of Dr Harrison's grave role as Christian censor and image of the Good Pastor.

Amelia gives a little more promise of assuming real life as a character, in her frankly feminine awareness of her own attractiveness, and, occasionally, in her response to her husband, as, for example, when she is refreshingly resentful – of course within the proper limits of a virtuous wife's submission – to her husband's unexplained command that she not accept the ticket to the masquerade (book 4, chapter 6). More often, though, we see her frozen in the conventional poses of virtuous womanhood, a sort of modern version of the Worthy Wife of Proverbs xxxi – embracing her innocent young ones, waiting loyally long into the night for the return of her wayward husband, pleading before the great to save him from destruction. 'Art thou really human,' Booth exclaims in one of his fits of adulation, 'or art thou rather an angel in human form?' (book 10, chapter 6), and the reader may be tempted to answer the rhetorical question with an irony that Fielding never intended.

The conception of both the heroine and the central situation of *Amelia* is, finally, parabolic, and unlike the biblical symbolism in *Joseph Andrews* or the submerged hint of allegory in *Tom Jones* (Tom in search of Wisdom, Sophia, whose handmaiden is Honour), the parable is not entirely assimilated to the novel form. Dr Harrison at one point refers to Amelia in terms which transparently reveal the kind of symbolic function she is meant to serve: 'She hath a true Christian disposition. I may call her an Israelite indeed, in whom there is no guile' (book 9, chapter 8). His words echo those addressed by Jesus to Nathanael in John i 47, and the allusion to John suggests an interesting imaginative affinity, for of all the Gospels, John is the one that consistently converts physical facts into spiritual symbols, and the one in which the central figure of Jesus is most transcendently divine, least sympathetically human. If Fielding had attempted before to present an Israelite indeed, in whom there was no guile, in the person of Abraham Adams, he also had a novelist's keen awareness that it can be a grotesque liability to be without guile in an un-redeemed world of cheats and hypocrites. His spiritual gravity as parabolist, however, leads him to suppress such awareness in the characterization of Amelia.

John iconically translates the flesh-and-blood Jesus into the Lamb of God, and Amelia, the true Christian, the sacrificial wife, the vulnerable innocent, is also a lamb of sorts. Why, the narrator asks rhetorically, should a poor wretch like Booth, imprisoned through the machinations of Colonel James, be the object of the colonel's envy? 'Because this wretch was possessed of the affections of a poor little lamb, which all the vast flocks that were within the power and the reach of the colonel could not prevent that glutton's longing for' (book 8, chapter 8). The allusion, of course, is to the parable of the poor man's lamb used by Nathan the prophet in his condemnation of David, who arranged the death of Bathsheba's husband so that he could have her for himself (II Samuel xii). Actually, there are indications in the biblical story that Bathsheba was not quite so innocent or helpless as the lamb of Nathan's parable: she might have made a more interesting heroine for a novel than Amelia, who too often is merely a symbolic figure in a tale told to prod conscience, not a credible personality whose story can open the imagination to the multifarious and nuanced possibilities of humanity in a particular society.

There is, moreover, an element of contradiction or at least tension between the conception of the novel as moral parable and the novelist's aims of social criticism. Although Fielding is obviously aware in *Amelia* that many of the institutions of society are not what they should be, he ultimately sees the pervasive corruption which is his subject as a derivative of the moral life of individuals. The vagueness of this viewpoint is apparent in an exchange between Booth and Amelia at the very end of book 10. 'Compassion,' Booth argues, is 'the fellow-feeling only of men of the same rank and degree of life for one another, on account of the evils to which they themselves are liable.' Booth would appear to be echoing the Mandevillian doctrine of self-love as the universal motive, though his words raise a question – which Fielding, with his fundamentally conservative imagination, never confronts – as to whether some other kind of social order might be possible, where men would not be so utterly alienated from each other by rank and degree. Amelia, in any case, responds to her husband's account of the inhumanity of society with a well-meaning moralism, clearly speaking for Fielding as she repeats the maxim of

Terence's which she has heard from Dr Harrison: '*I am a man myself, and my heart is interested in whatever can befall the rest of mankind.* That is the sentiment of a good man, and whoever thinks otherwise is a bad one.' It is worth noting that Dr Harrison's paraphrase of the Latin introduces one distinctly un-Roman notion – the interested heart. The world would be better, Amelia suggests, if every man would just have a Good Heart, if people would be good and not bad. Because Fielding tends to slip into this kind of pious moral generality, he never fully engages the social aspects of his subject: there is a hiatus between the private and public concerns which were announced in the first sentence of the Dedication as the subject of the novel.

That hiatus is probably most conspicuous in the dénouement. The comic happy ending, in which interlopers are banished, lovers harmoniously united, and undreamt of estates made to tumble down out of heaven, is entirely appropriate in *Joseph Andrews* and *Tom Jones*, for both those novels are consciously selective artifices which implicitly assure us, by the providential presence of the artificer, that all things rightful will be finally bestowed upon all the right people. Fielding's attitude, moreover, toward the conventional ending is more slyly ironic than most readers give him credit for; he surely means to tip us the wink, one last time, when at the end of *Tom Jones* he hastily marries off his paragon of crude female lust, Molly Seagrim, to the timorous Partridge, and the energetically sensual Mrs Waters to that most spineless of clergymen, Parson Supple. In *Amelia*, on the other hand, Fielding uses the happy ending as his Victorian imitators did and as hostile critics have imagined he did in *Tom Jones* – to clap together some conventional happiness for his protagonists which does not necessarily follow from the logic of the novel itself. Plots constructed, or at least concluded, in this way are, to borrow Ford Madox Ford's vehement phrase, 'dangers to the body-politic', for they evade the responsibilities of the moral issues which the novelist himself has raised.

Booth's conversion, as has often been observed, is hardly credible because it comes so suddenly, without any psychological preparation: the metamorphosis of Booth the deist into Booth the Good Christian is a final reflection of that tendency in *Amelia* to moral schematism which we have been considering. More to our present purpose, the miraculous recovery of Amelia's estate seems like too easy a way out here because the whole novel has been concerned with the absolute failure of the social system to recognize merit, and the apparently irreversible trend of the whole crooked system is to crush all poor innocents like Booth. Since there is no happy solution to Booth's predicament within the system, Fielding invokes another schematism, converting Booth's pagan Fortune to Providence with the hero's own conversion, and so he ends up using Dr Harrison as a fairy godfather to waft the Booths with a magic wand away from the really hopeless snares and delusions of London to their own true home in the country.

To complete this account of the weaknesses in *Amelia*, one aspect of the novel must be mentioned which is not so much a matter of uncertain artistic purpose as of unfortunate intellectual fashion. The moral view that informs this novel, as we have seen, places the locus of mankind's redemption in men's hearts, the potential goodness of which becomes a first principle of faith, and rather too heavy a load is put upon that frail organ from a novelistic as well as a moral point of view. Fielding alerts us at once, in the third paragraph of the Dedication, to the fact that this novel is directed to a special kind of reader: 'The good-natured reader, if his heart should be here affected, will be inclined to pardon many faults for the pleasure he will receive from a tender sensation.' Now, the 'sagacious reader' of *Tom Jones* was also credited with good nature and expected to be moved by scenes of virtue, but the conjunction here of heart, pleasure, and tender sensations is reaching toward a kind of experience alien to the comic spirit of Fielding's two previous novels. Much eighteenth-century literature, even that which is usually thought of as coolly intellectual, contains an undercurrent of craving for intense and sublime sensation: by the sixties and seventies, the undercurrent had become a mainstream in the literary vogue now generally referred to as the cult of sensibility. Fielding had already given intimations of his interest in effects of sensibility in the pathetic stories of the Andersons and the Millers in *Tom Jones*; now, in *Amelia*, sensibility becomes a central concern, and it is one which plainly militates against novel writing.

Surely one reason why so few good English novels were produced in the last decades of the eighteenth century was the predominance in that period of the cult of sensibility. For the novel, after all, begins with a lucid vision of familiar reality, seen in the varied richness of its concrete particulars, while the focus of writers of sensibility blurs into mysterious and limitless penumbras of experience, vaguely apprehended. The novel is founded on a supreme confidence in the power of language to incorporate reality; even kinds of experience which might seem to be beyond the limits of massive verbal reconstruction – daydream, fantasy, hallucination, fragmented memory, contradictory motivation, preconscious desire – become plastic subjects for novelistic manipulation. The cult of sensibility, on the other hand, insists on the primacy of the ineffable: the most desirable end to which a literary vehicle can convey us is to a love (or joy, or pathos) that passeth understanding and the limits of language as well.

Fielding intends a touchingly tender relationship between Booth and Amelia to be the imaginative center of his novel, but because his assumptions about representing the emotions are essentially those of the writers of sensibility, he constantly refuses to realize that relationship novelistically, in psychological or factual details, in particularizing language. The various narrators of *Amelia* repeatedly allude to the ineffability of the experiences they attempt to report – 'raptures not to be expressed', 'an ecstasy not to be described', and more of the like. 'Shall I tell you what I felt at that instant?' Booth asks Miss Matthews as he relates to her a painful leavetaking from Amelia. 'I do assure you I am not able. So many tender ideas crowded at once into my mind, that, if I may use the expression, they almost dissolved my heart' (book 3, chapter 3). The apology for the expression hardly dilutes its stickiness or mitigates its hyperbolic inadequacy. Later on, when the narrator confesses his inability to convey the pathos of Amelia, weeping with her children who have been bereft of their beloved father, he reveals his underlying semantic assumption: 'The scene that followed ... is beyond my power of description; I must beg the readers' hearts to suggest it to themselves' (book 8, chapter 3).

Where, we may wonder, does the heart get such marvelous knowledge to reach beyond the mystic borders of the inexpressible? Fielding's answer is simple enough: the heart knows by already having been there. Booth makes the point quite clear in concluding his description to Miss Matthews of the pathetic scene in which he parted from Amelia in order to join the expedition to Gibraltar:

'This I am convinced of, that no one is capable of tasting such a scene who hath not a heart of tenderness, and perhaps not even then, unless he hath been in the same situation' (book 3, chapter 2). And when he reports his and Amelia's reunion with the child they left behind in England – a kind of narrative inconvenience who has been complacently forgotten and now is introduced as an after-thought – he invokes the same principle of communication: 'The transports we felt on this occasion were really enchanting, nor can any but a fond parent conceive, I am certain, the least idea of them' (book 3, chapter 11).

Nothing could illustrate more clearly how the assumptions of the cult of sensibility go against the generic grain of the novel. The literature of sensibility generally takes it for granted that emotional responses to the universal human experiences are everywhere the same – that is why it so frequently draws upon stock situations and characters and fixed verbal formulas, the flow of sensibility naturally spilling over into the clichés of sentimentalism. The only significant variation in response to experience will be one of degree, depending upon the fineness of the individual sensorium, how tender the heart. Logically, then, the best way for a writer to convey a particular emotion is to point to a shared experience – you who are a parent must know what I felt – and without the shared experience, he can communicate little, for only the already loving heart can know love. The novel, on the other hand, that most imperialistic of genres, characteristically seeks to extend its domain to all the little nooks and crannies of both society and the mind, whether or not its readers have been there themselves. The novelist of course begins with the common humanity of us all, but what especially fascinates him is the endlessly varied differences by which men are distinguished from one another, and he often uses the power of imaginative language to transform the otherness of others into familiar objects of our own inner space. If we try to imagine Dostoyevsky writing, 'The exquisite mental torture which Raskolnikov felt, only one who has committed murder will understand', or Faulkner explaining that 'Only a true lunatic could have any idea of what went on in Benjy's mind at that moment', we can see how far the assumptions of the cult of sensibility lead us from the novelistic representation of individual experience. A good novel, to be sure, does not have to center on the representation of consciousness, but the new emphasis upon emotional experience in *Amelia* calls for a much closer approach to consciousness than Fielding's habits as a writer and his semantic assumptions will allow him to give us.

The cult of sensibility, finally, is a quest for sensation in itself, and since mere sensations are both impersonal and asocial, their cultivation in fiction tends to preclude that convincing representation of individual character implicated in society which is so essential to the novel. Most of the major characters of *Amelia*, with the exception of the worst villains, are on the lookout for exquisite feelings: that is why they are willing audiences to each other's lengthy narratives, so that they can participate in the evocation of what they themselves self-consciously refer to as 'tender scenes'. Even the beloved husband of a beloved wife does not rest happy in his matrimonial state without seeking moments when conjugal affection can be concentrated in exquisite sensation: Booth says of Balligard, the Frenchman who he learns had designs on his wife, 'To say the truth, I afterward thought myself almost obliged to him for a meeting with Amelia the most luxuriously delicate that can be imagined' (book 3, chapter 9). 'Luxurious delicacy' is the kind of phrase which in the earlier novels is used with a cunning satiric doubleness, to indicate, say, the carnal propensities of a Bridget Allworthy, but here there is no suspicion of irony.

One of the most revealing expressions of the shift in attitude toward sensation in Fielding's last novel is the peculiar fact of Amelia's feminine debility. In his earlier fiction, Fielding had been particularly happy in representing virtuous women who were vigorously energetic, and he gave only a few hints of a possible assent to the new literary fashion of polarizing humanity into rough though tamable males and delicate, hypersensitive, spiritually finer females. Amelia does retain a certain resiliency or at least forbearance in adversity, but she also exhibits a delicate female sensibility which registers small shocks as major quakes and brings her to the inevitable verge of fainting at several points in the novel. It may well be that Fielding was influenced by Richardson in this respect. He had been immensely impressed by *Clarissa*, which appeared three years before *Amelia*, and he may even have wanted to suggest he intended a more Richardsonian kind of novel by adopting the practice of Richardson's two published novels in using a virtuous heroine's name for the title.[1] In any case, the congenital debility of the virtuous female plausibly follows from the assumptions of the novel of sensibility: virtue itself is ultimately determined by the degree to which the character's heart is 'sensible', in the eighteenth-century sense of the term, and so the character that is to be the model of virtue is likely to possess an instrument of response to experience which is exquisitely sensitive and therefore somewhat fragile as well. All this heightened interest, then, in intense and supposedly virtuous sensations encourages schematic simplifications of human nature in the novel and leads the novelist away from the sphere most congenial to him – the solid, multifaceted, variously populated social world – into a private domain not so much of feeling as of the delectation of feeling, where language itself becomes a violation of the purity of emotion.

I do not want to suggest that *Amelia* is in any consistent way a novel of sensibility, or that the insistently didactic notes to which we have attended ring through the entire structure of the book. Most of what Fielding does in his last novel, bad and good alike, is done in spots and patches, and if this contributes to making *Amelia* a miscarried novel in some important respects, it means that the faults are not unrelieved. *Amelia* is certainly very far from being a general failure, unless we foolishly expect, as some critics have done, that it be another *Tom Jones*, something which Fielding himself clearly did not intend. It is not enough to say there are good things in *Amelia*; there are things in this book which one simply does not find in the English novel until it reaches a stage of greater technical sophistication, in the nineteenth century.

To begin with, Fielding's only partially successful attempt at making the novel a vehicle of practical, panoramic criticism of contemporary society is unique in kind until the end of the century. This aspect of Fielding's achievement against the background of his own age is brought into sharp relief by the tone and tendency of Richardson's expressed disapproval of *Amelia*:

I have not been able to read more than the first volume of *Amelia*. Poor Fielding! I could not help telling his sister, that

1 The similarity of titles was suggested to me by Hugh Amory, who also points out that one take-off on *Shamela*, Fielding's parody of *Pamela*, was called *Shamelia*.

I was equally surprised at and concerned for his continued lowness. Had your brother, said I, been born in a stable, or been a runner at a sponging house, we should have thought him a genius, and wished he had the advantage of a liberal education, and of being admitted into good company; but it's beyond my conception, that a man of good family, and who had some learning, and who really is a writer, should descend so excessively low in all his pieces. Who can care for any of his low people?[1]

Such appalling condescension was not, of course, typical of all eighteenth-century readers, but it does point up the real advantages as a novelist that Fielding's own social background and temperament gave him. For Richardson's distressingly narrow range of social and moral sympathy is precisely the opposite of the quality we like to associate with the novel as a genre. A profoundly bourgeois sensibility like Richardson's could contribute to the extension of realism downward, into the inner depths, but not outward, in social space. The rise of the novel is, of course, historically connected with the rise of the middle class; but – as the Goncourts argued in their preface to *Germinie Lacerteux* – it may be equally legitimate to consider the novel as the democratic rather than the bourgeois genre, impelled by a sense of responsibility to extend the 'franchise' of realistic representation to the underprivileged classes, the despised occupations, the neglected social settings. Fielding, to be sure, presents his lower-class people sympathetically but always from a carefully maintained distance – his final imaginative allegiance is to the traditional values of the landed gentry. He is free, however, of the constant uneasiness about social standing which in a self-made man like Richardson produces such morally paralysing snobbery.

What disgusted Richardson in *Amelia* belongs to the very substance of its original achievement. Fielding thrusts us into 'low' settings like Newgate and the bailiff's house not so much in the manner of Smollett, who used such locations to pay off personal scores and to tie together formal satiric vignettes, as in the manner of the later Dickens, for whom the institutions of justice and detention were

1 Samuel Richardson, *Correspondence*, ed. A. L. Barbauld, 1804, vol. 6, p. 154.

vivid illustrations and symbolic embodiments of the pervasive maddening perversity of society at large. Social panorama is clearly essential to Fielding's purpose in *Amelia*. He had also been interested in social panorama in his two previous novels, but here the lines of connection between the various parts of the big picture are drawn tighter. The noblemen and the turnkeys of *Amelia* are linked not only by a common moral posture – as, say, noblewoman and country wench are connected in *Tom Jones* – but also by the common role they play, at different levels, as functionaries of the same utterly cynical system of social and legal power. Fielding had perhaps given an intimation of this general approach in *Jonathan Wild*, but he makes its social implications more apparent in *Amelia* and comes closer to a particularized observation of contemporary institutions and practices.

Equally important, there are sections of *Amelia* which demonstrate that Fielding could attain a new subtlety in the presentation of character by leaving most of the commentary to the reader's imagination while preserving the ample balance achieved in his comic novels between shrewd satiric observation and humanely sympathetic imagination. The long encounter in prison between Booth and Miss Matthews (Books, 1, 2, 3 and the beginning of 4) is a tour de force of a sort scarcely attempted in the English novel for another century, and it nicely illustrates how Fielding was developing a new mode of fiction out of his old methods. The two regressive narratives – first Miss Matthews', then Booth's – derive technically from the interpolated tales of the comic novels, and may seem a little cumbersome to certain readers, but in their manner of drawing us dramatically into the lives of the protagonists, they anticipate the flashback techniques of later fiction, introducing the substance of the main action and not merely offering an analogy to it.

Necessary information is gradually disclosed with a fine sense of timing. At first, we are not even told that Booth is married; the first mention of it is from the mouth of Miss Matthews. Then Miss Matthews, still a somewhat enigmatic presence for the reader, recounts in detail her own fall from virtue, and finally we get to Booth and his tale of Amelia and their courtship and marriage. While all this rehearsal of the past is going on, Fielding uses a quieter, subtler version of the technique of breaking in upon interpolations which we observed in *Joseph Andrews* and *Tom Jones*: as the two old friends talk on in the privacy of Miss Matthews' cell, it slowly dawns on us that her sympathy for him is excessively animated, that she has a particular interest in him, that she is ogling him, that she is offering her immediate, experienced services as substitute wife. In the interplay, moreover, between genial naïf and congenial seductress, Fielding manages to maintain a nice balance of affectionate sympathy and satiric censure for both, so contriving the adulterous liaison that we can see its origins in a most understandable human weakness together with its morally reprehensible implications and even its comic aspects.

In the splendid figure of Miss Matthews, who lamentably is reduced later in the novel for didactic reasons to a venomous Rejected Mistress, Fielding hints at an ironic doubleness of attitude toward that very pursuit of sentiment which is undertaken elsewhere in the novel with distressing single-mindedness. Miss Matthews is presented to us as a reader, or rather listener, of sensibility *par excellence*. When Booth offers to omit from his narrative the description of a particularly tender scene between him and Amelia, she protests vehemently: 'Indeed I beg you will not . . . nothing delights me more than scenes of tenderness. I should be glad to know if possible, every syllable which was uttered on both sides' (book 3, chapter 1). The effect of attributing this delight in tender scenes to Miss Matthews of all people, given her past history and present motives, is to cast a teasing shadow of suspicion over the whole mode of sensibility which the writer himself seems to relish. Booth, invoking a familiar formula as he recalls Amelia's fainting at his first declaration of love, tells Miss Matthews, 'To describe my sensation till she returned to herself is not in my power.' And his listener's response would seem to illustrate nicely the dogma of sensibility that a word to the wise heart is always sufficient: ' "You need not," cried Miss Matthews. "Oh, happy Amelia! why had not I been blessed with such a passion?" ' (book 2, chapter 2). Does Miss Matthews have a sensible heart, or merely the superficial empathy of an envious one, the keen imagination of unsated desire? Fielding exercises sound artistic tact in leaving the doubt suspended as Miss Matthews goes on to suggest obliquely – she dares do no more – that the nobility of Booth's passion exceeds the worthiness of the object it has chosen in Amelia.

Just a little further on in Booth's narrative (book 2, chapter 4), the doubt about the candor of Miss Matthews' tender heart is almost resolved. Booth again apologizes for the ineffability of an experience, this time, having his beloved sister die in his arms: ' "The sensations I felt are to be known only from experience, and to you must appear dull and insipid" . . . Here Mr Booth stopped a moment, and wiped his eyes; and Miss Matthews, perhaps out of complaisance, wiped hers.' The characteristic strategy of the double irony in *Tom Jones* is here interestingly reversed. The narrator of *Tom Jones* would probably have had Miss Matthews wipe her eyes 'perhaps out of tender sympathy', a pointed irony which would lead us to infer that the character's motive was quite the opposite – or possibly, quite the opposite of the asserted motive and yet just a little like it. The 'perhaps' phrase which Fielding actually uses here evokes a similar suspension of absolute judgement, but with a shift in emphasis from satiric exposure to sympathetic reconsideration. In *Amelia*, Fielding is not interested in maintaining a consistent ironic elevation over his personages, and so here he states directly what we are by now prepared to infer in any case – that Miss Matthews' tears are a show put on for Booth. But – the strategic 'perhaps' makes us wonder – are they entirely that? We have already been given enough hints to guess that Miss Matthews throughout is preparing the way for the seduction of Booth, but, at least in this first part of the novel, she shows a warm sympathy and generosity which probably cannot be wholly explained away as stratagems of seduction. In the new, subdued presentation of character in *Amelia*, then, Fielding gives us a chastened version of his familiar inferential technique which leads us at once to a firm moral judgment of character and a tolerant recognition of the mixed nature of human motives.

As the narrator tends to withdraw from the action in *Amelia*, much of the inferential activity which is evoked by authorial comment in *Tom Jones* is now shifted to the uninterrupted exchanges between the characters. The novel, in short, becomes more purely dramatic. The best moments, for example, in the dialogue between Booth and Miss Matthews exhibit a deftness of comic revelation and a bold dramatic irony unparalleled in the earlier novels. Here is Miss Matthews, indignant over the discovery that Mandeville makes no provision in his philosophy for the greatest of passions:

'If he denies there is any such thing as love, that is most
certainly wrong. I am afraid I can give him the lie myself.'

'I will join with you, madam, in that,' answered Booth,
'at any time.'

'Will you join with me?' answered she, looking eagerly at
him – 'O, Mr Booth! I know not what I was going to say –
What – Where did you leave off? I would not interrupt you
– but I am impatient to know something.'

'What, madam?' cries Booth; 'if I can give you any
satisfaction –'

'No, no,' said she, 'I must hear all; I would not for the
world break the thread of your story. Besides, I am afraid to
ask – Pray, pray, sir, go on' (book 3, chapter 5).

A beautifully transparent exposure of character and motive is
achieved here through the most natural exchange of speech, with
none of the manifest stylization or comic heightening of dialogue
we noted in *Joseph Andrews* and *Tom Jones*. In the absence of the
narrator, the characters assume a new independence: we know them
for what they are by what they say and think, how each responds to
what is said and apparently thought by the other. The nature of the
relationship between Miss Matthews and Booth, which has been
revealed in stages through their long colloquy, is suddenly thrown
into sharp focus by Booth's inadvertent double entendre: Miss
Matthews pounces on the sexual implication with joyful anticipation,
then, confused in her excitement, hesitant at having moved too soon,
she quickly retreats, while the inveterately well-meaning, unsuspecting Booth sails blithely on to still another unwitting sexual pun,
promising to give his warm-tempered female companion 'any
satisfaction'. Sterne sometimes works double entendre into dialogue
in similar fashion, but without the same developing interplay of
character that culminates in the comic exchange here. To find
dialogue in an English novel that can generate this kind of revealing,
limpidly dramatic irony, one has to look to Jane Austen and beyond.
As with other artistic virtues of *Amelia*, it is something that comes in
flashes, not as a steady illumination, but its very presence in the book
is an indication of the author's undiminished originality and technical
command.

Fielding's last novel, in sum, with all its obvious unevenness, is still the work of a writer of genius; it offers some striking evidence that he was beginning, however uncertainly, to explore bold new possibilities for the genre he himself had already helped to bring to a brilliant first maturity. However, because Fielding was to leave *Amelia* without an artistic sequel, his new aims in it only partly realized, this last novel remains, finally, a fascinating and instructive anomaly. It is to *Joseph Andrews* and *Tom Jones* that we must look for the vividly achieved models of what could be made of this protean form called the novel by a writer balancing the claims of literary tradition and contemporary reality, of adherence to moral actuality in all its unseemly blemishes and devotion to the lovely unity of a perfected art.

(141–77)

Select Bibliography

Books or Articles on Fielding

Works anthologized in this volume are not normally included in this bibliography, unless they contain substantial material on Fielding in addition to the extracts I have reprinted.

Editions: Collections

Complete Works, ed. W.E. Henley, 16 volumes, Heinemann, 1903.
The Wesleyan Edition of the Works of Henry Fielding, ed. W.B. Coley et al., Clarendon Press and Wesleyan University Press, 1967–. Standard annotated edition, of which two volumes, *Joseph Andrews*, ed. Martin C. Battestin, 1967, and *Miscellanies. Volume One*, ed. Henry Knight Miller, 1972, are available so far.

Editions: Individual Works
Plays

The Author's Farce (1730), ed. Charles B. Woods, University of Nebraska Press, 1966; Edward Arnold, 1967 (annotated).
The Tragedy of Tragedies (1731; with earlier version, *Tom Thumb*, 1730), ed. James T. Hillhouse, Yale University Press, and Oxford University Press, 1918 (very fully annotated); another annotated edition of both versions, by L.J. Morrissey, Oliver & Boyd, 1970.
The Grub-Street Opera (1731), ed. Edgar V. Roberts, University of Nebraska Press, 1968; Edward Arnold, 1969 (annotated).
Covent-Garden Tragedy (1732), in *Burlesque Plays of the Eighteenth Century*, ed. Simon Trussler, Oxford University Press, 1969 (also includes *Tom Thumb*, 1730; some annotation).
The Historical Register for the Year 1736 and *Eurydice Hiss'd* (both 1737), ed. William W. Appleton, University of Nebraska Press, 1967; Edward Arnold, 1968 (annotated).

Novels

Joseph Andrews (1742), ed. Martin C. Battestin, Houghton Mifflin, 1961; Methuen, 1965. Available in England with, and in the USA with or without, *Shamela* (1741); also *Joseph Andrews and Shamela*, ed. Douglas Brooks, Oxford University Press, 1971 (both editions annotated; Battestin's introduction is particularly full and useful).

Jonathan Wild (1743; revised 1754). Several editions, none outstanding. The World's Classics edition, Oxford University Press, 1932, is unusual and useful in reprinting the first version of 1743, with an Appendix giving revisions of 1754. The Everyman's Library edition, Dent, 1932, also includes *Voyage to Lisbon*.

Tom Jones (1749), ed. R.P.C. Mutter, Penguin, 1966 (annotated).

Amelia (1751), 2 volumes, Everyman's Library, Dent, 1930. Originally with introduction by George Saintsbury, and in current reprints by A.R. Humphreys.

Other Works

The Female Husband and Other Writings (1746, includes among other things *The Masquerade*, 1728), ed. Claude E. Jones, Liverpool University Press, 1960 (slight annotation; a poor edition, but no other text easily available).

The True Patriot (1745–6), ed. Miriam Austin Locke, University of Alabama Press, 1964; MacDonald, 1965 (fully annotated).

Covent-Garden Journal (1752), ed. G.E. Jenson, 2 volumes, Yale University Press, and Oxford University Press, 1915 (very fully annotated).

Journal of a Voyage to Lisbon (1755), ed. Harold E. Pagliaro, Nardon Press, 1963 (annotation much indebted to Austin Dobson's editions, 1892, 1907); see also above, *Jonathan Wild*.

The Criticism of Henry Fielding, ed. Ioan Williams, Routledge & Kegan Paul, 1970 (collects a large number of critical essays and statements by Fielding, with some annotation).

Bibliographical Aids

The most up-to-date bibliographical guide to works by and about Fielding is by Martin C. Battestin in *New Cambridge Bibliography of English Literature*, ed. George Watson, vol. 2, 1971. The detailed bibliography of early editions of Fielding's works at the end of Cross's *History of Henry Fielding* is extremely useful. F.T. Blanchard's *Fielding the Novelist*, Yale University Press and Oxford University Press, 1926, is a very full survey of critical reactions to the novels from the 1740s to the early 1920s. Francesco Cordasco's *Henry Fielding: A List of Critical Studies Published from 1895 to 1946*, Long Island University Press, 1948, has many deficiencies.

Biography

Wilbur S. Cross, *The History of Henry Fielding* Yale University Press, 3 volumes, 1918.

F. Homes Dudden, *Henry Fielding: His Life, Works, and Times*, Clarendon Press, 2 volumes, 1952.

Criticism: General

Robert Alter, *Fielding and the Nature of the Novel*, Harvard University Press, 1968. One of the best critical studies.

Wayne C. Booth, *The Rhetoric of Fiction*, University of Chicago Press, 1961. Deals masterfully with problems of authorial intrusion and 'point of view'.

Leo Braudy, *Narrative Form in History and Fiction: Hume, Fielding and Gibbon*, Princeton University Press, 1970.

John Butt, *Fielding*, Writers and their Work, no. 59, Longman, revised edn 1959. An admirable short guide.

William B. Coley, 'The Background of Fielding's Laughter', *Journal of English Literary History*, vol. 26, 1959, pp. 229-52.

Frederick S. Dickson, Manuscript Indexes to several works by Fielding in Yale University Library, available in photocopy in certain other libraries.

Aurélien Digeon, *Les Romans de Fielding*, Hachette, 1923; trans. *The Novels of Fielding*, Routledge, 1925. Still a useful general study.

A.E. Dyson, *The Crazy Fabric: Essays in Irony*, Macmillan, 1965. Contains a good essay on Fielding.

Morris Golden, *Fielding's Moral Psychology*, University of Massachusetts Press, 1966.

Graham Greene, 'Fielding and Sterne', in *From Anne to Victoria*, ed. B. Dobrée, Cassell, 1937.

Glenn W. Hatfield, *Henry Fielding and the Language of Irony*, University of Chicago Press, 1968.

Maurice Johnson, *Fielding's Art of Fiction*, University of Pennsylvania Press, 1961.

Frank Kermode, 'Richardson and Fielding', *Cambridge Journal*, vol. 4, 1950, 106–14. An important, sharp essay. Reprinted in Spector (see below).

Arnold Kettle, *An Introduction to the English Novel*, 2 volumes Hutchinson, 1951–3.

George R. Levine, *Henry Fielding and the Dry Mock*, Mouton, 1967.

A.D. McKillop, *The Early Masters of English Fiction*, University of Kansas Press, 1956.

Henry Knight Miller, *Essays on Fielding's Miscellanies: A Commentary on Volume One*, Princeton University Press, 1961. Far more important and central than the title indicates. Excellent index worth looking up on any topic of interest to students of Fielding.

J. Middleton Murry, *Unprofessional Essays*, Jonathan Cape, 1956. Contains a good essay on Fielding.

Ronald Paulson (ed.), *Fielding: A Collection of Critical Essays*, Prentice-Hall, 1962. An excellent collection of essays of the last fifty years, including Ian Watt on *Shamela* and *Tom Jones*, Empson on *Tom Jones*, Mark Spilka and Maynard Mack on *Joseph Andrews*, Sherburn and John S. Coolidge on *Amelia*, and several other pieces.

Ronald Paulson, *Hogarth: His Life, Art and Times*, 2 volumes, Yale University Press, 1971.

Ronald Paulson, *Satire and the Novel in Eighteenth-Century England*, Yale University Press, 1967.

Ronald Paulson and Thomas Lockwood (eds.) *Henry Fielding: The Critical Heritage*, Routledge & Kegan Paul, and Barnes and Noble, 1969. A copious selection of eighteenth-century criticism of Fielding, mostly during his lifetime.

Martin Price, *To the Palace of Wisdom: Studies in Order and Energy from Dryden to Blake*, Doubleday, 1964.

C.J. Rawson (ed.), *Henry Fielding*, Profiles in Literature, Routledge & Kegan Paul, and Humanities Press, 1968. Selections with commentary designed to illustrate various features of Fielding's art.

C.J. Rawson, *Henry Fielding and the Augustan Ideal under Stress*, Routledge & Kegan Paul, 1972.

Sheldon Sacks, *Fiction and the Shape of Belief: A Study of Henry Fielding*, University of California Press, 1964.

Robert Scholes and Robert Kellogg, *The Nature of Narrative*, Oxford University Press, 1966. Contains a number of suggestive discussions of aspects of Fielding's art.

Arthur Sherbo, *Studies in the Eighteenth-Century English Novel*, Michigan State University Press, 1969.

George Sherburn, 'Fielding's Social Outlook', *Philological Quarterly*, vol. 35, 1956, pp 1–23. Reprinted in *Eighteenth-Century English Literature. Modern Essays in Criticism*, ed. James L. Clifford, Oxford University Press Inc., 1959.

Diana Spearman, *The Novel and Society*, Routledge & Kegan Paul, 1966. Inaccurate but often lively book, containing some discussion of Fielding and challenging some of the arguments of Ian Watt's *The Rise of the Novel*.

Robert D. Spector (ed.), *Essays on the Eighteenth-Century Novel*, Indiana University Press, 1965. Reprints Frank Kermode on 'Richardson and Fielding', Mark Spilka on *Joseph Andrews*, and R.S. Crane's 'The Plot of *Tom Jones*'.

Philip Stevick (ed.), *The Theory of the Novel*, Collier-Macmillan, 1967. An important collection of reprinted discussions of the novel-form.

Stuart M. Tave, *The Amiable Humorist: A Study in the Comic Theory and Criticism of the Eighteenth and Early Nineteenth Centuries*, University of Chicago Press, 1960.

Ethel M. Thornbury, *Henry Fielding's Theory of the Comic Prose Epic*, University of Wisconsin Studies in Language and Literature, no. 30, 1931. A useful study; reprints in an appendix the sale catalogue of Fielding's library, 1755.

Ian Watt, *The Rise of the Novel*, Chatto & Windus, and University of California Press, 1957. A seminal, highly provocative work.

Rebecca West, *The Court and the Castle: A Study of the Interactions of Political and Religious Ideas in Imaginative Literature*, Yale University Press and Macmillan, 1958. Contains a vivid and individual essay on Fielding, 'The Great Optimist', with some special emphasis on *Amelia*.

James A. Work, 'Henry Fielding, Christian Censor', in *The Age of Johnson: Essays Presented to Chauncey Brewster Tinker*, ed. F.W. Hilles, Yale University Press, 1949, pp. 139–48. An examination of Fielding's religious outlook.

Andrew Wright, *Henry Fielding, Mask and Feast*, Chatto & Windus, and University of California Press, 1965.

Ioan Williams (ed.), *Novel and Romance, 1700–1800: A Documentary Record*, Routledge & Kegan Paul, 1970. A collection of eighteenth-century statements about the novel-form.

Malvin R. Zirker Jr, *Fielding's Social Pamphlets*, University of California Press, 1966. A study of the legal-sociological writings of Fielding's last years, and an important account of his social outlook.

Criticism: The Plays

F.W. Bateson, *English Comic Drama 1700–1750*, Clarendon Press, 1929.

Ian Donaldson, *The World Upside-Down: Comedy from Jonson to Fielding*, Clarendon Press, 1970.

John Loftis, *Comedy and Society from Congreve to Fielding*, Stanford University Press, 1959.

Criticism: Jonathan Wild

Gerald Howson, *Thief-Taker General: The Rise and Fall of Jonathan Wild*, Hutchinson, 1970. A biography of the real-life Jonathan Wild.

W.R. Irwin, *The Making of Jonathan Wild: A Study in the Literary Method of Henry Fielding*, Columbia University Press, 1941. A very useful background-book.

John Preston, 'The Ironic Mode: A Comparison of *Jonathan Wild* and *The Beggar's Opera*', *Essays in Criticism*, vol. 16, 1966, pp. 268–80.

Allan Wendt, 'The Moral Allegory of *Jonathan Wild*', *Journal of English Literary History*, vol. 24, 1957, pp. 306–20. Interprets the novel in the light of comments in the Preface to the *Miscellanies*. See introduction to Part Three, above.

Criticism: Joseph Andrews and Shamela

Martin C. Battestin, *The Moral Basis of Fielding's Art: A Study of Joseph Andrews*, Wesleyan University Press, 1959. A very useful study of Fielding's moral and religious thought, and its background.

Douglas Brooks, 'Richardson's *Pamela* and Fielding's *Joseph Andrews*', *Essays in Criticism*, vol 17, 1967, pp. 158–68.

Douglas Brooks, 'Symbolic Numbers in Fielding's *Joseph Andrews*', in *Silent Poetry: Essays in Numerological Analysis*, ed. Alastair Fowler, Routledge & Kegan Paul, 1970, pp. 234–60. Interesting as the only full-scale numerological study of a work by Fielding.

Irvin Ehrenpreis, 'Fielding's Use of Fiction: The Autonomy of *Joseph Andrews*', in *Twelve Original Essays on Great English Novels*, ed. Charles Shapiro, Wayne State University Press, 1960, pp. 23–42.

Homer, Goldberg, *The Art of Joseph Andrews*, University of Chicago Press, 1969. A very useful study, which considers the novel in 'relation to its continental antecedents', in Cervantes, Scarron, Lesage and Marivaux.

Robert M. Jordan, 'The Limits of Illusion: Faulkner, Fielding, and Chaucer', *Criticism*, vol. 2, 1960, pp. 278–305. Contains an interesting discussion of *Joseph Andrews*.

Bernard Kreissman, *Pamela-Shamela. A Study of the Criticisms, Burlesques, Parodies, and Adaptations of Richardson's Pamela*, University of Nebraska Press, 1960.

Bernard N. Schilling, *The Comic Spirit: Boccaccio to Thomas Mann*, Wayne State University Press, 1965. Contains essays on *Joseph Andrews* and its Preface.

Criticism: Tom Jones

Robert Alter, *Rogue's Progress: Studies in the Picaresque Novel*, Harvard, 1964. Contains a chapter on *Tom Jones*.

Martin C. Battestin, 'Fielding's Definition of Wisdom: Some Functions of Ambiguity and Emblem in *Tom Jones*', *Journal of English Literary History*, vol. 35, 1968, pp. 188–217.

Martin C. Battestin, '*Tom Jones*: The Argument of Design', in *The Augustan Milieu. Essays Presented to Louis A. Landa*, ed. Henry Knight Miller and others, Clarendon Press, 1970, pp. 289–319.

Martin C. Battestin (ed.), *Twentieth-Century Interpretations of Tom Jones*, Prentice-Hall, 1968. Reprints discussions by Leavis, Watt, Empson, Crane, Booth and others.

Michael Bell, 'A Note on Drama and the Novel: Fielding's Contribution', *Novel*, vol 3, 1970, pp. 119–28.

Neil Compton (ed.), *Henry Fielding: Tom Jones: A Casebook*, Macmillan, 1970. Reprints discussions by Kettle, Van Ghent, Murry, Watt, Empson, Paulson, Preston and others, and some shorter extracts from earlier critics.

R.S. Crane, 'The Concept of Plot and the Plot of *Tom Jones*', in *Critics and Criticism, Ancient and Modern*, ed. R.S. Crane,

University of Chicago Press, 1952, pp. 616–47. An expanded version of an essay first published in 1950, and reprinted in its earlier form in Battestin's *Twentieth-Century Interpretations*, and in Spector, *Essays on the Eighteenth-Century Novel*.

Frederick S. Dickson, *An Index to the History of Tom Jones*, New York, 1913. A useful reference-work, existing only as a manuscript in the Yale University Library and in photocopy in some other libraries.

Irvin Ehrenpreis, *Fielding: Tom Jones*, Edward Arnold, 1964. An excellent short book.

Frederick W. Hilles, 'Art and Artifice in *Tom Jones*', in *Imagined Worlds. Essays on Some English Novels and Novelists in Honour of John Butt*, ed. Maynard Mack and Ian Gregor, Methuen, 1968, pp. 91–110.

Eleanor N. Hutchens, *Irony in Tom Jones*, University of Alabama Press, 1965.

Henry Knight Miller, 'The Voice of Henry Fielding: Style in *Tom Jones*', in *The Augustan Milieu: Essays Presented to Louis A. Landa*, ed. Henry Knight Miller and others, Clarendon Presss, 1970, pp. 262–88.

John Preston, *The Created Self: The Reader's Role in Eighteenth-Century Fiction*, Heinemann, 1970. A work of considerable originality and value, with two chapters on *Tom Jones*, one of which is reprinted in this anthology.

Dorothy Van Ghent, *The English Novel: Form and Function*, Holt, Rinehart & Winston, 1953. An important book, containing a good chapter on *Tom Jones*, from which a brief extract is reprinted in this anthology.

Criticism: Amelia

Sheridan Baker, 'Fielding's *Amelia* and the Materials of Romance', *Philological Quarterly*, vol. 41, 1962, pp. 437–49.

John S. Coolidge, 'Fielding and "Conservation of Character"', *Modern Philology*, vol. 57, 1960, pp. 245–59. Reprinted in Paulson, *Fielding*.

George Sherburn, 'Fielding's *Amelia*: An Interpretation', *Journal of English Literary History*, vol. 3, 1936, pp. 1–14. Reprinted in Paulson, *Fielding*. The first important extended critique of this novel, still very central and valid.

Acknowledgements

For permission to use copyright material acknowledgement is made
to the following:

To the *Forum* for 'The Profitable Reading of Fiction' by Thomas
Hardy; to Macmillan of London and Basingstoke for a note by
Thomas Hardy from *Life of Thomas Hardy* by F. E. Hardy; to
Penguin Books for the Preface to *Plays Unpleasant* by George Bernard
Shaw; to Miss Dorothy E. Collins and Darwen Finlayson for an
extract from *All Things Considered* by G. K. Chesterton; to Macmillan
of London and Basingstoke for a speech by Thomas Hardy from
Personal Writings edited by Harold Orel; to Macdonald & Co. for
an extract from *Henry Fielding: A Memoir* by G. M. Godden; to the
estate of H. G. Wells for an extract from *The Contemporary Novel*
by H. G. Wells; to Cassell & Co. Ltd for extracts from *Logbook of
the Coiners* by Andre Gide translated by Justin O'Brien; to the estate
of W. B. Yeats for extracts from letters by J. B. Yeats to W. B. Yeats
from *Letters to His Son* edited by Joseph Hone; to Laurence Pollinger
Ltd for an extract from 'Study of Thomas Hardy' by D. H. Lawrence
from *Phoenix: The Posthumous Papers of D. H. Lawrence* edited by Edward
D. MacDonald; to Russell & Russell for an extract from *The History
of Henry Fielding* by Wilbur L. Cross; to Editions Gallimard for
'Notes en Manière de Preface à *Tom Jones*' by Andre Gide from
Oeuvres Completes; to Edward Arnold Ltd for extracts from *Aspects
of the Novel* by E. M. Forster; to the Estate of D. H. Lawrence and
Laurence Pollinger Ltd for an extract from *A Propos of Lady Chatterley's
Lover* by D. H. Lawrence from *Phoenix II* edited by Warren Roberts
and Harry T. Moore; to David Higham Associates Ltd and Constable
for an extract from *The English Novel* by Ford Madox Ford;
to the Merlin Press for 'Tolstoi and the Development of Realism'
by George Lukács from *Studies in European Realism* translated by
Edith Bone; to the Merlin Press Ltd for extracts from *The Historical
Novel* by George Lukács translated by H. and S. Mitchell; to *Verve*
for an extract from 'Travels in English Literature' by Andre Gide
translated by Dorothy Bussy; to George Allen & Unwin Ltd for
extracts from *The March of Literature* by Ford Madox Ford; to Mrs
Sonia Orwell and Secker & Warburg for extracts from articles in
Tribune by George Orwell from *Collected Essays, Journalism and
Letters* edited by Sonia Orwell and Ian Angus; to the Clarendon Press

for an extract from 'Fielding's Irony: Its Methods or Effects' by
A. R. Humphreys from the *Review of English Studies*; to Chatto &
Windus Ltd for an extract from *The Great Tradition* by F. R. Leavis;
to Gollancz for an extract from *I Like It Here* by Kingsley Amis; to
Macmillan of London and Basingstoke for an extract from *The
Court and The Castle* by Rebecca West; to Jonathan Cape Ltd for
Love and Death in the American Novel by Leslie A. Fiedler; to Wayne
University Press for 'Endangering the Reader's Neck: Background
Description in the Novel' by D. S. Bland from *Criticism*; to Professor
Martin Price and Southern Illinois University Press for 'Fielding:
The Comedy of Forms' from *To the Palace of Wisdom* by Martin Price;
to Yale University Press for an extract from *Hogarth: His Life, Art
and Times* by R. Paulson; to The Clarendon Press for 'High and Low
Life and the Uses of Inversion' from *The World Upside-Down* by Ian
Donaldson; to Hutchinson Publishing Group Ltd for an extract from
Introduction to the English Novel by Arnold Kettle; to Macmillan of
London and Basingstoke for 'Fielding: Satire and Comic Irony'
by A. E. Dyson from *Modern Language Quarterly* reprinted in *The
Crazy Fabric*; to Wayne University Press for 'Language and Comic
Play in Fielding's *Jonathan Wild*' by Robert H. Hopkins from *Criticism*;
to Houghton Mifflin Co. for the Introduction to *Joseph Andrews and
Shamela* by Martin C. Battestin; to the English Association for 'Comic
Epic in Prose' by W. L. Renwick from *Essays and Studies*; to Chatto
& Windus for extracts from *The Rise of the Novel* by Ian Watt; to
University of Chicago Press for extracts from *Henry Fielding and the
Language of Irony* by Glenn W. Hatfield; to Cornell University Press
for an extract from *The Shaping Vision: Imagination in the English
Novel from Defoe to Dickens* by Robert Alan Donovan; to CBS
Education International for an extract from *The English Novel* by
Dorothy Van Ghent; to *Kenyon Review* and the author for 'Tom
Jones' by William Empson from *Kenyon Review*; to Edward Arnold
Ltd for an extract from *Fielding: Tom Jones* by Irvin Ehrenpreis; to
Journal of English Literary History for 'Tom Jones and the Pursuit of
True Judgment' by John Preston from *Journal of English Literary
History*; to Harvard University Press for an extract from *Fielding
and the Nature of the Novel* by Robert Alter.

Index

Extracts included in this anthology are indicated by bold page references.

Penguin English Poets

Instead of offering selections of the works of English and American poets, the Penguin English Poets will consist of the complete poems, in one or more volumes depending on the length of the *oeuvre*. The aim of the series is to provide a sound, readable text with helpful annotation which does not intrude on the text itself.

Already published

Robert Browning: The Ring and the Book
Edited by Richard D. Altick
Regents' Professor of English, Ohio State University

John Donne: The Complete English Poems
Edited by A. J. Smith
Professor of English Literature, University of Keele

Samuel Johnson: The Complete English Poems
Edited by J. D. Fleeman
Tutorial Fellow of Pembroke College, Oxford

John Keats: Complete Poems
Edited by John Barnard
Lecturer in English, University of Leeds

Christopher Marlowe: The Complete Poems and Translations
Edited by Stephen Orgel
Associate Professor of English, University of California at Berkeley

Andrew Marvell: Complete Poems
Edited by Elizabeth Story Donno
Associate Professor of English, Columbia University

Sir Gawain and the Green Knight
Edited by J. A. Burrow
Fellow of Jesus College and Lecturer in English, University of Oxford

William Wordsworth: The Prelude: A Parallel Text
Edited by J. C. Maxwell
Reader in English Literature and Fellow of Balliol College,
University of Oxford

Penguin Critical Anthologies

Emily Brontë
Edited by Jean-Pierre Petit

Geoffrey Chaucer
Edited by J. A. Burrow

Charles Dickens
Edited by Stephen Wall

Henrik Ibsen
Edited by James McFarlane

D. H. Lawrence
Edited by H. Coombes

Andrew Marvell
Edited by John Carey

Alexander Pope
Edited by F. W. Bateson and N. A. Joukovsky

Ezra Pound
Edited by J. P. Sullivan

Edmund Spenser
Edited by Paul J. Alpers

Wallace Stevens
Edited by Irvin Ehrenpreis

Jonathan Swift
Edited by Denis Donoghue

Leo Tolstoy
Edited by Henry Gifford

John Webster
Edited by G. K. and S. K. Hunter

Walt Whitman
Edited by Francis Murphy

Penguin Modern Poets

Already published

Pelican Biographies